D0173078

Honey, Hush!

OTHER WORKS BY DARYL CUMBER DANCE

Shuckin' and Jivin': Folklore from Contemporary Black Americans

Folklore from Contemporary Jamaicans

Fifty Caribbean Writers: A Bio-Bibliographical and Critical Sourcebook

Long Gone: The Mecklenburg Six and the Theme of Escape in Black Folklore

New World Adams: Conversations with Contemporary West Indian Writers

Honey, Hush!

AN ANTHOLOGY OF AFRICAN AMERICAN WOMEN'S HUMOR

Edited by Daryl Cumber Dance

FOREWORD BY NIKKI GIOVANNI

W. W. NORTON & COMPANY

NEW YORK LONDON

Copyright © 1998 by Daryl Cumber Dance
Foreword copyright © 1998 by Nikki Giovanni

Since this page cannot legibly accommodate all the copyright notices,
pages 665–73 constitute an extension of the copyright page.

All rights reserved
Printed in the United States of America

The text of this book is composed in Bembo
with the display set in Stuyvesant Open
Composition and manufacturing by the Haddon Craftsmen, Inc.
Book design by Chris Welch

Library of Congress Cataloging-in-Publication Data
Honey, hush! : an anthology of African American women's humor / edited
by Daryl Cumber Dance ; foreword by Nikki Giovanni.
p.   cm.
Includes bibliographical references.
ISBN 0-39304557-9
1. Afro-American wit and humor.   2. American wit and humor—
Women authors.   I. Dance, Daryl Cumber.
PN6231.N5H66   1997
817.008'09287'08996073—dc21   97-6772
CIP

W. W. Norton & Company, Inc., 500 Fifth Avenue, New York, N.Y. 10110
http://www.wwnorton.com

W. W. Norton & Company Ltd., 10 Coptic Street, London WC1A 1PU

4   5   6   7   8   9   0

Dedicated to the memory of three generations of supportive
women with whom I have shared love and laughter:

My grandmother, Sallie Brown Bell Brown (1875–1952),

My aunts, Emma Cumber Slade (1909–1960)
and Sarah Jacqueline Cumber Jenkins (1917–1991),

and

My dear friend, Clara Deese Lewis (1936–1994)

Contents

Foreword by Nikki Giovanni   *xix*

Introduction   *xxi*

Acknowledgments   *xxxvii*

CHAPTER I

"No Big Thing for 'Oman"

THE POWER AND STRENGTH OF THE BLACK WOMAN   1

MIMEOGRAPHED ITEM   Masterpiece   4

NIKKI GIOVANNI   Ego Tripping   4

ROXANNE SHANTÉ   Have a Nice Day   6

CAROLYN M. RODGERS   Living Water, IV   7

FRANCES ELLEN WATKINS HARPER   Learning to Read   8

HAZELLE   I Not Going to Stop til I Make It to de Top   10

MARGARET WALKER   Kissie Lee   14

MAGGIE POGUE JOHNSON   Old Maid's Soliloquy   16

BESSIE SMITH   Backwater Blues   17

CHRIS ALBERTSON   Bad Bessie   18

DONALD CLARKE   Billie Holiday   19

ETHEL WATERS   Whipping the Chorus Girls   20

IDA COX   Wild Women Don't Have the Blues   23

FOLK   How'd You Make Out?   24

FOLK   Queen Bee   24

VALERIE WILSON WESLEY   Devil's Gonna Get Him   25

ANONYMOUS   View de Land   31

MARILYN FULLEN-COLLINS   Mama   32

A. ELIZABETH DELANY   Getting the Last Word   35

MAMA SEZ   36

SISTER TO SISTER   36

CHAPTER 2

"Nice Girls Don't . . ."

MOTHERLY ADVICE   39

FANNIE BERRY   Ol' Enough   42

KATE RUSHIN   The Tired Poem   42

FOLK   An Hour of Pleasure   47

FOLK   Norfolk   47

TOI DERRICOTTE   Dildo   48

APRIL SINCLAIR   Prince Charming   50

APRIL SINCLAIR   ain't gonna be the same fool twice   50

PATRICIA J. WILLIAMS   In Search of Pharaoh's Daughter   54

JULIA A. BOYD   Got a Job to Do   63

BEBE MOORE CAMPBELL   Envy   64

KARLA F. C. HOLLOWAY   Nice Girls   78

JEANNETTE DRAKE   Yes M'am   79

DARYL CUMBER DANCE   You Rinate?   81

CAROLYN M. RODGERS   how i got ovah II/ It Is Deep II   82

SONYA BROOKS   Grandma Talk   83

MAMA SEZ   83

SISTER TO SISTER   88

CHAPTER 3

Mirror, Mirror on the Wall

THE BLACK WOMAN'S PHYSICAL IMAGE   90

BETYE SAAR	The Liberation of Aunt Jemima	98
THYLIAS MOSS	Lessons from a Mirror	99
ME'SHELL NDEGEOCELLO	Soul on Ice	100
BEBE MOORE CAMPBELL	Black Men, White Women	100
LOUISE MERIWETHER	A Happening in Barbados	106
APRIL SINCLAIR	Looking Out for the Children	115
FOLK	Ball It Up and Throw It to Me	116
AUDRE LORDE	Naturally	116
TRADITIONAL BLUES	I'm a Big Fat Mama	117
SARAH MARTIN	Mean Tight Mama	118
FOLK	Just a Cream Color	118
CAROLYN M. RODGERS	For Sistuhs Wearin Straight Hair	118
KARLA F. C. HOLLOWAY	The Long Way Home	119
ALISON WORKMAN	Grease	121
THYLIAS MOSS	A Reconsideration of the Blackbird	122
APRIL SINCLAIR	Here I Come, Ready or Not	123
FOLK	We Must, We Must, We Must	124
MIMEOGRAPHED ITEM	Ode to a Mammogram	125
BARBARA BRANDON	Where I'm Coming From	126
GLORIA WADE-GAYLES	Who Says an Older Woman Can't/Shouldn't Dance?	126
FOLK	Do You Remember?	128
MIMEOGRAPHED ITEM	Growing Wild	129
FOLK	Old Age Is Hell	130
FOLK	I Can't Remember	130
FOLK	Plenty Fire in the Furnace	131
FOLK	You Got an "F" in Sex	131
MAMA SEZ		132
SISTER TO SISTER		133

CHAPTER 4

Bronzeville U.S.A.

THE BLACK COMMUNITY 135

NAGUEYALTI WARREN   Down Home Sunday Blues   139
MOTHER LOVE   Dealing with Illness and Helpless Relatives   141
DORI SANDERS   Her Own Place   143
MIMEOGRAPHED ITEM   The Strongest Drive   150
FOLK   A Dentist's Jokes   150
TERRY MCMILLAN   Waiting to Exhale   151
PAULE MARSHALL   Talk Yuh Talk   154
VIRGIE M. BINFORD   Quilting Time   157
PRISCILLA JANE THOMPSON   An Afternoon Gossip   158
TRUDIER HARRIS   The Overweight Angel   162
MAGGIE POGUE JOHNSON   Meal Time   169
SARAH AND A. ELIZABETH DELANY   Having Our Say   170
MAGGIE POGUE JOHNSON   What's Mo' Temptin' to de
     Palate?   174
BECKY BIRTHA   Johnnieruth   176
TONI CADE BAMBARA   The Lesson   181
ETHEL MORGAN SMITH   The Spelling Bee   189
ZORA NEALE HURSTON   The Yellow Mule   191
GLORIA NAYLOR   Dr. Buzzard   194
MAGGIE POGUE JOHNSON   To See Ol' Booker T.   202
ANN PETRY   When I Mourns, I Mourns All Over   206
TINA MCELROY ANSA   Ugly Ways   217
MAMA SEZ   221
SISTER TO SISTER   222

CHAPTER 5

The Black Church and Churchgoers   225

OPAL J. MOORE   The Fence   227
JOYCE CAROL THOMAS   Young Reverend Zelma Lee Moses   238
MICHELE BOWEN-SPENCER   A Fool, a Girlfriend, a Husband
     and a Wife   257

HATTIE MAE DAWSON   The Preacher Tells a Lie   264
FOLK   The Minister's Fresh Air   265
FOLK   Open That Door   266
MAYA ANGELOU   The Reverend Howard Thomas   266
FOLK   He Remembered   267
FOLK   Under Suspicion   268
CAROLYN M. RODGERS   Jesus must of been some kind
  of dude   269
A. ELIZABETH DELANY   Praising the Lord   271
FOLK   Helping a Lady Out   271
FOLK   Shall We Gather at the River   272
FOLK   Gone to Meddlin'   273
FOLK   Prayer I   274
FOLK   Prayer II   274
BILLIE HOLIDAY   I'm Thinking It Over   274
MAMA SEZ   275
SISTER TO SISTER   276

CHAPTER 6

My Sweet Papa

COURTSHIP AND GOOD LOVING   277

ANONYMOUS   Sample of a "Courtship" Conversation   281
ANONYMOUS   A Difficult Courtship   284
PENNY WILLIAMS   Going Courting   287
VIOLET GUNTHARPE   The Happiest Minute   288
ZORA NEALE HURSTON   Jonah's Gourd Vine   288
ZORA NEALE HURSTON   Story in Harlem Slang   291
MARY CARTER SMITH   Cindy Ellie, a Modern Fairy Tale   292
RITA DOVE   Through the Ivory Gate   298
JESSIE REDMON FAUSET   Mary Elizabeth   307
MARY WESTON FORDHAM   The Coming Woman   314
RUBY DEE   To Pig or Not to Pig   316
JEANNETTE DRAKE   Conflict   318
BUTTERBEANS AND SUSIE   I Wanna Hot Dog for My Roll   318
SARAH AND A. ELIZABETH DELANY   We Ain't Dead Yet   320

MIMEOGRAPHED ITEM   The Mechanic   322

FOLK   May I Have This Dance   322

FOLK   The Next Time You Come . . .   323

MAMA SEZ   323

SISTER TO SISTER   323

CHAPTER 7

"My Daddy Won't Stop His Evil Ways"

PROBLEMS WITH HUSBANDS AND LOVERS   325

BARBARA BRANDON   Where I'm Coming From   329

PAULE MARSHALL   A Herb Most Bruised Is Woman   329

ALICE WALKER   The Color Purple   332

FOLK   I Can't Remember   333

MOMS MABLEY   The Good Ole Days   334

FOLK   Over the Hill   335

FOLK   The Fifteen–Inch Pianist   336

FOLK   Up   337

FOLK   Shortening   338

LOUISE BREWINGTON   The Laziest Man   338

FRANCES CRESS WELSING   The Language of Black Men   339

AMANDA SMITH   Brother Johnson's Search for a
Colored Wife   340

FLO KENNEDY   On Marriage   344

FOLK   A Man Won't Make a Fool of Me Twice   349

BARBARA BRANDON   Where I'm Coming From   350

NORMA MILLER   The Ladies   350

TERRY McMILLAN   It Ain't About Nothin'   351

COCO   Love Awaits   360

FOLK   I Figured He Could Fly   362

FOLK   Sexual Awareness   363

MIMEOGRAPHED ITEM   Cucumbers Are Better than
Men Because . . .   364

MIMEOGRAPHED ITEM   Chain Letter   365

MIMEOGRAPHED ITEM   Dear Ann Landers   366

MOTHER LOVE   How to Tell if Your Marriage Is in Trouble   366

BARBARA BRANDON   Where I'm Coming From   368
TONI CADE BAMBARA   The Johnson Girls   368
LISA JONES   Corporate Boys   371
BARBARA BRANDON   Where I'm Coming From   374
FLO KENNEDY   If You Won't Talk About What I'm Wearing   375
NTOZAKE SHANGE   lady in red   376
FOLK   Well, . . .   377
FOLK   She Didn't Ask about You   377
FOLK   I Ain't Dead   377
MIMEOGRAPHED ITEM   Woman Whacks Off Sleeping
   Husband's Penis, Then Throws It from Moving Car   378
ZORA NEALE HURSTON   Their Eyes Were Watching God   379
MAMA SEZ   381
SISTER TO SISTER   381

CHAPTER 8

"Just Like a White Man"

DICTIES   384

BONNIE ALLEN   Your attitude is politically correct if   386
GLORIA NAYLOR   Mama Day   388
BARBARA NEELY   Blanche among the Talented Tenth   389
DOROTHY WEST   The Wedding   397
BENILDE LITTLE   The Queen of Sheba Done Got Married   400
GLORIA NAYLOR   Linden Hills   406
APRIL SINCLAIR   Coffee Will Make You Black   412
DOROTHY WEST   The Living Is Easy   418
FOLK   Where Are You From?   422
FOLK   The Proper Word   422
FOLK   Fido   423
MIMEOGRAPHED ITEM   College Graduates   424
FOLK   The Lee Sisters   425
FOLK   Does It Come in White?   425
MAMA SEZ   426
SISTER TO SISTER   426

CHAPTER 9

My People, My People!

SELF-DENIGRATING TALES   428

FOLK	I Raised Hell while I Was There	431
MAGGIE POGUE JOHNSON	Superstitions	431
FOLK	I Been Sick	435
FOLK	We Ain't Dumb	435
FOLK	It Hasn't Been Used	436
FOLK	Jesus Wept	436
FOLK	Tongue and Teeth	437
FOLK	Why I Talk Like Dis?	438
FOLK	Am I Jewish or Am I Black?	438
FOLK	You Is What You Is	439
FOLK	Testimonials	439
MOMS MABLEY	Mom's First Plane Ride	440
FOLK	I'll Take Him	440
FOLK	You Know	441
FOLK	Ho-de-do	441
FOLK	O.J.'s Going to Cancun	442
FOLK	Country Guy and City Guy	442
JACQUELINE BRICE-FINCH	English 'Umor	443
VAL WARD	Pa'nella	443
FOLK	The New Rectum	444
FOLK	Stayman	444
FOLK	Hurry Up	445
FOLK	Playing in a Big Auditorium	445
NTOZAKE SHANGE	spell #7: geechee jibara quik magic trance manual for technologically stressed third world people	446
MIMEOGRAPHED ITEM	Blacks Application for Employment	453
MIMEOGRAPHED ITEM	Ebonics	454
MAMA SEZ		454
SISTER TO SISTER		455

CHAPTER 10

Fight, Kick, Bite

DEALING WITH A RACIST AND SEXIST AMERICA   457

LINDA BRENT   The Jealous Mistress   459
LINDA BRENT   Months of Peril   464
NAGUEYALTI WARREN   Butter 'n' Bread   467
FANNIE BERRY   Us Colored Women Had to Go through
  a Plenty   468
FANNIE BERRY   Sukie   468
MINNIE FOLKES   Serves 'Em Right   469
FORMER SLAVE   No Overseer Ever Downed Her   470
SOPHIA WORD   The Meanest Nigger   471
FORMER SLAVE   It's a Good Time to Dress You Out   472
FORMER SLAVE   Childhood   472
JULIA FRAZIER   Charlie   473
FANNIE BERRY   Fire Sticks   474
HANNAH PROSSER   Aunt Hannah Introduces Herself   475
SLAVE SONG   Old Satan Is Mad   477
SLAVE SONG   Marching up the Heavenly Road   478
SARAH BRADFORD   Harriet, the Moses of Her People   478
SOJOURNER TRUTH   While the Water Is Stirring I Will
  Step into the Pool   480
HARRIET E. WILSON   Our Nig   482
MATTIE J. JACKSON   The Soldiers, and Our Treatment
  during the War   485
CHARLOTTE FORTEN   Journal, October 28, 1862   488
ANNIE L. BURTON   Memories of Childhood's Slavery Days   489
ARMACIE ADAMS   You's Free   490
CHARLOTTE BROWN   Stomp Down Freedom   490
FANNIE BERRY   We's Free   491
FREEDOM SONG   Done wid Driver's Dribin'   492
PRISCILLA JANE THOMPSON   A Common Occurrence   492
JULIA GROVERNOR   I Ain't Know Nuttn'   495
FOLK   The Tar Baby   495
FOLK   You Gon' Make Bread Today   496

PAULINE GAY   Too Many Ups   497
SARAH AND A. ELIZABETH DELANY   I Would Rather Die
    than Back Down, Honey   498
ALICE CHILDRESS   Like One of the Family   502
ALICE CHILDRESS   The Pocketbook Game   504
ALICE CHILDRESS   Mrs. James   505
APRIL SINCLAIR   Never Trust a White Person   506
FOLK   I'll Go as Far as Memphis   508
FOLK   Gaining Respect   509
FOLK   'Sippi   509
MOMS MABLEY   Listen, Mame   510
KATHRYN L. MORGAN   Maggie's Stories   510
RUBY DEE   Mary Had a Little Lamb   512
FOLK   Some People Just Can't Tell Jokes   512
FOLK   At Least I Know Where I Am   513
MAMA SEZ   513
SISTER TO SISTER   513

CHAPTER 11

"From the Back of the Bus to the Back of the National Priority List"

THE CIVIL RIGHTS MOVEMENT, INTEGRATION, AND BEYOND   515

BONNIE ALLEN   We Are Overcome   518
LORRAINE HANSBERRY   A Raisin in the Sun   519
FANNIE LOU HAMER   Sick and Tired of Being Sick and
    Tired   524
MICHELE WALLACE   Black Macho and the Myth of the
    Superwoman   525
RUBY DEE   Jack and Jill   526
CAROLYN M. RODGERS   Yeah, I Is Uh Shootin Off at the
    Mouth, Yeah, I Is Uh Fairy Tale or Yeah, I Is
    Uh Revolutionist!   526
CAROLYN M. RODGERS   and when the revolution came   527
CAROLYN M. RODGERS   The Revolution Is Resting   530

OPAL J. MOORE   Git That Gal a Red Dress   531

ETHEL MORGAN SMITH   Come and Be Black for Me   532

ANN PETRY   The Bones of Louella Brown   538

LANI GUINIER   Female Gentleman   551

SHIRLEY CHISHOLM   I Didn't Come Here to Play   553

BERTICE BERRY   Getting to Know Me   554

BERTICE BERRY   Changing the Tapes   554

NIKKI GIOVANNI   Campus Racism 101   555

BARBARA BRANDON   Where I'm Coming From   559

BONNIE ALLEN   America   559

BENILDE LITTLE   The Interview   562

JILL NELSON   We Will Live the Life of the Cosbys   567

MIMEOGRAPHED ITEM   Affirmative Action in Heaven   573

SARAH AND A. ELIZABETH DELANY   I Know a Rascal
    When I See One   574

BARBARA BRANDON   Where I'm Coming From   575

SISTER TO SISTER   575

CHAPTER 12

Tidbits from the Laughing Barrel   577

JOHNNETTA B. COLE   Sister President   579

TONI CADE BAMBARA   A Sort of Preface   580

OPAL J. MOORE   A Happy Story   581

NIKKI GIOVANNI   Lorraine Hansberry   591

RITA DOVE   Nexus   594

FLO KENNEDY   To Whom It Concerns   595

ZORA NEALE HURSTON   The Map of Dixie on My Tongue   596

FOLK   How You Doing?   596

MARILYN NELSON WANIEK   Emily Dickinson's Defunct   597

SIBBY ANDERSON-THOMPKINS   Epitaph for Willie   598

WHOOPI GOLDBERG   Fontaine   599

MIMEOGRAPHED ITEM   Bill Clinton's Advisers and Cabinet   604

MIMEOGRAPHED ITEM   How You Can Tell When It's
    Going to be a Rotten Day   605

FOLK   O.J. Is Chilly   606
FOLK   Approach the Bench   607
BARBARA BRANDON   Where I'm Coming From   607
FOLK   Wait on de Lord   608
FOLK   Is the Coast Clear?   608
MIMEOGRAPHED ITEM   Retirement Policy   609
FOLK   Teachers on the Third Floor   610
MIMEOGRAPHED ITEM   Senior Citizens Beat Inflation   611
JACQUELINE BRICE-FINCH   Safe Sex   612
FLO KENNEDY   Women's Movement   612
MIMEOGRAPHED ITEM   West Virginia Medical Terminology
    for the Layman   613
FOLK   My Sympathy   614
MIMEOGRAPHED ITEM   The Birth of a Candy Bar   614
MOMS MABLEY   The Greatest Man   614
MIMEOGRAPHED ITEM   Best Rum Cake Ever   615
MOMS MABLEY   Helen Hunt   616
KATE RUSHIN   In Answer to the Question   616
MAMA SEZ   617
SISTER TO SISTER   618

Biographies of Contributors   619
Bibliography   653
Credits   665

Foreword

EVEN NOW, HOORAY FOR
THE BLACK WOMAN

Nikki Giovanni

I am a huge fan of the Black woman. I never hesitate to recommend her when times are bad or things go wrong. One of the reasons I personally like the word "Black" not as a description but as a sociological term is that we all can be Black women. In any given room everyone from blonde to redhead to silver-haired to bald can be a Black woman. Even a room full of men would benefit from saying once or twice a day to themselves, "I'm a Black woman; I can do anything." Oh sure, you laugh, who would want to be a Black woman if they didn't have to be? And that is my point exactly. If you could be anything at all without penalty or punishment why wouldn't you want to be a Black woman?

We are the folk who took rotten peaches and made cobbler; we took pieces of leftover cloth and made quilts; we took the entrails of pigs and cleaned them and rinsed them in cold water until the water ran clear then chopped up onions, shredded some red peppers, dropped a few fresh bay leafs and one large whole peeled potato in the pot to let it simmer over the open fire until we returned from the fields so that our families would have a hot meal at the end of the day. Every time something was taken away we took something else and made it work.

They took our language we made folk tales; they took our religion we took the Bible stories; they wouldn't let us waltz that was okay 'cause we could shimmy shimmy like my sister Kate. They withheld societal approval but we didn't care cause we looked to ourselves for our validation. And even now when Clarence Thomas lied on his sister whose only crime was to stay home and take care of the aunt who took care of them; when Bob Dole accepted medical help from the United States government as his due from his service as a soldier; when Newt Gingrich had his wife sign divorce papers favorable to him while she was receiving care for cancer; even now when the men who divorce and desert the women and children who have loved and served them well—we who understand the trials and tribulations of being women, let alone Black women, we find a way to laugh because we know that the only way to win this battle of life and liberty is with the pursuit of happiness. We find a way to get together with our green beans that need breaking or our dried beans that need picking through; our soaps for washing hair and hot combs for getting the kinks out; our files to smooth our fingernails or calluses on our feet and we talk about the world and how it won't defeat us. No way. 'Cause we start with that belly laugh and tears roll down our cheeks; we throw up our hands and all is right with the world.

Who wouldn't want to be a Black woman knowing nothing can defeat the indomitable spirit that is determined to love and laugh? Who can help but be a fan of the greatest, most wonderful creature on the planet. And when things are not going well with you, why not gather a few friends, fry a chicken or two and sit around a table saying: "I am a Black woman. I am the best thing on Earth." Then laughing your foolish head off. Yeah. We're wonderful. Honey, Hush!

Introduction

FUNNY
Sometimes laughter erupts
from deep volcanic soul space
surprising solemn moments like
blue crocuses in spring snow
—Nagueyalti Warren, from *Lodestar and Other Night Lights*

I f there is any one thing that has brought African American women whole through the horrors of the middle passage, slavery, Jim Crow, Aunt Jemima, the welfare system, integration, the O. J. Simpson trial, and Newt Gingrich, it is our humor. If there is any one thing that has helped us to survive the broken promises, lies, betrayals, contempt, humiliations, and dehumization that have been our lot in this nation and often in our families, it is our humor. Humor has often been defined as "God's aspirin to soothe the headache of reality." The formula for humor is said to be tragedy plus time, or pain plus time. African American women may not have had much *time*—time to reflect and to achieve some distancing—but we have had our share of tragedy and pain, and often even in the *midst* of that pain, we have found the relieving balm of humor. Humor hasn't been for us so much the cute, the whimsical, and the delightfully funny. Humor for us has rather been a means of surviving as we struggled. We haven't been laughing so much because things tickle us. We laugh, as the old blues line declares, to keep from crying. We laugh to keep from dying. We laugh to keep from killing. We laugh to hide our pain, to walk gently around the wound too painful to actually touch. We laugh to shield our shame. We use our humor to speak the unspeakable, to mask the attack, to get a tricky subject on the table, to warn of lines not to be crossed, to strike out at enemies and the hateful acts of friends and family, to camouflage sensitivity, to tease, to compliment, to berate, to brag, to flirt, to speculate, to gossip, to educate, to correct the lies people tell on us, to bring about change. Ultimately we recognize, as Toni Morrison has written in *Jazz,* "that laughter is serious. More complicated, more serious than tears."

The strength and creativity reflected in our humor is typical of a certain power that characterizes Black life in general—a power not only to cope and survive, but also to take the bitter lemons of our lives and make sweet lemonade. As Jessie Fauset has noted in her essay, "The Gift of Laughter," laughter has "its source in a wounded heart and in bleeding sensibilities. . . . The remarkable thing about this gift of [laughter] is that it has its rise . . . in the very woes which beset us." This is illustrated by numerous accounts in Patrice Gaines's *Laughing in the Dark,* including this brief summary of the banter among the women in her jail cell: "We went on like that for twenty minutes or so, talking shit, embellishing tales, joning, until we couldn't stand it anymore. Then we fell asleep, exhausted from our lies and our longings. We fell asleep contented too, in a way in which many of us had never been with our men. We gave each other laughter to help us through the night (117)."

As is obvious in Gaines's commentary, African American women's humor has been an *in-house* affair. There are a number of reasons that this humor was concealed from the public—especially the white public. One reason for this concealment was the requirement of "proper" behavior in the presence of whites. Thus raucous Negro behavior could not be allowed to offend the sensibilities of refined whites, especially white ladies. There is a popular old joke in the black community that Negroes in Southern towns were prohibited from laughing in the street. If they felt a laugh coming on, they had to rush and stick their heads into the laughing barrel marked "For colored" in order to protect whites from their loud, uproarious, and corrupting behavior. But of course, as with the music, and the dancing, and the fashions, and the other kinds of "niggerish" behavior that were below the dignity of white folks, those who were touched were lost.

Another reason for the concealment of African American women's humor is that it was not considered ladylike to tell jokes or even to laugh too loud publicly. The grandmother of Rita Dove's protagonist in *Through the Ivory Gate* explains to her how a proper lady should laugh: "Hold your hand over your mouth . . . hold it straight and a little to the side, like you're going to whisper something to someone next to you." *Ladies* are supposed to be quiet and reserved. Jokes are something shared in *male* company, often too coarse for the sensitive and delicate ears of women. This was even more an issue for black women than for white women since African American women have always had to contend with white America's derogatory image of them as laughing clowns, incapable of serious and tragic concerns. One wonders if this could possibly have anything to do with the popularity of an almost formulaic response to jokes, witty remarks, signifying comments and the like among black women, particularly Southern black women—"Honey, hush!" or "Hush yo' fuss!" It really isn't a suggestion that the person stop talking, but rather a friendly encouragement, a mild suggestion of playful disbelief, or a suggestion that one is telling truths that are prohibited.

Most of the public's introduction to so-called "Negro humor" has come in literature, plays, and films presented from a white perspective, with black females being portrayed in the most obnoxious and demeaning stereotypical roles, usually as loud, raucous, clownish and bossy mammies and Aunt Jemimas, stupid coons, or rump-shaking, oversexed wenches and whores. These despicable images of black women were (along with equally reprehensible images of black males) integral in plantation school literature and were the central attraction of the popular minstrel and vaudeville stages. Originally all black roles in minstrels were played by white males in blackface. White women in blackface and black men (also in blackface) eventually were allowed to participate, but it was later that black women joined them on stage. Ironically Thelma and Marjorie White, the Caucasian stars in the first version of the musical comedy *Topsy and Eva* in 1920, were billed as "The White Sisters." In the film version the popular white actress Mona Ray portrayed Topsy. To say that these and other white interpreta-

tions of black humor villified black men and women is an understate-
ment, which can be verified by viewing *Ethnic Notions,* a documentary
about racist stereotypes of blacks, produced by Marlon Riggs. Thus it was
deemed necessary here as in other areas of their lives for black women to
conceal their humor lest they lend credence to hated stereotypes perpet-
uated in white popular culture.

Despite all their efforts at concealment, I grew up believing that all
black women were comediennes—at least of the "behind-the-closed-
door" variety—for what I saw whenever the doors were safely closed was
African American women laughing—laughing about their men, laughing
about their hair, laughing about their white folk, laughing about their nation, laughing about their race. And even though much of this banter
might be described as tragicomic, sarcastic, absurd or sick humor, their reflections and philosophizing and just plain bad-mouthing were always en-
cased in hilarious jokes, witty proverbs, naughty blues, and in-your-face
dozens that provoked raucous laughter in their gatherings. Now I knew
that this comic image to which I was privy was rarely shared with the outside world, especially not the white world. Many of the most vocal of
those provoking laughter would be the first to malign the "loud" black
woman cracking jokes all the time and would whenever they were in public present the most sophisticated and reserved image imaginable.

Indeed this duality was first presented to me through my maternal
grandmother and her friends. At church, on occasional trips to the city,
even in the grocery store or the post office, they were as straightlaced as
Queen Victoria herself. Soft-spoken, quiet, reserved, their public personae
bore no similarity to the ladies whose repartee around the kitchen table
or in their sun parlors or on their front porches so enthralled me.
But upon their return to those private spaces, what a delight for me to
witness their magical transformation and hear them laugh and joke and
mimic everybody from the preacher to the President—big belly laughs,
tears rolling down their cheeks, arms reaching out to slap a shoulder,
screaming, "Pat, you know you lying," or "Stop that, girl, before you have
me rolling on the floor," or "Lawd, help me before this woman makes
me split my sides." No obscene language or sexual innuendos entered these
conversations, perhaps because even when they let their hair down in the
privacy of their homes they were ever aware of their image as college-

educated descendants of Abraham[1] and wives of Harvard lawyers and respectable gentleman farmers, or perhaps it was just because they were aware of my presence on the edge of the porch or sneaking something out of the icebox or pretending I was reading on the living room sofa. They would, however, in this protected and private company, throw around that hated epithet that would never darken their conversation in public: "Nigger!"[2] And their ever-proper language would drift into a slight dialect despite their attacks on "those Niggers who sprinkle 'aint's' throughout their speech or drop every 'g' as they murder the King's English."

When I remember being the fly on the wall during gatherings of my mother and her friends (which was a bit later in my life, when I was an adolescent and teen), their sessions were a bit more scurrilous, the language a bit more obscene, the subject matter often risque. But their hen parties were always marked by a constant stream of comic tales, outrageous anecdotes, new jokes, naughty sayings, and comic retorts. And when my Aunt Geneva visited, there was screaming before she reached the front door and the play attacks began:

1. Abraham Brown, the legendary free black from whom most of the members of my community and church were descended, was a proud and prosperous landowner and an active participant in the life of the third oldest black church in the United States, which he helped to found, for which he donated the land, and which he represented in meetings of Virginia's Dover Baptist Association from 1810 to 1825, rather an honor for a colored man of that day. His descendants, who include numerous prominent blacks, have always taken great pride in their distinguished forefather.

2. This term ranges in connotations from a term of endearment to a vilification, and it is used freely in conversations among many African Americans. Among upper-class blacks it tends more toward the pejorative. Blacks almost always consider "nigger" an offensive term when it is used by whites. Just how controversial the use of the term remains was suggested the day after I wrote the first draft of this chapter. The headline in the *Richmond Times-Dispatch* for November 2, 1996 (three days before the election) reporting the debate between Senator John Warner and his challenger Mark Warner was "Black Aide's Racial Slur Overshadows Debate." In conversation with Paul Gillis, president of the Virginia State Conference of the NAACP, Senator John Warner's African American aide had used the term "nigger," as had, he contends, the NAACP official. However, the aide's use of the term was the focus of the first question in the debate, and resulted in his immediate dismissal from Warner's staff. The aide contended that he and the NAACP official had both used the term in a joking manner, and he (and other members of the NAACP who spoke about it afterward) regarded it as a discussion that should have remained between the blacks involved in the initial conversation.

"Girl, do I see a gray hair in your head?"

"Not unless my hairdresser wants to get her tail whipped, but what you doing signifying on me, your baby sister? I know I see a whole lotta gray hairs in your head, girl! Haven't you ever met my friend, Lady Clairol?"

"Well, you know what they say, "Don't pay any attention to the snow on the mountain, cause it's still plenty fire in the furnace.""

"Honey, hush!"

And my mother's friend, Mrs. Evelyn Cotman, was, I thought when I was growing up and *know* now beyond a shadow of a doubt, the most hilarious comedienne to be found anywhere. Everybody sought her out to hear her "lie." Her comments, her responses, her gestures, her tales would literally have people rolling on the floor. Whatever I was doing, I would find some excuse to hang around when Aunt Geneva or Miss Evelyn was around—and even my efforts would be the cause of more humor:

"Chile, if you ever repeat what I said 'bout Ole Man————, I'll whup yo' ass good fo' you."

"Ronica, is this lil' womanish gal gon' sit here and hear us ole hens talk this trash?"

The friendly banter tinged with a few "colorful" (blue) words was, of course, a sign that I was being accepted as long as I remembered my place.

Similar scenarios continued through the years from my mother and her friends to my own generation, where humor has served to entertain, delight, heal, and create bonds for my friends and myself from elementary school through college and my adult life. And now I see myself in my daughter—a little shocked at the antics of some famous writer or doctor letting her hair down in a hen session, but trying to prove she's woman enough to at least hang around the fringes. When I reflect on these sessions (which I rarely do—I simply enjoy them), I'm happy that my daughter and her peers are sharing this tradition which is an education in life, in being black women, in dealing with the world, in deflecting the threatening blows, in relating to men, and loving (or at least not hating) themselves as blackbrownbeigecreamdamnnearwhitewomen with straightcurlybushy-kinkylongdamnneardowntothewaistmediumshorthair and breasts and hips of varied and sundry descriptions. I am happy that she is learning that laughter is not simply funny; it's serious medicine; it's righteous therapy. She who laughs . . . lasts.

Most African American women writers have been shaped by this "village" humor, though the earlier writers, fearful that they might reinforce stereotypes, were more restrained in revealing it than are their contemporary sisters. Still there are comic moments in many of the works of the early slave narrators, antebellum poets, and nineteenth-century novelists despite the fact that their primary tone is serious, tragic, and sentimental. Twentieth-century writers are much more freely reaching back to that traditional humor that has helped their mothers and their sisters to make it through the night, and are boldly and unabashedly using it to create a rich body of literature that frequently is characterized by its comic vein. The tone was set by Harlem Renaissance writer and personality Zora Neale Hurston, and continues with many of those established writers who have been on the scene for ten, twenty, thirty, forty, or more years, such as Dorothy West, Alice Childress, Maya Angelou, Paule Marshall, Louise Meriwether, Toni Morrison, Toni Cade Bambara, Ann Petry, Nikki Giovanni, Ntozake Shange, Gloria Naylor, and Carolyn Rodgers. And there are a whole host of more recent writers who promise us that we can continue to make it through the night. (Note that even their titles are often funny.) There are the hilarious essays in Bonnie Allen's *We Are Overcome* and Lisa Jones's *bulletproof diva;* there are the sometimes sidesplitting novels such as Tina McElroy Ansa's *Ugly Ways,* April Sinclair's *Coffee Will Make You Black* and *Ain't Gonna Be the Same Fool Twice,* Dori Sanders's *Her Own Place,* and Terry McMillan's *Waiting to Exhale;* there are the comic episodes in detective stories, such as Barbara Neely's *Blanche Among the Talented Tenth* and Valerie Wilson Wesley's *Devils' Gonna Get Him;* there are the frequently uproarious autobiographies, such as Flo Kennedy's *Color Me Flo,* Bebe Moore Campbell's *Sweet Summer: Growing up with and without My Dad,* Jill Nelson's *Volunteer Slavery: My Authentic Negro Experience,* and the Delany Sister's *Having Our Say;* there are the humorous advice books that include Mother Love's *Listen Up, Girlfriends!* and Julia Boyd's *Girlfriend to Girlfriend: Everyday Wisdom and Affirmations from the Sister Circle;* and miscellaneous other works, such as Ruby Dee's *My One Good Nerve*—all represented in this anthology, along with a number of other previously unpublished talents.

Black female singers also traditionally introduced some humor into their acts; the routines and lyrics of artists such as Josephine Baker and Billie Holiday and all of the blues greats were often comic, as were the acts of vaudevillians such as Sweetie May of Stringbeans and Sweetie May and Susie of Butterbeans and Susie—but these performances were not considered appropriate for respectable audiences—a number of black people still regard blues and jazz and the like as sinful music and their performers as the disciples of the devil.

There were limited dramatic opportunities for those black actresses who at least appeared to play into the popular stereotypes of the comic mammies, coons, and jezebels, such as Hattie McDaniel, Louise Beavers, Ethel Waters, Josephine Baker, Butterfly McQueen, and Ernestine Wade (who played Sapphire on the *Amos n' Andy Show*). Many of these earlier comic actresses, forced into demeaning roles, nonetheless found ways to speak a dual tongue and to maintain some dignity and provide some depth to their performances, thereby rising above the stereotype and injecting some authentic and often ironic Negro humor into their characters. Offstage, they also humorously reflected on the irony of their situation. In response to those who attacked her for accepting roles as a maid, Hattie McDaniel is reported to have retorted, "I can either *play* a maid for two hundred dollars a day or work as a maid for two dollars!"

The opportunities for the development of comediennes has been even more difficult than those for actresses and writers because of attitudes toward women and humor as well as women performing in nightclubs. Notwithstanding these and other problems, a few brave female comediennes broke the ice, comics such as Moms Mabley, and later LaWanda Page and Flo Kennedy. Even current day comediennes still face a number of hostile audiences—male and female, black and white—who resent women dealing with and joking about issues that they find completely acceptable from male performers. Nonetheless a number of comics have found wide audiences and some are making big bucks—a group headed by Whoopi Goldberg and including Marsha Warfield, Kim Coles, Kim Wayans, Phyllis Stickney, and Hazelle.

But these writers, comic actresses, and stand-up comediennes are but the beneficiaries and transmitters of the tradition of African American women's humor to the wider audience. The true creators, the authentic sources are to be found among the ordinary folk in the black communities where the comic vision was planted and Jes Grew.[3] And this vibrant folk tradition has been recorded by some collectors, including Zora Neale Hurston and myself.

Despite this rich history of humor in literature, on the stage, and in the folk tradition, African American women have been pretty much ignored in every kind of study of humor—American humor, women's humor, African American humor. It's not too much of an exaggeration to play on a previous observation and argue that insofar as treatments of humor are concerned, all the Americans are male WASPs, all the women are white, and all the African Americans are men. There are scores of studies of American humor; most barely mention either African American men or women; those that do often treat them as stereotypical objects of humor in white productions: Arthur Hudson's two-volume *Humor of the Old Deep South* (1936), for example, has one chapter titled "Darkies," with all of the selections taken from white authors—it apparently does not occur to him to look elsewhere for what he describes as "the authentic 'corn field Negro.' " Stephen Gale's 1988 *Encyclopedia of American Humorists,* which touts itself as "the most comprehensive and up-to-date reference text on American and Canadian humorists ever published" does not have one entry that I recognize as an African American woman.

There are scores of studies of varied aspects of American humor—sectional, thematic, etc.; here coverage of black women ranges from conspicuous absence in most to a paragraph or two in some (such as Ron Jenkins's *Subversive Laughter*), to a rare reasonable inclusion such as that in Roy Blount's *Book of Southern Humor.*

There are scores of treatments of women's humor (and these are rather recent): most of them say nothing about black women, and others give them short shrift. For just a few examples, Regina Barreca's *They Used to Call Me Snow White* gives one paragraph to black women; Gloria Kaufman and Mary Kay Blakely's *Pulling Our Own Strings* includes two poems by Nikki Giovanni and Sonia Sanchez and a couple of brief selections from Flo Kennedy; Nancy Walker's chapter on "The Humor of the Minority"

3. I play here on Ishmael Reed's use of Jes Grew in *Mumbo Jumbo* (influenced by James Weldon Johnson in his *The Book of American Negro Poetry*) to refer to the manner in which powerful and persistent aspects of African culture just grow and cannot be destroyed through legislation, violence, scurrilous attacks, or assimilation. Jes Grew continues to spring up all over the place and to "infect"/vitalize the souls that it inhabits.

in *A Very Serious Thing* looks at African-American and Jewish women's humor, treating Alice Childress and Zora Neale Hurston and not even giving a footnote to Moms Mabley and Dorothy West. Notable exceptions are John Lowe's analytical study of the humor in Zora Neale Hurston *(Jump at the Sun);* and the treatment of black women fully or in part in at least three essays in Gail Finney's *Look Who's Laughing.*

There are a few treatments of African American humor; they focus on African American men. The best of these, Mel Watkin's *On the Real Side,* mentions a number of women, but I doubt that more than twenty pages of his 652-page book deal with women. He lists only two women in his bibliography of fiction. In *The History of Negro Humor in America,* William Schechter spends more time on the Smothers Brothers than he does on black women; he has one paragraph on Moms Mabley and lists one woman in his bibliography.

In most of the studies and anthologies of humor, when African American women are included, they are considered in the narrow terms of the subject of the study, often ignoring other aspects of their being—in the studies of women's humor, they are viewed simply as women, ignoring their race; in the studies of African American humor, they are usually treated merely as African Americans, ignoring their gender; and so on with Southern humor or subversive humor, etc., etc.

It is certainly time to give some attention to that brand of humor that evolves from the unique culture/history/experience of the African American female in this nation. There is no previous anthology of African American women's humor, nor is there an analytical study of that body of humor. The goal of this book is to remedy that situation by presenting and briefly commenting upon all forms of African American women's humor from slavery to the present, incorporating representative selections from literature, popular culture, and folklore, including slave narratives, autobiographies, novels, short stories, essays, poems, plays, jokes, proverbs, comic routines, dozens, raps, blues, spirituals, cartoons, paintings, children's songs and sayings, acronyms, and mimeographed sheets.[4]

4. Alan Dundes and Carl R. Pagter have labeled this folk item "folklore from the paperwork empire." This is a new form of folklore that results, obviously, from the presence of copiers in the workplace and the home. Individuals make copies of a drawing, narrative, verse, cartoon, or tale for their friends and pass them around. Some individuals make changes, create new versions of these pieces, and copy and circulate them. As Dundes and Pagter point out, the individual creators of these copies are not known. Though sometimes

The experiences of the African American female have been comprehensive and her humor is wide ranging and inclusive. Several items here may be familiar to readers as material that is popular in their white, Jewish, black male, and varied other racial and ethnic groups. Folklore circulates broadly and occurs simultaneously among different peoples. It is quite clear that African American women like other groups have created and passed down as well as adopted and adapted many items that appear elsewhere. It is clear also that white Americans have shown a fascination with black humor and that they have consciously studied and copied that humor from slavery onward through the minstrels, the Uncle Remus tales, and, more recently, white comics who regularly visited the Apollo and other black clubs with their secretaries to record the material of black performers or to, as Jerry Lewis informs, study and emulate their routines, delivery, and timing. The fascination of white Americans with black humor is documented by numerous of their own accounts, such as this comment by J. Kennard in the *Knickerbocker Magazine* in 1845:

> Who are our true rulers? The Negro poets, to be sure. Do they not set the fashion, and give laws to the public taste? Let one of them, in the swamps of Carolina, compose a new song, and it no sooner reaches the ear of a white amateur, than it is written down, amended (that is, almost spoilt), printed, and then put upon a course of rapid dissemination to cease only with the utmost bounds of Anglo-Saxondom, perhaps with the world. Meanwhile, the poor author digs away with his hoe, utterly ignorant of his greatness.[5]

We know as well that blacks have taken the humor directed by whites toward them and "switched the yoke and changed the joke." The rationale for inclusion in this anthology is not origins (which would be impossible

---

a name appears on them, variants are often found with another name. Thus it is not possible to declare that these pieces *originate* with black women. However, the mimeographed items included in this anthology do circulate among and are popular with black women. I should also warn that many of the items from the paperwork empire are obscene and may be offensive in other ways to varied ethnic or gender groups. For a more detailed discussion of this folk form, see Dundes and Pagter's *Urban Folklore from the Paperwork Empire* and *When You're up to Your Ass in Alligators.*

5. Cited in Eileen Southern, *The Music of Black Americans: A History,* 103.

in most instances to determine) but popularity among African American women.

Thus, at times it may appear to the reader that the humor included here is more female than black; at other times it may appear more black than female; sometimes more American or Southern or white than either African or female. Occasionally, a selection simply reflects on the human condition without regard to race, gender, or place. Race and gender are paramount here because they are so consequential in our society, but everything black women laugh about does not center on these issues.

Now, having recognized that certain shared humorous pieces often remind us of how closely related we all are, it is important to recognize that we are dealing here with a distinctive body of humor, one that reflects the spirit of the African American female. This body of humor stems basically from what it is to be a black, a female, a human being in America; what it is to be a part of that long line of those who sailed in the hold of the ships on the middle passage, rode on the underground railroad, sat on the back of Southern buses, joined in the March on Washington and cheered on their brothers during the Million Man March. It includes variously all those other important identifying factors that make us what we are: an artist, mother, wife, sister, lesbian, who may be fat, skinny, tall, short, young, old, rich, poor, rural, urban, Northern, Southern, etc., etc. All of these come together in members of the sisterhood circle to create that special perspective on ourselves, our race, our gender, our family, our community, our nation, and our world that defines us and our humor. As a body of material, it reflects the *spirit* of African American women.

In addition to a propensity for subject matter and themes that most often speak to our experience in this nation, African American women's humor is often characterized by a certain style that includes a predilection for satire and irony, a delight in the irreverant, a vigorous sense of *force vitale,* an insistence on reality ("be real!"), a love of contest/challenge/debate, and a delight in drama and kinesics: the black woman worldwide is noted for that most atavistic of all African American gestures—cut-eye, suck teeth, an insulting gesture of disdain, eliciting one of the most vehement reprimands from black mothers: "Girl, don't you cut/roll your eyes at me!" The black woman is also noted for that arching of the eyebrow and "the stare," as well as some unique head bobbing, neck swiveling, hip swinging, finger pointing, hands on hips stances, and other gesticulations that form a dynamic vocabulary of their own. But the most distinctive aspect of the style of black women's humor is her language, which has moved me to end each chapter with a list of her sayings, proverbs, figures of speech, cracks, philosophical reflections, riddles, and other memorable aphorisms.

The literature, popular culture, and folklore of African American women reflect their love of musical, rhythmical language; their tremendous range of tonal inflections; their delight in rhyme, colorful metaphor, and simile, and pure sound; and their affinity for verbal play and name-calling. You will also observe that when African American women are joking around, they often slip into an idiom that is uniquely black, one that includes a propensity for double negatives, double comparisons, verbal nouns, and repetitions. In addition, our vocabulary is made interesting by black slang expressions, jive talk, stock phrases, and a few obscenities, as well as frequent biblical allusions and quotations. Even the most sophisticated raconteurs usually revert to Nation language[6] in closed company—indeed the stories, jokes, and proverbs lose much of their flavor in standard English. And when amid the laughter sparked by some tale or joke, you hear a playful entreaty, "Honey, hush!" then you *know* that you are in the midst of African American women.

This delight in experimentation with sound, imagistic phrases, musical expressions, and with the catchy rhythms of the old-fashioned church service has greatly influenced the style and language of our writers. As Paule Marshall has declared, "Language is the only homeland" (and here she is referring to the language of the "poets in the kitchen," those women whose conversations around the kitchen table shaped her writing). Asked about her language, Toni Cade Bambara asserted that she prefers "the language of Langston Hughes, the language of Grandma, the language of 'mama sez' ";[7] and Rosa Guy has noted that the speech patterns the female writers in the African Diaspora had sometimes ridiculed as children have now "be[come] our poetry."

African American women's humor like that of any other group is based on shared experiences, and on some levels, it is strictly in-group humor. But the reader who is not a part of this community will find that he/she likely

6. Phrase coined by Kamau Brathwaite to replace terms that have a derogatory significance, such as dialect, creole, patois, and broken English.

7. *First World* 2 (1980), 48.

shares some experiences with black women's concerns in their humor, whether those concerns deal with race, gender, sexual identification, economic and social class, occupation, politics, home and neighborhoods, school and education, family relationships, marital problems, or a host of other commonalities. And laughter is, after all, contagious. Now that I'm bringing it out of the laughing barrel, others might find themselves unable to resist the temptation to join in that laughter. Nothing more than mutual laughter can bind people together and build bridges of understanding, as Regina Barreca suggests in *They Used to Call Me Snow White:* "When you laugh with someone . . . [y]ou're connected. You're standing on the same turf. Laughing together is as close as you can get to a hug without touching."

Finally, laughter contributes to health—it relieves stress, lowers blood pressure, helps control pain, changes moods, helps you to deal with problems, develops a sense of empowerment, provides a more objective view of events, builds morale, and provides philosophical instruction. It is, doctors now tell us, an aerobic exercise and an internal massage, exercising the lungs and stimulating the circulatory system.

The reader should be warned that there is something in this anthology to offend everyone. There are off-color jokes, lewd language, ethnic and racist slurs and stereotypes. Everyone may at one point or another see him/herself as the target of insensitive gibes. But African American women's humor is an equal opportunity offender, as likely to target black women for vicious attack as white women, white men, black men, Jews, Southerners, homosexuals, fat people, old people, rural people, poor people, everybody, anybody! A few entries will undoubtedly offend your moral principals. At points in my introductory commentary, even I, in the interest of maintaining a tone appropriate to my subject, find myself sounding a blue note. Finally, humor is often unkind, unfair, and unjust. In *Jump at the Sun: Zora Neale Hurston's Cosmic Comedy,* John Lowe aptly notes, "The comic . . . walks a narrow [and I would add, constantly wavering] line between pleasurable surprise and uncomfortable shocks."

The material in this book is the natural delight of my life, what I grew up with, what created bonds of friendship for me, what I read whenever I get a chance, what helps me through the night, what I want to pass on to others. I see no need to summon Jung and Freud or even Fanon to discuss it (though I may occasionally drop their names here or there to make a few of my academic friends happy). I loved it just as much before I ever heard those names as I do now. All you linguists, theorists, psychoanalysts, structuralists, deconstructionists, feminists, womanists, black aestheticians, and Marxists are welcome to do what you want with this material, but as for me, I'm going to just plain have some good laughs and a healthy massage as I enjoy it anew with you, my new friends, 'cause I'm not metaphysical, and I expect you're not exegetical.[8]

Honey, hush!

No need to waste time with further introductions. The sisters are already here and gathered around the table—behind the closed door, of course. But I'm opening the door for you—men and women of whatever color or creed. Drop your inhibitions and sensitivities and prudishness at the door. Come on in and join the party!

8. I allude to Sterling Brown's response to Robert Penn Warren's line from "Pondy Woods": "Nigger, your breed ain't metaphysical"; Brown's response: "Cracker, your breed ain't exegetical." See Henry Louis Gates, Jr., *The Signifying Monkey.*

Acknowledgments

I would like to thank my editor, Ms. Amy Cherry, with whom I first shared the idea for this book in an unrelated telephone call, and whose enthusiasm and encouragement immediately took the idea out of the realm of a farfetched dream that one never mentioned to anyone and transformed it into a planned project with specific procedures and a due date.

My thanks also go to the Wintergreen Collective, the next to hear about this dream with a due date. They immediately sat down to share humor, suggested works to be included, promised contributions, and provided helpful ideas, and have remained ardent supporters and encouragers throughout. I am especially grateful to Ms. Nikki Giovanni, who at this early stage of germination readily agreed to my request that she write a foreword and who contributed generously of her own work to this collection. When this work was nearing completion and my publisher and I were preparing announcements, I still had not settled on a title. After much agonizing, I finally wrote to my Wintergreen friends and urgently solicited their help. Within a couple of days, I was being bombarded with excellent suggestions from these creative ladies. "Honey, Hush!" came from our founder, Dr. Joanne V. Gabbin, and the moment she said it in her inimitable way, I knew that I had the title to my book. Special kudos to you, Joanne!

I am greatly indebted to my graduate assistant, Ms. Alison Workman, whose contributions are too numerous to list. Suffice it to say that she is an energetic worker, a bright and efficient researcher, and a talented writer who generously shared her energies and her talents.

Other friends and acquaintances offered encouragement, performed tasks, shared tales, sayings, and anecdotes, suggested literature to include, provided information, gave me helpful advice, offered me reprieves from my labor, and in varying other ways contributed to this project. Among them are Dr. Deborah Smith Barney, Dr. Jill Busey, Mrs. Calvine Battle, Mrs. Dorothy Chambers, Ms. Clotilde Coleman, Mrs. Margaret Crews, Mrs. Elaine Crocker, Mrs. Carolyn Daughtry, Mr. J. Ghaphery, Mrs. Shirley Harris, Mrs. Bulinda Hereford-Crawley, Dr. James L. Hill, Mrs. Clara Hoggard, Mr. David Hoggard, Mrs. Marie Hunter, Dr. Mae C. Johnson, Dr. M. Thomas Inge, Mrs. Wendolyn Johnson, Mrs. Sylvia Lambert, Dr. John Lowe, Ms. Paule Marshall, Dr. Eddie Moore, Dr. Joyce Pettis, Mrs. Jo Ann Pugh, Dr. Margaret Reid, Mrs. Delores Robinson, Dr. Charles Wilson, and my mother, the late Mrs. Veronica Bell Cumber.

The above list of those who contributed to this project in progress does not include those whose influences throughout my life motivated this project and whose voices and tales still reverberate through my mind and echo throughout this work in various ways. It is impossible to list them all here: some I have never known personally; the names of others are lost to me; a few very prominent influences are mentioned in my introductory chapter.

The writers whose works appear in this book make the anthology possible, of course, and I thank them for enriching our literature and sharing their talents with me here.

I am indebted also to various libraries for special assistance. Some individuals deserve special notice, but lest I omit a few, let me simply offer inclusive thanks to the staffs of Boatwright Memorial Library at the University of Richmond, with special kudos to the Reference, Acquisitions, Interlibrary Loan, and Media Resource Center staffs; the University of Richmond Music Library; the James Branch Cabell Library at Virginia Commonwealth University; the Hampton University Archives; the Library of Congress; the Johnston Memorial Library at Virginia State University; and the Moorland-Spingarn Research Center at Howard University.

Finally, I thank my children who energetically support every project with the hopes that I'll get it out of the way and finally get to write the family history. I owe special thanks to my middle child, Allen Cumber Dance, who frequently spends his weekends and holidays setting up and repairing my office machinery, updating my computer equipment, and providing me guidance and instructions on understanding and working with all the newfangled inventions that I can't do without, but can't quite master, and who has been known to sit at the phone for hours to talk me through some problem I am having with my computer or printer or fax. My youngest, Daryl Lynn Dance, deserves particular acknowledgment for typing, filing, running to the library, suggesting pieces for this work, and providing much helpful information on contemporary humor and comics. Thank you also to my oldest children, Warren Carlton Dance, Jr., and Tadelech Edjigu Dance, who offer me a pleasant change of scenery whenever I need to get away (much of the early work on this project was begun at their Houston, Texas, home). My grandson, Yoseph Warren Dance, contributed nothing more than his appearance during the time that this project was in the works, but that was the greatest gift of all!

Honey, Hush!

CHAPTER 1

"No Big Thing for 'Oman"

THE POWER AND STRENGTH OF THE

BLACK WOMAN

[If a *woman* had been the first person on the moon, she would have declared,] "That's one big step for *mankind*, but no big thing for 'oman."
—Barbara Cloudon, Speech at the Trinidad Conference on Caribbean
Women Writers, St. Augustine, Trinidad, 1991

Though it is little known outside the African American female community, the bad men who are celebrated in black legends, such as Shine, Stagolee, The Great McDaddy, and John Henry, have their female counterparts, who share many of their "heroic" traits and superhuman exploits. The female superwomen too are ba-ad—that is they are often willing to violate the dictates of white America and the moral code of the "respectable" black community, and they certainly always succeed at tasks and achieve goals generally presumed beyond the power of females. Their "ba-adness," as with men's, is often seen in their uncommon strength, courage, guile, and aggressiveness. It is also seen occasionally in their *style,* in the way they walk that walk and talk that talk. Often, too, they are sharp tricksters, whose wit allows them to triumph over and to humiliate their enemies.

Analagous to the ba-ad men, the ba-ad women are often characterized

1

as irresistable and seductive Erzulies,[1] capable of phenomenal sexual exploits. Their allure is commonly expressed in blues lyrics such as Clara Smith's in which she declares that she has everything she needs to seduce men; and once she has them, she brags, "I'll treat them kind of rough / Then I'll show them how I can do my stuff." A similar confidence is expressed by Maya Angelou's speaker's in "Still I Rise": "I dance like I've got diamonds / At the meeting of my thighs."

But one of the most popular traits of the ba-ad woman is her verbal dexterity. Black women have always appreciated *Nommo*—the force of the word, the power of giving things their names and thereby bestowing upon them her life force.[2] One of the distinctive marks of the black woman's verbal power has been her *sassiness.* Both in her speech and in her behavior, the sassy female is impudent, saucy, vigorous, lively, smart, and stylish. Joanne M. Braxton, in *Black Women Writing Autobiography,* provides an etymology of the term:

> *Sass* is a word of West African derivation that is associated with the female aspect of the trickster. The *Oxford English Dictionary* attributes the word's origin to the poisonous "sassy tree." A decoction of the bark of this tree was used in West Africa as an ordeal poison in the trial of accused witches, women spoken of as being wives of Exu, the trickster god. In her 1893 *Autobiography,* Amanda Smith, an independent black missionary, wrote: "I don't know as any one has ever found what the composition of this sassy wood really is; but I am told it is a mixture of certain barks. They say that it is one of their medicines that they used for punishing witches so you cannot find out what it is. The accused had *two gallons* to drink. If she throws it up, she has gained her case." So, obviously, "sass" can kill.

As one might imagine, the worst thing a black woman could do to her master, the worst thing a black woman could do to her husband, the worst

---

1. Erzulie is the beautiful Vodoun goddess of love, whom Zora Neale Hurston describes as "the perfect female [who] must be loved and obeyed. . . . She is the ideal of the love bed. She is so perfect that all other women are a distortion as compared to her" (*Tell My Horse,* 144).

2. William H. Robinson, in his *Nommo,* points out that "Nommo is a term common to several African languages."

thing a black girl could do to her parents was *sass* those authority figures. Such a female was *bad*. But for those in the female community who sympathize and associate with the black female, these same acts of sassing elicit much celebration and admiration. Such a female is *ba-ad!*

Other indications of intellectual acumen and verbal dexterity also mark the ba-ad black woman; she can brag as brazenly as the man; she can sweet-talk as persuasively as the male seducer; she can play the dozens with any brother. Like her male counterpart she is often a sharp signifier, a rhyming rapper, and an inveterate liar. The female's engagement in verbal repartee has a long history going back to Africa, and it is, perhaps, most familiar to many in this century from female responses to males in many musical forms, including the blues and raps. Female blues singers for example have countered attacks on black women's color, hair, and size with traditional lines such as: "I ain't good lookin' / ain't got great long hair / But I got ways, Baby, that can take me anywhere"; and "I'm a big fat mama, meat shakin' on my bones / Everytime I shimmy, some skinny gal lose her home." Blues singers who applaud the "Wild Woman" (see p. 23) are among those who most often presented themselves as ba-ad.

Needless to say, when the black female personae are in contest with the broader society, the White male or female, the black male, or some less sympathetic black female, their independence, their impudence, their spunkiness, their physical power, their sass, their wit, their quick retort, their indestructibility provide much pleasure and pride and laughter to an African American female audience. This is, after all, a society and a community in which the black woman has historically been viewed as the least powerful among us. Yet the amazing reality is that despite the harsh realities of their existence, despite a long history of deprivation, repression, humiliation, and debasement, an impressive number of black women (historical and fictive) have asserted through their humor (and other means) a positive sense of self-identity, a healthy ego, and even frequently an outspoken, forthright assertion of superiority. They are *ba-ad!*

Honey, hush!

MIMEOGRAPHED ITEM

Masterpiece

Sure God created Man before Woman, but then you always make a rough draft before the Final Masterpiece.

Nikki Giovanni

EGO TRIPPING
(THERE MAY BE A REASON WHY)

from *The Women and the Men*

i was born in the congo
I walked to the fertile crescent and built
   the sphinx
I designed a pyramid so tough that a star
   that only glows every one hundred years falls
   into the center giving divine perfect light
I am bad

I sat on the throne
   drinking nectar with allah
I got hot and sent an ice age to europe
   to cool my thirst
My oldest daughter is nefertiti
   the tears from my birth pains

created the nile
I am a beautiful woman

I gazed on the forest and burned
    out the sahara desert
    with a packet of goat's meat
    and a change of clothes
I crossed it in two hours
I am a gazelle so swift
    so swift you can't catch me

    For a birthday present when he was three
I gave my son hannibal an elephant
    He gave me rome for mother's day
My strength flows ever on

    My son noah built new/ark and
I stood proudly at the helm
    as we sailed on a soft summer day
I turned myself into myself and was
    jesus
    men intone my loving name
    All praises All praises
I am the one who would save

    I sowed diamonds in my back yard
My bowels deliver uranium
    the filings from my fingernails are
    semi-precious jewels
    On a trip north
I caught a cold and blew
My nose giving oil to the arab world
I am so hip even my errors are correct
I sailed west to reach east and had to round off
    the earth as I went
    The hair from my head thinned and gold was laid
    across three continents

I am so perfect so divine so ethereal so surreal
I cannot be comprehended
    except by my permission

I mean . . . I . . . can fly
    like a bird in the sky . . .

Roxanne Shanté

HAVE A NICE DAY

Some people call me Shanny, some people call me Rox
Those who try to I just knocks them out the box
'Cause I'm Shanté an' y'all know the routine
An' here we go again so all hail the queen
I left for a while but it was worth the wait
Because it gave me just enough time to create
A funky rhythm that's guaranteed to move the world
Have the party people screamin' now, "Go on girl"
It's like Diana Ross, I'm the boss
An' those who disapprove you can go for yours
But to think a girl like me, ha, is easy to take
Treat me like Nell Carter, give me a break
'Cause I'm a super female that's called Shanté
And like Hurricane Annie I'll blow you away
Whenever I'm in a battle, yo, I don't play
So you best go about your way
An' have a nice day

A lot of M.C.s today really know how to please
But I gave birth to most of them M.C.s
So when it comes around to the month of May
Send me your royalty check for Mother's Day
Because, yo, ya know, ya can't deal with this

I'm Shanté, the microphone grand mistress
I pioneered like Lola Falana
With a name that stands big like Madonna
Speaking of Madonna, some girls on the mike
Rap like virgins and get real tight
But I get loose with the rhymes I produce
That's why I'm queen of the crew with the juice
'Cause I'm a super female that's called Shanté
And like Hurricane Annie I'll blow you away
Whenever I'm in a battle, yo, I don't play
So you best go about your way
And have a nice day

Shanté—the baddest around
And a name like that can't be broken down
As supreme highness or mighty noble topic exponent
An' any title for a girl you can't believe I own
'Cause to me there ain't none fresher
For me to rock—my pleasure
I'll pick up the microphone and start rockin'
Say the funky rhymes that have the people clockin'
Me, the S-h-a-n-t-é
Good lookin', never tooken' female M.C.

Carolyn M. Rodgers

LIVING WATER, IV

from how i got ovah

there IS a well in me
    if i open up i can
        flow forever
    i am surely a shout that can
        shimmy right on up to heaven

        i think sometimes
          when i write
        God has his hand on me
    i am his little black slim ink pen.

Frances Ellen Watkins Harper

LEARNING TO READ

from *Sketches of Southern Life*

Very soon the Yankee teachers
    Came down and set up school;
But, oh! how the Rebs did hate it,—
    It was agin' their rule.

Our masters always tried to hide
    Book learning from our eyes;
Knowledge did'nt agree with slavery—
    'Twould make us all too wise.

But some of us would try to steal
    A little from the book,
And put the words together,
    And learn by hook or crook.

I remember Uncle Caldwell,
    Who took pot-liquor fat
And greased the pages of his book,
    And hid it in his hat.

And had his master ever seen
    The leaves upon his head,
He'd have thought them greasy papers,
    But nothing to be read.

And there was Mr. Turner's Ben,
   Who heard the children spell,
And picked the words right up by heart,
   And learned to read 'em well.

Well, the Northern folks kept sending
   The Yankee teachers down;
And they stood right up and helped us,
   Though Rebs did sneer and frown.

And, I longed to read my Bible,
   For precious words it said;
But when I begun to learn it,
   Folks just shook their heads,

And said there is no use trying,
   Oh! Chloe, you're too late;
But as I was rising sixty,
   I had no time to wait.

So I got a pair of glasses,
   And straight to work I went,
And never stopped till I could read
   The hymns and Testament.

Then I got a little cabin—
   A place to call my own—
And I felt as independent
   As the queen upon her throne.

Hazelle

I NOT GOING TO STOP TIL I MAKE IT TO DE TOP

SCENE ONE

An obvious immigrant from the Caribbean, Hazelle's character Millie enters wearing a straw hat and carrying an American flag. Her hair is in dreadlocks. She is obviously being hassled by unseen immigration authorities.

Leave me bags alone. Leave me bags alone! I don't have no mangos in dere. . . .* Tank you, Jesus. I *finally* reach. Take a *long,* long time, but, honey, I *finally* reach. Dis is America. New York, where dey say plenty plenty money grow on trees. . . . Look at all de White people *[gesturing and waving towards the audience].* . . . Hello. . . . Hello. . . . Look at all de White people wit' dem *children.* Dey will be needing babysitters, and I am ready for dem. No work is too hard for me, honey. De Empire State Building, de Statue of *Liberteee!* God bless dis America, de land of de rich and de free. You know I don't know why in New York all dose damn nasty people want to live on de street: You too damn nasty. Get up from dere. You smelling like pee. Move. . . . Move *[hitting out at unseen homeless folks with her flag]!*

[Crossing arms in front of her] Honey, I not going to stop til I make it to de top. I going to get a job. . . . Maybe two. . . . Maybe tree. . . . You know I so glad I get to leave dat poor hurricane little country. I *just* miss de tornado. . . . But I must make it fast because my family is depending on me. I want everybody, everybody, everybody to come to America an' be free. God bless dis America. It is a *savior* for me. . . .

Taxi, Taxi! *[sound of car passing].* Wait. I wasn't going to tell all ye dis, but I gon' talk it. . . . when I did get off de plane, de policeman come with a damn dog to smell me up. . . . De dog was sniffin' me up, sniffin' me up all under my dress. Den dey take me in some lickle room and start to feel up

---

* Ellipses are used throughout to indicate pauses and not omissions.

my person. I start to feel *guilty*. I almost give dem de two mangos I was hiding in. . . . *[the end of the sentence is drowned out by the audience's laughter]*. But I didn't want dem export me. I just close my eyes and pray. Dey tell me deys lookin' for contraband. What de hell I doin' with contraband? All de White women and dem comin' trew wit' dere hair in braids. . . . Yes, honey, when dey come down to de island on vacation dey like to braid dere hair and run around wit' de Rasta men and dem. . . . We call it "Rent-a-Dread. . . ." *Nobody* ever stop dem for contraband. Dey come to harass *me*. I tell you dat ting give me such a bad feeling 'bout de place. But I tell myself I not gon' let dem break my spirit. No. I not gon' let dem stop me before I start. I come here to make it to de *top*, and dat is where I'm going—to de *top*, top, top. Taxi . . . Ta . . . *[sound of taxi passing]*. You know where I come from de taxi does have two and tree and four people. . . . In America, a big taxi waiting just for me. . . . Taxi, Taxi. . . . *[sound of passing taxi]*. Seem like de blasted taxi man don't want to stop for me. . . . Damn crazy . . . *[sucks teeth in disgust]*. I gon' see all you. De next time all ye see me I gon' be at de *top*. Even if I have to *walk*. Because dat is where I come here to go—to de *top*, top, top. All ye take care, take care. Tank you, Jesus. Tank you. Tank you.

[She exits]

SCENE TWO

[Millie enters wearing an apron]

How are ya doin'? Hello. I so glad I get to see all ye again. Excuse me, I don't talk to nobody without my hat and my glove. Wait. You know, de lady I work for, she give me dis hat an' de glove *[Millie puts on a big red hat]*. Wait. Let me ask you someting. What you tink about dis hat? You tink red is a good color for me? *[Audience responds, "Yeah"]* An', honey, she give me de glove. You know, she's a very nice lady. You know, some of dese people, you work for dem, dey don't give you a blasted ting. You know what I mean? You just work, work, work. But she always giving me some little ting. Honey, dese gloves is French lace. Dey come straight from France. What you tink? You like? *[laughter at the unmatched gloves]*. What is wrong with de blasted glove? Like de glove is a reject. You know, you can't trust dese damn people. . . . All de work I does do for she, you don't tink she coulda give me a decent pair o' glove? Anyhow, I not gon' let she upset me. I am doing very, very well. Honey, I tell you, I sent up for my husband, Boisie, and my two children, Brenda and Hezekiah. Everybody's in the States now. And I have a couple of good jobs, you know. I am night cleaning down on Wall Street. Den, I have a tree-day-a-week job babysittin' on Park Avenue. After dat, I does run down to de East Village to clean a doctor's office. Dey say running helps you to keep slim. And I don't want you to tink I am boasting, but . . . I have my *own* house now. *[Audience applauds].* Tank you, tank you, tank you, darling, tank you. . . . And a little used car. . . . *[one person claps].* . . . Tank you. *[Hands on hips and facing audience]* Why you was lookin' at me like dat? You want to know how I do all dis so fast, eh? I does save my money, honey. Ye ever hear about sous-sous? Passna? It's like a Christmas club. Every week, ten of us from de island does get together and pool our money. I'm not like dose girls I work wit'. Every night dey want to buy Chinese food. De Chinaman have dat fry rice dere since last year. . . . He does keep it in a ting—dey call it a wok. . . . You know why dey call it a wok? Because dey have to wok it up with de soy sauce. . . . Not me, darling. I does bring my food from home. Rice and peas, dumplings, ackee, saltfish . . . *[cheers from the audience].* Yes, honey, you know what I talkin' 'bout. Yes. Honey, when you see I eat dat food dere so, I can work straight trew for a week. And de next ting dose girls I work with like to do; they always want to go on *vacation.* Where dey going? St. Thomas? Barbados? What I want to go to dose places for? . . . All you seein' in dose places is bush and water. . . . I just *leave* de bush and water. . . . De hurricane leave plenty a water. . . . I almost get wash *way* in de water. . . . Not me, darling, I staying right here. Because I have *big,* big plans. I plan on going to night school to learn about real estate. *[Cheers]* Tank you, darling. Not fake estate, you know, real estate. Honey, let me tell ya, I gon' buy up de whole a Eastern Parkway in Brooklyn. . . . An' I gonna call it Millie's Parkway. What you tink about dat?

Anyhow, I have to go; it gettin' late. I have an interview for another part-time job. Dis one is in a nursing home. But de next time all ye see me, honey, I promise you, I gonna be at de top, top, top. Because dat is where I come here to go—to de *top,* top, top. Let me hear you say it. To de *top,* top, top. *[Audience repeats "To de top, top, top"]* All ye take care, take care. Tank you, Jesus, I gon' see ya.

[She exits spiritedly]

SCENE THREE

[Millie is down on her knees scrubbing. Her usually vibrant voice is now tired and defeated.]

Lord, Jesus, I can't take it any more. . . . I can't take it any more, Jesus. Dey're trying to kill me, Lord; dey trying to kill me, Jesus. *[She stands, notices the audience, and projects some of her usual agressiveness.]*

All you come back again? You don't have any place to go? I'm doin' fine, fine, fine. . . . *[Her voice breaks again]* My husband, my husband is gone, gone, gone. He run away with dat big, fat woman down de road dere. . . . She had big, big titties out to here *[illustrating]*. . . . Dey tell you to keep *slim* so you can keep *him*. I *run* everywhere, I run everywhere, trying to keep *slim* to keep *him*, . . . an' what he do? He run away with dat big, fat woman down de road dere. . . . I guess big is in. . . . An' I have *pain* all over my body. Look how my hand twist up *[holding hand out]*. When all ye did first see me, was my hand twist up so? *[Audience responds "No."]* No. I go to de doctor. He say I have art-writis. I am not an *artist*. I don't *write* anybody. How de hell I get art-writis? . . . De other day I wake up with a pain from de *top* of my head straight down to my little toe. I go to de hospital. . . . King's County. . . . *Don't* go dere! . . . Dey wouldn't even give me an aspirin. Dey want to know if I have insurance. A poor man was sitting dere. Blood running from de top of his head straight into his mout'. An' all he keep saying is "Lover's Lane—he wasn't in Lover's Lane. . . ."

It's like a hurricane come an' hit my life. An' I have *so* many bills to pay. *Bills,* bills, bills. And for what? . . . *[Voice becomes very depressed]* My husband is gone. De children is big men and women now; dey don't have uses for me again. I tink I should retire while I can still walk. But I must say one ting. God bless America. *[Assertive voice returns]* Yes, I gon' say it, man. All ye see what does happen aroun' de world when de people try to speak out and de government kill dem? In American, I can say any *damn* ting I please. I can tell Mr. Bush, "You was no *damn* good, I glad you're gone!" . . . So I say, God bless America. . . .

[Long pause and then she speaks in a soft, pensive tone] But I tinkin' 'bout heading back home, man. Dis going to de top, top, top is killin' me. . . . I rented my tree houses. I sell de little use car. I already buy myself a ticket. I am going home. . . . *[Audience signs sympathetically and she responds in more upbeat tone]* No, it's all right. It's all right. All ye need to come go with me

because when I look at all you, all you look like dey're killin' you here. . . .
You need a little vacation. So, if you ever decide to come down to my is-
land for a little vacation, ask anybody in de village for *me,* Miss Millie.
I buildin' a *big,* big hotel . . . by de bush, near de water. I gon' see all you.
All ye take care. Take care. Tank you, Jesus. Tank you. I gone. Tank
you, Lord.

    [She exits, limping and beaten]

Margaret Walker

KISSIE LEE

Toughest gal I ever did see
Was a gal by the name of Kissie Lee;
The toughest gal God ever made
And she drew a dirty, wicked blade.

Now this here gal warn't always tough
Nobody dreamed she'd turn out rough
But her Grammaw Mamie had the name
Of being the town's sin and shame.

When Kissie Lee was young and good
Didn't nobody treat her like they should
Allus gettin' beat by a no-good shine
An' allus quick to cry and whine.

Till her Grammaw said, "Now listen to me,
I'm tiahed of yoah whinin', Kissie Lee.
People don't ever treat you right,
An' you allus scrappin' or in a fight.

"Whin I was a gal wasn't no soul
Could do me wrong an' still stay whole.
Ah got me a razor to talk for me
An' aftah that they let me be."

Well Kissie Lee took her advice
And after that she didn't speak twice
'Cause when she learned to stab and run
She got herself a little gun.

And from that time that gal was mean,
Meanest mama you ever seen.
She could hold her likker and hold her man
And she went thoo life jus' raisin' san'.

One night she walked in Jim's saloon
And seen a guy what spoke too soon;
He done her dirt long time ago
When she was good and feeling low.

Kissie bought her drink and she paid her dime
Watchin' this guy what beat her time
And he was making for the outside door
When Kissie shot him to the floor.

Not a word she spoke but she switched her blade
And flashing that lil ole baby paid:
Evvy livin' guy got out of her way
Because Kissie Lee was drawin' her pay.

She could shoot glass doors offa the hinges,
She could take herself on the wildest binges.
And she died with her boots on switching blades
On Talledega Mountain in the likker raids.

Maggie Pogue Johnson

OLD MAID'S SOLILOQUY

from *Virginia Dreams/Lyrics for the Idle Hour*

I'se been upon de karpet,
    Fo' lo, dese many days;
De men folks seem to sneer me,
    In der kin' ob way.

But I don't min' der foolin',
    Case I sho' is jis as fine
As any Kershaw pumpkin
    A hangin on de vine.

I looks at dem sometimes,
    But hol's my head up high,
Case I is fer above dem
    As de moon is in de sky.

Dey sho' do t'ink dey's so much,
    But I sho' is jis as fine
As eny sweet potato
    Dat's growd up from de vine.

Dey needn't t'ink I's liken dem,
    Case my match am hard to fin',
En I don't want de watermillion
    Dat's lef' upon de vine.

Case I ain't no spring chicken,
    Dis am solid talk,
En I don't want anything
    Dat's foun' upon de walk.

Case ef I'd wanted anything,
    I'd hitched up years ago,
En had my sher ob trouble.
    But my min' tol' me no.

I'd rader be a single maid,
    A wanderin' bout de town,
Wid skercely way to earn my bread,
    En face all made ob frowns,—

Den hitched up to some numbskull,
    Wid skercely sense to die,
En I know I cud'n kill him,
    Dar'd be no use to try.

So don't let ol' maids boder you,
    I'll fin' a match some day,
Or else I'll sho' 'main single,
    You hear me what I say!

I specs to hol' my head up high
    En always feel as free
As any orange blossom
    A hangin' on de tree.

Bessie Smith

BACKWATER BLUES

Back in Black Mountain, a child will smack your face,
Back in Black Mountain, a child will smack your face,
Babies cryin' for liquor, and all the birds sing bass.

Black Mountain people are bad as they can be,
Black Mountain people are bad as they can be,
They uses gun powder just to sweeten their tea.

On the Black Mountain, can't keep a man in jail,
On the Black Mountain, can't keep a man in jail,
If the jury finds him guilty, the judge'll go they bail.

Had a man in Black Mountain, sweetest man in town,
Had a man in Black Mountain, the sweetest man in town,
He met a city gal, and he throwed me down.

I'm bound for Black Mountain, me and my razor and my gun,
Lawd, I'm bound for Black Mountain, me and my razor and gun,
I'm gonna *shoot* him if he stands still, and *cut* him if he run.

Down in Black Mountain, they all shoot quick and straight,
Down in Black Mountain, they all shoot quick and straight,
The bullet'll git you if you start to dodging too late.

Got the Devil in my soul, and I'm full of bad booze,
Got the Devil in my soul, and I'm full of bad booze,
I'm out here for trouble, I've got the Black Mountain blues.

Chris Albertson

BAD BESSIE

from *Bessie*

[Albertson relates several incidents illustrating Bessie Smith's ba-adness. In one she and several girls arrive at a raucous party and eagerly retreat to the kitchen to enjoy some of the soul food. A drunk and perspiring man suddenly disrupts them, leering at the girls.]

"C'mon, baby, let's dance." His tone of voice made it sound more like an order. As the girls retreated farther into their corner he approached, bent on grabbing at least one of them.

At this point Bessie shifted her attention from her plate to the man. Rising slowly, she struck a characteristic hands-on-hips pose and defiantly spit a small bone in his direction.

"We don't want to be bothered," she said, "so you just get back in there and let them alone."

"Who in the hell are *you?*"

Bessie's calm was deceptive. "Did that fucker say something to me?" she asked softly. Before anyone could respond to her question, she had jumped the intruder and hit him on the head with her two clenched fists. As stunned by surprise as by the blow itself, he fell to the floor.

Not waiting for a reaction, Bessie turned back to the table, sat down, and resumed eating. "This here sure is some delicious food, uhm, uhm, uhm," she said, as her victim got back on his feet and stumbled discreetly out of the kitchen.

Donald Clarke

BILLIE HOLIDAY

from Donald Clarke, *Wishing on the Moon*

[Pianist Bobby Tucker] said that one New Year's Eve a merchant marine turned to the bartender [in a nightclub] and asked, "Since when did you start serving nigger bitches?" She [Billie Holiday] was drinking brandy and white crème de menthe—those big long shot glasses—and she just worked his face all over with the end of that glass until he looked like a three-ring Ballantine thing (the beer company's logo of intersecting circles). . . .

[Vocalist Thelma Carpenter tells about the incident when some prejudiced soldiers and sailors stuck cigarettes to her coat and burned it, and they went outside to fight.] She gave me that coat to *hold.* And I wanna tell ya, she'd laid 'em *flat*—and I threw a few milk bottles at 'em—When the cops came, she got very feminine, and she says, "They *attacked* me." And the cops cracked up. Two sailors layin' out on the street, and she says, they *attacked* her. She put on her coat and went back into the club.

Ethel Waters

WHIPPING THE CHORUS GIRLS

from *His Eye is on the Sparrow*

While I was playing in *Africana* on Broadway I had a Locomobile and a love affair. I should have kept them well separated. But I couldn't drive, and my love affair could, so I put him in charge of the keys and the steering wheel.

Now I had a very liberal attitude and I told him, "Look, I know you are messing around with other girls. That is okay if you obey two simple rules. Don't fool around with the little chorus girls in my show. And I won't have you taking any chorus girl, or a girl of any other description, joy-riding in my car."

The idea that he was using my expensive Locomobile, not to mention gas, oil, and the usual wear and tear, to promote on-the-side romancing was just too much for me to take.

So one day I was in a taxi going down Seventh Avenue, when I saw my big beautiful Locomobile parked in front of an apartment house where I knew two of the little show girls in my show had an apartment. I got out of the taxi and went up there.

"Who is it?" asked one of the girls when I rang their bell.

"Western Union," I said.

She opened up.

"My boy friend is here, or maybe I should say our boy friend," I told her. She looked scared. "Oh no," she said, "he isn't here, Miss Waters."

"All I want is my car keys," I said. "Get them from him, will you?"

"But he isn't here, Miss Waters!"

"My car is parked downstairs, so I know he is here. Now get the keys."

Though she continued to deny he was there, she led me through the apartment so I could look for him. But there was one room with the door closed which she didn't show me. So I knew he was in that room.

Now this fellow of mine was a very nosy and inquisitive type. I had a hunch that he would be standing right there behind the door, listening to what I was saying.

I went to the door and pushed it open. I slammed it back hard against the wall. And he was hiding there all right. I crashed him so hard against the wall that he gurgled for breath and began to search himself all over for broken bones.

The other *Africana* chick was in the bed. She looked terrified, but I told her, "I don't intend to beat you up—today. But I'll get you some other time when I'm more in the mood. And it will be me and you. So you can relax—for the time being."

Then I got my car keys from him and left. It was now raining in the street, and the top of my Locomobile was down. I had never driven a car before. But I was so mad that day I got behind the wheel and drove it off right down Seventh Avenue.

Everything went better than I expected until I came to 126th Street. At that time the Fifth Avenue busses that went up Seventh Avenue turned there at 126th Street to go downtown again.

As I approached the corner I could see that a bus was turning. The Irish driver was swinging it wide. I yelled to him. "Get out of my way."

But that stupid Irish bus driver was stubborn, and he wouldn't stop. I guess he thought I knew how to stop, or at least turn the wheel. And all on account of his pigheaded stubbornness I crashed into him, wrecking my car.

An officious white copper, also Irish, of course, came rushing up. He was as dumb as the bus driver.

"And will you be getting your wreck of a car out of the way of my southbound traffic?" he yelled.

I remained cool and very much the lady. I just took the keys out of my ignition and handed them to him.

"I'll tell you a little secret, officer," I said. "I don't know how to drive."

"Will you listen to the talk of her?" he said to the bus driver. "She doesn't know how to drive! And is it news you're telling me, madam? As though I couldn't see that with the foine eyes the good Lord gave me. So get your car out of the way before you tie up traffic all the way to Pough-keepsie!"

I kept trying to hand him the keys, but he ignored them. I found out later the reason was that he didn't know how to drive himself, that dumb cop. But he wouldn't admit he didn't have the know-how. A big crowd was all around us, laughing, and the other car drivers who couldn't move were honking their horns like it was Armistice Day.

"Officer!" I said. "You are the one who wants the car moved. So you can move it. I own this car and I have my owner's papers right on me. I give you permission to move it. Or if you don't want to move it yourself, get somebody to do it—and I will pay him."

Nobody in that big crowd volunteered his services. Harlem people are like that. They were enjoying all the yelling, the cop's frustration, and the confusion too much to want it to end. I wasn't having such a bad time myself. I had bruised and rattled the bones of my two-timing man and I was glad I had wrecked my Locomobile—because now he couldn't drive any little girls around in it.

At the height of all the uproar, who should come along in a taxi but my battered, depressed Romeo himself. He got out, and when he saw the wrecked Locomobile he almost sobbed. But I made him get in and drive it and me off Seventh Avenue and down a side street where the repair people could get it. I was laughing at the top of my lungs.

And he could read what was in my mind. Not only had I wrecked the car for a long time, but I was gonna whip him when I got him home. However, when we did get home he got out his gun—and I had to about-face on the whipping for the time being.

I went out of there in a hurry. And when I returned to my apartment Pearl Wright called to say he was down at her place and to come and get him. I went and got him and gave him the whipping at home when he was defenseless.

But that was not the end of my revenge. With Betty Hardy and Tony Salemme, the sculptor, I dropped into the Nest, a place Mel Frazier was running on 133rd Street. And the little chorus girl who had been in the room with my boy friend that day was an entertainer in the show there.

In Harlem night clubs they have ways and means of protecting their entertainers. So I did nothing for a whole hour. I wanted that chorus girl to relax and think I wasn't going into action. She was small like all the girls this particular boy friend had two-timed me with.

Between shows I noticed that she was sitting at a table only a few steps from the ladies' room. And I waited—until the dance music started up and the customers were dancing. I knew that everyone else would be watching the dance floor.

Then I started for her. I gave her one of my short, hard lefts to the chops, then dragged her into that ladies' room. I locked the door, then just beat the living hell out of her.

I told her what I always tell girls who mess around my boy friends: "There takes two people to make one of these love affairs. And my pain goes along with his pleasure."

Then I'd whip 'em to illustrate my point.

Now when my love affair heard about my whipping one of his on-the-side girls he didn't take it in silence. And once he said, "But, Ethel, you just can't go around beating up everybody you don't like."

"No," I answered him, "but I can whip anyone *you* like. Because you like only little chorus girls. I'll whip 'em every time I catch you messin' around with them. And I'm gonna make you respect me if I have to cripple 'em all."

I was playing in Baltimore one week when I heard he was messing around with a popular Plantation chorus girl in New York. After my last show that Saturday night I took the train to New York and a cab from the station to the Plantation, giving the driver five dollars to wait for me.

"I'm waiting for my cousin," I said.

But before I could go inside she came out of the club. I rushed over and slugged and disabled her. Then I got back in the cab and told the driver to take me back to the railway station.

Ida Cox

WILD WOMEN DON'T HAVE THE BLUES

I've got a disposition and a way of my own,
When my man starts to kicking I let him find a new home,
I get full of good liquor, walk the street all night,
Go home and put my man out if he don't act right.
Wild women don't worry,
Wild women don't have the blues.

You never get nothing by being an angel child,
You'd better change your way an' get real wild.
I wanta' tell you something, I wouldn't tell you no lie,
Wild women are the only kind that ever get by.
Wild women don't worry,
Wild women don't have the blues.

Folk

HOW'D YOU MAKE OUT?

from Daryl Cumber Dance, *Shuckin' and Jivin'*

This old man and old lady were eighty years old, and they'd been together so long that they decided they wanted some younger person and have an affair. So they found a couple of twenty-year-olds. The boy was twenty and the girl was twenty. So the old man eighty took the twenty-year-old girl, and the old woman eighty took the twenty-year-old boy. So they went on and spent the night together.

The next morning when they came out, the older couple got together again. The old man said, "How'd you make out last night, honey?"

She said, "Well, you know twenty will go into eighty four times. How'd you make out?"

Folk

QUEEN BEE

[The following was recorded by me from a conversation between two young Black women.]

FIRST SPEAKER: You know the Queen Bee kills the male after she finish with him.

SECOND SPEAKER:That's right, use him and kill him.

FIRST SPEAKER:Yes, wham, bam, thank you sir. [Note the play on the well-known line about the sexual behavior of the male rabbit, "Wham, bam, thank you ma'am."]

Valerie Wilson Wesley

DEVIL'S GONNA GET HIM

So you're Tamara Hayle," said the tall, gaunt man who walked into my office without knocking. "DeLorca says you're the best P.I. in Essex County. I only do business with the best." He had flawless dark skin, thick silver-gray hair, and was dressed like a banker in a navy pin-striped suit and black wing-tipped shoes. But he had the dead eyes of a street thug. *Killer's eyes,* I thought to myself, even though I knew better.

Lincoln E. Storey was a legend in Newark, and I wondered why the photos that always ran in *Black Enterprise* and on the business pages of *The Star-Ledger* never captured the predatory glint in his eyes. I also wondered why DeLorca, chief of the Belvington Heights Police Force and my grumpy ex boss, had given me such a sparkling endorsement.

"Yes, I'm Tamara Hayle. Would you like to sit down?" I asked, extending a hand. He glanced at my offering but didn't take it. I reached for his overcoat, a dove-gray cashmere number that felt as soft as mink against my palm, and hung it up on the rocky coat rack in a dark corner of my office.

"I assume you know who I am," he said with an arrogant thrust of his chin.

"Is there anyone in the state of New Jersey who doesn't?" I hated the ingratiating sound of my voice, but it was too late to call it back. "What can I do for you, Mr. Storey?" I asked, trying hard to tone down my eagerness.

"I'll get to that," he snapped in a way that told me he was a man who was used to taking his own time and getting his own way. His tone caught me short, but I tossed him a sugary smile, deciding in that instant to listen to my pocketbook rather than my pride.

For "the best P.I. in Essex County," I was broke as hell. With a 1982 diesel Jetta that needed a new transmission and a big-mouthed teenage son to feed, being anything but pleasant to the biggest client who had ever graced my funky little office would be just plain foolish.

Spring had touched everything in Newark but me. The cherry trees were blossoming in Weequahic and Branch Brook Parks, and folks, sick and tired of the hawk and the harshest winter in fifteen years, were stepping out into the sun. My best friend Annie had fallen in love with her husband of the last ten years . . . again. After the worst year of his young life, my son Jamal had beaten down grief and discovered, with a vengeance, the opposite sex. And Wyvetta Green, the owner of Jan's Beauty Biscuit, the beauty salon downstairs, who I could always count on for her sweet spirit and sour words, had dyed her hair a hot-to-trot blond and was planning a week in Jamaica with her gold-toothed boyfriend Earl. But I was horny *and* broke, and I couldn't think of two worse things to be in spring which, up until this year, had always been my best season. It didn't bode well for the rest of the year. I'd been sitting at my desk, lamenting my sorry state, when Lincoln E. Storey had walked through my door. I wasn't about to let him walk out.

"Could I get you something to drink, Mr. Storey?" I asked. "A cup of tea?"

"I don't drink tea."

"How about some coffee?"

"Freshly brewed?"

"Sorry, I don't have a pot. Instant okay?" I asked. I don't like instant, but I keep it in my office to be polite.

"I don't drink that shit."

That "shit" business threw me for a minute, but I swallowed the urge to tell him to kiss my behind and watched him as he crossed his long legs and surveyed, I feared, the secondhand computer that separated us, the film on the window that dimmed the sun, and the streak of brown gravy that had found its way to the front of my blouse, when I'd shared some egg foo yong with Wyvetta for lunch. I also recalled the first time I'd seen him.

I'd been twelve years old then, one of maybe three hundred bored kids assembled in our junior-high auditorium to honor him on Black Heroes Day. Lincoln E. Storey, a local boy made good, had grown up on the mean streets of the toughest ward in Newark and made money's mama as one of the first black investment bankers on Wall Street. He was, as the principal told us in a flowery introduction, a young man who had studied hard, paid his dues and made his dreams come true.

This was the late 1960s, a time for dreams—and nightmares, too. The flames of the riot in '67 had charred the city's soul as hard as burnt wood. Everybody was looking for a hero, and Storey was made to order. He was in his twenties then, old by junior-high standards. He'd stood tall and stern in his charcoal gray suit and explained the market and how he'd learned to work it, and how if we studied hard, we could learn to work it, too. We didn't understand the market, but we understood rich and the reverent posturing of our principal and teachers, who gathered like spring hens around a young cock.

But later that night when I'd mentioned Storey to my father, his eyes had darkened.

"I remember Lincoln, Seafus Storey's boy," he'd said. "He lived in that dilapidated old tenement over there on Irvine Turner Boulevard, just off Avon, back in the days when Turner Boulevard was Belmont, before the big-time Negroes took over City Hall. His daddy used to whip that boy all up and down the avenue every time the mood hit him good. I always wondered what became of him."

I remembered my father's eyes as I watched Storey now and wondered how old he had been when the cruel lines around his mouth had settled in his face as deeply as dimples.

"How long have you been in this business?" Storey asked, snapping me from my memories.

"Five years going on six."

"You're licensed by the state?"

"Of course."

"What kind of things do you handle?"

"Anything that comes my way. Disappearances. Missing persons. Occasionally the Public Defender's will ask me to help on a homicide or larceny. Insurance fraud."

"And your rates?"

"Depends on the job, plus all my expenses."

"And you're worth the money?"

"That's what they tell me."

"Do you find this line of work hard for a woman, a black woman?"

"No harder than being a cop."

"You used to work for DeLorca, I take it."

"Six years ago."

"Why did you leave?"

"I got sick of it," I said, wondering how much DeLorca had told him about me.

"Sick of . . ."

"Sick of being called a nigger bitch by my brethren in blue every day of my beat," I said, the old anger surfacing again, coloring the edge of my words. Storey chuckled deep in his throat, and our eyes locked for a moment telling me he hadn't forgotten his roots. "So I take it you live in Belvington Heights?" I asked, knowing the answer but tired of answering his questions.

"You grew up around here?" he asked, changing the subject. His thin hand swept elegantly toward the window indicating that "around here" meant East Orange, Newark, and beyond.

"East Orange. Newark. The same ward as you."

A glint of something I couldn't read came and left his eyes.

"Discretion means as much to me as money," he said, out of nowhere.

"I know how to keep my mouth shut."

"You do surveillance work?"

"I've done it."

"You like it?"

"It depends."

"On?"

"On who I'm following and where they lead me."

He smiled a crooked smile that told me nothing. "I need to get some . . . information on somebody." He paused. "I need to know every bit of shit about this motherfucking cocksucker that I can possibly get. Do you understand me?"

It wasn't the words that got me. I've heard men curse before; my dead brother Johnny could belt them out harder than anybody I ever knew. But the way Storey's face broke when he spoke, the way he lost control and his lower lip trembled and his eyes squinted, was downright scary. Whoever the "motherfucking cocksucker" was, he had made Storey's shit-list big time.

"Is this person an employee?" I asked neutrally, cooling my voice against the heat I heard in his.

Storey smirked. "You could say that, I guess, depending upon how you define employee."

He was being cagey, and I wondered why he wasn't giving it to me straight.

"I take it this is somebody who has betrayed your trust?" I asked, stating the obvious.

"I want to know where he sleeps and who he fucks," he answered bluntly.

"Does he sleep with someone you know?" I asked innocently, making my voice sound caring, sister-gentle, willing to share a brother's pain. *Somebody you sleep with?* I didn't ask.

He straightened his back, uncrossed his legs, folded his hands. "My stepdaughter," he said after a minute. "I assume they're sleeping together. My stepdaughter Alexa is involved with this person, this character. I don't trust him. I suspect he likes my money more than he likes my stepdaughter, and I want to find out everything I can about him."

"So what's his name?"

"Brandon Pike."

"Brandon Pike," I repeated the name once softly, to myself, like I'd never heard it before, but it had hit me like a fast, hard punch in the gut—lower, because when I had known and loved him, that was where Brandon Pike had hurt me: my female center, the most vulnerable part of me.

Lincoln Storey studied my face, taking in the change that I knew was there.

"You know him, then?" He watched my eyes as they dropped. I forced them back up, confronting his.

"Years ago . . . Not well."

Storey seemed to buy it. "He has been seeing Alexa for about a year. She's twenty-three. Dropped out of school in upstate New York. Vassar. Trying to 'find' herself. He's, how old would you say? Thirty-something? He's come into her life. After my money, anyone can tell that. She's got nothing to offer him. He's that kind of man. My wife Daphne and I are very concerned." His eyes sought mine for a reaction, and then he continued. "If I can get something on him, I can confront her with it. It's clear she has nothing to give him."

What is he giving her? I asked myself because that had been Brandon's special talent, giving women what they thought they needed.

I had spent the years after our "affair" trying to figure him out. And all I really knew in the end was that I'd left my joke of a marriage to my ex, DeWayne Curtis, with my head high, and Brandon Pike had brought it low, lower than I'd ever let it fall for any man again.

"I want you to follow him. Find out what you can on him. See what he's up to. Report it to me," Storey continued.

I wondered for a moment if getting into Brandon's business was really an ethical thing for me to do. Was it right to use my professional skills to get even with somebody who had done me wrong? P.I.s are supposed to be objective, removed from the subject. Cool, detached. I wondered if I could be that way where Brandon Pike was concerned. But it had been three years since he'd left me—me wondering what I'd done wrong and if I'd failed him. He'd severed everything then. Professionally. Personally. Permanently.

And ethics aside, I truly needed the money. And on the real tip, the son of a bitch deserved it.

"What can you tell me about him now? I'll need a recent photo, current home address, work address?" I asked, slipping into my professional mode again, pushing back the personal.

Storey looked at me blankly.

"I know that he got an award a couple of years ago for *Slangin' Rock,* the documentary he did on kids dealing cocaine. Is he making any money yet? Is he still doing docs?"

"I thought you didn't know him well."

"I haven't seen him in about five years," I said, looking Storey in the eye. *Three years.*

"Do you have a recent photo?" I asked again. Maybe he *had* changed in three years.

"Why the hell would I carry around a photograph of Brandon Pike?"

"Why the hell would you come to my office wanting me to tail somebody and not have a picture of him?" I snapped back, deciding in that flash of a moment that maybe I didn't need Lincoln Storey's money after all, not bad enough anyway to put up with his bad attitude. Not bad enough maybe to rake up the embers of Brandon Pike.

Storey smiled what he probably thought was a charming smile. "I like a woman with spirit," he said.

"Mr. Storey, don't waste my time." Suddenly I was as sick of him as I'd ever been of anybody in my life.

"No. To answer your question, I don't have any photographs. And I can't tell you a lot about him because I don't know anything or I wouldn't be hiring you. But I'm giving a fund-raiser tonight, for Stella Pharr. Stella Pharr."

"Tonight?"

"Yes, for Stella Pharr," he said, repeating the name for the third time.

"Stella Pharr?" I asked. I'd heard the name before but couldn't place it. Storey certainly seemed to relish the sound of it.

"Yes. Deputy District Attorney. She's running for state assembly. Alexa, my wife, Daphne, Pike. They'll all be there. At Tate's. You know Tate's used to be on West Market, now it's on Fullbright in Belvington Heights."

"Yes, I know the place." Jackson Tate's ancient, elfin face quickly came to mind. Tate's had been the hottest new restaurant in the comeback of Newark. Tate had raised hackles and eyebrows all over town when he'd moved it to Belvington Heights, which needed another ritzy restaurant like another Lexus dealership.

Anonymous

VIEW DE LAND.

from M. F. Armstrong and Helen W. Ludlow, *Hampton and Its Students*. Courtesy of Hampton University Archives

Oh way over Jerdan, View de land, View de land—
Way over Jerdan, Go view de heavenly land.
I'm born of God, I know I am; View de land, View de land;
And you deny it, if a you can, Go view de heav'nly land.
I want to go to heaven when I die; View de land, View de land;
To shout salvation as a I fly, Go view de heav'nly land.

What kind o' shoes is dem-a you wear? View de land, &c.
Dat you can walk upon de air? Go view, &c.
Dem shoes I wear am de gospel shoes; View de land, &c.
An' you can wear dem ef-a you choose; Go view, &c.—*Cho.*

Der' is a tree in Paradise; View de land, &c.
De Christian he call it de tree ob life; Go view, &c.
I spects to eat de fruit right off o' dat tree; View de land, &c.
Ef busy old Satan will let-a me be; Go view, &c.—*Cho.*

You say yer Jesus set-a you free; View de land, &c.
Why don't you let-a your neighbor be? Go view, &c.
You say you're aiming for de skies; View de land, &c.
Why don't you stop-a your telling lies; Go view, &c.—*Cho.*

Marilyn Fullen-Collins

MAMA

"Mama, hi." "Come in, Child, I've been waiting for you." She stands on the old wooden landing that leads to the tattered screen door. She urges me to watch my step saying, "Mr. Jackson keep sayin' he gonna fix them steps. Shoot, he been saying that since Methuselah was a boy." She grins, big and safe. I reach for the splintered banister, lose my footing and stumble into Mama's arms. Powerful, henna-colored arms that held me even before my mother did. My eyes catch the never changing entirety of her life. Who my grandmother is is drawn in the vitality of her living room.

A makeshift altar rests near the entrance to her kitchen. She uses her best Christmas linen as altar cloths. White, starched creases that are ironed so sharp they could make you bleed. A three-foot-tall statue of Jesus stands guard over her apartment and her life. His sacred heart is swallowed by flames. His feet balance on top of a weary world. She keeps a white votive candle steadily burning in perpetual adoration of her Savior. A scarred, silver crucifix rests nearby, along with a copy of this month's *Catholic Digest,* her well-used indigo rosary is nestled in a saffron receptacle that contains Pope-blessed holy water, a dun-colored palm from last Palm Sunday, and a tiny splinter of wood said to be from the cross on Calvary. On the opposite wall is a grand portrait of Marcus Garvey in full military complement. Underneath, she keeps a small photo of the Black Star

Shipping Lines masthead as a reminder of her desire to go home to Africa.

Heading for the kitchen, my hand brushes against the back of her maroon horsehair sofa. I always thought I could fly when I jumped on it. Mama used to encourage me to jump for the stars. She always believed I'd make it. Even when I didn't. Pushing past the weighty kitchen door I am bombarded with a thousand smells coming from her old O'Keefe and Merritt stove.

"Sit down, Girl, your dinner be ready soon enough." I do as I'm told, and she places a cup of coffee before me strong with cinnamon and chicory. Grabbing a cup for herself she settles down in the chair facing me. "You know, Honey, we never had much, always a struggle just to keep food on the table." She laughs, deep in her throat, her intonations as sensual and sexy as a teenager's. "Your granddaddy always say I was too young and fine when he met me. Guess I was too, but times change and people change. Life puts lines in your face. Plugs up your ears, sometimes makes you feel like you all used up."

She rises from the table, tying her favorite apron around her abundant waist, the one she embroidered with the farmer's wife scattering grain to the chickens. She lifts the silver top off the big pot and steam rises up to blush her well-lived face. The hairs tucked into her bun break free and crinkle around her forehead and ears. She talks as she stirs teeny tabasco peppers in with the ham hocks and collards. "Yes, Child, people say, menfolks specially, that a woman's no good after twenty-five. Don't you believe it! Hell, I done my best living after fifty! Outlived your granddaddy didn't I?" She snickers as she dices onions, celery and baby bay shrimp that will make up her secret potato salad recipe. Mama brushes a thatch of gray hair out of her way with the back of her wrist. "Good God Almighty, old ain't no disease. It's proof you alive! I get so mad when I go into the Safeway and see these women buyin' hair dye." She measures her eyes on mine until I squirm in my seat. "Yes, I know you been thinkin' on buying some of that mess too cause you got a couple of strands of white hair. Shoot, Girl, if you didn't have that how you gonna prove you been alive? Each one of them hairs signifies somethin' important!"

After rinsing the shrimp smell from her hands she reaches for my hair. Gently she peels a strand away from the rest and pulls my head under the table lamp. "Now, lookee here. I can tell you when you got each one of these."

I look up. "Mama, you good, I'll admit, but not even you can tell me where I got this mess of gray on my head."

Her leathery hand chucks me easily under my chin. Cloudless eyes stare me down. "Girl, why I always got to prove you wrong, uh?" She laughs that laugh again and continues pulling threads of hair from my head. "You got this one when that boy, Tyrone Hicks, done stood you up for the St. Mary's prom. This one over here you got when your cat Bubba got runned over by a car on New Year's Eve. Sure was a sour year too. Now lookee here, see this cluster right here? All of it come up soon after you had that abortion." Tears bite my eyes. She sees them. Rocking me against that perfect breast, she says, "Oh Babygirl, I ain't namin' off no sin. It just be life that's all. Ain't nothin' happened to you, ain't happened to most women whether they care to admit it or not. You strong, Babygirl. You a woman. You gotta be."

That was eleven years ago. Yesterday we buried my Mama. Just the way she wanted too. Had the service over at Our Lady of Perpetual Sorrows, right there on Central Avenue. The church was packed with flowers, and resting at the foot of her bronze casket was the grandest spray of lavender African violets this town has ever seen. And poised against the pulpit was the picture of Marcus Garvey in full military complement. The Reverend Father Julian Mansfield pontificated about Bertha Lee's life as a living saint. Talked about all the good she'd done, the homeless she'd housed, the starving she'd fed, the forgotten children she'd loved. The congregation "uhhed" and "amenned" her right into heaven. There I sat, alone in the front pew, feeling like a motherless child until I looked up at the massive mahogany cross spotlighted in the sanctuary, and I saw her smile. Smile and nod and whisper, "Remember, Grand Babygirl, you strong, you a woman, you gotta be." And I finally understood.

A. Elizabeth Delany

GETTING THE LAST WORD

from *Having Our Say*

Now, honey, I get the blues sometimes. It's a shock to me, to be this old. Sometimes, when I realize I am 101 years old, it hits me right between the eyes. I say, "Oh Lord, how did this happen?" Turning one hundred was the worst birthday of my life. I wouldn't wish it on my worst enemy. Turning 101 was not so bad. Once you're past that century mark, it's just not as shocking.

You know what I've been thinking lately? All those people who were mean to me in my life—all those *rebby boys*—they have turned to dust, and this old gal is still here, along with sister Sadie.

We've outlived those old rebby boys!

That's one way to beat them!

That's justice!

They're turning in their graves, while Sadie and me are getting the last word, in this book. And honey, I surely do love getting the last word. I'm having my say, giving my opinion. Lord, ain't it good to be an *American*.

Truth is, I never thought I'd see the day when people would be interested in hearing what two old Negro women have to say. Life still surprises me. So maybe the last laugh's on *me*.

I'll tell you a little secret: I'm starting to get optimistic. I'm thinking: *Maybe I'll get into Heaven after all*. Why, I've helped a lot of folks—even some white folks! I surely do have some redeeming qualities that must count for something. So I just might do it: I just might get into Heaven. I may have to hang on to Sadie's heels, but I'll get there.

Mama Sez

"Yes, I've seventy-nine years old, and you don't see no wrinkles in my fore-head and no bags under my eyes, and, . . . here, feel how soft my hands are—my feet's just as soft and smooth. Every night I put some vaseline on my feet and sleep in socks. In the morning I use a slice of cucumber or wa-termelon rind on my face and put some grated white potato under my eyes." [one of the informants for *Shuckin' and Jivin'*]

You haven't lived until you've tasted my hot grits and Smithfield ham bis-cuits.

I passed by the schoolhouse do' even if I didn't go in.

If God had wanted me to fly, he would have given me wings.

Sister to Sister

Girl, we come from a long line of strong and going on women; we don't let nothing keep us down.

What you talkin' bout? Back out! Naw. We keep going . . . through rain, through snow, through hail, through blood—like de Lone Ranger say, "We gon' ride tonight."★

That's right, cause Black women are committed, not just involved: when you look at your breakfast of ham and eggs, you know the hen was in-volved, . . . but the pig was *committed*.

★Though this is a statement often collected among males with sexual connotations, it is used among women simply to suggest determination.

Like I tell my husband, "Yeah, the rooster crows a lot, but it's the hen that delivers the egg."

That's one up and coming woman.

Yeah, it's time for Black women to press on, and I don't mean false nails.

Gon' with yo' bad self, Girl.

You go, Girl.

Hey, Miz Thang, you got your act together.

She can walk that walk and talk that talk.

Now don't that just take the cake!

It's a poor dog that won't switch its own tail.

That's for me to know and you to find out.

You can read my letters, but you sure can't read my mind.

You can saddle me, but you can't ride me.

I wasn't born yesterday.

I laugh and joke, but I don't play.

"Violet don't take no tea for the fever." [doesn't take any stuff from any-one—from Benilde Little, *Good Hair,* 15]

"Don't mess with me! . . . I know how to be mean. I can put the itch in bitch." [Mother Love, *Listen Up,* xvi]

"You would rather run through hell in gasoline drawers than fool with me." [Mother Love, *Listen Up,* 8]

Don't mess wit' me when I got PMS—planning to murder somebody!

You might as well call a spade a spade.

Ain't but two things I *got* to do—die and stay black.

Put that in your pipe and smoke it.

I don't cotton to that.

I'll drop that man like a hot potato.

Yeah, if he don't . . . , he's history.

[Alluding to the fact that though she's married, she still enjoys flirting with men] "Just because I'm full doesn't mean I can't look at the menu." [Mother Love, *Listen Up*, 33]

CHAPTER 2

"Nice Girls Don't..."

MOTHERLY ADVICE

For young girls, there is nothing more boring, insulting, condescend-ing, restricting, old-fashioned, and just plain pain-in-the-neck than the advice with which mothers and other female authority figures constantly bombard them. These thousands of rules, guides, admonitions, and threats that older women rain down on female children from the time they wake them up in the morning until they tuck the blankets around their necks at night seem always to begin with, "Nice girls don't...." Life for girls seems to be a series of "No's"—all the thrills, excitement, pleasures of youthful abandon and adolescent exploration are prohibited to them. That, of course, is when they are growing up. Later in life, they are inclined to thank God that their mothers protected them from some of the pitfalls that befall so many women; or to bewail the fact that they did not listen to their mothers and therefore had to pay the price. Even later in life, they are very likely to quote their Mothers to their daughters: "My mother always warned me that nice girls don't . . . ," and thus the cycle begins anew.

Much of the advice-blitz that young African American girls endure is similar to that that all mothers of every race/place/age dispense, especially the admonitions on the woman's sexual vulnerability. These warnings often become more ominous, however, for the black female, who (especially in the South) has historically been the victim of legalized, random, and often ritualistic sexual exploitation. Thus, mothers are concerned about proper behavior, not only to help their daughters develop into socially acceptable individuals, but also to protect them from some of the dangers (sexual and otherwise) that threaten their security. These daughters must learn to recognize that many of the attractive possibilities presented for the White female by our society are unattainable and may even be entrapments for them—Cinderella may have been darkened by some cinders, but they could be washed off. Besides, black girls have no Fairy Godmothers and no Prince Charmings—and everybody knows their feet are too big to fit into the slippers. Thus for black girls, the necessary behavior is not just a matter of etiquette and amenities, but also often practical ways of defending themselves against commonplace disappointments, intimidations, and dangers from every possible source (the white community/the black community/white men/black men/white women/other black women, not to mention natural disasters, illnesses, and spells).

Clearly the worst thing that could happen to a girl was to get pregnant before marriage. This marked the end of any possible advancement in life, since until a few years ago, it meant that you were kicked out of school and couldn't return, that you were labeled sexually loose and no decent man would ever consider marrying you; and that your mother and the rest of your family were embarrassed that they had raised a slut that didn't know how to keep her dress down and her panties up.

Also common to the advice-blitz of all groups is the counsel about the "proper" behavior of a young woman, which can deal with everything from table manners to dress to the choice of friends. Again these warnings assume a special urgency when one recognizes that black females must also be trained to *counter* the racial assumptions that the broader society makes about them—they must dress or conduct themselves a certain way, not only because it is appropriate, but also because they must not reinforce stereotypes about the colors they wear, the manner in which they style their hair, the way they talk, the volume of their voice, and so on, ad infinitum.

All mothers, too, certainly censure their daughters about behavior that is too grown up—the most common retorts to such conduct in African American families often being that the child is acting too womanish or that she is a Miss Know-it-all. All sorts of threats are often dispensed about the disastrous consequences of such behavior.

Though similar training of girls occurs in most families, in black-American families, from slavery to the present, there was a greater possibility that the child would grow up in a female-dominated household. Even though it has also been more likely that the mother might work outside the home, most African American children grow up surrounded by those working mothers as well as grandmothers, great-grandmothers, aunts, great-aunts, cousins, friends, roomers, and sundry other mother-substitutes; like author Bebe Moore Campbell, many of these children probably felt that they "could have died from overexposure to femininity." Thus the African American female is likely to receive an even larger and more varied dose of motherly advice than others. The goal of these mothers, of course, is to keep their daughters safe and to provide them a little common sense and mother wit as well as religion and formal education—whatever resources will allow them to avoid the mistakes they made, and to enable their daughters to grow up to be healthier, happier, more secure financially, and better educated than they were.

As serious as this motherly advice is, it has often been dispensed with humor, designed no doubt to make it more readily swallowed, more sharply felt, and more memorable. Oftentimes the advice is not delivered in a straightforward way. As Iyanla Vanzant has noted in *The Value in the Valley,* "Granny and Momma did not come right out and tell us what they knew. Oh no! That would have made it too easy! Instead, the knowledge and wisdom is couched in old wives' tales, euphemisms, and innuendo." Much of this lore has become proverbial. Much of it is phrased in the most remarkable and memorable metaphors and similes and hyperboles. Some of it is made even more striking by the rhythms and rhymes in which it is presented. No session among grown African American women is more hilarious than one in which they share the lessons their "mothers" taught them.

Fannie Berry

OL' ENOUGH

from Charles L. Perdue, Jr., et al., eds., *Weevils in the Wheat*

I came to Petersburg, the first year of the Civil War. Den de comet had done bin here an' I wuz up in my teens. As ol' folks use to tell us, "You ain't got no business knowing yo' age." "Go away from here," my mother use to tell us when we asked 'bout our age. "Lemme be. All I know," she would say, "you are ol' enough to smell yourself." Ha, ha. Baby! Is you writing dat down?

Kate Rushin

THE TIRED POEM: LAST LETTER FROM A TYPICAL UNEMPLOYED BLACK PROFESSIONAL WOMAN

So it's a gorgeous afternoon in the park
It's so nice you forget your Attitude
The one your mama taught you
The one that says Don't-Mess-With-Me
You forget until you hear all this
Whistling and lip smacking
You whip around and say
I ain't no damn dog
It's a young guy
His mouth drops open
Excuse me Sister
How you doing
You lie and smile and say
I'm doing good
Everything's cool Brother

Then five minutes later
Hey you Sweet Devil
Hey Girl come here
You tense   sigh   calculate
You know the lean boys and bearded men
Are only cousins and lovers and friends
Sometimes when you say Hey
You get a beautiful surprised smile
Or a good talk

And you've listened to your uncle when he was drunk
Talking about how he has to scuffle to get by and
How he'd wanted to be an engineer
And you talk to Joko who wants to be a singer and
Buy some clothes and get a house for his mother
The Soc. and Psych. books say you're domineering
And you've been to enough
Sisters-Are-Not-Taking-Care-Of-Business discussions
To know where you went wrong
It's decided it had to be the day you decided to go to school
Still you remember the last time you said hey
So you keep on walking
What   you too good to speak
Don't nobody want you no way

You go home   sit on the front steps   listen to
The neighbor boy brag about
How many girls he has pregnant
You ask him if he's going to take care of the babies
And what if he gets taken to court
And what are the girls going to do
He has pictures of them all
This real cute one was supposed to go to college
Dumb broad knew she could get pregnant
I'll just say it's not mine
On the back of this picture of a girl in a cap and gown
It says something like

I love you in my own strange way
Thank you

Then you go in the house
Flip through a magazine and there is
An-Ode-To-My-Black-Queen poem
The kind where the Brother
Thanks all of the Sisters Who Endured
Way back when he didn't have his Shit Together
And you have to wonder where they are now
And you know what happens when you try to resist
All of this Enduring
And you think how this
Thank-you poem is really
No consolation at all
Unless you believe
What the man you met on the train told you
The Black man who worked for the State Department
And had lived in five countries
He said Dear
You were born to suffer
Why don't you give me your address
And I'll come visit

So you try to talk to your friend
About the train and the park and everything
And how it all seems somehow connected
And he says
You're just a Typical Black Professional Woman
Some sisters know how to deal
Right about here
Your end of the conversation phases out
He goes on to say how
Black Professional Women have always had the advantage
You have to stop and think about that one
 Maybe you are supposed to be grateful for those sweaty
 Beefy-faced white businessmen who try to

Pick you up at lunchtime
And you wonder how many times your friend had
Pennies thrown at him
How many times he's been felt up in the subway
How many times he's been cussed out on the street
You wonder how many times he's been offered
$10 for a piece of himself
$10 for a piece
So you're waiting for the bus
And you look at this young Black man
Asking if you want to make some money
You look at him for a long time
You imagine the little dingy room
It would take twenty minutes or less
You only get $15 for spending all day with thirty kids
Nobody is offering you
Any cash for your poems
You remember again how you have the advantage
How you're not taking care of business
How this man is somebody's kid brother or cousin
And could be your own
So you try to explain how $10 wouldn't pay for
What you'd have to give up
He pushes a handful of sticky crumpled dollars
Into your face and says

Why not
You think I can't pay
Look at that roll
Don't tell me you don't need the money
Cause I know you do
I'll give you fifteen

You maintain your sense of humor
You remember a joke you heard
Well no matter what
A Black Woman never has to starve

Just as long as there are
Dirty toilets and . . .
It isn't funny
Then you wonder if he would at least
Give you the money
And not beat you up
But you're very cool and say
No thanks
You tell him he should spend his time
Looking for someone he cares about
Who cares about him
He waves you off
Get outta my face
I don't have time for that bullshit
You blew it Bitch

Then
(Is it suddenly)
Your voice gets loud
And fills the night street
Your voice gets louder and louder
Your bus comes
The second-shift people file on
The security guards and nurse's aides
Look at you like you're crazy
Get on the damn bus
And remember
You blew it
He turns away
Your bus pulls off
There is no one on the street but you

And then
It is
                    Very
                    Quiet

Folk

AN HOUR OF PLEASURE

The Dean of Women was giving her usual lecture to the incoming freshman women about how to conduct themselves as Virginia Stateswomen, and she was especially warning them against sexual activity. After appealing to their religious teachings, their need to protect their health, and the threat of pregnancy, she ended dramatically, "Ask yourself if you ever feel tempted, 'Is an hour of pleasure worth a lifetime of regrets?' " to which one of the freshman girls inquired, "How do you make it last an hour?"

Folk

NORFOLK

[This verse, which is sung like a cheer, was very popular at Virginia State College and Norfolk State when I was in college in the 50s—at which time most of the students who finished the two year program at Norfolk State came to Virginia State to complete their degrees. A version that was given to me in 1996 by a Hampton alumna of my generation added "Virginia" at the end.]

We are the girls of Norfolk, Norfolk, Norfolk,
We don't drink, nor smoke, Nor-folk!

Toi Derricotte

DILDO

She had bought herself a very good-size rubber one, molded from an actual erect penis, with all the raised veins and details of the texture of the skin. It was ten inches long, and her thumb and index finger could barely fit around the circumference. It had balls, reddish dark, kind of pimply thick, with no backs, like a mask.

She had quickly brought in the box, which was waiting on the front steps. Thank God she had beat her husband and children home! She noticed with relief the return address said something innocuous, like Halcyon or Life Streams . . . Whatever it was, no way did it call up the open flood of female jism. She tore into it. Never in her Catholic life had she allowed herself to imagine! True, she had owned a wand once, a long, hard battery-operated thing that she had been afraid to put inside her for fear it would electrocute her. She had tried it a few times, but it soon rusted where the battery went in, probably from washing it!! That had been ten years ago. Lately, however, as her sexual encounters with her husband had become less frequent, less exciting, and after she had given up on an affair—scared off by AIDS and Catholic guilt—she had sent for a catalogue.

Inside the box there was another box, with a large-as-life astounding picture. Taking the dildo out and handling its rubber, not too stiff stiffness made her smile—as if she were a goddess looking down on herself from a distance, shaking her head. Of course she rushed upstairs to try it, and she was not disappointed! She was shocked by how quickly she responded, not even needing to be aroused first. She added a lubricant, stuck it in, and reached orgasm—a very deep orgasm—in about a minute, even though she hadn't touched her clitoris!

After, she worried. First, the box it came in was so big she couldn't get it hidden in the trash can. Her husband took out the garbage. The picture of the dildo loomed. The box was too thick to tear. Finally she turned it inside out, strapping it together with a rubber band, then folded it down tightly in the garbage and opened the step-on can several times to make sure the picture wouldn't pop out in his face.

Second, when she left the house shortly after, she noticed that the kitchen blinds were partway open. She had been so excited opening the box she had forgotten to close the blinds! Her neighbor had been out shoveling snow. She went out to check and found that one could see—if one were walking quickly—only a flash of the kitchen. Surely he wouldn't have stopped and stared! Well, maybe if he had, he would have thought it was something she and her husband had sent away for. It seemed less embarrassing if it was for conjugal purposes.

And there were other worries. Would she stretch so that her husband would notice? Would she enjoy sex with him less as a result? Would she go crazy for it, doing it several times a day? What if someone came home? What if the cleaning lady found it, the pet-sitter? What if her mother found it? She hid it in her sweater drawer in the second bedroom. But what if she died? Who would go through her drawers separating out the sweaters to give to friends, the sweaters to Goodwill?

If her husband found it, would he feel hurt, betrayed? If her son found it, would he feel repulsed, horrified? And if it was her mother, would she have a heart attack? Her mother hadn't slept with her father since she was born. She could see her mother's face—as if the dildo would jump out of the drawer and eat her alive!

She would just *tell* her husband. How would she put it? "I really enjoy sex with you, but I need a little something extra. It's in the second dresser drawer in the guest bedroom. If I die, please get it before my mother." Would she show it to him? Would he need a demonstration? That could be very bad for their sex life, which, though not perfect, was at least, let's face it, human.

Maybe, before she died, she'd outgrow the need, confess and throw it out—like Kafka burned his notebooks. But probably she'd have to stand up with it on the last day, before the complete heavenly host—John the Baptist, Peter and Paul, and all the saints, Bartholomew, Linus, and Cletus, the prophets, and even the pure angels, who are no doubt still pissed off after realizing what they *didn't* get in order to be smarter than us and immortal.

April Sinclair

PRINCE CHARMING

from Coffee Will Make You Black

[In the following selection Stevie, the adolescent heroine of *Coffee*, is having a conversation with her best friend's mother.]

"Stevie, promise me something."

"What?"

"Promise me you'll never put your trust in no man."

I didn't know what to say. I trusted my father and my uncle. Maybe Mrs. Perkins meant other men. Carla's mother didn't wait for me to answer. She just took a drag off her cigarette and threw her head back, and emptied the can of beer into her mouth.

"There is nobody out there for you," Mrs. Perkins shouted and pointed with her knife. "If you make it in this world you're gonna have to make it all by your lonesome. Do you hear me? Cinderella was not written about the negro woman. Do you understand?"

"Yes, I think so," I said, edging back a little from the knife. She was really getting worked up.

"Your Prince Charming ain't never gonna come! Do you hear me?"

"Yes, ma'm," I said. But I still planned to wait and see what would happen.

April Sinclair

AIN'T GONNA BE THE SAME FOOL TWICE

[In the following selection, Sinclair's heroine, Jean Heloise, who has moved to California and discovered her sexual bent, attempts to tell her mother that she is a lesbian.]

I'd decided to come out to Mama, if I could work it into the telephone conversation. Maybe seeing that there was hope for Jawea and her mother had given me courage. Artemis was in my lap. I wasn't sure if she was sticking around to give me moral support or if she was just being nosy.

"Today called, wanted to know if you were still out there with that man," Mama said, sounding resentful.

"Oh," I gulped. As far as Mama was concerned, I was out here checking into graduate schools and trying to find work.

"I just sent Today a postcard." But I'd kept it short and sweet. I hadn't given her the "411" on me.

"Jean, what man is this? I hope that you're not letting some man use you. You're not out there shacking up are you?"

"Mama, whatever I'm doing, I'm over twenty-one."

"Everybody feels like they have the right to do their own thing these days," Mama continued. "David announced that he's moving out of the dorm next semester, and Kevin has jumped up and joined the army."

"And I'm gay," I said, trying to casually complete Mama's sentence.

"What do you mean, you're gay?"

"I'm a lesbian."

"Jean, don't be ridiculous! There's no way that you're a homosexual. That doesn't run in our family."

"You make it sound like it's a disease."

"I read enough to know it's not a disease. It's a mental disorder."

"No, it's not, Mama, the American Psychological Association dropped homosexuality from its list of mental disorders two years ago."

"Why would they go and do a thing like that for?"

"Because it's not a sickness, that's why."

Mama sucked her teeth in. "They probably just couldn't come up with a cure. So they threw in the towel. They took the easy way out."

"There's nothing to cure."

"Hold on while I take a pressure pill." I felt my stomach tighten and I took a deep breath. At least we were talking about it. That was better than having to keep it all a big secret. But it was hard; I'd driven Mama to take a blood pressure pill. I tried not to feel guilty.

Mama had returned to the phone, but Artemis had jumped out of my lap. I guess she didn't want to be bothered with this conversation anymore. I was on my own.

"Well, Jean Eloise, you might be able to outwit the psychiatrists, but you can't outwit the Master. You can't go against God and Nature without paying the consequences."

"God made gay people too."

"God made everybody, including rapists and murderers."

"Mama, are you equating gays and lesbians with rapists and murderers?"

"I'm just saying that people make choices. And you can't blame God for your actions."

"What if people are born gay?"

"They still don't have to act on it."

"But straight people get to act on their feelings."

"Sin is wrong no matter who commits it."

"But we're not allowed to get married."

"Don't give me this 'we' stuff. You're not one of *them*. And I know for a fact that *you* weren't born gay."

"How do you know that?"

"Because I carried you for nine months, that's how. I knew you before you knew yourself. There has never been anything abnormal about you. You weren't even a decent tomboy. If you had some boy in you, I would've picked it up a long time ago."

"Mama, not all lesbians are diesel dykes."

"Well, I know that you're not a lesbian. You need to get your behind out of that crazy place and away from those sick people. That's why California is sliding into the ocean now."

"Why is California sliding into the ocean?"

"Because San Francisco is dripping with sin, that's why. I saw a piece on that 'Gay Parade' they had out there. It was just like Sodom and Gomorrah."

"It had nothing to do with Sodom and Gomorrah. The parade had to do with people standing up for their rights and celebrating themselves."

"Half-naked men dancing with each other; bare-breasted women kissing on one another. God could send an earthquake there anytime. We're in our final days. You need to read Revelations."

"We've been in our final days ever since I've known you."

"Jean, the signs are everywhere now."

"Hold on, there's somebody at the door, I don't know who it could be. I'm not expecting anybody. I'll be right back."

I returned to the phone.

"Who was it, Satan?" Mama asked with a touch of humor in her voice.

I had to laugh. "No, it was somebody dropping off something for my roommate. Anyway, it really bothers me that you won't accept me for who I am."

"That's not true."

"How can it not be true?"

"Because, I accept you just fine. It's you who doesn't accept yourself. You're the one who's going against your own nature."

"Mama, loving another woman *is* my nature."

"No it's not. You think rubbing your body up against another woman makes you a lesbian. Well, you're wrong. You're just going through a phase right now, that's all."

"A phase?"

"Yes, and all I ask is that you keep this mess to yourself. It would break your father's and your brothers' hearts if they knew. They might take this as a rejection of them."

"Mama, this is not about hating men. This is about loving women."

"And you certainly don't need to upset your grandmother," she continued. "Her blood pressure is higher than mine. You don't want to cause her to have a stroke, do you?"

"So I'm just supposed to pretend to everyone, live a lie?"

"I'm trying to protect you."

"Protect me?"

"Yes, because when you grow out of this mess, you'll look back at this time and thank me for not letting you make a complete fool of yourself with everybody."

"Mama, I am not going through a phase. I'll be twenty-two years old next month. I'm old enough to know what I want."

"Talk to me again when you're pushing thirty five. Then I'll give what you say more weight."

Pushing thirty-five! "Mama, I'm no virgin!" I blurted out. "I was never satisfied by a man."

"How many men have you been with? You sound like a streetwalker."

"I've had a few experiences, OK?"

"Jean, there's more to a relationship than just sex. And most of these young dudes out here don't know what they're doing anyway. You just haven't met the right man yet, that's all."

"Mama, there might not be a *right* man."

"When your father and I were newlyweds, I had problems."

"You and Daddy had problems?" I shouldn't have been surprised, since I'd never remembered them showing any affection for each other.

"I had trouble relaxing," Mama whispered, even though I was sure that she was alone. "The doctor told me to drink a glass of wine beforehand. It worked, and I have three children to prove it. That's what you need to do. Find you a good husband and drink a glass of wine beforehand."

"Mama, it's not that simple."

"Jean Eloise," Mama lowered her voice even more, "you're not doing anything oral, are you?"

"What's this about Kevin joining the army? Is he crazy? I know the Vietnam War is over, but still."

"Never mind about Kevin, I'm gonna say an extra prayer for you, just in case."

Patricia J. Williams

IN SEARCH OF PHARAOH'S DAUGHTER

Why are you doing this to yourself?" asked my mother dubiously when I began the process of adopting a child. "You're only forty. The right man could come along any day now. Women are having babies into their fifties these days." I had been hearing my mother say this since my thirtieth birthday, when women were said to be having babies well into their forties. Her quiet, unblinking slippage into the next decade made me realize that while *her* hope sprang eternal, I was starting to get stiff from all that sitting on the porch in ruffled sateen with the gardenia behind my ear.

My father was grumpier about the prospect: "I'll be a hundred years old before this child reaches college."

"No, you won't," I said sourly. "You'll barely be ninety."

The rest of my family was delighted but worried that I had not adequately taken into account how much having a child would cut into the indulgent Buppy lifestyle of which they so rightly accused me.

I have really hated disappointing everyone, but thus far motherhood has been the richest, most satisfying of rewards. While my son has indeed restricted my ability to eat in fancy restaurants, he has opened up the way to new and far better indulgences, like playing, like learning to be silly again. He has made walking the streets of New York unexpectedly inter esting: people smile at me—at him—more. They establish eye contact. They talk in streams of uncontrolled amiability. The other day as I stood waiting to cross the street, a young man with a ruby-hennaed mohawk and a ring through his nose said very gently, "What a cute baby. God bless you." My son, bless him indeed for I can take no credit in it, brings out the best in other people, even a hard case like me.

Yet for all the touted and mythic joys of motherhood, as the columnist Barbara Reynolds points out:

Across the USA, there are about 250,000 children without homes . . . In Alaska, the whales are being fawned over because of their intelligence, their lovability. Hourly reports measure the "terrible stress" on these endangered mammals . . . Our endangered homeless children are under greater stress. They are also intelligent and lovable, when given a chance . . . If we could bottle that national will and enthusiasm poured on the whales and sprinkle it on children in dangerous waters, they would be more grateful than Jonah was when a great whale spit him out rather than devour him.

In contrast, consider a small piece of the material world: when arson destroyed a home in an all-white section of Queens, New York, which had been scheduled for the placement of six "boarder" babies, then police commissioner Benjamin Ward said, "I do know most of the babies are minority babies. Maybe that's inside."

"Are they still going to be here when they grow up?" asked Richard Blasi, 11 years old. He meant the six babies . . . "This is heartbreaking," said Gretel Strump, a 46-year resident of the block. "Listen, we have nothing against babies. But the mothers, the dope addicts. My husband says, we will never be safe any more. It's nothing but dopists."

"I know it's a selfish kind of feeling but I moved here because it is the way it is," Mrs. Sawicki said. "I have my daughter here. These houses are worth a lot of money. There's got to be a better place for them than smack in the middle of here."

(I can't help noticing that the word "better" is quite a loaded term in the context of that sentence. Better does not seem to mean better for the babies, but better for the Sawickis: someplace "else," someplace where the daughters and houses are worthless. So better for the Sawickis means worse for the babies and vice versa. Better from the reference point of the babies, in other words, means not better at all, but worse.)

Fliers handed out to residents in opposition to making the house into any sort of a group home said, "We do not want our stabilized residential areas turned into garbage. We do not need more CRIME, VIOLENCE, BUR-GLARIES, TRANSIENT PEOPLE OR PROSTITUTION."

(Again the language is quite remarkable: the mere presence of six babies is a kind of reverse Midas-touch, a noxious contaminant, a garbagey breeding ground for flies, prostitution, and all the world's vices.)

The battle over the house began when the owners put it up for sale. John W. Norris, the head of a local civic association, the Auburndale Improvement Association, said the owners asked $325,000, about $100,000 more than the market price for other houses on the block.

In September, a private foster-care agency offered to buy the house and use it as a group home for six to eight girls ages 14 to 16. Human Resources Administration officials said the buyer, the Jewish Child Care Association of New York, changed their minds because of the community outcry.

The city signed a rental agreement last Friday to pay $2,400 a month for the house, which neighborhood residents said would bring about $1,100 on the open market.

Mr. Koch did not say why the city had agreed to that rent, other than to cite "supply and demand."

There is a peculiar and powerful inversion at work, in which "worthless" children drive up the price to corrupt or unattainable heights; the poorer and blacker the child, the higher the price rises. Meanwhile the more valuable legitimate daughters get to live in the high-rent district for cheap.

The market valuation of children reflected in this story is reiterated at every level of social and legal thinking. Recently, I was rereading an article by that great literary mogul of the University of Chicago's School of Law and Economics, Judge Richard Posner, and his associate Elizabeth Landes. In their short opus "The Economics of the Baby Shortage," newborn human beings are divided up into white and black and then taken for a spin around a Monopoly board theme park where the white babies are put on demand curves and the black babies are dropped off the edge of supply sides. "Were baby prices quoted as prices of soybean futures are quoted," the authors say, "a racial ranking of these prices would be evident, with white baby prices higher than nonwhite baby prices."

The trail of the demand curve leads straight into the arms of the highest bidder; the chasm of oversupply has a heap of surplus at the bottom of its pit. In this house of horrors, the surplus (or "second-quality") black babies will continue to replicate themselves like mushrooms, unless the wise, invisible, strong arm of the market intervenes to apply the wisdom of pure purchasing power. In a passage that some have insisted is all about maximizing the kindness of strangers, Landes and Posner argue:

> By obtaining exclusive control over the supply of both "first-quality" adoptive children and "second-quality" children residing in foster care but available for adoption, agencies are able to internalize the substitution possibilities between them. Agencies can charge a higher price for the children they place for adoption, thus increasing not only their revenues from adoptions but also the demand for children who would otherwise be placed or remain in foster care at the agency's expense. Conversely, if agency revenues derive primarily from foster care, the agencies can manipulate the relative price of adopting "first-quality" children over "second-quality" children to reduce the net flow of children out of foster care.

What these authors conclude, in an unsurprising rhetorical turn, is that the current "black market" for adoptive children must be replaced with what they call a "free baby market."

When this article first appeared almost twenty years ago, it created a storm of controversy. Since Judge Posner has reaffirmed its premises many times, most recently in his book *Sex and Reason,* the article has remained a major bone of contention. I will leave to economists a full-fledged critique of the models presented (as well as of the more sophisticated models and analyses of adoption markets proposed by the economist Gary Becker, from whom Posner borrows heavily). My purpose is resurrecting this piece here is to examine (1) the degree to which it is a reflection of what goes on in the world of not just adoption but reproduction in general; (2) the degree to which market valuation of bodies, even when for ostensibly noble purposes, exemplifies what is most wrong with community as well as family in America; and (3) the possibility that a shift in focus could help us imagine a more stable, less demeaning, and more inclusive sense of community.

When I decided to adopt, I was unprepared for the reality that adoption is already a pretty straightforward market. I was unprepared for the "choices" with which I was presented, as to the age, race, color, and health of prospective children. I was unprepared for the fact that I too would be shopped for, by birth mothers as well as social workers, looked over for my age, marital and economic status, and race. All that was missing was to have my tires kicked.

"Describe yourself," said the application form. *Oh lord,* I remember thinking, *this is worse than a dating service. What's appealing about me, and to whom? Responsible nonsmoking omnivore seeks . . . what? Little person for lifetime of bicycle rides, good education, and peanut butter sandwiches? Forty and fading fast so I thought I'd better get a move on?"* "You can't tell them you're forty," a friend advised. "No one will ever pick you." Okay, I sighed. "Very well rounded," I wrote.

"Describe where you live." At the time, I was still at the University of Wisconsin, even though I was visiting at Columbia, and traveling almost every week to places like Indiana and Georgia in a frenzied ritual of academic legitimation. I struggled, as I straddled worlds, with which side I should present in my "Dear Birth Mother" letter. *Chic New York apartment with expansive square footage, north-south exposure, and a refrigerator stocked with the leftovers of fifteen different types of ethnic take-out food? Your child will grow up riding the subways and knowing the finer shades of the chardonnay-and-caviar lifestyle of the middlebrow and not-so-famous? Or should I just offer a well-childproofed home in that friendly dairy center of the universe, Wisconsin, land o' butter, cream, and lakes?* "Your child will taste the world," I wrote.

"What age, what sex?" asked the social worker. "Doesn't matter," I said, "though I'd like to miss out on as little as possible."

"If you're willing to take a boy, you'll get younger," she replied. "There's a run on girls."

"What races would you accept?" asked the adoption agency. "And what racial combinations?" There followed a whole menu of evocative options, like Afro-Javanese, Sino-Germanic, and just plain "white." I assume that this list, so suggestive of the multiple combinations of meat offered at, say, Kentucky Fried Chicken, would make Elizabeth Landes and Richard Posner very happy indeed. They advise:

> The genetic characteristics of natural children are highly correlated with their parents' genetic characteristics, and this correlation could conceivably increase harmony within the family compared to what it would be with an adopted child. Nevertheless, there is considerable suitability between natural and adopted children and it might be much greater if better genetic matching of adopted children with their adoptive parents were feasible—as might occur, as we shall see, under free market conditions.

"Any," I wrote, knowing that harmony genes abound in my ancestral bloodlines—yet wondering if the agency really meant to address that question to black parents. Would they truly consider placing "any" child with me if this agency happened to have a "surplus" of white babies? Would I get a Korean baby if I asked? And for all of the advertised difficulties, what does it mean that it is so relatively easy for white American families not just to adopt black children but to choose from a range of colors, nationalities, and configurations from around the world? (And I do mean *relatively* easy— for all of the publicity about the "impossibility" of white people adopting black American children, doing so is still in most instances far easier than going to Eastern Europe or China, for instance. While there are well-publicized instances of white families who are barred by local social service office policies, in most states a waiting period of about six months is the biggest institutional hurdle they will face. In addition, there are a good number of reputable private adoption agencies that facilitate and even specialize in "interracial" adoptions.)

What does it reveal, moreover, about the social backdrop of such transactions that if I "chose" a "white" child, it might reveal something quite alarming about my own self-esteem? What does it mean that if a white parent chose a black child, many people would attribute it to an idealistic selflessness that—however misguided and threatening to cultural integrity some blacks might consider it—is not generally perceived as proceeding from a sense of diminishment? Is race-neutral adoption the answer—even to the extent of barring "mild preferences" for same-race placements, as the law professor Elizabeth Bartholet has suggested? While I very much agree with the impulse behind that solution, does the social reality of unbalanced race relations and racial power suggest some constraints on complete color-blindness as a possibility?

A number of studies claim to show that black children fare just fine when adopted into white families—and I have no doubt that this is true on any number of levels—but I am troubled by some of the conclusions drawn from such representations: the claims that such children have "unique" abilities to deal with white people, or that they are "more tolerant." I always want to ask, more tolerant of what, of whom? More tolerant *than* other blacks? Or than whites? More tolerant *of* whites? Or of other blacks?

I am particularly troubled by the notion that black children in white families are better off simply because they may have access to a broader range of material advantages by having white parents and living in the largely white and relatively privileged world. Such an argument should not, I think, be used to justify the redistribution of children in our society, but rather to bolster a redistribution of *resources* such that blacks can afford to raise children too. Moreover, assertions that black children actually do better in white homes play dangerously against a social backdrop in which slavery's history of paternalistic white protectionism still demands black loyalty to white people and their lifestyle as a powerful symbolic precedent for deeming black social organization "successful." Such assertions do not take into account the imbalance in the way state agencies intervene in the lives of poor women and women of color—particularly in view of the disproportionate rate at which children of color are removed from their homes and put into foster care or up for adoption, with little provision of the kinds of facilitative family counseling that are available at higher ends of the socioeconomic ladder.

In any event, I wonder how many social science studies there are about how white children fare in black homes.

"What color?" asked the form. *You've got to be kidding.* I looked quizzically at the social worker. "Some families like to match," she said. *You mean, like color-coordinated? You mean like the Louisiana codes? Like ebony, sepia, quadroon, mahogany? Like matching the color of a brown paper bag? Like red, like Indian, like exotic, like straight-haired, like light-skinned? Like 1840, is that what this means?* Like 1940, sighed my mother, when I mentioned this to her. *(And is this what the next generation will be sighing about, so sadly, in 2040?)*

"I don't care," I wrote. And with that magical stroke of the pen, the door to a whole world of plentiful, newborn, brown-skinned little boys with little brown toes and big brown eyes and round brown noses and fat brown cheeks opened up to me from behind the curtain marked "Doesn't Care."

"This is a cheap shot," says my friend the economist. "How can anyone criticize or take scholarly issue with the breathy mother-love of such descriptions? And what does any of this have to do with the price of tea in China?" It's a good question, I guess, and all I can do is remind the reader that I am trying, quite intentionally, to explode the clean, scientific way in which this subject is often discussed. And if it has little to do with tea or soybeans, just maybe the positioning of mother-or-any-other-love as some kind of irrelevant externality has a little something to do with the price of children in America.

My son, because he is a stylish little character, arrived at my home in a limousine. (Credit for this must be shared with the social worker, who was a pretty jazzy sort herself.) I had a big party and a naming ceremony and invited everyone I knew. I was so happy that I guess I missed that price tag hanging from his little blue knitted beanie. A few weeks later I got a call from the agency: "Which fee schedule are you going to choose?"

"What's this?" I asked the adoption agency, flipping madly through Landes and Posner for guidance: "Prospective adoptive parents would presumably be willing to pay more for a child whose health and genealogy were warranted in a legally enforceable instrument than they are willing to pay under the present system where the entire risk of any deviation from expected quality falls on them."

"Are you going with the standard or the special?" came the reply. There followed a description of a system in which adoptive parents paid a certain percentage of their salaries to the agency, which fee went to administrative costs, hospital expenses for the birth mother, and counseling. Inasmuch as it was tied exclusively to income, in a graduated scale, it clearly met the definition of a fee for services rendered. This, it was explained to me, was the standard price list.

"And the special?" I asked. After an embarrassed pause, I was told that that referred to "older, black, and other handicapped children," and that its fees were exactly half of those on the standard scale. Suddenly what had been a price system based on services rendered became clearly, sickeningly, a price system for "goods," a sale for chattel, linked not to services but to the imagined quality of the "things" exchanged. Although, as the agency asserted, this system was devised to provide "economic incentives" for the adoption of "less requested" children, in our shopping-mall world it had all the earmarks of a two-for-one sale.

I was left with a set of texts resounding in my brain, rattling with the persistence of their contradiction—a medley of voices like descriptions of Americans adopting children in Latin America and of having to hide for fear of kidnapping until they were back on the plane to the United States because "desirable" children are worth a great deal of money on the open adoption block. Or like the *New York Times Magazine* cover story of a white American couple who adopted a little girl from China: when the couple finally returned from Wuhan to New York City with the child, they felt as if they "had walked off with something of incalculable value—a baby—with the approval of everyone involved. What a coup, what a blessing—what a relief!"

What links these narratives for me is the description of a powerful emotional state that styles itself as theft, as a coup, a walking off with something right under the approving noses of everyone: "Sara and I regarded each other with a deep sense of disbelief." I am troubled; the theft of one's own body is a kind of trickster's inversion of one's life reduced to chattel status. But the acquisition of another for a sum considered as either a "deal" or a "steal," if not outright slavery, resembles nothing less than bounty hunting.

Julia A. Boyd

GOT A JOB TO DO

Careers are what white women have; jobs are what Black women do.
—*Zoey*

Leave it to Zoey to break things down in simplistic terms. Actually, girl-friend isn't too far off in her view of things. I know, because twice a month I have this recurring fantasy that goes like this: I was born rich, and some-where there is a secret document that proclaims me Queen Money, but—here's the hitch—I have to find the damn document and then my worries will be over. How's that for magical thinking? Like I said, twice a month, the day I pay bills and the one day a month when I desperately need but can't afford to take a break from the office, I allow myself the indulgence of the Queen Money fantasy. And then I go to work!

While I've never known my mother to work outside of our home, she mentally prepared her six daughters to take their places in the world. With firm sincerity, Momi always told us, "Don't expect a knight in shiny armor to sweep you off your feet; if anything, he'll hand you the broom."

———

Mama always told me that a dollar bill was a Black woman's best friend. Mama says a dollar don't give you no lip, it'll feed you when you're hungry, clothe you when you're cold, and keep the rain off your head. Yes ma'am, if you treat a dollar right, it multiplies, and if you don't it disappears, but if you got a dollar, you've got a friend for life.

—*Flo*

Bebe Moore Campbell

ENVY

from *Sweet Summer*

The red bricks of 2239 North 16th Street melded into the uniformity of look-alike doors, windows and brownstone-steps. From the outside our rowhouse looked the same as any other. When I was a toddler, the similarity was unsettling. The family story was that my mother and I were out walking on the street one day when panic rumbled through me. "Where's our house? Where's our house?" I cried, grabbing my mother's hand.

My mother walked me to our house, pointed to the numbers painted next to the door. "Twenty-two thirty-nine," she said, slapping the wall. "This is our house."

Much later I learned that the real difference was inside.

In my house there was no morning stubble, no long johns or Fruit of the Loom on the clothesline, no baritone hollering for keys that were sitting on the table. There was no beer in the refrigerator, no ball game on TV, no loud cussing. After dark the snores that emanated from the bedrooms were subtle, ladylike, little moans really.

Growing up, I could have died from overexposure to femininity. Women ruled at 2239. A grandmother, a mother, occasionally an aunt, grown-up girlfriends from at least two generations, all the time rubbing up against me, fixing my food, running my bathwater, telling me to sit still and be good in those grown-up, girly-girl voices. Chanel and Prince Matchabelli wafting through the bedrooms. Bubble bath and Jergens came from the bathroom, scents unbroken by aftershave, macho beer breath, a good he-man funk. I remember a house full of 'do rags and rollers, the soft, sweet allure of Dixie peach and bergamot; brown-skinned queens wearing pastel housecoats and worn-out size six-and-a-half flip-flops that slapped softly against the wood as the royal women climbed the stairs at night carrying their paperbacks to bed.

The outside world offered no retreat. School was taught by stern, old-maid white women with age spots and merciless gray eyes; ballet lessons, piano lessons, Sunday school and choir were all led by colored sisters with a hands on their hips attitude who cajoled and screeched in distaff tongues.

And what did they want from me, these Bosoms? Achievement! This desire had nothing to do with the pittance they collected from the Philadelphia Board of Education or the few dollars my mother paid them. Pushing little colored girls forward was in their blood. They made it clear: a life of white picket fences and teas was for other girls to aspire to. I was to *do* something. And if I didn't climb willingly up their ladder, they'd drag me to the top. Rap my knuckles hard for not practicing. Make me lift my leg until I wanted to die. Stay after school and write "I will listen to the teacher" five hundred times. They were not playing. "Obey them," my mother commanded.

When I entered 2B—the Philadelphia school system divided grades into A and B—in September 1957, I sensed immediately that Miss Bradley was not a woman to be challenged. She looked like one of those evil old spinsters Shirley Temple was always getting shipped off to live with; she was kind of hefty, but so tightly corseted that if she happened to grab you or if you fell against her during recess, it felt as if you were bouncing into a steel wall. In reality she was a sweet lady who was probably a good five years past her retirement age when I wound up in her class. Miss Bradley remained at Logan for one reason and one reason only: she was dedicated. She wanted her students to learn! learn! learn! Miss Bradley was halfway sick, hacking and coughing her lungs out through every lesson, spitting the phlegm into fluffy white tissues from the box on her desk, but she was *never* absent. Each day at three o'clock she kissed each one of her "little pupils" on the cheek, sending a faint scent of Emeraude home with us. Her rules for teaching children seemed to be: Love them; discipline them; reward them; and make sure they are clean.

Every morning she ran a hygiene check on the entire class. She marched down the aisle like a stormtrooper, rummaging through the ears of hapless students, checking for embedded wax. She looked under our fingernails for dirt. Too bad on you if she found any. Once she made David, a stringy-haired white boy who thought Elvis Presley was a living deity and who was the most notorious booger-eater in the entire school, go to the nurse's office to have the dirt cleaned from under his fingernails. Everybody knew that what was under David's fingernails was most likely dried-up boogies and not dirt, but nobody said anything.

If she was death on dirt and earwax, Miss Bradley's specialty was head-lice patrol. Down the aisles she stomped in her black Enna Jettick shoes, stopping at each student to part strands of blond, brown or dark hair, looking for cooties. Miss Bradley would flip through plaits, curls, kinks—the woman was relentless. I always passed inspection. Nana put enough Nu Nile in my hair to suffocate any living creature that had the nerve to come tipping up on my scalp. Nu Nile was the official cootie killer. I was clean, wax-free, bug-free and smart. The folder inside my desk contained a stack of spelling and arithmetic papers with As emblazoned across the top, gold stars in the corner. Miss Bradley always called on me. She sent me to run errands for her too. I was her pet.

When Mrs. Clark, my piano teacher and my mother's good friend, told my mother that Logan Elementary School was accepting children who didn't live in the neighborhood, my mother immediately enrolled Michael and later me. "It's not crowded and it's mixed," she told a nodding, smiling Nana. The fact that Logan was integrated was the main reason Michael and I were sent there. Nana and Mommy, like most upwardly mobile colored women, believed that to have the same education as a white child was the first step up the rocky road to success. This viewpoint was buttressed by the fact that George Washington Carver, my neighborhood school, was severely overcrowded. Logan was just barely integrated, with only a handful of black kids thrown in with hordes of square-jawed, pale-eyed second-generation Ukrainians whose immigrant parents and grandparents populated the neighborhood near the school. There were a few dark-haired Jews and aristocratic-looking WASPs too. My first day in kindergarten it was Nana who enthusiastically grabbed Michael's and my hands, pulling us away from North Philly's stacked-up rowhouses, from the hucksters whose wagons bounced down the streets with trucks full of ripe fruits and vegetables, from the street-corner singers and jitterbugs who filled my block with all-day doo-wahs. It was Nana who resolutely walked me past the early-morning hordes of colored kids heading two blocks away to Carver Elementary School, Nana who pulled me by the hand and led me in another direction.

We went underground at the Susquehanna and Dauphin subway station, leaving behind the unremitting asphalt and bricks and the bits of paper strewn in the streets above us. We emerged at Logan station, where sunlight, brilliant red and pink roses and yellow chrysanthemums, and neatly clipped lawns and clean streets startled me. There were robins and blue jays flying overhead. The only birds in my neighborhood were sparrows and pigeons. Delivering me at the schoolyard, Nana firmly cupped my chin with her hand as she bent down to instruct me. "Your mother's sending you up here to learn, so you do everything your teacher tells you to, okay?" To Michael she turned and said, "You're not up here to be a monkey on a stick." Then to both of us: "Don't talk. Listen. Act like you've got some home training. You've got as much brains as anybody up here. Do you know that? All right now. Make Nana proud of you."

A month after I returned from Pasquotank County, I sat in Miss Bradley's classroom on a rainy Monday watching her write spelling words on the blackboard. The harsh sccurr, sccurr of Miss Bradley's chalk and the tinny sound the rain made against the window took my mind to faraway places. I couldn't get as far away as I wanted. Wallace, the bane of the whole class, had only moments earlier laid the most gigunda fart in history, one in a never-ending series, and the air was just clearing. His farts were silent wonders. Not a hint, not the slightest sound. You could be in the middle of a sentence and then wham! bam! Mystery Funk would knock you down.

Two seats ahead of me was Leonard, a lean colored boy from West Philly who always wore suits and ties to school, waving his hand like a crazy man. A showoff if ever there was one.

I was bored that day. I looked around at the walls. Miss Bradley had decorated the room with pictures of the ABCs in cursive. Portraits of the presidents were hanging in a row on one wall above the blackboard. On the bulletin board there was a display of the Russian satellite, *Sputnik I,* and the American satellite, *Explorer I.* Miss Bradley was satellite-crazy. She thought it was just wonderful that America was in the "space race" and she constantly filled our heads with space fantasies. "Boys and girls," she told us, "one day man will walk on the moon." In the far corner on another bulletin board there was a Thanksgiving scene of turkeys and pilgrims. And stuck in the corner was a picture of Sacajawea. Sacajawea, Indian Woman Guide. I preferred looking at Sacajawea over satellites any day.

Thinking about the bubble gum that lay in my pocket, I decided to sneak a piece, even though gum chewing was strictly forbidden. I rarely broke the rules. Could anyone hear the loud drumming of my heart, I wondered, as I slid my hand into my skirt pocket and felt for the Double Bubble? I peeked cautiously to either side of me. Then I managed to un-wrap it without even rustling the paper; I drew my hand to my lips, coughed and popped the gum in my mouth. Ahhh! Miss Bradley's back was to the class. I chomped down hard on the Double Bubble. Miss Bradley turned around. I quickly packed the gum under my tongue. My hands were folded on top of my desk. "Who can give me a sentence for 'birthday'?" Leonard just about went nuts. Miss Bradley ignored him, which she did a lot. "Sandra," Miss Bradley called.

A petite white girl rose obediently. I liked Sandra. She had shared her crayons with me once when I left mine at home. I remember her draw-ing: a white house with smoke coming out of the chimney, a little girl with yellow hair like hers, a mommy, a daddy, a little boy and a dog standing in front of the house in a yard full of flowers. Her voice was crystal clear when she spoke. There were smiles in that voice. She said, "My father made me a beautiful dollhouse for my birthday."

The lump under my tongue was suddenly a stone and when I swal-lowed, the taste was bitter. I coughed into a piece of tablet paper, spit out the bubble gum, and crumpled up the wad and pushed it inside my desk. The center of my chest was burning. I breathed deeply and slowly. Sandra sat down as demurely as a princess. She crossed her ankles. Her words came back to me in a rush. "Muuuy fatha made me a bee-yoo-tee-ful dollhouse." Miss Bradley said, "Very good," and moved on to the next word. Around me hands were waving, waving. Pick me! Pick me! Behind me I could hear David softly crooning, "You ain't nothin' but a hound dog, cryin' all the time." Sometimes he would stick his head inside his desk, sing Elvis songs and pick his boogies at the same time. Somebody was jabbing pins in my chest. Ping! Ping! Ping! I wanted to holler, "Yowee! Stop!" as loud as I could, but I pressed my lips together hard.

"Now who can give me a sentence?" Miss Bradley asked. I put my head down on my desk and when Miss Bradley asked me what was wrong I told her that I didn't feel well and that I didn't want to be chosen. When

Leonard collected the homework, I shoved mine at him so hard all the papers he was carrying fell on the floor.

Bile was still clogging my throat when Miss Bradley sent me into the cloakroom to get my lunchbox. The rule was, only one student in the cloakroom at a time. When the second one came in, the first one had to leave. I was still rummaging around in my bookbag when I saw Sandra.

"Miss Bradley said for you to come out," she said. She was smiling. That dollhouse girl was always smiling. I glared at her.

"Leave when I get ready to," I said, my words full of venom.

Sandra's eyes darted around in confusion. "Miss Bradley said . . ." she began again, still trying to smile as if she expected somebody to crown her Miss America or something and come take her picture any minute.

In my head a dam broke. Terrible waters rushed out. "I don't care about any Miss Bradley. If she messes with me I'll, I'll . . . I'll take my butcher knife and stab her until she bleeds." What I lacked in props I made up for in drama. My balled-up hand swung menacingly in the air. I aimed the invisible dagger toward Sandra. Her Miss America smile faded instantly. Her eyes grew round and frightened as she blinked rapidly. "Think I won't, huh? Huh?" I whispered, enjoying my meanness, liking the scared look on Sandra's face. Scaredy cat! Scaredy cat! Muuuy fatha made me a bee-yoo-tee-ful dollhouse. "What do you think about that?" I added viciously, looking into her eyes to see the total effect of my daring words.

But Sandra wasn't looking at me. Upon closer inspection, I realized that she was looking *over* me with sudden relief in her face. I turned to see what was so interesting, and my chin jammed smack into the Emeraude-scented iron bosom of Miss Bradley. Even as my mind scrambled for an excuse, I knew I was lost.

Miss Bradley had a look of horror on her face. For a minute she didn't say anything, just stood there looking as though someone had slapped her across the face. Sandra didn't say anything. I didn't move. Finally, "Would you mind repeating what you just said, Bebe."

"I didn't say anything, Miss Bradley." I could feel my dress sticking to my body.

"Sandra, what did Bebe say?"

Sandra was crying softly, little delicate tears streaming down her face. For just a second she paused, giving a tiny shudder. I rubbed my ear vigorously, thinking, "Oh, please . . ."

"She said, she said, if you bothered with her she would cut you with her knife."

"Unh unh, Miss Bradley, I didn't say that. I didn't. I didn't say anything like that."

Miss Bradley's gray eyes penetrated mine. She locked me into her gaze until I looked down at the floor. Then she looked at Sandra.

"Bebe, you and I had better go see the principal."

The floor blurred. The principal!! Jennie G., the students called her with awe and fear. As Miss Bradley wrapped her thick knuckles around my forearm and dutifully steered me from the cloakroom and out the class-room door, I completely lost what little cool I had left. I began to cry, a jerky, hiccuping, snot-filled cry for mercy. "I didn't say it. I didn't say it," I moaned.

Miss Bradley was nonplussed. Dedication and duty overruled compassion. Always. "Too late for that now," she said grimly.

Jennie G.'s office was small, neat and dim. The principal was dwarfed by the large brown desk she sat behind, and when she stood up she wasn't much bigger than I. But she was big enough to make me tremble as I stood in front of her, listening to Miss Bradley recount the sordid details of my downfall. Jennie G. was one of those pale, pale vein-showing white women. She had a vocabulary of about six horrible phrases, designed to send chills of despair down the spine of any young transgressor. Phrases like "We'll just see about that" or "Come with me, young lady," spoken ominously. Her face was impassive as she listened to Miss Bradley. I'd been told that she had a six-foot paddle in her office used solely to beat young transgressors. Suppose she tried to beat me? My heart gave a lurch. I tugged rapidly at my ears. I longed to suck my thumb.

"Well, Bebe, I think we'll have to call your mother."

My mother! I wanted the floor to swallow me up and take me whole. My mother! As Jennie G. dialed the number, I envisioned my mother's face, clouded with disappointment and shame. I started crying again as I listened to the principal telling my mother what had happened. They talked for a pretty long time. When she hung up, ole Jennie G. flipped through some papers on her desk before looking at me sternly.

"You go back to class and watch your mouth, young lady."

As I was closing the door to her office I heard her say to Miss Bradley, "What can you expect?"

"Ooooh, you're gonna get it, girl," is how Michael greeted me after school. Logan's colored world was small, and news of my demise had blazed its way through hallways and classrooms, via the brown-skinned grapevine. Everyone from North Philly, West Philly and Germantown knew about my crime. The subway ride home was depressing. My fellow commuters kept coming up to me and asking, "Are you gonna get in trouble?" Did they think my mother would give me a reward or something? I stared at the floor for most of the ride, looking up only when the train came to a stop and the doors hissed open. Logan. Wyoming. Hunting Park. Each station drew me closer to my doom, whatever that was going to be. "What can you expect?" I mulled over those words. What did she mean? My mother rarely spanked, although Nana would give Michael or me, usually Michael, a whack across the butt from time to time. My mother's social-worker instincts were too strong for such undignified displays; Doris believed in talking things out, which was sometimes worse than a thousand beatings. As the train drew closer to Susquehanna and Dauphin I thought of how much I hated for my mother to be disappointed in me. And now she would be. "What can you expect?"

Of me? Didn't Jennie G. know that I was riding a subway halfway across town as opposed to walking around the corner to Carver Elementary School, for a reason: the same reason I was dragged away from Saturday cartoons and pulled from museum to museum, to Judimar School of Dance for ballet (art class for Michael), to Mrs. Clark for piano. The Bosoms wanted me to Be Somebody, to be the second generation to live out my life as far away from a mop and scrub brush and Miss Ann's floors as possible.

My mother had won a full scholarship to the University of Pennsylvania. The story of that miracle was a treasured family heirloom. Sometimes Nana told the tale and sometimes my mother described how the old Jewish counselor at William Penn High School approached her and asked why a girl with straight Es (for "excellent") was taking the commercial course. My mother replied that Nana couldn't afford to send her to college, that she planned to become a secretary. "Sweetheart, you switch to academic," the woman told her. "You'll get to college." When her graduation day approached, the counselor pulled her aside. "I have two scholarships for you. One to Cheyney State Teacher's College and the other to the University of Pennsylvania." Cheyney was a small black school outside of Philadelphia. My mother chose Penn. I had been born to a family of hopeful women. One miracle had already taken place. They expected more. And now I'd thrown away my chance. Michael, who was seated next to me on the subway and whose generosity of spirit had lasted a record five subway stops, poked me in my arm. "Bebe," he told me gleefully, "your ass is grass."

Nana took one look at my guilty face, scowled at me and sucked her teeth until they whistled. My mother had called her and told her what happened and now she was possessed by a legion of demons. I had barely entered the room when she exploded. "Don't. Come. In. Here. Crying," Nana said, her voice booming, her lips quivering and puffy with anger. When Nana talked in staccato language she was beyond pissed off. Waaaay beyond. "What. Could. Possess. You. To. Say. Such. A. Thing?" Embarrass-ingyourmotherlikethatinfrontof *those people!*" Before I could answer she started singing some Dinah Washington song, real loud. Volume all the way up. With every word she sang I sank deeper and deeper into gloom.

Later that evening, when my mother got home and Aunt Ruth, Michael's mother, came to visit, the three women lectured me in unison. The room was full of flying feathers. Three hens clucking away at me, their breasts heaving with emotion. Cluck! Cluck! Cluck! How could I have said such a thing? What on earth was I thinking about? Cluck! Cluck! Cluck! A knife, such a, a *colored* weapon.

"But I didn't do anything," I wailed, the tears that had been trickling all day now falling in full force.

"Umph, umph, umph," Nana said, and started singing. Billie Holiday this time.

"You call threatening somebody with a knife nothing?" Aunt Ruth asked. Ruth was Nana's middle girl. She was the family beauty, as pretty as Dorothy Dandridge or Lena Horne. Now her coral lips were curled up in disdain and her Maybelline eyebrows were raised in judgment against me. "They expect us to act like animals and you have to go and say that. My God."

Animals. Oh. Oh. Oh.

My mother glared at her sister, but I looked at Aunt Ruth in momentary wonder and appreciation. Now I understood. The unspoken rule that I had sensed all of my life was that a colored child had to be on her best behavior whenever she visited the white world. Otherwise, whatever opportunity was being presented would be snatched away. I had broken the rule. I had committed the unpardonable sin of embarrassing my family in front of *them.* Sensing my remorse and shame, Mommy led me out of the kitchen. We sat down on the living room sofa; my mother took my hand. "Bebe, I want you to go to your room and think about what you've done. I don't understand your behavior. It was very hard for me to get you in Logan." She drew a breath. I drew a breath and looked into the eyes of a social worker. "I'm extremely disappointed in you."

I didn't go straight to my room. Instead I sneaked into Michael's room, which overlooked Mole Street, the tiny, one-sided alley of narrow rowhouses that faced the backyards of 16th Street. Michael and I usually played on the "back street." Alone in Michael's room with the window open, I could hear Mr. Watson, our neighbor, hollering at one of his kids. Why had I said what I said? What had possessed me? Then I remembered. "Muuuy fatha made me a bee-yoo-tee-ful dollhouse for muuuuy birthday." Something pinched me inside my chest when I heard those words. Pain oozed from my heart like a tube of toothpaste bursting open, going every whichaway. Blue-eyes kept yapping away with her golden hair and her goofy little smile. Who cared what her fatha did? Who cared? I couldn't help it. When she came into the cloakroom I got mad all over again. When I said I had a knife, she looked just like Grandma Mary's chickens. Scared. And my chest stopped hurting. Just stopped.

Mr. Watson's baritone voice was a seismic rumble echoing with the threat of upheaval, violence. His words floated over Mole Street and into the bedroom window. Whoever was in trouble over there was really gonna get it. None of this "go to your room" stuff. None of this corny "I'm disappointed in you" stuff. Mr. Watson was getting ready to beat somebody's ass.

Adam's. He was the youngest and one of my playmates. I could tell by his pleading voice. "Please, Daddy. I won't do it anymore, Daddy. I'm sorry, Daddy."

Michael came into the room. "What are you doing?" he whispered.

"Shhh. Adam's getting a whipping."

"You better go to your room before Aunt Doris comes upstairs."

"Shhhh."

My playmate's misery took my mind off my own. His father's exotic yelling hypnotized me. From downstairs I could hear the hens, still clucking away. Michael and I sat quietly, not making a sound. Mr. Watson's voice sounded so foreign coming into our house. For a moment I pretended that his anger was emanating from Michael's bedroom, and I remembered how only last year he got mad and ran after all of us kids—Jackie, Jane and Adam, his own three, and me. His face was covered with shaving cream and he held a razor in one hand and a thick leather belt in the other. I don't recall what we had done, but I remember him chasing us and yelling ferociously, "This belt's got your name on it too, Miss Bebe!" And I recall that I was thrilled when the leather grazed my hiney with the vengeance of a father's wrath.

My mind drifted back a few years. The memory was vague and fuzzy. When I was four or five I was playing on Mole Street when my ten-year-old neighbor, a boy named Buddy, asked me to come inside his yard. He was sitting on an old soda crate. "Come closer," he told me. "Wanna play doctor?"

"Uh huh."

"You can examine me."

I told my mother, prattling on about the "game" I had played. She sat me down on her bed. "Did he touch your private parts?"

"Nope." Why was Mommy's face so serious?

"Did you touch his?"

"I touched his zipper." Had I done something wrong?

Nana went into hysterics, singing and screeching like a wild woman. "Mother, just calm down," Mommy told her.

Mommy was cool, every inch the social worker; she took my hand and we walked down the street to Buddy's house. He was in his yard making a scooter out of the crate. "Buddy," my mother said softly. When he saw the two of us, he dropped his hammer. "Buddy, I want to talk with you."

My mother questioned him. Calmly put the fear of God in him. Warned him of penalties for a repeat performance. And that was that. Not quite. Weeks, maybe months later, my father came to visit me, one of his pop-in, no-real-occasion visits. My mother, my father and I were sitting in his car and she told him about my playing doctor. His leg shot out in wild, uncontrollable spasms. His face became contorted and he started yelling. Nana's screeching paled in contrast. This was rage that my mother and Nana could not even begin to muster. And it was in my honor. This energy was for my avengement, my protection. Or should have been. But the sound of his fury frightened me. I remember angling away from my father, this man who was yelling like an animal in pain. I leaned toward my mother, and she put one arm around me and with the other hand tried to pat my father's shoulder, only he snatched away. He leaned forward and started reaching for his chair. "I may not be able to walk, goddammit, but I can tear that little son of a bitch's ass up."

My mother kept talking very softly, saying, "No, no, no. It's all right. He's just a kid. I took care of it. It's okay." I leaned away from my father's anger, his determination. He frightened me. But the rage was fascinating too. And after a while, when my father was shouting only a little, I moved closer to him. I wanted to see the natural progression of his hot words. If he snatched his wheelchair out of the backseat and rolled up to Buddy's house, what would he do? What would he do in my honor? My mother calmed my father. His shouting subsided. I was relieved. I was disappointed.

"Hey"—I suddenly heard Michael's persistent voice—"ain't you glad Mr. Watson ain't your father?" I felt Michael's hands, shaking my shoulder. "Ain't you?"

I didn't answer. I was thinking about Miss Bradley, Jennie G., Aunt Ruth, Nana and Mommy. All these women with power over me. I could hear Mrs. Watson telling her husband that enough was enough and then the baritone telling her he knew when to stop and Adam letting out another feeble little yelp. "Muuuy fatha made me a bee-yoo-tee-ful dollhouse." Maybe my mother would write my daddy and tell him how bad I had been. Maybe he would get so mad he would get into his car and drive all the way to Philly just to whip my behind. Or tell me he was disappointed in me. Either one.

The bosoms decided to forgive me. My mother woke me up with a kiss and a snuggle and then a crisp, "All right, Bebe. It's a brand-new day. Forget about yesterday." When I went to get a bowl of cereal that morning, my Aunt Ruth was sitting in the kitchen drinking coffee and reading the newspaper. She had spent the night. "Did you comb your hair?" she asked me.

I nodded.

"That's not what I call combed. Go get me the comb and brush."

She combed out my hair and braided it all over again. This time there were no wispy little ends sticking out. "Now you look nice," she said. "Now you look like a pretty girl, and when you go to school today, act like a pretty girl. All right?"

I nodded.

Last night Nana had hissed at me between her teeth. "If you want to behave like a little *heathen,* if you want go up there acting like a, a . . . *monkey on a stick . . . well,* thenyoucangotoschoolrightaroundthecorner-andI'llwalkyouthereandI'llwalkyoubackhomeandI'llcomeandgetyoufor lunchnowyou*behave*yourself!" But today she was sanguine, even jovial, as she fixed my lunch. She kissed me when I left for school.

On my way out the door my mother handed me two elegant letters, one to Miss Bradley and the other to Jennie G., assuring them that I had an overactive imagination, that I had no access to butcher knives or weapons of any kind, that she had spoken to me at length about my unfortunate outburst and that henceforth my behavior would be exemplary. These letters were written on her very best personalized stationery. The paper was light pink and had "D.C.M." in embossed letters across the top. Doris C. knew lots of big words and she had used every single one of them in those letters. I knew that all of her *i*s were dotted and all of her *t*s were crossed. I knew the letters were extremely dignified. My mother was very big on personal dignity. Anyone who messed with her dignity was in serious trouble.

I was only five when an unfortunate teller at her bank called her by her first name loud enough for the other customers to hear. My mother's body stiffened when she heard, "Doris, oh Doris," coming from a girl almost young enough to be her child.

"Are you talking to *me,* dear?" Her English was so clipped, her words so razor sharp she could have taken one, stabbed the teller and drawn blood. The girl nodded, her speckled green eyes wide and gaping, aware that something was going on, not quite sure what, and speechless because she was no match at all for this imperious little brown-skinned woman. "The people in *my* office all call me *Mrs. Moore."*

And she grabbed me by the hand and we swept out of the bank. Me and Bette Davis. Me and Claudia McNeil. People stepped aside to let us pass.

So I knew my mother's letters not only would impress Miss Bradley and

Jennie G. but also would go a long way toward redeeming me. After Miss Bradley read the note she told me I had a very nice mother and let me know that if I was willing to be exemplary she would let bygones be bygones and I could get back into her good graces. She was, after all, a dedicated teacher. And I had learned my lesson.

My mother wrote my father about the knife incident. I waited anxiously to hear from him. Would he suddenly appear? I searched the street in front of the school every afternoon. At home I jumped up nervously whenever I heard a horn beep. Finally, a letter from my dad arrived—one page of southpaw scribble.

> *Dear Bebe,*
>
> *Your mother told me what happened in school about the knife. That wasn't a good thing to say. I think maybe you were joking. Remember, a lot of times white people don't understand how colored people joke, so you have to be careful what you say around them. Be a good girl.*
>
>

Lots of love,
Daddy.
>

The crumpled letter hit the edge of the wastepaper basket in my mother's room and landed in front of her bureau. I picked it up and slammed it into the basket, hitting my hand in the process. I flung myself across the bed, buried my face into my pillow and howled with pain, rage and sadness. "It's not fair," I wailed. Ole Blondie had her dollhouse-making daddy whenever she wanted him. "Muuuy fatha . . ." Jackie, Jane and Adam had their wild, ass-whipping daddy. All they had to do was walk outside their house, look under a car, and there he was, tinkering away. Ole ugly grease-monkey man. Why couldn't I have my daddy all the time too? I didn't want a letter signed "Lots of love," I wanted my father to come and yell at me for acting like a monkey on a stick. I wanted him to come and beat my butt or shake his finger in my face, or tell me that what I did wasn't so bad after all. Anything. I just wanted him to come.

Karla F. C. Holloway

NICE GIRLS

from *Codes of Conduct: Race, Ethics, and the Color of Our Character*

The peach speech happened in the summer. We were in Eastern Market in Detroit—a large open air market that began our summer Saturday mornings and that my older sister Karen and I called Easter market. I was trying to pick our free stone instead of cling peaches and Grandmother Celia decided it would be a perfect time to give me and Karen the fuzz lecture. She had us "handle" a peach—passing it back and forth between us, rubbing it smooth and clear of its soft fuzz until the contrast between ours and the one she still held was evident. That, Grandmother said, is the difference between a nice girl and one that has been passed around. If we put the one we had passed between us back with the others, no one would choose the well-handled peach over the fresh ones. Karen and I looked. It was absolutely apparent which peach had been passed around. We shook our heads, agreeing with our grandmother. Then we went home and made cobbler.

Grandmother's other lesson, the one about red, had no touchable peach-like text. And there was no reward in pies. It was simply that nice girls do not wear red. And especially nice girls that are dark, like you Karla Francesca (my grandmother always called me by my two names). She eyed me over her coverlets where she lay in the front bedroom. It makes you look common.

Jeannette Drake

YES M'AM

(For My Grandmother on the Occasion of Her Ninty-fifth Birthday)

from *Daughter of Abraham*

Her name is Esther,
but they call her "Miss Sis."
M'am?
Yes M'am . . .
she says when I ask
what it was like when she was young
and she tells me in a voice, slow
and strong about girlhood:
"stayin' wid grandmammy Celie,"
while her momma worked,
'bout her step grandpoppa
(who had a "good" head of hair),
how she went to school "some"
and learned to read "some."

M'am?
Yes M'am . . .

How "grown folks didn't talk
in front of chullens"
but she asked many questions
anyway and heard " 'bout folks
turnin' over washpots
at prayer meetin' time."

M'am?
Yes M'am.

" 'Bout President Hoover
and how folks would 'vide
with one another to make a meal
and they just lived good
from one to another."

M'am?
Yes M'am.

And how girls would roll
their hair in brown paper
to make curls, not straighten it.

M'am?
Yes M'am.

M'am?
Yes M'am.

M'am?
Yes M'am.

"What? Talk lak' des chullens now?
You'd get a pop in your mouth!
If you don't honor me, who you gon'
honor?
If you honor me
If you honor me
You can honor somebody else
away from home.
You won't make me feel bad
when I'm dead and gone,
and that's that!"

M'am?
Yes M'am.

She called her husband, Mister Drake.
But when she made her mind up,
she got her own business straight . . .
"Lord, show me the right way,
what to do and how to do."
M'am?
Yes M'am.

In between naps,
Esther keeps going,
strumming me
music from her heart.
M'am?
Yes M'am.

M'am?
Yes M'am.
A queen at ninety-five,
is what I want to be,
slow, steadfast and strong
like Esther Lee.
M'am?
Yes M'am.

Daryl Cumber Dance

YOU RINATE?

I always used the proper names when I potty trained my daughter, so I would set her on the potty, and say, "Alright, sweetheart, urinate for mommy; come on now, urinate in the potty."

At first I was somewhat nonplussed when upon succeeding, she gleefully yelled, "I rinated, Mommy, I rinated in the potty." It was some time before I realized that she had understood me to say to her, "you rinate," and thus she was responding, "I rinated."

Carolyn M. Rodgers

HOW I GOT OVAH II / IT IS DEEP II

(for Evangelist Richard D. Henton)

from *how i got ovah*

just when i thought i had gotten away
my mother
called me on the phone
and did not ask,
but commanded me
to come to church with her.

and because i knew so much
and had "escaped"
i thought it a harmless enough act.

i was not prepared for the Holy Ghost.
i was not prepared to be covered by the
blood of Jesus.

i was not ready to be dipped in
                              the water. . . .

i could not drink the water turned wine.

and so i went back another day
trying to understand the mysteries
of mystical life the "intellectual"
purity of mystical light.
and that Sunday evening while i was
sitting there and the holy gospel choir
was singing
            "oh oh oh oh somebody touched me"

somebody touched me.
           and when i turned around to
see what it was whoever touched me wanted
my mother leaned over and whispered in my ear
    "Musta been the hand of the Lord"

Sonya Brooks

GRANDMA TALK

Ya say something botherin you . . .
Well, I hope it ain't money 'cause
I ain't got no money to put "gas in my tank."

I sho do hope it ain't "dofunny" 'cause
I can't come betwinxt no "bread and butter."
What is it chile? I ain't got all day, so
ya better shoot "straight from the hip."

If you got the "hibbijibbies," just pray
to the Lord for strength and understanding.

Chile, I don't know what's botherin you,
but whatever it is, always remember this,
"a closed mouth won't get fed."

Mama Sez

Her tongue knows no Sunday.

A whistling woman and a crowing hen never come to a good end.

A pullet always tells where she lays her first egg.

You ever see a fish what kept his mouth shut caught on anybody's hook?

Shut mouth don't catch no flies.

We can all sing together, but we can't all talk together.

The empty barrel makes the most noise.

A tattler keeps the pot boiling.

What eyes don't see, mouth can't talk about.

Never let your right hand know what your left hand is doing.

See and be blind; hear and be deaf.

Believe half of what you see and nothing that you hear.

Every shut eye ain't sleep; every good-bye ain't gone.

The bush has ears and the wall has a mouth.

You kin hide the fire, but what you gon' do with the smoke?

Chile, don't you raise yo' voice at me. Don't you ever forget, I brought you into this world and I'll take you out.

Chile, you kin cloud up, just so you don't rain.

Gal, don't roll your eyes at me!

No she didn't cut eye/suck teeth!

I raised her since she was knee high to a duck!

Dr. Brown ain't yo' mother. [reminder that the final authority whose advice is to be followed is always the mother—often said after a child has quoted a teacher or a doctor or even a minister]

You talk back to me, gal, I'll knock you into next week!

God don't like ugly!

Old Lady Know-it-all died last year.

A hard head makes a soft behind.

You got to crawl before you can walk.

A po' dog is glad of a whippin'.

There are three kinds of people in this world: those who make things happen, those who watch things happen, and those who wonder, "What happened?"

When you're down and out, raise your head high and shout, "I'm out o' here!"

What you don't have in your head, you got to have in your feet.

The chickens come home to roost.

When trouble sleeps, don't wake 'im up.

Feed the devil wit' a *long* spoon.

Heep a good cotton stalks get chopped up from 'sociatin' wid de weeds.

If you don't want to trade with the devil, keep out of his shop.

If you make yourself an ass, folks will ride you.

If you live with dogs, you learn to howl.

If you play with dogs, you get bitten.

You run with dogs, you get fleas.

A dog that will bring a bone will carry one.

Don't put the cart before the horse.

Don't swap the Devil for a witch.

An open door admits many visitors.

You made your bed, now lie in it.

If you make your bed hard, it's you gon' have to lie on it.

If you can't stand the heat, you better git outta the kitchen.

If you're wearing rags, stay away from the fire.

Live by the sword, you die by the sword.

Where there's smoke, there's fire.

Every tub must sit on its own bottom.

Look before you leap.

You have to take the fat with the lean.

Any poor dog will tuck his tail sometimes.

Even the biggest brook runs dry sometimes.

I don't keep nothin' hidden in the closet.

Don't ever forget on what side yo' bread is buttered.

One hand washes the other.

You scratch my back, I'll scratch yours.

We've got to all stand together or we will fall together. It's a whole lot easier to break a single stick than a bundle of sticks.

Nothing ventured, nothing gained.

A seldom visitor makes the best friend.

You can't hurry up good times by waitin' for 'em.

The first one to the spring gets the clearest water.

Naught from naught leaves naught.

Don't cry over spilt milk.

Don't worry. A dog wants a bone more than once.

You never miss your water till your well runs dry.

The sun ain't gon' shine in your door always.

It's six in one hand and a half-dozen in the other.

Robbing Peter to pay Paul.

The rich get richer and the poor get chirren.

He's not gon' buy the cow if he can get the milk for free.

You be safe long as you remember to keep your dress down and your drawers up.

Keep your drawers up and your knees shut.

If you give an inch, they'll take a foot.

He's a chip off the old block, and the chip don't fall too far from the block/the leaves don't fall too far from the tree.

Chip off the old block tastes like timber.

The gourd will follow the vine.

Where there's smoke, there's fire.

Pity the bee that don't make no mo' honey than she want.

The bird can't fly with one wing.

The littlest snow flakes make the deepest snow.

There's more than one way of skinning a cat.

It's a mighty bad wind that never shifts.

It don't rain every time the clouds gather.

Be careful what you pray for, cause you just might get it.

It takes two birds to make a nest.

It's many a slip between the cup and the lip.

Don't worry that the right man hasn't come along yet. Remember, there's a lid for every pot.

"If it don't fit don't force it." [Mother Love, Listen Up, 55]

Take what you can get until you get what you want.

Walk with a crooked stick until you can find a straight one.

Don't cut up more than you can eat.

Monkey see, monkey do.

Crow and corn can't grow in the same field.

If you gon' dig a hole for someone, you better dig two.

Gal, you can't spit in my face and call it rain. [spoken to one who is trying to deceive]

Boy, you can't piss on me and tell me it's raining.

Who the cap fit, wear it.

Don't shout before the spirit rises.

The dead man can't hire his own gravedigger.

The graveyard is the cheapest boarding house.

Sister to Sister

You may not get all you pay for, but you will damn sho pay for all you get.

I keep my money in my bra cause they're the only two suckers I can trust.

Don't let your mouth write a check your ass can't cash.

You got to play big to win big.

Whatever you do, be sure to C-Y-O. [cover your ass]

You run your mouth; I'll run my business.

Friends are few and far between.

Just cause you paranoid don't mean somebody is not after you.

Wait for you! I don't wait! Weight broke the mule's back/Weight broke the wagon down.

If you not gon' shit, git off the pot.

Girl, don't pay no tention to what dey call you. Labels are for canned goods and you sho don't sit aroun' on nobody's grocery shelf.

Girl, when you gonna wake up and smell the coffee!

All he's looking for is a one-night stand.

Don't let him tell you to play like Jack and Jill and go up the hill for no damn *water*. Water don't run up hill.

Remember what one strawberry said to the other: "If we hadn't gone to bed together we wouldn't be in this *jam* today."

[Speaking to women thinking of cheating] "You think the grass is greener somewhere else? If your grass is brown it's because you haven't been watering it, tending to it." [Mother Love, *Listen Up*, 127]

CHAPTER 3

Mirror, Mirror on the Wall

THE BLACK WOMAN'S PHYSICAL IMAGE

Mirror, mirror on the wall?
Who's the fairest one of all?

. . . .

Queen, you *were* the fairest, t'is true
But *Snow White* is a thousand times lovelier than you.

Those who saw the movie or read the novel *The Color Purple* can never forget the scene in which Alice Walker's Mister spits out at his wife Celie, "Look at you. You black, you pore, you ugly, . . . Goddam, . . . you nothing at all." How many black females winced at this excoriating denunciation of Celie, feeling its vehemence so keenly because they knew that it was not just an isolated and merely fictional attack of one angry husband on one unfortunate wife, but it reflected the bitter reality of the image they saw when they peered in the mirror held up to them by society? Certainly the black woman's negative self-image is reinforced when she looks at the ugly stereotypical images generally projected of her in movies, in literature, on TV, even in folk materials. She is certainly not Snow White, and therefore she can never be the "fairest one of all." One might wonder then of the black female, to paraphrase William Butler Yeats's "A Dialogue of the Soul":

> How in the name of Heaven can [she] escape
> That defiling and disfigured shape
> The mirror of malicious eyes
> Casts upon [her] eyes until at last
> [She] thinks that shape must be [her] shape?

One of the most revered images of the black woman in American society is that of the Mammy (the best known of which is Aunt Jemima), who is characterized as strong, bossy, religious, superstitious, and ever-loyal to her white masters. Physically the Mammy is fat, with a big bust, and old, with gray hair, often concealed in the trademark head-rag she has tied around her head; she is inevitably swathed in an apron, her big eyes shining, and a grin stretching across her face. So admired is she by the white public that the Daughters of the American Confederacy petetitioned Congress to erect a monument in Washington in her honor.[1] (One wonders if this group contributed anything to the present effort [in 1996] to raise funds to erect a Black Patriots Memorial in Washington, D.C., to honor the more than five thousand blacks who fought for American independence.)

If the black woman is young, the dominant historical image of her has been as a Jezebel, a rump-shaking, loud talking, sexually aggressive whore, obviously a descendent of the Venus Hottentot, the captured African, Saartjie Baartman, who was displayed naked and caged in circuses in Europe to reveal the "unusual" size of the derriere and genitalia of barbaric, jungle creatures, i.e., black women. So obsessed were the Europeans with the "sexuality" of African women that after her death they preserved Ms. Baartman's sexual organs, which remained on display at the Musée de L'homme in Paris well into the last quarter of the twentieth century.[2] That this image continues can be seen in the 1977 Coleman II album cover *Electric Savage*, which features a naked colored woman. Though the Jezebel is sometimes pictured as a mulatto, generally both the Mammy and the Jezebel have dark, shiny skin, a big mouth, glowing white teeth, and large

1. Deborah Gray White, *Ar'nt I a Woman?*, 165.
2. See Sander Gilman, *Difference and Pathology*, 85–90.

hips and breasts. This image of the black woman is always contrasted with that of the white woman, who is small, perfectly proportioned, delicate, soft spoken, with blonde hair and blue eyes.[3] Historically, there has been no image in American popular culture of a black woman as young, innocent, beautiful, and charming. If she is a child, she is a wild and heathenish pickininny—a stupid and unkempt urchin with the familiar black skin, thick lips, shining teeth, huge pop eyes, and a head of nappy hair or outlandish braids.[4]

That such mirror images have been devastating for black girls growing up in this society is indicated in every aspect of their lives and discussed in some detail by psychiatrists William H. Grier and Price M. Cobbs in "Achieving Womanhood" in their famous study of the black psyche, *Black Rage.* There is hardly a novel by a black woman that does not touch upon the issues of complexion, hair, and general physical appearance, i.e., beauty; and, as Gloria Wade-Gayles tells us in *Rooted Against the Wind,* pretty for black women means "not overweight, nor too dark, attractively coiffeured, well-dressed, and young-looking." In the earliest novels by black women, the "beautiful" heroines were always fair with "good" hair. The concern with the concept of physical beauty never wavered as can be seen in nov-

---

3. One realizes that women from other groups also suffer because they do not fit the model image, that even among whites, there are variations of complexion and hair and eye color that leave some white females feeling unattractive. Further, the obsession of white females with body shape and size and with a youthful appearance is too familiar to require commentary; however, my concern here is with black females, who tend as a group to be further from the image of the ideal female in America than others. It is true also that black males have been affected by the preference for fair skin and straight hair, but as psychologists Angela M. Neal and Midge L. Wilson point out, "Compared to Black males, black females have been more profoundly affected by the prejudicial fallout surrounding issues of skin color, facial features, and hair." Literary critic Mary Helen Washington concurs: "The color/hair problem has cut deep into the psyche of the black woman. It is that particular aspect of oppression that has affected, for the most part, only women."

4. Clearly such figures as Cicely Tyson, Lena Horne, and a few others have stood in contrast to these stereotypes for a number of years, and a number of recent films and TV shows, such as *The Cosby Show,* have also countered the stereotypes. But the fact remains that stereotypes die hard, and the loud mouth, hip shaking "bitch" in such current shows as *Martin, Living Single* and the now-rerunning *In Living Color* continue to be the darker woman; and rather than let go of Aunt Jemima there are efforts to update her with even such a popular figure as Gladys Knight appearing in a recent Aunt Jemima pancakes ad.

els from Zora Neale Hurston's *Their Eyes Were Watching God* (1937), right on through Gwendolyn Brooks's *Maud Martha* (1953) and Toni Morrison's *The Bluest Eye* (1970), to Benilde Little's *Good Hair* (1996). In the latter the major concern of the protagonist and several characters, especially in their judgment of women, is hair. Little's protagonist, Alice Andrews, though popular, is always worried that her hair is not "good" enough to hold certain men. When she is courted by an attractive doctor, she expects his mother won't approve because "my skin is a little too dark for her and my hair a little too bushy." In Toni Morrison's *Song of Solomon,* Hagar is literally driven to her grave by the realization that "He [her lover, Milkman] loves silky hair. . . . He's never going to like my hair."[5] In the spring 1996 special issue of the black journal *Callaloo,* "Emerging Women Writers," a number of the new writers continue to focus on the black woman's physical appearance: one writer treats the Venus Hottentot; at least three works deal at some point with nappy hair; and another story emphasizes dark skin, and big busts and hips. Similarly the recent collection of writings by young black women, *Black Girl Talk* (1995), has at least eight pieces that focus on hair and skin color.

Practically every autobiographical writing by a black woman focuses upon the impact of color and hair upon her, whether she is a fair woman with straight hair and Nordic features such as Toi Derricotte, who stands out because she is "different,"[6] or a dark woman with coarse hair and African features, such as Whoopi Goldberg, who declares that "Beauty is something we all want," but observes that she grew up realizing that "If you

5. An excellent discussion of attitudes toward hair in the black community and specifically in two works of literature may be found in Bertram Ashe, " 'Why don't he like my hair?' ": Constructing African-American Standards of Beauty in Toni Morrison's *Song of Solomon* and Zora Neale Hurston's *Their Eyes Were Watching God.* Anyone interested in pursuing this subject further should also see Kathy Russell, et. al. *The Color Complex: The Politics of Skin Color Among African Americans* (New York: Harcourt Brace, 1992).

6. While being "graced" with fair skin and straight hair is a mixed "blessing" within the black community, that creates another set of dilemmas and conflicts, as suggested in the constant battle in Spike Lee's *School Daze* between the "Wannabees," the light-skin girls with longer, straighter hair, and the "Jigaboos," the darker girls with short, nappy hair. I was recently teased about growing up in a church that required the "brown bag and comb test" for admission, a comment that is both an accusation and a compliment (the test requires that a person be no darker than a regular paper bag and that a comb go through his/her hair without any problem).

were like me, you knew you stood a better chance of winning the Nobel Prize than of waking up beautiful."[7]

Within the black community there are constant reminders of the ideal image, with popular sayings such as

> If you're white, you're right
> If you're brown, stick around,
> If you're black, step back.[8]

Then there is the familiar anecdote about the black man who declares that he loves *fat* white women because there's so much of them that's white; he loves *young* white women because they've got so long to be white; and he loves *old* white women because they've been white so long. Note that here, *whiteness* is the most significant item, overiding what would generally be considered shortcomings—age and obesity. Other folk sayings attributed to black males in the folk community include, "The only thing black I want is a Cadillac," "I don't haul no coal," and "The only thing a black woman can do for me is lead me to a white woman." This obsession of many black men with whiteness has led some observers to charge that such black men don't just want a white woman, they want to *be* a white woman, an accusation that finds credence in Dennis Rodman, who revels in his relationship with Madonna, boasts that he dates only white women,[9] and appeared in August, 1996, at a book signing dressed in a wedding gown and wearing a blonde wig.

Toni Morrison writes in *The Bluest Eye* that the idea of physical beauty is "the most destructive [idea] in the history of human thought." Nowhere is this more obvious than among those black women whose obsessive efforts to realize the unattainable ideal has been a subject of much humor that

7. Foreword to Beverly Johnson, *True Beauty* (unnumbered).

8. There are also some items in the folk lexicon that attack fair skins, such as a popular song that includes verses such as "I wouldn't marry a yellow woman / I'll tell you the reason why / Her neck's so long and stringy now, / I'm 'fraid she'll never die." [the singer may detail other reasons, such as "she wouldn't mend my britches."] However, the greater number of attacks by far are on Negroid attributes.

9. See his autobiography written with Tim Keown, *Bad As I Wanna Be*. New York: Delacorte, 1996.

they direct at themselves as they joke about their use of skin bleachers and other extreme measures to lighten their complexion, of cosmetic surgery to change their features, of colored contact lenses to achieve blue or gray eyes, of wigs to approximate white hair, and of a variety of often torturous hair treatments to dye, straighten, or otherwise change the texture and length of their hair.[10] In "hair always *and* forever," Lisa Jones quotes a legendary jazz singer who told her, "everything I've done with my hair explains everything I've done with my life and art," and Jones goes on to declare, "Hair is the be-all and end-all."[11] Life for all too many African American women is devoted to concealing all the kinks in their hair, including the kitchen (the hair at the back of the neck that is the most difficult to get at and straighten) and the edges (that short hair at the contour of the hairline that inspired the title of Ntozake Shange's collection of poetry *Nappy Edges.* So urgent is the need to keep one's hair from "going back" (reverting to nappiness)[12] that black women often forego many pleasures that might cause them to perspire, get their hair wet, or in any way destroy a difficult and expensive hairdo. The day before I wrote this introduction, a friend had me in stitches—her back and neck were killing her because for a week she had been sleeping in uncomfortable positions to avoid mussing her hairdo—"I rather suffer these pains than mess up the waves, Girl! Ain't it looking *good?*" . . . It was . . . She wasn't.[13] As Bonnie Allen has noted, no matter how much heat has been applied, our hair, with a "short, nappy little mind of its own," will not "melt down in the melting

10. These include bleaching, dyeing, straightening or pressing with a hot comb, curling with hot curlers, blow drying, teasing, braiding, cornrowing, locking (dreads), twisting, weaving, sculpting, and the application of chemical relaxers, permanents, Jheri curls, waves, wraps, and extensions.

11. *bulletproof diva,* 11.

12. In *Talkin and Testifyin: The Language of Black America,* Geneva Smitherman discusses that "whole category of terminology and concepts that precludes white usage . . . terms . . . limited in meaning to one particular black-based referrent . . . [many having] to do with hair, color, skin, and facial features of blacks." See pp. 64ff.

13. Though in humorous accounts the focus is usually on the discomfort of hair styling, it is important to note that some of the most pleasant memories of many black girls is of sitting between their mothers' or grandmothers' legs and having their hair fixed or of that rite of passage when they join their older sisters in visiting the beauty parlor and joining in the ritual of female communion there.

pot." Two recent books by Lonnice Brittenum Bonner humorously recount problems the author experienced with chemical treatments and offer advice for caring for natural hair. Playing on Shange's well-known choreopoem, *for colored girls who have considered suicide/when the rainbow is enuf*, Bonner's comic titles are *Good Hair: For Colored Girls Who've Considered Weaves When the Chemicals Became Too Ruff* (1991) and *Plaited Glory: For Colored Girls Who've Considered Braids, Locks, and Twists* (1996).

Some black women also torture themselves physically and emotionally about other aspects of their appearance, including their weight (particularly the size of their busts, waist, and hips), the size and shape of their lips and nose, and their age. Added to the concerns over which women of other ethnic groups agonize as a result of living in this youth-oriented culture, the black woman is faced with *nappy* gray hair and *black* wrinkled skin (though at times there is some pride in the fact that black skin does not wrinkle as early as pale skin). At a certain age, when she looks in the mirror, the black woman is likely to querry, "Mirror, mirror on the wall, who's the best preserved/most youthful of them all?" Even those black women who don't carry around a lot of extra pounds are often embarrassed by their high butts, frequently the subject of ridicule as in the song "Big Ole Butt" and the 2 Live Crew's album cover with its picture of a black woman's butt (no face or head is shown; we focus only on the butt).

One may ask how and why black women take this most painful subject and make it an item of humor among themselves. One theory about women's humor advanced by psychologist Paul E. McGhee might be argued to have some relevance to black women:

> [Several studies show] the puzzling finding that females actually prefer humor in which women are victimized.... [Female comics] offered self-depreciating humor significantly more often ... than did the males.... these findings may reflect the fact that females are typically less concerned than males with the issue of dominance and infallibility.

Whether this is true of black women or not, it is certainly true that their physical appearance—or perhaps, more significantly, black men's attitude toward their physical appearance—is just *one more* subject on which black women can either laugh or cry, and they refuse to do the latter. They laugh about their desire for long hair: one of Whoopi Goldberg's most poignant and hilarious routines is about a little black girl with a white shirt on her head, acclaiming "This is my long luxurious blonde hair. Ain't it pretty?"[14] They laugh about what they do to their hair and how they are restricted by it. They laugh about their beauty parlors: April Sinclair calls one of them the "No Naps Salon" in *Coffee Will Make You Black*. They laugh about their obsession with color: note the title of Sinclair's novel. They laugh about black men's obsession with whiteness: when I recently asked a friend why another friend's husband had left her, she laughed and tapped the back of one hand with another,[15] indicating that he had left for a white woman. They laugh about their wrinkles and their big hips. . . . And sometimes they proclaim their physical attributes more desirable, more captivating, more beautiful. For them, like Langston Hughes:

> Humor is what you wish in your secret heart were not funny, but it is, and you must laugh. Humor is your own unconscious therapy.

---

14. "Direct from Broadway," Whoopi, Inc., 1985.

15. Alluding to skin color and blue veins—an indication of whiteness. The society of those blacks fair enough to pass was called The Blue Vein Society (see Charles Chesnutt's *The Wife of His Youth*).

Betye Saar

THE LIBERATION OF AUNT JEMIMA

Mixed Media, 1972, University of California, Berkeley Art Museum.

Thylias Moss

LESSONS FROM A MIRROR

Snow White was nude at her wedding, she's so white
the gown seemed to disappear when she put it on.

Put me beside her and the proximity is good
for a study of chiaroscuro, not much else.

Her name aggravates me most, as if I need to be told
what's white and what isn't.

Judging strictly by appearance there's a future for me
forever at her heels, a shadow's constant worship.

Is it fair for me to live that way, unable
to get off the ground?

Turning the tables isn't fair unless they keep turning.
Then there's the danger of Russian roulette

and my disadvantage: nothing falls from the sky
to name me.

I am the empty space where the tooth was, that my tongue
rushes to fill because I can't stand vacancies.

And it's not enough. The penis just fills another
gap. And it's not enough.

When you look at me,
know that more than white is missing.

Me'shell Ndegeocello

SOUL ON ICE

My, my, master's in the slave house again.
Visions of her virginal white beauty
Dancin' in your head
Your soul's on ice
Your soul's on ice
Brother, brother, are you suffering from a social infection mis-direction?
Excuse me, does the white woman go better with the Brooks Brothers
suit?

. . . .

You no longer burn for the motherland brown skin.
You want blonde-haired, blue-eyed soul
Snow white passion without the hot comb.

Bebe Moore Campbell

BLACK MEN, WHITE WOMEN: A SISTER RELINQUISHES HER ANGER

There is a story that has been wending its way through the cocktail-and-house party circuit of middle-class African-American communities in large urban cities. Two wealthy black businessmen are strolling down the street and one says to the other, "Man, let's try to get a date with the next white women we see." His friend agrees and soon they notice two white women approaching them. One is young and pretty; the other is over seventy, not very attractive, and has difficulty walking. One of the men says quickly, "I want the old one." His amazed companion asks, "Why in the world do you prefer her?"

"Because she's been white longer."

In some circles "The White Girl Joke" is met with stony silence, considered not so much humorous as it is a searing social commentary that strikes far too close to home to evoke laughter. For many African-American women, the thought of black men, particularly those who are successful, dating or marrying white women is like being passed over for the prom by the boy of their dreams, causing them pain, rage, and an overwhelming sense of betrayal and personal rejection.

––––––––

Regardless of the statement black men with white women want to make, or even if they wish to make one, what many black women receive is a hurtful mixture of blatant sexism and eerie internecine racism: If you were good enough (if you looked like white women and didn't give me so much back talk), I wouldn't choose someone else. The message that they don't measure up makes some sisters want to scream.

I know the feeling.

Days after I first heard The White Girl Joke, some friends and I—all African-American women—were sitting in a trendy Beverly Hills restaurant having lunch when a good-looking, popular black actor strolled in. As an audible buzz of recognition traveled from table to table, my friends and I—restrained star-gazers all—managed to surreptitiously turn our heads toward the handsome celebrity without sacrificing one iota of our collective cool. That is, until we saw the blonde trailing behind him.

Our synchronized forks hit the plates on the first beat. An invisible choir director only we could see raised her hands: All together now. In unison, we moaned, we groaned, we rolled our eyes heavenward. We gnashed our teeth in harmony and made ugly faces. We sang "Umph! Umph! Umph!" a cappella-style, then shook our heads as we lamented for the ten thousandth time the perfidy of black men and cursed trespassing white women who dared to "take our men." The fact that I am married to my second black husband didn't lessen the fervor of my rendition of this same old song one bit. Had Spike Lee ventured in with a camera and recorder, he would have had the footage and soundtrack for *Jungle Fever Part II, III,* and *IV.* Before lunch was over I had a headache, indigestion, and probably elevated blood pressure. In retrospect, I think I may have shortened my life considerably. To add insult to injury, my last glimpse of the blonde and the brother revealed that they were so intent on gazing into each other's eyes that they were oblivious to our stellar performance.

As I drove home with my head pounding and my heart racing, I slowly came to a conclusion that I'd been avoiding for a long time: in the multiracial society that Americans live in, to feel that one has exclusive rights to the members of the opposite sex of one's race is a one-way ticket to Migraine City. I don't want to live there anymore. It is time for me to relinquish the wrath I feel toward black men and white women and move on.

Let me be clear: I'm not ashamed of my fury. The resentment and even hostility that I harbor are perfectly normal, and I believe that my sisters and I have conducted ourselves with ladylike dignity and enormous restraint. We're not slashing brothers' tires; we're not cutting off white girls' hair. We're just obsessing; anyone in our situation would do the same. "All races and even some ethnic and religious groups have a sense of proprietary rights over the opposite sex members of their society," says Belinda Tucker, Ph.D., who with a partner, Claudia Mitchell-Kernan, Ph.D., has conducted a study at UCLA of interracial dating patterns among African Americans. "These feelings are a form of social control." Immigrants from Ireland, Italy, Poland, and other countries experienced bitterness several generations ago in America when the first of their European clan began "marrying out." "Other people besides black women absolutely feel resentment," says Dr. Tucker. "It is difficult for anyone who identifies with just one group to see interracial dating and marriage and not worry."

In California, where most Asians reside, in some ethnic groups more than 80 percent marry out—more than any other people—to partners who are most likely white. Although some Asian women accuse their men of abandoning them for big-breasted, blue-eyed blondes, in direct contrast to African Americans, these Asian/white marriages are four times as likely to be between white men and Asian women. In a society where tall, muscular hunks are viewed as the ideal, Asian men say that their image has been neutered and they are angry about being abandoned. Antonio De Castro, forty, a Filipino photographer, says that lots of Asian men sit around and gripe about the trend. "They say, 'Why are all the fine Asian women going out with white guys?' There are Asian women who consciously choose not to date men like themselves because they believe being with white men elevates their social status or because they feel their biracial children will be more beautiful than Asian kids. You ask all of them why they're with white men and they'll say they just happened to fall in love. But something else is going on besides true love. It's an issue of self-contempt," says De Castro, who in the last two years has tried to woo back Asian women by publishing a beefcake calendar of well-muscled, scantily clad Asian men.

Asian women respond to accusations that they are abandoning their race by saying that their brothers are sexist and that white males don't put restraints on them. Some white women tend to view the phenomenon with resentment and suspicion, believing that they are being discarded because white men are attracted by the notion of subservient China dolls and geisha girls, preferring them to "feminist" Caucasians. There are white women who also react jealously when they see white males with African-American women.

In the Jewish community, where more than half of all marriages are interfaith, Orthodox and Conservative rabbis refuse to marry "mixed" couples. Some Jewish women believe that "their" men are programmed to prefer the "shiksa," or Gentile woman. "Many Jewish women will never have blond hair, narrow hips, and slender thighs," explains Robin Warshaw, forty-two, the author of *I Never Called It Rape,* who is married to a Christian. "When they see Jewish men who've chosen women like that, who dismiss them as nagging and materialistic Jewish-American Princesses, it stirs up resentment. You feel betrayed."

Bri Franchot, thirty-two, a casting director who grew up Christian, has long dark blond hair that has attracted Jewish men and the ire of some of those women. "I was at a party surrounded by Jewish women who were complaining that they couldn't find men of their religion to date, and I said it seemed as though that's all I met," says Franchot. "One of the women turned to me and said, 'You're what they want to date. You're the Shiksa Goddess.' I think there was some resentment in that remark."

"I go to conferences where there are intellectual Latino men, and they are all with white women," says Sandra Cisneros, thirty-seven, the author of *Woman Hollering Creek.* She declares that when Henry Cisneros (no relation), the former mayor of San Antonio, admitted to having an affair with a blonde, Mexican-American, women in the city were furious. She says, "Latina women always talk about brown men and white women among ourselves. Our rage is real and so is our pain. I think Latino men don't love us the way we love them."

African-American men, who according to Dr. Tucker's study are the most likely to date outside their race, aren't immune to expressing resentment when they see "their" women dating other men. On a recent "Arsenio Hall Show," black actress Rae Dawn Chong told the audience how the black owner of a barbecue restaurant ordered her and her white ex-husband out of his restaurant because he disapproved of the interracial couple. Throughout the history of this country, white males have reacted violently to even the implication that white women might consort with outsiders. "I am much more afraid of white male hostility than that of black women," says Jean Bernard, Michael Hughes's white lover. "I still think of white males as capable of violence."

But if my anger is within the range of predictable and acceptable group norms, it is increasingly uncomfortable for me personally, like a horrifying LSD trip I can't escape. Anger has become a habit, an addiction. And as with any quick high, I can get a fix almost anywhere. There are, of course, black women who couldn't care less about whom any man besides their man is with. And according to Dr. Tucker, black women are more likely to date outside their race than women of other groups. Still, almost every time I get together with two or more African-American women, the topic turns to "the problem." We're disgusted; we're fascinated. We're obsessing; we're PMSing. We operate on a blatant double standard, thrilling to tabloid gossip that Robert De Niro is "into sisters," but castigating black male celebrities who have deserted us. I'm tired of putting my mood at the mercy of chance encounters with strangers. I'm too old for this shit.

I want peace of mind. I am ready to relinquish my anger.

Yes, I want my people to date and marry each other and I don't think it will ever give me pleasure to see black men with white women, but my wanting it isn't going to make it happen. My being angry isn't going to make white women and black men stop choosing each other. The only thing I can control regarding this phenomenon is my response to it. My goal isn't to enjoy the fact that some black men prefer white women to the women of their own race. I'm simply trying to live with it, as sanely as I can. What I'm striving for is the same feeling I get whenever I run into my ex-husband: neutrality. I can acknowledge the man without giving up any energy or emotions. I worked for years to achieve that kind of peace of mind; it is a wonderful blessing.

I guess I'll have to retrain my mind, learn to take deep breaths when I see black men and white women, maybe even smile. Meditation might help and I'll try it, if I can sit still long enough. I suppose that what I must do is forgive those black men who've hurt me. All the New Age, spiritual books I read recommend this. They say forgiveness cleanses the spirit. I certainly want my spirit cleansed.

What is even more pressing than having a clean spirit, though, is passing on the right message to my fifteen-year-old daughter, Maia, who now finds herself contending with the same issues that have caused her mother and other older black women so much pain. Not long ago Maia went to a party. Her mood had been happy when she left, but when I picked her up, she was silent and gloomy. I asked the usual motherly questions. Was the party fun? Grunt. Did she have a good time? Grunt. Did she dance? Grunt. I was about to give up when she said suddenly, her tone venomous, "The black boys only asked the white girls to dance."

Looking at my child's crestfallen face, I contemplated all the things, both practical and soothing, that I could say to her. I thought about the legacies I wanted to pass on to her and the ones I didn't. I thought about the kind of woman I wanted her to be and the kind I didn't want her to become. And then I thought about my own childhood and a special woman who permeated it.

As a child, I remember sitting in my bedroom in the dark with a hair clip on my nose, trying to reduce the size of my wide nostrils. Later, when the teenage parties I attended grew hot and my hair turned "nappy," I would dash into the bathroom and attempt to repair the damage with a frail comb not up to the task, so the boys wouldn't see how ugly I was. While I was growing up I recall watching my grandmother make pancakes and seeing Aunt Jemima's face on the box. Aunt Jemima has a new, modern hairdo now, but she is still on the pancake box, a sturdy, sensible woman, not unpleasant to look at, but clearly one who is meant for servitude and not adoration. And what I knew then, I know now: when some people look at me, or any black woman, they see Aunt Jemima: a mammy, built to serve, not to adore. A few of those people are *my* men.

I can't change anyone's perception of me; I can only love myself better, hold all the facets of me in high esteem. The thing I like about Sister Jemima is this: she's a survivor.

I don't want my child or me held hostage by our own rage. I want us to endure through the decades, smiling and knowing that no one can reject us unless we give them permission to do so. So, what I finally said to Maia was this: "Don't get angry about it, honey. That's the worst thing you can do. People have the right to be with whomever they choose. Those choices don't have anything to do with you personally, unless you think they do."

Louise Meriwether

A HAPPENING IN BARBADOS

The best way to pick up a Barbadian man, I hoped, was to walk alone down the beach with my tall, brown frame squeezed into a skintight bathing suit. Since my hotel was near the beach, and Dorothy and Alison, my two traveling companions, had gone shopping, I managed this quite well. I had not taken more than a few steps on the glittering, white sand before two black men were on either side of me vying for attention.

I chose the tall, slim-hipped one over the squat, muscle-bound man who was also grinning at me. But apparently they were friends, because Edwin had no sooner settled me under his umbrella than the squat one showed up with a beach chair and two other boys in tow.

Edwin made the introductions. His temporary rival was Gregory, and the other two were Alphonse and Dimitri.

Gregory was ugly. He had thick, rubbery lips, a scarcity of teeth, and a broad nose splattered like a pyramid across his face. He was all massive shoulders and bulging biceps. No doubt he had a certain animal magnetism, but personally I preferred a lean man like Edwin, who was well built but slender, his whole body fitting together like a symphony. Alphonse and Dimitri were clean-cut and pleasant looking.

They were all too young—twenty to twenty-five at the most—and Gregory seemed the oldest. I inwardly mourned their youth and settled down to make the most of my catch.

The crystal-blue sky rivaled the royal blue of the Caribbean for beauty, and our black bodies on the white sand added to the munificence of colors. We ran into the sea like squealing children when the sudden raindrops came, then shivered on the sand under a makeshift tent of umbrellas and damp towels waiting for the sun to reappear while nourishing ourselves with straight Barbados rum.

As with most of the West Indians I had already met on my whirlwind tour of Trinidad and Jamaica, who welcomed American Negroes with open arms, my new friends loved their island home, but work was scarce and they yearned to go to America. They were hungry for news of how Negroes were faring in the States.

Edwin's arm rested casually on my knee in a proprietary manner, and I smiled at him. His thin, serious face was smooth, too young for a razor, and when he smiled back, he looked even younger. He told me he was a waiter at the Hilton, saving his money to make it to the States. I had already learned not to be snobbish with the island's help. Yesterday's waiter may be tomorrow's prime minister.

Dimitri, very black with an infectious grin, was also a waiter, and lanky Alphonse was a tile setter.

Gregory's occupation was apparently women, for that's all he talked about. He was able to launch this subject when a bony white woman— more peeling red than white, really looking like a gaunt cadaver in a loose-fitting bathing suit—came out of the sea and walked up to us. She smiled archly at Gregory.

"Are you going to take me to the Pigeon Club tonight, sugar?"

"No, mon," he said pleasantly, with a toothless grin. "I'm taking a younger pigeon."

The woman turned a deeper red, if that was possible, and, mumbling something incoherent, walked away.

"That one is always after me to take her some place," Gregory said. "She's rich, and she pays the bills but, mon, I don't want an old hag nobody else wants. I like to take my women away from white men and watch them squirm."

"Come down, mon," Dimitri said, grinning. "She look like she's starving for what you got to spare."

We all laughed. The boys exchanged stories about their experiences with predatory white women who came to the islands looking for some black action. But, one and all, they declared they liked dark-skinned meat the best, and I felt like a black queen of the Nile when Gregory winked at me and said, "The blacker the berry, mon, the sweeter the juice."

They had all been pursued and had chased some white tail, too, no doubt, but while the others took it all in good humor, it soon became apparent that Gregory's exploits were exercises in vengeance.

Gregory was saying: "I told that bastard, 'You in my country now, mon, and I'll kick your ass all the way back to Texas. The girl agreed to dance with me, and she don't need your permission.' That white man's face turned purple, but he sat back down, and I dance with his girl. Mon, they hate to see me rubbing bellies with their women because they know once she rub bellies with me she wanna rub something else, too." He laughed, and we all joined in. Serves the white men right, I thought. Let's see how they liked licking *that* end of the stick for a change.

"Mon, you gonna get killed yet," Edwin said, moving closer to me on the towel we shared. "You're crazy. You don't care whose woman you mess with. But it's not gonna be a white man who kill you but some bad Bajan."

Gregory led in the laughter, then held us spellbound for the next hour with intimate details of his affair with Glenda, a young white girl spending the summer with her father on their yacht. Whatever he had, Glenda wanted it desperately, or so Gregory told it.

Yeah, I thought to myself, like LSD, a black lover is the thing this year. I had seen the white girls in the Village and at off-Broadway theaters clutching their black men tightly while I, manless, looked on with bitterness. I often vowed I would find me an ofay in self-defense, but I could never bring myself to condone the wholesale rape of my slave ancestors by letting a white man touch me.

We finished the rum, and the three boys stood up to leave, making arrangements to get together later with us and my two girl friends and go clubbing.

Edwin and I were left alone. He stretched out his muscled leg and touched my toes with his. I smiled at him and let our thighs come together. Why did he have to be so damned young? Then our lips met, his warm and demanding, and I thought, what the hell, maybe I will. I was thirty-nine— good-bye, sweet bird of youth—an ungay divorcee, uptight and drinking too much, trying to disown the years which had brought only loneliness and pain. I had clawed my way up from the slums of Harlem via night school and was now a law clerk on Wall Street. But the fight upward had taken its toll. My husband, who couldn't claw as well as I, got lost somewhere in that concrete jungle. The last I saw of him, he was peering under every skirt around, searching for his lost manhood.

I had always felt contempt for women who found their kicks by robbing the cradle. Now here I was on a Barbados beach with an amorous child young enough to be my son. Two sayings flitted unbidden across my mind. "Judge not, that ye be not judged" and "The thing which I feared is come upon me." I thought, ain't it the god-damned truth?

Edwin kissed me again, pressing the length of his body against mine.

"I've got to go," I gasped. "My friends have probably returned and are looking for me. About ten tonight?"

He nodded; I smiled at him and ran all the way to my hotel.

At exactly ten o'clock, the telephone in our room announced we had company downstairs.

"Hot damn," Alison said, putting on her eyebrows in front of the mirror. "We're not going to be stood up."

"Island men," I said loftily, "are dependable, not like the bums you're used to in America."

Alison, freckled and willowy, had been married three times and was looking for her fourth. Her motto was, if at first you don't succeed, find another mother. She was a real-estate broker in Los Angeles, and we had been childhood friends in Harlem.

"What I can't stand," Dorothy said from the bathroom, "are those creeps who come to your apartment, drink up your liquor, then dirty up your sheets. You don't even get a dinner out of the deal."

She came out of the bathroom in her slip. Petite and delicate with a pixie grin, at thirty-five Dorothy looked more like one of the high school girls she taught than their teacher. She had never been married. Years before, while she was holding onto her virginity with a miser's grip, her fiancé messed up and knocked up one of her friends.

Since then, all of Dorothy's affairs had been with married men, displaying perhaps a subconscious vendetta against all wives.

By ten-twenty we were downstairs and I was introducing the girls to our four escorts, who eyed us with unconcealed admiration. We were looking good in our Saks Fifth Avenue finery. They were looking good, too, in soft shirts and loose slacks, all except Gregory, whose bulging muscles confined in clothing made him seem more gargantuan.

We took a cab and a few minutes later were squeezing behind a table in a small, smoky room called the Pigeon Club. A Trinidad steel band was blasting out the walls, and the tiny dance area was jammed with wiggling bottoms and shuffling feet. The white tourists trying to do the hip-shaking calypso were having a ball and looking awkward.

I got up to dance with Edwin. He had a natural grace and was easy to follow. Our bodies found the rhythm and became one with it while our eyes locked in silent ancient combat, his pleading, mine teasing.

We returned to our seats and to tall glasses of rum and cola tonic. The party had begun.

I danced every dance with Edwin, his clasp becoming gradually tighter until my face was smothered in his shoulder, my arms locked around his neck. He was adorable. Very good for my ego. The other boys took turns dancing with my friends, but soon preferences were set—Alison with Alphonse and Dorothy with Dimitri. With good humor, Gregory ordered another round and didn't seem to mind being odd man out, but he wasn't alone for long.

During the floor show, featuring the inevitable limbo dancers, a pretty white girl, about twenty-two, with straight, red hair hanging down to her shoulder, appeared at Gregory's elbow. From his wink at me and self-satisfied grin, I knew this was Glenda from the yacht.

"Hello," she said to Gregory. "Can I join you, or do you have a date?"

Well, I thought, that's the direct approach.

"What are you doing here?" Gregory asked.

"Looking for you."

Gregory slid over on the bench, next to the wall, and Glenda sat down as he introduced her to the rest of us. Somehow, her presence spoiled my mood. We had been happy being black, and I resented this intrusion from the white world. But Glenda was happy. She had found the man she'd set out to find and a swinging party to boot. She beamed a dazzling smile around the table.

Alphonse led Alison onto the dance floor, and Edwin and I followed. The steel band was playing a wild calypso, and I could feel my hair rising with the heat as I joined in the wildness.

When we returned to the table, Glenda applauded us, then turned to Gregory. "Why don't you teach me to dance like that?"

He answered with his toothless grin and a leer, implying he had better things to teach her.

White women were always snatching our men, I thought, and now they want to dance like us.

I turned my attention back to Edwin and met his full stare.

I teased him with a smile, refusing to commit myself. He had a lusty, healthy appetite, which was natural, I supposed, for a twenty-one-year-old lad. Lord, but why did he have to be that young? I stood up to go to the ladies' room.

"Wait for me," Glenda cried, trailing behind me.

The single toilet stall was occupied, and Glenda leaned against the wall waiting for it while I flipped open my compact and powdered my grimy face.

"You married?" she asked.

"Divorced."

"When I get married, I want to stay hooked forever."

"That's the way I planned it, too," I said dryly.

"What I mean," she rushed on, "is that I've gotta find a cat who wants to groove only with me."

Oh Lord, I thought, don't try to sound like us, too. Use your own, sterile language.

"I really dug this guy I was engaged to," Glenda continued, "but he couldn't function without a harem. I could have stood that, maybe, but when he didn't mind if I made it with some other guy, too, I knew I didn't want that kind of life."

I looked at her in the mirror as I applied my lipstick. She had been hurt, and badly. She shook right down to her naked soul. So she was dropping down a social notch, according to her scale of values, and trying to repair her damaged ego with a black brother.

"You gonna make it with Edwin?" she asked, as if we were college chums comparing dates.

"I'm not a one-night stand." My tone was frigid. That's another thing I can't stand about white people. Too familiar, because we're colored.

"I dig Gregory," she said, pushing her hair out of her eyes. "He's kind of rough, but who wouldn't be, the kind of life he's led."

"And what kind of life is that?" I asked.

"Didn't you know? His mother was a whore in an exclusive brothel for white men only. That was before, when the British owned the island."

"I take it you like rough men?" I asked.

"There's usually something gentle and lost underneath," she replied.

A white woman came out of the toilet and Glenda went in. Jesus, I thought, Gregory gentle? The woman walked to the basin, flung some water in the general direction of her hands, and left.

"Poor Daddy is having a fit," Glenda volunteered from the john, "but there's not much he can do about it. He's afraid I'll leave him again, and he gets lonely without me, so he just tags along and tries to keep me out of trouble."

"And he pays the bills?"

She answered with a laugh. "Why not? He's loaded."

Why not, I thought with bitterness. You white women have always managed to have your cake and eat it, too. The toilet flushed with a roar like Niagara Falls. I opened the door and went back to our table. Let Glenda find her way back alone.

Edwin pulled my chair out and brushed his lips across the nape of my neck as I sat down. He still had not danced with anyone else, and his apparent desire was flattering. For a moment, I considered it. That's what I really needed, wasn't it? To walk down the moonlit beach wrapped in his arms, making it to some pad to be made? It would be a delightful story to tell at bridge sessions. But I shook my head at him, and this time my smile was more sad than teasing.

Glenda came back and crawled over Gregory's legs to the seat beside him. The bastard. He made no pretense of being a gentleman. Suddenly, I didn't know which of them I disliked the most. Gregory winked at me. I don't know where he got the impression I was his conspirator, but I got up to dance with him.

"That Glenda," he grinned, "she's the one I was on the boat with last night. I banged her plenty, in the room right next to her father. We could hear him coughing to let us know he was awake, but he didn't come in."

He laughed like a naughty schoolboy, and I joined in. He was a nerveless bastard all right, and it served Glenda right that we were laughing at her. Who asked her to crash our party, anyway? That's when I got the idea to take Gregory away from her.

"You gonna bang her again tonight?" I asked, a new, teasing quality in my voice. "Or are you gonna find something better to do?" To help him get the message I rubbed bellies with him.

He couldn't believe this sudden turn of events. I could almost see him thinking. With one stroke he could slap Glenda down a peg and repay Edwin for beating his time with me on the beach that morning.

"You wanna come with me?" he asked, making sure of his quarry.

"What you got to offer?" I peered at him through half-closed lids.

"Big Bamboo," he sang, the title of a popular calypso. We both laughed.

I felt a heady excitement of impending danger as Gregory pulled me back to the table. The men paid the bill, and suddenly we were standing outside the club in the bright moonlight. Gregory deliberately uncurled Glenda's arm from his and took a step toward me. Looking at Edwin and nodding in my direction, he said, "She's coming with me. Any objections?"

Edwin inhaled a mouthful of smoke. His face was inscrutable. "You want to go with him?" he asked me quietly.

I avoided his eyes and nodded. "Yes."

He flipped the cigarette with contempt at my feet and lit another one. "Help yourself to the garbage," he said, and leaned back against the building, one leg braced behind him. The others suddenly stilled their chatter, sensing trouble.

I was holding Gregory's arm now, and I felt his muscles tense. "No," I said as he moved toward Edwin. "You've got what you want. Forget it."

Glenda was ungracious in defeat. "What about me?" she screamed. She stared from one black face to another, her glance lingering on Edwin. But he wasn't about to come to her aid and take Gregory's leavings.

"You can go home in a cab," Gregory said, pushing her ahead of him and pulling me behind him to a taxi waiting at the curb.

Glenda broke from his grasp. "You bastard. Who in the hell do you think you are, King Solomon? You can't dump me like this." She raised her hands as if to strike Gregory on the chest, but he caught them before they landed.

"Careful, white girl," he said. His voice was low but ominous. She froze.

"But why," she whimpered, all hurt child now. "You liked me last night. I know you did. Why are you treating me like this?"

"I didn't bring you here"— his voice was pleasant again—"so don't be trailing me all over town. When I want you, I'll come to that damn boat and get you. Now get in that cab before I throw you in. I'll see you to-morrow night. Maybe."

"You go to hell." She eluded him and turned on me, asking with in-credible innocence, "What did I ever do to you?" Then she was running past toward the beach, her sobs drifting back to haunt me like a forlorn melody.

What had she ever done to me? And what had I just done? In order to degrade her for the crime of being white, I had sunk to the gutter. Sud-denly Glenda was just another woman, vulnerable and lonely, like me.

We were sick, sick, sick. All fucked up. I had thought only Gregory was hung up in his love-hate, black-white syndrome, decades of suppressed hatred having sickened his soul. But I was tainted, too. I had forgotten my own misery long enough to inflict it on another woman who was only try-ing to ease her loneliness by making it with a soul brother. Was I jealous because she was able to function as a woman where I couldn't, because she realized that a man is a man, color be damned, while I was crucified on my own, anti-white-man cross?

What if she were going black trying to repent for some ancient Nordic sin? How else could she atone except with the gift of herself? And if some black brother wanted to help a chick off her lily-white pedestal, he was en-titled to that freedom, and it was none of my damned business anyway.

"Let's go, baby," Gregory said, tucking my arm under his.

The black bastard. I didn't even like the ugly ape. I backed away from him. "Leave me alone," I screamed. "Goddamit, just leave me alone!"

For a moment, we were all frozen into an absurd fresco—Alison, Dorothy, and the two boys looking at me in shocked disbelief, Edwin hid-ing behind a nonchalant smokescreen, Gregory off balance and confused, reaching out toward me.

I moved first, toward Edwin, but I had slammed the door behind me. He laughed, a mirthless sound in the stillness. He knew. I had forsaken him, but at least not for Gregory.

Then I was running down the beach looking for Glenda, hot tears of shame burning my face. How could I have been such a bitch? But the white beach, shimmering in the moonlight, was empty. And once again, I was alone.

April Sinclair

LOOKING OUT FOR THE CHILDREN

from *Coffee Will Make You Black*

[In the following two brief passages Jean, the young adolescent protagonist of *Coffee* shares some of her mother's views on color, features, and hair. It was rare for a dark woman like her mother to marry a lighter complex-ioned man like her father, and thus her mother always considered herself lucky to have a husband whom she often said she married "cause she was looking out for her children." In the first selection the mother is referring to Jean and in the second to one of Jean's friends who is visiting her. The references to "handing out color and hair" and standing in line allude to popular old black etiological tales explaining how colored people got their color and hair by standing in line as God gave out these items to all of the races. For illustrations see "Ball It Up and Throw It to Me," the next se-lection, and Chapter 1, "Etiological Tales," of my *Shuckin' and Jivin'*.]

Anyway, Mama says she doesn't know where I was when they were hand-ing out color and hair. She says I let my nine-year-old brother David get ahead of me in the hair line and my six-year-old brother Kevin get ahead of me in the color line. But at least I've got nice features, she's thankful for that, Mama always says. In other words, she's glad I don't have a wide nose and big lips like Grandma and some other colored people. And Mama likes that I have high cheekbones, of course.

Denise had some meat on her bones, large eyes, a wide nose, full lips, and was light-skinned. Mama would call Denise "yellow-wasted." That's what she called light-skinned people with hair nappy enough to be straightened and/or African features.

Folk

BALL IT UP AND THROW IT TO ME

from Daryl Cumber Dance, *Shuckin' and Jivin'*

All right now, we going to our races; we going to find out where the Black people got their hair from. . . . When it was time for the Lord to give hair, He called all three of these men, and this is what he said. Well, first he called the white man to come on and get his hair. All right, the white he went right on up there and got his hair. So the Lord called the Jew man to get his hair. So the Jew man went up there and got his hair, and said, "Thank you, Lord."

So when it got down to the Black man, the Lord called him. And do you know what the Black man said? Black man said, "Lord, ball it up and throw it to me." And it's been balled up ever since.

Audre Lorde

NATURALLY

Since Naturally Black is Naturally Beautiful
I must be proud
and, naturally,
Black and
Beautiful
who always was a trifle
yellow
and plain
though proud
before.

So I've given up pomades
having spent the summer sunning
and feeling
naturally
free
(and if I die of skin
   cancer
   oh well—one less
   black and beautiful me)
For no agency spends millions
to prevent my summer's tanning
and nobody trembles nightly
with a fear
of lily cities being swallowed
by a summer ocean
of naturally woolly hair.

But I've bought my can of
Natural Hair Spray—
made and marketed in Watts—
still thinking more
Proud Beautiful Black Women
could better make and use
Black bread.

Traditional Blues

I'M A BIG FAT MAMA

I'm a big fat mama, got the meat shakin' on my bones,
I'm a big fat mama, got the meat shakin' on my bones,
An' ev'y time I shake, some skinny girl loses her home.

Sarah Martin

MEAN TIGHT MAMA

Now my hair is nappy and I don't
           wear no clothes of silk
Now my hair is nappy and I don't
           wear no clothes of silk
But the cow that's black and ugly
           has often got the sweetest
           milk.

Folk

JUST A CREAM COLOR

The minister was preaching and sang out the old song, "Lord, wash me and I shall be whiter than snow."
    An old Sister say, "Just a cream color will do for me."

Carolyn M. Rodgers

FOR SISTUHS WEARIN STRAIGHT HAIR

me?
i never could keep my edges and kitchen
straight
even after
supercool/straighterPerm had burned

whiteness onto my scalp
my edges and kitchen didn't
ever get the message that they
was not supposed to go back home.
oh yeah. edges and kitchens
will tell that they know where
they nat'chal home is at!

Karla F. C. Holloway

THE LONG WAY HOME

from *Codes of Conduct*

First, we got a box of heavy flow, night-wear, super absorbency Kotex. This was before the days when the Kimberly-Clark folk filled super thin sanitary napkins with some kind of super absorbent crystals. When I was in junior high, absorbency of the kind we required meant an incredibly thick pad. After all, we needed to block all the water in the swimming pool at Fillmore Junior High School. Then, we stuffed these pads into a stocking with a run in it. This was before the age of panty hose too. After we had a stocking filled with enough Kotex to circle our heads, we put these into a plastic bag and wrapped it around our precious pressed hair. Only then would we leave the girls' locker room and enter the swimming pool area. Our only source of comfort was that it was seventh period.

We learned to be aggressive and assertive about class schedules in junior high. Black girls just had to have a seventh period, end-of-the-day physical education class. We'd even give up the elite chorus group, a late-day study hall, orchestra, and yearbook staff—all of which met during seventh period—the semester we were scheduled to swim. Priorities, you know. If all our trappings failed, we could leave school immediately after swimming and make certain that no one would see us because we could go home the long way.

It was one of the few times I was grateful for my older sister's presence in my school. Who else could have taught me how to stuff the Kotex into my swimming cap with as much consideration as she extended to me? After all, Karen didn't want my nappy-headed self embarrassing her on her way home. So it was mutually beneficial that she should wrap my head as thoroughly as she could. Our huddle in the corner of the locker room, checking each other's Kotex, stuffing escaped plastic back under our caps, making certain there were no gaps in the loop around our heads kept us there until Miss Zimmerman's very last whistle, when she insisted we close the locker-room doors and enter the swimming pool area.

The only time I really remember my preparations being a total failure was the time I was forced off the diving board. They thought I was sinking when I failed to come back to the surface and strike out for the side of the pool. But that wasn't it at all. It was the whoosh of water I felt when I jumped in that went right past my Kotex covered ears and started seeping through my scalp that paralyzed me. I could feel every strand of my hair react to the watery assault. Cold watery streams viciously attacked my roots, oblivious to the intensity of my locker-room efforts. I was so distressed over what I knew was going on under my cap that I forgot to stroke out from the jump. I just sank. It was when I felt the poke of the nine-foot metal pole that Miss Zimmerman kept for just such an emergency (drowning bodies, not drenched hair) that I remembered to grab hold. They dragged me to the side of the pool and she tapped me on my rubberized head as she always did when she wanted our attention. I think she knew the black girls had an extra hard time hearing with all that cotton, plastic, and nylon stocking-net around our ears. "What happened?" she asked. I shook my head. "Do you want to try it again?" I quickly climbed out, said no, and hurried for the locker room. The buzzer had rung anyway. I do not even remember how my hair looked after I removed the sopping mass from around my head. It is one of those repressed, childhood memories. Where was the age of baseball caps when you needed it? I do remember, however, that I took the long way home.

Alison Workman

GREASE

from *Tapestry: The Literary Magazine of Virginia State University*

REMEMBER HOW SHE WOULD
SIT
YOU
DOWN BETWEEN HER KNEES,
WRAP YOU TRAP YOU WITH
HER BIG MAMA LEGS
AROUND YOUR LITTLE DAHTA BODY AND
SHE'D GET OUT THAT JAR OF
GREASE
AND SOMETIMES
IT
WAS
THAT
DAX POMADE
AND SOMETIMES
IT
WAS
THE
"pink stuff" (YOU LIKED THAT ONE)
AND SOMETIMES
IT
WAS
THAT
TOO THICK PALMER'S SHIT
WHICH YOU ALWAYS CONFUSED WITH THE COCOA
BUTTER BECAUSE
THE JARS LOOKED THE DAMN SAME
AND SOMETIMES
SHE WOULD USE THE ONE THAT WAS BLACK AND
SMELLED LIKE TAR I

SWEAR TO GAWD THAT MESS SMELLED LIKE THEY
WAS PUTTING UP
A ROAD ON YOUR HEAD OR SOMETHING AND
IF YOU WERE *LUCKY*
SHE'D USE THE ONE THAT
SMELLED LIKE COCONUTS AND PROMISED TO
GROW YOUR HAIR
"stronger" "longer" "thicker" "faster"
AND YOU'D RUN OUTSIDE
WITH YOUR FRESHLY GREASED COCONUT-
SMELLING HEAD
AND
　　JUST
　　　　PRAY
　　　　　　THAT　　　UPWIND.
　　　　　　　THE　　WERE
　　　　　　　　BEES

Thylias Moss

A RECONSIDERATION OF THE BLACKBIRD

Let's call him *Jim Crow.*

Let's call him *Nigger* and see if he rises
faster than when we say *abracadabra.*

Guess who's coming to dinner?
Score ten points if you said blackbird.
Score twenty points if you were more specific, as in the first line.

What do you find *from here to eternity?*
Blackbirds.

Who never sang for my father?
The blackbirds who came, one after the other, landed on the roof
and pressed it down, burying us alive.
Why didn't we jump out the windows? Didn't we have enough time?
We were outnumbered (13 on the clothesline, 4 & 20 in the pie).
We were holding hands and hugging like never before.
You could say the blackbirds did us a favor.

Let's not say that however. Instead let the crows speak.
Let them use their tongues or forfeit them.

Problem: What would we do with 13 little black tongues?

Solution: Give them away. Hold them for ransom. Make belts.
Little nooses for little necks.

Problem: The little nooses fit only fingers.

Solution: Get married.

Problem: No one's in love with the blackbirds.

Solution: Paint them white, call them visions, everyone will want
one.

April Sinclair

HERE I COME, READY OR NOT

[This selection presents the reflections of the young adolescent protagonist,
Jean.]

I still thought breasts might be more trouble than they were worth. Growing up reminded me a little bit of Hide and Go Seek. When it was your

time to grow up, Nature said, "Here I come, ready or not." And Nature could always find you.

Folk

WE MUST, WE MUST, WE MUST

[When I recorded this verse on May 21, 1995, the singer told me she learned it in gym class in the 1950s, but as she sang a younger woman joined her, suggesting that it has passed along to the next generation.]

> We must, we must, we must,
> We must develop our bust.
>
> We must, we must, we must,
> We must develop our bust.
>
> The bigger the better,
> The tighter the sweater,
> The boys are depending on us.

MIMEOGRAPHED ITEM

Ode to a Mammogram

For year's n year's they told me,
"Be careful of your breasts.
Don't ever squeeze or bruise them,
And give them monthly tests.

So I heeded all their warnings
And protected them by law . . .
Guarded them very carefully,
And always wore a bra.

After 30 years of carefull care,
The doctor found a lump.
He ordered up a mammogram
To look inside that clump.

"Stand up very close" she said,
As she got my tit in line,
"And tell me when it hurts," she said.
"Ah yes, there that's just fine."

She stepped upon a pedal . . .
I could not believe my eyes
A plastic plate was pressing down,
My boob was in a vice!!

My skin was stretched 'n stretched
From way up by my chin
And my poor tit was being squashed
To a swedish pancake thin!!!!

Excrutiating pain I felt
Within it's vice-like grip
A prisoner in this viscious thing
My poor defenseless tit.

"Take a deep breath," she said to me.
Who does she think she's kidding?
My chest is smashed in her machine,
I can't breathe, and woozy I'm getting.

"There, that was good," I heard her saying
As the room was slowly swaying.
"Now lets get the other one,"
"Lord, have mercy, I was praying."

It squeezed me from the up and down;
It squeezed me from both sides,
I'll bet she's never had this done
To her tender little hide.

If I had no problem when I came in
I surely have one now . . .
If there had been a cyst in there,
It would have popped . . . ker-pow!!!

This machine was made by man,
Of this I have no doubt . . .
I'd like to get his balls in there
For months he'd go "without."

Barbara Brandon

WHERE I'M COMING FROM

Gloria Wade-Gayles

WHO SAYS AN OLDER WOMAN CAN'T/SHOULDN'T DANCE?

from *Rooted Against the Wind*

"How do you do it? You just don't look your age."
[Do what? Look how?]

"You're so playful so . . . so much fun. You don't act your age."
[I came out of my mother's womb playful, and pray tell me why I can't remain so at my age, and says who?]

"No gray hair? Come on now. I know you are using a rinse."
[Are you asking me or telling me?]

*"It's the natural! That's the magic. People do say a natural
takes years off a black woman's face. When I see how young
it makes you look, I seriously consider giving up my perm."*
[Give up your perm! You wouldn't go natural if
guidelines for the crowning of Miss America required
that the tiara be placed only on top of peppercorn.]

*"You're the kind of older woman who could drive a young
man crazy."*
[That's supposed to be a compliment? All he needs to
be is *young*, but I have to be some kind of special-old!
Exactly what bait am I using to get this so-called catch?]

"It's amazing. You still look sexy."
[You need a crash course in sexuality after fifty.]

*"Me. Personally, I prefer older women, unless they're fat.
Now that, even in a young woman, turns me off."*
[When was the last time you stepped on the scale,
I wonder.]

*"Girl, you're lucky. You don't have to worry about lying
on top."*
[Lying on top? What in the world is *that* about?]
"You know. When we lean over, our sag really sags."

When a woman reaches fifty, her age becomes "the talk of the town," and
most of the people doing the talking are other women, not men. To be
sure, men are curious about our age, but they express their curiosity in ways
allowed only to their gender. Some of them are bold enough to ask directly,
"How old are you?" We need not answer, for as the eyes undress us they
say, "You couldn't be more than . . . but it really won't matter when the
lights are out." In other words, men flirt. Women, however, pry, and un-
derstandably so because we know that asking a woman her age can be as
invasive as a gynecological exam. Consequently, we are forced, as men are
not, to use search-and-find techniques which would be offensive if they
weren't so transparent and silly.

We measure the number and length of wrinkles on a woman's face as if, like rings around a tree, they indicate the exact number of years lived. Laughter, however, throws off our computation, turning parallels into a thicket of lines we can neither count nor measure.

We conduct clandestine research on her life which aids us with our math. "Let's see now. Her children are _____ and that would make her at least _____, and since she graduated college in _____, . . ." Or, "She was in the class with _____, maybe a year ahead or behind, but definitely around the same time, and since _____ is _____, she would have to be at least _____."

We disclose in order to get a disclosure. For example, we share our disappointment in having been "done in" on our driver's license. Showing the unbecoming mug shot, but really the year beneath it, we ask, "Did they do you in, too?" I don't play show-'n-tell: "Worse, girl. Mine is so bad I won't let anyone see it, not even traffic cops."

Folk

DO YOU REMEMBER?

Two women were sitting around reminiscing about the old days of their youth. One asked the other if she remembered the waltz.

"Oh, yes, and that Johnny Miles was one smooth waltzer?"

"And the jitterbug, girl, do you remember the jitterbug?"

"Oh, yes, chile, I could cut me some rug on the jitterbug? . . . But I bet you don't remember the minuet."

"The men I et! Girl, I don't even remember the men I fucked."

MIMEOGRAPHED ITEM

Growing Wild

There was this guy who really takes care of his body, he liftsweights and jogs six miles every day.

One morning he looked into the mirror and admired his body, and noticed that he was suntanned all over with the one exception of his penis, which he readily decided to do something about.

He went to the beach, completely undressed and buried himself in the sand, except for his penis which he left sticking out.

Two old ladies were strolling along the beach, one using a cane. Upon seeing the thing sticking out of the sand she began to move it around with her cane, remarking to the other little old lady, saying, "There is no justice in the world."

The other little old lady said, "What do you mean by that?"
The first little old lady said, "Look at that . . .

When I was 20—I was curious about it.
When I was 30—I enjoyed it.
When I was 40—I asked for it.
When I was 50—I paid for it.
When I was 60—I prayed for it.
When I was 70—I forgot about it.

And now that I'm 80, the damn things are growing wild, and I'm too old to squat."

Folk

OLD AGE IS HELL

[found in handwriting among my mother's papers]

Body gets stiff, cramps in your legs;
Corns on your feet, big as hen's eggs.
Gas in your stomach, B.M. is poor
Take an Ex-Lax, but then you're not sure.
Teeth start decaying, vision gets poor,
Hair's falling out, and there is no cure.
Don't go to parties, don't dance anymore,
You are, in effect, one hell of a bore.
Liquor is out, can't take a chance,
Bladder is weak, might wet your pants.
Nothing to plan for, naught to expect,
Only the monthly social security check.
Now be sure your affairs are in order
And your will is made out just right,
Or on the way to your funeral,
There'll be one hell of a fight.
Just hope in the few years remaining,
That you will feel fairly well,
And thank the good Lord you are living,
Though as noted, Old Age is Hell.

Folk

I CAN'T REMEMBER

An eighty-three-year-old woman went to the doctor and asked to be impregnated since she had heard of all the advances in gynecology for older women. The doctor consented to performing in vitro fertilization for her, and she gave birth to a beautiful baby boy.

Her friends came to see her and asked to see the baby. She said, "Okay, but I'll have to wait until he cries."

The friends asked, "Why?"

She replied, "Because I can't remember where I put him."

Folk

PLENTY FIRE IN THE FURNACE

from Daryl Cumber Dance, *Shuckin' and Jivin'*

This ole lady, she was flirting with a young fellow, you know. She was standin' around there, and of course the young folks could see she was old, you know. Her hair was all gray and everything. So she say, "Oh, don't pay any attention about the snow on the mountain 'cause it's *plenty* fire in the furnace."

Folk

YOU GOT AN "F" IN SEX

This little boy was out shopping with his grandmother, and he looked up and asked her, "How old are you, Grandma?"

She said, "Oh, Johnnie, you must never ask a lady how old she is. That's not a very nice question for a little boy to ask a lady."

"Well, how much you weigh, Grandma?" he persisted. "No, no, Johnnie, nice boys don't ask ladies how much they weigh."

After a little pause, he looked up and he said, "Grandma, tell me then why you and Grandpa don't sleep together."

"Now, Johnnie, that certainly is not something you should ask about," she reprimanded him.

After a while, when the grandmother paid for a purchase with a check, the clerk asked for her driver's license. The little boy had an opportunity to see it, and when they walked off, he pulled his grandmother's hand, and proudly acclaimed, "I know how old you are, Grandma; you're fifty-five years old."

"How do you know that?" asked the grandmother.

"I saw it on your driver's license."

"Well, you mustn't tell anyone," she cautioned.

"I know how much you weigh too—175 pounds."

"How do you know that," asked the grandmother.

"I saw it on your driver's license."

"O.K., smarty pants. I ought to punish you for being so nosy. But you better not ever tell anybody how much I weigh."

"I know why you and Grandpa don't sleep together too," he boasted.

"Well, there's no way you can tell that from my driver's license," she laughed.

"Yes, I could too," he insisted.

"O.K. How could you tell that from my driver's license why Grandpa and I don't sleep together?"

" 'Cause you got an 'F' in Sex."

Mama Sez

Pot calling the kettle black, and the fryin' pan standin' up for witness.

Don't care how much you whitewash a pot, the black is still there.

You better stop drinking so much coffee. It will make you black.

Beauty is skin deep; ugly is to the bone.

When you a child, the minutes just tick away so slowly, but when you get old the hours fly by.

Sister to Sister

The blacker the berry, the sweeter the juice.

Her family so color struck and she went and married herself a pure-dee black Sambo.

Her Mama told her she don't want no tar brush in this family.

My grandmother was high yaller, and she always told me, "Don't marry no black nigger. Don't marry no black nigger." So I looked the earth over, and I saw this half-white nigger, and I say, "I got to have you, Baby!"

When I brought Ernest home to meet Mama, she looked at him and said, "Well, I guess it's gon' be gingerbread babies."

Ernest took Mama and me to the movies. She went to the bathroom and came back and sat on Ernest. Swore she couldn't see 'im.

She's blacker than midnight.

She's blacker than patent leather shoes.

She's so black that when she sweat, she sweat chocolate.

He was so black that we told him, "Max, you never be without a job cause the government's gon hire you to spit ink."

She was so black when I looked at her I thought I had my eyes closed.

Her baby so black the poleece arrested her for carrying round a blackjack.

Her child was so black and ugly that when she put him in the sandbox, the cats tried to cover him up.

That child had a face that only a mother could love.

If you're white, you're right
If you're brown, stick around
If you're black, step back.

Don't mess with me today. You don't want me to show my colors.

Her hair was so nappy she won a place in the Hair Hall of Shame.

Yeah I'm happy,
Cause my hair ain't nappy.

She got her hair dyed, fried, and laid to the side.

She got herself a real do [hairdo] today.

Yeah but her kitchen's [hair around the back of the neck] still nappy.

I done tol' so many lies about my age, I forget how old I really am. I'm thirty-nine and holding.

This weight sho sneaks up on you: I used to not even be able to pinch a inch; now I kin fold a roll.

It must be jelly cause jam don't shake like that.

She so fat you can't get your arms round her.

She so fat her boyfriend have to hug her on the installment plan.

She look like she done swallored a watermelon [is pregnant].

She's old as Methuselem.

She's old as dust.

Well, it's just one alternative to gettin' old. I'll take old any day. Bad as it is here, I'll take what I know to what I don't know nothin' 'bout. I know heaven's my home, but I ain't in no rush to go home.

I'm old, but I ain't cold.

Lucky black women don't wrinkle like white women—no, *black* don't *crack*.

She done mellowed in her old age.

Old kindlin' easy to catch fire.

The older the moon, the brighter it shine.

CHAPTER 4

Bronzeville, U.S.A.

THE BLACK COMMUNITY

"Oh, child, being colored can be a lotta fun when ain't nobody
looking."
—Missy, in Ossie Davis's *Purlie Victorious*

ertain aspects of the black world in the United States have always been
and remain segregated. These include (with a few exceptions) residential areas, schools, churches, barber shops, beauty parlors, juke
joints/beer gardens/nightclubs/bars, urban street corners, jails, chain gangs,
doctors' offices, funeral parlors, and graveyards. These and other institutions
in the black community have been the subject of a great deal of laughter
and even stereotyping in African American humor. While the personae, the
setting, the language, and the rhythms of the tales and sayings that focus on
the black community are black to the core, race is not always a direct issue
for the simple reason that when everything is black, one does not have to
focus on race as much as when one is dealing with white folks. Despite the
acknowledged problems in the black community, almost every black person has at some time proudly acclaimed that his/her community is char-

acterized by a joy, a gaiety, a free and unrestrained laughter that others covet. Thus it is that the White man in black folklore would do anything to enjoy the thrill of "being black on a Saturday night," partaking in all the joyous events that go on among blacks on the night before their one day off from work and away from the white world. At such times, among one's friends, among the laughter, the music, the fellowship and the jokes, the problems of life and work and segregation are forgotten. As Countee Cullen's Constantia Brandon declares in *One Way to Heaven,* "I could go white if I wanted to, but I am too much of a hedonist; I enjoy life too much, and enjoyment isn't across the line." Similarly, Nikki Giovanni, after relating the pain, disappointment, and poverty of her youth in her famous poem "Nikki-Rosa," declares that a white observer would only view her "hard childhood" and not realize that, being rich in "Black love," she was always "quite happy."

The black communities in most large cities are very well known and used to be sought out by Negroes traveling to those cities as well as by white voyeurs and thrill seekers—Sweet Auburn in Atlanta, Jackson Ward in Richmond, and numerous others.[1] Among the most famous of course are Harlem in New York and Bronzeville in Chicago. The latter was the birthplace or place of residence for such notables as Nat King Cole, Scott Joplin, Richard Wright, Jessie Owens, Joe Louis, and Redd Foxx. It was the home of Johnson Publishing company (the best known of all black publishing companies, whose most popular magazines are *Ebony* and *Jet*), site of The Chicago Bee Building (which housed several black newspapers), and the locus of numerous famed cafes and clubs where noted jazz musicians performed. Bronzeville was made even more famous by the poetry of Gwendolyn Brooks (*A Street in Bronzeville* [1945] and *Bronzeville Boys and Girls* [1956]), and through her work comes to symbolize similar communities of varying sizes throughout this nation.

The one thing that the Negroes in African American literature miss most if they in some way leave the black world by going abroad, passing, or simply "moving up" in society is their "Bronzeville." Typical is Helga Crane in Nella Larsen's *Quicksand,* who, after spending a few years in

---

1. Sometimes the areas are known by the most popular street, as Second Street in Richmond, State Street in Chicago, Lenox Avenue in Harlem, and Beale Street in Memphis.

Copenhagen where she was popular and lived in luxury and contentment, began to miss the Negro community. She then could understand her Negro father's desertion of her white mother:

> She understood his yearning, his intolerable need for the inexhaustible humor and the incessant hope of his own kind, his need for those things, not material, indigenous to all Negro environments.

Historically, one of the most popular community gatherings of black women was the quilting bees, one recalled in Dr. Binford's memorate (p. 157). Quilting bees were a popular practice among slave women that continued widely practiced in rural areas well into this century. At these social gatherings women of the community came together to assist one of their neighbors to create a quilt. As they quilted, they socialized, ate, told tales, shared anecdotes about the pieces of fabrics they were incorporating into their quilts, and gossiped. Many of their creations, some of them extant from the period of slavery, are exquisite works of art, valuable not only for their practical use (warmth) and aesthetic value, but also for their cultural, social, and historical commentary, evident variously in the materials used in the quilt, the cultural memories incorporated in them, and the message inherent in their designs. Numerous writers, most notably Gloria Naylor and Alice Walker, have made quilts and quilting important parts of the narrative, theme, and symbolism of their works, particularly Naylor's *Mama Day* and Walker's "Everyday Use."

Doing their hair has offered women in the black community another opportunity for socializing, whether it be families in the home scratching, shampooing, braiding, and pressing one another's hair, coeds in the college dorms setting, cornrowing, and styling each other's locks, or women in a beauty parlor getting a professional do. In such settings, African American women truly let their hair down and engage in some of the freest and most hilarious repartee to be found outside their kitchens and front porches. In recent years these gatherings have become even more comical because of the presence of coiffeurs, most of whom have been embraced by this female community. A number of them are homosexuals and/or transvestites, some styling their hair and dressing exactly like the female operators and sometimes sporting even tighter skirts, higher heels, heavier makeup and more exaggerated feminine gestures. Some of them will call themselves and each other girls. Their acceptance into this female community was made very apparent to me recently when, after listening to a tale generally shared only among women, one coiffeur laughed, tossed his head, and intoned, "Honey, hush!"

A visit to any but the more sophisticated beauty parlors remains a social occasion of eating, drinking, laughing, and gossiping, with some of the customers interacting for hours—the lengthy stays resulting from the fact that many hairdressers commonly overbook, some mothers and daughters come together, and some hairstyles take several hours—even occasionally a couple of days. This segment of the community was brought to the stage in 1987 and 1990 with Shelly Garrett's farcical and controversial *Beauty Shop* and *Beauty Shop Part 2,* plays ignored or blasted by the black intelligentsia and enthusiastically supported by a large segment of the black community that does not generally attend the theater.

Then there are the gatherings of professional women. In larger cities there are social clubs and professional organizations of black women. Teachers, writers, doctors, lawyers, politicians, entrepreneurs enjoy many of the same types of comic tales and jokes as do their less sophisticated sisters, though their professional lives offer a great deal of additional grist for the comedy mill. All of these vocations have a body of folklore focusing on their profession, as can be seen in "A Dentist's Jokes," given me by a Richmond dentist and "The Strongest Drive," popular with writers and English teachers. Lani Guinier, nationally known law professor who came to prominence when President Clinton picked her for an Assistant Attorney General and then withdrew her name, tells about one of her law professors at Yale who addressed each student as "gentleman," thus making her a "female gentleman."[2]

African American literature and folklore are full of accounts of women and men sitting around lying, joking, cracking up—on their front porches, at their quilting bees, in their barbershops and beauty parlors, in their juke joints, in their private social clubs, in whatever places a few of them are gathered. There they laugh about everything: their homes, their poverty, their schools, their church, their language, their names, their neighbors,

2. Lani Guinier, "Introduction of Professor Mari Matsuda," *Temple Political & Civil Rights Law Review* 3 (Fall 1993/Spring 1994) 3.

their jobs, their white folks, their illnesses and cures, and their deaths. They tell ghost stories and Brer Rabbit stories and tales about how things came to be. They play the dozens and signify and lie. They sing songs and recite toasts and poems. They recall these events with great pleasure and sentimentality in numerous autobiographies and recount them with uproarious glee in numerous works of fiction.

Nothing did these individuals laugh about more than their hardships. When Bertice Berry and her siblings asked their mother what was for dinner, if there were no food she would reply, "Poke, rolls, and grits. Poke your mouth out, roll your eyes, and grit your teeth, 'cause that's all you're getting." This ability to laugh has always helped African-Americans to deal with their deprivations. The bad times—and the good—are grist for the humor mill in the African American community.

Nagueyalti Warren

DOWN HOME SUNDAY BLUES:
MEMOIR OF A DAUGHTER GONE NORTH

from *Lodestar and Other Night Lights*

Chile, I used to wake up on Sunday mornings
With the smell of baking powder biscuits
Frying slabs of thick ham and smothered chicken
Beating me all upside my sleepy head.
Momma be cooking—coffee brewing, and daddy
Be shaving 'n' singing like he in the choir already.
June Bug be spit-shining his black church shoes.

Sun be sitting there, right over the rose bush
Looking in my window, askin' me why I'm so slow to move?
Daddy be singing loud! Loud!
Then momma join in
Her sweet soprano floating over and under
Daddy's baritone.

"Joleeen, gal, get yo' lazy be-hind out from that bed
And come sit this table!" Momma shocking me to my feet—
She ain't had to call but once.
It's Sunday morning in our house.
No work—cause momma done worked us to death
Saturday, washing clothes, cooking food, pressing hair—
Good food all day long
Sunday breakfast be like a meal
You ain't never seen.

Girl, down home on Sunday
I'd be dressed to kill
Hair plated with shiny red ribbons
Patent leather shoes, shined with a biscuit
Lace and crinoline slips—
In church we be singing hot loud songs
And sometimes momma cry
Me and June Bug slide down in our seats
For fear she will cut loose with a shout!

It was like that on Sundays
'Till the summer of '62
I seen him 'cross from the mourner's bench
Sister Thomas' nephew
From New York City
Lord have mercy, that man was fine:
Skin brown red like the wine served up
On Christmas day—
Eyes like hazel nuts
Hair black as coal

That summer was spent
On my front porch
Him eatin' my momma's Sunday lemon pies
Banana pudding, coconut cakes
And telling me about a world
Of high rise buildings and fine shops:
New York

Honey, when he left on that North bound train
I was right there with him
Made my momma cry
Broke my daddy's heart
But I was heading North
North, where love became a big belly
Birthing screaming mouths to feed
Where no gardens grow
And I can't see the sky
Where I can only dream about
What these food stamps won't buy!

Mother Love

DEALING WITH ILLNESS AND HELPLESS RELATIVES

from *Listen Up, Girlfriends!*

Remember when Auntie had cancer and we snuck those pork-shoulder sandwiches into the hospital? Yeah, she enjoyed the sandwiches, but what was more important was that we spent quality time with her. We read to her, we played cards with her, and we told silly jokes as we laughed with her.

Auntie would whisper in my ear, "Go over there and bother that doctor. Go on, girl, and give him a hard time 'cause he's working on my nerves."

In my family, when somebody is ill you don't just turn them over to the medical profession. The same is true with the elderly. We would never think of putting my eighty-eight-year-old great-grandmother into a nursing home. Well, mostly because she got kicked out of three of them.

So we had to take her in. Was she grateful?

Great-Grandmother: "I don't wanna live with none of y'all! You don't do what I want ya to do!"

What did she expect from us before she moved in? She expected us to come to her apartment and scrub the iron steps, scrub the concrete, and sweep the dirt.

My father was still alive when he and my mother decided to bring Great-Grandmother to our house to live. And she had her own room.

We'd all protest: "Why we got to have her live here with her old self? Why we got to comb that nappy blue hair of hers?"

Yeah, Great-Granny had blue hair. After it turned white she had it rinsed blue. And combing her hair was like combing steel wool.

It was long.

It was thick.

It was wiry—and to make it worse, she was tender-headed!

She could not stand for her hair to be combed, but she wanted it to be combed all the way through to its very end. When you washed her hair it just matted up like a big cotton ball on her head.

We had to use this old, thick-toothed comb and comb it in sections. If any of her hair came out she'd start screamin', "You're pullin' my hair out! You're pullin' my hair out! Get away from me!" Then she'd start smackin' whoever she could reach. It was a nightmare. But we couldn't put her off on anybody else.

My father said that we needed the influence of our great-grandmother, that we should know and respect our elders.

Excuse me?

Now here was a woman who chewed tobacco, smoked cigarettes, and dipped snuff. She could spit forty feet, without any of it dripping, straight into a spittoon. And she didn't use her spittoon just to catch her spit. She did all of her "business" in it and demanded that we empty it. Didn't matter to her that her bedroom was right next to the bathroom!

As far as I can remember she was eighty-eight her entire life. So she had to be about 112 when she finally died in her sleep. Why, she outlived my father!

We were taught that when someone was sick or going through hard times, you automatically entertained them or played with them. If someone was hospitalized they had a visitor every day. Regardless of who (and how unbearable they were), what, or why the crisis, our family always pulled together.

Dori Sanders

HER OWN PLACE

[The following selection comes well into the novel after our heroine Mae Lee has successfully raised her children; but finding the "golden years" lonely and empty, she has moved into town.]

Still, the decision to move to town had been a good one. So many of her old friends lived nearby now. The chairs on her front porch never remained empty for long. As soon as it was shaded from the summer's hot sun, Mae Lee would leave the air-conditioned comfort of her living room and sit out there, her very presence an open invitation to the neighbors, her porch a welcome mat. Through idle conversation spiced with gossip they reviewed the events of the day, and the years that brushed their lives, exposing and hiding faults as if they were removing layers of paint from old furniture or doing a touch-up job on the town.

"Poor Clairene's troubled again, Mae Lee," Ellabelle announced sadly one day even before she climbed the steps.

"How come you say that Clairene's troubled?" Mae Lee asked. She didn't look up, just kept on shelling peas.

"Can't you hear her? She's singing 'Amazing Grace' again." Ellabelle climbed the steps. "Get me a bowl, and I'll help you shell peas." She pulled a handful from a big brown paper bag. "You must be having the preacher for supper tonight."

"No, just me."

"It's enough for three families."

"I'll put what's left over in the freezer."

Ellabelle lifted her skirt to wedge a pot between her fat thighs.

"For goodness' sake, woman," Mae Lee fussed, "pull your dress down! You might excite somebody. As if it were possible," she added.

Ellabelle grunted, "Huh, it's possible all right, and that's exactly what I want to do, or run 'em crazy, one. Just might snare me an old nighthawk. He'll be good for the night and can fly off in the morning. This old tired body could stand a little tune-up. My engine parts have been neglected too long."

"Hush up," Mae Lee laughed. "You are going to mess around and start talking dirty. With the state of mind you're in, it wouldn't be safe for old man Sheets Cannon to walk by."

Ellabelle grunted. "I know you don't mean Sheets. My body engine parts are not that much in need of repair. Poor Cannon was born troubled. His mama had to be also, to have a last name like Mills and then turn around and name her son Cannon. How could he escape being called Sheets? Especially the way he keeps his head tore up. Poor thing, he's always three sheets in the wind."

Mae Lee laughed. "I guess it's better than being called Pillow Case or Towels. They say he was fired last week from the textile mill where he was working."

"I thought he retired when he was sixty-five."

"He did, Ellabelle. He was just doing odd jobs part-time. They say when he got his walking papers he asked to speak to the head man to thank him for being able to work there for so many years. Well sir, they said, Sheets took off his cap and sort of bowed, 'I want to thank you, sir, want to thank your kinfolk, but most of all I want to thank your mother for doing something nobody else has *ever* done, and that's birth a SOB like you!' Then the tipsy fool started singing, 'What you gonna do, when the river go dry . . . sit on the bank and watch the catfish die . . .' and then he truck-danced out of the office."

Ellabelle laughed until she cried, then she took off her glasses and lifted the edge of her wide skirt to wipe the tears from her eyes.

"There you go again," said Mae Lee. They laughed some more. She grew serious. "At least while he lives with his sister he won't go hungry for something good to eat. Sheets's sister is a good cook. Cooked for years for some of the richest people in Rising Ridge."

"*Was* a good cook," Ellabelle corrected. "She's getting old now. Last year she forgot to remove the plastic bag from the inside of her Thanksgiving turkey. Poor thing. She just wasn't at herself that day. She's a good woman." She glanced at the early summer's sky. "Before you know it we will be hearing the honking Canadian geese streaking across the skies. My daddy said it was going to be a cold, cold winter if they formed letters when flying. For me they spell 'almost turkey time.' "

Mae Lee reached for more peas. "How can you think that far ahead? It's after mid-October when they fly through."

"These peas are making me hungry, that's how."

After they'd cooked and eaten a Sunday dinner on a weekday they returned to the front porch.

Mae Lee took a long sip of iced tea. "I swear this is my last glass." She swallowed hard. "We got to stop eating so much. We're pushing our bodies way out of shape. Did you see Janet Dalton's fancy picture in the paper today? She sure looked good."

"I would too," Ellabelle pined, "if I had her money. She probably uses what my daughter said most of Them use nowadays, something I think she said called Night Repair. She works at the cosmetic counter in Dillard's department store, you know. According to my daughter, a little bottle no bigger than my thumb is very expensive!"

"If it's the size of your thumb, honey, it's a pretty good-sized bottle," Mae Lee chuckled.

"Look who's talking, child, you must still be looking at your body in your high school mirror."

Mae Lee laughed. "It's pitiful the way we've let ourselves go. Maybe we need some of that night cream."

"A lot of us widows need it, especially poor old Miss Austin who runs the jewelry store on Main Street. For all I know she might be using it. If the stuff does work, its repair job sure doesn't last, because by daybreak it's broken down and needs to be fixed all over again." Ellabelle shook her head.

"I almost hate to go in her store anymore," Mae Lee said. "She is so anxious to find a friend, before she even waits on her customers she'll ask, 'Do you know of any good unmarried men around?' I guess she's teasing, though."

Ellabelle poured iced tea from a pitcher. "Like hell she is. I was in there to get a battery for my watch and with my own ears I heard her tell a customer that she'd heard that old Clay Lewis had started taking some high-powered pep pills, so she said, 'I called up Mr. Clay Lewis one evening, and I said to him on the telephone, come on over. I'm a-sitting here all alone with nothing on but my TV.' "

"Poor thing, she's still searching for love. The likelihood of finding it, though, is about as good as a dry dandelion flower staying on its stem during a windstorm," Mae Lee said sadly.

Clairene's singing was slicing through the still night air again, her voice clear and mournful: ". . . I once was lost, but now I'm found . . ."

They listened, and from a distance quietly shared her sadness.

Ellabelle wiped away tears. "Lord, Lord, Clairene can sing."

She'd hardly finished speaking when Clairene's husband, Joshua, slowly drove by, his arm in the open car window. From a radio turned up too loud for a man his age, a mellow voice offered the blues. She watched him snapping his fingers to the beat.

Mae Lee shook her head sadly. "Poor Clairene, I'll bet her old man has gone and overbit too big a chew of tobacco again. She's going to have to sing more than 'Amazing Grace' to hang on to that big new white Lincoln he's tooling around in all over town."

"I don't know how I even have time to fill my head with someone else's problems," Ellabelle said, "I'm up against so much. My children are putting me through right much now. You got good children, Mae Lee." Ellabelle seemed really sad. "Guess it does no good to talk about it, though."

"Children always seem to offer some problems," Mae Lee mused. "I heard my Taylor's spoiled wife Bettina threatened to pack up and go back to her mother's." Mae Lee drew a deep breath. "I am careful not to interfere with my daughter-in-law and my grandchildren. The only problem, to tell the truth, that I'd have with Bettina leaving is that she'd soon be running right back to my son. Taylor is not only a fine schoolteacher, he's a fine husband!"

Mae Lee softly fingered the pin on her dress. A découpage photo of a grinning little boy, her grandson, Dallace's child, lay enshrined in a pseudoantique cameo pin wreathed in tiny plastic pearls. A printed nametag was never necessary for Mae Lee. The picture of her grandson was her identity, her reason for being. Mae Lee was the grandmother of Tread Wallace.

Mae Lee offered no apology for singling out her grandson for extra praise. He was the firstborn male of her grandchildren, not to mention being very special besides. She thought of the times when, as a youngster, he would beg and cry to come stay with her, beg and cry to not have to leave. She loved his little sister Shella, too, but disapproved of the way she was being raised. She was a spoiled brat. "She is a precocious little girl," her daughter Dallace had tried to explain. Her daughter may have had a lot of learning to be able to become Dr. Wallace, Mae Lee thought, but she sure raised a rotten kid in the process.

Unlike Ellabelle, Mae Lee had not used her tears for Clairene's singing.

She needed them now. "My grandson," she moaned softly, cupping her hand over his picture, "my fine baby boy. He's got an earring in his ear. An earring. And you know something, his mama is to blame. Yes, my daughter Dallace is at fault."

"For heaven's sake, Mae Lee, the boy is almost fourteen years old. You know how these teenagers go out for these stylish fads," said Ellabelle.

"Style? You know deep down in your heart what people think."

"People don't think nothing if it's in their left ear."

"All I know is for the first and only time in my entire life, I'm not sorry that my mama is dead. I never believed I would or could ever say this, but I know if my mama wasn't dead, this would kill her. Would kill her for sure."

"Mae Lee, I'm gonna tell you like they do on TV—'You can see what it's doing to someone else, but you can't see what it's doing to you.' Let it go. Listen to me, somebody who knows."

Mae Lee looked at her friend. She believed Ellabelle remembered everything she'd seen and heard on TV. But she couldn't always put too much stock in some things she had to say. How could she? There is not much there for a woman who answers when asked if she has a middle initial, "I don't know whether I have one or not. I have a middle name, though. Maybe you could use it instead." It seemed Ellabelle's chest of knowledge was filled entirely with what she'd learned from watching television shows.

For a few moments, Mae Lee was lost in thought. Indeed, she was a little disturbed that she could blame her daughter, with all the unhappiness she was going through. Dallace was struggling under a load of problems too heavy for her to face alone at her age. She knew all too well how much Dallace needed her counsel—far and beyond what she even realized. It didn't matter that Dallace was over forty now; in the mothering department there are no age limits.

She had been startled, but not overly saddened, by her daughter's decision to divorce her husband. When Dallace told her about the child's picture she'd accidentally found in her husband's wallet, Mae Lee wished she'd been more understanding, more so than her mama, Vergie, had been with her. But she'd been angry, angry that her daughter in all her years of marriage had considered herself too proper and high-class to look through her husband's wallet every now and then. That was just one more form of the night work a wife had to perform. All she had to do was not have a headache, and she would be sure of a free chance to search his pockets and wallet when he fell asleep. Her mama had taught her all those kind of things long ago. But back then, daughters listened to their mamas.

Even if she had told her, Mae Lee didn't believe her daughter would have listened. Her guarded daughter was, after all, Dr. Dallace Wallace, a professional person who claimed she always respected a person's privacy. So she'd found the picture only when her husband asked her to hand him his wallet and it fell out, a picture of a little boy whose Asian heritage could not be denied, nor could it disguise the genes of her husband.

When she confronted him, he readily admitted that, yes, that was his son. Mae Lee thought of her grandchildren, the mental image of the missing-tooth smile of her pretty, ponytailed granddaughter, Shella, and the imp-ish grin of her little Tread, with his second-growth of buckteeth, flashed before her.

Lately Mae Lee's daughters had always been reminding her that her thinking was not on the "same page" as theirs. Well, in that case she wanted to tell her daughters that on her "page," and on the same for her friends, the child was a "you-know-what." In her eyes the father was no longer married to her daughter. As far as she was concerned, her daughter's mar-riage had ended when her husband slept outside his marriage bed. This is the eighties, she wanted to say; be a smart young woman.

She wanted personally to hurt her son-in-law for what he'd said to her daughter Dallace about the braces that were so badly needed for his son Tread's teeth. He had said that the money spent on the outside son was bet-ter served. After all, he didn't want to alter their son's looks; "He's a spit-ting image of his old man," he had laughed, adding with a roguish wink, "he'll have some pretty young thing as wild over him as you are over me."

It pained her that in recent years her precious daughter had been hang-ing on to such worthless trash. Changing to crazy hairstyles, spreading lay-ers of makeup on her face, as if she were competing with a seven-layer pineapple cake, and of course there were the miniskirts. A wife trying to force a chaser of miniskirted females to turn around and chase her. Dallace's saving grace was her legs; she had great legs, legs like her mama's.

Poor Dallace. It didn't matter that she had "doctor" before her name, or "Ph.D." after it, or wherever they put it. She was a pitiful woman. Dallace had been stricken with a "mother's affliction," thorns in a mother's side. Mae Lee wanted so desperately to gather her child and grandchildren to her side, and give them the down-home grandma comforts, sunshine-fresh ironed sheets that smelled of the fragrant lilac talcum powder she always sprinkled on mattress covers; her home cooking; long hours on the front porch.

Ellabelle offered more advice. "Remember, when we were coming along we did plenty, plenty of stuff that would have worried our parents to death, but we turned out all right."

"Speak for yourself," Mae Lee retorted. But then she relented. "It's true," she finally agreed. "But for the most part they didn't know about it. I wonder which is better, to know or not to know? I think not knowing keeps your hair black longer."

"Or else, not allow a gray hair in the county and do like you're doing, buying out the drugstore to cover the gray," laughed Ellabelle. She slapped her arm; a whining mosquito raised itself. "These mean old boogers are starting to act nasty. They say only the females bite. That figures. Guess I'll head home and turn in. Oh, Lordy," she groaned, "I can tell I'm getting old. I'm starting to get pains where I didn't even know I had a place."

"You're going to end up on a kidney machine if you don't start drinking more water. The only liquid you get comes from a can."

"How do you know that all I drink is soft drinks?"

"It's all I ever see you drink. I don't believe you can swallow water. You even take your blood pressure pills with Pepsi."

"Well," Ellabelle said, "you won't have to worry about it no more. I'll never bring my cans of soda again. Not as long as I live on the face of this earth. You are sitting here talking behind my back. I can't stand that."

"Ellabelle, we are face to face," Mae Lee reminded her.

When they finished laughing, Ellabelle said, "I've been aiming to tell you I saw Fred Rivers's widow the other day. She's nothing but skin and bones. Going down fast, she's going to worry herself to death over. . . ." Her voice trailed off. "I know where we all need to take our problems. I know exactly where I'm taking mine."

Mae Lee grunted, thinking, if you're planning on taking them to the Lord tonight, be prepared to wait a spell for help. Because with just the calls coming in from Rising Ridge alone, I don't think he could handle them, even with "call waiting."

MIMEOGRAPHED ITEM

The Strongest Drive

The strongest drive

is not Love or Hate.

It is one person's need

to change another's copy

Folk

A DENTIST'S JOKES

I.

Question: What do you call a man who still has his baby teeth?
Answer: Dentally retarded.

II.

Question: What time is it when you have to go to the dentist?
Answer: Tooth-thirty.

III.

A man called a plumber to come over and look at his leaky faucet. The plumber came in and in five minutes, tightened a bolt and said, "That will be a hundred dollars."

The man was aghast and exclaimed, "You've got to be kidding. That's more than I have to pay my orthodontist!"

The plumber said, "Yes, that's why I got out of orthodontics."

Terry McMillan

WAITING TO EXHALE

"I hope the party's not over *now*," Robin said. "I'm just getting worked up here."

"Hey, why don't you all spend the night?" Gloria said. "As a matter of fact, I don't think any of you should be driving, with all this champagne in your system."

"She's right," Robin said. "So let's get sloppy drunk!"

"Where's my glass?" Savannah asked.

Robin gave everybody a refill. For the next hour, they played old records and got so drunk they couldn't laugh anymore. By the time Robin managed to get Smokey Robinson's "Tracks of My Tears" on, they all had their heads down. "I told you I didn't want to cry," Savannah said. "I'm so sick of this shit, I don't know what to do. Can somebody tell me what we're doing wrong?"

"What are you talking about now?" Bernadine asked.

"I want to know why I'm thirty-six years old and still single. This shit is not right. What ever happened to the good old days?"

"What good old days?" Gloria wanted to know.

"You know. When a man saw you in a crowd, smiled at you, flirted, and came over and talked to you. Not one has asked me for my phone number since I've been here. Why not? There's nothing wrong with me. Shit, I'm smart, I'm attractive, I'm educated, and my pussy's good, if I do say so myself. What happened to all the aggressive men? The ones that aren't scared to talk to you? Where the fuck are they hiding?"

"They're not hiding. They're just scared to make a damn commitment," Robin said.

"They're with white women," Bernadine said.

"Or gay," Gloria said.

"Or married," Savannah said. "But you know what? They're not all with white girls, they're not all homosexuals, they're not all married, either. When you get right down to it, we're talking five, maybe ten percent. What about the rest?"

"They're ugly."

"Stupid."

"In prison."

"Unemployed."

"Crackheads."

"Short."

"Liars."

"Unreliable."

"Irresponsible."

"Too possessive."

"Dogs."

"Shallow."

"Boring."

"Stuck in the sixties."

"Arrogant."

"Childish."

"Wimps."

"Too goddamn old and set in their ways."

"Can't fuck."

"Stop!" Savannah said.

"Well, shit, you asked," Robin said.

Savannah reached inside her purse in slow motion. She was trying to find some Kleenex, because something was in her eye. She wasn't successful. Robin handed her a handkerchief. "Here, girl," she said.

"And stop crying," Bernadine said. "This is too pathetic."

"I'm not crying. Something's in my damn eye. Shit, I can't help it if I'm sick of *being* by myself, *doing* everything by myself, and I don't know what to . . . Oh oh," she said, and struggled to get up.

"Get her to the bathroom," Gloria said. All of them helped Savannah up, dragged her to the bathroom, and as soon as she got inside the door, she threw up all over the floor.

"That champagne'll do it every time," Robin said. "Who's gonna clean this mess up?"

"I will," Gloria said.

"Not on your birthday," Bernadine grumbled. "Get me some old rags, and lay her down on the couch."

Bernadine cleaned the floor on her hands and knees. By the time she finished, she couldn't get up, let alone stand, so she crawled back into the living room. Savannah had long since passed out on the couch. Gloria went to the laundry room to empty the pail. She'd planned to get Savannah a blanket, but she was moving so slow by the time she dropped the pail in the utility sink, she had to stand there for a few minutes to get her bearings. She forgot what she was getting ready to do next.

Robin and Bernadine heard a key in the front door. A burglar with his own key. Now, that was a good one, Bernadine thought, and wanted to laugh, but she'd lost the ability. Robin's eyes were half closed, but she could tell it was Tarik, who was shocked to see his mother's friends sprawled out on the living room floor and one—unconscious—hanging over the edge of the couch. The room was a total disaster. Albums and tapes were everywhere. At least five empty bottles of champagne were on the coffee table, as well as plates of dried-up, half-eaten slices of pizza. "Hi," he said, with some reservations.

"Hi, Tarik," Robin and Bernadine mumbled.

"You're getting taller by the day," Bernadine whispered, and let her head drop.

Tarik could see they were all toasted. "So you guys did it up, I see."

"You only turn thirty-eight once," Robin muttered.

He looked at the cake. It hadn't been cut. "Where's my mother?"

Bernadine and Robin looked at each other. "Isn't she in this room with us?" Bernadine said.

Tarik realized this was a waste of time. "Well, good night," he said, and on his way toward the stairs, he saw his mother feeling her way through the kitchen. Tarik started laughing. He could see she was drunk too. He tried to wipe the smirk off his face, but Gloria didn't even see him. "Yo, Ma. You all right?" he said.

Gloria waved her hand toward the floor and said, "Un hun."

Tarik ran on upstairs. Gloria finally remembered what she was supposed to do. Once she found the linen closet, she fell inside it and grabbed some blankets. When she got back to the living room, somebody had dimmed the lights—at least they looked dim. Robin and Bernadine were on the floor, dead to the world. Gloria dropped a few folded blankets on top of her friends and headed for the stairs. She stopped at the foot and looked up. At first it looked like an escalator, but then the steps stopped moving. She blinked, grabbed hold of the banister, and looked up again. Not tonight, she thought, and found herself an empty spot near the front door. She made a pillow out of a stack of albums, pulled her dress up over her shoulders like a blanket, and went to sleep. Gloria didn't feel the cold tile against her legs and thighs or the spider crawling over her right foot. She didn't hear Smokey Robinson, either, still singing his heart out.

Paule Marshall

TALK YUH TALK

from *Brown Girl, Brownstones*

On Saturdays the kitchen was filled with fragrances, for Silla made and sold Barbadian delicacies: black pudding, which is the intestines of the pig stuffed with grated sweet potato, beets, animal blood and spices until it is a thick sausage, then tied at the ends and boiled; also souse, which she made by pickling parts of the pig; and coconut or sweet bread, a heavy bread with coconut running in a rich vein through the center.

From early one Saturday Selina and Ina had been grating until, by noon, their fingers were torn and their blood mixed with the shreds. The bell rang, relieving them, and a shaft of wind brought voices and a feel of the snow crusted hard along the curbs.

"Dear-heart, the pudding and souse smell too sweet! How?" Iris Hurley entered, her wide nostrils stiff with cold. She was tall and big-boned like Silla, with smooth black skin, high hard facial bones, evasive eyes.

"Iris, I still here," Silla said and turned to the other woman. "Florrie, how?"

"Suffering, soul!" Florrie Trotman's short legs carried her chunky body as if it was an unfair burden. She had dull yellow skin, oblique eyes, an innocent mouth and huge breasts that swelled over her brassière so that it appeared that she had four breasts instead of two. Sometimes Silla affectionately called her "Bubby-Island."

"Come soul, sit, do." She motioned her to a chair. "You's blowing like a whale."

Florrie Trotman sat heavily; her bosom heaved. "We ain staying Silla-soul. We just stop to see if you was still living or dead. Wha'lah I din see the children." She twisted around to them. "C'dear, I never see girl-children so features their father as these two, Silla."

"They's his all right—frighten for work just like he."

Florrie struggled out of her coat and swung her pocketbook high on her arm. "But in truth these New York children don like work. They soft. Look that half a man I got there. All day his head does be up in a radio listening to jazz like he's some jazz fiend or the other. Only yesterday I had to up hand and give a cuff that near kill him."

"You best watch that heavy hand," Silla said, " 'cause this is New York and these is New York children and the authorities will dash you in jail for them."

"Never mind that! They want licks!" Florrie shouted. "You got to wash their tail in licks. You remember what the old people home did tell us: hard ears you wun hear, own-ways you'll feel."

Iris Hurley spoke for the first time. "But c'dear, I don does have no trouble with mine. Maybe if you two would of send the children to church . . ."

"But Iris, who ask you?" Silla flared. "You always bringing up the church in everything. Don you think I sent the little beasts to Barrow's Church and they was up there reciting the 'Little Lord Jesus lay down his sweet head' and thing so! You think that change them?"

"As for you! It's years since you darken the door-mouth of a church," Iris said.

"And years to come!" Silla added, "And you know why, Iris? It's not that I's some heathen or the other, but that my mind turn from the church. I see too many hypocrites prostrating themself before the cross each Sunday. The same ones buying house by devious means. Lemme tell you, Iris, you don see God any better by being sanctified and climbing the walls of a church and tearing off your clothes when you's in the spirit, or even when you's up in the so-called High Church, choking on the lot of incense and bowing and kneeling for hours and singing in various tongues. Not everyone who cry 'Lord, Lord' gon enter in . . .'"

"I gon pray for you, Dear-heart."

"Don waste breath, Iris. Each man got to see God for himself."

Florrie Trotman sucked her teeth, annoyed. "But why wunna two hard-back women always arguing 'bout the church. . . . Silla, those new curtains?"

"Woman, who can be buying anything new with all this war and foolishness going on?"

Iris Hurley sent a blast through her wide nostrils. "But do you read how many thousand upon thousand they killing out each day? But c'dear, these white people getting on too bad. They say that Hitler put all the Jews in a gas chamber. But you know, somebody oughta take up a gun so and shoot down that man so, 'cause he's nothing but the devil-incarnate."

"In truth," Silla said with bowed head and her face drawn with sadness. Suddenly she cried, her voice tremulous with anger, "It's these politicians. They's the ones always starting up all this lot of war. And what they care? It's the poor people got to suffer and mothers with their sons."

"Oh Jesus-Christ-God, Silla!" Florrie shuddered. "Don speak do. Livingston's due to go, y'know. He ain no good but he's my only son."

"They'd never get a child of mine in no army," Iris said. "I'd make him eat soap each day to make the heart beat fast first. Wait, no . . ." She paused. "I might if he was gon fight direct for England and the crown."

"But Iris you's one ignorant black woman!" Silla said softly. "What John Bull ever did for you that you's so grateful? You think 'cause they does call Barbados 'Little England' that you is somebody? What the king know 'bout you—or care? You best stop calling the man name like you and he does speak. You think the king did care when you was home heading canes? Or when the drought come and not a pot stir 'pon the stove for days . . . ?"

"Dear-heart," Iris said placidly, "you like you come to read the burial service over me."

"You deserve to dead," Silla cried, her face working and her eyes boring into Iris, who remained unmoved and unimpressed. Silla leaned across the table to her, whispering, "Iris, you know what it is to work hard and still never make a head-way? That's Bimshire. One crop. People having to work for next skin to nothing. The white people treating we like slaves still and we taking it. The rum shop and the church join together to keep we pacify and in ignorance. That's Barbados. It's a terrible thing to know that you gon be poor all yuh life, no matter how hard you work. You does stop trying after a time. People does see you so and call you lazy. But it ain laziness. It just that you does give up. You does kind of die inside . . ."

"It's the God truth," Florrie whispered.

"I ain saying that we don catch *H* in this country what with the discrimination and thing and how hard we does have to scrub the Jew floor to make a penny, but my Christ, at least you can make a head-way. Look how Roosevelt come and give relief and jobs. Who was one the first Bajan bought a house? You, Iris. When they pass this law to hire colored in defense plants who was the first up in the people face applying? Your husband, Iris. Even I gon apply for one those jobs. So c'dear, give credit where it due, nuh," she pleaded softly, then as Iris still ignored her, she lashed out, "You's an ungrateful whelp."

"Dear-heart," Iris laughed, "I ain able for you to kill me with words!"

Florrie had listened rapt, respectful to Silla, and now she said solemnly, "Talk yuh talk, Silla! Be-Jees, in this white-man world you got to take yuh mouth and make a gun."

Virgie M. Binford

QUILTING TIME

During my preschool years, I was one of the official volunteers as a "Needle-Threader" for my grandmother and her team of neighborhood quilters in rural Mississippi. Each member of the team hosted the group on a rotating basis for completion of sewing the quilt after the design was stretched in a frame.

Each quilter had at least two needles. The job of the volunteers was to keep a needle threaded for each participant. In addition to providing warmth for covering in the winter for beds of sleepers, the activity provided joyful communication for these snuff-dipping ladies. They had developed a language known to them but supposedly foreign to the pint-sized needle-threaders.

During one session they were talking about the sadness of a pregnant girl. Instead of saying what had happened, a "snuff-dipper" used her spittoon to release the fluid that had drained from her stuffed lower lip of the brown powdered tobacco product and said "Guhls, listen to the latest news! Don't you know that little ole Patty dun gone and broke her leg!"

My grandma replied, "how do you know Susie? Don't be gittin dysentery of the mouth puttin that gossip out on that po guhl!" In an effort to support my loving grandmother, I replied, "I know Patty's leg is not broken because I saw her."

Instead of being complimented for sharing what I thought was factual information, I was punished for "sticking my nose in grown folks' bizness" and lost my job as needle-threader.

Priscilla Jane Thompson

AN AFTERNOON GOSSIP

from *Gleanings of Quiet Hours*

Is that you sistah Harris?
    I knowed you when you knocked;
Jest keep right on a-pushing,
    The ole door isn't locked!

Ole white man's been forgetting,
    Each day since first I sent;
He's got a pow'ful mem'ry,
    When comes the time for rent.

Now, sit down; Whut's your hurry?
   You have no work to do;
I'm mos' done with my i'ning;
   You always beats me through.

You aint no bother to me!
   Jest sit here where its cool;
Hush fretting 'bout them child'en!
   You know they're safe in school.

Now, whut's the news, Amanda?
   Hearn some 'bout Flora Ann;
Jest take this little rocker,
   And reach that pa'm leaf fan.

I hearn she's gone and married,
   That trifling Louis Bird;
Says I to Abe this mo'nin',
   Don't b'lieve a single word.

Hush woman! Whut's you sayin'?
   How can that news be true?
Flo Ann wus sot on Jasper,
   She never keered for Lou.

Well people! Don't that beat you?
   Gone married Lou fo' spite;
The Lo'd have mussy on her!
   She's trapped herse'f for life.

Guess what ole Jeems been doin'?
   Can't guess to save my life;
Aint took a crazy notion,
   To git another wife?

Fo' land-sakes! sister Harris,
  Ha! ha! ha! aint I beat?
That man's jest buyin' hosses
  Fo' crows an' dogs to eat.

Now, you know well as I do,
  He loses ev'ry one:
They're half dead when he gets them;
  I 'spect he thinks it's fun.

'Twus jest a week last Tuesday;
  Abe made me break my side,
Telling how the marshal fined him,
  For half bur'ing one that died.

I hearn 'bout Sister Curtley?
  Why Sistah Harris, no!
Fell down and broke her ankle?
  Good Lo'd! You don't say so?

Fell down them ole back do' steps!
  She told me they wus broke;
Ole Smith put off the fixing:
  I'd make that white man smoke!

I must git round and see her;
  Hope God will bring her through;
We must pray for her, Mandy,
  And see whut we can do.

We must not shirk our duty,
  And linger in the lurch,
But help, in tribulations,
  A sistah in the church.

You say you're feeling poorly?
    Then course you couldn't go;
Yes, Sistah Riley told me,
    That you wus feeling slow.

Now hush your 'pologizing!
    I know your heart is true;
Whut sistah did more shouting,
    Last 'vival time than you?

You wa'n't out to meeting,
    When they 'churched' Riah Brown?
You'd broke your sides a-laughing,
    How Elder called him down.

The Elder riz and asked him,
    To take a seat in front;
So, up the aisle he shuffled,
    And sot down, with a grunt.

Then, spoke up Elder Mitchell,
    "Now, whut have you to say?
You know the charge against you,
    For the evil of your way.

"You've walked the way of sinnahs,
    Used church funds for your gain,
And when 'cused by Deacon Riley,
    Took the name of God, in vain."

Ef evah in your lifetime,
    You've seen a good whooped hound,
With head and tail a-dragging,
    You then saw Riah Brown.

"And therefore," said the elder,
   His voice was loud and stout;
"We want no wolves among us;
   I move to turn you out."

Poor sistah Brown wus crying,
   Riah wus sniffling too;
Yet seemed no sad occasion,
   Jest spite of all I'd do.

I know 'twa'n't like no christain,
   The feeling that I had,
For ev'ry where around me,
   The sistahs looked so sad.

But 'pon my word, Amanda,
   Since my eyes first saw light;
I never felt more tickled,
   Than I did Tuesday night.

Trudier Harris

THE OVERWEIGHT ANGEL

from *Obsidian: Black Literature in Review*

Aun Sis was one of the angels who got misplaced. Instead of coming from the right side of the throne and descending down to the miry clay of the earth, she got coughed up from the devil's furnace and never made it more than six inches off the ground. You see, she miscalculated her historical time periods and somehow got the idea that Satan was still as angelic as the day he was booted out from up there and she wouldn't get tainted from the association. Starting out with this basic misconception, she took it upon herself to right the wrongs of the world, which to her was our tiny neighborhood in Tuscaloosa, Alabama. The community consisted of one street and perhaps thirty houses and a grocery. Not being one to admit even a potential for mistakes, Aun Sis continued on her shaky foundation until her charges in our neighborhood moved, got married and disappeared, died or otherwise removed themselves from her influence.

She was nobody's aunt in particular. At least none of us could trace any bloodlines directly back to her side of the oven, but she delighted—sometimes to our chagrin—in claiming all of us. Not only "us," meaning the children, but our parents as well. Some of the women her age were even calling her "Aun" Sis and the title did seem to add a bit of authority—warped though it may be—to the huge woman who made it her business to tend the business of our lives. She must have been all of two hundred fifty pounds. When she stood up she was an easy six feet barefooted. You can well imagine why she succeeded in passing out so much free soul saving. She towered over everybody, including her diminutive husband, whom the neighbors fell into the habit of calling "Mr." Sis.

It was amazing how Aun Sis managed to get into so much of her neighbors' business without leaving her seat on her front porch. But she did. That was partially because she lived across the street from the grocery and any self-respecting family in the area had to make at least four trips to that store per day. So Aun Sis would sit there bombarding them with questions or drawing them onto her porch with the sheer force of her voice. If you didn't get over there fast enough, she'd let out with: "Well, there, Miss Frosty, didn't know you wuz gittin' above yo kinfolk these days. 'Cose I 'member the time when you ain't had a pot to piss in nor a window to th'ow it out of. But since you big enough to know where fertilizer come from, I guess you don 'preciate relatives no mo." Believe me, it was the scum of the community for a week who would let her finish that speech.

Poor Mrs. Johnson, who couldn't hear very well, should have thanked the Lord that she couldn't at times. Aun Sis would start in on her when she was a good forty feet away from the store.

"Hear tell that boy of yourn got in trouble with the law again," Aun Sis would say. "Tried to tell that fool he ain't the President's son, but naw, he wouldn't listen. How much time he git this time, Bertha?"

Mrs. Johnson would continue making her way slowly to the entrance of the store and lean more heavily on her walking stick. She was already slightly bent and seemed to go over further doing that last thirty feet or so. Maybe her bending was natural because it was a known fact that Mrs. Johnson left her hearing aid home in order to escape the remarks she knew would be hurled from Aun Sis's porch. Or her bending might simply have been from the knowledge of entering Aun Sis's territory.

When Mrs. Johnson offered no response to Aun Sis's comment, the silence by no means stopped the assault.

"Bertha," Aun Sis would bellow, "I know you hear me talkin' to you. Been tellin' that lie to everybody for years like you can't hear, but I know better. I knew you when you could hear a gnat piss twenty feet away. So jes cut that deef mess out!"

Mrs. Johnson would wait until she got to the store and directly across from the porch, then she would look up and say "How you, Sis?" turn abruptly and walk into the store, not allowing Aun Sis a chance to catch her eye and respond.

As soon as she saw Mrs. Johnson coming out, Aun Sis would start again.

"When that boy of yourn git outta jail, Bertha, you brang him to Sunday School and church. Teach him to turn from the ways of the wicked. You tell him I said he oughta pray while he there in jail. Be good for his soul. And don't forgit to brang him to church."

The attack never ended until Mrs. Johnson was completely out of earshot, even if she had been able to hear.

Another way Aun Sis stayed in everybody's business was through the frequent trips Cut'n Coot made to her house. Cut'n Coot lived at the far South end of the street, around the one and only bend in the road and she kept Aun Sis posted on that neck of the woods. Cut'n Coot was Aun Sis's twin in every way except height. Aun Sis also towered over her and it was felt that she even threatened her into bringing news from around the bend. A gossip flunky, that's what Cut'n Coot was. But it didn't seem to matter very much. The voice and its echo were perfectly harmonized.

I remember once when I was fourteen and Momma sent me to take some canning jars to Aun Sis. The two of them were sitting on the porch taking people apart with their lip service. Aun Sis never would cease her attacks when children were around because she felt that if they knew how grown-ups acted, they wouldn't grow up to be that way.

"Chile," she was saying to Cut'n Coot, "I wuz sittin' here and she come walkin' down that road right out there. Jes 'a switchin' her tail as drunk as you please. Musta spent the night at Bootleg Gert's."

"Lawd, naw," came the echo's reply. "You hush yo mouf. Did she have on that little bobtail black dress again?"

"Um huh, so short you could see her tail feathers."

I tried to interrupt.

"Momma said she sent these jars for you to put your canning in."

"Jes put 'em down over there. . . . And you know, she dared to raise her voice and try to speak to me—me, a church goin' woman. You know I don cotton to that kind of thang."

I put the jars down and listened almost against my will. Aun Sis continued:

"And she wuz draggin' that little whimperin' snotty nosed young'un behin' her. Had on a t-shirt and nothin' else. Hollerin' to the top of his voice. 'Cose you know they say it ain't her husband. Look jes like that man what live next door to her. You know the one."

"I sho do. Umh, umh, umh. Ain't that scandalous?"

The conversation continued as I descended the steps and started home. It was only one of many about Mrs. Taylor, our neighborhood drunk and scene thrower. And Aun Sis always fell just one short of saving Mrs. Taylor's soul by delighting so much in discussing her sins.

Aun Sis was worse than the mail service. Rain, shine, sleet or snow she was sitting on that porch. Only a blizzard could have driven her inside, but such phenomena are unknown in that part of Alabama. When it was a mere eighteen or nineteen degrees, Aun Sis put on her light overcoat and survived off her fat. In fact, if you stepped on her porch on the coldest of days, there seemed to be a certain amount of warmth exuding from the great lady. Perhaps that was due to her origins. Anyway, she would sit there and keep up her various tirades against the neighbors.

Aun Sis continued her bullying and misdirected soul saving throughout my junior high school years, but the year I started to high school was the year she met her pepper salt. It came in the form of a pint-sized runt by the name of Sary Jane Rebecca Addison (named for two grandmothers and an aunt). Sary moved into the neighborhood and transferred to the local high school. Her family occupied the house that Mrs. Johnson used to live in, thus suggesting it was destined from the beginning that she not get along with Aun Sis. Sary's mother had died six months before and perhaps Aun Sis felt a special obligation toward her since she had no children of her own. But Sary didn't feel particularly like returning the obligation. This showed the first time she made a trip to the now famous store across from Aun Sis. It was the beginning of Spring, on a Saturday afternoon, and Aun Sis was sitting there busily trying to force a couple of flowers to grow when she saw Sary switching up the street. She had on a bikini top and a pair of short shorts. Aun Sis swiftly concluded that the devil was in our midst and that this child needed her soul saved.

" 'Roun' here," she directed to the fast approaching Sary, "we dress accordin' to our family."

"Well, I'm sure glad my family isn't from around here," the impish Sary replied. "I don't take to sheets very well." It was obvious that Sary had been warned about Aun Sis and obvious too that Aun Sis had *not* been warned about Sary. The big woman almost rose from her seat in a show of surprise, but changed her mind half-way up. She couldn't let the devil get the upper hand. Mustn't let the child know of her startled reaction. She sank back into her chair, more determined than ever that she should save Sary from the throes of the wicked, and come Judgment Day, present her soul a shining offering on the altar of the Lord. Thus determined, she decided to take a new approach with Sary. Instead of insults, threats or insinuations, she would use logic.

"What I meant, Sary," she tried again, "wuz that the little boys often git the wrong ideas when girls don cover up their bodies. Goin' 'round' 'sposed like that might cause 'em to think you easy."

"Didn't cause Daddy to think that way about Momma and this was her favorite outfit."

And that's probably why you so backwards, Aun Sis undoubtedly thought—no home training—but she didn't say a word. And for that woman to be speechless was in itself something miraculous. The miracle was only momentary, however.

"Didn't yo mama teach you no respect for yo elders?" Aun Sis asked.

"Sure she did and she told me to be especially respectful to Aun Rebecca cause she gets a bit trying sometime."

Unwilling to be led or pushed from her course, Aun Sis responded.

"What about strangers? Didn't she tell you to be kind to 'em? What about that?"

"My Momma," said Sary, looking directly at Aun Sis and pausing for emphasis, "told me not to talk to strangers." With that, she turned and walked into the store. The interval gave Aun Sis time to revamp her attack or her rescue, depending on the point of view. She had a long reverie because what she didn't realize then was that Sary had a part-time job at the store on weekends. Cut'n Coot provided her with this bit of information when she joined Aun Sis on the porch. They were both there to greet Sary when she came out of the store three hours later.

"Hear tell you got a job over there," Aun Sis started in. "Mighty fine thang for young'uns to learn the value of work at a early age."

"That's what Momma always said, Miss Sis." Sary had also rejected the kinship title. "But from what I can see, some folks didn't get the proper training when they were growing up. Momma always said idle minds were the devil's playthings and there seem to be a lot of them around here."

"You wouldn't be tryin' to git sassy, would you girl?" Cut'n Coot asked. "We can take any little sassy tail in this community and whup her butt good."

"Now, now Coot," Aun Sis cautioned. "Ain't no need to threaten the chile. She wuzn't tryin' to make it personal . . . wuz you Sary?"

"No m'am, Miss Sis, but Momma always said it was a good practice to apply the truth of a thing to yourself once you saw it. See y'all later, Miss Sis." Sary made a fast exit down the road and around the bend, leaving the two ladies no further along on their crusade than they had been before.

The fireworks between Aun Sis and Sary became so well established that idle spectators would try to find their way near the scene with one excuse or another whenever the two were scheduled to confront each other, which was almost every day. For almost two years the war continued with Aun Sis trying to convert, moralize and otherwise change Sary and Sary resisting almost effortlessly. Aun Sis forgot that she had other charges in the neighborhood and concentrated all her energies on Sary. We suspected that deep down they probably liked each other because they made such an effort to disagree, insult and otherwise maim each other.

Sary succeeded fairly well in starting a new trend in the community. All newcomers during that two year period invariably called Aun Sis by her recently bestowed appellation—Miss Sis. Other ladies in the area were accustomed to such address, but you could see Aun Sis's displeasure whenever it was applied to her. That is, you could see it every time any of the new people used the title, but not when Sary used it. Aun Sis was still very much determined that Sary would never see her upset, angry or in any way displeased.

The final scene between the two occurred on the day of our graduation from high school. Sary refused to take off her gown after the ceremony and we soon found out why. Upon reaching home, she put down her diploma, took off her shoes and started up the street. She didn't have to work that day and could have only one destination in mind.

When she reached the spot directly across from Aun Sis's porch, she stopped. Aun Sis was sitting there as usual. She had seen Sary coming and waited in anticipation. She knew that Sary must have something to say and held her tongue to give the heathen first go.

"Hey, Miss Sis!" Sary called, as if Aun Sis might have been thirty yards instead of thirty or so feet away. The greeting was unnecessary because she already had Aun Sis's attention. Perhaps she wanted to emphasize the distance between them; she had never once set foot on Aun Sis's porch. The present arrangement had always been the normal talking space between them.

"Miss Sis," Sary addressed her again. "I just wanted you to be the first to know that I'm leaving this neighborhood. Getting out of this town. Going away forever. You're not going to have me to yell and scream at anymore. And I wanted you to know, too, that I'm going unconverted. That church stuff was too much. Doggone bunch of hypocrites. Always telling people, 'Go cleanse yourselves,' and never looking at their own morals, and their own souls. I am sick and tired of that. I am sick and tired of do-goodies trying to straighten out my morals when they're already straight. I am sick and tired of this old narrow-minded neighborhood. But mainly, *I am sick and tired of you*. That's what I came to tell you too, but that doesn't matter anymore cause I'm leaving."

Aun Sis, somewhat immunized to Sary's backtalk by now, simply asked: "Where you goin' Sary?"

"Up to Knoxville to college," she answered in a "I've got something on you" kind of voice, and turned and made her departure.

Aun Sis bowed her head and smiled.

Maggie Pogue Johnson

MEAL TIME

from *Virginia Dreams / Lyrics for the Idle Hour: Tales of the Time Told in Rhyme*

Liza! call dat chile
    En make her wash her face
En cum on to de table
    So Pap can say de grace.

You let de chillun hab der ways
    And soon dey'll manage you,
Ef you don't try to check dem,
    Come on, Bob en Sue!

Yo'all set up to de table,
    'Twill take a ha'f a day
To get y'all to yo' meals,
    Cumin in dat way.

Don't make sich noise wid dem stools!
    Does you hear me, Jane?
Ef 'twarn't fer we ol' folks
    You chillun wud raise Cain.

Set up straight dar, Jimbo!
    We all is ready, Pap!
Stop dat whisperin' Lisha!
    En pull off dat air cap.

Yo' all cud'n sho keep still
    'Till Pap cud say de grace;
I don't know what's gwine to cum
    Ob dis young cullud race.

Sal! git de spoon en git mo' hash—
  Don't spill it on de flo';
Take up all de co'n cakes,
  I t'ink Pap wants some more.

Abe, don't stuff yo' mouf so full,
  You sho kin git some mo';
Be kerful wid dat buttermilk—
  Don't spill it on de flo'.

En pass de cakes aroun',
  Don't t'ink all 'bout yo' self;
Try to l'arn some manners,
  You ugly little elf.

You kids done eat enuf!
  Git up from dat table
En clean dem dishes up
  As fas' as you is able.

En you sweep de kitchen good,
  Be quick about it, too;
'Twill be time fer anodder meal,
  Befo' you chaps git thro'.

Sarah and A. Elizabeth Delany

HAVING OUR SAY

Bessie and I have been together since time began, or so it seems. Bessie is my little sister, only she's not so little.

She is 101 years old, and I am 103.

People always say they'd like to live to be one hundred, but no one really expects to, except Bessie. She always said she planned to be as old as

Moses. And when Bessie says she's going to do something, she does it. Now, I think Moses lived to 120. So I told Bessie that if she lives to 120, then I'll just have to live to 122 so I can take care of her.

————

One thing Sadie and I do is stay away from doctors as much as possible. And we avoid hospitals because, honey, they'll kill you there. They overtreat you. And when they see how old you are, and that you still have a mind, they treat you like a curiosity: like "Exhibit A" and "Exhibit B." Like, "Hey, nurse, come on over here and looky-here at this old woman, she's in such good shape. . . ." Most of the time they don't even treat you like a person, just an object.

One time, some doctor asked Sadie to do a senility test. Of course, she passed. A year later, he asked her to do it again, and she said, "Don't waste your time, doctor." And she answered all the questions from the year before, before he could ask them. And then she said to me, "Come on, Bess, let's get on out of here."

————

[In the next selection the sisters recall their young adulthood.]

Here I was, traveling around the countryside, a grown woman with professional responsibilities. Yet Papa was still in charge of my social life. He didn't want me to go out with any fresh boys, so he selected my gentleman friends. When I had a caller, we would sit in the parlor to talk. That was about all we were allowed to do. Papa would sit in the other room and read his newspaper and I am quite sure he was listening to every word.

I had one beau named Frank who was particularly fond of me. He was a fellow student of Lemuel's, studying medicine at Shaw University. Papa used to get kind of annoyed with Frank because he talked too much, and would keep talking even when Papa thought it was time for him to leave. Lights went out at the school at ten o'clock, and Papa couldn't stand the idea of our house still having lights on past that hour. It didn't look good. So one time I remember Papa called to me, and I left Frank in the parlor, and Papa said to me, "Are you going to tell him to leave, or am I?" And I said, "Oh, Papa, I can't tell him to leave! I don't want to hurt his feelings!" So I didn't, and neither did Papa. Instead, Papa just cleared his throat and stomped around, hoping Frank would get the hint. We used to have to practically shove Frank out the door.

Now, I liked Frank a lot, but then one day, Papa told me, "Sadie, you won't be seeing any more of Frank for now." It seems Lemuel had reported to Papa that Frank had been linked to some scandal involving a young nurse. Well, Frank was never able to clear his name to Lemuel's and Papa's satisfaction. I guess he really was involved somehow but I never learned the details. All I know is that I never saw Frank again.

Well, here I am an old maid. Ooops, I shouldn't say "old maid" 'cause it makes Bessie mad. Bessie says we're "maiden ladies." Well, whatever we are, I have no regrets about it. I think Frank would have worried me to death. I've had a good life, child.

———

I suppose Lemuel and Papa thought they were doing the right thing by Sadie, forbidding her to see Frank anymore, but I don't think it was right. She was a grown woman. She should have had a say. It was her choice to make, not theirs!

Oh, I don't know what she saw in old Frank, anyway. He was kind of dull and he talked too much, though I guess I shouldn't say that, because I can outtalk anyone. Yes, sir! I don't know how Sadie's put up with this old flabbermouth for the past one hundred years.

Don't you go thinking because we are maiden ladies that Sadie and I didn't have lots of beaus. We were popular, good-looking gals, but I think we were too smart, too independent for most men. This was especially true for me when I went to teach in Boardman, North Carolina. Honey, when you get to be one hundred years old, you look back and see things very clearly. And I can see I kind of overwhelmed those boys in Boardman, North Carolina, back in 1911!

[In the following selection the Delanys return to their present lives at the time they were completing *Having Our Say.*]

I don't think Mama would have been at all surprised that Sadie and I have kept living this long. We learned a lot from her about being old. Mama set a good example. She took care of herself, and she was surrounded by love.

I'll tell you something kind of funny. It had annoyed Mama that when Manross died, they made his wife return the pension check he had in his pocket. She thought that was mean. So she said, "If I die and I have a check in my pocket, Sadie, you must promise me that you will run to the bank and cash it, and keep that money!"

So, while Mama was ailing, Sadie did just that. And do you know that the pension company sent a letter immediately? They had seen Mama's obituary in *The New York Times*—that Bishop Delany's widow had died— and they sent a letter that said, "Please return the last check." And Sadie wrote to them, "Sorry, but it was cashed."

We always did what Mama asked.

———

Some white folks believe that Negroes bring down a neighborhood because they don't keep up their property. Well, in our case, we had the neatest, spiffiest-looking yard on the block! Sadie and I set out to have the best garden you could find, and it has given us a great deal of pleasure. For many years, these little old white gals would walk over from this white retirement home, just to look at it, every day. Of course, we had lots of flowers, roses, you name it; but we also grew vegetables, like Kentucky wonder-beans, which we would eat or can for the winter months.

I'll tell you a funny thing that happened with our garden. A beautiful plant with a star-shaped leaf started growing there, and we couldn't figure out what it was. It annoyed us because we thought we knew everything about gardening and we hadn't seen this plant before. It got bigger and bigger, and we covered it faithfully each winter. Whenever we had visitors to the house, we would say, "Do y'all know what kind of plant that is?" And none of our visitors ever knew, either. Finally, our young nephew said, "Aunt Bessie! Aunt Sadie! What in the world are y'all doing with a marijuana plant in your garden?" Well, we surely were surprised. And I said, "Sadie, we had better get rid of it immediately, because we are breaking the law!" Don't worry, we got somebody to take care of it.

Maggie Pogue Johnson

WHAT'S MO' TEMPTIN' TO DE PALATE?

from *Virginia Dreams/Lyrics for the Idle Hour: Tales of the Time Told in Rhyme*

What's mo' temptin' to de palate,
    When you's wuked so hard all day,
En cum in home at ebentime
    Widout a wud to say,—
En see a stewin' in de stove
    A possum crisp en brown,
Wid great big sweet potaters,
    A layin' all aroun'.

What's mo' temptin' to de palate,
    Den a chicken bilin' hot,
En plenty ob good dumplin's,
    A bubblin' in de pot;
To set right down to eat dem,
    En 'pease yo' hunger dar,
'Tis nuffin' mo' enjoyin',
    I sho'ly do declar.

What's mo' temptin' to de palate
    Den a dish ob good baked beans,
En what is still mo' temptin'
    Den a pot brimfull ob greens;
Jis biled down low wid bacon,
    Almos' 'til dey's fried,
En a plate ob good ol' co'n cakes
    A layin' on de side.

What's mo' temptin' to de palate
    Den on Thanksgibin' Day
To hab a good ol' tuckey
    Fixed some kin' o' way;
Wid cranber'y sauce en celery,
    All settin' on de side,
En eat jis 'til yo' appetite
    Is sho' full satisfied.

What's mo' temptin' to de palate,
    Den in de Summer time,
To bus' a watermillion
    Right from off de vine;
En set right down to eat it
    In de coolin breeze,
Wif nuffin' to moles' you,
    Settin' neaf de apple trees.

What's mo' temptin' to de palate,
    Den poke chops, also lam',
En what is still mo' temptin'
    Den good ol' col' biled ham;
Veal chops dey ain't bad,
    Put de mutton chops in line,
I tell you my ol' appetite,
    Fo' all dese t'ings do pine.

What's mo' temptin' to de palate,
    When you cum from wuk at night,
To set down to de fiah,
    A shinin' jis so bright,
De ol' 'oman walks in,—
    Wid supper brilin' hot,
En a good ol' cup ob coffee,
    Jis steamin' out de pot.

'Tis den I kin enjoy myse'f,
   En eat dar by de fiah,
Case puttin' way good eatin's
   Is sho'ly my desire;
Dar's nuffin dat's so temptin',
   Dat to me is a treat,
Den settin' at a table
   Wid plenty good to eat.

Becky Birtha

JOHNNIERUTH

from *Lovers' Choice*

Summertime. Nighttime. Talk about steam heat. This whole city get like the bathroom when somebody in there taking a shower with the door shut. Nights like that, can't nobody sleep. Everybody be outside, sitting on they steps or else dragging half they furniture out on the sidewalk—kitchen chairs, card tables—even bringing TVs outside.

Womenfolks, mostly. All the grown women around my way look just the same. They all big—stout. They got big bosoms and big hips and fat legs, and they always wearing runover house-shoes, and them shapeless, flowered numbers with the buttons down the front. Cept on Sunday. Sunday morning they all turn into glamour girls, in them big hats and long gloves, with they skinny high heels and they skinny selves in them tight girdles— wouldn't nobody ever know what they look like the rest of the time.

When I was a little kid I didn't wanna grow up, cause I never wanted to look like them ladies. I heard Miz Jenkins down the street one time say she don't mind being fat cause that way her husband don't get so jealous. She say it's more than one way to keep a man. Me, I don't have me no intentions of keeping no man. I never understood why they was in so much demand anyway, when it seem like all a woman can depend on em for is making sure she keep on having babies.

We got enough children in my neighborhood. In the summertime, even the little kids allowed to stay up till eleven or twelve o'clock at night—playing in the street and hollering and carrying on—don't never seem to get tired. Don't nobody care, long as they don't fight.

Me—I don't hang around no front steps no more. Hot nights like that, I get out my ten speed and I be gone.

That's what I like to do more than anything else in the whole world. Feel that wind in my face keeping me cool as a air conditioner, shooting along like a snowball. My bike light as a kite. I can really get up some speed.

All the guys around my way got ten speed bikes. Some of the girls got em too, but they don't ride em at night. They pedal around during the day, but at nighttime they just hang around out front, watching babies and running they mouth. I didn't get my Peugeot to be no conversation piece.

My mama don't like me to ride at night. I tried to point out to her that she ain't never said nothing to my brothers, and Vincent a year younger than me. (And Langston two years older, in case "old" is the problem.) She say, "That's different, Johnnieruth. You're a girl." Now I wanna know how is anybody gonna know that. I'm skinny as a knifeblade turned sideways, and all I ever wear is blue jeans and a Wrangler jacket. But if I bring that up, she liable to get started in on how come I can't be more of a young lady, and fourteen is old enough to start taking more pride in my appearance, and she gonna be ashamed to admit I'm her daughter.

I just tell her that my bike be moving so fast can't nobody hardly see me, and couldn't catch me if they did. Mama complain to her friends how I'm wild and she can't do nothing with me. She know I'm gonna do what I want no matter what she say. But she know I ain't getting in no trouble, neither.

Like some of the boys I know stole they bikes, but I didn't do nothing like that. I'd been saving my money ever since I can remember, every time I could get a nickel or a dime outta anybody.

When I was a little kid, it was hard to get money. Seem like the only time they ever give you any was on Sunday morning, and then you had to put it in the offering. I used to hate to do that. In fact, I used to hate everything about Sunday morning. I had to wear all them ruffly dresses— that shiny slippery stuff in the wintertime that got to make a noise every time you move your ass a inch on them hard old benches. And that scratchy starchy stuff in the summertime with all them scratchy crinolines. Had to carry a pocketbook and wear them shiny shoes. And the church we went to was all the way over on Summit Avenue, so the whole damn neighborhood could get a good look. At least all the other kids'd be dressed the same way. The boys think they slick cause they get to wear pants, but they still got to wear a white shirt and a tie; and them dumb hats they wear can't hide them baldheaded haircuts, cause they got to take the hats off in church.

There was one Sunday when I musta been around eight. I remember it was before my sister Corletta was born, cause right around then was when I put my foot down about that whole sanctimonious routine. Anyway, I was dragging my feet along Twenty-fifth Street in back of Mama and Vincent and them, when I spied this lady. I only seen her that one time, but I still remember just how she look. She don't look like nobody I ever seen before. I *know* she don't live around here. She real skinny. But she ain't no real young woman, neither. She could be old as my mama. She ain't nobody's mama—I'm sure. And she ain't wearing Sunday clothes. She got on blue jeans and a man's blue working shirt, with the tail hanging out. She got patches on her blue jeans, and she still got her chin stuck out like she some kinda African royalty. She ain't carrying no shiny pocketbook. It don't look like she care if she got any money or not, or who know it, if she don't. She ain't wearing no house-shoes, or stockings or high heels neither.

Mama always speak to everybody, but when she pass by this lady she make like she ain't even seen her. But I get me a real good look, and the lady stare right back at me. She got a funny look on her face, almost like she think she know me from some place. After she pass on by, I had to turn around to get another look, even though Mama say that ain't polite. And you know what? She was turning around, too, looking back at me. And she give me a great big smile.

I didn't know too much in them days, but that's when I first got to thinking about how it's got to be different ways to be, from the way people be around my way. It's got to be places where it don't matter to nobody if you all dressed up on Sunday morning or you ain't. That's how come I started saving money. So, when I got enough, I could go away to some place like that.

Afterwhile I begun to see there wasn't no point in waiting around for handouts, and I started thinking of ways to earn my own money. I used to be running errands all the time—mailing letters for old Grandma Whittaker and picking up cigarettes and newspapers up the corner for everybody. After I got bigger, I started washing cars in the summer, and shoveling people sidewalk in the wintertime. Now I got me a newspaper route. Ain't never been no girl around here with no paper route, but I guess everybody got it figured out by now that I ain't gonna be like nobody else.

The reason I got me my Peugeot was so I could start to explore. I figured I better start looking around right now, so when I'm grown, I'll know exactly where I wanna go. So I ride around every chance I get.

Last summer, I used to ride with the boys a lot. Sometimes eight or ten of us'd just go cruising around the streets together. All of a sudden my mama decide she don't want me to do that no more. She say I'm too old to be spending so much time with boys. (That's what they tell you half the time, and the other half the time they worried cause you ain't interested in spending more time with boys. Don't make much sense.) She want me to have some girl friends, but I never seem to fit in with none of the things the girls doing. I used to think I fit in more with the boys.

But I seen how Mama might be right, for once. I didn't like the way the boys was starting to talk about girls sometimes. Talking about what some girl be like from the neck on down, and talking all up underneath somebody clothes and all. Even though I wasn't really friends with none of the girls, I still didn't like it. So now I mostly just ride around by myself. And Mama don't like that neither—you just can't please her.

This boy that live around the corner on North Street, Kenny Henderson, started asking me one time if I don't ever be lonely, cause he always see me by myself. He say don't I ever think I'd like to have me somebody special to go places with and stuff. Like I'd pick him if I did! Made me wanna laugh in his face. I do be lonely, a lotta times, but I don't tell nobody. And I ain't met nobody yet that I'd really rather be with than be by myself. But I will someday. When I find that special place where everybody different, I'm gonna find somebody there I can be friends with. And it ain't gonna be no dumb boy.

I found me one place already, that I like to go to a whole lot. It ain't even really that far away— by bike—but it's on the other side of the Avenue. So I don't tell Mama and them I go there, cause they like to think I'm right around the neighborhood someplace. But this neighborhood too dull for me. All the houses look just the same—no porches, no yards, no trees—not even no parks around here. Every block look so much like every other block it hurt your eyes to look at, afterwhile. So I ride across Summit Avenue and go down that big steep hill there, and then make a sharp right at the bottom and cross the bridge over the train tracks. Then I head on out the boulevard—that's the nicest part, with all them big trees making a tunnel over the top, and lightning bugs shining in the bushes. At the end of the boulevard you get to this place call the Plaza.

It's something like a little park—the sidewalks is all bricks and they got flowers planted all over the place. The same kind my mama grow in that painted-up tire she got out front masquerading like a garden decoration— only seem like they smell sweeter here. It's a big high fountain right in the middle, and all the streetlights is the real old-fashion kind. That Plaza is about the prettiest place I ever been.

Sometimes something going on there. Like a orchestra playing music or some man or lady singing. One time they had a show with some girls doing some kinda foreign dances. They look like they were around my age. They all had on these fancy costumes, with different color ribbons all down they back. I wouldn't wear nothing like that, but it looked real pretty when they was dancing.

I got me a special bench in one corner where I like to sit, cause I can see just about everything, but wouldn't nobody know I was there. I like to sit still and think, and I like to watch people. A lotta people be coming there at night—to look at the shows and stuff, or just to hang out and cool off. All different kinda people.

This one night when I was sitting over in that corner where I always be at, there was this lady standing right near my bench. She mostly had her back turned to me and she didn't know I was there, but I could see her real good. She had on this shiny purple shirt and about a million silver bracelets. I kinda liked the way she look. Sorta exotic, like she maybe come from California or one of the islands. I mean she had class—standing there posing with her arms folded. She walk away a little bit. Then turn around and walk back again. Like she waiting for somebody.

Then I spotted this dude coming over. I spied him all the way cross the Plaza. Looking real fine. Got on a three piece suit. One of them little caps sitting on a angle. Look like leather. He coming straight over to this lady I'm watching and then she seen him too and she start to smile, but she don't move till he get right up next to her. And then I'm gonna look away, cause I can't stand to watch nobody hugging and kissing on each other, but all of a sudden I see it ain't no dude at all. It's another lady.

Now I can't stop looking. They smiling at each other like they ain't seen one another in ten years. Then the one in the purple shirt look around real quick—but she don't look just behind her—and sorta pull the other one right back into the corner where I'm sitting at, and then they put they arms around each other and kiss—for a whole long time. Now I really know I oughtta turn away, but I can't. And I know they gonna see me when they finally open they eyes. And they do.

They both kinda gasp and back up, like I'm the monster that just rose up outta the deep. And then I guess they can see I'm only a girl, and they look at one another—and start to laugh! Then they just turn around and start to walk away like it wasn't nothing at all. But right before they gone, they both look around again, and see I still ain't got my eye muscles and my jaw muscles working right again yet. And the one lady wink at me. And the other one say, "Catch you later."

I can't stop staring at they backs, all the way across the Plaza. And then, all of a sudden, I feel like I got to be doing something, got to be moving.

I wheel on outta the Plaza and I'm just concentrating on getting up my speed. Cause I can't figure out what to think. Them two women kissing and then, when they get caught, just laughing about it. And here I'm laughing too, for no reason at all. I'm sailing down the boulevard laughing like a lunatic, and then I'm singing at the top of my lungs. And climbing that big old hill up to Summit Avenue is just as easy as being on a escalator.

Toni Cade Bambara

THE LESSON

from *Gorilla, My Love*

Back in the days when everyone was old and stupid or young and foolish and me and Sugar were the only ones just right, this lady moved on our block with nappy hair and proper speech and no makeup. And quite naturally we laughed at her, laughed the way we did at the junk man who went about his business like he was some big-time president and his sorry-ass horse his secretary. And we kinda hated her too, hated the way we did the winos who cluttered up our parks and pissed on our handball walls and stank up our hallways and stairs so you couldn't halfway play hide-and-seek without a goddamn gas mask. Miss Moore was her name. The only woman on the block with no first name. And she was black as hell, cept for her feet, which were fish-white and spooky. And she was always planning these boring-ass things for us to do, us being my cousin, mostly, who lived on the block cause we all moved North the same time and to the same apartment then spread out gradual to breathe. And our parents would yank our heads into some kinda shape and crisp up our clothes so we'd be presentable for travel with Miss Moore, who always looked like she was going to church, though she never did. Which is just one of things the grown-ups talked about when they talked behind her back like a dog. But when she came calling with some sachet she'd sewed up or some gingerbread she'd made or some book, why then they'd all be too embarrassed to turn her down and we'd get handed over all spruced up. She'd been to college and said it was only right that she should take responsibility for the young ones' education, and she not even related by marriage or blood. So they'd go for it. Specially Aunt Gretchen. She was the main gofer in the family. You got some ole dumb shit foolishness you want somebody to go for, you send for Aunt Gretchen. She been screwed into the go-along for so long, it's a blood-deep natural thing with her. Which is how she got saddled with me and Sugar and Junior in the first place while our mothers were in a la-de-da apartment up the block having a good ole time.

So this one day Miss Moore rounds us all up at the mailbox and it's puredee hot and she's knockin herself out about arithmetic. And school suppose to let up in summer I heard, but she don't never let up. And the starch in my pinafore scratching the shit outta me and I'm really hating this nappy-head bitch and her goddamn college degree. I'd much rather go to the pool or to the show where it's cool. So me and Sugar leaning on the mailbox being surly, which is a Miss Moore word. And Flyboy checking out what everybody brought for lunch. And Fat Butt already wasting his peanut-butter-and-jelly sandwich like the pig he is. And Junebug punchin on Q.T.'s arm for potato chips. And Rosie Giraffe shifting from one hip to the other waiting for somebody to step on her foot or ask her if she from Georgia so she can kick ass, preferably Mercedes'. And Miss Moore asking us do we know what money is, like we a bunch of retards. I mean real money, she say, like it's only poker chips or monopoly papers we lay on the grocer. So right away I'm tired of this and say so. And would much rather snatch Sugar and go to the Sunset and terrorize the West Indian kids and take their hair ribbons and their money too. And Miss Moore files that remark away for next week's lesson on brotherhood, I can tell. And finally I say we oughta get to the subway cause it's cooler and besides we might meet some cute boys. Sugar done swiped her mama's lipstick, so we ready.

So we heading down the street and she's boring us silly about what things cost and what our parents make and how much goes for rent and how money ain't divided up right in this country. And then she gets to the part about we all poor and live in the slums, which I don't feature. And I'm ready to speak on that, but she steps out in the street and hails two cabs just like that. Then she hustles half the crew in with her and hands me a five-dollar bill and tells me to calculate 10 percent tip for the driver. And we're off. Me and Sugar and Junebug and Flyboy hangin out the window and hollering to everybody, putting lipstick on each other cause Flyboy a faggot anyway, and making farts with our sweaty armpits. But I'm mostly trying to figure how to spend this money. But they all fascinated with the meter ticking and Junebug starts laying bets as to how much it'll read when Flyboy can't hold his breath no more. Then Sugar lays bets as to how much it'll be when we get there. So I'm stuck. Don't nobody want to go for my plan, which is to jump out at the next light and run off to the first bar-b-que we can find. Then the driver tells us to get the hell out cause we there already. And the meter reads eighty-five cents. And I'm stalling to figure out the tip and Sugar say give him a dime. And I decide he don't need it bad as I do, so later for him. But then he tries to take off with Junebug foot still in the door so we talk about his mama something ferocious. Then we check out that we on Fifth Avenue and everybody dressed up in stockings. One lady in a fur coat, hot as it is. White folks crazy.

"This is the place," Miss Moore say, presenting it to us in the voice she uses at the museum. "Let's look in the windows before we go in."

"Can we steal?" Sugar asks very serious like she's getting the ground rules squared away before she plays. "I beg your pardon," say Miss Moore, and we fall out. So she leads us around the windows of the toy store and me and Sugar screamin, "This is mine, that's mine, I gotta have that, that was made for me, I was born for that," till Big Butt drowns us out.

"Hey, I'm goin to buy that there."

"That there? You don't even know what it is, stupid."

"I do so," he say punchin on Rosie Giraffe. "It's a microscope."

"Whatcha gonna do with a microscope, fool?"

"Look at things."

"Like what, Ronald?" ask Miss Moore. And Big Butt ain't got the first notion. So here go Miss Moore gabbing about the thousands of bacteria in a drop of water and the somethinorother in a speck of blood and the million and one living things in the air around us is invisible to the naked eye. And what she say that for? Junebug go to town on that "naked" and we rolling. Then Miss Moore ask what it cost. So we all jam into the window smudgin it up and the price tag say $300. So then she ask how long'd take for Big Butt and Junebug to save up their allowances. "Too long," I say. "Yeh," adds Sugar, "outgrown it by that time." And Miss Moore say no, you never outgrow learning instruments. "Why, even medical students and interns and," blah, blah, blah. And we ready to choke Big Butt for bringing it up in the first damn place.

"This here costs four hundred eighty dollars," say Rosie Giraffe. So we pile up all over her to see what she pointin out. My eyes tell me it's a chunk of glass cracked with something heavy, and different-color inks dripped into the splits, then the whole thing put into a oven or something. But for $480 it don't make sense.

"That's a paperweight made of semi-precious stones fused together under tremendous pressure," she explains slowly, with her hands doing the mining and all the factory work.

"So what's a paperweight?" asks Rosie Giraffe.

"To weigh paper with, dumbbell," say Flyboy, the wise man from the East.

"Not exactly," say Miss Moore, which is what she say when you warm or way off too. "It's to weigh paper down so it won't scatter and make your desk untidy." So right away me and Sugar curtsy to each other and then to Mercedes who is more the tidy type.

"We don't keep paper on top of the desk in my class," say Junebug, figuring Miss Moore crazy or lyin one.

"At home, then," she say. "Don't you have a calendar and a pencil case and a blotter and a letter-opener on your desk at home where you do your homework?" And she know damn well what our homes look like cause she nosys around in them every chance she gets.

"I don't even have a desk," say Junebug. "Do we?"

"No. And I don't get no homework neither," say Big Butt.

"And I don't even have a home," say Flyboy like he do at school to keep the white folks off his back and sorry for him. Send this poor kid to camp posters, is his specialty.

"I do," says Mercedes. "I have a box of stationery on my desk and a picture of my cat. My godmother bought the stationery and the desk. There's a big rose on each sheet and the envelopes smell like roses."

"Who wants to know about your smelly-ass stationery," say Rosie Giraffe fore I can get my two cents in.

"It's important to have a work area all your own so that . . ."

"Will you look at this sailboat, please," say Flyboy, cuttin her off and pointin to the thing like it was his. So once again we tumble all over each other to gaze at this magnificent thing in the toy store which is just big enough to maybe sail two kittens across the pond if you strap them to the posts tight. We all start reciting the price tag like we in assembly. "Handcrafted sailboat of fiberglass at one thousand one hundred ninety-five dollars."

"Unbelievable," I hear myself say and am really stunned. I read it again for myself just in case the group recitation put me in a trance. Same thing. For some reason this pisses me off. We look at Miss Moore and she lookin at us, waiting for I dunno what.

"Who'd pay all that when you can buy a sailboat set for a quarter at Pop's, a tube of glue for a dime, and a ball of string for eight cents? "It must have a motor and a whole lot else besides," I say. "My sailboat cost me about fifty cents."

"But will it take water?" say Mercedes with her smart ass.

"Took mine to Alley Pond Park once," say Flyboy. "String broke, Lost it. Pity."

"Sailed mine in Central Park and it keeled over and sank. Had to ask my father for another dollar."

"And you got the strap," laugh Big Butt. "The jerk didn't even have a string on it. My old man wailed on his behind."

Little Q.T. was staring hard at the sailboat and you could see he wanted it bad. But he too little and somebody'd just take it from him. So what the hell. "This boat for kids, Miss Moore?"

"Parents silly to buy something like that just to get all broke up," say Rosie Giraffe.

"That much money it should last forever," I figure.

"My father'd buy it for me if I wanted it."

"Your father, my ass," say Rosie Giraffe getting a chance to finally push Mercedes.

"Must be rich people shop here," say Q.T.

"You are a very bright boy," say Flyboy. "What was your first clue?" And he rap him on the head with the back of his knuckles, since Q.T. the only one he could get away with. Though Q.T. liable to come up behind you years later and get his licks in when you half expect it.

"What I want to know is," I says to Miss Moore though I never talk to her, I wouldn't give the bitch that satisfaction, "is how much a real boat costs? I figure a thousand'd get you a yacht any day."

"Why don't you check that out," she says, "and report back to the group?" Which really pains my ass. If you gonna mess up a perfectly good swim day least you could do is have some answers. "Let's go in," she say like she got something up her sleeve. Only she don't lead the way. So me and Sugar turn the corner to where the entrance is, but when we get there I kinda hang back. Not that I'm scared, what's there to be afraid of, just a toy store. But I feel funny, shame. But what I got to be shamed about? Got as much right to go in as anybody. But somehow I can't seem to get hold of the door, so I step away for Sugar to lead. But she hangs back too. And I look at her and she looks at me and this is ridiculous. I mean, damn, I have never ever been shy about doing nothing or going nowhere. But then Mercedes steps up and then Rosie Giraffe and Big Butt crowd in behind and shove, and next thing we all stuffed into the doorway with only Mercedes squeezing past us, smoothing out her jumper and walking right down the aisle. Then the rest of us tumble in like a glued-together jigsaw done all wrong. And people lookin at us. And it's like the time me and Sugar crashed into the Catholic church on a dare. But once we got in there and everything so hushed and holy and the candles and the bowin and the handkerchiefs on all the drooping heads, I just couldn't go through with the plan. Which was for me to run up to the altar and do a tap dance while

Sugar played the nose flute and messed around in the holy water. And Sugar kept givin me the elbow. Then later teased me so bad I tied her up in the shower and turned it on and locked her in. And she'd be there till this day if Aunt Gretchen hadn't finally figured I was lyin about the boarder takin a shower.

Same thing in the store. We all walkin on tiptoe and hardly touchin the games and puzzles and things. And I watched Miss Moore who is steady watchin us like she waitin for a sign. Like Mama Drewery watches the sky and sniffs the air and takes note of just how much slant is in the bird formation. Then me and Sugar bump smack into each other, so busy gazing at the toys, 'specially the sailboat. But we don't laugh and go into our fat-lady bump-stomach routine. We just stare at that price tag. Then Sugar run a finger over the whole boat. And I'm jealous and want to hit her. Maybe not her, but I sure want to punch somebody in the mouth.

"Watcha bring us here for, Miss Moore?"

"You sound angry, Sylvia. Are you mad about something?" Givin me one of them grins like she tellin a grown-up joke that never turns out to be funny. And she's lookin very closely at me like maybe she plannin to do my portrait from memory. I'm mad, but I won't give her that satisfaction. So I slouch around the store bein very bored and say, "Let's go."

Me and Sugar at the back of the train watchin the tracks whizzin by large then small then gettin gobbled up in the dark. I'm thinkin about this tricky toy I saw in the store. A clown that somersaults on a bar then does chin-ups just cause you yank lightly at his leg. Cost $35. I could see me askin my mother for a $35 birthday clown. "You wanna who that costs what?" she'd say, cocking her head to the side to get a better view of the hole in my head. Thirty-five dollars could buy new bunk beds for Junior and Gretchen's boy. Thirty-five dollars and the whole household could go visit Granddaddy Nelson in the country. Thirty-five dollars would pay for the rent and the piano bill too. Who are these people that spend that much for performing clowns and $1,000 for toy sailboats? What kinda work they do and how they live and how come we ain't in on it? Where we are is who we are, Miss Moore always pointin out. But it don't necessarily have to be that way, she always adds then waits for somebody to say that poor people have to wake up and demand their share of the pie and don't none of us know what kind of pie she talkin about in the first damn place. But she ain't so smart cause I still got her four dollars from the taxi and she sure ain't gettin it. Messin up my day with this shit. Sugar nudges me in my pocket and winks.

Miss Moore lines us up in front of the mailbox where we started from, seem like years ago, and I got a headache for thinkin so hard. And we lean all over each other so we can hold up under the draggy-ass lecture she always finishes us off with at the end before we thank her for borin us to tears. But she just looks at us like she readin tea leaves. Finally she say, "Well, what did you think of F.A.O. Schwartz?"

Rosie Giraffe mumbles, "White folks crazy."

"I'd like to go there again when I get my birthday money," says Mercedes, and we shove her out the pack so she has to lean on the mailbox by herself.

"I'd like a shower. Tiring day," say Flyboy.

Then Sugar surprises me by sayin, "You know, Miss Moore, I don't think all of us here put together eat in a year what that sailboat costs." And Miss Moore lights up like somebody goosed her. "And?" she say, urging Sugar on. Only I'm standin on her foot so she don't continue.

"Imagine for a minute what kind of society it is in which some people can spend on a toy what it would cost to feed a family of six or seven. What do you think?"

"I think," say Sugar pushing me off her feet like she never done before, cause I whip her ass in a minute, "that this is not much of a democracy if you ask me. Equal chance to pursue happiness means an equal crack at the dough, don't it?" Miss Moore is besides herself and I am disgusted with Sugar's treachery. So I stand on her foot one more time to see if she'll shove me. She shuts up, and Miss Moore looks at me, sorrowfully I'm thinkin. And somethin weird is goin on, I can feel it in my chest.

"Anybody else learn anything today?" lookin dead at me. I walk away and Sugar has to run to catch up and don't even seem to notice when I shrug her arm off my shoulder.

"Well, we got four dollars anyway," she says.

"Uh hunh."

"We could go to Hascombs and get half a chocolate layer and then go to the Sunset and still have plenty money for potato chips and ice-cream sodas."

"Uh hunh."

"Race you to Hascombs," she say.

We start down the block and she gets ahead which is O.K. by me cause I'm goin to the West End and then over to the Drive to think this day through. She can run if she want to and even run faster. But ain't nobody gonna beat me at nuthin.

Ethel Morgan Smith

THE SPELLING BEE

Big Mama and Aunt Tiny stitched Rose a pumpkin-colored jumper with a small row of daisies around the hemline for her to wear to the spelling bee. Her blouse was light blue with a smaller row of the daisies around the collar. "Stand still," Big Mama yelled, as she pinned the jumper on her for fitting.

Aunt Tiny had cut the pattern from newspapers on her dining room table. She was a stout, dark-skinned woman with gold-trimmed front teeth; one even had a star on it. Rose never knew how Aunt Tiny could find anything in her cluttered house; but she knew where to put her finger on everything.

Aunt Tiny couldn't sew well, but she had a new zigzag sewing machine that she had ordered from Sears on time payments. She started sewing when her three daughters were young. Her dream was for them to marry well. "The nicer they dress the more chances they had to snatch a good one," she asserted as she snapped thread through her gold teeth. When her daughters took home economics, they learned to sew and increased their chances of marrying well.

To get to the spelling bee contest by 7:00 P.M., Rose had to spend the night with Mrs. Wright, her math teacher. Mrs. Wright didn't talk much, just smiled a lot. Her front teeth were like Peter Rabbit's. She was knock-kneed with shoulder-length thin hair; and she smelled like "Evening in Paris" cologne.

"You've done very well, Rose. Try and not get too nervous. You have a good chance of winning. And if you win, you'll be in the newspaper."

"Yes, ma'am; I'll try my hardest."

Mr. Wright, the principal at the Mt. Zion School, three towns over, arrived home two hours later.

"You have time to take a bath and relax a little before supper," Mrs. Wright smiled.

"Yes, ma'am" Rose answered.

The bathroom was roomy with wallpaper that was splashed with tiny pink and blue flowers. The towels were different shades of pink. A giant jar on the toilet lid was filled with pink bars of Dove soap. A basket of magazines and newspapers was on the left side of the toilet seat, and a small space heater was in the other corner. White cotton throw rugs covered most of the cold floor. Rose took a long hot bubble bath and pretended she was getting ready to be on television.

The jumper was a perfect fit. With her penny loafers spit-shined, a generous layer of Vaseline on her legs, and knots in her stomach, Rose was ready for the spelling bee.

For supper they ate meat loaf with cheese whiz on top, soggy mashed potatoes, canned green beans, and two slices of toasted Wonder bread. They drank a glass of milk to wash the supper down. Mr. Wright said grace and asked God to remember their contestant in the spelling bee. Rose wondered how God would know which contestant to bless, since Mr. Wright didn't mention her name. The food made the knots in her stomach churn like making fresh butter.

Mr. Wright was a rotund, red-brown man who walked with a crutch. He didn't talk much either. Rose thought the reason that Mr. & Mrs. Wright didn't talk much was because they didn't have any children. They quietly drove to the school.

There were twelve students in the contest. Rose didn't know any of them. Her principal and his family were there, along with several white folks, which made her even more nervous.

Rose thought that if she didn't win, maybe she could get a boyfriend, since all of the boys were taller than she was. There was a refreshment line with strawberry flavored Kool-Aid in a clear punch bowl and store-bought chocolate chip cookies. A huge bulletin board at the front door said: GOOD LUCK FROM THE RED DEVILS!

"Everyone, it's time to get started. This is an occasion we can all be proud of. These young people have worked so very hard. I would like to congratulate each of the twelve finalists and say to each of you, you're already winners," glowed Mr. Corbin, the superintendent of the county. "Without further ado, I would like to introduce our narrator for the evening, our own, Mrs. Opal Britt."

Mrs. Britt was considered the hardest English teacher in the county. Students could tell her mood by the shade of red of the wig she sported on a particular day. If it were deep red, they were in real trouble. Her daughter was going to 'Bama, home of the "Crimson Tide" to study engineering because she had made the highest test score ever recorded in the state.

When the spelling bee finally came down to the wire, Rose could feel the sweat on her waist where the rubber of her half slip was. She was scared to look down because she thought her socks had slipped down into her shoes. And the Vaseline felt like lead on her legs. Three contestants were left: Nathaniel Thornton from Riverview, Josephine Haynes from Dillion County Training, and Rose.

The next thing she remembered was being on the floor and people standing around her. "ROSE, ROSE," she heard.

"Rose, R-O-S-E," she spelled. With a hit of smelling salts and the spelling of xenophobia she had won second place. Nathaniel Thornton won first place and her heart. The three finalists were on the front page of *The Montgomery Advertiser* the next day.

Zora Neale Hurston

THE YELLOW MULE

from *Their Eyes Were Watching God*

Every morning the world flung itself over and exposed the town to the sun. So Janie had another day. And every day had a store in it, except Sundays. The store itself was a pleasant place if only she didn't have to sell things. When the people sat around on the porch and passed around the pictures of their thoughts for the others to look at and see, it was nice. The fact that the thought pictures were always crayon enlargements of life made it even nicer to listen to.

Take for instance the case of Matt Bonner's yellow mule. They had him up for conversation every day the Lord sent. Most especial if Matt was there himself to listen. Sam and Lige and Walter were the ringleaders of the mule-talkers. The others threw in whatever they could chance upon, but it seemed as if Sam and Lige and Walter could hear and see more about that mule than the whole county put together. All they needed was to see Matt's long spare shape coming down the street and by the time he got to the porch they were ready for him.

"Hello, Matt."

"Evenin', Sam."

"Mighty glad you come 'long right now, Matt. Me and some others wuz jus' about tuh come hunt yuh."

"Whut for, Sam?"

"Mighty serious matter, man. Serious!!"

"Yeah man," Lige would cut in, dolefully. "It needs yo' strict attention. You ought not tuh lose no time."

"Whut is it then? You oughta hurry up and tell me."

"Reckon we better not tell yuh heah at de store. It's too fur off tuh do any good. We better all walk on down by Lake Sabelia."

"Whut's wrong, man? Ah ain't after none uh y'alls foolishness now."

"Dat mule uh yourn, Matt. You better go see 'bout him. He's bad off."

"Where 'bouts? Did he wade in de lake and uh alligator ketch him?"

"Worser'n dat. De womenfolks got yo' mule. When Ah come round de lake 'bout noontime mah wife and some others had 'im flat on de ground usin' his sides fuh uh wash board."

The great clap of laughter that they have been holding in, bursts out. Sam never cracks a smile. "Yeah, Matt, dat mule so skinny till de women is usin' his rib bones fuh uh rub-board, and hangin' things out on his hock-bones tuh dry."

Matt realizes that they have tricked him again and the laughter makes him mad and when he gets mad he stammers.

"You'se uh stinkin' lie, Sam, and yo' feet ain't mates. Y-y-y-you!"

"Aw, man, 'tain't no use in you gittin' mad. Yuh know yuh don't feed de mule. How he gointuh git fat?"

"Ah-ah-ah d-d-does feed 'im! Ah g-g-gived 'im uh full cup uh cawn every feedin'."

"Lige knows all about dat cup uh cawn. He hid round yo' barn and watched yuh. 'Tain't no feed cup you measures dat cawn outa. It's uh tea cup."

"Ah does feed 'im. He's jus' too mean tuh git fat. He stay poor and raw-bony jus' fuh spite. Skeered he'll hafta work some."

"Yeah, you feeds 'im. Feeds 'im offa 'come up' and seasons it wid raw-hide."

"Does feed de ornery varmint! Don't keer whut Ah do Ah can't git long wid 'im. He fights every inch in front uh de plow, and even lay back his ears tuh kick and bite when Ah go in de stall tuh feed 'im."

"Git reconciled, Matt," Lige soothed. "Us all knows he's mean. Ah seen 'im when he took after one uh dem Roberts chillun in de street and woulda caught 'im and maybe trompled 'im tuh death if de wind hadn't of changed all of a sudden. Yuh see de youngun wuz tryin' tuh make it tuh de fence uh Starks' onion patch and de mule wuz dead in behind 'im and gainin' on 'im every jump, when all of a sudden de wind changed and blowed de mule way off his course, him bein' so poor and everything, and before de ornery varmint could tack, de youngun had done got over de fence." The porch laughed and Matt got mad again.

"Maybe de mule takes out after everybody," Sam said, " 'cause he thinks everybody he hear comin' is Matt Bonner comin' tuh work 'im on uh empty stomach."

"Aw, naw, aw, naw. You stop dat right now," Walter objected. "Dat mule don't think Ah look lak no Matt Bonner. He ain't dat dumb. If Ah thought he didn't know no better Ah'd have mah picture took and give it tuh dat mule so's he could learn better. Ah ain't gointuh 'low 'im tuh hold nothin' lak dat against me."

Matt struggled to say something but his tongue failed him so he jumped down off the porch and walked away as mad as he could be.

Gloria Naylor

DR. BUZZARD

from *Mama Day*

[In the first selection hoodoo doctor and general trickster Dr. Buzzard is confronted by Miss Miranda, generally called Mama Day, the wise healer and great-aunt of Cocoa, the protagonist of the novel. Mama Day is warning Dr. Buzzard against working any conjure on Bernice Duvall, a young woman in the neighborhood who is desperately trying to overcome her barren condition.]

"Now, Mama Day, when folks come to me seeking help, my conscience don't allow me to turn 'em away."

"Your conscience ain't got nothing to do with it, Buzzard—it's the money. And if you really had a conscience, you wouldn't be selling them hoodoo bits of rags and sticks—and that watered-down moonshine as medicine, passing yourself off as a—"

"I am just what I say I am. You do things your way and I do 'em mine. And it hurts my feelings no end that you won't call me *Doctor* Buzzard— I gives you respect."

"There ain't but one Dr. Buzzard, and he ain't you. That man is up in Beaufort County, South Carolina, and he's *real*. You may fool these folks in Willow Springs, but ain't nobody here older than me, and I remember when your name was Rainbow Simpson. And you can change that all you want, but you can't change the fact that you still nothing but an out-and-out bootlegger and con man. But what you do ain't none of my business . . ."

"If Bernice comes to me for help, I'm helping her." He throws the suit-cases into the back of the truck real hard. "And in all due respects, like you said, it ain't none of your business."

"It ain't, Buzzard, it really ain't. And that's why it would cause me no end of sorrow to make it so. 'Cause the way I see it, you been walking round on this earth a long time and got just as much right as the next fella to keep walking around, healthy and all—living out your natural life."

"I believe you're threatening me, Mama Day."

"Now, how could I do something like that? What could a tired old woman like me do to a powerful hoodoo doctor?"

————

[The following selection is narrated by Cocoa's husband, a Northern city boy whom she has brought to meet her family and friends in Willow Springs, South Carolina, one of the remote South Sea Islands. Here he comes up against Dr. Buzzard in a poker game.]

I was showing a pair of nines with an ace kicker, and twenty cards out with no one else showing higher than kings and not a possible straight in sight. I called and raised, got a five in the last deal, which didn't worry me too much with my ace in the hole—that's right, the proverbial ace in the hole—and he still beat me. My pair of aces and nines went down to Dr. Buzzard's full house. And that's when I was *sure* he was cheating. Even if we forgot the odds for that hand (they had been running six to one for me; fourteen to one for him), it was pretty hard to believe that an entire game could render one player three of a kind or better through the last twelve hands. But no one else was having problems believing it; they had gotten to his campsite talking that way.

He had said around eight, but I was the first to arrive. There was an open fire going and lanterns had been hung in the trees so the top of an oak stump we'd be using for a table was well lighted. Most folks sit on the ground or pull up a rock, he said, but he had borrowed a special canvas chair for me. I appreciated that because my thighs and legs were still sore from following Miss Miranda, but the south woods were a playground, considering what I'd been through that morning. Here I only had to follow his instructions and stay on a well-worn path that led me straight to his campfire and still. And since I wasn't a drinking man, he said, there was a six-pack he had cooling down in the stream. Budweiser. He shrugged his shoulders. Nothing but grown-up Kool-Aid, but he wouldn't feel right not having a little something for all his guests.

"You got my nachos?" Parris, the barber, was the first to arrive, his bald head gleaming under the kerosene lanterns. Keeping it shaved off was good for business, he had told me a few days before.

"Yeah, I got your damn nachos." Dr. Buzzard grinned.

"And I got your number tonight." Parris jingled a bulging pocket full of change. "I ain't losing more than two dollars if I'm losing a dime."

"Buy one of my gambling hands and you'll cut your losses even more."

"Nigger, I don't need your gambling hands. You're talking to a man who's played with the best in the Ninety-second Division. We had colored boys there from Miss-is-sip who could make a card cry."

Parris asked me how much I was planning to lose. And when I told him that actually I was planning to *win,* he and Dr. Buzzard found that very funny. Parris took his place, leaning back against the trunk of an old palmetto—facing east was good for his luck—while Dr. Buzzard brought him his bag of nacho chips and poured him a paper cupful of clear liquid from an earthen jug.

"In honor of the city boy, y'all getting my best stuff tonight—no second run of mash here."

"I'll remember that and take pity when you're howling about only two dollars from me."

Junior Lee was next to arrive, accompanied by a man who was introduced to me as Rickshaw. I had already met Junior Lee when he came to your grandmother's with his wife. He wouldn't be much competition—"I don't care how much I looose, I'm rolling in moneeey toniiight"—a good poker player needed sharpness if anything. This man was so soft, he was eerie. The one with him was a bit different, dark skinned and tall but eager, much too eager for a nickel-and-dime game. Did I know Reema—she ran the ladies' beauty parlor? No, I didn't. Well, he was husband to Reema's oldest gal. Dr. Buzzard asked Rickshaw how Carmen Rae was doing—heard their baby was down with the croup. Rickshaw said yeah, it was pretty terrible for a while. He was doing better now, thanks to Mama Day. It was a good thing she never took no payment, he wouldn't have as much to spare tonight. And he hated leaving a game early.

It was totally amazing: each in his own way expected to lose. Rickshaw was the only one who wanted to buy a "gambling hand." Dr. Buzzard said he'd sell him one for only a dollar tonight. He might need medicine for his baby. Rickshaw said he'd rather pay full price—he didn't want no half-assed gambling hand. Dr. Buzzard said no, it would be a good one—live frog and all. I was told the chamois bag had lodestone, sugar, black pepper, and cayenne in it. It definitely had a frog, because the thing kept croaking while we played. All of it was beyond ridiculous to me. The man, Rickshaw, was actually happy with his little red bag since he'd lost only a dollar fifty by the sixth hand. He was normally a much worse player, he confided to me, but look at how he knew to fold even showing a queen high on a possible pair before the third deal. The whole night was boiling down to that: how quickly do you fold—give up the dream—a battle between yourself and the possibility of the ever elusive royal flush. A straight flush, maybe. It was *never* a question of you against the man with rooster feathers in his hat, jumping up to refill cups, bringing in new bags of nachos, padding Rickshaw's seat with his sleeping blanket—and probably hiding jacks between his thighs. Parris finally took a pot with four of a kind. You should have seen the jubilation.

But I had gotten awfully angry by the twelfth hand. Stud poker was my game—with my experience, there was no way for me to come out less than even and I had lost more than anyone so far. I had learned to play at Columbia in a mathematics course dealing with game theory. I came out of that course with an A and a solid grounding in analyzing problems of conflict by abstracting common strategic features from an infinite number of conflict situations. And once you had distilled those handfuls of strategic features, you devised methods that could give you what is called "a most favorable result." The dozens of matrix charts I had labored over in graduate school proved that, all things being equal, there *is* a payoff matrix within the axis of maximizing a minimum result and minimizing a maximum result. In short, if Dr. Buzzard wasn't palming jacks between his thighs, stacking the deck, or marking the cards—whatever he was doing—I wouldn't have lost consistently for twelve hands and been out five dollars and twenty cents. I had played and bet in absolute proportion to the odds.

But I had learned something else in that math course: the study of game theory includes learning the principle of "extensive form"—a branching diagram in which at each juncture a player has several options to continue a course of play. The bizarre type of poker we were playing fit right into that. The pure strategy I'd been using wouldn't work to my advantage against him; I needed to introduce the formulas for behavior strategy. I had to discover exactly how he was cheating in each hand and then weigh those variables out to my advantage. In a way, the other guys were doing that, but to minimize their losses. I was going to win.

It took a little while. If my first show card wasn't the highest, I'd call whatever the bet was and always fold after the second deal—once even with three of a kind—to sit there and watch. I soon found out the cards were definitely marked, but that could only help Dr. Buzzard when he was the dealer. It was too shadowy for him to see the nick he had made in the left corner of the aces on our hole cards when someone else dealt them out. I asked him for another beer, although I'd barely touched the first one, and while he went down to the stream, I made a pretense of idly toying with the cards and nicked all the deuces in their left-hand corners. This cut his advantage in half at least, and more than that until he figured out what had happened. With Dr. Buzzard dealing, I played the next round through and Junior Lee won with two pairs—one pair was my deuces.

The next pot went to Parris, holding only a king high, the next to me with a pair of jacks. When Rickshaw took the next with three aces, a pall began to fall over our circle. They all looked toward Dr. Buzzard, extremely puzzled.

"Well, what is happening heeere?" Junior Lee let out a low whistle.

"Beats me." Dr. Buzzard shrugged. "Y'all wanna change the cards?"

"We better do something," Parris said. "This mess is becoming a mess."

Dr. Buzzard snapped the rubber bands off a new deck. He extracted the two jokers—and a seven of hearts. I had him now. I adjusted the odds for a fifty-one-card game with no seven of hearts in any hand but his. And with stud poker always showing four cards, it wasn't too hard to see when that seven could possibly help him and hurt me. Slowly, I broke even and then began to win. Now all eyes were on me—and were they, I thought with amazement, suspicious? Afraid? Yes, a bit of each. The joking ended completely then. No one talking to or kissing their cards. No joy when Rickshaw came up with a full house. He raked in the pot to his corner as if the coins were dirty. The crackling of the dying fire and the shuffling of the cards were the only things punctuating our silence. The calling went on by rote, everyone folding early in the next hand except for me and Dr. Buzzard.

The others became so still they could easily have not been there. Just myself and the old man with deep lines of concentration added to the others in his forehead, a slight quiver in his tightened bottom lip. But I was paying more attention to his hands, waiting for him to exchange his hole card with the hidden seven of hearts. His fingers were long and delicate, the palms callused with hardened ridges along each joint. Dancing hands. You could imagine them supporting his lean body in a handstand, moving to music. But they were sweating now, little flickers of moisture staying on the surface of the coins he fed into the pot. I called and raised him after my third card was dealt. The aces were running in my favor again. With the third deal I was showing two of them and had an eight of clubs in the hole. Dr. Buzzard was showing only a deuce, a six, and a jack high, but all were hearts. With his hidden card that meant the possibility of a definite flush; with his real hole card that could be anything from a lower pair than mine to a legitimate flush if it was a heart. The fourth cards were dealt: a deuce of clubs for me, a ten of *diamonds* for him. Gone. Gone. Gone. I called and raised—big. Rickshaw let out a long expulsion of air, Junior Lee started to hum, and Parris leaned forward in a fervent whisper, running his palm over his shaved head. "What ya got working there, Buzz? What ya got working?"

But his eyes never left mine as he called that bet. Their clear brown caught the reflection from the hanging lanterns and they were actually pitying me. I had to blink and look at our cards again just to be sure: No, any way he cut it, I was winning. But my throat was dry until he dealt out the last cards with those long delicate fingers. A ten of hearts for him, an eight of spades for me. He was showing a pair of tens against my aces. But we were up to three calls and a raise—three. And each time I kept doubting what was in front of my face, even doubting the eight of clubs in the hole that gave me *two* pair. No, there was absolutely nothing he could have in the hole, legitimate or otherwise, to win this hand. My mind knew it, but somehow the message hadn't reached my gut because the fourth time he met my bet the strain was enough to make me fold. My voice cracked as I called and raised the fifth time—all of three dollars and fifty cents on the table and my hands were shaking. If he called and raised me again— well, damn it, maybe he's palmed two cards (as unrealistic as that could be) and I'll just fold with my aces and eights. Then he smiled—a brilliant, brilliant smile. Slow, even, and gleaming it spread over his face. He made a motion toward his money as if he were going to see my bet, and with that same shade of pity in his eyes, he flipped over his hole card—the king of hearts. I sat there staring at it stupidly, wondering why he didn't pick up the pot. Then with a wave of disappointment I realized he had not won.

But that's not why I came home drunk. It was the clapping. Dr. Buzzard started it off, his callused palms meeting each other with the rhythm of dirge as he looked straight into the eyes of the other men. His lone clapping echoed loudly into the night, persistent and slow. One by one, they joined in. At first it was for me. The small sip of beer did nothing to dissolve the lump in my throat. Neither did the next or the next. So I drained the can. And then the rhythm of their clapping shifted slightly and this time it was for him. Dr. Buzzard took off his feathered hat and the necklace of bones. He emptied his overall pockets of crumpled tissues, bits of stone, a rabbit's foot. The clapping continued between the deep baritone of Parris's voice:

> Take my hand, Precious Lord.

He slipped out of his sneakers and with a huge grunt he was swaying upside-down on his hands.

> Lead me on. Let me stand.
> I am tired. I am weak. I am worn.

Each syllable was beat off in time with their hands while his raised small clouds of dust on the ground—

> Through the dark. Through the night.
> Lead me on to the light.

I didn't understand the rhythm and I refused to spoil it by attempting to join in. Perhaps if I had known that I only had to listen to the pulse of my blood—

> Take my hand, Precious Lord
> And lead me home.

How long could he stay that way? His palms and muscled forearms balancing his body so that through the shadows his feet seemed to stretch up to the stars. I wanted it to go on forever—

When my way grows drear
Precious Lord, linger near.
When my life is almost gone
By the river I will stand.
Guide my feet, hold my hand.
Take my hand, Precious Lord
And lead me home.

I wanted his feet anchored up there in the sky. The clear liquor in the paper cup that was pushed toward me burned every part of my body it touched. But it didn't touch as deeply as the rhythm being pounded into my ears.

Sometimes stumbling
Sometimes falling
Sometimes alone . . .

After the first cupful it stopped burning entirely. And through my watery eyes his body *was* stretching up into the stars—they outlined and illuminated the soles of his feet.

Take my hand, Precious Lord
And lead me home.

I said I fell asleep, you said I passed out. But when I woke up, I was holding on to the post of your grandmother's fence for dear life. It seemed the logical thing to do: her front yard had been replaced by a huge cavern and I needed to get to the three of you sitting up there on the porch without falling in. My pockets were loaded down with change and I was afraid that the weight of the coins would throw me off balance and straight down into that gaping hole. I was aware that I was a little tipsy, but if I held on long enough to get my direction around that cavern, I could make it up to the porch with a modicum of dignity. I didn't want your grandmother and Miss Miranda thinking that you'd married a drunk. I just hadn't tasted beer in over seventeen years and I'd never tasted moonshine before. So I was just going to hang on there, both arms wrapped around the fence post, and think my way through this.

"Honey, ain't you coming up on the porch?" Miss Abigail asked me.

"No, there's money in my pockets."

My answer was reasonable and I had concentrated carefully to avoid slurring my words, but after a moment of stillness, soft laughter encircled me before three pairs of even softer arms were guiding me up the steps.

Twice in less than twenty-four hours you ended up sprawled out on the bed with me having to undress you, and it was getting to be a bit much. That mess Dr. Buzzard brewed up was known to take paint off a wall—it had to be almost two hundred proof *after* he cut it down. What could have possessed you? Trying to be macho, no doubt. But you woke up after your wild drinking spree feeling a lot better than you deserved to. You had Mama Day to thank for that: she said just force two aspirin and a pint of water down your throat and you wouldn't have a hangover in the morning. Personally, I wanted you to suffer, especially when you got up arrogant and lying through your teeth about the condition you'd been in. Yes, I was always exaggerating and downright spiteful because you had gone out and had a little fun alone without clinging to my side. And, oh, now, you weren't going to humor me by having tea and dry toast for breakfast. You felt fine this morning because there had been absolutely nothing wrong with you last night. You insisted on pancakes and I *soaked* them with butter. You didn't stay arrogant long, did you. I didn't even bother repeating myself about your stomach muscles being paralyzed—you couldn't have heard me anyway with your head buried in the toilet.

Maggie Pogue Johnson

TO SEE OL' BOOKER T.

from *Virginia Dreams/Lyrics for the Idle Hour: Tales of the Time Told in Rhyme*

> Way down Souf whar de lillies grow,
>   Is the lan' I wants to see,
> En to dat lan' I specs to go,
>   Jis to see ol' Booker T.

I specs to take my faithful mule
   En hitch him to de cart,
En fo' dat famous cullered skool
   I's gwine to make a start.

I'll take a box and pack my lunch
   En start wid my ol' mule,
Case I know 'twill be a long time
   Fo' I reach dat Cullered Skool.

I wont get tired on de way,
   But sing en feel so free,
Jis longin' fo' de day
   To see ol' Booker T.

I hopes dat my ol' mule
   Wont gib out on de way,
Befor' I reach dat skool,
   Case I tell you dat wont pay.

Case dis feeble ol' man
   Ain't no lad, you see,
But befo' I leabes dis lan'
   I mus' see Booker T.

So I pray de Lawd to keep
   Bof me en my ol' mule,
En spar us till we git
   To dat Cullered Skool.

En gib our eyes de light,
   Dat we can cle'rly see,
Dat Alabama lan' so bright,
   En dear ol' Booker T.

I wonder ef he'll be at home,
    Case I heahed he'd been to sea,
En all de fer off lan's did roam,
    Dis same Booker T.

Dat eben kings en queens so great
    Did strive to shake his han'
En welcome Booker T.
    To der native land.

Now, you know he mus' be great;
    Well, I's gwine dar to see,
En ef I git dar soon or late,
    I'll ax fo' Booker T.

Dey say dat is de bigges' skool
    De same as eny town,
En neber was so many chaps
    Eber seen aroun'.

Day teaches you all kin's ob wuk,
    En how to write en read,
En figger in de 'rithmetic,
    En ebery t'ing you needs.

Dey teaches you to plant de co'n,
    En eben how to plow;
I tell you, man, as sho's you born,
    I'm on my way dar now.

En when I near dat skool,
    En all dem chaps I see,
Dey better had keep cool,
    En not make fun at me.

I sho' will bus' der heads,
    Case my only plea
Is dat fo' I's dead
    I mus' see Booker T.

Right in his office I will go,
    En dar I'll take a seat,
En ax fo' Booker T., you know,
    En res' my w'ary feet.

I'll tell him I has jis now 'rived,
    From ol' Virginny lan',
En took dat long en lonesom' drive
    To shake his willin' han'.

En dar I'll set en look at him,
    En he will look at me,
En fo' my eyes get dim,
    While I kin cl'erly see.

I'll take his gracious han'
    Widin my trimblin' grasp,
En praise de Lawd I reached de lan',
    I's finished up my tas'

"I's seen dis great, great cullered man,
    I's ready now to go;
You've done a great wuk in dis lan',
    Is why I lubs you so."

So now my eyes I clos' to res',
    I's happy, yea, so free;
I's took de journey, stood de tes'
    En seen ol' Booker T.

Ann Petry

WHEN I MOURNS, I MOURNS ALL OVER

from *The Narrows*

J.C. said, delight in his voice. "That's them bastids Kelly and Shapiro." Two small boys rolled over and over, on the sidewalk, shouting at each other, their voices muffled.

"Kick him in de ass. Kick him in de ass," J.C. yelled, jumping up and down.

"J.C.!" Abbie said sternly, pulling him along. "How many times have I told you that you simply cannot use that kind of language when you're with me. I simply will not have it."

"Yes'm," he said.

Then she pulled him across the street, crossing Franklin Avenue though they would only have to recross it when they reached the corner of Washington Street. But she had seen Cat Jimmie propelling himself along on his little wooden wagon. She couldn't bear to walk near that creature on the wagon, it wasn't just the smell of him, it was the whole horrible degenerate look of him, his eyes, and the mutilated flesh on the stumps of legs and arms, exposed even now on this cold windy afternoon. Pass by on the other side, she thought. "If you believe the Lord looks after and cares about a sparrow, then you must of necessity also believe that He looks after and cares about Bill Hod." That's what the Major had said. And she supposed that he would feel the same way about Cat Jimmie. The Major had a capacity for including all men in his sympathy, his understanding, that had sometimes annoyed her, sometimes surprised her. But Cat Jimmie—"there came down a certain priest that way: and when he saw him, he passed by on the other side. And likewise a Levite, when he was at the place, came and looked on him, and passed by on the other side. But a certain Samaritan . . . when he saw him, he had compassion on him."

Fall of a sparrow, she thought. Bill Hod? Compassion? For Hod? And that inhuman creature on the wagon? Mouth open, eyes like the eyes of a trapped animal, fierce, crazed. She turned and looked back, and he was lying down on the wagon, looking up under a woman's skirts, and the woman jumped away from him, went running up Franklin Avenue. Oh, no, she thought, he is no longer human, he is an animal, and it does say, "A certain man went down from Jerusalem to Jericho, and fell among thieves——" fall of a sparrow   Bill Hod—compassion—Cat Jimmie.

Once she'd stopped to speak to that creature on the wagon, something in her, pity, compassion, something, made her stop. She saw his eyes, horrible, the whites were red, and she turned away, mounting the steps of her house, and looked back and the pity, the compassion, vanished, replaced by revulsion, because he had propelled himself close to the bottom step and was looking up, trying to look under her skirts, panting, his mouth working, the eyes fierce, vengeful. For a moment she was so overcome by nausea that she couldn't move, and then she ran up the last two steps, hurried inside the house, and slammed the door.

They walked as far as Washington Street and then crossed Franklin Avenue again.

J.C. said, "What we cross over Franklin for, Missus Crunch?"

She hesitated, thinking, Evasion? outright lie? the truth? Truth. She said, "I didn't want to walk near that man on the little cart."

J.C. looked back, down Franklin Avenue. "Aw, him!" he said, contempt in his voice. "Mamie say he don't hurt nobody. She say he can't git it no other way but lookin'. And she say seein's dat's the only way he can pleasure himself, best thing to do is just let him go ahead and look."

I know what I'll do with you, young man, she thought, I'm going to leave you with Miss Doris. Miss Doris was Frances' maid, housekeeper, cook, whathaveyou, and Miss Doris' husband, whom she called Sugar, mowed the lawn, looked after the garden, and made all the repairs. Miss Doris could have a white cloth tied around her head, and have on very worn, very faded, but very clean, slacks, and be down on her hands and knees weeding a flower bed, and when she looked you over, she could make you feel as though your hair were uncombed and there were runs in your stockings.

When they turned in at the F.K. Jackson Funeral Home, J.C. tugged at Abbie's hand, again. "Is we goin' to a funeralizin', Missus Crunch?"

"I am," Abbie said. She looked down at his upturned face. His eyes were sparkling with excitement, pleasure. "But you're not. You're going to stay with Mrs. King until I come back."

Hand in hand, they climbed the front steps. Abbie rang the bell. The door opened almost immediately.

"Good afternoon, Mrs. Crunch," Miss Doris said. She had a white cloth wrapped tight around her head, a shorthandled dust mop in her hand.

Abbie thought she looked more than ever like a statue, short, wide, not fat, but bulky. Her flesh had the hard look of metal, and her voice was hard, cold, suggesting metal, too.

"I were not told to expect you so soon," Miss Doris said, reproach in the hard metallic voice. "Or I would have been in a state of preparation."

Abbie said, apologetically, "I'm early, Miss Doris. But I wanted to ask a favor of you. Will you look after this little boy for me, until after the funeral?"

Miss Doris and J.C. eyed each other with suspicion. Miss Doris said, "All right, boy. Come in." She frowned. "I see you brought your lollipop with you."

Abbie looked at J.C. He was sucking his thumb again but he didn't have a lollipop.

J.C. took his thumb out of his mouth. "Ain't got no lollipop," he said indignantly. Then put the thumb back in his mouth.

"What's that in your mouth?" Miss Doris said, sharply.

No answer. Scorn in his eyes. He cocked his round, hard head on one side, studying her.

"Come on, boy. I can't stand here all day," Miss Doris prodded J.C. with the shorthandled mop, pushing him inside the door.

Abbie turned away, quickly. She heard J.C. say, "You take dat mop off my clothes," and then the door closed.

The F. K. Jackson funeral parlor occupied the basement floor of the building where Frances lived, a building that reminded Abbie of the brownstone-front houses in New York. She and the Major had spent their honeymoon in a house very much like this one, same long flight of steps leading to the first floor, same type of basement with a separate entrance, at street level.

Howard, Frances' assistant, was standing just inside the door of the office.

Abbie said, "Miss Jackson asked me to see that everything—to—asked me to come over," faltering, remembering Frances' brusque voiced statement, "Howard's a fool."

Looking at him now, as he hovered in the doorway, she thought he was built like a eunuch, or what she thought a eunuch would be built like, very tall, very fat, soft fat, too broad across the hips, and he had a waddling kind of walk. He came waddling toward her, holding out his hand, and he bowed over her hand, then straightened up and looked into her eyes. He said, gravely, "Ah, yes, Mrs. Crunch. So very kind of you. Miss Jackson couldn't have found a more impressive representative."

The skin on his face was like a baby's skin, a kind of bloom on it. Amazing skin. A peculiar color. Almost the exact color of the fuzzy redbrown hair, not much of the hair left, he was getting bald, hairline receding, so that seen close to, without a hat, and she had never seen him hatless before, he appeared to have a high domeshaped forehead, a forehead that just never ended. And he had a moustache, a feather of a moustache, which seemed to have just taken rest, for a moment, over what in a woman would have been an incredibly pretty mouth. Baby's skin. Woman's mouth.

He said, "There are always so many details. I almost forgot your gloves. We'll put them on in Miss Jackson's office." His manner confidential, his eyes widening a little.

Abbie smiled at him, feeling as though he had just shared a delightful secret with her. She leaned toward him, ever so slightly. Then she checked the bend of her body, stiffening, straightening up, no longer smiling, frowning a little, thinking, Why the man's a hypnotist.

The glistening of his eyes told her he was waiting for this leaning response of her body, had known it would come, that he was practised in this business of subtly conveying the idea that here were his strong masculine shoulders, and the whole long smooth-skinned length of him, for widows, for orphans over sixteen, to lean on, to find solace in the leaning.

In the office, he helped her put on a pair of black gloves. He smelt ever so faintly of liquor and she thought of the Major—and that day he died. Frances' hands were long and bony and hers were short and plump. But they got the black gloves on and then he escorted her to a seat midway in the chapel. She sat staring at the ends of the glove fingers, black, empty, wiggled them once, thought they looked like the armless sleeves of a scarecrow, that a child would be frightened by these empty glove fingers, wondered what J.C. and Miss Doris were doing.

But she was here to see that everything was all right, went all right. The chapel was filling up with people, there were flowers in the embrasure where the casket stood in front of the windows, drawn curtains and shaded lights that cast a mournful pinklavender light. An airless room. Too hot. And filled with the heavy toosweet smell of roses.

The family came in. The widow was heavily veiled, there was a uniformed nurse in attendance, pallbearers in gray gloves. Everything seemed in order. Everything in order except the pressure, the feeling of tremendous pressure about her head.

The service started on time. Then the Baptist minister, Reverend Ananias Hill, grown older these last years, gaunter, slower of movement, even his voice had changed, the thunder had gone out of it to be replaced by a quality that was sad, sorrowful, spoke of the late Deacon Lord, and prayed for his immortal soul, and read from the Bible: "Thou shalt love the Lord thy God with all thy heart . . ."

A tremulous old man with an old man's voice. Mamaluke Hill's father. Queer the things you remembered about people. For years The Narrows had conjectured about Reverend Hill's wife, trying to decide whether she was white or whether she was colored. Nobody ever really knew. They said Reverend Hill didn't know himself whether she was white. The child's name, Mamaluke, would suggest that she was colored. She finally died in a rooming house, on Dumble Street. The fact that she left Reverend Hill, no longer lived with him, was a minor scandal.

Abbie heard Reverend Hill say that the late Deacon Lord had loved God, and had loved his neighbor as himself, and then she stopped listening to him. She began thinking about Dumble Street. About Link. About the night the Major died.

The Major had said, "Abbie, the house, the house." And she could smell the morning, the river, see fog blurring the street, feel it wet and cold against her face, drifting in in waves from the river, fog undulating, blurring the sidewalk, and once again she leaned over, blinked her eyes, wiped her eyes, so that she could read what had been written on the sidewalk, in front of her house, "At her feet he bowed, he fell—"

Reverend Hill said, again, "Thou shalt love the Lord thy God with all thy heart." And the pressure, the feeling of pressure increased. All of us, she thought, young and old, all of us here in this funeral chapel were brought up on the King James version of the Bible, all able to quote it, part of our thinking, part of our lives, and we keep moving away from it, forget about it. Even though we go to church. But we attend a funeral and something in us is fascinated, and afraid, and we keep going back into the past, trying to find ourselves or what we believe to be ourselves, a part of us lost somewhere back in the past.

Someone screamed. She thought for a moment that it was she who had screamed. Then she saw that the relatives, the family, were filing past Deacon Lord's coffin. It was the widow who had screamed, not so much screamed as wailed. She was a large woman, dressed in black, wearing a black veil so long, so thick, that it was like a curtain, a drapery over her face. Abbie thought of the Major and his favorite joke, "When I mourns, I mourns all over."

"I won't let him go," Mrs. Lord wailed. "I won't let him go, I won't let him go. Hubborn, come back, come back." The "come back" sounded as though it were being sung, on one high note, sustained, repeated.

Mourn all over, she thought. People do, in one way or another.

Then, very quickly, they were all outside on the sidewalk, standing there, and Howard and two other men were shepherding the people into the proper cars, darting in and out, just like sheepdogs, impatiently nosing a group of slowmoving and very stupid sheep over a stile.

Howard turned to Abbie, "Ah, yes, Mrs. Crunch," he said, taking her by the arm. "Miss Jackson always rides in front with me. So if you'll get in here. But first," he opened the back door of the car, "Mrs. Lord, this is Mrs. Crunch. She's Miss Jackson's personal representative. She'll be riding in the front seat with me."

Mrs. Lord said, "Glad to meet you," and reached out a blackgloved hand and shook Abbie's blackgloved hand. It was a surprisingly firm handshake.

"And this is Mr. Angus Lord," Howard said. "Deacon Lord's brother."

"My compliments," Mr. Angus Lord leaned forward, bowed. Then he sat back and sucked his teeth.

Abbie sat in the front seat of the car, close to the door. She was waiting for Mrs. Lord to start that weird wailing sound again, the back of her neck cold with waiting, her hands in the long fingered black gloves clenched into fists, hands tense with waiting. Howard started the car, pulled off, following close behind the hearse. Silence in the back seat.

Then Mrs. Lord said petulantly, "Angus, I can't remember whether I locked my back door."

Mr. Angus Lord said, "I locked it. It don't matter anyway. That big dog would keep anybody out ceptin' a blind man, who was a deaf man, too. A deaf blind man wouldn't be robbin' nobody's house." Pause. "A lot of folks at the funeral."

"I didn't see his cousin. Was she there?"

"I dunno. I ain't seen her in years." Pause. "By the way, I'd like his gold watch. For a keepsake."

"I'm keepsakin' it myself." Reproof in Mrs. Lord's voice. "I figure to keepsake it the rest of my life. Hubborn never give me nothin' while he was alive and now he's dead, he can start in. I aims to keepsake his gold watch and his diamond stickpin."

"He ain't in his grave," Mr. Angus Lord said, voice scornful. "You can wait awhile before you start puttin' bad mouth on him."

Abbie wondered if the scorn was due to disappointment or to fear of disparaging a dead man, fear so old no one really knew its source. Mrs. Lord had criticized the deacon, "Hubborn never give me nothin' while he was alive—" Speak no evil of the dead.

She turned her head to look at Mrs. Lord. The heavy black veil still concealed her face, but she had removed the black gloves, had rolled them up into a ball, and was kneading them with one hand, just as though the gloves were a ball of black dough. Mr. Angus Lord was staring out of the window, watching the traffic.

When they slowed down in order to turn in between the gates at the entrance to the cemetery, Abbie found herself thinking about the Major again, and his story about Aunt Hal who had ridden to a funeral astride the hearse, and how the rest of the Crunches, shouted, "Whip up them horses! Ride her down! Ride Hal down!"

Then the Reverend Ananias Hill was intoning, "Ashes to ashes—" voice sorrowful, voice sad, voice old, and Mrs. Lord wailed again, "Hubborn, come back, come back to me," and Reverend Hill went right on intoning, "Dust to dust—"

About five minutes afterwards, Howard was helping Mrs. Lord into the long black car, the nurse was hovering close by. Howard said, "Here, drink this—no—drink it right down—and you'll feel better—it's brandy." Then they were off, leaving the cemetery, going faster and faster.

Mr. Angus Lord said, "I'll have a little of that likker, young man." He sucked his teeth, waiting.

Howard stopped the car, reached in the glove compartment, got out the flask, a package of paper cups, handed them back to Mr. Angus Lord, and then started the car, driving even faster now.

Mr. Lord said, "Ah!"

Abbie turned, saw that he was drinking out of the flask, and that he was apparently emptying it; he paused for a moment in his drinking, and then said "Ah!" again.

"Now what might that have been, young man?" he asked.

Howard glanced at Mr. Angus Lord in the mirror. "Hennessy's Five Star brandy."

"Five stars. Stars. Thought so," he said. "Tasted like it." He smacked his lips. "Was that a colored cemetery, young man?" he asked companionably.

"No," Howard said. "But in another ten years or so we'll have that, too. We've got two practically colored schools and we've got a separate place for the colored to live, and separate places for them to go to church in, and it won't be long before we'll work up to a separate place for the colored to lie in after they're dead. It won't be long, brother. Then you'll feel right at home here in Monmouth. It'll be just like Georgia except for the climate."

Howard must be angry about something, Abbie thought. That's no way to talk to a customer. Customer? The customer was dead. They'd just left him there under the hemlocks. Well, it was no way to talk to the customer's family. Surely Mrs. Lord would resent the reprimanding, sarcastic voice Howard had used. Howard. What was his last name? How many people have I ever known that I called by their first names? What's his last name? I'll ask Frances. Maybe he didn't have one. Maybe he came into the world, broad of hips, fullgrown, fullblown, in his cutaway coat and striped trousers, with his flask of brandy and his derby hat and his gray gloves, and his feather moustache, above that delicatelyshaped, moistlooking, thirsty-looking mouth. What had made him angry? Why, the brandy, of course. The late Deacon Lord's brother had drunk up every drop of Howard's Five Stars. Then she thought, This whole thing has made me lightheaded, because she was rhyming again, saying over and over, Stars in his crown, to his renown, stars in his crown, to his renown.

The late Deacon Lord's brother must have been mellowed by the brandy, warmed by it, slightly intoxicated by it, because just as Abbie turned to look at him, he laid his hand on Mrs. Lord's large wellfleshed knee and said, "I spose you'll be lookin' around for another man—"

Mrs. Lord snorted. "Another man? Me? Another man? I could tell you things about Hubborn that would make your hair straighten out just like white folks' hair." Pause. "And I'll thank you to take your black hand off'n my leg."

Howard said smoothly, "Mind if I turn on the radio?" Music filled the swiftly moving car, jazz music, loud, strongly accented.

By the time they pulled up in front of Mrs. Lord's house, on the edge of Monmouth, a one-story shingled affair, glassed-in porch across the front, she had removed the black veil and the black gloves. She got out of the car, unassisted, handed Howard a white box edged with black.

Abbie thought, That's where she put the veil and the gloves.

Mrs. Lord said, "Goodbye, Mrs. Crunch, and thank you. Tell Miss Jackson everything was fine," and walked heavily toward her front steps, the late Mr. Lord's brother trailing along behind her.

Howard turned toward Abbie. "Drop you at Number Six?"

"No, thank you. I'll go back to the funeral parlor with you. I want to see Miss Jackson. She said she'd be back after the service."

She wondered what J.C. and Miss Doris were doing. Something intractable about Miss Doris. Even the way she used the word "were," pronouncing it as though it were "wear," and using it constantly. She was short but not stout, bulky, bulk of a statue. Her face and body looked like wrought iron, both as to color of skin, and an almost metallic hardness of the flesh. Flesh on the face, flesh on the forearms, like iron. Thin legs. Splay feet. She planted her feet flat on the ground when she walked. Even the voice hard and cold.

J.C. and Miss Doris? He'd be all right. If he could survive Mamie Powther and Shapiro and Kelly, he'd survive Miss Doris too.

"Tell me," she said to Howard, raising her voice against the sound of the radio. "Why did Mrs. Lord call Deacon Lord 'Hubborn.' I thought his first name was Richard."

"She couldn't say 'husband.' Hubborn was the nearest she could come to it in that loosepalated, liverlipped speech of hers." He turned the radio off.

He's still angry about his Five Stars, she thought. "Was she really upset? She seemed so calm, and then all of a sudden she was shrieking like a banshee."

Howard said, "Yes and no. She didn't want him back. If by lifting a finger she could bring him back, she'd tie her hands together, bind them, so the fingers couldn't move, even by reflex action. He was an old devil and she'd been married to him for forty years, married to a little black man who was mean and stingy and malicious. That was Hubborn. Mean.

"When her old mother died, a few years back, he wouldn't pay for the funeral. The city buried her. He knew a couple of ward heelers and he hollered poor mouth so Mrs. Lord's mother was dumped into what amounts to an open lot. The old lady had insurance. All these old folks have enough insurance to give 'em a pretty good funeral. They save pennies and nickels to pay for their insurance, pay for it by the week. Well, anyway, Mrs. Lord's old mother got a pine box, no extras, just a box. The city paid for it and we took care of the arrangements. That's how I know about it. The old lady got a plain pine box and the box was put in potter's field. Hubborn took the five hundred dollars from the insurance and bought himself a diamond and had one of the local jewelers set it in a gold stickpin.

"He was a great man for gold, Hubborn was. He was a thirty-third-degree Mason, too, and he kept the colored Masons in such a state of confusion and muddlement that they've never been able to buy a home. They rent one of those storefronts one night a week, and on the other nights the members of the I Will Arise and Follow Thee Praise the Lord for Making Me Colored and Not White Church sing hallelujah in it.

"No, she wouldn't bring him back. But he was alive one minute with his gold teeth flashing, and his gambler's cufflinks gleaming, ten-dollar gold piece in each one, and his diamond stickpin glittering, and his bright yellow ties shining and the next minute he was dead. So Mrs. Lord now has his gold cufflinks and his undeaconly diamond stickpin and his gold watch tucked in her black bosom—for keepsakin'."

He stopped talking, lit a cigarette, and Abbie thought he had finished. Then he said, indifferently, "Maybe she screamed because she was afraid she was dreaming, afraid that she would wake up and find that Hubborn was still alive. Or perhaps she saw herself as she would ultimately be, very dead, very cold, lying in a coffin, a satin-lined one, of course."

He gave her a sly sidewise glance, and she thought, This is an assumed callousness and I shall ignore it. He is trying to give me the impression that he is so accustomed to the idea of death that he can speak of coffins and satin linings, and go on smoking, and looking around him as he drives, as though none of it really mattered, as though it had nothing to do with him.

They were going down Franklin Avenue. The street was still filled with people, mostly women, all of whom were carrying bundles, or packages. They had finished their Saturday shopping, had finished exchanging a week's wages for clothes, groceries, liquor.

When he stopped the car in front of the F. K. Jackson Funeral Home, she got out quickly, before he could help her, deliberately ignoring his outstretched hand.

"By the way," she said abruptly, "what is your last name?"

"Thomas. Good old Anglo-Saxon last name. All of us black sub rosa Anglo-Saxons are named Stevens, Jackson, Williams, Smith, King."

"I'll tell Miss Jackson how well you managed everything, Mrs. Thomas." Heavens, what kind of a slip of the tongue was that? She started to say, What could I have been thinking of, I mean *Mr.* Thomas; but he appeared not to have noticed. He was kicking one of the front tires, trying to dislodge the mud that had spattered on its white walls.

"Muck," he muttered. "Graveyard muck."

Then he opened the door of the car, reached deep inside the glove compartment, took out a package, tore off the green paper wrappings, then the thin white paper underneath, clawing at it in his haste, got a corkscrew out of his pocket, pulled the cork out of the bottle.

"Can't do this on the job," he said, "but if you'll excuse me." He gave a slight shudder and poured half the contents of the bottle down his throat in one great swallowless draft. She walked away from him so that she would not see the second great draft go down his throat, the draft that would unquestionably empty the bottle.

Tina McElroy Ansa

UGLY WAYS

Look at them, stretched out there on my screened porch smoking cigarettes and drinking my husband's liquor. Even talking about smoking that marijuana like some kind of damn black girl hippies. And me laying up here in Parkinson Funeral Home with this ugly-assed navy-blue dress on. Talking about me like I ain't in my grave yet. Hell, I ain't in my grave yet. It just goes to show you what they gonna be like when I really am buried and gone.

Trifling! Trifling women! After all I did to raise them right. Well, alright. Maybe I didn't do a lot to raise them, not after the baby was five or so, but I did raise them. I did see to it that they were raised. And raised right. Even if they did have to half raise themselves.

Taught them how to carry themselves. How to keep that part of themselves that was just for themselves to themselves so nobody could take it and walk on it. Tried my best to make them free. As free as I could teach them to be and still be free my-self.

How many times did I tell Emily, my middle girl, to pull up that chin, tie up that chin. Look to the stars, I would tell them. Look to the stars. Don't let the whole town see you walking with your head down, like you got something to be ashamed of.

Lord knows this damn little-assed town did try to make them think that. That they had something to be ashamed of. Me mostly. Umph. It's funny really. The one thing in life that they could always look to with pride, a mother who set an exam-ple of being her own woman, was the thing that everyone wanted them to be ashamed of.

Well, one thing I can say for them, I don't think they were ever ashamed of me, or embarrassed by me. Never once.

It sure is nice and quiet in here. The Parkinsons always did run a nice estab-lishment. I had forgotten how lovely this old building is. Nice and quiet. Just the way the house used to be at night when I liked it best. Course, 'cause I got my beauty sleep much of the day, I could enjoy the night the way most people couldn't.

In the summer, it was too hot during the day to even think about stirring before four or five o'clock in the afternoon. By the time it got dark, I would have had a good long bath and taken care of myself, hair and stuff. And I would have gotten myself something to eat and looked at a little television. The girls or Ernest would have come home by dark and done whatever I needed doing. And I would have had a little company if I felt like it.

Usually, there would be enough time for a little nap in the evening before I went out to do my gardening. That way I'd be nice and refreshed for my work. What with taking my own time and stopping to rest and admire my work and coming into the house for coffee and to eat something, before you know it, there'd be streaks of color in the sky. And I'd come in and look at movies on videocassettes or early-morning television. Then, lay back down before the girls get up for school.

And in the winter, it was too depressing getting up earlier than afternoon. See-ing the sunlight outside and knowing it wouldn't even be strong enough to warm you if you was to walk out in it. Then, before you know it, the day would start to fade and it would be nighttime. But that didn't do any good because it would be too cold to do any gardening.

But then, in the summertime, it would take so long to get dark enough for me to go outside and get my work done. Oh, well, like the old folks say, "If it ain't one thing, it's three."

I don't seem to be able to feel the daylight on my skin in here the way I used to, but I am adaptable. Shore am gonna miss my plants, though, my flowers the most, I think. I just planted vegetables that made pretty plants. Collards as big as a small child line the walk to the back door. There's a tangle of mint and lavender by a old painted swing, that has mixed and mated so much that their flowers are variegated shades of purple and lavender and it makes your mouth water to brush by it. My patches of old elephant ears were so big and velvety, almost khaki, they held two and three cups of water when it rained.

In the full burst of spring and early summer, the place was a paradise.

Besides my separate rose garden, I had bushes scattered all through the garden. Delicate ones, big showy ones, trailing, climbing, grown in hedges and bushes and over trellises. Tea to cabbage.

I did so love to dig in the dirt. I was just a born gardener. I could taste the soil and tell whether it was acid or alkaline. When I woke up with dirt under my fin-gernails, it was some of the happiest moments for me.

My garden is a beautiful thing. This time of year I have as many flowers grow-ing almost as in May. Still got begonias and butterfly weed and cannas blooming along with dahlia, big wide dahlias, and delphiniums and Stokes' asters and chrysan-

themums. None of the herbs seem to know it's close to winter yet and with some kind
of herb planted at every crossway, turn, or corner of the garden, it's a pleasure just
to walk through and brush by 'em.

I guess my garden is the thing I'm most proud of.

Other than seeing my girls do so well, of course.

I also taught them how to be ladies. How to do the things that women need to
know how to do in this world. How to sew and clean and take care of a house. Make
a beautiful centerpiece out of whatever was growing in the nearest yard or field. Even
as a little thing, the baby Annie Ruth could step outdoors and come back in with
an armful of fall leaves and branches and make a right nice arrangement. I taught
'em that.

They took care of that house a whole lot better than I ever did or ever wanted
to. And when things needed taking care of personally, Betty could handle those white
bastards down at the gas company or those hinkty folks at Davison's Department
Store as well as lots of grown women. Finally even told that old cracker who used
to sit in the lobby entrance from store opening to closing to kiss her black ass when
she called her names once too often. I was proud of her for that. I probably told her
so.

I even taught them to take care of themselves. Many's the time I'd make sure they
bought Ivory liquid or Palmolive liquid so when Emily washed dishes she didn't ruin
those pretty hands of hers. She does have the prettiest hands. And it was me, nobody else, who taught those three girls how to take care of what they've been given.

How many girls their age know so much about moisturizing their skin as they
do? I never let 'em use soap on their faces and made sure there was always some
Pond's cold cream in the house. How many other mothers can say the same?

I never was one for lying. At least, I never was after things changed, so I'd tell
them right out what their best attributes were and what failings they didn't even need
to waste their time on trying to improve.

I didn't coddle 'em and cuddle 'em to death the way some mothers do. I pushed
'em out there to find out what they was best in. That's how you learn things, by getting on out there and living. They found their strengths by the best way anybody
could: by living them.

From the looks of this here dress they bought to bury me in—went out to the
mall and bought it out at Rubinstein's, too, know they paid good money for it, the
price tag is probably around here somewhere—you can tell they holds a grudge for
something though. What in God's name would possess them to go out and spend

good money on this navy-blue monstrosity—and they know navy blue is not my color, they know how pretty I look in pastels—when I had all those beautiful bed jackets at home. Hell, some of my old stuff might be a bit outdated, since I ain't had any need for street clothes in a number of years, but even it look better than this shit. They ought to be ashamed. Knowing how those girls love beautiful clothes, I can't believe they weren't trying to say something by picking this thing for me to lie in for all eternity. Them girls got ugly ways about 'em sometimes.

Well, at least it ain't cheap. I never could wear cheap clothes. You know, some people can wear cheap clothes and look right nice in 'em. I never could. If I ever put on anything cheap, it would stand away from my body like paper-doll clothes and just scream, "Cheap! Cheap! Cheap!" My girls couldn't either, wear anything cheap. When they was teenagers, they'd try to imitate they little friends and go down to Lerner's or one of them shops and get some outfit or other. It would be cute in the bag, but as soon as they put it on, it would start screaming, "Cheap! Cheap! Cheap!" and they'd have to give it to one of their cheap-clothes-wearing friends.

Knowing Annie Ruth, she gonna go through my bed jackets and personal things before the funeral to see what she can take back to that Los Angeles, maybe my pink satin quilted bed jacket, to wear with some tight jeans or expensive evening dress.

I can hear her now. "Oh, yes, this was my Mudear's. I just had to have something of hers." Little witch.

God, them girls got ugly ways about 'em sometimes. They must get them from their father's people.

You would think them girls were mad at me for something.

Just like them to be mad at me for something I don't even know. Just like with the damn telephone. They knew good and damn well that I didn't answer the phone unless I felt like it. Never did anything else but that in their memory. But wouldn't they get pissed off with me when they came home from school or one of those little piece of jobs they messed around with and I was nice enough to tell them that the phone had been ringing off the hook all day.

"Hope wasn't nobody expecting no calls," I'd tell them, nice like, too. Then, they would get fighting mad. Well, not really "fighting" mad because then they'd be mad enough to fight they ma and don't none of us play that. I guess I got that to be thankful for, too.

Just the other day I was looking at some talk show, coulda been Oprah, that was talking about these children. Call them Fragile X. They all looked a certain way, long faces and big ears, and they all had the tendency to fight their mothers. I know it wasn't funny, but I had to laugh. Of course, Ernest didn't see the humor of it when

I shared it with him later that night. But he's just about lost all his sense of humor over the years.

I have always tried very hard not to judge my girls too harshly. For one thing, everybody ain't me. I learned that years ago.

For another, they were too young to remember how it was before. To remember it and appreciate how much better things were after that cold, no-heat-and-no-lights-in-that-freezing-assed-house day when I was able to be what I am. A woman in my own shoes. And they don't hardly remember their daddy any other way than his meek, quiety self he is now.

I guess you can't completely blame the girls because they don't know what their Mudear has done for them. Practically all their lives—to show them a good example.

Wait a minute! What did she just say? "Mudear, now, she the kinda 'ho . . ." What the hell kind of thing is that to say about me, their own Mudear. Have they lost their minds or did they actually find some of that marijuana they wanted?

They ought to know that dope make you crazy!

Mama Sez

It's six in one hand and a half dozen in the other.

Blood is thicker than water.

The fruit don't fall too far from the tree.

I tell my children that children and groceries both have expiration dates—and when they get a certain age, they leaving this house.

This child has to learn that every day is not Christmas!

You better look out for them. They'll sell you down the river.

You have a son till he marries a wife;
You have a daughter for all of your life.

Two bulls can't reign in one fence.

Two cocks can't crow in one yard.

Girl, don't ever let nobody sweep a broom cross your feet—cause if you do, you'll never get married.

Don't wash clothes on New Year's Day. You'll wash somebody out of the family.

Don't ever go to anybody's house early on New Year's Day. It's bad luck all year if a woman is your first visitor on New Year's.

When you comb your hair, burn it all up so won't nobody get it and work a root on you.

After you comb your hair, take all the hair out the comb and burn it up to keep a bird from using it to make a nest, 'cause you will have a headache until the bird's eggs hatch.

It's good luck to eat blackeye peas and hog jowl on New Year's Day.

Right hand itching mean you gon' get some money.

Eye itching mean company must be coming.

Sister to Sister

I used to pretend I had a cold so my grandmother would fix me a hot toddy with bourbon, sugar, water, lemon, and spices. Then she rub some Vicks on my chest and let me sleep in her big bed so I would stay covered up. But then when she start dispensing cod liver oil for my symptoms, I soon stopped pretending I was catching a cold.

The Jews own this town, the Irish run it, and the Negroes enjoy it. [folk reflection on New York]

The joint was jumping.

Ain't nothin' jumpin' but the peas in the pot
And they wouldn't be jumpin' if the water won't hot.

[Noting a male homosexual] Another good man lost to the Sisters!

They are kissing cousins.

She got knocked up.

Well, I guess they'll jump the broomstick now [marry].

I'd like to be a fly on the wall when she tells him she's pregnant.

Me . . . I'm just a fly on the wall.

The shit hit the fan!

I usually tell a new mother what a cute baby she has. I can find something to say: "Look at his cute little nose," "look at that pretty smile," "Oh, what pretty eyes he has." But if the baby is too ugly to find anything to compliment, I just say, "My, look how he's growing."

When his daughter won that award, that was the last button on his coat [he was so proud].

They don't do nothing but scratch and save/skimp and save. That's the god-honest truth.

They have to live from pillar to post.

Lord I got all these nappy-headed children
and they won't listen to me.
I got seven children, I should have stopped at three. [Bertice Berry's mother would sing this jokingly to her children, *The World According to Me,* 67]

Well the eagle flies on Friday [get paid].

She's my ace boon coon.

If I'm lying, I'm flying.

I laugh and joke, but I don't play.

I'm just laughing to keep from crying.

Compared to my problems, yours don't 'mount to a pimple on a mosquito's ass.

Hush yo' mouf [mouth]!

No fool, no fun.

Tell the truth, snaggle tooth.

What's your story, morning glory?

See you later, alligator.
After while, crocodile.

My neighbor took sick and went away from here.

She kicked the bucket.

We all got to go when the wagon comes.

CHAPTER 5

The Black Church and Churchgoers

N o historical institution has been more instrumental in the black community than the church. No individuals have been more powerful
than church leaders. From the early days of slavery until the present,
blacks have flocked to their meetinghouses (or spaces) to sing praises to the
Lord, to respond to animated sermons, to be possessed by the spirit, to join
in holy dances, and to do a few other more secular things such as gossip,
meddle, show off, flirt, and signify.

Inspired by original African practices, African American worship services
are designed to uplift and to create a sacred community. All participants in
the worship are active participants—the minister, the deacons, the choir,
and the congregation. The music is an important component in the worship. In the black church, music calls the spirits, and through music one may
also become possessed. This music includes song and instrument, as well as

dance—which is inseparable from music and which is also a part of so many rituals in African life. As noted psychiatrist and prominent figure in the Negritude Movement Frantz Fanon wrote in *The Wretched of the Earth,* in dance and possession "may be deciphered as in an open book the huge effort of a community to exorcise itself, to liberate itself, to explain itself." African Americanist scholar Patrick Taylor in *The Narrative of Liberation* further informs, "dance has a symbolical meaning that unifies the group, however unconscious it may be. Rather than being a merely cathartic process, dance is a celebration of the story of the community in opposition to the colonizer." In the church, of course, where dancing per se is forbidden, it is the holy dance that is a part of the service. In many churches, music is used throughout the sermon to reinforce and enhance it. It helps, along with the sermon, to establish the rhythm of the worship. This rhythm is expressed through various body movements: the nodding of heads, swaying of bodies, tapping of feet, clapping of hands, jerking of the body, and holy dancing.

The rituals of the black Church are often reenacted in other aspects of black life. The psychic, emotional, and physical renewal that we seek in the church is expressed in daily struggles. The church played an important role in most black movements for freedom and Civil Rights in the Americas, including Toussaint L'Ouverture's rebellion in Haiti, the Nat Turner rebellion in Virginia, and numerous other slave rebellions in the United States and the Caribbean. The Garvey Movement is often seen as the genesis of Rastafarianism. Malcolm X, Martin Luther King, Jr., Jesse Jackson, and Louis Farrakhan, all ministers, have led the biggest movements and demonstrations of black Americans in the second half of the twentieth century. The rituals of the black Church were brought to bear in the Civil Rights demonstrations of the 1960s and in later campaigns where people met in churches to inaugurate movements; wherever they were they joined hands, formed circles, and sang songs, swaying together. Those who participated will tell you how such rituals provided spiritual strength, conquered fear, and created a sense of community and commitment.

Despite the historical significance of the church in their lives, black women (and men) have nonetheless directed much of their humor at the church and the church folk. All of their rituals may after services become the subject of much humor—the theatrics of the minister during his sermon, the boring repetitions of the deacon's interminable prayer, the histrionics of the choir director, the antics of an old sister possessed, the enthusiasm of some voice raised in song, the holy dancer who got carried away and failed to keep his feet on the floor. A whole host of comic types stem from the church and become the butt of many jokes: the egotistical, hypocritical, promiscuous, and gluttonous minister; the self-righteous deacon (who is frequently in competition with the minister for women, booze, and food), and the gossipy and sanctimonious old sister.

Perhaps more than the men, African American women relish lampooning the ministers and the deacons, the power brokers in the church who serve in positions that are generally denied women, who are typically relegated to ushering, singing in the choir, and, at best, becoming a deaconness, an official who rarely exercises any real authority in the church's governance. Aside from their roles in the church services, women are expected to do the cooking and serving for church functions, to keep the communion service cleaned and polished, to launder the communion cloth, to baby-sit in the nursery, and to provide all of the other "domestic" services. Is it any wonder then that some of these hard-working and long-suffering ladies might get together and talk about such provocative subjects as the deacon's tomcatting and the minister's drinking. Now, when some incensed sister brings to light what these distinguished gentlemen have done in the dark, her enraptured audience can only exclaim, "Honey, hush!"

It is important to emphasize here that the tales on the church are popular among the churchgoers as well as the backsliders and disbelievers. African American women, like other groups throughout history, enjoy satirizing their religious leaders and revealing the moral defects of those who set themselves up as exemplars and chastise the weaknesses of others.

Opal J. Moore

THE FENCE

Again? Seems like we were just out there. To Deacon's house. Why do we have to go every year? Why do we have to go at all is what I want to know, all the way out in the Boondocks . . . to the big deal sub urbs. So he's got a house. Big deal. My mother says to watch my smart mouth. I'm not grown yet. Then she says, It wouldn't be like your father if we didn't have to go traipsing out to the Boondocks for no good reason on the hottest day of the decade.

Well, do we have to go straight from church in stupid dresses? Why can't we go home first? I say.

Ask your father, she says. But then I remember it's Sunday and you can't wear shorts on Sunday anyway.

Why can't we go tomorrow? I say.

Ask your father, says my mother. She don't care I guess since she wears stupid dresses every day of the week. So it's "jubilation day," because Deacon lives in a house in the sub-urbs and we live in a small flat in the city like everybody else we know. So we should be impressed by his success. I am not impressed by Deacon's house. But I still have to go.

Deacon is not really a deacon. We, I, call him that behind his back. His father is head of the Deacon's Board at church, but that's not like he was a king or anything. But the father seems like a very nice old man, especially when he reaches in his pocket and gives me a quarter, or sometimes just a nickel, but none of that rubbed off on Deacon. Sometimes, my mother says, quality skips a generation. And so, when we go to Deacon's house, my mother does not look like jubilation day. She looks like a pin cushion, steel pins ready to fly at a word.

The high-speed expressway that will take the city folk out to the Boondocks faster will be done in about three more years, people say. My mother gives them ten years, which is about when she will be ready to go to Deacon's house. But right now, we stop-and-go for it seems like hours. Before we're started good, I can feel the car-air shrinking and my stomach starts reaching for the back of my throat, and I don't know if I can make it all the way without throwing up.

I concentrate on not throwing up. Then I figure out how I will throw myself across the lap of my sister, Sharin, and hang my head out the window if I have to. I imagine the vomit hitting the wind and blowing back into my face and onto my clothes and onto both Sharin's and Karin's clothes and how they will be so mad and almost never forgive me. Thinking of this, I concentrate on not throwing up. I tell my father I am going to be sick, and ask him if he will stop the car please please please. He says, We're almost there. But we're not. We are not almost there. That's just what my father says instead of No. We're almost there, he singsongs, almost there . . . almost there . . . he will say almost there until we are there.

My stomach feels like the treeless dusty sunbaked streets of the Boondocks. The houses are not red or brown brick like ours. These houses look weightless. They are colors like green, pale blue, yellow. They look like Monopoly houses all in their rows of aqua and beige and pink trimmed in white with trees so weak they need two sticks with wires to hold them up, or down. They look like houses in books, flat, with no backside.

Especially his house. Deacon's.

See Deacon's house, sub-urban, see his vomit-green window shutters that don't shut or open, his initials in cursive metal on the front door screen, swinging open, see him step through the crack, a dark slant cut into sunlight. My head is tight, swirly, dusty. The earth turns slowly. If I stare and stare at his black shoes like ink wells, like small black puddles, I can make it stop. Make the world stop moving, make my ears stop ringing, make my gut let go the back of my throat.

When I look up there are two flamingos standing in the yard. They look as if they might highstep out of here except, like the trees, they are stuck to the spot. A thin rod penetrates their bellies. It's supposed to be invisible, the rod, but I can see it from here. I can see it from every angle. Anyway, you see it once and you know it's there.

Inside are coordinating flamingo "cocktail" tables and pink shingle lamps. Mrs. Deacon hurries us kids into the kitchen as if we are about to spill ourselves on her light colored rug that is properly called carpeting (says my mother) because it covers the whole floor, not just part of it, but is crisscrossed anyway with plastic runners, so why is she worried?

In the kitchen we get watery Kool-Aid, grape, which is the worst flavor of all, especially if you mix it with something stupid like lime which gives you mud which is what this looks like, and on top of that mistake, not enough sugar, and I guess they ran out of ice just before we came so it's warm as tap water. It's good manners to say thank you, even if it's for brown tap water. So we all say thank you thank you thank you one after the other as we look at each other knowing we will have to take this mess outside and feed it to the flamingos who looked a little desperate.

These are the rules: My father will sit with Deacon in the living room laughing and talking and having a great time. My brother Jerome will take off with Deacon's son Leonard who is his age, twelve. My mother will sit in the kitchen with the wife "being sociable," pins lying sociably flat, mostly. Deacon's one daughter is "gotten pregnant and gone," so me and Karin and Sharin will be on our own. No place to go. No one to show us anything out here in the desert. In the Boonies.

We always walk to the edge of the yard or walk to the corner and back. We can't jump rope because it's Sunday and you can't play on the Lord's Day unless you are men sitting in the living room, and you can't sweat on the Lord's Day, unless you are women in a steamy kitchen chopping onions which is what we will end up doing if we hang around too long. And we can't go far because what's the point? Twenty minutes and we'd look like three Buckwheat Jesuses forty days in the wilderness. Plus this is the Boonies—you have to watch out for hidden dangers like grasshoppers as big as your fist, spiders, and white people looking at you like they're trying to remember something. My mother says they're trying to remember how we got here. How did we get here? I say. Never mind, she says. You're here. Be grateful.

So Sharin and Karin and I are sitting on the back step like three tarbabies in the sun when my brother slips by to whisper to my mother that they, he and Leonard, are going somewhere. She looks up at him, deciding. Without knowing where to, I want to go. I say it—I want to go . . . so what else is new? My brother rolls his eyes. Here is the rule: Whatever boys do, girls shouldn't be doing. Why? Never mind. Be grateful.

Mother looks at me. She says I can go. Jerome is stunned, but recovers in a split second because we know better than to argue. Come on, he says. Sharin and Karin want to come to. Sharin has to comb her hair. Karin has to use the toilet. Come on, says Jerome. Come on, then. And he and Leonard take off out the door running and I'm right behind them because I don't care how my hair looks and the flamingos got my Kool Aid.

They run without stopping. Leonard looks over his shoulder, laughing, running faster when he sees me. Karin and Sharin yell after us to wait. They yell for mother to make them wait. But my mother won't make them wait. She would say we got what we asked for. If we want to go with them, we have to go on their terms. Karin and Sharin run to the bathroom and shove open the window fussing and shouting threats but we are turning a corner, the boys ahead, and then me. And finally I hear nothing but my heart pounding and my breath still coming light.

When Leonard and my brother look over their shoulders, there I am, still there, still running my heart out to be with them, to be away from Deacon's house, away from back step sitting, away from the heat of onions and kitchens and Deacon-eyes smearing you with sin like fried chicken grease rising up in clouds of steam seeping into everything, covering everything with an invisible slickness.

We run down a hill, then up one. I feel free and alive, running as fast as I can but still falling behind. Then the boys come to a tall wooden slat fence. They give a whoop and, in what seems to be an impossible leap, they scramble up, then disappear over the top.

I run to the fence and jump. I jump again. I look around, quick, tip a crate, cardboard box, sideways, run, step, up! and grab the splintery top edge, then heave, pull, work one leg across. I inch to the top, my heart pumping, my lungs beating and dry in the dusty hot air; I cling to the narrow fence like a caterpillar to a willow. Carefully, I turn my head, and I can just see my brother and Leonard escaping across a field.

I scream at them to help me, to not leave me, that I can't get down, thinking they will pity me and come back. I watch them disappear into the distance. I hear, Come on! Come on! Jump! Jump! but they never slow down. They are gone and I see how high up I am, and the box is tumbled away and crushed anyway. I start to wonder if I can get down. I grip the fence tighter. They will come back. They have to come back.

They're not coming back. And I'm scared. I'm scared of falling . . .

Well, ok. Really I just have to let go and drop to the ground, but somehow I can't let go. I've come up wrong. My chest is balanced on my wrists pressed against the narrow fencetop. If I let go, I might topple over sideways. I might fall forward on my head. Why do you always want to go where you're not wanted? I should have stayed on the back step. Or in the kitchen.

People ought to keep to where they're wanted.

What if you hate being there?

I think of the Deacon's pink flamingos balancing circles of glass on their wings; I think of the Deacon peeping around doorways at church whispering my name, his eyes cutting me out of the fold like Clint Eastwood on *Rawhide* cuts a runt out of the herd. I realize only now that Clint must be invisible to the cows who mill about the horse's slender legs. Cows never look up. The Deacon is invisible like that, riding so high up on his

Daddy's back. I'm afraid of him because he is invisible, to them, and I am not. And because he is not Clint Eastwood.

The rough wood bites into the soft meat of my palms. My wrists hurt. My arms are shaking. If they keep shaking I'll topple over on my head. I look at the hardness of the dirt beneath me. I can't feel my hands. If I roll back off of my wrists, my hands might not catch me. My fingers might slip, numb, off the fence top. I pull one leg half over the top. Cling. I think of a vocabulary word: teetering.

I can't get down.

The ground is moving farther and farther away from me. Or the fence is getting taller. The longer I wait, the farther the fall. I know why I'm here. Because I can't do things like hit a softball. And I can't run fast. At school they say I can only catch a basketball pass with my face. My grandmother says I'm too thin but Lisa Harris is skinnier than I'll ever be and she can hit a softball out of the park, better than the boys who think they're so great. My grandpapa can't look at me without giving me a dollar and sending me for ice cream—one pint of New York Cherry for him and one Strawberry for me. But that's not it, being skinny. I'm not tough. That's what.

So get tough, says Lisa Harris. Let the basketball / hit you / in your damn face (Lisa curses) 'til you learn how to receive it (she says *receive* like the boys, instead of *catch* like I would say). You gotta take your damn licks, she says. Don't be a punk.

The longer I wait, the farther the fall. It is so hot. Gritty dirt and wood crumbles make glue in a skim of sweat. If I look up, the sky lurches and turns making me dizzy, so I have to grip the narrow fence even tighter. My wrists ache and shiver. Be tough says Lisa Harris leaping over the fence in a single bound and sauntering off in the same direction as my brother.

I can't get down.

Punk, says Lisa.

The sun drops an inch closer to the slatted wall, burns larger. The fence's shadow grows. On either side, I'm scared the same. Behind me is Deacon's house. Deacon appears in a doorway, shuts the door. Come 'ere girl, he says, come 'ere. What's wrong with giving your Uncle a kiss? Is there anything wrong with that? Come 'ere then . . .

They should have come back to help me, that's all. They should have known . . . they knew I couldn't make it over the fence. That's why Leonard came this way. They knew and laughed and kept on running, Jerome my brother, and his friend.

The sun burns straight on me. My shadow clings to the wall. Help me, I whisper. I scream inside my head. Somebody help me. To myself. Tears squeeze out of my eyes. Through the tears, the sun wobbles and shakes. I pray somebody will come to help me. I pray no one will come and find me stuck on top of a fence. My mouth trembles. The sun is cooking a hot spot on the top of my head. My palms are sticky with sweat, dirt, grit from the crumbly wall. I try to readjust my grip on the fence top. I have nowhere else to go but to Deacon's house. I have to . . .

Don't be a punk . . . Bein' scared is the problem. You gotta stop bein' so scared all the time. What's the big deal anyway? Grow up, for heaven's sake. It's mind over matter. It's how you think, see. You thinkin' you can't do it. You gotta think like you Bill Russell, somebody. Like you can do anything, see. Like you can fly like a bird.

If I was a bird I would know how to sit on a fence and not fall off. A bird, bluejay or robin or even just a plain brown sparrow, ready to take off . . . what does the sparrow think of? She laughs at the cock on a weathervane, stuck in one place and can't get down. She laughs. Flits up and along the fence top daring the cock to fly off of that stick stuck in its belly, dares him to leave that house and fly. I am the sparrow. Brown and plain. I could fly if I knew something else. I've no stick that pins me down. I could fly if I would, and look out over everybody's heads down there, counting the crosses on the church tops, counting the Deacons on their knees . . .

I could see . . . see where my brother went. And fly there. He'll be surprised when I show up and sing down to him, I don't want to go with you or Leonard, I've got better places to go. And then he sees I am flying—suddenly I am flying. Backwards, flying backwards. The sky swoops, hits me upside my head—am I screaming? screaming . . . the sky swerves, hits me upside my head once like a wooden board . . . black. Blackness. Dark.

I'm not dead . . . the darkness is my skirt over my head blocking the light because that's what gravity does when you hang by one knee upside down on a fence.

Blood in my face . . . swelling, inside my head . . . hot . . . dark as the sun blood red seeping through a dark curtain . . .

Push the skirt up out of your face, fool . . . do something with that spare leg waving in the air . . . go fishing . . . caught a whole fence . . . can you sit up? . . . grab the top . . . sit up (light) . . . grab it . . . missed (dark) . . . one hand to grab, one to keep my dress up (or down) to cover my pale-pink-for-Wednesday-even-though-it's-Sunday underwear . . . up! (light) . . . missed . . . down (dark)
    Again.

Something starts to shake . . . it's me . . . it's inside me . . . wet rolls off my eyelids . . . tears run off my forehead . . . splashdown in the tan dust over my head . . .

My head . . . big . . . like a big rock . . . heavy like a rock . . . raise up . . . raise up, rock! missed . . . above me, waiting, is the hard dirt . . . when I fall . . . when? sometime . . .

My eyes squeeze shut tight . . . please nobody come to see me hanging stupid upside down nobody

Nobody comes . . . didn't think so . . . good . . . nobody can hear me from those houses way over there . . . if they look out of their windows they will see . . . they will see a brown thing . . . won't know it's me (me who? me-myself-and-I) . . . won't see me . . . won't know it's me . . . it's me it's me it's me oh lord standin in the need of prayer . . .

Call somebody . . . can't call nobody for help . . . fences . . . good fences make good girls . . . and sun . . . red hot in a white sky is like hell you know is upside down . . .

Cry . . . can't . . . good . . . arms too heavy to reach . . . too heavy to keep my dress down . . . up . . . over me . . . heavy to hold my dress draped over my face (pull that dresstail down girl!) cools my face from the straight burn of the sun . . . hanging . . . dresstail over my head (with your fast-tail self!) . . . erase the little houses way over there white people peek out they see black me hanging upside down on a fence reminds them of something they can't remember . . . I can't remember how did I get up here on this fence? . . . never mind. Be grateful!

Who put this fence here anyway . . . to leave me back to push me back to Deacon's house to get away from me away in the dark I see him them sitting on a step drinking cold Nehi purple right out the bottle they've got penny candy mintjuleps wine candy sours banana bikes taste like salt like snot . . .

Sorry trees turned upside down brown dry skinny trees like me hanging in the heat . . .

Hate . . . I hate. I hate Leonard and my brother with their Nehi pop I hope / they trip / on a po-ta-to chip / and drown up / side down / in / a / bot / tle of pop! . . . my last wish . . .

I wish wish wish / to hypnotize this dish dish dish / yellow dirt over my head head head / make me a feather bed bed bed / to fall into instead stead stead . . .

The ugly big-nosed man on TV just happens to pass by my fence. He says: Whut uh revoltin' development dis is! and stretches his eyes . . .

When I fall I might die quick or I might just pop my head open pink inside strawberry ice cream or like that watermelon rolled off the edge of grandpapa's porch smack on the concrete step rind split open crooked and red water leaked off the step . . .

Hanging from my stem like green blackfruit on a tree. Like apple trees in Mrs. Johnson's yard. Her apples never fall, just rot on the limb. Gone straight from green to bad, she says. Like Deacon's daughter. Blackfruit. Green inside and gone to rot.

Well, girl, it could be worse. Just keep your knees together, eyes open. Hands up and open like this. Palms open. If he tries any tongue action keep your teeth closed. Keep everything closed. Except your eyes. And then, and then, well, it's nothing to worry about. Can't nothing happen then. So don't be a punk, ok?

I wouldn't want to have to tell my mother that I've gone and broken my neck. That would be hard to do because she would be frightened for me and in pain for me and have to take off work to take care of me and the worst part would be when she'd say, What were you doing up on a fence? and when I told her she'd say, You don't have the sense God gave you.

I let myself hang, loose. Last tears drop slip out of my eyes. I can feel the world's slow spin. Slow, barely moving.

A breeze. One. I feel cool in this slow motion like a world spin so I can catch the fence top with my flying foot heel heel heel then ankle pull slow but moving in the dark pull pull inch inch gaining the fence top scrape scrape little blood little blood on the wall on the wall will not fall will not fall up light up light take the fencetop. Hooray.

Simple. To bend at the waist, grip the top of the wall, skin my legs down sideways, push off from the fence, drop to the ground. My knees give out. I just stay down, on my knees, forehead to the wall, face hot, eyes sticky. Just for a minute. Wait. Just till I don't hear my heart. Wait. After a minute, or more, maybe? An hour. I climb to my feet, walk shakily toward Deacon's house. Before I turn the first corner and I know he will be waiting for me.

Where you been? Why you run off like that? Hardly had a chance to see you and you were gone . . .
    (Where is my father?) . . .
    Went to the store, for some ice . . . he'll be back . . .
    Hair, slicked back, dull in the late sun with old oil and dust. His narrow face is still and bland as the air behind a barn.
    How come you didn't give your Uncle a kiss when you came. You come to your Uncle's house and he can't get a kiss?
    I put my hands up, fists. Deacon thrusts his tongue against my firmly

clenched teeth. The backs of my knees ache from where the coarse wood of the fence has pressed and scraped. With my eyes open I see his eyes are open too. He forces open one clenched fist, presses my palm against the lump always between his legs. The cloth rubs rough against new bruises in my palm, ache and burn.

The air is quiet. I can hear the dust rising. I can hear a caterpillar creeping on a limb over there. I hear the far off creak and slap of the screen door to Deacon's kitchen and my mother calling Sharin and Karin because if they're just standing around they can come in this kitchen and make themselves useful. But mostly I hear silence shaped like the triangles of spaces between my fingers, hands palms up and open, knees together and slightly flexed, the proper way to receive the basketball muscled at you hard because if you play with the boys you better learn how to take it and stop whining and for God's sake don't be such a sissy.

Later there will be glasses of blue Kool Aid cooled with ice and fried chicken and some kind of potatoes but not potato salad because you can't trust mayonnaise on a day like this, it's just too hot, and some kind of canned peas.

It is almost dinner when Leonard and my brother get back from wherever they've been. I am sitting on the back step, still and quiet like a Tarbaby. I will not speak to them

Hey, says Jerome. What happened to you? Why you didn't come with us? We waited for you! Then he grins and looks at Leonard. They both laugh. I cut my eyes at Leonard and laugh with them thinking how it's too bad quality has skipped two generations. But really I'm looking at my brother, my mouth laughing, but I do not speak one word to him. I am looking at him. I am looking for something inside of him. I do not see what I am looking for. Me? They don't see me. Till they want to get by me, get into the house, him and that ugly Leonard, and I won't let them come by me. They see me then . . . they see my smile is not smiling, really. They see I mean it. They see me raise my hands too, so they can't step over me either and stunt my growth.

If they want to get in, they will have to go around to the other door, to the front door, have to go past the pink flamingos where my dark water still gleams at their feet and ring the doorbell so Mrs. Deacon has to disturb herself from whatever she's doing, has to walk to the front door thinking it must be someone, another guest, another place to set, make Mrs. Deacon walk from back to front, and it's only them, have to come past two pink birds balancing circles of glass on their wings, and track their dust past her and the birds, and let her ask them why in heaven's name they are tracking again through her front door, and are they too grown now to come through the back? And how they answer her will be their own damn business because today I am a fence with no gate. And I am not moving. Not today. No way. Yes, I am here. But I will not be grateful.

Joyce Carol Thomas

YOUNG REVEREND ZELMA LEE MOSES

A hoot owl feasted round eyes on the clapboard building dipped in April shadow at the edge of a line of magnolia and redbud trees.

The owl peered through the budding branches until he focused on the kitchen, in which a mother, brown and fluffy as buttermilk biscuits, stood by the muslin-draped window, opening glass jars of yams, okra, tomatoes, spinach, and cabbage and stirred the muted colors in a big, black cast-iron pot. Then she raised the fire until she set the harvest green and red colors of the vegetables bubbling before fitting the heavy lid in place and lowering the flame.

She watched the blaze, listening to the slow fire make the food sing in low lullaby.

When it was time, she ladled the stew onto warmed platters, sliced warm-smelling red-pepper corn bread into generous wedges, and poured golden tea into three fat clay mugs.

"Dinner!" her voice sang.

"Coming, Mama," said tall Zelma, who was leaning over stoking the fire in the wood fireplace. Her shadow echoed an angular face, backlit by the light from the flames.

When she turned around, her striking features showed misty black eyes in a face which by itself was a chiseled beauty mark. Indeed, she gave the phrase "colored woman" its original meaning. She was colored, with skin the sugar brown of maple syrup.

At the kitchen table she sat between her aging parents. Her father, his earthen face an older, darker, lined version of Zelma's, his hair thick as white cotton and just as soft and yielding to Zelma's touch, started the blessing.

"We thank thee for this bountiful meal. . . ."

"May it strengthen us in our comings and goings," Zelma continued.

"Lord, do look down and watch over us for the work that lies ahead," chanted the father and daughter together.

"And bless the hands of the cook who prepared this meal."

"Amen," said the mother.

They ate as the quiet light outside their window began to fall in whispers. Zelma told time by how long the fire in the fireplace at their backs danced. She counted the dusky minutes in how long it took to clear the table, to clean and place the dishes in their appointed places in the cabinet, to scrub the black cast-iron pot until it gleamed black as night.

Then it was the hushing hour, the clock of the trees and the sky and the flying crickets said, "Come, let us go into the house of the Lord." And they started out, hands holding hands, down the red clay dusty road together.

Before long they were joined by Mother Augusta, a pillar of the community and cornerstone of the church.

The eighty-year-old Mother Augusta, who like a seer was frequently visited by psychic dreams, enjoyed a reputation as the wrinkleless wonder because her face was so plump no lines could live there, causing folks to say, "She either a witch or she been touched by God." Today Mother Augusta kept up a goodly pace with her wooden cane. Augusta and her late husband had broken the record for the longest continuous years of service as board members to the church. She was a live oak living on down through the years and keeping up the tradition now that her husband was gone on.

Today as the family walked along, Mother Augusta smiled at Zelma, thinking it was just about wedding time for the young woman. The older Mother Augusta's head flooded with memories of Zelma and how she had always been special, but one memory stood out from the rest. One April memory many years back.

The Bible Band of preschoolers had come marching into the church that Easter looking so pretty, and all the children serious, strict-postured,

the girls with black braids laced with ribbons like rainbows. A few with
hot-iron curls.

Each of the ten children had stepped forward and given a biblical recitation, a spring poem, a short song. The church house nodded, a collection
of heads in a show of approval as one child with pink ribbons sat down.

Another reciter in a little Easter-egg-yellow child's hat stood up and delivered an age-old poem. Finishing, she gave a sigh of relief, curtsied, and
took her seat.

Then Zelma, pressed and curled, stepped forward, her maple hands
twisting shyly at the sleeves of her lavender-blue and dotty-green organdy
dress. In white cotton stockings and ebony patent leather shoes so shiny and
carefully walked in no mud scuffed the mirror bright surface, her feet just
wouldn't stay still. Zelma couldn't get settled; she nervously listed from one
foot to the other.

She started her speech in an expressionless, singsong tone. No color
anywhere near it. It was a typical Bible Band young people's performance
that the whole church endured, as yet another duty, as yet another means
of showering encouragement upon the young.

Zelma recited:

> "It's raining, it's raining;
> The flowers are delighted;
> The thirsty garden greens will grow,
> The bubbling brooks will quickly flow;
> It's raining, it's raining, a lovely rainy day."

Now instead of curtsying and sitting herself down, Zelma stared suddenly at the crucifix above the sanctuary door.

She stared so hard until every head followed her gaze that had settled on
the melancholy light beaming on the crucifix.

Then in a different voice she started to speak.

"And Jesus got up on the cross and He couldn't get down."

Mother Augusta had moved forward in her seat as if to say, "Hear tell!"

And Zelma went on like that, giving her own interpretation of the cru-
cifixion, passion making her voice vibrate.

An usher moved forward to stop her, but Mother Augusta waved the
usher back.

"Well?" said Mother Augusta.

"If He could have got down, He would've," Zelma supposed.

Zelma talked about stubbing her toe, about how much it hurt, and she reported the accident she had of once stepping on a rusty nail.

"If one nail could hurt so bad, how painful the Christ nails piercing Him in His side must have been," Zelma decided.

"And so I think He didn't get down, because you see," she added in a whisper, "something was holding Him there.

"It was something special."

"Yes?" called Mother Augusta just as a deacon moved to herd the child to her pew. Bishop Moses waved the deacon back.

"I know He wanted to get down. Why else would He have said, 'My Lord, my Lord, why hast Thou forsaken me?' "

"Amen," said the first usher.

"But you see," said Zelma, "something was holding my Lord there, something was nailing Him to that old rugged cross, and it wasn't just metal nails."

Now the entire church had gotten into the spirit with young Zelma.

"Wasn't just metal nails," sang the church in response.

"It was nails of compassion."

"Nails of compassion," repeated the church.

"He was nailed with nails of sorrow," Zelma preached.

"Nails of sorrow," the church rang out.

"Nailed for our iniquity," Zelma called.

"Nailed," the church responded.

"He was nailed, he was bruised for our transgression."

Then Zelma let go. "The nail, the nail that wouldn't let Him down, the nail that would give Him no peace, the nail that held Him there was the nail of love."

"Love," shouted the church.

"Jesus," Zelma said, in a lower muted voice, "Jesus got up on the cross and He couldn't get down, and because He couldn't get down, and because He couldn't get down, He saved a world in the name of a nail called Love!"

It was all told in rhythms.

As the church went ecstatic with delight, somebody handed Zelma her guitar.

Another child hit the tambourine.

And the music started talking to itself.

"She been called to preach," announced Mother Augusta.

Bishop Moses, scratching his getting-on-in-years head, was as thunderstruck as the other members of the congregation. He flitted from one to the other as they stood outside in the church yard to gossip and to appraise the service.

One of the elder deacons opened his mouth to object, starting to say something backward, something about the Bible saying fellowship meant fellows not women, but the eldest sister on the usher board proclaimed, "God stopped by here this morning!"

Who could argue with that?

This evening as Augusta walked along with Zelma's family skirting the honeysuckle-wrapped trees of the Sweet Earth woods, they eagerly approached that same church, now many years later. Two mockingbirds singing and chasing each other in the tulip trees just by the tamed path leading into the church house reminded Mother Augusta that it was almost Easter again.

Spring was lifting her voice through the throats of the brown thrashers and the wood thrushes and the wild calls coming from the woods.

And in the light colors of bird feathers, beauty spread her charm all over the land.

Inside the church a wine-red rug stitched with Cherokee roses led the way down the center aisle around a pot-bellied stove and continued up three steps. Behind the lectern sat three elevated chairs for Bishop Benjamin Moses, Zelma Lee Moses, and any dignitary who might come to visit. Then behind the three chairs perched seats for the choir members who filled them when the singers performed formally and on Sundays.

The church had been there so long that the original white paint on the pew armrests had been worn and polished by generations of the members' hands until in spots the pure unadulterated rosewood peeked through.

The Bishop opened the weeknight service by saying a prayer. All over the building the members stood, knelt, sat, waiting for the rapture.

Soon Testimony Service was over and the congregational singing had been going on for some time before they felt that special wonder when the meeting caught fire. First they felt nothing and then they all felt the spirit at one time.

The soul-thrilling meters, the changing rhythms, the syncopated tambourine beats trembled inside every heart until they were all of one accord.

Stripes of music gathered and fell across the people's minds like lights.

Melodies lifted them up to a higher place and never let them down.

The notes rang out from the same source: the female, powerhouse voice of Zelma Lee Moses. She bounced high on the balls of her feet as she picked the guitar's steely strings, moving them like silk ribbons. The congregation felt the notes tickling from midway in their spines and on down to the last nerve in their toes.

Zelma gave a sweet holler, then lowered her voice to sing so persuasively that the people's shoulders couldn't stay still, just had to move into the electrifying rhythm and get happy.

Zelma gospel-skipped so quick in her deep-blue robe whirling with every step she took, somebody had to unwrap the guitar from around her neck. She was a jubilee all by herself.

And the people sang out her name, her first two names, so musically that they couldn't call one without calling the other: *Zelma Lee.*

Perfect Peace Baptist Church of Sweet Earth, Oklahoma, sat smack-dab in the middle of a meadow near the piney woods. This zigzag board wooden building with the pot-bellied stove in its center served as Zelma Lee Moses's second home.

Here she sang so compellingly that shiny-feathered crows from high in the treetops winged lower, above the red clay earth, roosted on black tupelo tree branches, peeked in the church window and bobbed their heads, flapped their glossy feathers, cawing in time to the quickened-to-perfection, steady beat.

Reverend Zelma Lee Moses closed her eyes and reached for the impossible note made possible by practice and a gift from God. Row after row of worshippers commenced to moaning watching her soul, limited only by her earthly body, full and brimming over, hop off the pulpit. She sang, "Lord, just a little mercy's all I need."

And she didn't need a microphone.

"Look a yonder, just a skipping with the gift and the rhythm of God." Mother Augusta over in the Amen Corner clapped her hands in syncopated time. At home, Sister Moses, Zelma's blood mother, was the woman of the house, but in the sanctuary Mother Augusta, the mother of the church, was in charge.

Zelma began and ended every sermon with the number "Lord, Just a Little Mercy's All I Need."

The sound tambourined and the Sweet Earth sisters swooned and swooned, the ushers waved their prettiest embroidered handkerchiefs under the noses of the overcome, but they couldn't revive the fainting women as long as young Reverend Zelma Lee Moses dipped into her soul and crooned,

> *"Lord, just a little mercy's all I need.*
> *If I have sinned in any way,*
> *Down on my knees I'll stay and pray,*
> *Lord, just a little mercy's all I need."*

How her silver voice swooped over the words, coloring them a mystery color that did not exist except in the mind which received it, forgot it, then gave it back.

Daniel, a newcomer who'd only been in town for one year, wanted Zelma to pay him some attention; how she had stayed unattached puzzled him. He knew the statuesque Reverend Zelma Lee Moses easily attracted men. On this third visit to church Daniel saw how men flocked like butterflies to Zelma's color-rich flower garden, to the sunbows in her throat every time she opened her mouth to preach or sing. Out flew the apricot hues of hollyhock. The gold of the goldenrod, the blue pearl of Jacob's ladder. Daniel got a little jealous watching Zelma study the fellows, her camera eyes pausing on one young man's skin that rivaled the brown feather colors of a red-tailed hawk. Her admiring gaze directed briefly at the young man made Daniel itch around the collar. He turned neon red inside watching her watching him.

But it was on Daniel that Zelma's camera stopped scanning and focused. She saw his skin flirting with light, his inky hair accepting the brilliance like a thirsty canvas accepts a crown of black beads dabbed by a painter's shimmering brush.

His eyes shone with such a joy-lit intensity of sparkling double black flecked with the silver crescents of the moon that looking into them made her want to die or live forever.

Now Zelma, already so touched with talent that limousined producers from New York came down and waved rock and roll contracts in front of her, wanted to ask Daniel his opinion of the intricate offers.

"What do you think about this here music contract," she asked him one night after service.

"Rock and roll? I don't know. Seems to me you ought to keep singing gospel. But take your time," he advised after studying the papers.

"Time," she said thoughtfully, and when she looked in Daniel's eyes, she knew he was just thinking about what was best for her.

"Think I'll write gospel right next to rock and roll," she said.

"Makes sense to me," said Daniel.

"What you studying to be?" she asked.

"How do you know I'm studying anything?" he teased.

"You're getting lots of books in the mail."

"Oh that! I'm studying to be an electrician or a bishop like your daddy," he said, handing the music recording agreement back to her.

"So that's why you're always carting the Bible and those big mail-order books around!"

"That's the truth," he acknowledged with a grin.

"An electrical bishop."

"An electrician-bishop," said Daniel.

"Uh-hm," said Zelma Lee in her most musical speaking voice.

When she took her time about signing the contracts, the producers resorted to recording her mellifluous gospel voice to see if they could find someone else to match it who wouldn't study too long over the words in their contracts. But they never could.

Nobody else had that red clay memory in her throat, fat gold floating in the colored notes.

So they returned to try again and again until the young singer, after understanding as best she could all the small print and inserting the part about gospel, took pen in hand and signed the document.

That night her voice rivered out melodies so clear that when the music company visitors from the outside world heard the rhythms rinsed in some heavenly rain, they either thought of art or something dangerous they could not name.

Since the producers were coming with music on their minds, they only thought of songs and never perceived the threat.

The producers seemed so out of place in that place that welcomed everybody, common and uncommon, that they sometimes giggled suddenly without warning and thought that instead of stained glass they saw singing crows dressed in polka dot hats looking in the windows.

When they packed up their recording gear and stood on the outside of the church by the side of the road where the wild irises opened their blue mouths, Mother Augusta, leaning on her cane, bent an ear to the limousine and commented, "Say, good sirs, that motor's running so soft on this long machine you can hear the flowers whisper. Umph, umph, umph!"

"What?"

The music merchants leaned back in their accordion cars and waved the chauffeur forward. They eased on down the road shaking their heads, couldn't figure out what she was talking about.

One said to the other, "Whispering flowers? Another one of those old Oklahoma fogeyisms."

"No doubt," agreed his partner, hugging the hard-earned contract to his breast.

Reverend Zelma Lee Moses only sang so the people could rejoice.

"A whole lot of people will rejoice when you sign this contract," the producer had said.

"Will?" said Zelma.

"Of course I'll be one of them." The record company man smiled as he extended the pen.

And more people did rejoice about a year after she'd signed the contract.

The echo of colors flew across the airwaves. The song "A Little More Mercy" made women listening to the radio as they pressed clothes still their irons in the middle of rough, dried collars, watching the steam weave through the melody.

Daniel, in his pine thick backyard chopping wood, his head awash in the sound, wondered at the miracle of vinyl, catching a voice like that and giving it back so faithfully, reached inside the open kitchen window and turned up the homemade radio he had assembled with his own hands. The sound flowed out to him even more distinctly. He raised the ax, chopping more rhythmically, clef signs scoring the wood.

More and more people rejoiced.

Both Zelma's mothers, Augusta and her natural mother, ended up with limousines, if they wanted them, turning the dials to their favorite gospel stations, which always played their favorite artist to the additional accompaniment of limousine tires dancing down the road.

Zelma only sang so the people could rejoice.

And therein lay the danger. Preachers who had that kind of gift had to be around folks who loved them, for the devil stayed busy trying to stick the old pitchfork in. Zelma kept herself too wrapped up with her gift to notice the devil's works; those around her had to be aware, wary, and protective.

She preached one Sunday 'til her voice rang hoarse with power and her guitar hit a note so high it rang heaven's doorbell. And all up and down the rows, women stood up, their tambourines trembling like rhinestones.

Palm Sunday, the Sunday when visiting congregations from as far away as New Orleans, Louisiana, arrived with their clothes speckled with the Texas dust they passed through to get to Sweet Earth, Oklahoma, and the new gospel recording star; the visiting Louisiana choir, hot from their journey, crowded the choir stands to overflowing and mopped sweat from their curious brows.

Palm Sunday in Sweet Earth at Perfect Peace Baptist Church, the deacons with trembling hands, babies sucking blisters on their thumbs, folks so lame they had to wheel themselves in in wheelchairs, eyeglassed teachers, and farmers with weed cuts persisting around their scrubbed nails, all stepped out, in shined shoes, pressed suits, spring dresses, and assorted hats, coming to hear the female preacher perform on Palm Sunday, and she didn't disappoint them; she preached until her robe stuck to her sculptured body, wringing wet. She preached until dear Daniel, in an evergreen shirt of cotton and linen, Daniel so handsome she could squeeze the proud muscles straining against his shirt sleeves, until Daniel who had been tarrying for a year on the altar, dropped his tambourine and fell out in the sanctuary overcome by the holy spirit.

A cloud of "Hallelujah's" flew up like joy birds from the congregation when Daniel got religion. Still the Sweet Earth saints in front of Zelma with their mouths stretched open on the last syllable of Hallelujah, had not shouted, had not danced in the spirit.

Only one mover shook loose in the whole flock of them. And that was dimpled Daniel, an earth angel dressed in light and leaf green and smelling of musky sweet spring herbs, stepping all up and down and inside the gospel beat, a human drum.

It was just about time for Zelma to wind up the sermon and finish with the song "Lord, Just a Little Mercy's All I Need."

And she felt as if she hadn't done her job at all if she couldn't get ten sisters and several deacons moved from their sanctified seats.

The visiting choir voices behind her had sunk and their volume diminished. She was used to more call and response and certainly much more shouting.

"Why's this church so cold?" she asked.

Stopped in the middle of her sermon and asked it.

What she could not see behind her were the visiting choir members being carried off the stage one by one. The entire soprano section of the New Orleans New Baptist Church Youth Choir had danced until they fainted, until only one or two straggly alto voices were left.

The Sweet Earth congregation gazed so amazed at the rapture and the different shouting styles of the Louisiana choir that they settled back and, instead of joining in the commotion, sat transfixed on their chairs like they were in a downtown theater watching a big city show on tour.

Nobody told Zelma she had preached so hard that she had set a record for the number of folks falling out in one sermon.

She wasn't aware of the record she'd just broken because she couldn't see the Louisiana choir behind her, she only saw dear Daniel in a golden trance, speaking in tongues, Daniel who made her feel like an angel every time she beheld his face.

When she pronounced Daniel "saved" and accepted him into the church, she made a silent promise, looking into Daniel's deep dark gaze, finding her passion in the curve of his molasses colored lips.

Before the week-long revival was over Daniel would be proud of her.

And then it came to her, not from God but from the soft place in the center of her soul-filled passion.

She would do what nobody else had done.

Come Sunday, the crowning day of the revival, young Reverend Zelma Lee Moses would fly.

"On Easter Sunday," she announced, talking to the Church but looking Daniel in the eyes, "on the last day of the revival, on the day Christ came forth from the tomb, Church, it's been given me to fly."

Their opened mouths opened even wider.

The New Orleans New Baptist Youth Choir, scheduled to be in concert in Louisiana on Easter Sunday, took a vote and sent back word that their Oklahoma stay would be extended and that the Sunday School Choir would have to sing two extra numbers instead to make up for their absence.

Since the Reverend Zelma Lee Moses's voice had moved over them like a mighty wind, knocking them from their perches in the choir stand and rendering them senseless from the mighty impact of her spirit, they could not leave, even if they wanted to.

"Young Reverend Zelma Lee Moses's gonna fly come Sunday evening," the ecstatic choir director chanted over the Oklahoma-to-Louisiana telephone wires.

That very night, beneath her flower garden patched quilt, Mother Augusta dreamed. First she saw Zelma Lee inside the church, making the announcement about flying, then she saw a red-dressed she-devil down in her hell home listening to Zelma's promise to fly on Sunday. Slack-jawed, the devil looked up at the church and the people being moved like feathers and got jealous.

"Flying on Sunday? Zelma Lee's gonna fly!" The next day these two phrases lit up the telephone wires in Sweet Earth.

The funny thing about all of this, of course, was that passion was playing hide-and-seek.

Daniel wanted Zelma as much as Zelma wanted him, but she did not know this.

"I want this Zelma," Daniel whispered to himself in the still hours of the night when the lightning bugs flew like earth stars outside his window. It was then he spoke, forgetting his Sweet Earth enunciation, in the lyrical thick accent of the swamp place from which he came.

As experienced with women as Daniel was he had never seen anybody like Zelma, and so he studied her carefully; he slowly wondered how to approach her. He didn't want to make even one false move.

Just seeing her was sometimes enough to take his breath away. Zelma had already stolen his heart when he saw her sitting in the pulpit between the visiting evangelist and Bishop Moses that first Sunday he visited Perfect Peace.

Because the visiting evangelist preached, Zelma was not required to speak or sing. It was her presence alone that had attracted him. He didn't even know she could talk, let alone sing. Even quiet she was a sight.

Hearing her sing on his second Sunday visit brought him to his knees. Folks thought he had fallen down to pray.

Eventually he did kneel to pray all the subsequent Sundays, but his belly still quivered like Jell-O even now remembering what the woman did to his mind.

And Zelma had never had so much as one boyfriend before. Since she was a preacher's daughter, she was expected, when it came to passion, to wait 'til her appointed time. Music had been her passion; music had been enough.

Then came Daniel. When she looked at Daniel, her heart opened on a door to a God she had not known was even there.

Daniel she wanted to impress even though he was already smitten.

Anything she did beyond being who she already was was needless, was superfluous, but young Zelma didn't know this.

As Mother Augusta might have said, "Humph. The devil found work."

The first thing Zelma did wrong was she built a short platform out of the wrong wood and didn't ask the deacons of the church to help her out.

"Didn't ask nobody nothing," complained Deacon Jones, he was so mad his trembling bottom lip hung down almost to his knees. "Got to drive a nail in at the right angle or it won't hold!"

Second thing Zelma did wrong was she went downtown to some un-sanctified, whiskey-drinking folks and had them sew some wings onto her robe; looking like vultures roosting, they sewed crooked, leaving tobacco smoke lingering in the cloth.

"You don't tell sinning people nothing sacred," Mother Augusta clucked in a chastising voice to whoever's ears were free to listen.

"Sinning people! They nature is such that they misunderstand the mysteries.

"If they see trumpets on your head, they refer to them as horns.

"Now and then you run across an exception, but half the time they don't know *what* they looking at," said Mother Augusta.

And too, the seasoned women in the church primped their mouths and got offended, because for as long as they could remember they had personally sewn the sacred robe with the smoke blue thread that had been blessed and sanctified in a secret ritual that nobody discussed, lest a raven run away with their tongue.

"Who knows what them drunk people put in them wings?"

Mother Augusta, the human *Jet* and *Ebony* combined, kept a running oral column going among the older people all the revival days approaching Easter Sunday.

In the meantime Mother Augusta wanted to have words with the young preacher, but the members of the New Orleans New Baptist Youth Choir kept Zelma so occupied the female preacher didn't even have time for her own Sweet Earth congregation.

Even her own father, the retired Bishop Benjamin Moses, couldn't get a word in edgewise. Between counseling the New Orleans young folk, Zelma studied the Bible in the day and slept in the church house at night after falling out exhausted from continuous prayer. In the wee hours of the morning she slipped home, where her mother had prepared steaming hot bathwater and laid out fresh clothes. She refused her mother's platters of peppergrass greens, stewed turkey wings and Sunday rice, including her favorite dewberry biscuits. She was fasting and only took water.

But the community fed the Louisiana visitors. The gray-haired, white-capped mothers of the church, mothers of the copper kettles and porcelain pans, kept their kitchens bustling with younger Sweet Earth women. They instructed these sisters of the skillet in the fine art of baking savory chicken-and-dressing and flaky-crusted peach cobblers.

"Put a little more sage in that corn bread.

"Make that dumpling plumper than that," Mother Augusta ordered, throwing out to the birds a pan of dough that didn't pass her inspection.

She personally turned over each peach, seeing with her farsighted eyes what stronger, younger eyes often missed.

The young Louisiana people stood around, underfoot, mesmerized by Zelma, but Mother Augusta saw what they couldn't see and what Zelma's mother's eyes wouldn't see.

She prayed, Mother Augusta did.

Zelma prayed, but her love for Daniel had her all puffed up and half drunk with passion.

Come Easter Sunday she would fly, then after church she would offer Daniel her hand, and if he held it much longer than friendly, they would be companions.

Every night she preached and promised to fly on Sunday.

Every night the crowd got thicker.

By Sunday night the standing-room-only audience pushed and elbowed each other in competition with the cawing crows for a low, window-level place on the tupelo branches above the clay by the window.

Oh, the crowd and the crows!

The church house sagged, packed to the rafters. And Mother Augusta ordered the carpenter to check the floor planks because they might not be able to take the whipping she knew Zelma was going to give them once she got started stomping the floor and making the Bible holler.

"Tighten that board over yonder," she ordered.

Another sound that added to the clamor was the hum of more buses arriving from New Orleans. Some members back home in the Louisiana church were so intrigued by the choir's decision to remain in Sweet Earth that they boarded yet another bus and struck out for northeast Oklahoma to see what the excitement was all about, driving on through the sleepless night so they could reach Perfect Peace in time for Sunday service and the promised night of miracles.

The New Orleans contingency was so glad to have made it in time, they entered the church swaying down the aisle, fingers circling circles in the air, uncrossed feet whipping up the holy dance.

As the evening lengthened, something softened in the air. Maybe it was the effect of the full moon.

The Reverend Zelma Lee Moses preached about wings that Sunday night.

The soft shadows cast by the full moon looked like veils hanging over the sanctuary.

She took her text from Psalms.

"Read, Brother Daniel!"

Daniel opened his Bible and quoted, "Keep me as the apple of thy eye, hide me under the shadow of thy wings.

"And He shall cover thee with his feathers, and under his wings shalt thou trust: his truth shall be thy shield and buckler."

"Read!"

Daniel found the next Psalm and continued, "Be merciful unto me, O God, be merciful unto me: for my soul trusteth in thee: yea, in the shadow of thy wings will I make my refuge. . . ."

"Read!"

". . . Who layeth the beams of his chambers in the waters; who maketh the clouds his chariot: who walketh upon the wings of the wind."

Now the great flying moment the Sweet Earth people had been antic-ipating for a whole week arrived. The spectacle that the New Orleans vis-itors awaited was here at last.

As she approached the platform, the young Zelma Lee Moses began to sing the closing number, "Lord, just a little mercy's all I need."

One sister let out a long, low holler. Transfigured, a ghost took over her throat, and it was like a special spirit had flown in through the open church window; like the miracle of the cross, Christ ascending into heaven would be repeated in another way.

It was too crowded for the people to cut loose. They swayed backward, swooned; and the crush of their numbers held each member up.

Now Zelma Lee Moses approached the foot of the launching platform, the platform built without consulting the deacons.

She mounted it and spread the arms of her robe, revealing the drunk-people-made wings.

And the congregation hushed.

Neither crowd nor crows flapped.

Young Zelma Lee Moses leaped!

But instead of being taken up by a mighty wind into the rafters above the gaping crowd, she plopped, sprawled, spread out on the oak floor at the feet of the frowning deacons, under the scrutinizing gaze of Mother Au-gusta, dragging her wings in the sawdust.

"The hem's crooked. And the thread's red wrong." Mother Augusta pointed, almost choking.

"Caw!" sang a crow.

Zelma scrambled back up, sure that the Lord had not forsaken her.

Maybe all she needed was a little speed to prime her wings: Recalling the way kites had to be hoisted, remembering her long adolescent legs run-ning down the weed fields fast and far enough before the kite yielded to the wind and took off, she opened her hands and spread her wings.

And with her long arms out as far as she could fling them, she ran, up and down the aisles, her arms moving up and down, her hands making cir-cles. Up and down the aisles.

Up. Down.

Fast, faster.

Up. Down.

Fast. Faster.

She ran past her future sweetheart-to-be and Daniel saw that she could not fly.

And she could not fly.

Finally her mother said, "Daughter?"

And the people got mad.

"Limp-winged!" somebody said in an un-Christian voice.

They chased her on out of the church house. Out across the weed field like a carnival of people chasing a getting-away kite. They ran her under the full moon, under the crows shadowing and cawing above them and on into the woods. She disappeared right through a grove of white oak and yellow pines. The last thing Daniel saw was Zelma's left foot, looking like a wing, as she slipped farther into the piney woods.

The people stopped right at the lush wildness, which was a curtain of green forest pulled like a secret against the place where unknown lakes and streams flowed and where wild foxes and all sorts of untamed creatures roamed.

Daniel was the only one who could have followed her there into the wildness, for he knew wild places like the back of his hand. But the look Zelma had shot him had said No.

And then he remembered that the piney woods was a natural bird refuge. There also doves flew in the thicket, marsh hens strutted proud, and quail called across the muddy and winding Sweet Earth River. He saw Zelma trembling there among the white and golden lilies and the singing crows. And Daniel knew this red earth of willow trees, dogwoods, and redbuds could hypnotize a person like Zelma who had wings in her feet, until it would be difficult for her to leave its allure.

As the church people ended their chase, he also stopped. It seemed as if she had been gone for weeks already. But instead of following her, he did the best thing: He turned back with the others.

Mother Augusta now raised her trembling hand and directed the choir to sing Zelma's favorite number, "Lord, Just a Little Mercy's All I Need," which they began singing softly, and she conducted the song so that it slowed down to a soothing pace. Finally the Louisiana choir dispersed, gathered their belongings, got on board and continued their sweet, wafting music on the midnight bus as they started out for home and Louisiana.

"She'll be back," Mother Augusta promised Daniel, who was sitting by the altar, head sadly bowed, looking long-faced, sifting the sawdust through his fingers, sawdust Zelma Lee Moses made rise by pounding the oak into powder while doing one of her gospel-skipping holy dances.

"She'll be back," Mother Augusta repeated in a knowing voice, then added as she took apart the launching platform, "This church is full of God's grace and mercy. Zelma's seen to that." She was remembering Zelma's invisible flight of the soul every time she looked at Daniel.

"When?" asked Daniel in that deep baritone voice.

"In three days," Mother Augusta answered, mumbling something about God making humans just a little bit lower than the angels.

"Being a little spryer than a timeworn woman, she didn't know she couldn't fly," sighed Mother Augusta. "Yet we hear her flying every Sunday morning on the radio."

"Well then why did the people come if they knew she couldn't fly?" asked Daniel, forgetting the miracle of the sawdust in his hand and the clef notes in the wood he chopped that radio afternoon when Zelma's first record came over the airwaves.

"Listen," said Mother Augusta.

"I'm listening."

"They came for the same reason they got mad," answered Mother Augusta. "They didn't want to miss it just in case she could." The elderly woman paused, then added, "When she realizes she already can fly, she'll be back. Take a lesson from the crow. Why should a bird brag about flying—that jet bird just spreads two easy wings. When Zelma knows that lesson, and she will know it, she'll return, she'll sure enough return."

The next day the women gathered in the morning pews and Mother Augusta offered up a prayer of early thanks.

The deacons joined in, serving the women broomwheat tea, gathering the cloth to help the sisters in the sanctuary sew a new gown fit for a child of God.

Somebody started lining a hymn.

It started out as a low moan.

Then it grew until it was full to bursting.

It exploded and the right word dropped from a mouth, scooted along the floor, lifted its head, flapped in place, flew up and became a note hanging from the light bulb in the rafters of the church.

A moan. A lyric.

And it went on like that, from moan to lyric

Until the song was fully realized.

Three long days passed with the people sitting, waiting, sewing, singing.

Mother Augusta was lining a hymn and she was lining a hem.

And on the third day, and on the third day they heard the crows gathering around the church.

But they did not open their beaks.

The hymn stopped, circled the light bulb above their heads.

The sound of silence.

The sound of waiting.

Then the next sound they heard was the door of the church opening softly.

"Who is it?" Daniel asked.

"Sh!" Mother Augusta whispered.

Nobody turned around except the waiting silence.

The silence stood up and opened its welcome arms.

Zelma.

Zelma Lee.

Zelma Lee Moses.

On the third day Zelma Lee Moses, looking a little down at the heel, stepped through Perfect Peace, paused and put on her long sanctified robe of invisible wings, picked up her guitar, mounted the steps to the pulpit, opened her mouth, and began to sing a crescendo passage in a higher voice with light wings glittering in the fire-singed notes, "Lord, just a little mercy's all I need."

And she looked at Daniel with a look that some folks claimed she got from talking to the devil for three days. But this was not true.

The look was all mixed up with angels, mockingbird flights, burnished butterflies, and tree-skimming kites.

After the service Daniel took her hand and held it longer than friendly.

When Zelma glanced up at the crucifix it seemed to her that Jesus, through a divine transformation, was winking through His pain. Or maybe it was just the effect of the morning sun kindling His expression, beaming only on those muscles of the mouth that brightened the corners of His lips.

As they left the church they walked under the crucifix over the doorway.

As if he too saw the same expression on the Christ, Daniel squeezed

Zelma Lee's hand tighter. And she could feel electricity pulse back and forth from his fingers to hers.

And they flew away to a place where wings grew from their ribs.
    And they were standing still flying.

Michele Bowen-Spencer

A FOOL, A GIRLFRIELD, A HUSBAND AND A WIFE

Precious sat at her desk in the business office of The Purgatory—the brothel that had been so named because its patrons believed it was the perfect halfway point between heaven and hell. As one of two bookkeepers, she was responsible for adding up the daily costs and cash intake, as well as calculating the women's weekly salaries.

Precious, who rarely found bookkeeping tedious, didn't feel like doing any work this evening. She had been sitting at her desk, idle, for more than ten minutes and was still reluctant to go back to adding up the day's receipts. Precious rubbed her temples for several seconds to ease the beginning of a headache. When she finally forced herself to resume working, she pounded the keys of the adding machine so hard until she knocked off a sparkling red Lee Press on Nail.

"Damn. I knew I shouldn't have used that cheap shit," Precious thought as she put her throbbing finger into her mouth—dried, nasty-tasting glue and all.

Actually, her throbbing finger gave her just the excuse she needed to cry—cry over what she had heard thirty minutes ago when she had gone to knock on Marcel's office door. Precious could not believe what she heard—her man, Marcel, and some hollering, moaning, fool of a woman. Precious grabbed a tissue from the box on her desk and dabbed at her eyes. She hated crying at work because she hated messing up her makeup.

"Damn you, Marcel," she whispered to herself. "How could you cheat on me like that—and right under my damn nose? Damn dawg."

Precious blew her nose and painfully replayed the sounds of what she'd heard coming out of Marcel's office in her head. And, she knew it was him because what she heard was the exact same groan he released when he was with her—lying and saying it belonged only to her. That only, she, Precious, could make him groan like that. Precious wiped away another tear, taking care not to smear her makeup.

"Damn dawg," she thought again and went back to her receipts, adding them up so fast that she feared she had missed something. "Shit, serves his ass right if I mess up these damn books tonight," she mumbled. "That damn dawg."

The office door opened and Marcel walked in. He wanted to make sure that Precious was busy working and had not been walking around looking for him. Not that he didn't think she was a good worker, he thought she was his best worker. But he had just finished up a rather vigorous session with Quita Jones, his only female trustee member.

Marcel had selected Quita to serve on the church's Board of Trustees solely for the emotional and physical hunger she wore on her face like a neon-lighted poster. In fact, the first time Marcel had seen Quita, she looked to him like she had 'take me to the Ramada Inn' blinking on and off of her forehead. And, Marcel had quickly seen that hunger—blinking on and off at him—as something he could easily manipulate whenever he needed someone to cast a deciding vote on his behalf at a Trustee meeting.

Marcel, however, had to go farther than he had planned to go with Quita this evening—just to make sure she would vote for his latest set of changes at Freedom Temple when the Board of Trustees met next week. He had underestimated Quita, failing to even think about how calculating she might be. Marcel hadn't even considered that Quita would make sure she got more than the flirting and feeling around he had planned to do with her this evening. He had not wanted anything else to happen because that neon-lighted hunger unnerved him a little and she wasn't his type—he like big butts and Quita's behind was just too tight and narrow for his taste.

When things got out of hand—at least in Marcel's opinion—he became doubly upset with Quita because she was so loud. But, he shouldn't have been too upset—Quita was one of the few people in the congregation who said or expressed anything during his dry and uninspiring sermons.

Marcel looked up and almost sighed out loud when he thought about how much work was involved in pastoring a big church. But, then, he quickly remembered to also count his blessings. Quita had been so full, so satiated, when she left his office that Marcel was confident she wouldn't tell a soul about The Purgatory. Somehow he knew that Quita had suffered famine too long to risk losing what little repast she could get to subdue her gnawing hunger.

Quita had been so loud, though, until Marcel was a bit anxious that Precious could have heard them if she had decided to stop by for her daily dose of hugs and kisses. He liked Precious a lot—better, in fact, than most of the other, other women in his life. And, he wasn't ready to fall out with her just yet. Its just that her assumption that she could drop by his office anytime, was at times a bothersome presumption. He really hoped that she had kept her behind in this office while he was with that big mouth Quita Jones.

Marcel looked at Precious's bare, Crayola crayon brown back and her sweet smelling shoulders. She had the sweetest and softest shoulders Marcel had ever tasted and touched. She was wearing his favorite outfit this evening—a stretchy, leopard print halter top, black satin hot pants, black lace stockings, and black patent-leather high heeled boots that came up to her knees. She wore her big, curly Afro up in a cute Afro puff on top of her head—holding it in place with a thick, black band and a black patent-leather bow. The hairstyle, with the dark, curly tendrils escaping to frame Precious's face, showed just how sweet and round it was.

Marcel walked over to Precious and planted a warm kiss on her shoulder. It tasted like honeysuckle. He ran his tongue from her shoulder to her neck. "Precious, Precious, Precious," he murmured in between planting soft kisses at the nape of her neck. "What am I going to do with you, baby, with your fine, sweet self? You taste so good until I think I want the whole meal rather than this snack."

Normally, Precious would have just melted inside at the kisses and those words. But not tonight. She stopped working on the adding machine, making sure that she felt composed enough not to betray her feelings to Marcel. Something told her to just play this one by ear.

Precious sighed softly and then took a deep breath and let it out like an even more longing sigh. She wanted to smell Marcel without him knowing it. She couldn't believe he didn't have a trace of that woman on him.

"His ass musta made a beeline for that shower he had put in his office," she thought.

Precious swiveled her chair around to face Marcel, who was now sitting on the edge of her desk. She had to admit that he was looking exceptionally good tonight in a golden brown, tailor-made leisure suit, that hugged just the right amount of his shoulders, chest, and hips. She batted heavily mascaraed eyes at him and parted very red lips—lips that were full in size but small in width—into that pouting smile she was so famous for.

"Honey-baby," she purred, almost choking on those words. "Honey-baby, why you in here, with me stuck with so much work, tryin to run up my temp-ture?"

She watched Marcel through the mask she was wearing as he carefully searched her face for any hints that she might suspect something. "Honey-baby, you looking at me like, all funnylike. Somethin' wrong?"

Marcel felt confident that he was hiding his anxiety with that cool, seductive smile he used when he wanted something, almost anything from a woman. He lowered his soft, flat voice down to that decibel that almost always got him what he wanted.

"Nothing's wrong. Or rather, the only thing that is wrong is that you are looking at me with that sweet face, running my 'temp-ture' up," he said in an imitation of Precious's voice that under other circumstances would have made her want to jump into his lap.

Precious stretched her body—arching her back, reaching her hands up in the air and then back behind her head, stretching out her plump legs then folding them back with her knees slightly parted, and poking out her pelvis—like she always did when Marcel was getting to her. She was amazed at her own performance.

Marcel lowered his long, inky-black lashes down over his butternut brown eyes and ran the point of his tongue slowly across his top lip—a signal that Precious was getting to him. He turned her chair back around and put soft, golden-tan colored, and cool fingers on the back of her neck. He rubbed the tense muscles with expert hands.

"Precious, you have been working too hard. Your neck is so tight." He slid his hand down her neck and rubbed her bare back. "Baby, your back is tight, too. Maybe I should order you to take a break and give that sweet brown body the attention it needs."

Precious couldn't believe Marcel. Here he was rubbing all down her back like he hadn't just gotten what sounded to her like a very good piece from a very loud woman. She was so mad she could spit tacks. But, Precious was not about to let go of this charade, not yet. She wanted to see just how far he would go. She moved her head around like she was really enjoying Marcel's massage and leaned her head back so that he could see her face.

She smiled and said. "Honey-baby, I got too much bookkeeping to go off with you this evening. If I don't balance these books, none of the girls will get their money on time. And, we both know that wouldn't do, don't we. I'm gonna have to take a raincheck and let you, with yo' sexy self, take care of me at another time. Ok, honey-baby?"

Marcel smiled what he hoped was a disappointed but acquiescent smile. He was more than relieved that Precious didn't take him up on his offer. He was in his late thirties and well past the point in his life where he could please two women in less than two hours time. He didn't know what he would have done if Precious had said yes and he wasn't able to deliver the goods.

"Well, Precious, if you say so. I guess I'll just go hop in that cold shower and hope that I can cool down long enough to last until tomorrow. You wouldn't want me tipping out, would you?"

Precious wanted to smack him. While Marcel was talking she had taken a quick glance at his pants—there was no action going on in that area of his body. "The only thing working up anything on that lyin' ass nigger is his damn mouth." She thought bitterly. "Damn dawg."

Marcel kissed her on the cheek and walked over to the door. Precious turned toward him and blew a kiss. As soon as the door closed and she heard his footsteps retreat down the hall, she pulled her purse out of one of the desk drawers and onto her lap. She dug around in her purse among a large supply of makeup and slipped her hand down under the lining at the bottom. It took her several seconds to feel that tiny piece of paper. She pulled it out of the bag and read the numbers written on the paper to herself before putting it back in her purse.

Precious zipped the purse back up and put it on the floor under the desk. She picked up the telephone and dialed the number Marcel had told her never to call. Precious had not known what she was going to do to Marcel until he had the nerve to try and get her all excited—as if promising some action (action she knew he couldn't deliver on) would cover his messy tracks.

"I should have made him try and give me some," she thought with a laugh. "But, this is so much better."

Precious removed a huge black and gold earring from her ear and put the receiver back up to her ear just in time to hear, for the first time, the voice she had been wondering about for months.

"Hello."

Precious lost her nerve at the exact moment of hearing that cultured, crisp, and very Southern sounding voice on the other end of the telephone.

"Hello."

Precious hung up the phone, rubbed her forehead and took three deep breaths. She had not counted on Saphronia sounding so properly intimidating. She had been going with Marcel for about six months—six very hot months. Precious knew that Marcel couldn't possibly be taking care of home with any decency, spending that much time with her. And, she had just imagined that a woman who wouldn't fight her man over some love time would be kind of weaklike, easily intimidated. She never dreamed that it would be her who was intimidated by a voice that was so cold, it could freeze ice.

Precious sat on her hands for three more minutes. They were cold and shaking. Sitting on her hands always made her feel better, in control, when her life got so crazy until it gave her the shakes. Precious looked back over her shoulder at the clock on the wall beside the door. In just twenty minutes, Laymond would come in for a cup of coffee and whatever treat the cook had left him for the evening. And, since he was Marcel's right-hand henchman, she certainly couldn't call that Sapphire woman with his nosey self hovering around like some vulture.

Precious took a very long and deep breath. She blew the air filling up her lungs out real slowlike. She moved her now calmed hands back to the telephone and dialed the number again. This time the hand on the other end snatched the phone off of the hook, and this hello was so cold until Precious swore she saw smoke come out of the phone—the kind of smoke that one sees on the most frigidly cold mornings.

"Uh, Uh, Honey, you don't know me but yo' husban' is cheatin' on us."

"I beg your pardon." Saphronia said in a voice that was so cold and mean that Precious almost hung up the phone again.

"I sayed that, Hun–ney . . . yo . . . huzzbannddd . . . is . . . cheat-in' . . . on . . . us. Did you hear me, Sapphire?"

"I do not have the slightest idea concerning who you are and what you are talking about. But, I am certain that you are an improper-talking nuisance who has, in a moment of extreme confusion, dialed the wrong telephone number."

"Sapphire, wait. Pleaz don't hang up the phone."

"Why not? You do not even know me. You are trying to reach Sapphire and my name, slow woman, is Saphronia. Can you say that? Sa-phro-ni-a."

"Shit." Precious thought. "How in the hell could I have mistaken this cold-ass bitch for a Sapphire?"

"Look, Miz Brown. That is yo' name ain't it?"

Saphronia didn't answer and she didn't hang up the telephone either.

"Uh-huh. I thought so. Now, like I just sayed."

"I know, I know. My husband is allegedly having conjugal relations with a woman other than you or I." Saphronia said in a bored voice.

Precious thought to herself, "What in the hell is she talkin' 'bout." And she said, "Yea, right."

Look, is yo' man named, Marcel? Rev. Marcel DeMarcus Brown?"

"That is correct."

"Well then let me tell you a few things about yo' Reverend. In fact, you and me needs to talk, cause I just caught his ass red-handed in the act, if you know what I mean."

Saphronia started to laugh silently to herself. Of all the telephone calls she expected to get, she never thought she would get one from the latest link in Marcel's chain of fools. And, now this woman, who had laid up with a married man, had the audacity to be angry about his philandering. Didn't that poorly spoken fool know that lusting and satisfying that lust was more Marcel's calling than being a minister would ever be?

Saphronia was shaken out of these thoughts when in the midst of Precious's tirade, Precious said, "And, you know Sapphire, I mean, Saphronia, I think we needs to get together and fix Marcel's bumpin 'n grindin' ass."

This time, Saphronia laughed out loud. It was a refined kind of laugh—one that sounded like crystal when it connected with itself. She had to admit that Marcel had definitely gotten his "bumping and grinding" behind in some hot water when he cheated on this woman. Her voice had a sliver of warmth in it when she said, "Your complaints about Marcel are quite valid. But, before we continue with this conversation, I need to at least know your name."

Precious sighed with relief—she had managed to get through to this woman. She looked back at the clock and realized that she was out of time. She lowered her voice and said hurriedly, "My name is Precious, Precious Powers. But, Sapphir . . . I mean, Saphronia, I gotta go right now. I'm at work. Call you later when I get off, okay?"

Precious hung up the telephone just as she heard Laymond's heavy footsteps in the hall. She held onto the sides of the chair to calm her hands down. She was so glad he hadn't been in the hall just seconds before. Precious was kind of scared of Laymond and didn't know what he would do if he found out she had called Marcel's wife. Laymond was always trying to preach to her and the other women at The Purgatory, about not crossing the line that separated the good church women from the bad ones in the street. Laymond opened the door and gave her that ugly-looking smile of his. Precious looked at him, thinking that he could sit up in Marcel's church twenty-four hours a day and still be just as lowdown and dirty as he could be.

"Humph, Laymond's ugly ass the one that should be throwed out the church away from the real church folk and right onto the street." Precious thought as she picked up a receipt and tried to finish balancing the books before her shift ended.

Hattie Mae Dawson

THE PREACHER TELLS A LIE

from John A. Burrison, ed., *Storytellers: Folktales & Legends from the South,*

This is a li'l story about three li'l boys. An' one of 'em had a dog, an' the othah two they didn't have a dog but they wanted one. An' every Sunday mo'nin' their parents would get 'em up an' get 'em ready ta go ta Sunday school. So, this particular Sunday they didn't want ta go ta Sunday school.

So. They got 'longside the road an' one said, "I don' wanna go ta Sunday school."

Othah un say, "Me neither."

Othah un say, "Me neither." He say, "What can we do?"

One say, "Oh, I know what we can do." Say, "We can tell a story; one tell the biggest story gits the dog."

The othah un say, "Yeah!"

The othah li'l boy he say, "Yeah!"

So. By that time the preacha come along. The preacha got there, he says, "Why-h-h-y, son. Why ain' y'all in Sunday school? Sha-a-ame, sha-a-ame! Mmm, mmm, mmm!" [Clicks tongue after each "mmm"]

An' says, "Well, Preacha, we 'as sittin' here an' the one tell the biggest story gits the dog."

He says, "Mmm, mmm. Sha-a-ame, sha-a-ame. Why, I never tol' a lie in my life."

One of 'em jump up an' say, "Give 'im the dog!"

Folk

THE MINISTER'S FRESH AIR

One Sunday the minister was preaching, and he had the people happy and everything. And all of a sudden he stop preaching, he say, "Sing a little song and say a little prayer, while the preacher goes out to get some fresh air."

And he went on out and came back, and he was preaching, just preaching! Then he stopped and say, "Sing a little song and say a little prayer while the preacher goes out to get some fresh air."

So two deacons looked at each other, say [whispering], "What is this fresh air he's talking about?" Say, "Let's go out there and check it." So they followed him out there and saw he was getting a little nip from a bottle of liquor he had hidden out there. So when he went back in they grabbed his bottle.

In the meantime, he's back in church now, just preaching, just raging—

got it going real good. Then he say, "Sing a little song and say a little prayer while the preacher go get some more fresh air."

So when he went out there, he came back in church, he say, "Don't sing another *damn* song, and don't say another *damn* prayer, cause some sonovabitch has stole my *damn* fresh air!"

Folk

OPEN THAT DOOR

This church was over on Twenty-fifth Street and the preacher was *just-t-t-t* preaching. He say, "Open that door and open it *wide-e-e-e;* let my voice ring *outside!*"

About that time one o' those coons out there threw a brick at his head. He say, "Close that door and close it quick, some sonovabitch done hit me with a brick!"

Maya Angelou

THE REVEREND HOWARD THOMAS

from *I Know Why the Caged Bird Sings*

[This selection treats the childhood of Maya Angelou when she was living in Stamps, Arkansas, with her grandmother (Momma) and brother Bailey.]

Reverend Howard Thomas was the presiding elder over a district in Arkansas that included Stamps. Every three months he visited our church, stayed at Momma's over the Saturday night and preached a loud passionate sermon on Sunday. He collected the money that had been taken in over the preceding months, heard reports from all the church groups and shook hands with the adults and kissed all small children. Then he went away. (I used to think that he went west to heaven, but Momma straightened me out. He just went to Texarkana.)

Bailey and I hated him unreservedly. He was ugly, fat, and he laughed like a hog with the colic. We were able to make each other burst with giggling when we did imitations of the thick-skinned preacher. Bailey was especially good at it. He could imitate Reverend Thomas right in front of Uncle Willie and never get caught because he did it soundlessly. He puffed out his cheeks until they looked like wet brown stones, and wobbled his head from side to side. Only he and I knew it, but that was old Reverend Thomas to a tree.

His obesity, while disgusting, was not enough to incur the intense hate that we felt for him. The fact that he never bothered to remember our names was insulting, but neither was that slight, alone, enough to make us despise him. But the crime that tipped the scale and made our hate not only just but imperative was his actions at the dinner table. He ate the biggest, brownest and best parts of the chicken at every Sunday meal.

Folk

HE REMEMBERED

from Daryl Cumber Dance, *Shuckin' and Jivin'*

This Minister could not find his hat, and he finally decided that one of the members of his church must have stolen it. He was very disturbed, and he decided to talk to his Deacon about what he should do. The Deacon suggested, "Why don't you preach on the Ten Commandments next Sunday, and then when you come to 'Thou shalt not steal' really lay it on, so that the guilty person will repent and return your hat." The Minister said, "That's a good idea. I'll try it."

So the next Sunday he got up in the pulpit and he was really laying it on strong on those Ten Commandments. He preached on "Honor thy father and thy mother"; then he preached on "Thou shalt not commit adultery." Then—he cut his sermon short.

After the service the Deacon said to him, "Reverend, you were doing so well, but you never did get to the main part of your sermon. What happened?"

He say, "Deacon Jones, I didn't need to use that part 'cause when I got to 'Thou shalt not commit adultery,' I remembered where I left my hat."

Folk

UNDER SUSPICION

Two neighborhood boys were very bad and always misbehaving. Their mother asked her minister to have a talk with them and maybe their behavior would improve. The minister decided to talk with them individually. He told the first boy about the merits of good Christian behavior. Then he asked, "Where is God?"

The boy did not answer, so the minister repeated the question more forcefully, "Where is God?"

The boy still made no reply. Then the minister grabbed him by the shoulders and demanded, *"Where is God?"*

The boy jumped up and ran home with his brother close behind. The brother asked, "What happened? Why did you run away?"

He replied, "God is missing, and they think we did it!"

Carolyn M. Rodgers

JESUS MUST OF BEEN SOME KIND OF DUDE

(for James and Esther Mitchell and family)

from *how i got ovah*

Jesus must of been
some kind of dude
even though they crucified
him
I think he whipped game on em
though
cause he strutted on up and out
again
　　after three days
　　one day for resting
　　one day for mourning
　　and one day for just getting on up

Yeah, he must of been some kind
of dude, I'm telling you
he must a been a real mean actor
walking on top of the water
feeding thousands of folks with
five loaves of bread and two little fishes
raising folks up from the dead
changing water to wine
making the dumb to talk and the blind to see

Jesus was a militant dude sisters.
A revolutionary cat brothers,
a whole lot of members saw and touched him
he was sho'nuff fuh real but remember ole
doubting Thomas who had to stick his finger in
Jesus' side before he would believe?

And Jesus had a boss black natural too
they say it was natural like lambs wool
and feet—like burnt brass

And remember when Peter and all the others was in that
ship and the wind and water was cutting up cutting em
down and they saw somebody walking on the water
      Peter thought it was a vision
      He say I gots to be seeing things now,
who done spiked the holy wine?
How this dude Jesus gon walk on
      some WATER!

But Jesus was cool and his rap was heavy, he just pulled
      Peter on
          out and don't you know
Peter walked out on the water too!

Wow, they was some
          badddd dudes. . . .

And Black men say sister loves what do you want us to do
      how you want us to be
And we say be like medgar
          a love rock like Jesus
  be like martin
        a love rock like Jesus
  be like malcolm was be–coming
          a love rock
            like Jesus

Jesus keep coming, knocking at our doors
and we don't even recognize him when we see him.

Stand up brothers and sisters and let Jesus come into
    yo heart.

A. Elizabeth Delany

PRAISING THE LORD

from *The Delany Sisters' Book of Everyday Wisdom*

BESSIE: When we walk into our house—whether we're coming back from a long trip or just from seeing the neighbors—the first thing we say is, "We're home. Praise the Lord." We do that to honor Him, to thank Him for watching over us.

Of course, there are times when I wish the Lord *wasn't* watching, like when I run my mouth or lose my temper. I try to do right; I try not to stray. As Sadie says, "If you want to climb that ladder to Heaven, you've got to treat every day as if it's Judgment Day."

I think God understands that I'm only human. He gave me this mouth, He gave me a temper, and so I'm bound to err. I'm sure I must be getting credit for trying! But every once in a while, just to keep on His path, I try to take in an old-fashioned fire-and-brimstone sermon. I'm an Episcopalian, and I appreciate the thoughtful preaching in my Church but there's nothing like fire and brimstone to set me straight

Fight fire with fire, I always say!

Folk

HELPING A LADY OUT

This man came into town and he went to see his buddy. He say, "I don't want to sound like a begger, but I'm going to move here eventually and I came to take some exams. May I spend some time with you?"

He say, "Yeah, you kin stay here thirty days if that will help you."

He say, "O.K. I just want to ask you one thing. Where are the churches?"

And the guy say, "We have one on every corner. It depends on what you want." He say, If you want that 'Humn-humn-humn' [proper and sedate humming] church, that's over there." And he say, "If you want that *'Eeee-owwww!'* [loud and abrupt] church, you can find that on every other corner."

He say, "Well, that's the one I want—if you're referring to the Baptist church."

So he went to church this particular Sunday, and he came home, he had a black eye. The roommate say, "Excuse me?"

He say, "I'm sorry, man, the church wasn't air-conditioned; the unit was broken, and we got up to sing a hymn. And the big fat lady in front of us stood up, . . . and her dress was stuck up in between her legs [illustrating it stuck in her crotch] and everybody behind her was laughing, and I felt sorry for her, and I reached over and pulled it out, and she turned around and knocked the *living* hell outta me!"

The man say, "Don't you know you don't touch women, strange women, and in church, and old women?" He say, "Man, you got so much to learn."

He say, "Well, I know better now."

Went back to the same church and came back home—the other eye was black.

He say, "I don't want to hear it."

He say, "You ain't gon believe it. The air-conditioning unit has not been fixed. Same woman. Same dress. . . . Same hymn. . . ." And say, "The dress was *way-y-y* up in her crotch [illustrating], and everybody laughing, and the man next to me felt sorry for her, and he reached over and pulled it *out*. I know she didn't want it out, so I reached over and put it back in [illustrating]."

Folk

SHALL WE GATHER AT THE RIVER

from Daryl Cumber Dance, *Shuckin' and Jivin'*

One Sunday the Preacher got up in the pulpit and he started to preachin'. He say, "For my part, you can take *all* the whiskey and throw it in the river."

A old Deacon in the front say, "A-A-A-MEN!"

He say, "For my part, you can take all the *wine* and throw it in the river."

The Deacon said, "A-A-MEN!" again.

He said, "For my part, you can take *all* of the alcohol and throw it in the river!"

The Deacon say, "A-A-A-MEN!"

So he ended his sermon.

The Deacon jumped up. He say, "Let us sing page 392, 'Shall We Gather at the River.' "

Folk

GONE TO MEDDLIN'

from Daryl Cumber Dance, *Shuckin' and Jivin'*

The Preacher was preaching one Sunday, and he was talking about the youngsters. And this Old Sister was sitting up there with a big ball of snuff in her mouth. Say the Minister said, "Yes, these youngsters now days, you can't do anything with 'em. They drink; they smoke; they stay out all late hours of the night."

The Old Sister say, [mouth obviously full of snuff] "Dat's right! [Chewing.] Pweach it, Reverend, you jes' pweach it!"

So, all of a sudden, he say, "Yeah, and some of these Old Sisters walking 'round here with snuff in their mouth and comin' to church and sittin' up here gossipin'."

She say, [mouth still full] "Shee dat," say, "now, he done stop pweachin' and gone to meddlin'."

Folk

PRAYER I

The minister said to one of the deacons, he say, "Brother, why don't you come and go with me hunting?"

So the deacon said, "Okay, I'll go with you."

And they went out hunting, and they run up on a bear. The minister said to the deacon, say, "Let's pray."

The deacon say, "A prayer is alright in a *prayer* meeting, but it ain't worth a damn in a *bear* meeting."

Folk

PRAYER II

So they went on down the road, and the deacon turned around and looked, and the preacher was praying. And the bear was behind him with his hands like this [pressed together as in prayer].

The preacher said to the deacon, "See I told you that you could calm a bear."

The bear say, "Calm shit, I'm saying grace cause I'm gon' eat your ass."

Billie Holiday

I'M THINKING IT OVER

recounted in Donald Clarke, *Wishing on the Moon*

When Billie Holiday was hospitalized with her last illness, Louis McKay, her former husband, came to visit and read her the Twenty-third Psalm. She told *New York Post* journalist Bill Duffy, "I've always been a religious bitch, but if that evil motherfucker believes in God, I'm thinking it over."

Mama Sez

You got to take God at his word. If you can believe it, you can receive it.

Those who wait to seek God at the eleventh hour, usually die at ten-thirty. [Iyanla Vanzant, *The Value in the Valley*]

The Lord helps those who help themselves.

It's better to have a star in your crown than a dollar in your pocket. After the dollar is gone, the star shines on.

What God intends for you, you'll get.

If God had meant for us to go to the moon, he'd have given us wings.

God may not give you what you ask for, but I know He answers prayer in His own way and time.

The Lord don't give you more burdens than you can bear.

She's in the right church, but the wrong pew.

Let your conscience be your guide.

You reap what you sow.

God don't like ugly.

An idle mind is the devil's workshop.

Lawd have mercy!

Lawd a mercy!

Lawd, take the day!

Lord today!

Do Jesus!

Sister to Sister

White folks go to church
They never crack a smile.
Black folks go to church
And you hear them laugh a mile.

You know he done pissed in the churchyard now [he has offended someone who has been helpful to him].

CHAPTER 6

My Sweet Papa

COURTSHIP AND GOOD LOVING

A ccounts of loving suitors and mates tend to be realistic or sentimental rather than comic, but there are a few hilarious exceptions. This
chapter presents those rituals, stories, tales, and verses that humorously
reveal or acclaim the loving qualities of the male. It is, however, a short
chapter, for the above reasons and because there are admittedly more humorous items that lament and berate the shortcomings of men.

There are in the African American community many humorous rituals
that detail a man's approaching a woman, flirting, courting, sweet-talking,
and making up after a quarrel. Sometimes these humorous commentaries
take the form of a verbal contest between two men about which one loves
and appreciates a woman's attractive qualities more or which one would do
more for her if she would choose to encourage his attentions. A number
of humorous items take the form of verbal duels between a man and a

woman, but instead of harsh putdowns and sarcastic attacks, such exchanges are often humorous rituals in which each tries to express his/her sentiments in allegorical and metaphorical language. They are made even funnier by the coy suggestion, usually on the part of the woman, that she does not understand what her suitor is suggesting. Such courtship rituals have existed from slavery to the present.

In January 1895 the *Southern Workman* published the text of a speech by folklorist Frank D. Banks to the Hampton Folk-Lore Society, in which he described the ritual of courtship among slaves on the plantation, and the journal also requested that readers send in additional information on similar rituals with which they were familiar. Mr. Banks noted the importance of the courtship rituals and the prominent role played by the experienced old slave on the plantation who instructed the young men in the art of courtship. Uncle Gilbert, the counselor to the young men on the plantation where Mr. Banks grew up, instructed his pupils thusly:

> "[A] young man mus' tes' an' prove a gal befo offerin' her his han.' Ef er gal gives a man as good anser as he gives her question, den she is all right in min.' Ef she can look him squar in de face when she talks to him, den she kin be trusted; and ef her patches is on straight, an' her close clean, den she is qwine ter keep de house straight and yer britches mended. Sich er ooman is wuth havin." [the location of apostrophes and the spelling are consistent with the original.]

Thus the man may ask the woman the traditional question in a courting ritual, "Are you a standin' dove or a flyin' lark?" (see "Sample of a 'Courtship' Conversation," p. 281 and the Hurston selection from *Jonah's Gourd Vine,* p. 288). If she responds that she is a *standin'* dove, then she is informing him that she is already involved in a relationship; however, if she describes herself as a *flyin'* lark, then she is free. He can, therefore, through this ritualistic query, approach her without the risk of receiving a direct rejection as a suitor. Furthermore, as Uncle Gilbert suggests above, her response will indicate whether she is witty enough to equal him in this ritualistic exchange.

That similar verbal banter continues in popularity in more recent times is shown through the following conversation in which Claudia Mitchell engaged with one male among a group of her interviewees for her study on signifying and other aspects of language in the black community:

ɪ: Mama, you sho is fine.

ʀ.. That ain no way to talk to your mother.

> (Laughter)

ɪ: You married?

ʀ: Um-hm.

ɪ: Is your husband married?

> (Laughter)

ʀ: Very.

---

i: Baby, you a real scholar. I can tell you want to learn. Now if you'll just cooperate a li'l bit, I'll show you what a good teacher I am. But first we got to get into my area of expertise.

ʀ: I may be wrong but seems to me we already in your area of expertise.

> (Laughter)

ɪ: You ain't so bad yourself, girl. I ain't heard you stutter yet."

["Language Behavior in a Black Urban Community"]

In this familiar ritual, the interviewee has learned that the researcher is not available, but the nature of the conversation prevents her response from being a direct rejection of his attentions; indeed he has been given tacit permission to continue the game at which he observes that she is equally adept. Here, as is often the case, a significant factor in the verbal contest is the presence and response of the audience (the other male interviewees who are the source of laughter during the above exchange).

No author has made more extensive use of the traditional courtship routines than the noted folklorist and novelist Zora Neale Hurston, who has dramatized scenes of the teasing banter between couples in several of her novels, short stories, and plays (notably *Their Eyes Were Watching God, Jonah's Gourd Vine,* "The Gilded Six-Bits," "Story in Harlem Slang," and *Mule Bone* [coauthored with Langston Hughes]). Similar rituals of flirtation and courtship, familiar to the black folk community, have found their way into vaudeville acts, folk musical forms (such as the blues), and the works of literary writers. They have been observed and recorded as well by numerous folklorists and anthropologists, some of the most interesting accounts appearing in the *Southern Workman* in 1895 and 1896 and in Hurston's anthropological work *Mules and Men*.

Courtship rituals also often advance to sharper duels in which the couples sometimes playfully attack each other for a variety of shortcomings, a practice that Barbara Monroe labels "post-courtship." Obviously the line between the playful romantic banter designed to win affection and the increasingly hostile banter designed to denigrate and defeat is not always clear cut. There is no question, however, that the aggressive and bitter repartee that characterizes the dozens[1] has moved to the other side of the line. This chapter focuses upon the more loving and romantic verbal banter, that designed, in the words of Hurston, to "deny affection but in reality flaunted it," while that intended to deflate and to wound is found in Chapter 7.

Other popular humorous forms rely on a play on words. One is the romantic brag. When brags are designed to build up one's lover, they are included here. When they are designed to assert one's superior verbal dexterity and sexual potency at the expense of the partner, they are placed in the following chapter. There are also the accounts of the efforts of blacks to imitate in their courtship rituals romantic exchanges that they have overheard; these turn on the fact that they invariably make the most ridiculous errors in their efforts to emulate their more sophisticated white masters and mistresses.

One special form of black humor that makes use of verbal duels, romantic brags, and courtship rituals deserves special mention here: male/female vaudeville teams developed their own unique blend of comedy in the first quarter of this century. They were an obvious outgrowth of plantation minstrels and later white minstrelsy in blackface, which imitated and modeled itself on the former. The most popular of these acts were among the

---

1. The dozens is the most recognized term for a popular form of verbal duel common throughout Africa and the African diaspora, in which the combatants exchange insults, often in rhymed couplets and most often directed toward the opponent's mother. The goal in the game is to maintain your cool while responding with a greater and more humorous and more eloquent and more obscene insult. In the United States the following terms are sometimes used to describe similar duels: snapping, busting, woofing, cutting, chopping, downing, capping, slipping, sounding, ranking, signifying, cracking, dissing, bagging, hiking, joning, ranking, and ribbing.

best paid performers on the T.O.B.A. circuit, notorious for its harsh demands and its low pay (T.O.B.A. stood for Theater Owners Booking Association, but those on the circuit often joked that it stood for Tough on Black Asses). Teams such as Stringbeans and Sweetie May and later Butterbeans and Susie danced and sang and verbally attacked and challenged each other, using risque lyrics and provocative gestures that provoked criticisms of obscenity and stereotypical comedy. At times their exchanges were quite menacing and agonistic and they frequently threatened to leave each other. In one routine when Susie declares she is leaving, Butterbeans warns, "A ground hog will deliver your mail," and goes on to declare, "There'll be flowers and you won't smell 'em on the day you change your name, baby![2] Despite such bluster, the sense of their love for each other often was obvious, with Butterbeans declaring in one routine that for love of Susie, "I'd fight all the animals in the jungle or even in the zoo, [sic] I'd grab a lion and smack his face and tear a tiger in two!"[3]

Thus though African American women know that love may not always be perfect, they derive a great deal of pleasure from laughing about a Sweet Papa who, whatever his flaws, can ultimately be counted on to *TCB—take care of business!*

Honey, hush!

Anonymous

SAMPLE OF A "COURTSHIP" CONVERSATION

from *Southern Workman*

He. My dear kin' miss, has you any objections to me drawing my cher to yer side, and revolvin' de wheel of my conversation around de axle of your understandin'?

She. I has no objection to a gentleman addressin' me in a proper manner, kin' sir.

2. Cited in "Butterbeans and Susie," *Ebony,* 61.
3. Cited in Marshall and Jean Sterns, "Frontiers of Humor," 231.

He. My dear miss, de worl' is a howlin' wilderness full of devourin' animals, and you has got to walk through hit. Has you made up yer min' to walk through hit by yersef, or wid some bol' wahyer?

She. Yer 'terrigation, kin' sir, shall be answered in a ladylike manner, ef you will prove to me dat it is not for er form and er fashion dat you put de question.

He. Dear miss, I would not so impose on a lady like you as to as' her a question for a form an' a fashion. B'lieve me, kin' miss, dat I has a pertickler object in ingagin' yer in conversation dis afternoon.

She. Dear kin' sir, I has knowed many a gentleman to talk wid wise words and flatterin' looks, and at de same time he may have a deceivin' heart. May I as' yer, kin' gentleman, ef you has de full right to address a lady in a pertickler manner?

He. I has, kin miss. I has seen many sweet ladies, but I has never up to dis day an' time lef' de highway of a single gentleman to foller dese beacon lights. But now, kin' miss, as I look in yer dark eyes, and sees yer hones' face, and hears yer kind voice, I mus' confess, dear lady, dat I would be joyous to come to yer beck and call in any time of danger.

She. Den, kin' sir, I will reply in anser to your 'terrigation in de fus place, sence I think you is a hones' gentleman dat I feels dat a lady needs de pertection of a bol' wahyer in dis worl' where dere's many wil' animals and plenty of danger.

He. Den, kin' honored miss, will you condescen' to encourage me to hope dat I might, some glorious day in de future, walk by yer side as a perteckter?

She. Kin' sir, ef you thinks you is a bol' wahyor I will condescend to let you pass under my observation from dis day on, an' ef you proves wuthy of a confidin' ladies' trus', some lady might be glad to axcept yer pertection—and dat lady might be me.

———

[1.] Kin' lady, are yo' a standin' dove or a flyin' lark? Would you decide to trot in double harness and will you give de mos excrutish pleasure of rollin' de wheels of de axil, accordin' to your understandin'? If not my tracks will be col' an' my voice will not be heard aroun' your do! I would bury my tomihawks an' dwell upon de [word unclear] of mos' any T.

[2.] Kin' lady, ef I was to go up between de heavens and de yeath an drop down a grain of wheat over ten acres of land an' plow it up wid a rooster fedder, would you marry me?

———

[3.] Kin' lady, s'pose you was to go long de road an' meet a pet rabbit, would you take it home an' call it a pet o' yourn?

[4.] Good lady, ef you was to come down de riber an' you saw a red stran' o' thread, black o' white, which one would you choose to walk on? (In the answer, the color of the thread given is the color of the man she would accept.)

———

[5.] Kin' lady, since I have been travlin' up hill, vally an mountain, I nebber seed a lady dat suit my fancy mo' so dan you does. Now is you a towel dat had been spun, or a towel dat had been woven. (Answer—If spun, single.)

[6.] Good lady, I was in a garden in my dream an' I saw de lovelies' table an on de table was a fine cake an' a glass of wine, an' a beaut ful lady was walkin' in de garden, and you were de lady. Ef you saw a peas hull in de garden which one would you choose,—one wid one pea in it or a hull full of peas. (Answer, The hull with one pea is a single man, the hull full of peas is a widower with children.)

———

Are you a rag on the bush or a rag off the bush? (Answer—If a rag on the bush, free, if off, engaged.)

I saw three ships on the water, one full rigged, one half-rigged, and one with no rigging at all. Which would you rather be? (Full rigged, married; half-rigged engaged; no rigging, single.)

Sometimes the girl wishes to find out her friends' intentions. *If so* it may be done without loss of dignity through the following circumlocution:

"Suppose you was walkin' by de side o' de river an dere was three ladies in a boat, an' dat boat was overturned, which lady would you save, a tall lady or a short lady or a middle-sided lady?"

If the young man declares his desire to save a lady corresponding in height to his questioner she may rest assured that his intentions are serious. He may perhaps add the following tender avowal:

"Dear miss, ef I was starvin' an' had jes one ginger-cake, I would give you half, an' dat would be de bigges' half."

Should a girl find herself unable to understand the figurative speech of her lover she may say "Sir, you are a huckleberry beyond my persimmon," and may thus retire in good form from a conversation in which her readiness in repartee has not been equal to her suitor's skill in putting sentimental questions.

Anonymous

A DIFFICULT COURTSHIP

from *Southern Workman*

This is a conversation between a young lady and a gentleman. The girl's father wants her to marry a man with an education, so she consults with her father about the young man who is coming to see her.

SCENE I.

The first call.

HE.—"Good evening, kind miss."

SHE.—"Good evening, sir."

HE.—"Large circumstances (circles) round the moon."

SHE.—"Sir?"

HE.—"Kind miss, your eyes look like terriable dog eyes," (turtle dove eyes).

SHE.—"Oh, no sir."

HE.—"Oh, kind lady, you have gained my heart."

SHE.—"Yes, sir."

HE.—"Lady, may I have the pleasure of coming from my residence to your happy home to gain your heart and mind?"

SHE.—"Oh, sir, you will have to ask my father."

HE.—"Do your father allow you to keep company, lady?"

SHE.—"Yes, sir, with a gentleman of education."

HE.—"I shall call some other evening, lady, to see you again. Good bye."

He goes away to get some one to teach him some large words and how to use them, when he calls on the young lady another time.

S C E N E I I .

The girl is consulting with her father.

SHE.—"Father, have you any objections to my getting married?"

FATHER.—"To whom, daughter?"

SHE.—"To the milkman on Mars George plantation."

FATHER.—"Is he got any learning?"

SHE.—"Yes, father, you just ought to hear him split dick," (dictionary.)

FATHER.—"Yes, daughter, when will he be here?"

SHE.—"This evening, I think. He was here last night."

S C E N E I I I .

(Daughter alone. Father in next room where he can hear the conversation. Young man raps at the door and enters.)

SHE.—"Good evening, sir."

HE.—"Good evening, kind miss. Seems as if I have seen you several times during the past, and your bewildering countenance has taken such impression on my heart, till necessity compels me to ask you one question."

SHE.—"Oh, kind sir, have you come from the plantation to-night?"

HE.—"Yes, miss, all the way by the marl spring."

SHE.—"It is no use for you to come from your residence to my home to gain my heart and mind, because the chunk is gone out and you can't kindle it, the road is grown up and you can't clear it, the spring is gone dry and you can't get any water out of it."

(Then she turns and goes out to supper, leaving her caller in the room. While at supper she and her father converse together.)

FATHER.—"Help yourself, daughter."

SHE.—"I have eaten sufficiently. Any more would be conbunctious to my system."

FATHER.—*(Not understanding the large words)* "Have you been out fishing?"

SHE.—"No, eaten a plenty."

FATHER.—"Caught twenty? Why, we had better have some for break-fast."

(The girl now goes back into the room and the conversation between her and her visitor begins again.)

HE.—"For several times I have attempted, my heart failing me each time. Now with the greatest and last resolution that ever human was en-dowed with, I again ask you for your heart, your hand and your all."

SHE.—"Wait until I see my father. *(Goes out.)* Father, the young man wants my heart, my hand and my all."

FATHER.—"What does he want? Wait a minute, and I will go and get them for him."

(Father goes and gets his brass rasp, (meaning the heart) a turkey wing, (for the hand) and the shoe awl. These he gives to his daughter.)

SHE.—"Oh, father, he means me."

FATHER.—"You are too young to marry, daughter send him away."

(She goes out and tell the young man all the conversation between her father and herself. Then she recites to him these lines.)

When I become of age
　I promise to marry thee,
If father won't consent
　I'll run away with you.

(After this the young man goes off to sea and stays a long while or until the girl becomes of age. Then he writes her the following letter.)

Dear Pollie:

　　　I will now write you a few notes, and if your heart is willing, some day I will be at your house.

You ask your dear old father,
　The sad and story tell
That I am the one that loves you,
　Oh, yes, I love you well.
And if he says you can marry
　The man he turned away,

If not too young to marry
    Will you write the wedding day?
Still land and sea divides us,
    Your face I can not see,
Still I am the man that loves you.
    Pollie, do you love me?
I love you as I foresaid,
    Morning, mid-day and night:
You are the rainbow on my port bow
    And the light-house on my right.
Pollie, my dear, good night.
    J.

Penny Williams

GOING COURTING

from George P. Rawick ed., *North Carolina Narratives.* vol. 15 of *The American Slave.*

"Dar wus some nigger mens what 'ud go coutin' spite of de debil, an' as de marster ain't gibin' dem no passes dey goes widout 'em. Mr. Whitaker, he whups, an' whups, but dat ain't stop 'em. At las' Marster Lawrence 'cides ter hang cowbells on dere necks so's he can hyar dem if'en dey leabes de place atter night.

"I'se tellin' you chile, dem niggers am gwin' anyway. Dey ain't got sense nuff ter put dere han's in de bell ter keep de clapper from ringin', but dey does stuff de bell wid leaves an' it doan ring none, 'sides dat dey tears deir shirts, or steals sheets from missus clothes line an' fold dem ter make a scarf. Dey ties dese 'roun' deir necks ter hide de bell an' goes on a-courtin'.

"Dey ain't got no pins ter pin de scarf on, but dey uses thornes from de locust tree or de crabapple; an' dey hol's fine.

Violet Guntharpe

THE HAPPIEST MINUTE

from Belinda Hurmence, ed., *Before Freedom*

My mammy stay on with the same marster till I was grown, that is fifteen, and Thad got to looking at me, meek as a sheep and dumb as a calf. I had to ask that nigger right out what his intentions was, before I get him to bleat out that he love me. Him name Thad Guntharpe.

I glance at him one day at the pigpen when I was slopping the hogs. I say, "Mr. Guntharpe, you follows me night and morning to this pigpen; do you happen to be in love with one of these pigs? If so, I'd like to know which one 'tis. Then sometime I come down here by myself and tell that pig about your affections."

Thad didn't say nothing but just grin. Him took the slop bucket out of my hand and look at it, all round it, put upside down on the ground, and set me down on it. Then, he fall down there on the grass by me and blubber out and warm my fingers in his hands.

I just took pity on him and told him mighty plain that he must limber up his tongue and ask something, say what he mean, wanting to visit them pigs so often.

Us carry on foolishness about the little boar shoat pig and the little sow pig, then I squeal in laughter. The slop bucket tipple over and I lost my seat. That ever remain the happiest minute of my eighty-two years.

Zora Neale Hurston

JONAH'S GOURD VINE

Out on the porch John said softly, "Meet me tuhmorrer 'cross de branch by dat swee' gum tree 'bout fo' o'clock."

"Aw right. Aincha goin'tuh stay and have some dinner wid us?"

"Naw, Ah don't choose none. Dey got baked chicken at de big house and Ah eats from dere whenever An wants tuh. You gointer be sho' tuh be at our tree?"

"Unhunh."

"Sho now?"

"Unhunh."

"S'pos'n yo' mah uh some of de rest of 'em ketch yuh?"

Lucy threw herself akimbo. "Humph, dey can't do nothin' but beat me, and if dey beat me, it so won't kill me, and if dey kill me dey sho can't eat me. Ah'll be dere jus' as sho as gun's iron."

" 'Bye den, Lucy. Sho wisht Ah could smack yo' lips."

"Whut's dat you say, John?"

"Oh nothin'. 'Bye. Doan let de booger man ketch yuh."

"Don't let ole Raw-Head-and-Bloody-Bones waylay yuh neither."

John was at the tree long before Lucy. He was sitting on the knurly-roots tying his handkerchief into a frogknot when he saw her coming diffidently down the hill on the Potts side of the branch. Presently she was standing before him.

" 'Lo, Lucy."

"Hello, John. Ah see you fixin' tuh make soap."

"Whut make you say dat, Lucy?"

"Ah see yuh got yo' bones piled up."

She pointed to his crossed legs and they both laughed immoderately.

"Miss Lucy, uh Lucy, whyn't yuh have some set down?"

"Unrack yo' bones den and make room."

Lucy sat down. John untied his handkerchief and Lucy plaited rope-grass. John attempted another knot but fumbled it nervously. Lucy caught hold of the handkerchief also.

"Lemme he'p yuh wid dat, John. Ah know how tuh tie dat. Heah, you take dem two corners and roll 'em whilst Ah git dese fixed."

They both held the handkerchief taut between them. But before the knot could be tied John pulled hard and made Lucy lean towards him.

"Lucy, something been goin' on inside uh me fuh uh long time."

Diffidently, "Whut, John?"

"Ah don't know, Lucy, but it boils up lak syrup in de summer time."

"Maybe you needs some sassafras root tuh thin yo' blood out."

"Naw, Lucy, Ah don't need no sassafras tea. You know whuss de matter wid me—but ack lak you dumb tuh de fack."

Lucy suddenly lost her fluency of speech. She worked furiously at the love-knot.

"Lucy, you pay much 'tention tuh birds?"

"Unhunh. De Jay bird say 'Laz'ness will kill you,' and he go to hell ev'ry Friday and totes uh grain uh sand in his mouf tuh put out de fire, and den de doves say, 'Where you *been* so long?' "

John cut her short. "Ah don't mean dat way, Lucy. Whut Ah wants tuh know is, which would you ruther be, if you had yo' ruthers—uh lark uh flyin', uh uh dove uh settin'?"

"Ah don't know whut you talkin' 'bout, John. It mus' be uh new rid-dle."

"Naw 'tain't, Lucy. Po' me, Lucy. Ahm uh one wingded bird. Don't leave me lak dat, Lucy."

Suddenly Lucy shouted, "Look, John, de knot is tied right, ain't it pretty?"

"Yeah, Lucy iss sho pretty. We done took and tied dis knot, Miss Lucy, less tie uh 'nother one."

"You got mo' han'kerchiefs in yo' pocket?"

"Naw. Ah ain't studyin' 'bout no hankechers neither. De knot Ah wants tuh tie wid you is de kind dat won't come uh loose 'til us rises in judgment. You knows mah feelings."

"How Ah know whut you got inside yo' mind?"

"Yeah yuh do too. Y'all lady people sho do make it hard fuh us men folks. Look me in de eye Lucy. Kiss me and loose me so Ah kin talk."

There was an awkward bumping of mouths. Lucy had had her first kiss.

"Lucy, Ah looked up intuh Heben and Ah seen you among de angels right 'round de throne, and when Ah seen *you,* mah heart swole up and put wings on mah shoulders, and Ah 'gin tuh fly 'round too, but Ah never would uh knowed yo' name if ole Gab'ull hadn't uh whispered it tuh me."

He extended his hands appealingly.

"Miss Lucy, how 'bout changin' frum Potts tuh Pearson?"

"Yeah, John."

"When?"

"Whenever you ready fuh me. You know mo' 'bout dat dan Ah do."

"How 'bout on yo' birthday, Lucy? Us kin make merry fuh uh heap uh things den at de same time."

"Aw right, John."

Zora Neale Hurston

STORY IN HARLEM SLANG

[Jelly and Jam, two young Harlem jive cats, are hanging out on a street corner, bragging about their women and their escapades when they look up the Avenue and notice a young lady coming.]

Both went into the pose and put on the look.

"Big stars falling!" Jelly said out loud when she was in hearing distance. "It must be just before day!"

"Yeah, man!" Sweet Back agreed. "Must be a recess in Heaven—pretty angel like that out on the ground."

The girl drew abreast of them, reeling and rocking her hips.

"I'd walk clear to Diddy-Wah-Diddy to get a chance to speak to a pretty lil' ground-angel like that," Jelly went on.

"Aw, man, you ain't willing to go very far. Me, I'd go slap to Ginny-Gall, where they eat cow-rump, skin and all."

The girl smiled, so Jelly set his hat and took the plunge.

"Baby," he crooned, "what's on de rail for de lizard?"

The girl halted and braced her hips with her hands. "A Zigaboo down in Georgy, where I come from, asked a woman that one time and the judge told him 'ninety days.' "

"Georgy!" Sweet Back pretended to be elated. "Where 'bouts in Georgy is you from? Delaware?"

"Delaware?" Jelly snorted. "My people! My people! Free schools and dumb jigs! Man, how you going to put Delaware in Georgy? You ought to know dat's in Maryland."

"Oh, don't try to make out youse no northerner, you! Youse from right down in 'Bam your ownself!" The girl turned on Jelly.

"Yeah, I'm *from* there and I aims to stay from there."

"One of them Russians, eh?" the girl retorted. "Rushed up here to get away from a job of work."

That kind of talk was not leading towards the dinner table.

"But baby!" Jelly gasped. "Dat shape you got on you! I bet the Coca Cola Company is paying you good money for the patent!"

The girl smiled with pleasure at this, so Sweet Back jumped in.

"I know youse somebody swell to know. Youse real people. You grins like a regular fellow." He gave her his most killing look and let it simmer in. "These dickty jigs round here tries to smile. S'pose you and me go inside the café here and grab a hot?"

Mary Carter Smith

CINDY ELLIE, A MODERN FAIRY TALE

Once upon a time, over in East Baltimore, there lived a happy family: Sam Johnson, his wife Lula, and their daughter Ellie. Lula was good and kind; a quiet, church-going woman but mighty puny and sickly. One day Lula called Ellie to her bedside. "Child, Mama ain't feeling so well. One of these days I might leave you." "Oh, Mama, don't say that," Ellie said with tears in her eyes. "Don't cry, child. All of us go sometime, and I'd rather it be me than you. So there are a few things I want to tell you. Always mind your daddy. Stay in church, go to school, and learn that book. Remember what I'm telling you." "All right, Mama, I'll remember."

One day, not long after, the poor woman just up and died; real peaceful-like and quiet.

Honey, let me tell you, they had a beautiful funeral. Sam sure put her away nice. The Senior Choir turned out full force. The Junior Choir was there. And the Gospel Chorus just sung their hearts out! The church was crowded! Folks all on the outside, with loudspeakers going. Lula's lodge sisters was there in their white dresses, and them purple sashes all edged in gold. Ellie was on the first row beside her daddy. Just as cute as she could be in a white dress and her hair in a fine bush. Ellie was one purty young black sister, her skin like black velvet.

Child, let me tell you, that poor woman's body wasn't hardly cold before them church sisters was after Sam Johnson like flies after honey! 'Cause he had a good job down Sparrow's Point, with lots of seniority. And they had just paid for one of them pretty, big houses on Broadway, with them pretty white marble steps. It was a lovely block; won first prize in the AFRO Clean Block three years running!

That poor man, like so many good men, was weak for a pretty face and big legs and big hips. One huzzy, the boldest of 'em all, had a heart as hard as a rock. The milk of human kindness had curdled in her breast. But she did have a pretty face, big legs, and great big hips. Ooh-wee! She could put on! Made like she loved Ellie so, and was always bringing good barbecued ribs, collard greens, cracklin' bread, and jelly-layer cake to Ellie and Sam. Well, that fool man fell right into that woman's trap. She had that man cornered and married before you could say, "Jackie Robinson."

Then bless my soul. You ain't never seen such a change in nobody! First off that woman went down to Souse Car'lina for her two big-footed, ugly gals her Mama'd been keeping. Brought them back to Baltimore, and put poor Ellie out of the pretty room with the canopied bed and let her ugly gals sleep in that pretty room. Made poor little Ellie sleep on a pallet in the cellar.

Now Ellie's mama had been wise. When everybody else was converting they furnaces to oil and gas, she said, "Uh-uh. One day they gone be hard to get." She had kept her coal furnace. Poor little Ellie had to do all the cooking, cleaning, washing, and ironing. She had to scrub them marble steps twice a day and wait on them ugly gals hand and foot. Not only that, but in the winter she had to keep the fire going and clean out the ashes and cinders. So they got to calling her Cindy Ellie.

Tell you the truth, I believe that woman had put some roots on that man! 'Cause no matter how she mistreated Cindy Ellie, he never said a word, just *crazy* 'bout that big-legged woman.

That November, the good white folks, the good Asian folks, and the good black folks all turned out and voted for a good black brother, running for mayor. And he won the election by a landslide! He was having his inauguration ball down at the convention center. So many folks voted for him that they had to hold it for two nights running. The mayor's son had come home from college to go to the ball.

Oh, them stepsisters was primping and buying designer gowns to go to the ball. Poor Cindy Ellie had to give one a perm, the other a jheri curl, and both of them facials; not that it helped much. Honey, them gals was ugly from the inside out!

"Cindy Ellie, don't you wish you could go to the ball?" they asked her.

"Oh, you are making fun of me," Cindy Ellie said.

So Cindy Ellie's daddy, her stepmother, and then two ugly gals all went to the ball and left poor Cindy Ellie home.

Now Cindy Ellie had a godma. She had been her dear mama's best friend, and she still had a key to the house. She came to the house, as she often did, to sneak food to poor Cindy Ellie and found the child lying on her hard pallet, just crying her heart out!

"Why are you crying, child?" she asked her.

"Be–because I want to go to the ball."

Now this godma had been born with a veil over her face, down in New Orleans. She knew a thing or two about voodoo and hoodoo. Besides that, she had a High John the Conqueror Root that she always used for good. The godma told Cindy Ellie, "Go upstairs to the kitchen, child. Look in the kitchen cabinet drawer and bring me the biggest white onion you can find." Cindy Ellie was an obedient child. She didn't ask, "Why?" She just did what her godma told her to do. Cindy Ellie brought her the onion. She gave it to her godma. Then they went out in the backyard. The godma laid that onion on the ground. Then she stepped back and waved that root over that onion! And right before their eyes that onion turned into a long white Cadillac that parked itself in the back alley!

"Cindy Ellie go up on the third floor and bring me that mouse trap." Cindy Ellie brought it down. There were two little black mice trapped in a little cage. She told Cindy Ellie to open the door and them mice started out. But that godma waved that root over them and they turned into two six–foot–tall black chauffeurs dressed in shining white uniforms with fancy white caps! And they had on long black boots! And they was bowing and scraping. "All right, Cindy Ellie, you can go to the ball now."

"But, godma, look at me. I'm clean but I'm ragged."

"Don't worry 'bout it," her godma said. Then she stepped back and waved that root over Cindy Ellie. Her rags turned into a dazzling dress of pink African laces! Her hair was braided into a hundred shining braids, and on the end of each braid were beads of pure gold. Her eyes were beautifully shaded and her skin was shining like polished ebony! Golden bracelets covered her arms clean up to her elbows! On each ear hung five small diamond earrings. On her tiny feet were dainty golden sandals encrusted with dazzling jewels! Cindy Ellie was laid back!

As one of the chauffeurs helped her into the white Cadillac her godma told her, "Be sure you leave before midnight or you'll be as you was. Your Cadillac will turn back into an onion, your chauffeurs into mice, and your clothes into rags." Cindy Ellie promised her godma that she would leave before midnight. Away she went, as happy as could be.

The mayor's son heard that a beautiful girl had arrived who looked like an African princess. He came out to see and said to himself, "This sure is a fine fox!" He asked her, "May I escort you into the ballroom?" Cindy Ellie replied in tones soft and low, "I don't mind if you do." He helped her out of her limousine and escorted her into the ballroom and to the head table where he was sitting. Every eye was on Cindy Ellie. You could have heard a pin drop. Then voices could be heard, "Gorgeous," "Lovely," "Devastating," "Elegant," etc. Even the mayor himself could not take his eyes off her. His wife agreed that she was indeed a charming young woman. The other ladies were looking at her clothes and wishing they had material in their gowns as beautiful as that in Cindy Ellie's.

Although the table was loaded with sumptuous food, Toussaint, the mayor's son, couldn't eat a bite! Just busy looking at Cindy Ellie. In her honor, the band played the Ghanian High-Life. Cindy Ellie and Toussaint danced it as if they had been dancing together all their lives. Cindy Ellie was friendly and courteous to everyone she met. She even sat beside her stepsisters (who had no idea who she was) and invited them to come back the next night. For Toussaint had begged Cindy Ellie to return for the second night of the ball.

Then Cindy Ellie heard the clock strike forty-five minutes after eleven! She murmered to Toussaint, "Really, I must be getting home." And she rushed out as fast as she could go.

As soon as she was home Cindy Ellie called her godma and thanked her for such a splendid time. The doorbell rang and she heard her stepsisters' voices: "Hurry, stupid! Open the door!" Cindy Ellie came, yawning and rubbing her eyes, as if she'd been asleep. "Did you have a good time?" she asked. "Oh, it was all right, but we didn't get to dance with the mayor's son. He danced only with some new girl. No one had seen her before. She had on some old African clothes. But on her they did look good. She did have the good sense to recognize what quality people we are, and she had the mayor's son invite all of us tomorrow night. "What was her name?" asked Cindy Ellie. "No one knows. The mayor's son is dying to find out who she is." Cindy Ellie said, "You don't mean it. Oh, how I wish I could go to the ball tomorrow night. Lillie, won't you lend me your old blue gown so I can go also?" They almost split their sides laughing. "You, with your ragged self, going to the inauguration ball? Wouldn't that be something else! Of course not. Come and help us get undressed and turn back the covers on the bed so we can go to sleep."

As on the night before, poor little Cindy Ellie was left behind while the rest of them went to the ball again. Her godma came in and heard the child crying again. "Why you crying, child? You want to go to that ball again?" "Yes, ma'am." "I thought so. You've been a good child all your life, and you always respect your elders. So don't worry. You can go to the ball again. Now dry your eyes and get your face together. Look in that kitchen cabinet drawer and bring me the biggest yellow onion you can find." Cindy Ellie came back with the biggest yellow onion you ever laid your eyes on. Then they went out in the backyard. The godma laid that onion on the ground. Then she stepped back and waved that root over that onion! And right before their eyes that onion turned into a solid gold Mercedes-Benz about half a block long! And it parked itself in the back alley.

"Cindy Ellie, go up on the third floor and bring me that rat trap." Cindy Ellie brought it down. There were two big white rats trapped in a big wire cage.

That family lived so close to Johns Hopkins Hospital that mice and rats used to escape from them laboratories up there. They took that cage out in the backyard. She told Cindy Ellie to open the door and them rats started out. But that godma stood back and waved that High John the Conqueror root over them, and they turned into two seven-foot-tall white chauffeurs dressed in shining gold uniforms with fancy gold caps! And they had on shining white boots! And they was bowing and scraping.

"All right, Cindy Ellie, you can go to the ball now."

"But godma, look at me. I'm clean but I'm ragged."

"Don't worry 'bout it," her godma said. Then she stepped back and waved that root over Cindy Ellie. Her rags turned into a dress made of pure silk kente, that royal cloth from Ghana! Worth thousands of dollars! On her head was a geelee of the rarest of taffeta, standing tall and stiff and just gorgeous! Her big pretty eyes were beautifully shaded, and her skin was shining like polished ebony. Golden bracelets covered her arms clean up to her shoulders! On each ear hung five small diamond earrings. On her tiny feet were dainty golden sandals encrusted with dazzling jewels. She was cool!

As one of the chauffeurs helped her into that gold Mercedes-Benz, her godma told her, "Be sure you leave before midnight or you'll be as you was. That Mercedes-Benz will turn back into an onion, your chauffeurs into rats, and your clothes into rags." Cindy Ellie promised her godma that she would leave before midnight. Away she went, as happy as could be.

As they drove up, Toussaint was waiting for her. She went into the ball-room draped on his arm. Oh, they was having such a good time laughing and talking and cha-cha-chaing and waltzing and boogeying! That poor child forgot all about time! Then she heard the clock as it began to strike twelve! She ran out of there as fast as her legs would carry her. She ran so fast, she ran out of one of those sandals. She put the other in her hand and ran on. Toussaint ran behind her, but he couldn't see where she had gone. He picked up the golden sandal.

He asked the security people, "Did you see an African princess run by you?" "No. We did see a girl dressed in rags run out of the door. We thought she had stole something. But that chick was gone!"

That night when the family came home from the ball they told Cindy Ellie, "Something mighty strange happened tonight. As the clock on city hall began to strike twelve that African princess began to run like crazy! She ran so fast, she ran out of one of her golden sandals. The mayor's son found it and kept it. He just kept looking at it. He's really upset over that sister."

Child, the next day the mayor's son came on television, came on the radio, and announced to every paper in Baltimore that he would marry the girl whose foot would fit that sandal he had picked up. Now a lot of folks who had supported the mayor lived in the places surrounding Baltimore. So first all them sorority girls and debutantes and folks like that tried to fit their foot in that sandal. Wouldn't fit none of them girls in Columbia, Cockeysville, Randallstown, and places like that. Then they went to them rich folks' houses up on Cadillac Row and places like that. Wouldn't fit none of them girls neither. Then they went to all them condominiums downtown by The Inner Harbor and them fancy town houses. Wouldn't fit none of them neither. Finally they come to East Baltimore. Length and long they came to Broadway and knocked at the Johnsons' residence. The mayor's men came in with that golden sandal on a red velvet pillow. Them two stepsisters tried their best to put on that shoe! They pushed and they jugged. But their big feet would not get into that shoe. No way, Jose! "May

I try?" asked Cindy Ellie. "No, stupid. It's not for the likes of you." "Yes, you may try on the sandal," the mayor's representative said. "For the proclamation issued by the mayor said that any girl in Baltimore and surrounding areas may try." He spoke kindly to Cindy Ellie. "Sit down, miss, and see if it fits you." And do you know, that sandal just slid on Cindy Ellie's little foot as smooth as silk. Then she pulled from the pocket in her clean but ragged dress the other sandal. As soon as she put it on her foot, right there before their very eyes, Cindy Ellie was transformed into the African princess they had seen the nights before! Them two stepsisters had a fit! "Oh, Cindy Ellie, we didn't mean no harm! Oh, Cindy Ellie, please forgive us!" They was on the floor rolling round and carrying on.

Cindy Ellie told them, "Get up off that floor and stop all that whooping and hollering. I forgive you."

Then Cindy Ellie was transported to the mayor's mansion in his private limousine. Toussaint was there waiting to welcome her with open arms. Cindy Ellie was true to her word, for she not only forgave her stepsisters in word but in deed. She found them two ugly councilmen for husbands. Toussaint and Cindy Ellie were married in the biggest Baptist church in East Baltimore, and the reception was held in the convention center. And they lived happily, happily forever after.

Rita Dove

THROUGH THE IVORY GATE

"Now that you're here, you might as well get a little advice from someone who knows what's what. You think you know everything just 'cause you've been to the university and all those fancy places people think mean something. They don't mean a thing to me."

"Grandma—"

"Shhhh! Listen, 'cause these might be my last words, child!" She smiled but immediately grew serious again. "I haven't had a chance to help raise you, really, and I know good and well I can't make up for it now. But I'm gonna tell you some things now that I've got a chance, and it's up to you to take it or leave it. Coffee?"

Virginia nodded. "I can make it, Grandma," she offered.

"No, no, child," she said, rising from the love seat with a grunt. "I need to move around some. Makes me feel natural." She shuffled toward the kitchenette.

"Now," she threw back over her shoulder. "There's a way for a lady to act and there's a way not to. Take laughing; there's a way to laugh. Miss Allen in the choir used to say, 'A woman laughs like a saloon, a lady like a music box.' When you laugh, hold your hand over your mouth. Don't clap it over like you're about to burp—hold it straight and a little to the side, like you're going to whisper something to someone next to you. And no whistling. No lady's got no business walking down the street in broad daylight pursing her lips as if there weren't nothing to be ashamed of. Everything in its place, and that ain't the place for that. What my mother told me was good advice and I'll tell it to you:

> *A whistling woman and a cackling hen*
> *Will never come to a good end.*

"Mark that. You're a big girl now, that's why I'm telling you all this. Nice legs and pretty eyes too—wide-set like Belle's. They fill up your face without being cow-ey. You're a good-looking young lady."

She filled the kettle at the stainless-steel sink and turned on the front burner. "Just be careful with them eyes when you get mad. It's got something to do with dark skin and the contrast. When your mama was a little girl, I took her to the park once and told her not to do something, I forget what, and she knew better than to sass me but she rolled them whites at me and I beat her little rump. She claimed she was just looking at me from the side-like, but it sure looked like rolling. So be careful with them. They'll get you into trouble when you least expect. Nowadays, though, no one seems to think about such things. Saucy women, running around with their skirts halfway to their necks and their eyes all blacked with makeup! I never liked it. I didn't like it when they started it, back in the twenties. I saw some movie star on the TV yesterday with one of those mini-skirts on . . . terrible! Knees looked like a couple of turnips."

Virginia had to smile. It was true—knees *were* ugly on white people.

"You're more like me. I feel it. A name ain't just decoration, you know. It's got destiny in it. That's why I told Belle to give you a good one. And she knew what to do. Yes! She did the best thing she could have done. You ain't my namesake for nothing. You like your name, don't you? It's a pretty name. Long and dignified, with a lilt. Not one of those short, bobbed–off names that sound like people's ashamed of saying them. People got to think twice before they say ours. Take their time: Vir-gin-i-a. Couldn't stand it when someone tried to shorten it—like some floozy, Gina or Ginny."

"Your neighbors here don't seem to realize that," Virginia couldn't help saying.

"What do you mean?" Grandma Evans cocked her head to one side again, a spoonful of Folger's suspended over the thick lip of a cup whose red trim seemed dimly familiar. Virginia told her about Amy Kepler.

"Hummph," she said. "This place is full of disrespectful people. You can't teach these white folks nothing. I remember how your grandpa said it when he first got a conversation going with me. Set his guitar down real slow. 'Miss Virginia,' he said, 'you're a fine piece of woman.' Seems he'd been asking around. Knew everything about me. Knew I was bold and proud and didn't cotton to no silly niggers. Vir-gin-ee-a, he said, nice and slow. Almost Russian, the way he said it. Right then and there I knew this man was for me. That's how you pick 'em, honey. Listen how they say your name. If they can't say that right, there's no way they're going to know how to treat you proper, neither."

Virginia watched her pour the water in without spilling a drop. Even the cups had survived all those years.

"They've got to take time with it. Your granddad took his time. He knew this lady wasn't going to be pushed over like any old applecart. He courted me just inside a year, came by nearly every day. First I wouldn't see him for more than half an hour. I'd send him away, and he knew better than to try to force me. Fellow did that once, kept coming by when I said I had other things to do. I told him he do it one more time, I'd be waiting at the door with a pot of scalding water to teach him some manners. Fool didn't believe me—I had the pot waiting on the stove and when he came up those stairs, I was standing in the door. He took one look at my face and turned and ran. He was lucky those steps were so steep. I only got a little piece of his pant leg. No, your granddad knew his stuff. He'd come on time and stay till I told him he needed to go.

"Did I ever tell you how I met him? I was out at Summit Beach one day. That was a place then! Clean yellow sand all around the lake, and an amusement park that ran from morning to midnight. I went there with a couple of other girls. They were younger than me and a little silly—you know how girls are. But they were sweet. I was nineteen then. 'High time,' everyone used to say to me, but I'd just lift my head and go on about my business. I weren't going to marry just any old Negro. He had to be perfect."

Virginia slipped off her shoes and settled back into the cushions, tucking up her legs. She remembered this tone: Grandma was on her talking seat, and there was no stopping her until the story was told.

"There was a man was chasing me around about that time, too. Tall dark nigger. Sterling Williams was his name; pretty as a panther. Married, he was—least that's what people said. Left a wife in Washington, D.C. A little crazy, the wife, and poor Sterling was trying to get a divorce.

"Well, Sterling Williams was at Summit Beach that day, too. He followed me around, trying to buy me root beer. We loved root beer that summer. Root beer and vanilla ice cream—the Boston Cooler. But I wouldn't pay him no mind. People said I was crazy—Sterling was the best catch in Akron, they said. 'Not for me,' I said. 'I don't want no secondhand man.' But Sterling wouldn't give up. He kept buying root beers and having to drink them himself.

"Then I saw your granddaddy. He'd just come up from Tennessee. Folks said his best friend had been lynched down there and he turned his back on the town and said he was never coming back. Well, when I saw this cute little man in a straw hat and a twelve-string guitar under his arm, I got a little flustered. My friends whispered around to find out who he was, but I acted like I didn't even see him.

"He was the hit of Summit Beach. Played that guitar like a devil. We'd take off our shoes and sit on the beach toward evening. Those girls sure loved James. 'Oh, Jimmy,' they'd squeal, 'play us a *looove* song!' He'd laugh and pick out a tune:

> *'I'll give you a dollar if you'll come out tonight,*
> *If you'll come out tonight,*
> *Come out tonight!*
> *I'll give you a dollar if you'll come out tonight*
> *And dance by the light of the moon!'*

All the girls would grin and sigh, 'Jimmy, you oughta be 'shamed of yourself!' He'd sing the second verse then:

> *'I danced with a girl with a hole in her stockin',*
> *And her heel kep' a-rockin',*
> *And her heel kep' a-rockin'.*
> *I danced with a girl with a hole in her stockin',*
> *We danced by the light of the moon!'*

They'd all priss and preen their feathers and wonder which would be best—to be in fancy clothes and go on being courted by dull factory fellows, or to have a hole in their stocking and dance with James. I never danced at all. I sat a bit off to one side and watched them make fools of themselves.

"Then one night near season's end we were all sitting down by the water, and everyone had on sweaters and was in a foul mood because the cold weather was coming and there wouldn't be no more parties. Someone said something about hating to have the good times end, and James struck up a nice and easy tune, looking across the fire straight at me:

> *'As I was lumb'ring down de street,*
> *Down de street, down de street,*
> *A han'some gal I chanced to meet,*
> *Oh, she was fair to view!*
>
> *I'd like to make dat gal my wife,*
> *Gal my wife, gal my wife.*
> *I'd be happy all my life*
> *If I had her by me.'*

"I knew he was the man. I'd known it a long while, but I was just biding my time. He called on me the next day; I said I was busy canning peaches. He came back the day after. We sat on the porch and watched the people go by. He didn't say much, except to say my name like that. 'Vir-gin-ee-a,' he said, 'you're a mighty fine woman.' I sent him home a little after that. He came back a week later. I was angry at him and told him I didn't have time for playing around. But he'd brought his guitar along, and he said he'd been practicing all week just to play a couple of songs for me. I made him sit on a stool while I sat on the porch swing. I can still remember those songs—silly little things, and I knew he hadn't been up all week trying to learn them. That's when I realized he was proud, too. I liked that.

"He sang the first one. It was a floor thumper:

> 'There is a gal in our town,
> She wears a yellow striped gown,
> And when she walks the streets aroun'
> The hollow of her foot makes a hole in the groun'.
>
> 'Ol' folks, young folks, cl'ar the kitchen.
> Ol' folks, young folks, cl'ar the kitchen.
> Ol' Virginny never tire.'

I got a little mad then, but I knew he was baiting me. Seeing how much I would take. Now mind you, I'm no highfalutin fool would cut off her nose to spite her face. I knew he wasn't singing about me, and I'd already heard how he said my name. It was time to let the dog in out of the rain, even if he shook his wet all over the floor. So I leaned back and put my hands on my hips, real slow. 'I just *know* you ain't singing about me,' I said.

" 'Virginia,' he said with a grin would've put Rudolph Valentino to shame, 'I'd *never* sing about you that way.' Then he pulled a yellow scarf out his trouser pocket. Like melted butter it was, with fringes. 'I saw it yesterday and thought how nice it would look against your skin,' he said. That was the first present I ever accepted from a man. Then he sang his other song:

> 'I'm coming, I'm coming!
> Virginia, I'm coming to stay.
> Don't hold it agin' me
> For running away.
>
> 'And if I can win ya,
> I'll never more roam.
> I'm coming, Virginia,
> My Dixieland home.'

"I was gone for him. But not like those girls on the beach: I had enough sense left to crack a joke or two. 'You saying I look like the state of Virginia?' I asked, and he laughed. But I was gone.

"I didn't let him know it, though, not for a long while. Even when he asked me to marry him, months later, he was trembling and thought I just might refuse out of some womanly whim. No, he courted me proper, every day for a little while. We'd sit on the porch until it got too cold and then we'd sit in the parlor with two or three bright lamps on. My mother and father were glad I'd found a beau, but they weren't taking any chances. Everything had to be proper.

"He got down, all trembly, on one knee and asked me to be his wife. I said yes. There's a point when all this dignity and stuff get in the way of destiny. He kept on trembling; he didn't believe me.

" 'What?' he said.

" 'I said yes,' I said. I was starting to get angry. Then he saw I meant it, and he went into the other room to ask my father for my hand in marriage, and that was that.

"Now you'll learn, Virginia, that you can't hide nothing from nobody in this world. You do something vile and noaccount, no matter how well you think you've covered it up, there's going to be someone somewhere going to find you out. James came all the way up from Tennessee and that should have been far enough, but he couldn't hide that snake anymore. It just crawled out from under the rock when it was good and ready.

"The snake was Jeremiah Morgan. Some fellows from Akron had gone off for work on the riverboats, and it seems some of these fellows heard about your grandpa. That twelve-string guitar and straw hat of his made him pretty popular. Anyway, story got to town that James had a baby somewhere. And joined up to that baby—but long dead and buried—was a wife.

"You'll find out soon enough in life, child, that nobody'll tell you nothing till everyone else's got wind of it. We'd been married six months and I wager half the town knew it before the honeymoon was over; but I found out from sweet-talking, side-stepping Jeremiah Morgan, who never liked me nohow after I laid his soul to rest one night when he took me home from a dance. I always carried a brick in my purse—no man could get the best of me! Well, Jeremiah must have been the happiest man in Akron the day he found out. He found it out later than most of them—seems things like that have a way of circulating first among those people know how to keep it from spreading to the wrong folks—then, when the gossip's gone the rounds, it's handed over to the one who knows just what to do with it.

" 'Ask that husband of your'n what else he left in Tennessee besides his best friend,' was all Jeremiah'd say at first. But no no-good nigger like Jeremiah Morgan could make me beg for information. I wouldn't bite.

" 'I ain't got no need for asking my husband nothing,' I said, and walked away. I was going to choir practice. He stood where he was, yelled after me like any old common person.

" 'Mrs. Evans always talking about being Number One! Looks like she's Number Two after all.'

"My ears burned from the shame of it. I went on to choir practice and sang my prettiest; and straight when I was back home I asked him.

" 'What's all this Number Two business?'

"He broke down and told me the whole story. How he'd been married before when he was seventeen, and his wife died in childbirth and the child not quite right 'cause of being blue when it was born. And how when his friend was strung up he saw no reason for staying. And how when he met me, he found out pretty quick what I'd done to Sterling Williams and that I'd never have no secondhand man, and he had to have me, so he never told me.

"I took off my coat and hung it in the front closet. Then I unpinned my hat and set it in its box on the shelf. Then I reached in the back of the closet and brought out his hunting rifle and the box of bullets. I didn't see no way out but to shoot him.

" 'Put that down!' he shouted. 'I love you, Vir-gin-ee-a.'

" 'You were right not to tell me,' I said to him, 'because I sure as sin wouldn't of married you. I don't want you *now*.'

" 'Virginia!' he said. He was real scared. 'How can you shoot me down just like that?'

"He had something there. I couldn't shoot him when he stood there looking at me with those sweet brown eyes, telling me how much he loved me. 'You have to sleep sometime,' I said, and sat down to wait.

"He didn't sleep for three nights. He knew I meant business. I sat up in this very chair with the rifle across my lap, but he wouldn't sleep. He sat at the table there and told me over and over that he loved me and he hadn't known what else to do at the time.'

" 'When I get through killing you,' I told him, 'I'm going to write to Tennessee and have them send that baby up here. It won't do, farming a child out to any relative with an extra plate.' I held on to that rifle. Not that he would've taken it from me—not that that would've saved him. No, the only thing would've saved him was running away. And he wouldn't run, either.

"Sitting there, I had lots of time to think. He was afraid of what I might do, but he wouldn't leave me, either. Some of what he was saying began to sink in. He had lied, but that was the only way to get me, I could see that. And except for that, he was perfect. It was hardly like having a wife before at all. And the baby—anyone could see the marriage wasn't meant to be, anyway.

"On the third day about midnight I laid down the rifle. 'You will join the choir and settle down instead of plucking on that guitar anytime anyone drops a hat,' I said. 'And we will write to your aunt in Tennessee and have that child sent up here.' Then I put the rifle back in the closet.

"That child never made it up here—it had died a month before Jeremiah ever opened his mouth. That hit James hard. He thought it was his fault and all, but I made him see the child was sick and was probably better off with its Maker than it would be living out half a life.

"He was a good man, your granddaddy. He made a good tenor in the choir. The next spring I had your mother and we decided to name her Belle. That's French for beautiful. And she was, too."

Grandma Evans nodded once, satisfied, and finished her gone-cold coffee in one decorous gulp.

Jessie Redmon Fauset

MARY ELIZABETH

from *The Crisis*

Mary Elizabeth was late that morning. As a direct result, Roger left for work without telling me good-bye, and I spent most of the day fighting the headache which always comes if I cry.

For I cannot get a breakfast. I can manage a dinner,—one just puts the roast in the oven and takes it out again. And I really excel in getting lunch. There is a good delicatessen near us, and with dainty service and flowers, I get along very nicely. But breakfast! In the first place, it's a meal I neither like nor need. And I never, if I live a thousand years, shall learn to like coffee. I suppose that is why I cannot make it.

"Roger," I faltered, when the awful truth burst upon me and I began to realize that Mary Elizabeth wasn't coming, "Roger, couldn't you get breakfast downtown this morning? You know last time you weren't so satisfied with my coffee."

Roger was hostile. I think he had just cut himself, shaving. Anyway, he was horrid.

"No, I can't get my breakfast downtown!" He actually snapped at me. "Really, Sally, I don't believe there's another woman in the world who would send her husband out on a morning like this on an empty stomach. I don't see how you can be so unfeeling."

Well, it wasn't "a morning like this," for it was just the beginning of November. And I had only proposed his doing what I knew he would have to do eventually.

I didn't say anything more, but started on that breakfast. I don't know why I thought I had to have hotcakes! The breakfast really was awful! The cakes were tough and gummy and got cold one second, exactly, after I took them off the stove. And the coffee boiled, or stewed, or scorched, or did whatever the particular thing is that coffee shouldn't do. Roger sawed at one cake, took one mouthful of the dreadful brew, and pushed away his cup.

"It seems to me you might learn to make a decent cup of coffee," he said icily. Then he picked up his hat and flung out of the house.

I think it is stupid of me, too, not to learn how to make coffee. But, really, I'm no worse than Roger is about lots of things. Take "Five Hundred." Roger knows I love cards, and with the Cheltons right around the corner from us and as fond of it as I am, we could spend many a pleasant evening. But Roger will not learn. Only the night before, after I had gone through a whole hand with him, with hearts as trumps, I dealt the cards around again to imaginary opponents and we started playing. Clubs were trumps, and spades led. Roger, having no spades, played triumphantly a Jack of Hearts and proceeded to take the trick.

"But, Roger," I protested, "you threw off."

"Well," he said, deeply injured, "didn't you say hearts were trumps when you were playing before?"

And when I tried to explain, he threw down the cards and wanted to know what difference it made; he'd rather play casino, anyway! I didn't go out and slam the door.

But I couldn't help from crying this particular morning. I not only value Roger's good opinion, but I hate to be considered stupid.

Mary Elizabeth came in about eleven o'clock. She is a small, wizened woman, very dark, somewhat wrinkled, and a model of self-possession. I wish I could make you see her, or that I could reproduce her accent, not that it is especially colored,—Roger's and mine are much more so—but her pronunciation, her way of drawing out her vowels, is so distinctively Mary Elizabethan!

I was ashamed of my red eyes and tried to cover up my embarrassment with sternness.

"Mary Elizabeth," said I, "you are late!" Just as though she didn't know it.

"Yas'm, Mis' Pierson," she said, composedly, taking off her coat. She didn't remove her hat,—she never does until she has been in the house some two or three hours. I can't imagine why. It is a small, black, dusty affair, trimmed with black ribbon, some dingy white roses and a sheaf of wheat. I give Mary Elizabeth a dress and hat now and then, but, although I recognize the dress from time to time, I never see any change in the hat. I don't know what she does with my ex-millinery.

"Yas'm," she said again, and looked comprehensively at the untouched breakfast dishes and the awful viands, which were still where Roger had left them.

"Looks as though you'd had to git breakfast yoreself," she observed brightly. And went out in the kitchen and ate all those cakes and drank that unspeakable coffee! Really she did, and she didn't warm them up either.

I watched her miserably, unable to decide whether Roger was too finicky or Mary Elizabeth a natural-born diplomat.

"Mr. Gales led me an awful chase last night," she explained. "When I got home yistiddy evenin', my cousin whut keeps house fer me (!) tole me Mr. Gales went out in the mornin' en hadn't come back."

"Mr. Gales," let me explain, is Mary Elizabeth's second husband, an octogenarian, and the most original person, I am convinced, in existence.

"Yas'm," she went on, eating a final cold hot cake, "en I went to look fer 'im, en had the whole perlice station out all night huntin' 'im. Look like they wusn't never goin' to find 'im. But I ses, 'Jes' let me look fer enough en long enough en I'll find 'im,' I ses, en I did. Way out Georgy Avenue, with the hat on ole Mis' give 'im. Sent it to 'im all the way fum Chicaga. He's had it fifteen years,—high silk beaver. I knowed he wusn't goin' too fer with that hat on.

"I went up to 'im, settin' by a fence all muddy, holdin' his hat on with both hands. En I ses, 'Look here, man, you come erlong home with me, en let me put you to bed.' En he come jest as meek! No-o-me, I knowed he wusn't goin' fer with ole Mis' hat on."

"Who was old 'Mis,' Mary Elizabeth?" I asked her.

"Lady I used to work fer in Noo York," she informed me. "Me en Rosy, the cook, lived with her fer years. Ole Mis' was turrible fond of me, though her en Rosy used to querrel all the time. Jes' seemed like they couldn't git erlong. 'Member once Rosy run after her one Sunday with a knife, en I kep 'em apart. Reckon Rosy musta bin right put out with ole Mis' that day. By en by her en Rosy move to Chicaga, en when I married Mr. Gales, she sent 'im that hat. That old white woman shore did like me. It's so late, reckon I'd better put off sweepin' tel termorrer, ma'am."

I acquiesced, following her about from room to room. This was partly to get away from my own doleful thoughts—Roger really had hurt my feelings—but just as much to hear her talk. At first I used not to believe all she said, but after I investigated once and found her truthful in one amazing statement, I capitulated.

She had been telling me some remarkable tale of her first husband and I was listening with the stupefied attention, to which she always reduces me. Remember she was speaking of her first husband.

"En I ses to 'im, I ses, 'Mr. Gale,—' "

"Wait a moment, Mary Elizabeth," I interrupted, meanly delighted to have caught her for once. "You mean your first husband, don't you?"

"Yas'm," she replied. "En I ses to 'im, 'Mr. Gale! I ses—' "

"But, Mary Elizabeth," I persisted, "that's your second husband, isn't it,—Mr. Gale?"

She gave me her long-drawn "No-o-me! My first husband was Mr. Gale and my second is Mr. *Gales.* He spells his name with a Z, I reckon. I ain't never see it writ. Ez I wus sayin', I ses to Mr. Gale—"

And it was true! Since then I have never doubted Mary Elizabeth.

She was loquacious that afternoon. She told me about her sister, "where's got a home in the country and where's got eight children." I used to read Lucy Pratt's stories about little Ephraim or Ezekiel, I forget his name, who always said "where's" instead of "who's," but I never believed it really till I heard Mary Elizabeth use it. For some reason or other she never mentions her sister without mentioning the home, too. "My sister where's got a home in the country" is her unvarying phrase.

"Mary Elizabeth," I asked her once, "does your sister live in the country, or does she simply own a house there?"

"Yas'm," she told me.

She is fond of her sister. "If Mr. Gales wus to die," she told me complacently, "I'd go to live with her."

"If he should die," I asked her idly, "would you marry again?"

"Oh, no-o-me!" She was emphatic. "Though I don't know why I shouldn't, I'd come by it hones'. My father wus married four times."

That shocked me out of my headache. "Four times, Mary Elizabeth, and you had all those stepmothers!" My mind refused to take it in.

"Oh, no-o-me! I always lived with mamma. She was his first wife."

I hadn't thought of people in the state in which I had instinctively placed Mary Elizabeth's father and mother as indulging in divorce, but as Roger says slangily, "I wouldn't know."

Mary Elizabeth took off the dingy hat. "You see, papa and mamma—" the ineffable pathos of hearing this woman of sixty-four, with a husband of eighty, use the old childish terms!

"Papa and mamma wus slaves, you know, Mis' Pierson, and so of course they wusn't exackly married. White folks wouldn't let 'em. But they wus awf'ly in love with each other. Heard mamma tell erbout it lots of times, and how papa wus the han' somest man! Reckon she wus long erbout sixteen or seventeen then. So they jumped over a broomstick, en they wus jes as happy! But not long after I come erlong, they sold papa down South, and mamma never see him no mo' fer years and years. Thought he was dead. So she married again."

"And he came back to her, Mary Elizabeth?" I was overwhelmed with the woefulness of it.

"Yas'm. After twenty-six years. Me and my sister where's got a home in the country—she's really my half-sister, see Mis' Pierson,—her en mamma en my step-father en me wus all down in Bumpus, Virginia, workin' fer some white folks, and we used to live in a little cabin, had a front stoop to it. En one day an ole cullud man come by, had a lot o' whiskers. I'd saw him lots of times there in Bumpus, lookin' and peerin' into every cullud woman's face. En jes' then my sister she call out, 'Come here, you Ma'y Elizabeth,' en that old man stopped, en he looked at me en he looked at me, en he ses to me, 'Chile, is yo' name Ma'y Elizabeth?'

"You know, Mis' Pierson, I thought he wus jes' bein' fresh, en I ain't paid no 'tention to 'im. I ain't sed nuthin' ontel he spoke to me three or four times, en then I ses to 'im, 'Go 'way fum here, man, you ain't got no call to be fresh with me. I'm a decent woman. You'd oughta be ashamed of yoreself, an ole man like you.' "

Mary Elizabeth stopped and looked hard at the back of her poor wrinkled hands.

"En he says to me, 'Daughter,' he ses, jes' like that, 'daughter,' he ses, 'hones' I ain't bein' fresh. Is yo' name shore enough Ma'y Elizabeth?'

"En I tole him, 'Yas'r.'

" 'Chile,' he ses, 'whar is yo' daddy?'

" 'Ain't got no daddy,' I tole him peartlike. 'They done tuk 'im away fum me twenty-six years ago, I wusn't but a mite of a baby. Sol' 'im down the river. My mother often talks about it.' And, oh, Mis' Pierson, you shoulda see the glory come into his face!

" 'Yore mother' he ses, kinda out of breath, 'yore mother! Ma'y Elizabeth, whar is your mother?'

" 'Back thar on the stoop,' I tole 'im. 'Why, did you know my daddy?'

"But he didn't pay no 'tention to me, jes' turned and walked up the stoop whar mamma wus settin'! She was feelin' sorta porely that day. En you oughta see me steppin' erlong after 'im.

"He walked right up to her and giv' her one look. 'Oh, Maggie,' he shout out, 'oh, Maggie! Ain't you know me? Maggie, ain't you know me?'

"Mamma look at 'im and riz up outa her cheer. 'Who're you?' she ses kinda trimbly, callin me Maggie thata way? Who're you?'

"He went up real close to her, then, 'Maggie,' he ses, jes' like that, kinda sad 'n tender, 'Maggie!' And hel' out his arms.

"She walked right into them. 'Oh,' she ses, 'it's Cassius! It's Cassius! It's my husban' come back to me! It's Cassius!' They wus like two mad people.

"My sister Minnie and me, we jes' stood and gawped at 'em. There they wus, holding on to each other like two pitiful childrun, an he tuk her hands and kissed 'em.

" 'Maggie,' he ses, 'you'll come away with me, won't you? You gona take me back, Maggie? We'll go away, you en Ma'y Elizabeth en me. Won't we, Maggie?'

"Reckon my mother clean fergot my step-father. 'Yes, Cassius,' she ses, 'we'll go away.' And then she sees Minnie, en it all comes back to her. 'Oh, Cassius,' she ses, 'I cain't go with you. I'm married again, en this time fer real. This here gal's mine and three boys, too, and another chile comin' in November!' "

"But she went with him, Mary Elizabeth," I pleaded. "Surely she went with him after all those years. He really was her husband."

I don't know whether Mary Elizabeth meant to be sarcastic or not. "Oh, no-o-me, mamma couldn't a done that. She wus a good woman. Her ole master, whut done sol' my father down river, brung her up too religious fer that, en anyways, papa was married again, too. Had his fourth wife there in Bumpus with 'im."

The unspeakable tragedy of it!

I left her and went up to my room, and hunted out my dark-blue serge dress which I had meant to wear again that winter. But I had to give Mary Elizabeth something, so I took the dress down to her.

She was delighted with it. I could tell she was, because she used her rare and untranslatable expletive.

"Haytian!" she said. "My sister where's got a home in the country, got a dress looks somethin' like this, but it ain't as good. No-o-me. She got hers to wear at a friend's weddin',—gal she was riz up with. Thet gal married well, too, lemme tell you; her husband's a Sunday School sup'rintender."

I told her she needn't wait for Mr. Pierson, I would put dinner on the table. So off she went in the gathering dusk, trudging bravely back to her Mr. Gales and his high silk hat.

I watched her from the window till she was out of sight. It had been such a long time since I had thought of slavery. I was born in Pennsylvania, and neither my parents nor grandparents had been slaves; otherwise I might have had the same tale to tell as Mary Elizabeth, or worse yet, Roger and I might have lived in those black days and loved and lost each other and futilely, damnably, met again like Cassius and Maggie.

Whereas it was now, and I had Roger and Roger had me.

How I loved him as I sat there in the hazy dusk. I thought of his dear, bronze perfection, his habit of swearing softly in excitement, his blessed stupidity. Just the same I didn't meet him at the door as usual, but pretended to be busy. He came rushing to me with the *Saturday Evening Post,* which is more to me than rubies. I thanked him warmly, but aloofly, if you can get that combination.

We ate dinner almost in silence for my part. But he praised everything,—the cooking, the table, my appearance.

After dinner we went up to the little sitting-room. He hoped I wasn't tired,—couldn't he fix the pillows for me? So!

I opened the magazine and the first thing I saw was a picture of a woman gazing in stony despair at the figure of a man disappearing around the bend of the road. It was too much. Suppose that were Roger and I! I'm afraid I sniffled. He was at my side in a moment.

"Dear loveliest! Don't cry. It was all my fault. You aren't any worse about coffee than I am about cards! And anyway, I needn't have slammed the door! Forgive me, Sally. I always told you I was hard to get along with. I've had a horrible day,—don't stay cross with me, dearest."

I held him to me and sobbed outright on his shoulder. "It isn't you, Roger," I told him, "I'm crying about Mary Elizabeth."

I regret to say he let me go then, so great was his dismay. Roger will never be half the diplomat that Mary Elizabeth is.

"Holy smokes!" he groaned. "She isn't going to leave us for good, is she?"

So then I told him about Maggie and Cassius. "And oh, Roger," I ended futilely, "to think that they had to separate after all those years, when he had come back, old and with whiskers!" I didn't mean to be so banal, but I was crying too hard to be coherent.

Roger had got up and was walking the floor, but he stopped then aghast.

"Whiskers!" he moaned. "My hat! Isn't that just like a woman?" He had to clear his throat once or twice before he could go on, and I think he wiped his eyes.

"Wasn't it the—" I really can't say what Roger said here,—"wasn't it the darndest hard luck that when he did find her again, she should be married? She might have waited."

I stared at him astounded. "But, Roger," I reminded him, "he had married three other times, he didn't wait."

"Oh—!" said Roger, unquotably, "married three fiddlesticks! He only did that to try to forget her."

Then he came over and knelt beside me again. "Darling, I do think it is a sensible thing for a poor woman to learn how to cook, but I don't care as long as you love me and we are together. Dear loveliest, if I had been Cassius,—he caught my hands so tight that he hurt them,—and I had married fifty times and had come back and found you married to some-one else, I'd have killed you, killed you."

Well, he wasn't logical, but he was certainly convincing.

So thus, and not otherwise, Mary Elizabeth healed the breach.

Mary Weston Fordham

THE COMING WOMAN

from *Magnolia Leaves*

Just look, 'tis a quarter past six, love—
And not even the fires are caught;
Well, you know I must be at the office—
But, as usual, the breakfast 'll be late.

Now hurry and wake up the children;
  And dress them as fast as you can;
"Poor dearies," I know they'll be tardy,
  Dear me, "what a slow, poky man!"

Have the tenderloin broiled nice and juicy—
  Have the toast browned and buttered all right;
And be sure you settle the coffee:
  Be sure that the silver is bright.

When ready, just run up and call me—
  At eight, to the office I go,
Lest poverty, grim, should o'ertake us—
  " 'Tis bread and butter," you know.

The bottom from stocks may fall out,
  My bonds may get below par;
Then surely, I seldom could spare you
  A nickel, to buy a cigar.

All ready? Now, while I am eating,
  Just bring up my wheel to the door;
Then wash up the dishes, and, mind now,
  Have dinner promptly at four;

For to-night is our Woman's Convention,
  And I am to speak first, you know—
The men veto us in private,
  But in public they shout, "That's so."

So "by-by"—In case of a rap, love,
  Before opening the door, you must look;
O! how could a civilized woman
  Exist, without a man cook.

Ruby Dee

TO PIG OR NOT TO PIG

from *My One Good Nerve*

[Jesse B. Simple is a famous character created by the late Langston Hughes. The following two stories are attempts to write about Simple as Mr. Hughes might have.]

"I am in the doghouse now," said Simple. "Let me take that back. The truth of the matter is that I am under the doghouse, if I am not the mangy dog."

"Why's that?" asked the bartender.

"Well, the other day I brought home some pork chops and Joyce started in on me. Made me so mad yak yakking about this and that, and that if I don't lay off my pork chops, I'm gonna get a case of cholesterol, turn to worms and die with a heart attack."

"Lots of people are giving up the hog and trying to eat less meat altogether. Raw food seems to be the big thing now," ventured the bartender.

"Now you bad as Joyce," said Simple. "What I look like walking up to a raw cow and taking a bite."

"You know I don't mean raw cow. Although some people do eat raw cow. Of course, it's all ground up with onions and spices. It's called steak tartare. However, I was referring mostly to raw vegetables."

"Refer on," said Simple. "Like I told Joyce, I do not like and will not eat raw vegetables or any other kind of rabbit food. I know I'll die from something, so it may as well be from something I love like pork chops—fried or smothered in onions with gravy or baked in a roast with tomatoes and little potatoes swimming on the side. It is better to die with your stomach happy than to be hit by a truck or to poison myself just breathing. And then she hit on my ignorance. I say it's my ignorance so just leave it alone."

"Stubbornness [or] ignorance is a bad thing," said Joyce, "so you just take your chops back to the store or else cook them yourself."

"Now, I am not too good in the kitchen," Simple continued, "but a wise man does not let a woman think he can't do for himself if he has to. I just told her to move on out the way. I'd cook my own damn chops. Then she come pushing me out the kitchen, saying I can't cook no pig parts in her pots because she would have to decontaminate everything. Then I did it again. I asked her 'You got anything to decontaminate your ugly, mean self? Look in the mirror and you'll see that you and my pork chops have a lot in common. You both come from pig.' "

"That was an unforgiveable thing to say. How can you possibly call her ugly?" asked the bartender. "Joyce is a fine looking woman."

"I know it," said Simple. "She is *my* woman. True, she is not ugly, but Gawd a'mighty she *can* be mean at times. Let me teach you something, my man. When you don't have all night and you need to win an argument real fast, just call *any* woman ugly and you got it made."

"It's a wonder she didn't hand you your head."

"No, she just sat down, swelled up and started crying. I told her I was sorry and to please forgive me, but she wouldn't say nothing. Just steady crying. I felt bad. I said, 'Okay, Joyce I don't have to have those chops. Come on, Baby, let me take you out to eat.'

She said, 'But I already fixed our dinner. It's in the icebox. Then she whipped into action. Set the table and brought out this big bowl of cold raw vegetables arranged like some kind of flower. First we had some soup with little scraps of chicken in it, and then we ate gobs and gobs of that vegetation. Oh, she liked that. She even apologized for screaming at me about my ignorance. Said she did it because she loves me and hates to think of my veins getting clogged up with cold fat, because she wants me to live and be with her always. Said if I just had to have some pig, maybe she'd cook me some pig liver New Year's Eve."

"Sounds like you made a good compromise," said the bartender. "For your own good, I might add."

"Wait, now, let me tell you the rest," said Simple. "You see, late that night, when I thought Joyce was asleep, I got hungry, got up, got my chops ready, and put them in the pan to cook. I guess I must have dozed off, because the next thing I knew, look like the stove had caught fire and Joyce was hollering. 'Get the baking soda. Open the windows.' Oh the smoke was everywhere, and Joyce burnt her hand getting rid of my burnt chops, and then the phone started ringing and people come banging on the front door. What got me, though, was when I heard the fire truck. If the house was on fire—"

"It's comforting to know that the fire department responded so quickly—especially in Harlem," interrupted the bartender.

"Now I don't know what to do. Since that little grease fire, Joyce stopped speaking to me. Hasn't said a word to me in two days."

"I can see you are in trouble. Would you consider telling her that you'll ease into eating raw vegetables, if she'll cook you some chops say maybe once a month? It's cold in the doghouse, I imagine," suggested the bartender.

"Eating like that is asking an awful lot from love," said Simple. "I started writing her a song though, and soon's I finish it, I'm gon' sing it to her. It's called 'Don't Let Pig Part True Love.' "

"That might make matters worse," said the bartender.

"Oh, no," said Simple, "Joyce likes it when I hold her and sing softly in her ear."

Jeannette Drake

CONFLICT

from *Pods and Peas: Summer Meditations*

Chickens and roosters may share
the same kernel if each looks
the other in the eye and makes
less noise.

Butterbeans and Susie

I WANNA HOT DOG FOR MY ROLL

[While there are a few spoken lines, this is a lively ragtime tune, most of which is sung. The basic melody is carried by Susie, and her lines rhyme, even when Butterbeans interjects a question or a comment.]

B—Hot dogs! Hot dogs! Here come the hot dog man.

S—Hey, come here.

B—What is it, lady?

S—I see you got a hot dog stand.

B—You know something, Sue, I'm known now as the hot dog man. Yes, suh, hot dogs.

S—Listen, I want a dog without bread, you see.

B—Why, what's the matter?

S—Because I carries my bread with me.

B—Now, Sue, you peculiar, and that's the natural thing.

S—Yes, and if I like your dog, why I'll come back.

B—I *know* you will.

S—How much is it? I'm here to play.

Satisfy me, listen while I say,

B—What is you got to say?

S—I want a hot dog for my roll.

B—Well, here it is, here it is.

S—I want it hot, I *don't* want it cold,

B—My dog's never cold,

S—Give me a big one, that's what I say,

I want it so it will fit my bread.

B—Now here's a hot dog for your roll

S—Now, is it young?

I don't want it cold [possibly "old" is meant here].

B—My dog's never cold.

S—I sure will be disgusted if this dog ain't full of mustard.

Don't want no excuse,

It must have lots of juice.

I want a hot dog for my roll.

B—Come here, let me straighten you out

Now here's a dog that's *long* and lean

S—Unn-un! That ain't the kind of dog I mean.

B—Now here's a dog, Sue, that's short and fat.

S—I sure need something different from that.

Now, here's my roll.

B—Where's your roll?

S—Now where's your dog?

B—Unn-un, sister, that roll you got will hold a half a hog, yes suh!
S—Now listen, Butter, can you fit it?
B—Why sure I can.
S—Why, Butter?
B—Why, Sue, I'm known now as the champion hot dog man.
Now here's a hot dog for your roll.
S—It must be hot,
I don't want it cold.
B—My dog's never cold.
S—Give me a big one, that's what I say,
I want it so it will fit by bread.
B—Now here's a hot dog for your roll.
S—Now, is it young?
I don't want it old.
B—You know my dog's never old.
S—I sure will be disgusted if this dog ain't full of mustard.
Don't want no excuse,
It must have lots of juice.
I want a hot dog for my roll.
B—Hot dog man is gone, I'm gone. Hot dogs!

Sarah and A. Elizabeth Delany

WE AIN'T DEAD YET

from *The Delany Sisters Book of Everyday Wisdom*

SADIE: We're still enjoying menfolks, too! Recently, my doctor said to me, "I have a patient—a man—who is 102 years old. Would you like me to introduce you?" And I said, "No thanks, doctor. How about somebody your age?"

Then when I was in the hospital with a broken hip, Bessie came to visit me. A man there asked her if she fixed her own hair, and Bessie told him,

"Why, yes, I do." "Well, it surely looks nice," he said. Bessie was just tick-led to death over that.

BESSIE: Well, I'm surely not too old to get crushes on men! One time, Sadie and I were on live television and the host, Regis Philbin, went and kissed me right on the mouth! That shocked me, but someone said, "You sure looked like you enjoyed it!" And I said, "Well, maybe I did and maybe I didn't."

Another time, we were being interviewed on *Good Morning America* and we could not take our eyes off one of the cameramen. He was a tall red-haired man with a handlebar mustache. Finally, I said, "Excuse us for staring, but we haven't seen a mustache like that since Teddy Roosevelt was president!" Later, someone teased us, "Aren't you two something, flirting with that man like that." And I said, "Child, we ain't dead yet!"

MIMEOGRAPHED ITEM

The Mechanic

I have been married to eight (8) different men.
Let me tell you what was wrong with them—to begin with:

My 1st. was a Musician. All he wanted to do was sing to it.

My 2nd. was a Doctor. All he wanted to do was examine it.

My 3rd. was a Politician. All he wanted to do was make promises to it.

My 4th. was a Psychiatrist. All he wanted to do was talk to it.

My 5th. was a Painter. All he wanted to do was paint pictures of it.

My 6th. was a Policeman. All he wanted to do was keep it under lock and key.

My 7th. was a Cook. All he did was taste it and tell me how salty it was.

My 8th. husband is the one I am married to now, and I like him the best.

He is a Mechanic. He tore it up the first night and has been working on it every since.

Folk

MAY I HAVE THIS DANCE

A girl from the city and a girl from the country were sitting there near each other, and this fellow came by, say, "May I have this dance?"

The city girl say, "Oh, I'm concentrating on matrimony, and I rather sit it out."

So he went over and asked the country girl, say, "Can I have this dance?"

She say, "I'm constipated on macaroni and I rather shit it out."

Folk

THE NEXT TIME YOU COME . . .

One day this maid overheard her mistress and her boyfriend talking. When the man was leaving, the lady smiled up at him and said, "The next time you come I'll gratify your wishes." The man looked so happy.

When the maid went on her next date with her boyfriend, she decided that she would repeat those same magic words. So when her boyfriend said good-night to her, she declared, "The next time you come I'll grab it out yo' britches."

Mama Sez

Still water runs deep.

A bird in the hand is worth two in the bush.

Cut some hair out of your man's head and put it in a jar in a hole under your step. That'll keep him coming. *(Shuckin' and Jivin')*

Sister to Sister

I always keep me a sweet back door man on the side.

It's good to have a candy man [lover on the side].

He's as sharp as a 'squito's [mosquito's] peter, . . . and that's sharp at both ends.

He's sharp as a tack.

He's as cool as a cucumber.

That man could talk a 'possum out a tree.

That man can TCB [take care of business].

That man can make my love come down.

He can take me to the moon.

He can light my fire anyday.

He's got me hot and ready to trot.

My train has come in today!

She told me it was a sin to be having sex with Joe unless we were trying to make a baby, and I told her, "Well, I'll see you in hell."

I knew the sun was gon' shine in my backdoor some day!

Let the good times roll.

He's a credit to the race.

Don't buy your man no new shoes. Do, he'll sho walk away from you.

CHAPTER 7

"My Daddy Won't Stop His Evil Ways"

PROBLEMS WITH HUSBANDS AND LOVERS

If we laugh at each other we won't kill each other.
—Ralph Ellison[1]

No conflict has been more long-standing or more complex than that between men and women, beginning, at least from a Judeo-Christian perspective, with Adam and Eve, when Adam, like many a male in many a creation myth, implied that God made one mistake: God created woman and *she* caused him to disobey God: "The woman whom *thou* [my emphasis] gavest *to be* with me, she gave me of the tree, and I did eat."[2] The

1. Quoted in John F. Callahan, "Frequencies of Memory: A Eulogy for Ralph Waldo Ellison," 298.
2. Genesis 3:12. In some myths women open a box and unleash plagues and evils in the world, talk too much and betray critical secrets, seduce men and cause them to make love against the will of the Supreme Being, etc., etc. Ultimately they disobey God and create chaos. The male is usually punished, but the female is usually given a graver punishment. The woman is usually created by the man or from some part of the man (his rib, his toe);

love/hate relationship between the genders has, of course, been a major theme in literature and folklore from time immemorial. No subject has caused more tears—or provoked more laughter.

The woman has frequently been the victim of cruel and malicious humor among men in almost every racial and cultural group. As Regina Barreca has noted, "Many jokes about women are more hostile than any of us would like to face."[3] Such material has been generally accepted with little controversy—it is, after all, simply humor—can't men enjoy a little harmless laughter? However, when women begin attacking men, there is often some concern about this "hostility" shown by these obviously maladjusted females. One of the most common attacks on the women who show any aggressiveness or hostility toward men is the accusation of lesbianism, one met with a quick rejoinder by comic Florynce Kennedy when a male heckler called out to her: "Are you a lesbian?" to which she immediately responded, "Are you my alternative?"[4]

Among no group has the black female been treated more savagely than in the humor of some African American males, and among no group has the humor of women directed toward black males been the cause of more vituperative, defensive commentary; in other words, they can give it but they can't take it. Obviously, one must recognize that both the black male and female are and have been manipulated by the politics and mass media of the larger society, and one might write volumes on the negative impact of racism on the relationships within the black community. Yet, when both continue to embrace and perpetuate some of the hated stereotypes of a racist society, especially in this more enlightened age, one recognizes that the prevalence of these hostile comic materials is not merely the result of the devices and designs of the white society.

In order to set the humor of African American women in context, one must recognize that there is a long tradition of tales, verses, rhymes, sayings,

---

Mineke Schipper cites a myth from Tanzania in which one of the two original men slips with an axe and cuts off his companion's penis, leaving a bleeding wound—thus woman (*Unheard Words: Women and Literature in Africa, the Arab World, Asia, the Caribbean and Latin America,* 24). There are, of course, a few contrasting myths in which the women are the original inhabitants of an Edenic world and the introduction of man disrupts it, such as the creation myth of the Ekoi of Nigeria, also cited by Schipper (p. 39).

3. *They Used to Call Me Snow White,* 78.

4. Quoted in Regina Barreca. *They Used to Call Me Snow White,* 96.

and graffiti popular among black males (and some black females) that attack black women with greater hostility and more obscene invectives than
that directed against whites. In the dozens, in the toasts,[5] in the blues, in
raps, in other forms, black women are commonly portrayed as bitches,
tricks, and hos (whores),[6] whose only good or acceptable feature is that they
humbly submit to complete sexual domination and physical brutality from
their men. Generally they are pictured as unfaithful bitches who must be
beaten and killed, often in a sexual contest. Sometimes the women are
killed in ritualistic fucking contests, but frequently their demise requires little fanfare as they are casually shot to death for the most insignificant of
acts. That such treatment of women is seen as a natural, everyday thing is
suggested in one of the most popular of the toasts, "Stackolee," when the
judge tells him:

> Well, now, Stackolee, you've led a simple life,
> fucked your sister and killed your wife.[7]

In this body of folk and popular literature the black women's sexuality
is always perverse: she is sexually insatiable; she can be satisfied only by a
beast; she is uncouth and sexually promiscuous; she is ugly and never as desirable as her white sister; her breasts, hips, sexual organs, menstrual period,
etc., are the subjects of much vicious lampooning. The only thing the
black male could possibly desire from her is sex, but he would never consider marriage or any other commitment to her. Those who attack the malicious treatment of women in current raps are evidently not familiar with
the blues, the dozens, and the toasts, many of which, by comparison, make
the raps look mild.[8]

It should be no surprise then that women have not suffered all of these
attacks quietly, but they have come out fighting. Blues singers, rappers, sig-
nifyers/crackers, and storytellers have in many instances provided direct re

5. Long, narrative poems in rhyming couplets popularly recited by black males, toasts
usually focus on street and prison culture and portray a world ("jungle") of con men,
pimps, whores, bad niggers, drug peddlers, junkies, winos, and cops.

6. By the count of one critic in 1980, 2 Live Crew referred to women as bitches and
whores 163 times in their albums to date (*People Magazine,* July 2, 1980, 90).

7. Bruce Jackson, *"Get Your Ass in the Water and Swim Like Me,"* 51.

8. For examples of the toasts and dozens, see my *Shuckin' and Jivin'*.

sponses to some of the insults leveled at them by black males. They often attack their victims for comparable shortcomings in humor that is nearly as coarse and spiteful: thus, for one of many (mild) examples, the problem in sexual relationships is not that the female's genitalia are so large, but rather that the male penis is too small. Just as in the most crude male humor women are referred to as bitches and hos; in the harshest of the women's humor, men are frequently labeled dogs. Men are criticized for a variety of shortcomings (often similar to those for which the women have been attacked), including sexual impotence, insensitivity, and ineptitude, laziness, immaturity, ignorance, age, physical appearance, body odors, egomania, unfaithfulness, and their attraction to white women. Women brag about "dogging" men and dropping them. They create and lampoon certain comic types: old men, lazy bums, conniving leeches, corporate boys/dicties/conservatives, homosexuals, and white men.

To many outsiders, much of this humor seems cruel and vindictive; to some men it is viewed as bitter antimale hysteria; to some psychoanalytic types it reveals a plethora of neuroses, but to the women who get together for some male bashing, it is a chance to reflect on some conflicts, share some painful experiences, achieve some release of anger and frustration and just plain had-it-up-to-here with the men in their lives, and slip the yoke and change the joke. They experience the same catharsis as the females in Toni Morrison's *Jazz,* who in a moment of fear and bitterness, burst out in laughter; Morrison writes, "they felt . . . better. Not beaten, not lost. Better." They learned "that laughter is serious. More complicated, more serious than tears." Or as Muhammad Ali put it, "My way of joking is to tell the truth. That's the funniest joke in the world." These women are joking, but they are telling the truth about their problems with their husbands and lovers, and if you challenged any one of them, I know she would respond, "If I'm lying, I'm flying."

Honey, hush!

Barbara Brandon

WHERE I'M COMING FROM

Paule Marshall

A HERB MOST BRUISED IS WOMAN

from *Brown Girl, Brownstones*

"Going home already, Miss Thompson?" one of the beauticians called as she passed.

"Yes indeed, honey," she nodded absently, "I done worked round the clock, did more work in twenty-four hours than these good-timing niggers out here on Fulton Street done for the year, and I'm headed for my bed . . ."

> *"Of all things upon the earth that bleed and*
> *grow, a herb most bruised is woman."*

As Miss Thompson trudged down Fulton Street looking, in her severe black dress, like one of the saved sisters who gathered in the store-front churches each night sobbing and shouting for Jesus, Silla sat in the grave house beyond the park, her stunned eyes encountering nothing, her hands still clutching the chicken feathers.

"But look how trouble does come," she whispered, straining forward as though addressing some specter-shape. "Look how it does come . . . What is it," she demanded with sudden fierceness, "that does give what little luck there is to fools . . . ? Not a soul ever give me nothing a-tall, a-tall. I always had to make my own luck. And look at he! Somebody dead so and he got ground so. Got land now!" She broke off and slowly lapsed into a dull be-wilderment. Her entire body gave way to it so that she seemed either drunk or drugged or so tired that she had fallen into a sodden sleep. After a long time, the chicken feathers slowly wafted from her limp hand, and the silence when they settled was like the kitchen, sterile and rigid and splin-tered with white light.

She remained like this until a voice blustered through the hall and a round, almost white face emerged from the darkness there like a moon from behind a rack of dark clouds. Virgie Farnum entered the kitchen, bearing her swollen stomach with a slightly startled expression—as though it was an enormous ball which someone had shoved in her hands and left her holding.

"Silla-gal, you still cleaning chicken and night near falling?" her voice boomed in the quietness. "How?"

"I here, soul," Silla said listlessly. "Sitting and thinking hard-hard." She surveyed Virgie with amusement and concern, "But how, Virgie?"

"Suffering."

"No doubt. You like you gon bring the child before the night out. But look at you," she said with tender disapproval. "You's a disgrace to come tumbling big so soon after the last one."

"C'dear, what I must do? It's the Lord will."

"What Lord will?" Silla sucked her teeth in disgust. "Woman, you might go hide yourself. These ain ancient days. This ain home that you got to be always breeding like a sow. Go to some doctor and get something 'cause these Bajan men will wear you out making children and the blasted chil-dren ain nothing but a keepback. You don see the white people having no lot."

"I know, soul." Virgie's pale skin flushed. "And this one's the worse. The little demon does get on inside me like it got nettle."

"It's a girl-child. They does do so. Both these I got did kick like horses inside me. But the boy, God rest him in his grave, did lay easy-easy inside me. Y'know," she said wistfully, her hand groping for Virgie's as the memory of him softened her face, "he was a child who look like he never knew a sick day. But the heart wasn't good." Her hand trailed from Virgie's. "The heart wasn't good."

"I know, soul. A boy-child is a hard thing to raise."

"And then the wuthless father had to take him out in a piece of old car and shake up his insides so it near kill him . . ."

"Silla, hush. It don do no good to reef up."

"Reef up? Virgie, I has never forgot," she said solemnly. Virgie's gray eyes flitted uneasily over Silla's numb face. A pain struck and she clutched her stomach, the blood draining from her thin lips and the broad nose spread across her face as the one sign of her scant Negro blood. "Oh there it go, the little whelp lan'ing me hell inside and gon land me more outside."

There was no response from Silla, but although her eyes remained abstracted she took up a newspaper from the table and carefully fashioned two fans and handed one to Virgie. Slowly the blood filtered back to Virgie's skin as she fanned. She tucked the dress under her stomach and called loudly, "Where he is?"

"Who?" Silla lifted remote eyes.

"The beautiful-ugly Deighton. Upstairs?"

"Upstairs, what! You know every Sat'day he does run bird-speed to the concubine to lick out what's left from his pay."

"But Deighton oughta stop." Virgie roared her disapproval. "Nobody din say he can't have the hot-ass woman but, c'dear, his own got to come first."

"Ah Virgie, you does talk sense. Who in the bloody hell care how many women he got. Those women ain got nothing but a man using them. But his own got to come first." And then remembering the land, she added bitterly, "Yes, they gon be spreeing tonight over the land."

"Wha'? Wha' land?" Virgie's body slumped over her huge stomach, straightened with interest. "Wha' land?"

"He got piece of ground home, soul."

"Deighton? Who give he?"

"The schoolteacher sister that dead left him."

"How much ground?"

"Near two acres. A good piece of ground, he say."

"But hey-hey!" Amazement struck Virgie's broad features. "That Deighton is a lucky something, nuh?"

"In truth." The same amazement scored Silla's voice. "That's what I was thinking when you came. How there don seem to be no plan a-tall, a-tall to this life. How things just happen and don happen for no good reason. I tell you, it's like God is sleeping."

Alice Walker

THE COLOR PURPLE

Dear God,

Harpo wanted to know what to do to make Sofia mind. He sit out on the porch with Mr. _____. He say, I tell her one thing, she do another. Never do what I say. Always backtalk.

To tell the truth, he sound a little proud of this to me.

Mr. _____ don't say nothing. Blow smoke.

I tell her she can't be all the time going to visit her sister. Us married now, I tell her. Your place is here with the children. She say, I'll take the children with me. I say, Your place is with me. She say, You want to come? She keep primping in front the glass, getting the children ready at the same time.

You ever hit her? Mr. _____ ast.

Harpo look down at his hands. Naw suh, he say low, embarrass.

Well how you spect to make her mind? Wives is like children. You have to let 'em know who got the upper hand. Nothing can do that better than a good sound beating.

He puff on his pipe.

Sofia think too much of herself anyway, he say. She need to be taken down a peg.

I like Sofia, but she don't act like me at all. If she talking when Harpo and Mr. _____ come in the room, she keep right on. If they ast her where something at, she say she don't know. Keep talking.

I think bout this when Harpo ast me what he ought to do to her to make her mind. I don't mention how happy he is now. How three years pass and he still whistle and sing. I think bout how every time I jump when Mr. _____ call me, she look surprise. And like she pity me.

Beat her. I say.

Next time us see Harpo his face a mess of bruises. His lip cut. One of his eyes shut like a fist. He walk stiff and say his teef ache.

I say, What happen to you, Harpo?

He say, Oh, me and that mule. She fractious, you know. She went crazy in the field the other day. By time I got her to head for home I was all banged up. Then when I got home, I walked smack dab into the crib door. Hit my eye and scratch my chin. Then when that storm come up last night I shet the window down on my hand.

Well, I say, After all that, I don't spect you had a chance to see if you could make Sofia mind.

Nome, he say.

But he keep trying.

Folk

I CAN'T REMEMBER

An elderly man was seated on a park bench sobbing and weeping uncontrollably. When a passerby asked what had saddened him to this extent, he replied, "I married a beautiful young woman last week, and she's home waiting for me."

"But why should that make you sad?" the surprised passerby asked. "I should think that would make you very *happy*.

"I can't remember where I live," the old man cried.

Moms Mabley

THE GOOD OLE DAYS

"Let Mom tell you what happened to me in the good old days. You couldn't do *nothing* you want to do—and you better not open your mouth. If you did they'd *knock* your *brains* out. . . . Everything your parents picked for you to do—who you to love, who you to go out wit, who you even to *marry!* Think o' somebody pickin' somebody you got to spend the rest o' your days wit! Make no difference what conditions it was—if Daddy said so, that was it. And I wasn't nothin' but a chile. Nothin' but a chile foteen—foteen, goin' on fifteen years old. And just as cute as I wanna be. *Hair* hanging down my *back*. . . . See I'm half Indian. And the other half, the beauty parlor takes care o' that."

And this *o-o-o-l-d-d-d-d-d-d-d dead-d-d-d-d, pu-u-u-u-u-n-y, moldy* man. I mean an *o-o-o-o-ld-d-d-d* man! Santa Claus look like his son. He was older than his *mother!* He was so old that his sister died and we went to the funeral. After the funeral the minister walked over to him and tapped him on the back, say, "How old are you, Pops?"

He sez, "Ninety-one."

He say, "Ain't no need you goin' home!"

And his brother was *older* than he was . . . and married a girl *thirteen!* He ain't live but *five* days. Took three undertakers a week to get the smile off his face. . . . He layin' up there . . . [dramatizing his big smile]

My *daddy* liked him. I had to marry that old man. My *daddy* shoulda married 'im. He de one liked 'im. The nearest thing to *death* you've ever seen in you life! His shadow weighed more 'n he did. He got outta breath threading a *needle*. And *UG-G-G-G-LY!* He was so ugly he hurt my feelings. He was just so ugly he had to tip up on a glass to get a drink o' water. He was so ugly he had a job at a doctor's office standing beside the door makin' people *sick!* One day I said to 'im, I said, "You get that number?"

He say, "What number?"

I say, "The number o' that *truck* that run over your *face!*"

One night I said to 'im, I said, "Come on, darling, let's be sociable." He went out and bought a case of Pepsi-Cola.

I thought he *never would die!* Rat poison agreed wit 'im.

I never will forget when we went up to get married. We standin' up there in front the man. The man looked at me, said, "Will you take this man?"

Some undertaker jumped up and said, "I will."

Oh, I thought he never would die. I shouldn't talk like that about 'im, though. . . . He dead. They say you mustn't say nothin' bout the dead less you kin say somethin' good. . . . He dead—*good!* I know he's dead cause I had 'im cremated. I burnt 'im up. I was determined he was gon' get *hot* one time anyhow. Don't you know the undertaker had the nerve to call me up, talkin' bout do I want the ashes. I say, "Hell naw, burn them up too. I don't want *nothin!*"

Folk

OVER THE HILL

[This is the only folk item included in this book that I recorded from a male. "Over the Hill" is, however, most commonly recited by women and was often performed by Moms Mabley.]

It's not the gray hair that makes a man old,
Nor that faraway stare in his eyes, I am told.
But when his mind makes a contract that his body can't fill.
He is—over the hill, over the hill.

Now, life is a conflict, and the battle is keen.
There are just so many shots in the old magazine.
When he has fired the last shot, and he just can't refill.
then he is . . . over the hill, over the hill.

He should salvage his energy while he can,
Because Lydia Pinkham can't help a man.
You can't get a new gland from the little pink pill,
So you're over the hill, over the hill.

He can fool the dear wife with the tenderest of lies,
He can shear that poor lamb and pull the wool over her eyes.
But when she calls for an encore, and he pretends that he's ill,
Then he's . . . over the hill, over the hill.

Now his sporting days are over, and his tail light is out,
And what used to be his sex appeal now is just his water spout.
So that's the story, alas and alack,
When he's squeezed out the toothpaste, he just can't squeeze it back.

So if you want to make whoopie, don't wait until . . .
You get . . . over the hill, over the hill.

Folk

THE FIFTEEN-INCH PIANIST

Well, . . . there was this man who came to this farm, and he was at this farm
with all the other people. And they were standing around him, and he, all
of a sudden, pulled out of his pocket this little piano. He put the piano on
the bar, and they said, "Oh, that's an interesting little piano. Where did you
get that little piano there?"

He said, "Oh, I have something even more amazing than that." And he
reached in his pocket and he pulled out this little man—no more than fifteen inches tall, and he put the man down there, and the man started playing the piano.

And they said, "This is amazing. How did you do this?"

He said, "Well, I got it out of a bottle." He said, "You want to see the
bottle?"

Everybody said, "Yes."

So he pulled out the bottle, and they said, "How did you get that? How
did you get the piano and the man?"

He said, "Well, this genie in the bottle told me that if I wanted to make
a wish, I can, you know, have my wish." So one of the men said [excitedly],
"Well, can *I* try this?"

So this man sitting next to him told the genie, "I want a *million bucks*," and so the genie responded, and, all of a sudden, there were flying overhead a million *ducks!*

The man say, "I didn't ask for a million *ducks*, I said a million *bucks.*"

And the man who originally brought the piano in said [in a dejected tone], "Man, I know how you feel. You think I asked for a fifteen-inch *pianist?*

Folk

U P

This man went to the doctor, and he said, "Doctor, I'm having serious problems. I'm forty-five years old, and I'm not pleasing my wife, and it's driving me crazy."

Doctor say, "I've got some ointment for you. Let's try it three times—this ointment is good for three times, but you've got to help it. Now, I'm going to put the ointment on. But you control it. When you're ready, you go 'Up-p-p-p' [raising his hand as high as possible], and it goes up. And when you're ready to finish, you go 'Phew-w-w' [whistling sound]. Simple. You got it?"

He say, "Yeah . . ."

He say, "Un-un, don't say it now. Wait til you get home cause you only have *three* times to do it."

So my boy comes on out of the doctor's office, and they standing there waiting, and the elevator door opens, and the lady say, "You goin' *up?*"

It came up (illustrating). He say (in amazement), "Phew-w-w!" It went right down. He say, "Oh, Jesus! There go one time already."

Say he got out of the cab, paid the driver. He say, "Wait a minute, let me give you a tip."

A old lady come by, she say, "Scuse me. You going *up*town?" Went up again (gesturing).

He say, "Oh, shit! I can't even get in the house." So he got in the house. He told his wife, say (breathless voice), "Hurry up, I ain't got but one time," and he went on to explain to her.

So he say, *"UP!"* And it came up. She hadn't seen it up in so long, she say (incredulously), *"Pheew-w-w-w!"*

Folk

SHORTENING

Big John had a big one, and naturally all the women were crazy about him. Little Joe was so envious. He say, "Goddamn, I wish I had a big one like that. I would be hell on wheels." Say, "Big John, how you get such a big one?

Big John say, "Just stretch it and grease it, stretch it and grease it, and it'll grow."

So Little Joe ran home and he started stretching and greasing, stretching and greasing. And he worked religiously at it, day in and day out, but nothing happened. When he saw Big John, he say, "Man, I've been stretching and greasing, stretching and greasing for *six* weeks, and ain't nothin' happened!"

Big John say, "What you greasing it with, man."

Little Joe say, "Wesson oil."

Big John say, "Man, that's shortening!"

Louise Brewington

THE LAZIEST MAN

from John A. Burrison, ed., *Storytellers*

There was a man—lazy. But, oh, he was the laziest man! And some of 'em, they decided they would bury him alive, because he was so lazy. So, they had him in the wagon, goin' on with him.

Say, "What you gonna do with him?"

Say, "We gonna bury him alive. He's too lazy to cook and eat."

So one lady said, "Well, don't bury him alive." Said, "I'll give him [food]; he won't work." Say, "I'll give him a bushel of corn."

He raised up and said, "Shelled?"

So she said, "No."

So he say, "Well, drive on."

So another one wanted to know and they told her, say, "Well, he just is so lazy he won't work, won't do anything." Say, "He too lazy to even' eat."

So she said, "Well, I'll give him a peck of meal." Say, "Don't bury him alive."

He raised up again, said, "Is it cooked?"

Say she said, "No."

Say he said, "Drive on."

And so it went on 'til he got near 'bout to the cemetery. And they asked what they were gonna do with him. And said, "He's just so lazy, he won't do anything. Too lazy to cook. You give him food, he's too lazy to cook it."

Say the one said, "Well, I'll give him some food that's already cooked." Say, "I got cornbread, black-eyed peas, and baked potatoes." And say, "The potatoes is peeled, and the bread is broke." And say, "I'll give him all of that if you don't bury him alive."

And say he raised up, said, "You gonna chew it?"

She said, "Man!" Says, "No."

Say he take that a little while, he say, "Well, all right. Bring it on, then. I guess I can chew it."

Now do you know that was some lazy!

Frances Cress Welsing

THE LANGUAGE OF BLACK MEN

[The following is a reproduction from rough notes of comments by Dr. Welsing at the National Conference on the Black Family in the American Economy, in Louisville, Kentucky, March 28, 1976.]

Blacks ask, "What's happening," because we really don't know what's going on. The Black man's language reflects his powerlessness in the face of

White supremacy. The "man" refers to the White man. The Black man re-
volted against being called "boy," and now they call each other "baby." The
Black man calls the Black woman "mama," he calls his house a "crib," and
he calls himself a "motherfucker."

Amanda Smith

BROTHER JOHNSON'S SEARCH FOR A COLORED WIFE

from *An Autobiography*

[In her *Autobiography,* Mrs. Smith recounts her service as a missionary in
several countries in Africa. The following selection is an account of an
event in Sierra Leone. She, along with other missionaries from the United
States, was staying with Sister Harmon, while two other new missionaries
were staying elsewhere, but have been invited to Sister Harmon's to have
tea with their colleagues.]

On Monday afternoon I invited Brother Johnson and Brother Miller to
take tea with the other brethren. Of course, these were my own country
people; they had left their home and went to work among my people in
Africa. So we did our best for them.

I got Sister Harmon to make some nice, old-fashioned, Maryland biscuit (which she knew as well how to do as I did myself, and I used to be
considered an expert, once upon a time), and we had nice fried chicken,
and all else we could get, and that in abundance; that is the way we generally had it in Africa, when we were in for a big thing!

Of course, we could not go at that speed every day. But thank God, I
never saw a day in Africa that I did not have plenty to eat. And when at Ma
Payne's, in Monrovia, for days my meals would be sent to me in my room,
when I was not able to go down, and as nicely served on a waiter as if I
had been at a nice boarding house, or at my own home in America.

After tea was over we were all talking and having a pleasant time; the
brethren seemed so to have enjoyed their tea, and we were all pleased.

Brother Johnson had been expressing in the most flattering terms his delight and appreciation of the splendid tea, and especially the biscuit. He said the lady who made them must have been a wonderfully nice lady, and if she was not married, she ought to be; for a lady that could make such biscuit ought to have a good husband. Well, we all laughed, and passed it off in a joking manner. I felt pretty safe, as I had not made the biscuit.

Sister Harmon was a nice looking woman, but was older than I, and had sons grown and married, and grandchildren; so she had no fear of anything, save the embarrassment of the question and answer, if it really came to that. So Brother Johnson said to me:

"Mrs. Smith, I would like to speak to you privately."

"Very well," I said; "we will excuse these brethren, and you can see me just here."

So the three brethren arose and withdrew to the parlor. I had watched and listened to Brother Johnson, and had taken his measure pretty thoroughly while he was talking, and I felt in my mind that he was going to play the fool.

"Now, Brother Johnson," said I, "proceed. What is it you want to say?"

He straightened up and smiled, and acted a little embarrassed; then got red in the face and all down his neck, till his beautiful white necktie seemed as though it was about to get pink, too.

I thought, "Dearie me, what will he say?" For I looked him squarely in the eye, and with the look of the rock of Gibraltar, if Gibraltar ever looked. I said, "It cannot mean that he is going to propose to me; he has just come; has not been here three days." After clearing his throat, he said:

"Well, Sister Smith, or *Mrs.* Smith," (emphasizing the Mrs.).

"Yes," I said.

"Well, I have come to Africa, and expect to make it my future home. I have not come to go back. I expect to die here."

Then I spoke and said, "I don't think you need die here any sooner than you would in the United States. One need only use his common sense, and go a little slow while he is acclimating." Then I waited for the next shot.

"I thought," he continued, "I would ask you if you knew of any nice colored woman that you think would make me a good wife. I could have married before I left my country, or America," (he was a Swede); "but I chose to wait till I got here; and I thought it would be better for me to marry a woman of the country, who is already acclimated. If I were to marry a white woman, she would all the time be crying to go home to see her aunt or uncle, or her mother," with a pretty smile.

I groaned, being burdened, to give vent to my mingled feelings. But then I controlled myself; for, during the time he talked, I was reading him, and I said to myself: "There is nothing in this man; he is as full of self as he can be, and he is going to be a failure, if not a disgrace, to Bishop Taylor's mission here." For the work was just starting, and was new, and needed much careful guiding and management, with all the American and African prejudices against this new, self-supporting movement.

"Mr. Johnson, I know some very nice women here, who, I think would make good wives for somebody; but I would not recommend anyone that I know, to do what I would not do myself; and I, myself, would not marry you, or any other man, if you were gold; a rank stranger, just come from another country, and have not been here three days; no one knows anything about you; you know nothing about the people. You are entirely premature. You will need to be here some time, and know Africa and the people. Then, besides, Bishop Taylor's self-supporting mission is in its infancy, and every eye is upon these first missionaries, both here and at home, and we must be careful that we do nothing that will hinder or hurt it in the start."

I saw that my version of things did not take very well with Brother Johnson. But I did not know until Wednesday what had gone before.

Mr. Pratt's wife's sister, a very nice girl, had gone to help in the house, as Mrs. Pratt was sick. She took a great fancy to Mrs. Harnard and the children, and had offered herself to Mrs. Harnard, to go with her, to take care of the children.

It appeared that when Mr. Johnson came ashore on Saturday, and saw this girl at Mrs. Pratt's, he was struck clear through at first sight, and had proposed; and she, poor thing, thought it was splendid. She judged from outside appearances; for Mr. Johnson was a very nice looking man, nicely dressed, patent leather boots, shirt, collar and necktie exquisitely beautiful, and she thought she had a fish of the first water. I suppose she had; but it was bony.

They were to be married on Thursday, and would have been, if Mr. Pratt had allowed it. When he found it out, he sent the girl home to her father, and managed to hold Brother Johnson in check for two weeks.

So that was the meaning of the private conversation that Mr. Johnson wanted with me Monday evening. But he did not come straight out and tell me. I was glad afterward that I did not know anything about it, and that I talked just as I did. And, notwithstanding all that, they tried to say that I was favorable to it.

They were married at the Methodist Church, by somebody, I don't remember now by whom; but I know Brother Harnard did not marry them. I never went near; because I was so busy with my sick missionaries, and I did not care anyhow, to see the beginning of the thing; I was more interested about how it was going to come out.

Well, it turned out just as I said. After a week or so he carried the poor thing up into the country to their station. She had nothing, and he had nothing, only his mission supplies; and they had used the best part of those for their marriage feast, no one made them any feast, or gave them any presents, as they do in this country. In this they both seemed to be greatly disappointed.

Mr. Johnson seemed to think if he only married a colored girl, he being a white man, it would be such a standing proof to the colored people that he really loved them, that they would take him right into their arms, and lavish upon them their wealth and gifts; especially as he had married into one of the most respectable families in Cape Palmas; the daughter of the Hon. Mr. H. Gibson. My! he thought he had it. And so he had.

Poor girl! I knew her well. She had been converted and sanctified in one of the meetings that I had held, and had grown in grace, and was developing so nicely, and was one of our good workers in the Band of Hope Temperance work.

When I knew that the decree was passed to marry Mr. Johnson, I confess I was disappointed in her; for I really gave her credit for having more sense. So I never opened my head to her on the subject.

Her joy and delight were of short duration. He got fever and was down sick. They came back to the Cape. I went to see him, and did what I could.

When he got better they went again up to their station. The natives received them gladly, and gave them a bullock. They had their mission house built to go into. But everything was so different from what it was in America. He got down with fever again, and again they returned to the Cape. I, with Brother Pratt, did everything I could for him till I left.

After some months of going back and forth, and getting down with fever, he came back to the Cape again, and took the first steamer for home, and left his wife there, to live or die.

Flo Kennedy

ON MARRIAGE

from *Color Me Flo*

In the late Fifties I acquired a partner, Don Wilkes, and a husband, Charlie Dye, both of whom ultimately proved disastrous. I married Charlie in 1957, when he was 31 and I was 41. He was a Welsh science-fiction writer, and a drunk. Joy always teases me about marrying Charlie, because for all my talk against marriage, the fact is that he was one of the very few men in my entire life who at all seriously suggested we get married. She thinks I would have married whoever came along, that my whole rap against marriage is a crock, and that I am really a secret romantic. It's true that when I was younger I used to get crushes on all kinds of people, mostly beyond my reach, but maybe that's wiser, since marriage means getting a crush on someone within your reach. Anyway, I married this dude.

He had come to a party we gave, where he fell for a friend of ours, Eleanor Martell. Ellie probably took one whiff of that stale liquor breath, spotted him for what he was—his teeth by this time were decaying and he wasn't all that appetizing—said, "No, thank you very much," and split, whereupon he got a tremendous crush. He would go into a tailspin over anyone who rejected him, and would come around sniveling and crying to me, and I'd try to get him together with Ellie. And then it developed that he had also been rejected by another friend of ours, Stella Halpern, a classical pianist. Supposedly she had broken his heart, but I remembered that she had once called me to report that he had met her after they'd broken up, and had brought her an Easter bunny. When she refused to go back with him, or even out with him, he pushed her down the subway stairs and threw the chocolate bunny after her. I had helped her threaten to arrest him, and stopped his assholery, so I realized that he was a crock and I should have been warned.

It turned out that he was the type of person who will latch on to people to whom he feels somewhat superior, and then when they reject him, thereby establishing his inferior status, he goes into fits of depression and rage. Charlie used to go up to Stella's house and try to get her to let him in, and she told me she was getting scared of him. I don't know if he was anyone to be afraid of, but he certainly managed to make a terrible nuisance of himself most of the time.

So this was the prize. Fortunately, I never took marriage very seriously; it just seemed to me that he wanted to be married more than I wanted not to be married. I never thought it would last very long, but finally, I guess just to see what it was all about, certainly not with any idea of a serious marriage, I gave in. We were married in the sunken living room in Leonard Cohen's apartment by Judge George Stark, a friend of his. Charlie was blind drunk. We couldn't get a cab from his apartment on Second Street and Avenue C, but he wouldn't go by bus, which was exactly across the street—he forced me to walk to the subway, and I got soaking wet. And of course none of these things persuaded me not to go through with it, so I guess I am not as immune as I like to think from society's brainwashing about marriage.

That very night we had a party up in Harlem where he got still drunker and grabbed crotches and did whatever else he could think of that was totally outside the pale. Joy thinks if I could marry a creep in that condition, I certainly had to be in love with him. Maybe a lot of women marry men they don't think any more of than I did of Charlie, but I certainly had no illusions about being in love with him. Don't ask me why I did it—that's just how it was.

I more or less moved in with him, still spending a certain amount of time at my place, and periodically, after I'd get tired of his drunken nonsense, I'd take all my clothes that I couldn't get into a cab, leave them at a cleaner's on Second Street and split, after he had gone to the bank. He worked at Irving Trust Company down near Wall Street as a security guard, which meant he carried a gun; but fortunately he didn't bring his gun home, because drunk and crazy as he was, I am not at all sure he wouldn't have shot me in one of his rages. And the idea of a man in his perpetually drunken condition working as a security guard gives you an idea of the kind of people we trust with guns.

On the plus side, though, he was a wonderful story-teller and he could be very amusing. Not amusing enough for me to put up with the rest of him, obviously, but anyway I did. When I first knew him, he would laugh at me because I got dressed, as he put it, to go to bed—he didn't think people should wear anything to sleep in. One Christmas I got him a pair of pajamas because it did occasionally get fairly cold in the apartment, and when he put them on he loved them so much he would hardly take them off for me to wash them. That was the way he was: he would say one thing and then be just the opposite when it came down to the wire. I also bought him a really beautiful pair of shoes, because I enjoyed shopping for him and he was such a ragamuffin when I first met him; that is, I called him a ragamuffin, but he thought of himself as an elegantly seedy author.

He didn't like to take baths, so much so that he would go in the bathroom and turn on the water in the shower without getting in. After I caught on, I'd make him come over and let me feel his skin to check up on him. He got cleaner and neater the longer we were together, but it always amuses me when people talk about the special odor of women, and their special problem. When I married Charlie, his socks were practically standing up in the closet. (It is funny, though, that neither Charlie nor my Dad, who also wasn't crazy about bathing, ever actually smelled.)

Although he drank constantly, he was not always mean when he was drunk. He drank Gallo muscatel for the most part, but sometimes Thunderbird, which was another of my names for him. Just about every night he would drink a quart, and more than a gallon over the weekend. At night he would sit on the floor, usually with no clothes on, and play his records. He was a big jazz fan, and whenever he sold a piece to a magazine, even if we had broken up, which we often did, he would call me up and we would go to Birdland. He was smart enough to stay away for weeks at a time, though, after I'd left him.

He had a tiny studio apartment, just one room with a little kitchen and bathroom and a small clothes closet where he kept his pornography collection. He said it was worth $1,500, which it well may have been, but it wasn't worth anything at all to me, and I threw so much into the incinerator after he died that I put the fire out.

In spite of everything, he was interesting to me because while he was terribly damaged merchandise, he had been at some point a quality person, and he was a peach all through my crisis with Don Wilkes's larcenous abandonment.

Wilkes had been the great white hope of one of the major Wall Street law firms. He thought he was so smart he could represent poor people as successfully as he had conducted the multimillion dollar case of Ford against Ferguson. But what he didn't know, which I understood very well, and which really flipped him out, was that there is no justice for Black people, or nigger-loving lawyers. We took on four or five big negligence cases, and in order to hurry them to trial he waived the jury, and to his shock always got dismissals and/or minimal damages.

We had a case where a woman was crushed between two cars when she got out to help a car which had stalled on the Long Island Expressway. One leg had to be amputated and the other was virtually useless, and Wilkes took the case to the judge without a jury, because he refused to believe me when I told him you could actually lose such a case. But of course it was fixed, and the judge tried to browbeat us into accepting minimal damages and ultimately gave us, as I recall, a verdict of maybe $20,000. The insurance company paid the limit of the policy, but that amounted to only $10,000, so this legless woman in a wheelchair with one leg gone and the other useless only got a pittance, which was heartbreaking.

Wilkes's work with the Wall Street firm had been brilliant, but he didn't have the strongest character in the world, and what he didn't understand was that his brilliance meant little or nothing in the crooked courts of New York, and that he would lose not only that case—in effect—but also a case where a woman slipped in water from a clogged drain in her own basement and suffered a fractured skull and damage to her eyesight. But there again, thinking he had a sure shot, he brought the case to trial without a jury, and again we got no recovery, although there was a statute that clogged drains were a no-no, and complaints had been made to the landlord. They called it contributory negligence on her part, as though she could have walked four inches above the floor.

Then there was the Moriarty case, where a man who worked for National Gypsum had been driving one of those go-cart arrangements around the factory. It got out of control and he was smashed to death. It was established that there was some sort of mechanical defect, but again there was a judgment for National Gypsum and the Butler Bin Company, which made the go-cart.

The pressure of these defeats finally drove Wilkes around the bend. He'd been spending money the firm didn't have, based on what he assumed was coming in, but he was so naive he didn't realize how racist the courts here were, and when he lost one case after another he finally flipped out. He ran away with $57,000 of the firm's money, leaving about $5,000 in the bank to cover bills amounting to over $50,000.

This was the worst crisis I had to face, and it was then that I developed my theory that you never have problems bigger than you can handle, and if you just don't panic you will make it. Two or three weeks after Wilkes had absconded, someone came in and offered me $100 for an electric typewriter I had recently paid $600 for. But I thought, "If I sell my typewriter I won't be able to type up any papers, and the $100 isn't going to do much good anyway. This is not a distress sale, and I am just not going to take such a loss." And that's when I began to realize that the greater disaster is panic, and that it was my business not to panic—that was my job, at that moment. If I could just keep my little boat from toppling over, I would probably be able to weather the storm, and that's what happened.

All through this bad period I owed a lot to Charlie; after Wilkes ran away Charlie came into the office and typed and answered the phones, and generally kept my spirits up. Actually, during that time he drank less and behaved better than he did at any time before or after; apparently it was easier for him to be decent when I was on my ass, because when things got better Charlie began to go to pieces. He got very sick, and the doctor told him he had a bad liver and would have to give up drinking if he intended to live. Naturally I mentioned Alcoholics Anonymous, but he wasn't interested. I was very much into laissez-faire, and took the position that if he wanted to drink himself to death, okay, as long as he didn't treat me too badly or try to complicate my life, which of course he did. So whenever my cup got too full, I would just leave.

That summer we took a place on Fire Island, where he had constant tantrums and insulted everybody and was generally impossible, and finally I got to the point where I decided that was it. I left him on Fire Island and moved all my stuff out of his apartment. When he came back in September he would vacillate between crying like a helpless baby and invading the office, drunk as a lord. Finally I called the police, who took him to jail, where he stayed overnight. The next morning when I had to go to court he looked so pale and pitiful, I felt really sorry for him. Soon after that he died, which I suppose was as good a disposition of the case as could be expected.

I sent his body to California to his mother, and heard from her later only in connection with his Social Security, which she got. I was dead broke at the time and entitled to it, as his widow. But she wanted it, and I figured that with all the hassle, it would be worth about as much as fishing around in an unflushed toilet to recover a ballpoint pen.

Folk

A MAN WON'T MAKE A FOOL OF ME TWICE

LeaElla and Deal were hanging out they daily wash one morning, when Deal was moved to ask LeaElla a personal question. "Ella, I don't mean to pry. But, girl, I been wondering, why did you have seven children by different mens and not marry a one o' them?"

LeaElla snorted, "A man won't gonna make a fool of me twice."

Barbara Brandon

WHERE I'M COMING FROM

© 1992 Barbara Brandon/Distributed by Universal Press Syndicate

5-24

Norma Miller

THE LADIES

from Redd Foxx and Norma Miller, *The Redd Foxx Encyclopedia of Black Humor*

I've been single so long, I'm a senior single. . . . Take it from me, Bill Bailey never is coming home. Last time I saw him, he was strolling down Hollywood Boulevard holding hands with his new interest. I said, "There they go—Romeo and Romeo!" . . . Men today are getting more face-lifts than women, but what they *should* have lifted, they *don't*.

Today *he* is the sex object. The competition out here today is very keen; women are outnumbering men almost five to one, and what's left we've got to share with? Homosexuals, bisexuals, transexuals—and I'm a heterosexual. There's nothing worse than being heterosexual and having nobody to heterosex with!"

Terry McMillan

IT AIN'T ABOUT NOTHIN'

from *Waiting to Exhale*

I opened the door for Troy. Good God almighty. This man is past gorgeous. He was holding a lit cigarette between his fingers. I wish he didn't smoke, but I guess I can live with one bad habit. "Hey, sugar," he said. He was wearing a pale-blue polo shirt with some navy-blue baggy pants and Ray-Ban sunglasses, even though it was dark outside. His beeper was clipped to his shirt pocket. Troy does not look at all like he's forty years old. He's in great shape. Hallelujah. His waist is probably the same size as mine, and he moves those narrow hips like he's still twenty.

He gave me a sloppy kiss. It was good. When he went to put his hand underneath my blouse, I thought about what Bernadine had said. The truth was, I didn't know all that much about Troy, and tonight might be a good time to find out. So I backed away.

"What's wrong, baby?" he asked, and took a puff of his cigarette.

"Nothing. Have a seat." I went to find an ashtray, then sat down on the couch. Troy walked over to my stereo.

"How about some music," he said, and pressed the buttons on my cassette player like he'd been doing it for years. It was hard to believe I'd only known him three days.

"What would you like to do tonight?" I asked.

"Whatever makes you feel good," he said. "This sister can blow," he said, after Vanessa Williams started singing "Dreaming." Troy jumped up, put his cigarette back in his mouth, turned toward me, and pretended like he was slow-dancing with somebody.

"How about a movie?" I said.

"I'm not in the mood for a movie," he said, and started pacing around the room. "Ask me what I want to do."

"What do you want to do?"

"Spend the night making sweet love to you."

He rushed over to the end table, crushed out his cigarette, and flopped down next to me on the couch. I inched away. "That's all we've been doing, Troy. I'd like to get out of the house, and I'd like to get to know you better—standing up."

"Oh, I get it," he said, grinning. "We're getting serious, are we?"

"You're not serious?"

"Don't I act serious?"

"I can't tell for sure yet."

"You mind if I get a glass of wine?"

"I'll get it," I said, and stood up. I went over to the kitchen, poured us both a glass, brought the bottle back, and set it on the table.

Troy had lit another cigarette. He drank his wine down in one gulp and poured himself another one. "So what'd you have in mind?" he asked, and got back up.

"Are you nervous about something?" I asked.

"No. Got a lot of things going on, that's all." His beeper went off. "Can I use the phone for a minute?"

"Yep. There's one in the kitchen."

He got up and pulled the cord over by the sink. I heard him say, "Yeah, man, I'll check on you in a few minutes. I'll have a lady friend with me. She's cool." He hung up, walked behind the couch, and kissed me on the forehead. I almost died. But I wanted to see if I could control myself. For once in my life. "I need to run by one of my partners' for a few minutes. You feel like taking a drive?"

"Why not."

"Cool. He lives in Scottsdale. He's a lawyer. Nice people. You'll like him. Plus, I want you to get to know the kind of people I deal with."

Sounded good to me. "Can you give me a minute to do my face?"

"You look good enough," he said, and lit another cigarette.

"It'll only take a minute." I took my makeup kit out of my purse and went on into the bathroom. I brushed on a little more blush, a coat of lipstick, picked my hair out, and grabbed a fresh handkerchief from my drawer. When I came out and said, "I'm ready," Troy looked like he'd just seen a ghost.

His car was deep. It was a 1978 Cadillac. I didn't know he was the Cadillac-driving type. The interior was gray leather, and it smelled good, like jasmine. It was coming from that yellow felt Christmas tree dangling from the rearview mirror. We drove through Tempe and on up toward

Scottsdale Road. The closer we got to the hills, the darker the streets got. "You mind if I crack the window? The smoke is making my eyes water."

"No. Go right ahead," he said.

"Whereabouts do you live, Troy?"

"Seventeenth, right off Baseline."

"Do you live by yourself?"

"Not anymore."

"You don't?"

"No. My mother and son live with me."

"Oh," I said. That bit of information put a real damper on things. The man was forty years old. And his mother still lived with him? I bet *he* lives with his mother. Either way, I couldn't believe it. Maybe there was more to this than I understood. Considering I just met the man, I didn't want to get all into his business, but I had to ask something. "How old is your son?"

"Sixteen."

"Is his mother here in Phoenix?"

"She's in Detroit. He was having some problems a while back, so I took him off her hands. He's a good kid. Just got mixed up with the wrong people."

"What about your mother?"

"What about her?"

"What's it like, living with your mother?"

"Convenient. She cooks and cleans and basically runs the house. She gets her social security checks, plays a little bingo, and goes to church. I couldn't ask for a better situation, really. She's only sixty-eight but kind of scared about living by herself. She's got asthma. But since she's been out here, she's only had three attacks where she had to be hospitalized."

"How long has she been out here?"

"Four years."

"She's been living with you for four years?"

"Yeah."

"What's that like?"

"I told you, it works out for everybody. She's not all in my business or anything, and I can bring a lady friend home with no problem. You'll see."

"I will?"

"Yeah. I already told her about you. I want you to meet both of them."

Well, I thought, how refreshing. Right now I was hoping we'd get where we were going, because I had to go to the bathroom. Bad. We pulled into this long driveway that led to a beautiful Santa Fe house with a big oak door. After we rang the doorbell, Troy bent over and kissed me. "You'll like Bill," he said. "He's real cool people."

When Bill answered the door, he didn't look like any lawyer to me. He was wearing a Mike Tyson T-shirt, but Mike's face was almost gone. Bill had two gold earrings in one ear, and a raggedy Jheri-Kurl. He was probably handsome at one time, but there were pockmarks all over his face. The sockets under his eyes were puffy, and his lips were chapped. He could stand some dental work. And his bluejeans were clearly too big. He was skinnier than my daddy.

"Come on in," he said, ushering us. Bill acted like he was in a hurry. He moved so fast, I almost broke my neck trying to catch up to him and Troy on that marble floor. It eventually led to a sunken living room. The whole house was done in black and white, that high-tech look, and he had Kenny G blaring. There were four other men sitting in the family room, and the TV was on, but it didn't look like anybody was watching it. That's when I smelled the reefer and saw the glass pipe sitting on the coffee table, with a flame burning underneath. Oh, shit, I thought, not crack.

I sat down. Bill introduced me to the other four men, whose names and faces I wasn't going to remember. Why didn't he ask me if I did this stuff, or if I minded being around it? Why didn't he give me some clue he was into this? "May I use your bathroom?" I asked.

"Be my guest," Bill said, and pointed down the hall.

When I came back out, they were crouched around the same spot, passing the pipe. Troy sounded like he was choking.

"You want a hit?" Bill asked.

"No, thanks," I said.

"How about some wine?"

"I don't think we have time, do we?" I said, looking at Troy.

"We've got time for a glass of wine," Troy said, and winked at me.

I sat there listening to them talk about some fight that had been on HBO, while they passed the pipe back and forth. One of the guys lit another joint, and I felt like running out the front door. This was so boring. And these men were old enough to know better.

I drank my wine and then the "transaction" was done. Troy handed Bill a hundred-dollar bill, and Bill handed him a white piece of paper shaped like a triangle. When Troy said we had to be going, I pretended like it was really good to have met them and looked forward to seeing them all again.

When we got in the car, Troy was wired up. "You feel like stopping by the Jockey Club and having a drink? I feel like doing something. Didn't you say you wanted to hear some music? I think Patti Williams is singing somewhere tonight. We could get a paper or stop by a phone booth and I could call around to check. She's good. You heard her before?"

"No," I said dryly. I didn't know where to start, since he obviously didn't feel weird about what I'd just witnessed. But then I blurted out, "I wanna go home."

"Is something wrong, baby?"

"I didn't know you were into this kind of thing."

"I just do it sometimes for recreation, that's all. Does it bother you?"

"Yes, it does."

"Then I won't do it around you. How's that?"

"I don't usually deal with men who mess around with drugs. Drugs scare me."

"You're making it sound like I'm an addict or something. All I did was took a few hits, picked up a little package, and to be honest, I don't *have* to do this. I swear. I like you, Robin, and I don't want something like this to come between us when I'm just starting to get to know you."

"I don't feel good about this, Troy. How can you do drugs, considering what you do for a living?"

"What I do in my private life is completely separate from what I do at work. Look, if I was into this shit that heavy, do you think I'd be in such good shape?"

He had a point, because he was in tip-top shape, which was another thing that baffled me. I was wondering how he could do this junk and work out without having a heart attack or something.

"Look," he said. "My mother is barbecuing some ribs tomorrow evening, and I told her I'd bring you over. What time do you get home from work?"

"About six."

"I'll pick you up about six-thirty. And hey, we can deal with this. It's really not as much of a problem as you're making it out to be. It ain't about nothin'."

He smiled at me and winked. I knew I was probably being a fool, but no man had asked me to meet his mother in centuries, so I figured *maybe* he wasn't into it so much and *maybe* if we got to know each other better— once he saw that I didn't need drugs to enjoy myself—*maybe* I might be a good influence on him. So I told him yes, I'd love to come over to his house and meet his mother and son.

When we got to my apartment, I let him get back into my bed. We did it for what seemed like hours. Troy didn't act like he was satisfied. He was still hard as a rock, but I was tired and had to call it quits. I had to get up and go to work in a matter of hours. I thought he fell asleep right after I did, but when I heard the phone ring and reached over to answer it, that's when I noticed Troy was gone.

"Hi, baby," he said.

"Troy?"

"In the flesh," he said. "How'd you sleep?"

"Good, I guess. When did you leave?"

"About five."

"Are you at home?"

"Yep. Just reading and listening to some Coltrane. You ever listen to Coltrane?"

"No, I don't."

"You should. He's deep, so deep I can't even understand him sometime. How's my baby?"

I didn't quite know how to answer that, but I said, "Fine."

"Good. How are those luscious titties of mine this morning?"

"They're mine, not yours, but they're fine."

"Come on, Robin. Help me go to sleep, baby."

"You haven't been to sleep yet?"

"I felt like reading. You had me so lit up last night, I couldn't get enough of you. But when I saw you were wiped out, I figured I should just go on home and read and let you get your rest."

"Thanks for being so considerate," I said.

"Open your legs for me, baby."

"What?"

"Open those long brown legs for me and touch yourself until you get slippery."

"Troy, I don't like this."

"Come on, baby, do it for me."

"I'm not doing anything. But what I am about to do is hang up this phone if you don't change the tone of your voice and this whole conversation. I mean it."

"Okay, okay. I was just having a little fun. Damn, I'm hard as ice, baby. See what kind of power you have? See what you can do to a grown man over the telephone? Does that tell you what kind of woman you are?"

"Not really."

Then the tone of his voice changed. He got serious all of a sudden. "I'll pick you up at six-thirty. My mother's already made the potato salad. Okay?"

"Okay," I said, but I didn't know what I was getting into.

"What should I do?" I asked Savannah. I spent half the morning telling her what had happened. I was at work.

"I wouldn't go. Especially knowing he's into crack."

"I know. But he said he only does it sometimes."

"What'd you expect him to say? That he's a crackhead? Give me a break, Robin. Stop being so gullible."

"What time is it?"

"A little past eleven."

"I should go ahead and call him and cancel, then, huh?"

"I would, but you do what you want to do. What I want to know is, what's with him wanting you to meet his family, and you haven't even known him a week? I'd be skeptical if for no other reason besides that. What have you done with this man besides fuck him that would make knowing you so deep that he wants to bring you home to his mama already?"

"I know, girl."

"Call him, and call me right back."

"I don't know his number at work."

"Call his mama and get it."

When I called, his mother answered the phone. "Hi there," she said. "We're really looking forward to meeting you. Troy's told me all about you. It isn't very often that he wants me to meet a lady friend, so I figure you must be awful special, which is why I told him I'd have this little barbecue for you. Give you a chance to meet the rest of the family what lives here in Phoenix."

"You mean this barbecue's for me?"

"He didn't tell you? We want to welcome you to the family. Make you feel at home."

"That's very thoughtful of you, ma'am. Could you give me Troy's work number?"

"He didn't go to work today."

"He didn't?"

"I think he's coming down with a cold."

"Well, is he there?"

"Nope."

"You think he'll be back soon?"

"I couldn't tell you, baby. Sick or not, that boy moves at eighty miles an hour. He don't stop too long for nothing. If he comes back anytime soon, you want me to have him call you?"

"Would you? I'm at work. He has the number."

"I sure will. Looking forward to meeting you. This ain't nothing fancy, so don't go getting all dressed up and everything. Just a few of his cousins, his brother and three sisters'll be here. That's all."

"Well, I'm looking forward to meeting all of you too," I said. "I'll see you a little later, ma'am."

"Bye, baby," she said, and hung up.

What the hell was going on here? I didn't know he'd planned a family reunion. Why didn't he let me in on this? What kind of man was I dealing with? Lord, help me.

I didn't feel like going out for lunch today, so I ordered a ham-and-cheese sandwich from the deli downstairs. When the boy delivered it, I reached inside my purse to get my wallet. It wasn't there. I took everything out and piled it on top of my desk. It wasn't there. I was trying to remember the last time I took it out for something. While I sat there going over this in my mind, Marva realized the boy was waiting for his money, so she lent me four dollars. I paid him. Then I tried to think again, where I could've dropped it, or if I forgot and left it at home.

I walked in my front door at ten after six. I looked between the cushions of the couch, the bathroom, under the bed—everywhere in that apartment—and still didn't find my wallet.

Troy showed up at six-thirty on the dot. His eyes were red, and he smelled like wine. He had a growth of hair on his face. He did not look so hot. He bent over to kiss me, and I wanted to gag. "You ready, baby?"

"I'm not going."

"What?"

"I said I'm not going."

"Why not?"

"Because I don't like this."

"You don't like what?"

"How you've done this."

"What are you talking about?"

"Troy. First of all, I don't feel good about any of this. I hardly know you, and you definitely don't know me, or you would've had the common courtesy to ask me if I indulged in drugs, or minded if you did, before you took me over to some crackhead's house, and then on top of that to call me up in the middle of the night talking all vulgar and then giving your mother the impression that we're almost engaged, and here I am thinking I'm going over to your house for a friendly barbecue and come to find out the whole affair's been staged for me."

"What's wrong with that?"

"I don't know you well enough to be meeting your mother and son yet."

"Says who?"

"Says me. This is moving too fast for me, and I can't deal with it."

"Oh, so what am I supposed to tell my mother and son and the rest of my family that's sitting over at my house right now waiting for *you?*"

"Anything you want to."

"And I'm just supposed to accept this."

"You don't have a choice. You should've asked me first."

"I did ask you."

"No you didn't. You told me."

"Look. Do you know how many women would love for me to bring them to my house to meet my mother?"

"I can about guess."

"I want you to come anyway."

"I said I don't want to, and I'm not going."

"You know what? You black bitches are all alike. First you complain that don't nobody want your asses or know how to treat you, and then when a man shows a genuine interest in you, you act simple. And y'all wanna know why we go out with white women."

I guess this was supposed to hurt my feelings, but it didn't. A white woman could have his sorry ass. "Are you finished?" I said.

"I guess I am," he said, and turned toward the door. "You know something?" he said.

"What's that?"

"You need to be more careful about who you pick up in grocery stores."

When he closed the door, I stood there fuming. I ran over to the phone, called Savannah, and told her everything. She wasn't the least bit shocked. "So I guess you know who's got your wallet?"

"You think he stole my wallet?"

"Bye, Robin," she said, and hung up.

Coco

LOVE AWAITS

from Courtney Long, ed., *Love Awaits*

I've had one interracial relationship. I had just graduated high school. He was thirty-six, a self-made millionaire. He was retired and he dated only Black women. He said he never, ever dated a white woman. His mother, his friends, his sister, all verified it. He said he finds Black women more appealing and more satisfying. Spiritually and sexually.

Wait, I gotta interrupt.

I know what you're gonna say, but I had just graduated high school. I hadn't formulated U.S. history, myth, racial solidarity, and I'm now sounding double standard and hypocritical, this was a bygone era. So, anyway. We had started out as friends and things progressed. He wanted to step up the relationship. He wanted to take me on a safari to Kenya. He wanted to lavish and spoil me like I've never been. I found out that he did that for every

Black woman he's dated. He's taken them to Africa. My mother wouldn't let me go.

But you were eighteen.

But my mother didn't want me to go.

And you didn't go?

Never seen the continent, but I've gotten all this other stuff I don't use. I have a pair of Jet Skis sitting in Seattle collecting dust. I don't know if he was try'n to make up for something with this Black woman thing, guilt complex or what, but, Africa, gifts, this was what he was doing for Black women.

As far as sex, we never had any. We never had full intercourse. He was very much content with just performing oral sex. And as far as the myth goes about men compensating through oral sex for not having a large penis, that wasn't the case. He was in there.

Why was he content with only oral sex?

Well, he knew at the time I was young and I wasn't ready for sex.

Were you a virgin?

No.

Then why was he content with only oral sex?

He also knew that's what I liked. See, that's a difference between Black men and white men. White men will make sure you're satisfied. Black men seem more concerned with their own satisfaction and that's it.

You're tell'n me he had no desire to enter this young, beautiful Black sister? A tight, dancer's body. He loves Black women. He dates only Black women. They're more appealing and satisfying. He has an energetic, fresh-out-of-high-school eighteen-year-old, and he's satisfied with just oral sex?

Well, then fuck it. To tell you the God's honest truth, it wasn't him, it was me. The thought of having sex with him turned me off. I only told him I wasn't ready to have intercourse. It wasn't so much that he was white, but he was white, white. He just wasn't sexually appealing. Had he a tan, and worked out, I may have been attracted.

Folk

I FIGURED HE COULD FLY

This old couple had been married fifty years, and she say [soft, appealing tone], "You know, you oughta do *something* for me."

He say [mean, cruel tone], "I give you shelter and food. What the hell you want?"

She say [conciliatory tone], "I just thought maybe we could go to Atlantic City."

"What the *hell* you going to Atlantic City for?"

She say, "Just for the sport of it—to celebrate fifty years . . ."

He say, "Aw shit, alright."

He fussed all the way to Atlantic City. When they got there the man say, "We have a room for you on the fifth floor."

He say, "Why we got to stay on the fifth floor? Why can't we stay on the first?"

She say, "Because the lobby's on the first floor, asshole. Nobody stays on the first floor. We gon' stay on the *fifth.*"

He cussed all the way up to the room.

She say, "Now the first thing you do when you go to Atlantic City is walk on the *Boardwalk.*"

He say, "You walk on the fuckin' Boardwalk. I'm gon' watch television."

"Fine."

So when she came back the chain was on the door. She couldn't get in. . . . [pause]

So the Coroner asked her, "What happened?"

She say, "It took me fifty years to get him to come here, and I put up with his attitude, which was just totally negative . . ."

He say, "Yes, go on."

She say, "I asked him to walk out on the Boardwalk with me, and he said no." She say, "He hasn't slept with me in years. But when I did push the door open and he was fucking the maid, I threw his ass out the window."

The man said, "Why?"

She say, "I figured if he thought he could fuck, he could fly."

Folk

SEXUAL AWARENESS

Sexual awareness comes so early now. A baby boy was lying next to a baby girl in the crib, and the baby girl started screaming, "Rape! Rape!"

"Oh, shut up," the baby boy responded—"ain't nobody bothering you. You just rolled over on your pacifier."

Cucumbers Are Better than Men Because . . .

The average cucumber is at least six inches long.

Cucumbers stay hard for a week.

A cucumber never suffers from performance anxiety.

Cucumbers are easy to pick up.

You can fondle cucumbers in a supermarket . . . and you know how firm it is before you take it home.

Cucumbers can get away any weekend.

A cucumber will always respect you in the morning.

A cucumber won't ask: Am I the first?

Cucumbers don't care if you're a virgin.

Cucumbers won't tell other cucumbers you're a virgin.

Cucumbers won't tell anyone you're not a virgin anymore.

With cucumbers you don't have to be a virgin more than once.

Cucumbers don't have sex hang-ups.

You can have as many cucumbers as you can handle.

You only eat cucumber when you feel like it.

Cucumbers never need a round of applause.

Cucumbers won't ask:

. . . Am I the best?

. . . How was it?

. . . Did you come? How many times?

A cucumber won't mind hiding in the refrigerator when your mother comes over.

A cucumber will never make a scene because there are other cucumbers in the refrigerator.

No matter how old you are you can always get another cucumber.

A cucumber will never give you a hickey.

Cucumbers can stay up all night . . . and you won't have to sleep on the wet spot.

Cucumbers won't leave you wondering for a month.

Cucumbers won't tell you a vasectomy will ruin it for them.

A cucumber never forgets to flush the toilet.

A cucumber doesn't flush the toilet when you're in the shower.

Cucumbers don't compare you to a centerfold.

Cucumbers don't tell you they liked you better with long hair.

A cucumber will never leave you for:

. . . another woman

. . . another man

. . . another cucumber

You always know where your cucumber has been.

Cucumbers don't have mid-life crises.

Cucumbers don't play the guitar and try to find themselves.

A cucumber won't tell you he's outgrown you intellectually.

Cucumbers never expect you to have little cucumbers.

It's easy to drop a cucumber.

No matter how you slice it, you can have your cuke and eat it too.

MIMEOGRAHED   ITEM

Chain Letter

Dear Friend,

This chain letter was started by a woman like yourself, in hopes
of bringing relief to tired and discontented women. Unlike most
chain letters, this one does not cost anything.

Send a copy to five of your friends who are just as tired of it
all as you; then pack up your husband and send him to the woman
whose name is at the top of the list. Then add your name to the
bottom of the list.

When your name comes up, you will receive 16,478 men, and some of
them are really dandies! Have faith and don't break the chain. One
woman broke it and got her own son-of-a-bitch back.

Sincerely,

A Discontented Wife

P.S. At the time of this writing, a friend of mine had received
183 men. They buried her yesterday, but it took three undertakers
36 hours to take the grin off her face.

MIMEOGRAPHED ITEM

Dear Ann Landers

Dear Ann Landers,

     I am writing to tell you my problem. It seems that I have been married to a sex maniac for the past 22 years. He makes love to me regardless of what I am doing. I can be ironing, washing dishes, sweeping or anything and I would like to know if there *[illegible]*

[several lines illegible handwritten text]

     Please *[illegible]*

[illegible signature]

Mother Love

HOW TO TELL IF YOUR MARRIAGE IS IN TROUBLE

A few pointers:

     You go to the bank and there ain't no money in your joint account.

     When the power company turns off your electricity and he hands you a change-of-address card for the post office. Could it be that he's trying to tell you that he doesn't want to live with you anymore? Take the hint, Girlfriend!

When you're washing his laundry, your laundry, and her laundry.

When you got a "wife-in-law." This is the other woman—ya know, the mistress.

When you find out he's got a couple of kids you never knew about who live around the corner . . . and you had been thinkin', *Don't all those kids resemble my husband?*

When her marriage starts coming to your house.

When his laundry is beginning to look a little sparse—where did all his clothes go? You know he can't be outgrowing them, so he must be leaving them somewhere else.

When he changes his aftershave.

When he's so preoccupied that he's forgotten to feed his dog (who you don't like) for a week. Now that dog is sniffin' around you, probably thinking, *Breakfast.*

When the dog you raised from a puppy starts barking at you, or he's barkin' more than usual at your Girlfriend, maybe he's trying to tell you something.

When your dog starts sniffin' your husband's crotch.

When you want to do the wild thing and he don't show up!

When everything you look at looks like a phallus and your husband looks like a tadpole.

When you're gettin' yourself all pretty and fancy and you ain't doing it for him.

Bottom line? You know your marriage is in trouble when things have changed—and not for the better. What do you do? If he's the one cheating (yeah, I know it really hurts), I'd be direct, open, and honest about it. See how he responds. Does he want to remain married to you? If so, he's going to have to end his affair. Is he willing to go to a marriage counselor with you so that you can both learn what's not working in your relationship?

While you may eventually forgive him, or he will eventually forgive you, this is a period in your marriage that neither one of you will ever forget. But look at yourself in the mirror, Girlfriend, and ask yourself: Is it worth fixing? And if it is, it's gonna be the hardest row you've ever hoed, but you can fix it if it means enough to you.

Barbara Brandon

WHERE I'M COMING FROM

Toni Cade Bambara

THE JOHNSON GIRLS

from *Gorilla, My Love*

[In this scene the "Sisters" are helping their friend Inez pack her clothes to go to Knoxville to bring her errant lover Roy home and lamenting the problem of having to live "à la carte." An indirect goal of this conversation is to teach the younger "Sister," who is the narrator, "the ways of menfolk."]

"Leave the door open, sweetheart," Sugar say to me. "Don't want to miss the bell."

"Whatshisname picking you up here, Sugar?" Gail say. "I don't know what you see in that ugly old man. Got no dough and no politics neither." Sugar just look at Gail and they all bust out laughing. "That cat in the suede hat you had with you at Marcy's opening was fine. Whatcha want with Whatshisname is beyond my brain." Sugar give Gail that same look and they fall out again. "Now seems to me Leon would catch your eye. He thinks you shit diamonds and pee Chanel Number Five, the way he knocks himself out every time you ask him to do something. Ain't too heavy in the mind department, but he looks as though he might be able to keep up with his own socks and fix a leaky faucet or something."

"I love a handy man," sigh Marcy, posing in the closet like she'd grown up worshippin toolboxes and hacksaws and shit, dream-walking through lumberyards questing the plumber prince or something. We just look at her, Marcy Stevens, sculptress in a trance, leaning against Inez's shoerack with a long velour purple knit tunic up against her like it was the fairy-princess gown. Then the bell rings and it's the man with the heroes, and Sugar with her plump self scoots back with the piles of stuff they all fall on so fast, all I get is two plastic cups of cole slaw and half a hero, mostly sauce and onions.

"One day," say Sugar, lickin the tomato sauce off her arm, "what I want's goin to be on the menu. Served up to my taste and all on one plate, so I don't have to clutter up the whole damn table with a teensy bowl of this and a plate of extra that and a side order of what the hell." She shimmy her buns on top of the dresser and plants her feet in the bottom drawer. "Cause let Sister Sugar hip you bitches, living à la carte is a trip."

"Tell it all, Sister Sugar," say Gail.

"First, you gotta have you a fuckin man, a cat that can get down between the sheets without a whole lotta bullshit about 'This is a spiritual union' or 'Women are always rippin off my body' or . . ."

"Amen," say Marcy.

"Course, he usually look like hell and got no I.Q. atall," say Sugar. "So you gots to have you a go-around man, a dude that can put in a good appearance so you won't be shame to take him round your friends, case he insist on opening his big mouth." Inez laugh her first laugh of the day and lean back in the chair to do her nails.

"Course, the go-round man ain't about you, he about his rap and his wardrobe and his imported deodorant stick with the foreign ingredients listed there at the bottom in some unknown tongue. Which means you gots to have a gofor."

"A gopher?" I ask, and they all look me over carefully to make sure I am finally old enough for these big-league sessions.

"Like when you crazy with pain and totally messed around and won't nobody on earth go for your shit, you send for the gofor cause he go for it whatever it is."

"Rah–rah for the gofors," say Marcy, flapping a sea–green paisley vest in the air.

"You gots to have your money man, that goes without saying. And more importantly, you got to have you a tender man."

"I loves me a tender man," sigh Marcy, who's beginning to sound fickle to me cause she sighin just as sexy as she did for the handyman dude.

"A tender man who can tend to your tenderest needs. Maybe it means painting your bedroom a dumb shade of orange, cause just so happens you need that dumb shade of orange in your life right now. Or holding your head while you heave your insides into the toilet on account you been tryin to drown some jive ass sucker in alcohol, and knowin all the while it won't wash."

"Speak on it, Dame Sugar," say Gail.

"Or maybe it's just spoon-feeding you and putting on your pink angora socks and rubbin your tired feet while you launch into some sad-ass saga about peeing in your pants in the second grade and how that set you on the wrong course of life forever after and . . ."

"He's beginning to sound like the gopher," I say, and then I'm sorry. Cause they all lookin at me, even Inez with her left hand rotating and glistening red, like I am indeed that pitiful babe stumblin into Great Ma Drew's dynamite shaft without a candle to my name.

"Oh but honey," Sugar say, shoveling in the green peppers, "one day I'm gonna have it all and right on the same plate. Cause à la carte is a bitch."

"Being a together woman is a bitch," say Marcy.

"Being a bitch is a bitch," say Gail.

"Men a bitch," is my two cents, which seems to get over.

"But one day my prince will come," sings Marcy, waltzing around with Inez's black sequined sweater. Sugar look at her like she crazy. Inez smile that slow smile. But Gail get up off the bed for a closer look at the hole in Marcy head.

"Prince? You waiting for a prince? That's anti-struggle, sister," say Gail and they all crack, "counter-revolutionary and just plain foolish. Princes do not come. Frogs come. And they are never the enchanted kind. And they are definitely not about some magic kiss. They give you warts, sister."

"That's right," say Sugar, jumping down from the dresser and poking up her belly and swellin up her cheeks till I thought I'd die.

"It's either à la carte or half a loaf," Inez say real serious.

Lisa Jones

CORPORATE BOYS

from *bulletproof diva*

Deandra, my crazy friend the photographer, is scoffing down rice and beans at a Cuban restaurant on Flatbush Avenue and talking about Negroes. Most of my straight women friends in their late twenties are grumbling about the one-in-four problem (one out of every four black men in this city is in jail, to which we add: number two is on drugs, number three prefers gentlemen or blondes, and number four already has ten women), but not Miss One and a Half. She always has a Negro or two on hand. Girl, *let me tell you* (Deandra loves to milk it), I've got myself a corporate boy. I drop my fork.

In college, Miss Bohemia wouldn't have been caught dead with a Negro in an alligator shirt and Levi's, and now she's dating corporate boys? I still believe in revolution, Deandra assures me, it's just, Che Guevara doesn't turn me on anymore. Revolution or no revolution, Deandra's attracted to power, so her taste in men changes with the political forecast: Today Huey Newton, tomorrow Ron Brown.

Deandra confesses that she's been watching corporate boys for a while. The ones who ride the iron horse into the city from buppie enclaves like Fort Greene, Prospect Heights, and Park Slope. They went to the right schools, and now they have the right jobs and the right cars (though between student loan payments and Amex bills, repossession is around the corner). And, of course, the right suits. (They work those suits, don't they? It's not about the suit making the man, it's about how the man is filling out the suit.) Something about their swagger and confidence started ringing my bells, Deandra says, Girl, forget about the dreadlocks and the dashikis, just give me a clean head and a Brooks Brothers charcoal gray (or even a Crick-eteer, I'm not a purist).

Deandra goes on about corporate boys and how the suit is such a loaded symbol in their lives. It's their badge of honor (stamps their professional degrees on their sleeves), their passbook to the white-collar world (even gets them a cab sometimes), and immediately "neutralizes" their skin color in the company of what corporate boys call their "majority brethren."

And, Deandra tells me, they have such a way with language. In familiar company they speak a creole of King's English and blacker-than-thou neologisms. You know, girl, they have to prove they're down all the time (lest we think they're sellouts), so they come up with the most endearing homeboyisms. Check out hommie's wig, my corporate boy said to me the other day, why doesn't he comb it? Looks like Nipsey Russell got lost in the African rain forest. It's that fascinating mix of extreme self-love and seething self-hatred that middle-class blacks do so well. Enough already, I tell Deandra, fix me up with some of your corporate boy's friends.

Lunch with bachelor number one is in the corporate dining room of a major commercial bank. Needless to say, he and I are the lone spots of color in the place. The only son of a large West Indian family from Bedford-Stuyvesant, Keith Browning (names changed to protect corporate identities), twenty-four, went to an Ivy League school to learn how to be a banker. Keith's staid blue and black suits are custom-made by his father, a tailor, and he is quite proud of how they fit him, unlike the "off-the-rack polyester jammies" worn by the lower level management types who work a couple of floors below him. Being a "custom man" is not so much a question of ego. Like many black men, he's a hard fit. "If you have a high behind," Keith says, "pants will ride up on you and ruin the line of the suit." As we nosh on our bow-tie pasta, I can't help staring at the knot of Keith's paisley tie, which is slightly askew. "You can't look too good," he tells me. "Then you're perceived as a threat. You already stand out as a minority. And I definitely do because I'm six-foot-four and most of the majorities I work for are Lilliputians."

Bachelor number two receives me in his Prospect Heights duplex: exposed brick, Levolor blinds, every electrical appliance known to mankind. The walk-in closet I pass on the way to the john is a virtual gallery: creamy leathers, mossy suedes, and a few dozen or so Cosby-style sweaters. And this is the *casual clothes* closet, mind you. Wonder where he keeps his suits.

Damon Givens, twenty-eight, grew up in the South Bronx, went to college out of state on a basketball scholarship, and is now a second-year attorney at a Madison Avenue firm. He tells me that going to college with fifteen pairs of sneakers and checking out his wealthy white roommate's closet (loafers, snow boots, and a pair of track shoes held together with duct tape) taught him a lot about priorities. Instead of high tops, now he collects Italian suits. Damon says his Armanis ("Manies," he calls them) and Hugo Bosses ("Hugues") make him something of maverick at the firm, but they're a better fit. He can get a way with a lot more in terms of cut than color because in the corporate world "it's about avoiding anything threatening. And color is threatening psychologically."

In his Toyota Celica ("just lean back and pretend it's a 280 SL"), bachelor number three takes me on a tour of the Brownsville housing project where he spent the first thirteen years of his life, before winning a scholarship to a Massachusetts prep school. After B-school, Michael Geffens, twenty-eight, worked at an investment bank until last year when he was laid off in the crunch. This is how Michael bought his first suit: He took the annual report of a company he wanted to work for to Barney's and matched a suit in a photo with one on the rack. Today he wears custom jobs by a guy named Rock out of California. Rock comes to Manhattan several times a year to hold fittings at the Waldorf Astoria, then sends the measurements to Hong Kong. The suits come back with the label: "designed exclusively for Michael Geffens." Michael and his boys share this same tailor and they refer to their suits as "rocks."

Michael describes the cockiness he feels as a young black man in an expensive suit. He savors the reactions he gets. Older black women smile at him like he's their son; young guys in kente-cloth kufis size him up, he feels, like "Who's the wannabe in the suit? Doesn't he know that he's still a nigger?" At work once, Michael changed to sneakers and jeans in the bathroom. A co-worker, one of his majority brethren, was shocked to run into him in such an altered state: "Gosh," his co-worker marveled, "if I saw you in the street with that on, I'd never think you're as intelligent as you are."

Deandra calls later in the week to ask how I did with the corporate boys. They talk a good game, but girlfriend, how do you get past the elitism? One bachelor kept going on about "mutants" (any "homeboy in a Gumby fade who's not rolling nine to five") and "perpetrators" who hang out in buppie watering holes like Honeysuckle's and B. Smith's but have to go home first to change into a suit. Deandra wants me to meet her corporate boy because, naturally, he isn't like that. (Not only does Deandra get the Negroes, she gets the exceptions.) Dodd Hicks treats us to a Thai meal on the Upper East Side.

Rising close to six-foot-three with the beginnings of a paunch and back-set hairline, Dodd reeks power. He humors us by engaging in the type of mock self-deprecation that only the truly confident can afford. Dodd tells us about the "who's-that-other-nigger-in-a-suit look" he gives and gets from other young black men on Wall Street. "White people have done a good job of convincing us that opportunities extended to others limit our own," Dodd says, fingering the lapels of his Hugo Boss. Deandra looks up at him like he's the best thing since the Afro pick. What could be more attractive than nationalist rhetoric from a boy in a suit?

Barbara Brandon

WHERE I'M COMING FROM

Flo Kennedy

IF YOU WON'T TALK ABOUT WHAT I'M WEARING

from *Color Me Flo*

Clothes are like packages—sometimes they are indicative of the contents: for example, in a rape situation, a jury can be made to believe a woman almost invites rape when she's wearing tight pants or jeans, whereas a man in an expensive coat doesn't suggest he should be mugged, and wearing a diamond doesn't mean you are inviting robbery. And women supposedly invite rape by wearing miniskirts. I am sure that nobody in our society is absolutely free of that feeling, but it would not occur to anyone seriously to suggest that a bank invites robbery by having all that money there.

When women began wearing pants there was a tremendous backlash. I can remember—I was still practicing law at that time—going to court in pants and the judge's remarking that I wasn't properly dressed, that the next time I came to court I should be dressed like a lawyer. He's sitting there in a long black dress gathered at the yoke, and I said, "Judge, if you won't talk about what I'm wearing, I won't talk about what you're wearing," because it occurred to me that a judge in a skirt telling me not to wear pants was just a little bit ludicrous. It's interesting to speculate how it developed that in two of the most anti-feminist institutions, the church and the law court, the men are wearing the dresses.

Ntozake Shange

LADY IN RED

from *colored girls*

without any assistance or guidance from you
i have loved you assiduously for 8 months 2 wks & a day
i have been stood up four times
i've left 7 packages on yr doorstep
forty poems 2 plants & 3 handmade notecards i left
town so i cd send to you have been no help to me
on my job
you call at 3:00 in the mornin on weekdays
so i cd drive 27 1/2 miles cross the bay before i go to work
charmin charmin
but you are of no assistance
i want you to know
this waz an experiment
to see how selfish i cd be

if i wd really carry on to snare a possible lover
if i waz capable of debasin my self for the love of another
if i cd stand not being wanted
when i wanted to be wanted
& i cannot
so
with no further assistance & no guidance from you
i am endin this affair

this note is attached to a plant
i've been waterin since the day i met you
you may water it
yr damn self

Folk

WELL, . . .

This woman had gone shopping, and so when she got home her husband wanted to know what she had bought. And so she said, "Well, I needed some new bras, and I got these."

And he said, "Well, why in the world would you buy any bras? You don't have anything to put in 'em."

And she say, "Well, you wear shorts, don't you?"

Folk

SHE DIDN'T ASK ABOUT YOU

This man's wife had gone in for her annual physical. And so she came home; she was *so excited!* She told her husband, "My doctor says I've got the body of an eighteen-year-old; I've got the breasts of a twenty-one-year old, and I've got the pussy of a twenty-five-year-old."

And he say, "Did she say anything about your ass?"

And she say, "No, she didn't ask about you."

Folk

I AIN'T DEAD

The old Baptist minister went to reprimand one of the women in his congregation. He say, "Sister, I heah tell you gon' have a baby! How in the world is you gon' be havin' a baby and yo' husband been dead more dan a year!"

"He might be dead," she retorted, "but I ain't."

MIMEOGRAPHED ITEM

Woman Whacks off Sleeping Husband's Penis, Then Throws It from Moving Car

Don't laugh, it's true and it could happen to you!

Right now, thousands of agitated, irate women have read that head-line and are contemplating taking that action against you the next time you make an unwanted sexual advance or look at them the wong way, or just piss them off in general (not to mention PMS and "that time of the month").

MEN, protect yourselves, NOW!!!

If you find yourself a victim of "CLIP and FLIP SYNDROME," could you be sure that the appropriate authorities would find your clipped member in time and intact? Could you be sure that the penis they find is REALLY YOURS?

Sign up now for our low-cost PENIS PROTECTION PLAN. We'll regis-ter your penis and scrotum and tattoo them with their own unique registration numbers, insuring that in case of separation, you'll get a perfect match every time!!

Or for just a little more money, you can join our JURASSIC PRICK program, in which we'll take a CELL SAMPLE from your penis and clone replacement parts for you in case a tractor trailer runs over your severed penis or some wild animal mistakes your detached member for chew toy, or DOWN THE HATCH, even!!

Don't get caught short. SIGN UP NOW

FOR THE JURASSIC PRICK PROGRAM

Zora Neale Hurston

THEIR EYES WERE WATCHING GOD

[At age thirty-five Janie's life is completely unfulfilled. Though she has material comforts, she feels beaten down by her husband Jody, but never expresses her emotions. For her, life is reduced to "nothin' but uh store and uh house." Things become even worse as her older husband begins to physically deteriorate. He tries to draw attention away from *his* potbelly, *his* aching back, and *his* sagging muscles by talking about his wife's aging. She meekly endures his humiliating commentaries as she labors quietly in his store . . . until the following episode.]

Steve Mixon wanted some chewing tobacco and Janie cut it wrong. She hated that tobacco knife anyway. It worked very stiff. She fumbled with the thing and cut way away from the mark. Mixon didn't mind. He held it up for a joke to tease Janie a little.

"Looka heah, Brother Mayor, whut yo' wife done took and done." It was cut comical, so everybody laughed at it. "Uh woman and uh knife—no kind of uh knife, don't b'long tuhgether." There was some more good-natured laughter at the expense of women.

Jody didn't laugh. He hurried across from the post office side and took the plug of tobacco away from Mixon and cut it again. Cut it exactly on the mark and glared at Janie.

"I god almighty! A woman stay round uh store till she get old as Methusalem and still can't cut a little thing like a plug of tobacco! Don't stand dere rollin' yo' pop eyes at me wid yo' rump hangin' nearly to yo' knees!"

A big laugh started off in the store but people got to thinking and stopped. It was funny if you looked at it right quick, but it got pitiful if you thought about it awhile. It was like somebody snatched off part of a woman's clothes while she wasn't looking and the streets were crowded. Then too, Janie took the middle of the floor to talk right into Jody's face, and that was something that hadn't been done before.

"Stop mixin' up mah doings wid mah looks, Jody. When you git through tellin' me how tuh cut uh plug uh tobacco, then you kin tell me whether mah behind is on straight or not."

"Wha—whut's dat you say, Janie? You must be out yo' head."

"Naw, Ah ain't outa mah head neither."

"You must be. Talkin' any such language as dat."

"You de one started talkin' under people's clothes. Not me."

"Whut's de matter wid you, nohow? You ain't no young girl to be get- tin' all insulted 'bout yo' looks. You ain't no young courtin' gal. You'se uh ole woman, nearly forty."

"Yeah, Ah'm nearly forty and you'se already fifty. How come you can't talk about dat sometimes instead of always pointin' at me?"

"T'ain't no use in gettin' all mad, Janie, 'cause Ah mention you ain't no young gal no mo'. Nobody in heah ain't lookin' for no wife outa yuh. Old as you is."

"Naw, Ah ain't no young gal no mo' but den Ah ain't no old woman neither. Ah reckon Ah looks mah age too. But Ah'm uh woman every inch of me, and Ah know it. Dat's uh whole lot more'n *you* kin say. You big- bellies round here and put out a lot of brag, but 'tain't nothin' to it but yo' big voice. Humph! Talkin' 'bout *me* lookin' old! When you pull down yo' britches, you look lak de change uh life."

"Great God from Zion!" Sam Watson gasped. "Y'all really playin' de dozens tuhnight."

"Wha—whut's dat you said?" Joe challenged, hoping his ears had fooled him.

"You heard her, you ain't blind," Walter taunted.

"Ah ruther be shot with tacks than tuh hear dat 'bout mahself," Lige Moss commiserated.

Then Joe Starks realized all the meanings and his vanity bled like a flood. Janie had robbed him of his illusion of irresistible maleness that all men cherish, which was terrible. The thing that Saul's daughter had done to David. But Janie had done worse, she had cast down his empty armor before men and they had laughed, would keep on laughing. When he pa- raded his possessions hereafter, they would not consider the two together. They'd look with envy at the things and pity the man that owned them. When he sat in judgment it would be the same. Good-for-nothing's like Dave and Lum and Jim wouldn't change place with him. For what can ex- cuse a man in the eyes of other men for lack of strength?

Mama Sez

The rooster does all the crowing, but it's the hen what lay the egg.

What's fair for the goose is fair for the gander.

You can take a horse to water, but you can't make him drink;
You can send a fool to school, but you can't make him think.

Leopards don't change their spots.

Remember, all that glitters is not gold.

You can take him outta the gutter, but you can't take the gutter outa him.

His mouth ain't no prayer book.

Men are like buses—you miss one, there's another one coming.

Don't jump out the frying pan into the fire.

Before you marry, keep both eyes open; after you marry, it's a good idea to shut one.

Sister to Sister

He's had his B.S. degree for a long time—bullshit.

That A.B. degree don't mean nothing but that he knows the first two letters of the alphabet.

Them lazy mens round here just itching to get in on my gravy train.

That man o' mine always gits everything assbackwards.

He ain't wrapped too tight.

How I gon' sleep with that husband o' mine callin' hogs [snoring] all night long?

When a group o' men get together, all they do is beat their chops about ball games.

That triffling nigger don't do diddly-squat/crow's squat around the house.

He's one of those "bip-bap, thank you ma'am" men [lovemaking is over as quickly as it is with rabbits in the folklore].

It's hard to find a man these days. They all either too young or too old! You either got to *teach* them how or try to *remind* them how.

This nigger come up, askin' me, "Are you a lesbian or somethin'?" I say, "No, but if you the alternative, I'll try it."

This old, gray-haired, bald-headed, stooped-over man come up in my face, trying to talk some stuff to me. I say, "Look here, man, I don't want nothin' old but some money."

That jive mother sure screwed up.

He just gits on my last nerve.

That man can just kiss me where the sun don't shine.

Nigger, puleese!

Every time I go out with that nigger, he reckless eyeballing some other woman.

"[My husband] was a rolling stone, all right. Couldn't keep his eye in his socket and his thing in his pocket." [Faye McDonald Smith, *Flight of the Blackbird*]

That nigger she's married to is a out and out dog. And she done let him run loose too long. He ain't changed in all these years they been married cept to a *old* dog.

Yeah, but he gon' find out one day that every dog has his day.

He goes up side her head any time he feel like it.

I told him he bet' not never put his cotton-picking hands on me.

I let him know that I'm a tough titty.

I let him know that I won't born yesterday.

I don't give a diddly squat if that jive turkey don't never darken my door again.

That jiggaboo better straighten up and fly right, cause I'm ready to put on my traveling/walking shoes.

Yeah, I'm ready to make like a banana and split/make like a paper doll and cut out.

She flew the coop.

I never was run out of a pond by a tadpole yet.

Well, you know, when the cat's away, the mouse will play.

He one of those young boys done start smelling hisself.

He sho opened up her nose. Yeah, he got her in the go-long.

He won't even give her the time of day now, and a few weeks ago look like he was gon' eat her up.

He just like all these other no-good mens, trying to deny that he's the F.O.B. [father of the baby].

If you want to get rid of yo boyfriend, take a picture and put it up face bottom in your shoe, and he'll fade away from you. [*Shuckin' and Jivin'*, p. 310]

"A woman without a man is like a fish without a bicycle." [Flo Kennedy, in Gloria Kaufman and Mary Kay Blakely, eds., *Pulling Our Own Strings: Feminist Humor & Satire,* 16]

CHAPTER 8

"Just Like a White Man"

DICTIES

Mr. Hartnett . . . blew his brains out just like a white man. Everybody
was a little proud of his suicide.
—Dorothy West, *The Living Is Easy*

From slavery to the present those Negroes who know no boundaries in their efforts to ape white people have always been the object of the most vehement assaults in the humor of African Americans—male and female. They bleach their skin to make it white; they suffer the most painful procedures to make their hair straight; they wear clothespins on their noses to make them straight; they hold their lips in to make them appear thin; they repudiate their emotional Baptist churches to become strait-laced Episcopalians; they wouldn't be caught dead eating a watermelon, but acclaim their love of peaches flambé; they repudiate spirituals and embrace Wesley's hymns; they deny the blues and jazz and claim an affinity for classical music; they castigate the drums and praise the violin; they ridicule the Negro dialect and pride themselves in speaking the King's English; they flee from the slums and aspire to a house in the suburbs with all white neighbors; they speak softly and cannot endure the loud, boisterous behavior they consider typical of unsophisticated Negroes. Their main goals in life are a big house in a white neighborhood, a Cadillac in their driveway, a mink coat on their backs, and acceptance into white homes and clubs where they will probably suffer constant affronts. In their efforts to raise their status in American society, they repudiate everything associated with the Negro and embrace anything suggestive of whiteness, no matter how ridiculous. They are more prejudiced against their darker skinned sisters and brothers than many white racists. One of Dorothy West's Boston mulatto bourgeoisie, Mr. Binney, was always the first to leave when other Negroes moved into the neighborhood: "Mr. Binney could say with pride, right up to the day of his death, that he had never lived on a street where other colored people resided."[1] In a more recent novel, *The Wedding,* West pictures a striving schoolteacher of the first generation after Emancipation who carefully plots her advancement in society, beginning by marrying a fair-skinned Harvard doctor and then devoting herself to the Episcopal church: "It was she who saw to the altar flowers, she who sent her girl to help at church suppers, she who gave a stained-glass window in her mother's name in the hope that it would help her Baptist soul move over to the Episcopalian side of heaven." Of this group of strivers, often labeled Dicties, E. Franklin Frazier has written in *Black Bourgeoisie:*

> Since the black bourgeoisie live largely in a world of make-believe, the masks which they wear to play their sorry roles conceal the feelings of inferiority and of insecurity and the frustrations that haunt their inner lives. . . . In attempting to escape identification with the black masses, they have developed a self-hatred that reveals itself in their depreciation of the physical and social characteristics of Negroes.

It is no surprise then that the hincty, saddity, uppity Dicty is the butt of much humor whether she (and sometimes he) be a Miss Ann (one who tries to act like a white woman), an Aunt Jemima (the female version of the humble Uncle Tom), a Dr. Thomas (an Uncle Tom type who is highly educated), a Blue Vein (a fair-complexioned Negro who attempts to act white), a Niggerati (one who makes a special pretense at intellectualism),

1. *The Living Is Easy,* 128.

a Socialite (one who aspires to acceptance in elite society), or a black Conservative (one whose political persuasion aligns him/her with Bush and Reagan and Dole). All of them at varying times in the second half of the twentieth century have been called an Oreo (black on the outside and white on the inside), a Wannabe (want to be white), a Bougie (member of the black bourgeoisie), a Buppie (black urban professionals; the black version of Yuppie), or, Politically Correct, as Bonnie Allen labels them in the first selection in this chapter, which defines the type better than I ever could.

Bonnie Allen

YOUR ATTITUDE IS POLITICALLY CORRECT IF

from *We Are Overcome*

You are embarrassed that you got your Ivy League acceptance through racial quotas, even though George Bush was never embarrassed that he got his Yale acceptance through the legacy quota that makes room for below-average descendants of above-average wealth.

You are embarrassed that you got your job through affirmative action, even though no one of your particular ethnic persuasion ever got your particular job through fair employment practices.

You worry that your white colleagues laugh at your qualifications behind your back despite the fact that you're overqualified.

You regret your close personal relationship with Huey P. Newton during the excessively turbulent and misguided sixties and sincerely understand that Barry Goldwater was a choice, not an echo.

You tried to resurrect Young Americans for Freedom at Morehouse College.

You are an editor at the *Dartmouth Review.*

You are a Whiffenpoof.

You fell in love with the law after the Bakke decision.

You fell in love with the law because of the Clarence Thomas hearings.

You fell in love with the law the moment Earl Warren stepped down.

You live in Simi Valley.

You're the only nonwhite member in your Episcopal congregation.

You're the only nonwhite resident in your neighborhood.

You're the only nonwhite resident in your home.

It is your opinion that LA Police Chief Daryl Gates was not tough enough on crime.

It is your opinion that we are not building enough prisons.

It is your opinion that Marion Barry should be executed for embarrassing the race and, while we're at it, we should nuke the boyz 'n the 'hood.

It is your opinion that the Rodney King jury showed extraordinary insight.

You feel the decline of Western civilization began with the advent of Afro-American studies.

You feel the decline of Western civilization began with the advent of women's studies.

You feel the decline of Western civilization began the day rapper Flava Flav became a clue in the *New York Times* daily crossword puzzle.

It is your opinion that welfare mothers, including the one who bore you, are just too lazy to work.

It is your opinion that welfare mothers, except for the one who bore you, would be better off with forced sterilization.

You tried to make Nancy Reagan an honorary Alpha Kappa Alpha.

You practice benign neglect.

You sound like William Buckley.

Since Ronald Reagan no longer has the capacity to remember how he devastated the Black community with his policies, neither will you.

Gloria Naylor

MAMA DAY

But when all the laughing's done, it's the principle that remains. And we done learned that anything coming from beyond the bridge gotta be viewed real, real careful. Look what happened when Reema's boy—the one with the pear-shaped head—came hauling himself back from one of those fancy colleges mainside, dragging his notebooks and tape recorder and a funny way of curling up his lip and clicking his teeth, all excited and determined to put Willow Springs on the map.

We was polite enough—Reema always was a little addle-brained—so you couldn't blame the boy for not remembering that part of Willow Springs's problems was that it got put on some maps right after the War Between the States. And then when he went around asking us about 18 & 23,★ there weren't nothing to do but take pity on him as he rattled on about "ethnography," "unique speech patterns," "cultural preservation," and whatever else he seemed to be getting so much pleasure out of while talking into his little gray machine. He was all over the place—What 18 & 23 mean? What 18 & 23 mean? And we all told him the God-honest truth: it was just our way of saying something. Winky was awful, though, he even spit tobacco juice for him. Sat on his porch all day, chewing up the boy's Red Devil premium and spitting so the machine could pick it up. There was enough fun in that to take us through the fall and winter when he had

★18 & 23 refers to the year 1823, a significant year in the life of this family. In that year their forebear, the African Sapphire Wade, killed Bascom Wade, the white man she had married and whom she had persuaded to deed all of his land to his slaves. After this act, people would use the expression "18 & 23" as a verb to mean a number of things reflecting their relationship and her action: passion, sex, children, conflict, and violence; for one example, to 18 & 23 someone might imply that you defeated, outwitted, or conjured him/her. Indeed the term becomes a double-voiced signifier that can mean whatever the speaker wants it to: "it was just our way of saying something." See Chapter 1 of the novel.

hauled himself back over The Sound to wherever he was getting what was supposed to be passing for an education. And he sent everybody he'd talked to copies of the book he wrote, bound all nice with our name and his signed on the first page. We couldn't hold Reema down, she was so proud. It's a good thing she didn't read it. None of us made it much through the introduction, but that said it all: you see, he had come to the conclusion after "extensive field work" (ain't never picked a boll of cotton or head of lettuce in his life—Reema spoiled him silly), but he done still made it to the conclusion that 18 & 23 wasn't 18 & 23 at all—was really 81 & 32, which just so happened to be the lines of longitude and latitude marking off where Willow Springs sits on the map. And we were just so damned dumb that we turned the whole thing around.

Not that he called it being dumb, mind you, called it "asserting our cultural identity," "inverting hostile social and political parameters." 'Cause, see, being we was brought here as slaves, we had no choice but to look at everything upside-down. And then being that we was isolated off here on this island, everybody else in the country went on learning good English and calling things what they really was—in the dictionary and all that—while we kept on calling things assbackwards. And he thought that was just so wonderful and marvelous, etcetera, etcetera . . . Well, after that crate of books came here, if anybody had any doubts about what them developers was up to, if there was just a tinge of seriousness behind them jokes about the motorboats and swimming pools that could be gotten from selling a piece of land, them books squashed it. The people who ran the type of schools that could turn our children into raving lunatics—and then put his picture on the back of the book so we couldn't even deny it was him—didn't mean us a speck of good.

Barbara Neely

BLANCHE AMONG THE TALENTED TENTH

The size sixteen shorts slipped easily over her hips. Blanche gathered the excess material at her waist and admired the contrast between her deep black skin and the nearly colorless cloth. She turned and looked over her shoulder at her substantial behind. A comfortable fit. She bought her pants and skirts at least a half size too large to give herself room to move and breathe and eat. She used to buy larger clothes because she thought they made her look slimmer. That was back when she'd believed she needed to be a woman-in-a-boy's-body to be attractive, even though big butts were never out of style in her world. Nowadays, all she wanted was the strongest, most flexible body she could maintain. She was hoping to be using it for at least another forty-two years.

She took off the shorts, folded them and packed them in the open suitcase on her bed. Clothes would be important at Amber Cove. Black people, even well-off black people, seemed to believe in looking good. She'd cleaned and cooked for plenty of rich white people who dressed like they got a kick out of being mistaken for a homeless person. No black people she'd ever known or worked for played that stuff. She'd once asked a black psychologist whose house she'd cleaned on Long Island about black people's attachment to clothes. She'd told Blanche it probably was partly due to African peoples' belief in body adornment in a spiritual way, and partly because, consciously or unconsciously, black people in America hoped clothes would make them acceptable to people who hated them no matter what they wore. She hadn't said which reason carried the most weight. In either case, Blanche knew Taifa would be mortally embarrassed if Mama Blanche didn't look just so. It wasn't an attitude the child got from her, but Blanche had made sure that the sand-beige, washable silk skirt and shirt, the off-white linen dress and slacks with matching jacket and Bermuda shorts, the pastel floral print sundress and the dressy, pale blue halter dress with its bolero jacket all had designer tags and were all so conventional and, originally, so expensive, they would undoubtedly meet with Taifa's approval.

She checked her list. Everything was packed except her robe, slippers and sponge bag. She gathered those last items. Outside, the scream of a police siren was quickly followed by the squeal of brakes. As the sound died out, someone drove down her street with their radio pumped up to maximum volume. The bass made her floor vibrate. She sighed and waited for the tiny silence that comes after a loud noise, before the regular, pushed-aside noises move back in. She breathed in the silence and let it ease some of the tension in her neck and shoulders. Was she ever going to get used to the sounds of city life again? She'd lived in Harlem for more than fifteen years; surely it was not as noisy here in Boston as it was there. But between New York and Boston, she'd been spoiled by living back home in North Carolina. It hadn't taken her a full day in Farleigh to grow re-accustomed to the sounds of birds singing and wind moving through the pine trees. Her readjustment to noise was taking longer. She'd been living in Roxbury—as this part of black Boston was called—for over a year. It would be good to be out of town, in the green world, by the sea, even if Amber Cove wasn't a place she'd choose to visit if the choice were hers to make. She folded her robe, packed it and tucked her slippers in the suitcase. She turned to the phone a millisecond before it rang. She put the receiver to her ear and started speaking before her caller had a chance to say a word.

"You found that Amber Cove article didn't you? It's about time!"

"What kinda way is that to answer the phone, girl! I coulda been one of your customers or a wrong number."

"Ardell, don't I always know when it's you? Now tell me what the article says."

"Why you got so much attitude, girlfriend?"

Blanche felt her face flush. "I'm sorry, Ardell." She sat on the bed next to her suitcase. "You know how packing can get on my nerves."

"Hummm," Ardell said. "I think you got more to worry about than how many pairs of drawers to pack."

Blanche waited for Ardell to go on.

"I got a bad feeling about this trip."

"Why?" Blanche wanted to know.

"Hummm. Well, this article on the place got a picture with some folks sittin' on a terrace by the ocean. I swear, I can smell the money just looking at this picture. And all the people in it could be models for the after pictures in a skin-lightener ad, even the men. Anytime you get this many light-skinned black people together at least half of them are going to be light-skinned folks who *act* light-skinned. On top of that, I think the man who built the place made his money . . ."

Blanche could hear Ardell flipping magazine pages.

"Wait a minute. Let me find it." Ardell turned more pages.

Blanche knew what Ardell meant. It wasn't natural for a picture of black people in a public place to all be the same complexion, unless somebody wanted it that way. But then, folks in Amber Cove were rich. The women who were mistresses of the few rich black homes where she'd cleaned or cooked didn't look like her, regardless of their husbands' complexions. She assumed there must be some black-black rich women in the country, but she'd never seen one; so she wasn't expecting to find her eggplant-black self mirrored at Amber Cove. But color wasn't the only way she'd be different. She doubted anyone in the Amber Cove picture had, like her, worked four parties to raise the money to spend two nights at the Inn. She could have stayed in the Crowley's cottage—they'd taken the children out on their new boat and wouldn't be back until Sunday. She'd move into their place next week, after they left the children in her care and went off for their ten days alone. When she'd turned forty, she'd promised herself as many little treats in life as she could afford, since the big ones were well beyond her reach.

"I can't find the part I'm looking for." Ardell's voice had that distracted lag that goes with reading and talking at the same time. "About the man who started the place, I mean." Ardell went back to turning pages.

Blanche waited with as much patience as she ever could. She was curious about Amber Cove. She'd never heard of the place until her kids were asked to spend their summer there. Her mind slipped backward a few months:

"You know Miss Christine said she'd love to have us, Mama Blanche!" Taifa's voice was as clear in Blanche's head as it had been when Taifa spoke three months ago, including that touch of wheedling in her tone that Blanche couldn't stand. But it was the little girl's eyes that had held her.

"This is really important to you, isn't it, Sugar Babe?"

Taifa had jerked her head up and down at an alarming rate. She'd been so focussed on what she wanted, she hadn't even reacted to Blanche's use of her now-despised nickname.

"And what about you?" Blanche had put her hand on Malik's shoulder.

"Casey's dad's got a new boat and he's going to teach me how to sail! If you let us go."

And, of course, she had agreed. How could she have refused them an opportunity for a summer by the sea, especially since they'd made it clear they didn't want to spend the summer in North Carolina with their grandmother? "Wack," is what they'd called that idea.

Blanche looked at the clock by her bed: It was after ten. Her bus left at quarter to midnight and she hadn't finished dressing. She was about to point this out, when she heard Ardell clear her throat. Blanche shifted the phone to her other ear.

"OK, here it is." Ardell's voice took on a reading-aloud tone:

" 'Many people are surprised to learn of a black resort on the coast of Maine. In fact, the Maine coast is rich in black history. Many runaway African slaves passed through Maine on their way to freedom in Nova Scotia. When slavery officially ended, some of them, and/or their children, migrated down into Maine . . .' OK, wait, this is about blacks in the state . . . "Now, wait a minute." Silence again.

"Ardell, please! I got a bus to catch."

"OK, OK. Let me see . . . All right, listen to this, 'Amber Cove was built in 1898 by Josiah Coghill, a black tycoon who made his fortune on Coghill's Skin Lightening Creme, Coghill's Silky Straight, a lye-based hair straightener for black men, and related products. The Coghill Mansion, now Amber Cove Inn, was built after Coghill was refused admittance to a wealthy white resort on Cape Cod. Coghill built spacious cottages on the Mansion's extensive grounds and sold them to friends and business associates, thereby creating his own exclusive summer resort. The Coghill Mansion became Amber Cove Inn in 1939. In its early days, guests at the Inn had to be related to or recommended by one of the Amber Cove cottage owners. In 1968, Amber Cove dropped this exclusive policy. The Inn continues to be owned by members of the Coghill family. Most of the cottages are also still owned by descendants of the original owners'. See what I mean?" Ardell added.

"I guess there won't be a lot of guests sittin' around talkin' about how beautiful black is." The sarcasm in Blanche's voice was sharpened by memories of past rejections and jeers because of her blackness and the knowledge that in black America, "exclusive" very often related not only to wealth or social position, but also skin color.

"Call 'em up and tell 'em you can't come," Ardell said.

Blanche saw herself getting on the phone, making up some lie, listening to Christine Crowley be nice about having to find someone to keep her kids and Blanche's for the ten days Blanche had promised to stay with the children while Christine and David got some time alone on their new boat. "No, it's too late for that. And it's only fair. They'll have Taifa and Malik for practically the whole summer."

"Yeah, but it ain't like you asked them to do it."

Blanche thought about the freedom the Crowleys were giving her. "Even if it was their idea, I gotta do something for 'em besides buy 'em a vase. You know how it is, Ardell."

Blanche slipped her hand in the side pocket of her suitcase and took out a small bundle wrapped in one of her grandmother's handkerchiefs. "And I got something to do there, remember? That's why I'm leaving tonight instead of tomorrow night." She held the phone between cheek and shoulder and untied the handkerchief to make sure she'd tucked Madame Rosa's instructions inside.

"Hummm. That's right. You need to get that dream business figured out. And you don't have to socialize with those people."

Blanche could hear the edge in Ardell's voice and knew what caused it. They were the same in that way—more angry about what hurt their friends than their friends sometimes were, certainly for longer. Blanche still didn't speak to Rose Carter because she once called Ardell a crazy bitch. And distance had no effect on their closeness. They still talked to each other on the phone at least three times a week, even though Blanche was in Boston and Ardell down in Farleigh, NC.

Blanche glanced at the clock again. "Anything else?"

"Yeah. Here's another picture. Of the Inn itself. Like a big old white plantation without pillars. Right on the ocean. Cottages look nice, too. Big, with porches. They only show the outside. Pretty."

Blanche didn't try to visualize the place. She could tell it would be different from the black resorts where she'd stayed before—places with erratic plumbing, rickety furniture and greasy but abundant food. In those spots the evenings rang with shouts and laughter from bid whist and tonk tables while B. B. King's voice slid from the sound system to float on the bar-b-que-scented air. She had no such high hopes for a place where a couple of doctors had a summer cottage.

"Well, I better get moving if I'm going to make this bus."

"Hummm. There ain't a place in the world I'd ride ten hours on a bus to reach. I hope it's worth it," Ardell told her.

"Me, too." She put her sponge bag in the suitcase and closed it. "If nothing else, I get to the sea, get some of my stuff worked out, maybe."

"Well, kiss Taifa and Malik for me, and tell them Aunt Ardell said not to give you no mess."

"Yeah." There was a heaviness in Blanche's tone.

"They're good kids, Blanche."

Both women were silent. Given how she'd gotten the money to send them to Wilford Academy, it would have been better all around if she hadn't had the wherewithal. But as soon as she'd realized those white folks in North Carolina were going to pay her for not putting their nasty business in the street, she'd known she'd use the money to buy Taifa and Malik the best education she could. She wanted them to have every opportunity and advantage a first-rate education could provide. But whatever they parlayed their educations into, she didn't want them to develop any dumb ideas about a lawyer or a doctor being a better person than someone who hauls garbage.

Blanche wondered if Ardell was thinking of the heated disagreements they'd been having recently about the children and how they were changing. Blanche was considering taking them out of Wilford Academy, where she thought they were picking up hincty ideas. Ardell was positive the move wasn't necessary. Blanche hoped Ardell was right, that she was making a boil out of a pimple, but she kept remembering the look Taifa had taken to giving homeless people; and the way Malik laughed at how some people in the neighborhood talked. They were eleven and nine now. What would they be like at sixteen and fourteen? She'd been regularly asking the ancestors to please not let Taifa and Malik be up in Maine acting in ways that would make her ashamed. A recent phone call in which Taifa suggested Blanche should get her hair straightened before she came to Amber Cove had confirmed her concern. Taifa had whispered over the phone so as not to be overheard by Christine Crowley and her daughter, Deirdre, neither of whose hair required straightening in order to be kink-free. Blanche hadn't straightened her hair since she was nineteen and had yet to agree to allow Taifa to straighten hers. She remembered hanging up the phone and railing against her dead sister for getting cancer, for dying of it, for insisting Blanche take her children—for putting her in a position where she now loved them too much to even complain about having to put up with their bullshit, even if they could be a pain in the ass and a worry to boot.

"Blanche," Ardell's voice was firm. "You raised 'em decent. They'll be fine."

"Yeah, I know. Thanks, Ardell. And listen, I'm sorry about snapping you up earlier."

"If you didn't snap me up, how would I know it was you? Now you listen. It's gonna be OK. You been black long enough to handle whatever them fools at Amber Cove got to hand out."

"I ain't worried about handling it. I'm just damned sick of having to. For just once in my life, I'd like to get through a whole week without having to deal with some fool, white or black, who's got an attitude about the way I look."

"Hummm. Well, in this world, in this time, you got as much chance of that happening as you do of having a limousine come up through your toilet."

"Don't I know it?" Blanche agreed. "Everybody in the country got color on the brain—whitefolks trying to brown themselves up and hate everything that ain't white at the same time; black folks puttin' each other down for being too black; brown folks trying to make sure nobody mistakes them for black; yellow folks trying to convince themselves they're white."

"Hummm. It's a mess girl, but it's all the mess we got and it ain't no gettin' away from it."

Blanche sighed. "Yeah, I know. But it would be nice just for a week to have our color be like tonsils, or toenails, or something else nobody really gives a damn about. We don't even know what it would feel like, do we?"

They were silent for a few moments, trying to imagine a life as foreign to them as life in a monastery.

Ardell spoke first, in a cheery voice. "Well, hell, just 'cause this picture is full of light-bright folk, don't mean the place is color struck."

Before Blanche could comment, Ardell went on: "And who knows, maybe they'll be givin' away money up there and they'll give you a couple million to pass on to me."

People passing by her building probably heard Blanche laughing. When she stopped, Ardell went on:

"I know the kids and the trip ain't all that's buggin' you, Blanche." Ardell hesitated for a beat or two. "I saw Leo yesterday. He asked about you. He . . ."

"Ardell, you know it ain't really about Leo. Anyway, it's gettin' late. I gotta go. Be cool, girlfriend. I'll call you in a couple days."

As soon as Blanche hung up the phone, she trapped the Leo thing behind a door in her mind and propped a foot against it. There would be time for that when she got to the sea. She closed the suitcase and slipped on her long, wide skirt—much more efficient than pants in those little toilet stalls on the bus. She carried her suitcase down the hall and sat it near the door along with her folded poplin coat and her canvas bag. She was standing in the vestibule when the cab driver blew his horn.

Dorothy West

THE WEDDING

[In this early section of *The Wedding,* members of the elite Ovalites (wealthy African-Americans living in the exclusive Oval [patterned after Martha's Vineyard]) are preparing for the wedding of the most beautiful daughter of one of the most prestigious families in this exclusive community—all that is except Adelaide Bannister, whose absence is exacerbated by the fact that she has compromised the social laws and rented to a tenant unacceptable to her fellow Ovalites.]

That Liz had married a dark man and given birth to a daughter who was tinged with her father's darkness had raised the eyebrows of the Oval. But at least she had married a man in medicine, in keeping with the family tradition that all men were created to be doctors, whose titles made introductions so easy and self-explanatory.

But how Shelby, who could have had her pick of the best of breed in her own race, could marry outside her race, outside her father's profession, and throw her life away on a nameless, faceless white man who wrote jazz, a frivolous occupation without office, title, or foreseeable future, was beyond the Oval's understanding.

Between the dark man Liz had married and the music maker Shelby was marrying, there was a whole area of eligible men of the right colors and the right professions. For Liz and Shelby to marry so contrary to expectations affronted all the subtle tenets of their training.

Though Shelby might have been headstrong in her choice of a husband, at least she had let her mother dissuade her from following Liz's lead and eloping. Her wedding would have the Oval setting that Corinne had promised Miss Adelaide Bannister on a golden afternoon in her daughters' teens. Addie, breathing hard behind the bulging stays that tormented and squeezed the unsuitable flesh of her thin existence, had sat stuck to her chair on the glassed-in porch that drew the sun and made the heat hotter, fanning herself with the limp hand that waved in her face whenever there was nothing else to stir a breeze.

Though money was as important in the Oval as in any other upper-class community, it was not the determining factor in distinguishing between majors and minors. The distinction was so subtle, the gradations so fine drawn, that only an Ovalite knew on which level he belonged, and an outsider sometimes wasted an entire summer licking the wrong boot.

Occasionally, over recent years, an Ovalite flush enough to vacation abroad, or not flush enough to vacation anywhere, had rented his cottage to a family with the right credentials, who valiantly lived up to all expectations. This standard the Oval had set for itself was strictly adhered to until, of all ill-timed defaults, the summer of the wedding, when every cottage but Addie Bannister's was part of the preparations.

That Addie, a major Ovalite, should be the transgressor, Addie, whose impoverished heart had laid the groundwork for the wedding, that she had let down the class bars and unlocked her door to someone nobody knew but everybody knew about, was so plainly a symptom of her sickness that she had to be forgiven because, after years of false alarms, she was finally dying.

This time there was no doubt even in those doubting minds that had never entirely believed in Addie's bad heart. The few Bostonians who had seen her through the winter said that Addie looked awful, thin as paper and weak as water. They were not surprised that she had rented her cottage. Indeed it was a blessed relief not to have Addie sick on their hands when all hands were needed to help with the wedding.

All the same, Addie had betrayed her own code, which counted money as the least of social accomplishments. With all the lovely people, friends of her closest friends, who would have been glad to rent her cottage the summer of the wedding, she had sold out to the highest bidder, someone to whom no one else would have rented a cottage for a million dollars.

But no one else was in Addie's shoes. She was mired in debt to her doctor and druggist for needles and pills that tried and failed, and to her patient grocer for the food on his shelves that failed too. These were debts of honor she could not bear to leave behind unpaid. And there was her funeral, likely come fall, with her small insurance not enough to cover it, and God knew she did not want to lie disgraced in a coffin for which some well-meaning meddler had passed the hat among his friends.

Her only salvation had been to rent her cottage, accepting the first extravagant offer, not caring, too frightened to care, whose signature was on the check, so long as the bank would honor it.

[Here we share the reflections of Gram, the very fair, ninety-eight-year-old great-grandmother of the bride to be, who is pleased that her great-granddaughter is marrying a White man. However, her greatest concern is with what will happen to her in her last days.]

Gram had got out of bed and knelt beside it to pray. She had not been down on her knees in years, the way there and back being too long, too perilous. But she wanted to humble herself before God so that He would see that her faith surmounted her frailty.

Our Father, who art in heaven, Gram prayed with pious hands, there is death in the Oval. The spread of its wings will darken the sky and cast a shadow on the house intended. You know, as I do not, whose turn it is to enter into the glory of Thy kingdom. Don't let it be me. I am not ready. Once I was ready, and You did not see fit to take me. You sent me to live in a foreign land, You set me down in the midst of strangers and savages. I bore my burden, I never complained.

My back is bent with the burden of living colored. Lift it from me in my last days. Make my great-granddaughter Your instrument. She's marrying a man true white. Put it in her listening mind to live like white. Put it in her loving heart to carry me home to die. With all her life before her, she won't refuse her poor old Gram with all her life behind her.

I don't mean to meddle in the mystery of Your ways, O Lord, but they say Addie Bannister is doomed to die. If You want Addie Bannister, her house is down the road a way. I know the choice is Thine, not mine. But I wanted You to hear my side. Praise God for His goodness. Amen, amen.

Benilde Little

THE QUEEN OF SHEBA DONE GOT MARRIED

from *Good Hair*

It was a brilliantly sunny June day, complete with local saunalike humidity. The perfect D.C. day for Laura and Jeffrey's wedding. Clair Russworm's soprano carried "Ave Maria" throughout the cathedral, Blessed Sacrament, which looms over D.C. border into Bethesda, Maryland. Clair had been an opera major at Howard when she had met Jack's father, who had been completing his medical studies. She had dropped out of school because they'd had to get married.

Laura looked appropriately radiant in a cap-sleeved, hoop-skirt wedding gown that was undoubtedly couture. The guys wore morning suits and top hats. The bridesmaids wore pink.

The reception was at the Regency, a newish hotel near downtown D.C. with a picturesque courtyard at its center. We were served champagne and hors d'oeuvres by gloved waiters as the bridal party posed for pictures in front of a man-made waterfall. Jack was the best man, so I was pretty much left on my own. I wandered around, smiling at strangers and eavesdropping. There was a cluster of Laura's overly powdered aunts who were providing commentary on everything from Laura's hairstyle, which was a simple bone-straight pageboy, to the flowers, white roses, to the bridesmaid's pumps, stilettos.

"Where did Laura say Jeffrey was from?" said Aunt One.

"He's from Brooklyn," said Aunt Two.

"Well, where in Brooklyn?" asked Aunt Three.

"I don't believe it was Stuyvesant Heights," Aunt Two said. "I think he's from, well, Brooklyn Brooklyn. He was a scholarship student."

"Well, it's just too bad that she couldn't have snagged that Scoffield boy, from that family. *He* would have been a catch," Aunt One said.

I wished that I had brought my tape recorder. Jack would never believe me if I told him what I heard. He was constantly trying to pretend that the class divisions were a thing of the past. I looked around the courtyard, and there seemed to be a thousand light-skinned men with light brown wavy hair and blue or green eyes escorting women who looked like their sisters, drinking Cook's as if it were water and debating about whether Martha's Vineyard was better than Highland Beach. The men looked like magazine ads for Polo and Britches in their kelly green, blue, and tan linen jackets, light socks, expensive shoes, and quiet ties. The women wore conservative chic jewel-toned outfits with coordinating shoes and purses in matching spring colors. I wore a funky olive-drab silk knit long skirt and matching short-fitted belted jacket, classic, clunky black Stephane Kelian pumps, and a satin backpack. One of the couples made their way over to me and introduced themselves.

"So, you must be from New York." I guess my wild hair, made more like Foxy Brown's 'fro thanks to the infamous humidity, and my offbeat-for-this-crowd outfit were clues.

"Yeah, I'm from New York. And you're from here?"

"Yes," they said simultaneously. "Three generations," he added, sounding satisfied, as if he'd just told me that he'd owned D.C. for three generations.

"Oh, that's nice," I said, not knowing how else to comment.

"I'm Chris Swift," he said, and extended his hand. "And this is my wife, Stephanie."

"I'm Alice Andrews."

"So you're with Jack?" she put in.

"Yes? You know Jack?"

"Yes, from the Vineyard. I think everybody knows Jack or who he is," she said.

"So, where do you live in New York?" Chris asked.

"Um, the Upper West Side. Do you know New York?"

"Very well. I went to Columbia Law school. Couldn't wait to get back to D.C."

"Yeah, well, you know, New York's not for everybody."

"And what do you do there?" he pressed.

"I'm a reporter."

"For?" he demanded to know.

"You must know Sharon Strong?" Stephanie piped in before I could answer.

"Uh, her name is familiar—"

"She's at *The Wall Street Journal*," Stephanie said.

"Uh-huh, I've met her before."

"Um, I think she's like a copy editor or something. We went to Spelman together," Stephanie continued.

"Oh yes. We've met. We know a few people in common."

I wanted to get back to the everybody knowing Jack comment. I realized that Stephanie was probably a champion Negro Geography player and could be a great resource.

"So, Stephanie, you've known Jack awhile?"

"Oh, I've known him forever, you know, summers on the Vineyard, just hanging out."

"How do you know Jack?" Chris asked with that same prosecutor's tone.

"From New York—"

"Well, how'd you meet?" he wanted to know.

"We met on a plane."

"Really. Oh, that's nice. My cousin Tracy met her boyfriend on a plane and—"

I cut Stephanie off. I could see she was also a champion of the non sequitur. "You know, I see someone I need to say hello to. It was nice meeting you both."

I got away from them before Chris launched into a full interrogation and Stephanie proved her Negro Geography prowess. Folks from the tribe, D.C. being its capital, were amazing that way. They'd take the most tangential morsel and want to make a connection. "Oh, you shop at Safeway. Well, do you know so-and-so . . ." It was beyond tiresome. And the family tree questions were considered appropriate party chatter. Once at Holyoke, my freshman suite mate, who was from D.C., asked me a few days after meeting me, after she'd given up trying to guess my social class, what my grandfather had done for a living. I had to say I had no idea. She'd thought that was strange. No one my age had ever asked me what my father did, much less my grandfather. I would later realize that I'd entered into a new world, where that kind of question was pertinent. Initially when my suite mate told me about the Black middle class, I thought that I'd finally found my long-lost milieu. I had no idea then how far off that mark I was.

I wandered around the courtyard some more, hoping to meet someone who had read a book or even watched a nature special; judging by what I overheard, those things were not discussed. As far as I could tell, this group didn't even have a lively race discussion going, which was unusual for a gathering of more than three Black people, especially ones who didn't know each other very well. This place was a humid desert speaking not only meteorologically, but for ideas as well. Once again I was back on Fenton Avenue, not fitting in.

I found Jeff's mother, who was looking more out of place than I was feeling. Obviously no one had told her about the brutal D.C. heat. She was wearing a long-sleeved gold satin-and-lace waltz-length gown, white lace stockings with a pearl design on the ankle, and pearl-studded gloves. Beads of sweat formed a line above her lip.

"Mrs. Doran, are you having a good time?"

"Oh yes, baby. Everything's beautiful. I'm fine, just fine, 'cept my feet is about killin' me."

I looked down at the puffs of skin rising from dyed-to-match pumps. I felt for her and on some level imagined what she must've been feeling. Laura's family virtually ignored her, and there wasn't enough of Jeff's side there to make her feel comfortable.

"How you doin', baby?" she asked me. I walked her over to an empty wrought-iron-and-glass café table and had her sit with me. The waiter brought us flutes of Cook's, which we both downed as though it were lemonade.

"So, what'd you think of the ceremony?" I asked. What I really wanted to ask was what she thought of her new daughter-in-law.

"Oh, it was just the most beautifulest thing I ever did see."

"Yes, it was."

She looked around, seeming like a junior high school girl at her first dance. I was personally invested in her feeling more comfortable; her level of belonging directly connected to my own.

"So you must be so proud of Jeff."

"Oh yeah. My Jeffrey. Always said he was gonna make me proud."

"That's nice."

"You got a nice fella there, that Jack."

"Yes, he is."

"Y'all gonna get married?"

"I don't know. We haven't been together that long."

"How long?"

"About eight months."

"Humph. Jeffrey ain't known Laura no mo' than three or four."

"Yeah, I know. I guess some people just know what they want."

"Yeah, and some people's just good at gettin' what they want."

Her comment took me by surprise. I'd slept Jeff's mother, underestimated her, but she didn't miss a thing. She was like the women in my old neighborhood who could size a person up in minutes, read them like the newspaper.

Jack was trying to make his way over to Jeff's mother and me but was being dragged around by his mother. When he broke free of her, he was still stopped continuously by revelers who seemed to want nothing more than to touch his hem. He was a celebrity in this crowd. Several older women in hats kissed his cheeks, patted his hair, and chatted him up. I hadn't been with Jack in a crowd like this before, so I'd never seen the Russworm thing in action. They treated him like Prince Russworm of the long-lost tribe of Freeborns.

"Whew, it's really hot, huh?" he said, plopping down on a wrought-iron chair after he'd finally made his way through the throngs. "Hope we're going inside soon. You having a good time?" he said.

"Oh yes, everything is just perfect."

"How about you, Mrs. Doran? Can I get you something?"

"Naw, I'm fine, baby."

"Are you done with the pictures?" I asked.

"Yeah, looks like it, at least for now. It's fun seeing all these old faces. That woman over there was a patient of my grandfather's, and her daughter is married to one of my dad's med school classmates. And my mother and that woman are club members—"

"That's nice. So they didn't need Jeff's mom to be in the pictures?" I whispered to Jack.

"Guess they're doing family pictures later."

"But I saw Laura's mom with you guys—"

"Mmm. I don't know." He brushed off my observation.

I wanted to have a good time for Jack. I felt like this was yet another test for me that I needed to pass, not for Jack, but for me. I needed to figure out how to do this without losing myself, but everyone seemed so focused on the exterior. How could a people, Black people, actually seriously adopt attitudes that our former masters had fed us for the sole purpose of dividing us and therefore keep us fighting with, disliking, and distrusting each other? It seemed insane to me that a people, twelve generations from one of the most inhumane systems of slavery in history, could actually be so cruel to one another. Maybe I was just too crazy for Jack. He probably needed somebody like that Stephanie woman, who seemed perfectly nice and had probably never had a bad mood or original thought in her entire life.

"There you are, dear, I wanted to introduce you to—Oh, Alice dear, forgive my manners. I didn't know you were here. How are you?"

"Oh, I'm fine, thank you, Mrs. Russworm, and you?"

"Wonderful. Mrs. Doran? Wasn't the ceremony lovely?"

"Yes, it was somethin'."

"So, Jack, Judge Carter is here and wants to say hello. Come with me." Jack turned to me. "I'll be back."

We moved inside the hotel for a sit-down dinner, but before dinner would be served, we'd have to see the bride and groom have their first dance and the bride would have to dance with her father. I worried about Mrs. Doran dancing in uncomfortable shoes, but she did fine. It was Laura's mother I should've worried about. Laura's father, a pleasant enough, unimpressive sort, made his way through a clichéd toast about long life. Obviously not satisfied with his stamp on the couple, Laura's mother, the social engine of the family, who'd made more than a few trips to the bar, got up and stood before the microphone.

"I just wanna say to you all, dear friends and family, thank you for coming and blessing our Laura as she makes her new life with this charming man, Dr. Jeffrey Doran. I've waited all my life for this day. Ever since Laura was a little baby, I knew what I wanted for her. This is a fine young man, with an honorable profession. Take care of my baby." With that tears began flowing, and Laura and Jeff had to walk her mother to her seat.

I was seated at the table with other girlfriends, boyfriends, and spouses of the bridal party. The champagne was flowing, and so were the tongues.

"Well, I'm glad that's finally over," said Laura's sister's husband to another brother-in-law.

"The Queen of Sheba done got married."

"Man, be cool," said the brother-in-law, laughing.

Both men were wearing gray suits. The one doing the talking also had on a gray tie and gray shoes. He was married to Laura's older sister. Laura was the youngest child and, from what I could put together, had been groomed to marry a doctor. In many Black families, being a doctor, or marrying one, is what becoming a priest is in Italian families. It's as good as it gets. Nirvana. The men in gray both worked for the federal government. One was a GS-12 or -13. I figured, by the way they told me this, that it was something of an accomplishment, but they'd been treated like pigeon-do by Laura's mother because of what they weren't. I figured resentment had to be pretty deep for them to go on in front of me and the other strangers at the table.

"All I can say is, I'm glad they ain't gone be livin' here," the second man in gray said.

"Yeah, seems like our loss is Westchester County's gain. Look at her. She in hog heaven," the first man in gray said, referring to Laura's mother.

I wanted to pull out my pad and ask them questions about the family, but I resisted. Instead I went to the bar to get a club soda. The Cook's had given me a headache.

I went to the ladies' room to remove some of the oil that was now covering my face. Thankfully a bathroom attendant had a bottle of Drug Fair aspirin. I sat in front of a mirror after taking the pills to let them get to work. I looked at my hair, which was big and bushy. I looked not only as though I were from out of town, in this crowd, I seemed to be from outer space. No one here would let their hair "go back" like this. I thought it looked kinda good, but two of the bridesmaids in pink who stood in front of the mirror next to me, with perms so straight they were afraid to revert, looked at me as though I had asked for spare change.

Gloria Naylor

LINDEN HILLS

[In this passage, Gloria Naylor gives a view of the black elite who live in or aspire to live in Linden Hills through the eyes of two "commoners" who are working as waiters at a wedding reception.]

"Now I want you boys to try and stay out the way of them folks carrying the trays." The stoop-shouldered old man led Willie and Lester to a corner of the large utility kitchen. He pointed to a pair of double swinging doors. "They gonna be coming through there like greased lightning 'cause they'll be over two hundred folks to serve. And don't want no accidents with all them high muckety-mucks out there."

"Don't worry, Mike, we'll be careful," Lester said.

"Good. I appreciate your help 'cause, fact is, I should be scraping them platters and hauling the garbage myself, but I don't know how they expect me to do all that alone with my rheumatism."

"They should have the waiters pitch in and give you a hand," Willie said. "That's what they're getting paid for."

"Naw suh." Mike threw up his hands. "The office come talking to me about some union—it ain't in they contract to scrape no plates and dump garbage. White folks got it good, don't they—even them waiting on tables. The realty company never worried 'bout me having no union, and I got six of these buildings to tend. Bad enough I get run ragged all during the week with a thousand fix-this and do-thats, they even wants me here on my day off to clean up after 'em. The least drip in the faucet, they banging on my door talking 'bout they nerves. A stray piece of paper and they calling the office on me— I'm letting the neighborhood run down. I never saw such a bunch of finicky niggers in all my life."

"As if they really cared about Second Crescent Drive," Lester said. "Everybody knows they come here and pay all those fancy rents, hoping for the first chance to beat it out of here and get into a home down the hill."

"That's just it, son. With the realty office sitting at the end of the street, they gotta show how good they take care of these here premises so they get a shot at something better later on. So they wear me to the bone. Pure slavery's all it is."

The old man kept complaining to Lester, and Willie went to the swinging doors and looked through the oval glass. The reception hall was beginning to fill up and the sixteen-piece band was playing soft background music. Large round tables, holding huge silver centerpieces of carnations and poinsettias, lined both sides of the room. The unoccupied bridal table sat on a raised and carpeted platform facing Willie across the long polished floor. Reflections from the crystal-tiered chandeliers glimmered on the silver patterns in the wallpaper, the sprays from the champagne fountain, the brass buttons of the waiters as they moved between the tables and the bar.

"Some setup, huh?" Lester stood behind Willie.

"I'm telling you." Willie nodded. "Look at the size of that cake."

The four-foot wedding cake held miniatures of the bridal party on two sets of golden stairways that ran up each of its sides. A tiny spray of liquid sugar rose mysteriously from its center and sprinkled the small bride and groom at regulated intervals.

Lester sucked his teeth. "It's disgusting."

Willie didn't think so. He secretly felt a bit proud that someone black could afford all this. That cake alone must have cost a small fortune—and then all this other getup. Even if they had to go into hock for this reception, it must really be something to be in a position to make that kind of debt. This was definitely no fried-chicken-and-potato-salad affair. The waiters were coming into the kitchen and unwrapping trays of marinated shrimp, stuffed artichokes, caviar, and some kind of cheese that Willie didn't recognize, so he knew it must be expensive.

And the clothes on those sisters. Willie couldn't tell the difference between the Halston minks and Saint Laurent fox capes out there, but the way those black women floated into the banquet hall like glittering birds of paradise spelled sable to him, sable beauty. The impeccable makeup, the manicured hands and custom-made hairdos were only rivaled by the sculptured attire of their male escorts. At first he watched in awe as the room filled and the waves of people mingled and separated into variegated patterns of silk, cashmere, and brocade. But even as glass after glass was refilled from the champagne fountain and the talk and laughter took on a flushed energy, Willie couldn't help feeling that something was missing from the jeweled sparkle in the air. Then he happened to notice a woman sitting to his left in a pink satin suit. She had bent her head forward to listen to a pepper-haired man across the table. And just as she went to throw her head back in a smooth arc of laughter, the white fur on the back of her chair slipped toward the floor. Her hand shot out to retrieve it, halted a fraction of a second, and then made an uninterrupted swing to come to rest on her bosom as her head finally lay back on her shoulders. The laughing woman with the apparently ignored fur trailing on the floor now told Willie what he'd missed from that room: spontaneity. His eyes flew around the long hall again over lifted glasses, backslaps, and nibbling mouths. And he could see that he hadn't been alone in his awe of all that splendor. He was actually watching them watch themselves having this type of affair. The soft strains of a slow waltz drifted through the doors and Willie made a mental bet that they'd dance to nothing more exciting than that the entire afternoon. These niggers would be afraid to sweat.

The music suddenly stopped and there was a slow drum roll and the far doors were swung open for the wedding party. Each couple was announced over the microphone by the maître d'. Each was greeted with a round of applause, and the announcement of Mr. Luther Nedeed escorting Miss Rosalyn Tyler brought a sustained ovation and some guests even stood up to clap.

"So that's Nedeed." Willie peered through the glass panel. "Pretty, ain't he?"

"Yeah," Lester said. "That face would stop a clock."

Willie felt an inexplicable twinge at those words and found himself asking aloud, "I wonder what his old lady looks like?"

"You know, it's funny. I've seen her a couple of times but I couldn't pick her out in that room right now. She's got the kind of face that wouldn't stand out in your mind—sorta average."

The bride and groom finally entered, bowed to the cheers of their guests, and went to the center of the floor officially to begin the first dance. The waiters began to stream back into the kitchen with their trays. But Willie and Lester had nothing to do except remove a few loose toothpicks and crumpled napkins. As the trays kept returning completely empty, Willie felt his stomach growling and sighed. They might look like birds of paradise, but they sure ate like vultures. So he and Lester went back to the door to watch the dancers.

"Well, ol' Winston did all right by himself," Lester said as the couple waltzed around the room. "She's not bad-looking."

"Nice eyes, but too skinny for me." Willie shook his head. "I like my women with some padding on 'em so when you go in for a landing, you don't get stuck on a pelvis bone."

"It's not bothering Winston none—he's just grinning away."

Willie's head followed the circling couple and he imagined himself and Ruth gliding out there on the polished oak floor. She would be looking up into his eyes just like that woman was, all dewy and covered with cream lace. And he would hold her around the waist and smile down at her just like that guy was doing now. But no—something about Winston's face didn't quite fit into Willie's daydream. No, he could never imagine himself smiling at Ruth like that. Why, that guy looks like someone had punched him in the stomach and his lips sorta froze up that way.

When the dancers left the floor, Lester poked Willie in the side. "Hey, get that, over in the corner. It's that douche bag, Xavier."

A tall man, with a face the shape and color of a brown egg, sat with his arm thrown over the chair of a young, blond woman. He playfully offered her a bit of cheese and she ate it from his fingers. Then he bent over and whispered in her ear and they laughed.

"That mother," Lester spit out. "He told Roxanne he wasn't invited to this shit and now he shows up with that pink job. I oughta go out there and smash him in his face."

"Shit, lay light." Willie pulled at his arm. "It's none of your business."

"It is my business." Lester pulled his arm away. "He came slobbering over my sister just last night, but she's not good enough to come here with him when it's broad daylight. I just wanna go out there and let him see me. Then he'll know his game is up."

The waiters hurried back through the swinging doors and Lester started to go out, but Willie grabbed his arm again. "You wanna get Mike in trouble? You know we ain't supposed to be here," he whispered. "You start something and that nice old guy loses his job for trying to help us."

That stopped Lester for a moment. "But why would he *do* that, Willie?"

Willie saw the hurt in his eyes. "I don't know. Some guys just like to go that way, I guess. And you don't know, it might have nothing to do with Roxanne. Maybe that woman's one of his business friends or something," he offered hopefully, but not believing it.

"Yeah, sure." Lester sighed.

Willie looked at his friend's face, which would probably be lighter than that blond woman's when she was suntanned. "Les, you ever been with one?"

"Why would you ask me that?" There was a defensive edge in his voice.

"I don't know." Willie shrugged. "I was just wondering."

"Well, yeah, a coupla times." Then he went into an exaggerated whisper. "But never in broad daylight." They smiled at each other. "When I used to read my stuff at the coffeehouses in the city, they'd come up to me afterward and we'd start talking, ya know?"

"Well, I never have. But I always sorta wondered—" Willie glanced at the waiters pouring soup into silver tureens at the other end of the kitchen. "Are they really different?"

"Nah." Lester shook his head. "But I'll tell you something, they're easier."

"Yeah?" Willie's eyes widened. "Ya know, I've heard guys say that."

"It's true. They don't put you through the rain dance that the sisters do. I use to think that was really something. It made me feel special, you know what I mean? But then once . . ." Lester's voice dropped off. "I never told you this, but . . ." He looked at the floor. "I met this girl once—after reading at this jazz session—and then we went to her place and got stoned. God, she had some good weed in that fancy pad. And then after the whole thing had gone down, she rolled over in the bed and started stroking my arms and stuff and said, 'That was nice, so I can imagine how great it would have been if you were really *black*.' "

"Christ!" Willie whistled.

"I swear to you, White." Lester stared off in space. "That was the first time in my life that I wanted to hit a woman."

They heard another slow drum roll, and a crash of cymbals brought the reception hall to a muted hum. The maître d' stuck his head in the kitchen and told the waiters to hold the soup until after the toasts. Lester and Willie went back to the door and Luther Nedeed was mounting the bandstand. The room was totally still as he adjusted the microphone and delicately cleared his throat.

"Gentlewomen, gentlemen. Before we settle into the marvelous repast that is awaiting us, pray bear with me as I extend our warmest regards to the nuptial union of Mr. and Mrs. Winston Alcott."

"God," Willie whispered, "does he always talk like that?"

"Yup, straight out of a gothic novel. He spoke at my high school graduation and you know what he called black folks? 'We denizens of the darker hue.' Made it sound like a disease. That nigger's unreal."

Luther had taken two small velvet cases out of his jacket pocket. "As an old friend of the Alcotts, I was honored to be an intimate part of this wedding party. And as the president of the Tupelo Realty Corporation, this occasion gives me unspeakable joy because Winston Alcott has been an outstanding member of this community, doing it great pride and showering it with his talents and vitality. And now today, he has taken the step which will insure the stability and growth of Linden Hills. I applaud you, Winston Alcott. We all applaud you."

There was a healthy response from the room.

"For somebody who is so full of *unspeakable* joy, he's sure got a lot to say," Lester said.

"Shhh," Willie said.

"But I feel that a moment like this requires more than applause. Yes, much more. So it does me great pleasure to announce that after you return from your nuptial retreat, you will not be bringing the new Mrs. Alcott back to Second Crescent Drive. You have proven your dedication to Linden Hills, and now Linden Hills will open its arms to you." Luther unsnapped the velvet cases and held them up. "The Tupelo Realty Corporation has decided to give you a mortgage on Tupelo Drive."

There was a loud gasp from the room and then wild and thunderous applause as Luther turned full circle on the bandstand, with his arms lifted high above his head, displaying the contents of the cases. There was a platinum-and-diamond key-shaped necklace in one and matching cuff links in the other.

"Well, I'll be damned!" Lester whistled. "Winston must be pissing happy over that one."

April Sinclair

COFFEE WILL MAKE YOU BLACK

I couldn't believe it, me and Mama were actually sitting across from Terri and her mother, sipping on orange frappe and eating fried chicken and potato salad in a far corner of the church basement. I'd recognized Terri immediately, despite her stylish haircut and the fact that she was taller.

All of us were stepping. Terri and her mother were wearing matching gold-colored knit suits that set off their light-brown complexions. I had on a simple, but sophisticated, rose-colored linen dress. Mama was wearing a jade outfit, and my brothers were off running around somewhere in their blue suits. Grandma was all decked out in chiffon that was almost the same color as the orange sherbet she was mixing with ginger ale at the main table.

"Stevie, I would've recognized you a mile away. You look the same, except you've gotten rid of your ponytail, and you've got a shape now."

Terri wasn't straight up and down anymore either, I noticed. We both had some breasts and booty to speak of.

"Even with your perm, you look like the same Terri."

"Have you thought about getting a perm, Stevie?"

"I just always get a press and curl. Carla's mother does my hair. Carla's my best friend now. You remember Carla Perkins, don't you?"

"Barely." Terri sounded like she might not want to remember her.

"Carla said she saw you and your mother coming out of Sears last year, around Easter."

Terri hunched her shoulders like it wasn't something worth remembering, even if she did.

"We don't even darken Sears' door now," Mrs. Mathews jumped in, picking at her little plate of food.

"We're regulars at Field's these days," she continued. "That's where we got these outfits." Mrs. Mathews stood up and turned around so that we could take in her clothes. I knew Mama was envying her slim figure.

Grandma walked over and set a sweet-potato pie on our table. I turned my attention to it.

"Did I hear you say Marshall Field's?" Grandma asked.

"Yes, ma'm."

"My, my, y'all must be eating pretty high off the hog these days."

Mrs. Mathews took a sip from her coffee and looked up at Grandma. "Mother Dickens, I've learned that expensive is the cheapest way to buy."

"I'm scared of you!" Grandma teased.

"By the way, Terri, is Reggie still cute?" I asked.

Terri frowned at me. "Thinks he's fine. He's six feet tall, the girls won't leave him alone."

"You see David's over there, grinning in some girl's face." I pointed.

"I still can't believe that's little David," Mrs. Mathews insisted.

"Little David is eating us out of house and home." Mama laughed.

"Where's your brother, Terri?" I asked. "I thought I would get to see Reggie."

"Reginald and Terrence are out on the golf course," Mrs. Mathews answered. "Reginald is caddying for his father."

"A black golfer, my, my, y'all sho have arrived, huh?"

"Mother Dickens, there are a number of black golfers at Washington Park these days. By the way, where is Mr. Stevenson today?"

"He's working," Mama answered.

"Is he still at the hospital?"

"Yes."

"Is he still a janitor?" Terri asked and then looked embarrassed.

Mama swallowed. "Yes, he's still a janitor. He applied to be an assistant supervisor in the housekeeping department, but he didn't get it."

"They gave it to a white man, right in off the street," I explained. "They don't even have any black supervisors."

"And they don't plan to have any," Grandma snapped.

"They seem to always be hiring at the post office," Mrs. Mathews said with a phony smile.

"I'll tell Ray to look into it," Mama said, without enthusiasm.

"Stevie, you never answered my question. Have you ever thought about getting a perm? Everybody has a perm these days."

"I guess the thought has crossed my mind, sure."

"You can get a perm," Mama cut in. "We can afford it."

"Half the girls at my school are wearing their hair in afros now. Even Carla has one," I said as Grandma handed me a piece of pie.

"You know, Madame Walker inventing the straightening comb was the best thing that happened to the negro next to Emancipation," Mrs. Mathews declared. She shook her head and put her hand out to keep Grandma from giving her any pie.

"We learned about Madame C. J. Walker in Afro-American History class. She was the first black woman to become a millionaire," I informed everyone.

"How could the straightening comb be more important than the freedom fighters and the Civil Rights Movement?" Grandma asked.

I glanced up at the banner on the wall, WE AS A PEOPLE WILL GET TO THE PROMISED LAND, and the picture of the late Dr. Martin Luther King.

"Yeah," I agreed. "And plus I think the natural looks good on some people."

"Well, I've yet to see it improve anyone's appearance," Mrs. Mathews said coldly.

Mama sighed, "I don't care for the natural look either."

"My Afro-American History teacher, Brother Kambui, says that if the white woman can wear her hair in its natural state, the black woman should be free to do the same."

"I thought the negro's name was Johnson."

"His name used to be Mr. Johnson, Mama, but he changed it because he said Johnson is a slave name."

"Honey, don't you listen to Brother Watusi . . ."

"Brother Kambui," I corrected Mrs. Mathews.

"Whatever, anyway you keep right on straightening your hair, honey. Men don't want to be running their fingers through a bunch of naps, trust me."

Mama nodded. "You sisters will be walking around here nappy-headed with rings through your noses and next thing you know Brother Kambui will be marrying some blonde."

"Brother Kambui is a revolutionary, Mama."

"Why do they let him teach at your school?" Terri sounded concerned instead of excited.

"Revolutionaries are the main ones who are talking black and sleeping white," Mama whispered.

"What's sleeping white mean?" Kevin had sneaked up on us.

"Never mind. Here, get a big piece of your grandma's sweetpotato pie."

"Terri, are you still planning to join the Peace Corps?"

"The Peace Corps? Why, I'd forgotten all about that. Boy, that seems ages ago."

"Remember, we were going to teach in Africa? We couldn't decide between Kenya and Ethiopia, remember? I've still got my application."

"Stevie, you haven't changed, you're still so . . . idealistic."

"Terri's dad wants her to major in Accounting when she goes to college. He says that's where the money is. And he's with the IRS, he ought to know."

"Mom, you know, I really want to be an airline stewardess and travel all over the world until I meet a rich man."

Mom? Since when did Terri call her mother "Mom"? What happened to "Mama"?

"Stevie, what do you want to be now?"

"Oh, I can't decide between a newspaper reporter and an actress. I'm in the Drama Club at school."

"Ray wants Jean to become a lawyer, he says *that's* where the money is." Mama probably didn't want to be outdone, I thought, because Daddy wanting me to be a lawyer was news to me.

"Today, you can be anything you put your mind to. The opportunities are there like they've never been before."

"Yes," Mama agreed with Mrs. Mathews.

"Hey, when I grow up, I'm gonna be rich," Kevin said, finishing his pie. "I'm gonna have me a place looking out over the ocean."

"Which ocean?" Terri asked.

"The one we got right here in Chicago."

"Boy, you know we don't have an ocean in Chicago!" Mama shouted.

"It looks like an ocean, I know it's not a sea."

"Kevin, you mean Lake Michigan," I said gently, not wanting my brother to feel like a fool in front of people.

"Oh, yeah, Lake Michigan," Kevin mumbled, staring down at his lap.

"A friend of Terrence's sells encyclopedias; you might want to invest in a set. If you don't live in a neighborhood with good schools, an encyclopedia set can make all the difference in the world."

"We have an Encyclopedia Britannica and a big Webster's dictionary," Mama snapped at Mrs. Mathews.

Grandma wrapped her arms around Kevin and turned toward Mrs. Mathews. "I hear y'all's area is pretty much all black now," she said, smiling. "It sure did change quickly, huh? Soon y'all will be right back in the ghetto again, huh?"

Mrs. Mathews cleared her throat. I knew Grandma's dig had gotten to her.

"So far we've been able to keep the lowlife out." Mrs. Mathews raised her eyebrows. "I pray that we can continue to hold the line."

Grandma cut her eyes at Mrs. Mathews. I knew that she wanted to read her chapter and verse, but she had to be polite since we were in the church.

"Kevin, baby, come help Grandma, I need somebody strong with muscles to carry the punch bowl to the kitchen."

Kevin jumped up and made a muscle like Popeye and followed Grandma to the main table.

"Mother Dickens, your sweet-potato pie is screamin'!" A woman in a fur stole shouted from across the room. "You put your foot in it!" she added.

"Thanks, Sister Little." Grandma beamed.

Telling a cook she'd put her foot in a dish was a very high compliment.

"I see Mrs. Little still looks and sounds like a Baptist," Mrs. Mathews said, sighing.

Mama nodded.

"Stevie, do you have a boyfriend?"

"Not really, Terri, do you?"

"Not yet, but I'm working on it."

I glanced over at Mama. "I'm not allowed to date until I'm sixteen. Let's see, I've got eleven months, one week and how many days, Mama?"

"Now, Jean Eloise is just being silly, she's not really all that boy-minded. I'm thankful for that. I'd hate to have a daughter who was boy crazy."

"Well, Terri Ann isn't boy crazy, I mean she likes boys, which is natural at fifteen."

Mama cleared her throat, "Well, Jean Eloise likes boys, I didn't mean to imply otherwise."

"Otherwise." The word hung in the air like laundry with too much starch in it, I thought.

"Your Jean gives every indication of being normal. I think it goes without saying that we both want the best for our daughters."

I let out a breath after being pronounced normal.

"I've always been impressed with Stevie, ever since she was a little girl," Mrs. Mathews continued. "I was particular about who my children associated with from day one. That's why I'm about to go out on a limb now."

"Thank you, Mrs. Mathews. I'm just sorry that Jean Eloise has never made another close friend that came up to Terri."

I frowned at Mama.

"Please call me Regina. After all these years we should be on a first-name basis."

"And call me Evelyn. Anyway, Regina, you were saying, about going out on a limb?"

"Oh, yes, you see, it's so important that young people don't get mixed up with the wrong crowd."

"And these days it's more important than ever," Mama added.

"Yes, well, to make a long story short, some of the girls in our area have formed a club . . ."

"It's called Charisma," Terri interrupted.

"Yes, well, the girls are meeting to plan the first get-together, and I don't see why Stevie couldn't be included."

Mama was grinning and nodding and Terri was smiling. Hey, maybe we could be tight again.

"Will the get-togethers be coed?" Mama asked.

"Yes, Evelyn, but the young men are all gentlemen. And there is always adult supervision. These are college-bound young people, all from good homes."

"Is Reggie going to be at the get-together?" I asked.

"Of course." Terri winked.

"Sounds good to me." I winked back.

"Regina, I like the situation that you've described. Who knows, I might just be willing to lower the dating age, under the right circumstances."

"Well then, it's set," Mrs. Mathews said, reaching for her handbag.

The program was about to start. A large woman in a flowery dress was calling for everyone's attention.

"You remember Roland Anderson, don't you, Terri?" I asked.

"Yeah, he was always on the honor roll, wore glasses."

"We've gotten to be friends."

"Well, the whole family's gone militant. Roland and his sisters and brother don't even come to church anymore," Mama whispered.

"Roland just loaned me *The Autobiography of Malcolm X.*"

Mrs. Mathews shook her head, "And they used to be such fine people."

"Well, all good things must end. Stevie, Terri Ann will be giving you a call," she added.

"Cool," I said, smiling. "I'll walk you all to the door."

I stood on the church steps, waving goodbye and watching Terri and her mother pushing against the wind to get to their big, shiny car.

"Come on, Terri Ann, let's get out of here before dark. This is Boogaville, remember."

I could have sworn I heard Terri say, "I sure hope she doesn't tell anybody her father is a janitor." Or did the wind distort her words?

I stared at the setting sun. My stomach was in knots as I watched it change colors.

Dorothy West

THE LIVING IS EASY

[In this selection from *The Living Is Easy,* the social climbing Cleo Judson is going with her dark daughter Judy to look for a home in an exclusive white neighborhood.]

She was dark. She had Papa's cocoa-brown skin, his soft dark eyes, and his generous nose in miniature. Cleo worked hard on her nose. She had tried clothespins, but Judy had not known what to do about breathing. Now Cleo was teaching her to keep the bridge pinched, but Judy pinched too hard, and the rush of dark blood made her nose look larger than ever.

A little white dog with a lively face and a joyful tail trotted down the street. Judy grinned and screwed around to follow him with her eyes.

Cleo hissed in her ear: "Don't show your gums when you smile, and stop squirming. You've seen dogs before. Sit like a little Boston lady. Straighten your spine."

The trolley rattled across Huntington Avenue, past the fine granite face of Symphony Hall, and continued up Massachusetts Avenue, where a cross-street gave a fair and fleeting glimpse of the Back Bay Fens, and another cross-street showed the huge dome of the magnificent mother church of Christian Science. At the corner of Boylston Street, within sight of Harvard Bridge and the highway to Cambridge, Cleo and Judy alighted to wait for the Brookline Village trolley.

Cleo saw with satisfaction that she was already in another world, though a scant fifteen-minute ride away from the mean streets of the Negro neighborhood. There were white people everywhere with sallow-skinned, thin, austere Yankee faces. They had the look that Cleo coveted for her dimpled daughter. She was dismayed by Judy's tendency to be a happy-faced child, and hoped it was merely a phase of growth. A proper Bostonian never showed any emotion but hauteur. Though Cleo herself had no desire to resemble a fish, she wanted to be able to point with the pride of ownership to someone who did.

The Village trolley came clanging up Boylston Street, and Judy clambered up the steps, pushed by her mother and pulled by the motorman. Cleo was pleased to see that there were no other colored passengers aboard. The occupants of the half-filled car were mostly matrons, whose clothes were unmodish and expensive. All of them had a look of distinction. They were neither Cabots nor Lowells, but they were old stock, and their self-assurance sat well on their angular shoulders.

They did not stare at Cleo and Judy, but they were discreetly aware of the pair, and appreciative of their neat appearance. Boston whites of the better classes were never upset nor dismayed by the sight of one or two Negroes exercising equal rights. They cheerfully stomached three or four

when they carried themselves inconspicuously. To them the minor phenomenon of a colored face was a reminder of the proud rôle their forebears
had played in the freeing of the human spirit for aspirations beyond the
badge of house slave.

The motorman steered his rocking craft down a wide avenue and settled back for the first straight stretch of his roundabout run. Cleo looked
at the street signs, and her heart began to pound with excitement. This was
Brookline. There wasn't another colored family she knew who had beaten
her to it. She would be the first to say, "You must come to see us at our new
address. We've taken a house in Brookline."

————

There were no stoop-sitters anywhere, nor women idling at windows, nor
loose-lipped loiterers passing remarks. Her friends who lived in Dorchester,
or Cambridge, or Everett had nice addresses, of course. But Brookline was
a private world.

She stopped and glanced down at her daughter to see if her ribbed
white stockings were still smooth over her knees, and if the bright ribbons
on the ends of her bobbing braids were as stiff and stand-out as they had
been when she tied them. She scanned the small upturned face, and a rush
of protective tenderness flooded her heart. For a moment she thought she
had never seen anything as lovely as the deep rich color that warmed
Judy's cheeks. She herself had hated being bright-skinned when she was a
child. Mama had made her wash her face all day long, and in unfriendly
moments her playmates had called her yaller punkins. Now her northern
friends had taught her to feel defensive because Judy was the color of her
father.

"Don't speak unless you're spoken to," Cleo warned Judy, and mounted
the steps of the house before which they stood.

In a moment or two a colored maid responded to her ring. She looked
at Cleo with open-mouthed surprise, then her look became sly and secret.
"Y'all come see about the house?" she asked in a conspiratorial whisper.

"I beg your pardon," Cleo said coolly. "I've come to see Mr. Van Ryper."

The maid's face froze. She knew these stuck-up northern niggers.
Thought they were better than southern niggers. Well, all of them looked
alike to the white man. Let this high-yaller woman go down South and
she'd find out.

"Step inside," she said surlily. "You're letting in flies."

"I'm sorry," Cleo said sweetly. "I see a big black fly got in already." With a dazzling smile she entered the house, and instantly drew a little breath at sight of the spacious hall with its beautiful winding stairway.

"What's the name?" the maid asked briefly. If this woman wanted to be treated like white folks, at least she wasn't going to be treated like quality white folks.

"The name is Mrs. Judson," Cleo said readily. She had been asked a proper question, however rudely, and she was perfectly willing to answer it. This peevish incivility was much less insulting than the earlier intimacy. If she had wanted to gossip with the servant before seeing the master, she would have used the back door.

"Wait here," the woman said, and began a snail-pace ascent of the stairs, with her rocking buttocks expressive of her scorn.

"Always remember," said Cleo loudly and sweetly to Judy, "that good manners put you in the parlor and poor manners keep you in the kitchen." The maid's broad back seemed to swell the seams of her uniform. "That's what I'm paying good money to your governess for," Cleo added impressively. "So you won't have to wear an apron."

Judy stared down at her shoes, feeling very uncomfortable because Cleo's voice was carrying to the woman on the stairs. Miss Binney always said that a lady must keep her voice low, and never boast, and never, never say anything that might hurt somebody's feelings.

"She heard you," said Judy in a stricken voice.

Cleo gave her a look of amiable impatience. "Well, I expected her to hear. Who did you think I was talking to? I certainly wasn't talking to you."

Her eyes grew lively with amusement as she studied her daughter's distress. Sometimes she wondered where she had got Judy. Judy had no funny bone. Thea was probably responsible. She had no funny bone either. Their diversions were so watery. What was the sense in Judy's taking delight in a dog's wagging tail if she was going to miss the greater eloquence of that woman's wagging rear, and then look shocked when her mother talked back at it? You really had to love Bostonians to like them. And the part of Cleo that did love them was continually at war with the part of her that preferred the salt flavor of lusty laughter.

Her eyes clouded with wistfulness. The more the years increased between the now and the long ago, the more the broad A's hemmed her in, the more her child grew alien to all that had made her own childhood an enchanted summer, so in like degree did her secret heart yearn for her sisters. She longed for the eager audience they would have provided, the boisterous mirth she would have evoked when she flatfooted up an imaginary flight of stairs, agitating her bottom. Who did she know in the length and breadth of Boston who wouldn't have cleared an embarrassed throat before she got going good on her imitation?

Sometimes you felt like cutting the fool for the hell of it. Sometimes you hankered to pick a bone and talk with your mouth full. To Cleo culture was a garment that she had learned to get into quickly and out of just as fast.

She put on her parlor airs now, for Mr. Van Ryper was descending the stairs. Her eyebrows arched delicately, her luscious mouth pursed primly, and a faint stage smile ruffled her smooth cheeks.

Folk

WHERE ARE YOU FROM?

One friendly and outgoing girl walked up to another female at a cocktail party and tried to start a conversation, inquiring, "So, where are you from?"

The stuck-up woman that she approached looked down her nose at her and huffed, "Don't you know better than to end a sentence with a preposition?"

The first girl replied, "Well, then, where are you from, *bitch?*"

Folk

THE PROPER WORD

This girl had just come back from her first semester at college, and she was appalled at her parents' speech. At breakfast she could take it no longer when her father said he had "done et seven slices of bacon."

"Daddy!" she exclaimed, "you don't say 'et.' The proper word is 'ate.' "

"Okay," he smiled proudly at his daughter. "If you say so. I done et *eight* slices."

Folk

F I D O

These dogs. . . . This mongrel walks by and say [rough, street tone], "Hey, baby!"

[Very properly] "It's Mimi—M-i-m-i."

He say, "Okay, M-i-m-i. And your sister?"

She say, "I'm Fifi—F-i-f-i."

He say, "Well, good for you."

"And what's your name?"

He said, "Fido—P-h-y-d-e-a-u-x . . . bitch!"

M I M E O G R A P H E D   I T E M
College Graduates

COLLEGE GRADUATES AND THUS PROSPECTIVE TEACHERS ARE NOT WHAT THEY USED TO BE. THAT IS—THEY COMMUNICATE WITH A SOMEWHAT CHANGED VOCABULARY. I RECOMMEND THAT THIS LIST OF WORDS BE ADDED TO ALL TEACHER APPLICATIONS. A NEEDED REVISION IS OBVIOUS WHEN YOU STUDY ABOUT A COLLEGE GRADUATE WHO:

1. SPENT FOUR DAYS IN SEARS LOOKING FOR WHEELS FOR A MISCARRIAGE.
2. TOOK HIS EXPECTANT WIFE TO A GROCERY STORE BECAUSE THEY HAD FREE DELIVERY.
3. LOOKED IN A LUMBER YARD FOR A DRAFT BOARD.
4. TOOK A ROLL OF TOILET TISSUE TO A CRAP GAME.
5. PUT IODINE ON HIS PAY CHECK BECAUSE HE GOT A CUT IN PAY.
6. WAS SO LAZY HE MARRIED A PREGNANT WOMAN.
7. WAS FEELING SO LOW HE GOT HIS FACE SLAPPED.
8. LOST HIS GIRLFRIEND BECAUSE HE COULDN'T REMEMBER WHERE HE LAID HER.
9. THOUGHT ASPHALT WAS RECTUM TROUBLE.
10. WOULDN'T GO OUT WITH HIS WIFE BECAUSE HE HEARD SHE WAS MARRIED.
11. THOUGHT A SANITARY BELT WAS A DRINK FROM A CLEAN SHOT GLASS.
12. WORE A UNION SUIT BECAUSE HIS WIFE WAS HAVING LABOR PAINS.
13. THOUGHT "NO KIDDING" MEANT BIRTH CONTROL.
14. THOUGHT PETER PAN WAS SOMETHING TO PUT UNDER THE BED.
15. THOUGHT HIS TYPEWRITER WAS PREGNANT BECAUSE IT MISSED A PERIOD.
16. THOUGHT MOBY DICK WAS A VENEREAL DISEASE.
17. WHO SMELLED GOOD ONLY ON THE RIGHT SIDE BECAUSE HE COULDN'T FIND THE "LEFT GUARD."
18. STUDIED FOR FIVE DAYS TO TAKE A URINE TEST.
19. BOUGHT HIS WIFE A WASHER AND DRYER FOR CHRISTMAS. IT WAS A DOUCHE BAG AND TOWEL.
20. WENT IN THE OUTHOUSE, PUT ONE LEG IN EACH HOLE, AND SHIT IN HIS PANTS.
21. THOUGHT A MUSHROOM WAS A PLACE TO NECK.

Folk

THE LEE SISTERS

These three women came into a party, strutting like they thought they looked good! So this lady they tried to snub say, "Well, there are the Lee sisters."

She say [in a very proper tone of voice], "No we are not!"

Lady say, "Yes you are, you *Ug* . . . , you *Home* . . . , and you *Unforgod*. . . ."

Folk

DOES IT COME IN WHITE?

Well this brother had a *terrible* accident, and in the accident he was deprived of his penis. But they told him, like Bobbitt, he could get one put on. And they recommended this physician.

The physician say, "Now *first* of all, you got to get your mind on straight. You worried." He say, "But, I can help you. You'll be all right. It'll take a little time."

He say, "That's what I don't have."

He say, "Well, you might as well." So he showed him *all* of these various sizes, gorgeous penises."

He say, "None of them is what I want, . . . since I'm getting a second chance." He say, "Money is no object."

The doctor say, "I know, but this is . . . Wait, wait, wait, *wait* a minute, here, I've got another box." So he pulled out this box.

"Yep! *That!* That's the one! . . . But does it come in *white?*"

Mama Sez

The higher you climb, the farther you have to fall.

It's never too late for the raccoon to wear a rough-dry shirt.

The cow's gon' need her tail agin' in fly-time [against a fair-weather friend].

The higher monkey climb, the more you see his behind.

Monkey better know what he gon' do wit' his tail before he buy his trousers.

No matter how high the bird flies, he have to come back down to the ground to eat.

She livin'/eatin' mighty high up on the hog.

Sister to Sister

They nigger rich.

He's got money's mammy.

"He was born on third and thinks he hit a triple." [one born into a wealthy family who acts as if he did something to deserve it—from Benilde Little, *Good Hair,* 109.]

She act so stuck-up, you'd think her shit don't stink.

She's got a sho-nuff attitude.

She sure is hincty/siddity.

She always walking around with her ass on her shoulder [acting superior].

She got her ass so high on her shoulders she can't even speak.

She think she the H.N.I.C. [head nigger in charge] at her job.

He's a Ph.D. you know—posthole digger.

All you could hear when their first son graduated was, "Oh, James graduated Summa Cum Laude"; they were bragging just as loud when their second one graduated Magna Cum Laude; but they ain't have so much to say 'bout this last one. You know he graduated Lawdy, Lawd, Lawdy/Thank you, Lawd!

They sho' in nigger heaven!

Think she's somethin' cause she's ridin'round in that hog [Cadillac]/deuce and a quarter [Buick Electra 225].

She's one o' those high yallers.

She's light, bright, and damn near white.

No matter how light you are, you got to keep the color [refuse to pass for white/remain in the race].

CHAPTER 9

My People, My People!

SELF-DENIGRATING TALES

In her book of essays, *bulletproof diva*, Lisa Jones writes about "a friend's cousin who since grade school had gone by [the name] 'Niggerman.' He died in the electric chair. His crime? Shooting a white man for calling him 'nigger.' " The response to that in the black community would be, "My people, my people!" It is the familiar lament among a people who say the worst things about themselves, but are quick to take offense if someone else dares offer similar criticism.

Some black people view this self-denigration with embarrassment and insist that only racist whites make such comments about African Americans. There is no question that this body of material is in-house humor, and that the same items that can cause raucous laughter among an all-black audience would be very painful to a black person in a mixed audience, who would likely respond with awkward silence and resentful anger. Novelist

John Oliver Killens notes that his daughter was upset when she went to Fisk University to find that "the password [among the girls in her dormitory was] 'a nigger ain't shit,' " and adds, "the same password was prevalent in my college days."[1] Obviously, a white student who made that comment in either dorm would do so at the risk of his life. Among blacks, appelations such as "bad-ass nigger," "bad nigger," and "my nigger" are generally positive and complimentary terms.[2] In his definition of "Nigger," Clarence Major writes:

> When used by a white person in addressing a black person, usually it is offensive and disparaging—and has been so since the end of the Civil War; used by black people among themselves, it is a racial term with undertones of warmth and goodwill—reflecting, aside from the irony, a tragi-comic sensibility that is aware, on some level, of the emotional history of the race."[3]

Major's commentary is applicable to much of the humor of the "My People, My People" variety. This is definitely tragicomic, in-house humor in which the principals laugh about behavior that reinforces hated stereotypes that are applied by racists to all members of the black community, and for which all members of the race continue to feel responsible. Thus, on one level, as Zora Neale Hurston points out in her essay of the same title,[4] the exclamation "My people, my people!" "is forced outward by pity, scorn and hopeless resignation." On another level, I would suggest that it is also a distancing technique, one suggested even more in the reversal sometimes playfully made, "Your people! Your people!" Certainly there are those blacks who view themselves as apart from and superior to these "other"

---

1. "Rappin' With Myself," in *Amistad 2,* ed. John A. Williams and Charles F. Hann (New York: Random House, 1971), 117–18.

2. There are, of course, members of the African-American community who will never use the term *nigger.* There are many more who publicly assail others for using it, but sling it around with impunity in private.

3. *Juba to Jive,* 320.

4. In *Dust Tracks on a Road,* ed. Robert Hemenway (Urbana: University of Illinois Press, 1984 [originally published: Philadelphia: Lippincott, 1942). I read this work for the first time when I was over thirty; and having heard and used the phrase all of my life, I have not felt the need to attribute my title to Hurston.

Negroes whose behavior can only be viewed condescendingly with the phrase, "My people, my people!" One should note parenthetically that the term also has widespread currency with positive connotations, as in Margaret Walker's classic poem, "For My People" or in common boasts about what "My people" (usually referring to the race, but also to family) have achieved; the context in which the phrase is used and the intonation of the speaker's voice will make quite clear the proper interpretation of "My people!" in either case.

Common among the self-denigrating jokes on this subject are those focusing on the Monkey, who is always associated with the Negro, though not in the positive sense that Henry Louis Gates, Jr., details in *The Signifying Monkey* as descendant of Esu Elegbara and his descendant, The Signifying Monkey, divine interpreter, divine linguist, master signifier. Instead, in this body of literature, the Negro's association with the monkey focuses on his ugly physical appearance, his tendency to ape others, and his weakness. One might speculate that the term *jiggaboo* is derived from *guije* or *jigue*, terms that, Gates indicates, are used to refer to a small black man and a monkey in Afro-Cuban mythology and that derive from the Efik-Ejagham word for *monkey, jiwe.* As used in the United States from slavery until the present, *jiggaboo* is much more negative than *guije* or *jigue*. Both emphasize the color black and both are associated with the monkey, but in the United States, as Clarence Major's *Juba to Jive* indicates, the term is "always pejorative." (Major traces *jiggaboo* to *tshikabo,* the Bantu word meaning a meek or servile person, and defines the term's usage here as "a very dark-skinned African-American of pure African descent.")

Among the characteristics bewailed with the response "My People, my People!" are embarrassing appearance (dress [design, color, and fit], skin color, hairstyle, makeup, size), loud and disruptive behavior, bad manners, tardiness, laziness, poverty, ignorance, nongrammatical speech, use of malapropisms and mispronunciations, religion, superstitions, greed, violent and criminal proclivity, and any other behavior that reinforces hated stereotypes. Any indications of these characteristics may cause black onlookers to look to the sky, drop their eyes, or roll their eyes at a companion in a gesture of resignation. Only when they get to the privacy of their homes, beauty parlors, and other all-black gatherings will they recount the event, laugh uproariously, and loudly proclaim, "My people, my people!"

Folk

I RAISED HELL WHILE I WAS THERE

from Daryl Cumber Dance, *Shuckin' and Jivin'*

This guy died and went to heaven, and when he got up there, say, all the angels were 'round at the table, you know, and he wanted to show off. So he ran around. He did the left-wing dive and the right-wing dive—all kinds o' stunts. So some of 'em had told 'im, you know, to stop because if he didn't he was gon' turn the table over. So finally he kep' on and kep' on until the table went over, and when the table went over, then they put him out of heaven. So after they put him out of heaven, they say he said, "Well, they put me out," he says, "but, HEY! HEY! I raised hell while I was there."

Maggie Pogue Johnson

SUPERSTITIONS

from *Virginia Dreams/Lyrics for the Idle Hour: Tales of the Time Told in Rhyme*

I ain't superstitious,
　　But dis I sho' do know,
Dat ef a rooster walks his se'f up
　　En crows right in y'o do',
Dar's sho' someone a comin'
　　Say jis what you might,
Dar'll be a stranger at yo' hous'
　　Fo' de cumin' ob de night.

I ain't superstitious,
    But dis I know is tru',
Say what you will, en do what you'll do;
    Ef yo' lef' han' itches,
You may t'nk it funny,
    But you sho' soon gwine er git
A little sum ob money.

I ain't superstitious,
    'Tis ignance I'll vow,
But sho's you're born,
    Dis is tru' some how,
Dat ef you starts a place,
    En has to turn back,
En fo'gits to make a cross,
    En spit right in yo' track,

Some bad luck sho' will follow,
    Dis t'ing sho' is tru',
Ef you don't believe me,
    I tell you what to do:
Jis go some whar fo' fun,
    En den turn back to see,
Some bad luck sho' will follow,
    'Tis tru' as it kin be.

I ain't superstitious,
    But I tell you what I've seen,
Ef you eats at a table
    Whar dar's jis thirteen,
You min' what I say,
    As sho's dar's a sky
One ob dat thirteen
    Will be sho to die.

I ain't superstitious
    But here's annoder fact,
En dis t'ing sho is tru'
    No matter whar you's at,
Dat if you starts a place
    En a black cat crosses you
'Tis sho en sartin bad luck
    No matter what you do.

I can't be superstitious
    En sho I ain't to blame
But if you cum in one do' ob de hous'
    En don't go out de same
Your min', it sho is bad luck,
    You kin turn dis way en dat
But bad luck sho will follow
    No matter whar you's at.

I ain't superstitious
    But some t'ings I do know,
Ef you sweeps yo' hous' out arter dark
    'Tis bad luck fo' you sho,
En please don't spill no salt,
    It jis as sho is tru'
Dat sumpin's gwine to happen,
    Min' what I say, too.

I ain't superstitious
    But I tell you fus en las'
It sho is awful luck
    To break a lookin' glass;
Bad luck fo' seven years
    Is de title read;
Dat sho is one t'ing dat I fears—
    One t'ing dat I dread.

I ain't superstitious
 But dis ain't no lie,
Ef a bird flies in de hous'
 Dars some one gwine to die;
'Tis jis as true as it kin be
 En when you see de bird
Some one's gwine to leabe dat hous',
 Case die am de word.

I ain't superstitious
 But let yo' lef' eye quiver,
Trouble sho will follow,
 You jis well 'gin to shiver;
En let yo' lef' foot itch
 'Tis jis as tru' fo' sho,
You jis well pack yo' satchel,
 Case on strange lan' you mus' go.

I ain't superstitious,
 But dis I sho do know,
In de ebening arter dark
 Ef you hears a rooster crow
Hasty news am cumin,
 'Tis tru' as it kin be,
En you jis well wa'r a long face
 En set en wait to see.

I ain't superstitious,
 It's ign'ance, 'tis a fact;
It jis sho's, too,
 Dat fo' 'telligence you lack,
But when settin at de table,
 La sakes! don't sneeze,
It's a sho sign ob death,
 Say what you please.

I ain't superstitious
　　En eberybody knows
Dat I ain't superstitious
　　Eny whar I goes,
But y'all sho kin tell
　　En read between de lines,
I ain't superstitious
　　But I do beliebe in signs.

Folk

I BEEN SICK

The animals had a meeting and they were trying to decide who was the ugliest. The Lion spoke up and declared, "You know I'm not the ugliest, cause I'm the King of the Jungle."

The Bear declared, "You know I'm not the ugliest because I stand up straight and tall."

And so on and on it went until they came to the Monkey, and they all looked at him. He say, "I don't know what you looking at me for. I'm not the ugliest. I just been sick."

Folk

WE AIN'T DUMB

A group of black girls went up to complain to the principal. They say, "We's the colored girls at this school, and we wants to know how comes we ain't on the cheering squad. We wents out there and yawl did not even gives us a chance to be on the cheering squad. And we kin cheer. We been cheerin' all our lives. . . ."

The lady say, (conciliatory tone) "Well, we have a game Friday night. Maybe . . ."

"*Don't* tell us when we ain't gon' be ready. We gon' be ready."

And so they got out there and they got ready to cheer:

> "One, two, three, go.
> Fried chicken, watermelon, Cadillac *car,*
> We ain't as dumb as you think we . . . is."

Folk

IT HASN'T BEEN USED

This white man was sick and the only thing that would save him was a brain transplant. So the doctors told him he had three choices. They could give him a brain from a white man for $1,000; they could give him a brain from an Asian man for $2,000; or they could give him a brain from a black man for $10,000.

The patient was incredulous: "Why is the brain from a *black* man so much more expensive than the brain from a white man?" he asked.

"Because it hasn't been used," the doctors replied.

Folk

JESUS WEPT

This woman had this underground house during the war where soldiers came and got a free meal, but they had to quote a verse of scripture. So this nigger came in there every day talkin' bout, "Jesus wept." Monday, Tuesday, Wednesday, and Thursday. She say, "Listen, son, do you know any story in the Bible?"

He say, "No, Ma'am."

She say, "Well, you keep saying 'Jesus wept.' Jesus did something else. He was a very wonderful man. Let me tell you a story. You a tall, strong man. There was a strong man in the Bible named Samson. Samson's strength was in his hair. He was a great warrior, and he didn't have guns and things in those days, so he took the *jawbone* of an ass and slew *thousands* of Philistines. And that's how they found out just how strong he was with his bare hands and with the jawbone of an ass just beating and whipping people to death." She say, "Now tomorrow, when you come for dinner, tell me that story about Samson, the strongest man. You got it?"

"Yas, Ma-a-a-m, I got it."

So the next day he came for dinner. One guy came by and said, "The Lord is in His holy temple. Let all the earth keep silent before him." Say "Paul wrote a letter to Corinthians, and on the road to Damascus, he was reborn."

She say "Fine, go eat your dinner."

So here come this nigger: "Jesus wept."

She say, "I told you a story yesterday."

He say, "Yaas, Maam, you did, you did, you did. . . . I got it right." He say, "Nigger named Sam from Pittsburg slipped up on his ass and broke his jawbone!"

Folk

TONGUE AND TEETH

from Daryl Cumber Dance, *Shuckin' and Jivin'*

Mr Charlie, he was the boss man. He had a lot of slaves. He had one of 'em, he told everything he knew. One day he was coming through the woods; he walked up on a skeleton, and he saw the skeleton layin' down. He kicked 'im. He say, "Skeleton, what are you doing here?"

The skeleton tol' him, "Tongue and teeth brought me here and gon' bring you here."

So he goes home and he tells his master 'bout this skeleton down in the woods talking. And the master said, "I tol' ya 'bout lying to me!"

But he swore that he was right.

His master said, "I'm going down there with you, and if that skeleton don't talk I'm gon' kill ya."

He picked up his shotgun and the two went on back in the woods and ask the skeleton what he was doin' there. He asked 'im three times, kicked 'im, but the skeleton wouldn't say a thing. Master drawed out the shotgun and shot 'im [the slave].

The skeleton say, "I tol' ya tongue and teeth brought me here, bring you here too!"

Folk

WHY I TALK LIKE DIS?

This little boy went to his mama, and he say, "Ma-ma-ma-mama, why I t-t-t-talk like dis?"

She say, "Go long and play, boy."

He went to his daddy, say, "Wh-why-why-why I t-t-t-talk like dis?"

He say, "Go long and play."

The next day the iceman came by. He say, "Mi-mi-mi-ster Iceman, how come I t-t-t-talk like dis?"

He say, "Wh-wh-wh-what you t-t-t-trying to do? Get somebody in tr-tr-tr-trouble?"

Folk

AM I JEWISH OR AM I BLACK?

John was the son of a Jewish mother and a black father. One day, when he was about twelve years he came running to his mother, and he asked, "Am I Jewish or am I black?"

"You're multicultural, Johnny."

"No, but I've got to know am I Jewish or am I black," Johnny insisted.

"Why do you ask?" his mother inquired.

"I've got to know what I am," he desperately insisted; "Am I Jewish or am I black."

"Well," his mother replied, "if you tell me why it is so important for you to know, I'll try to tell you."

"Well," John said, "Billy's got a bike he wants to sell for fifty dollars, and I need to know whether to try to jew him down to thirty-five or wait until after dark and steal it.

Folk

YOU IS WHAT YOU IS

A Zebra got to heaven and he asked St. Peter to help him resolve a dilemma that had tormented him all of his life: was he white with black stripes or black with white stripes? St. Peter sent him to talk with God about it, but when he saw him later, the Zebra seemed as disturbed as ever. St. Peter asked him if God had resolved his problem for him, and the Zebra said, "No, I'm as confused as ever. God just said to me, 'You are what you are.' So I still don't know whether I'm white with black stripes or black with white stripes."

"Oh," St. Peter smiled, "that means you are white with black stripes. If you had been black with white stripes, God would have told you, 'you is what you is.' "

Folk

TESTIMONIALS

"If my husband won't so stupid he wouldda had a good job as doorman down at the Jamaica Club. You know they have to wear bermuda shorts, so the lady what interviewed him asked to see his ankles. So he pulled up his trousers a little bit and showed her his ankles. Then she asked to see his knees, and he hitched up his pants up pass his knees. Then she said, "You look like you will look fine in our outfits. So the job is yours if your testimonials are in order. May I see your testimonials please?"

"Well, did he get the job?"

"Hell, no, that fool pulled down his pants and showed her his 'testimonials' and they threw his ass out."

Moms Mabley

MOM'S FIRST PLANE RIDE

The first time I was in a plane, it done me up so bad. I didn't get up no higher than this building . . . before both my ears stopped up. I couldn't hear *nothin'!* Oh, you talk about somebody being miserable! The attendant come by, . . . I said, "I can't hear *nothin'!*"

She say, "Chew this gum. Maybe that'll unstop your ears."

I chewed. I chewed. I couldn't hear nothin'! I say, "Honey, do something for me. I'm *dying!* I can't hear nothin."

She say, "Mom, drop your jaws."

. . . And I misunderstood her . . . I did.

I caught a terrible cold, I did.

Folk

I'LL TAKE HIM

There was a church meeting one night. The ushers took up collection and saw a hundred-dollar bill in the plate. Thinking it had been placed there in error, one usher passed the minister a note, and he asked the congregation if anyone had put in one hundred dollars through mistake—"If so, raise your hand and we'll return it so that you can put in what you intended."

A little old lady raised her hand and said, "I intended to put in that hundred dollar bill."

So the minister said, "To show our appreciation we shall give you a rising vote of thanks and three *hymns* of your choice. Which hymns would you like?"

To this the lady arose and, pointing her finger, said, "I'll take him . . . and him . . . and him."

Folk

YOU KNOW

When the Richmond City schools integrated, this white teacher had these little black children. And she said, "Well, I don't know whether they know how to use words in sentences but I'm gon' give them a chance." So she told this lil fellow that his word was "Dear."

"Dear?"

She say, "Yes, you know, what your mother calls your father when he comes home in the evening."

He say, "Oh! You mean 'son-of-a-bitch.' "

Folk

HO-DE-DO

What has eight legs and goes "ho-de-do, ho-de-do, ho-de-do"?
Four niggers running for the elevator.

Folk

O.J.'S GOING TO CANCUN

The guard went to get O.J. And he was all dressed up in his tennis short and tennis shirt, and he had his tennis racket, tennis shoes, and everything. And the guard say, "What are you dressed like that for?"

He say, "You said I'm going to Cancun."

He say, "Naw . . . I said, 'You going to the *can,* Coon.' "

Folk

COUNTRY GUY AND CITY GUY

This country guy came to the city to visit his cousin and they were invited to dinner. So he told his cousin, he say, "I don't know about going to dinner because I don't know how to act at a dinner table."

And he say, "Well, just follow me. Whatever I do, you do. If I pick up a fork, you pick up a fork. Whatever I say, you say."

So he say, "Awright."

So this lady invited them to dinner and he was watching his city cousin . . . he picked up his salad fork and then his dinner fork and . . . so when dinner was over, this city guy told the hostess, "Oh, I have dined elegantly sufficient."

And this country guy say, "Oh, I have dined the elephant and gone fishing.

Jacqueline Brice-Finch

ENGLISH 'UMOR

My mother was always unfailingly polite to the stream of school friends I brought home from college. One night she met Andrew, a guy from St. Croix who graduated as salutatorian from his high school but spoke with a heavy Crucian accent. He was married with a young son. Mom asked him what was his son's name. When he answered, she wondered why he was calling the boy a turd. She carefully repeated his statement, "He's a turd?" while trying desperately not to offend.

Andrew nodded, "Yes, I'm the second. He's the tird. Andrew Lawrence Martin, the Tird."

Val Ward

PA'NELLA

Once when I was a girl about seven and a half years old, growing up in the Mississippi Delta, I went with my older sister, Josie, to spend the weekend in the country with my grandmother, Sarah, whom we all called "Mother." While visiting awhile, Josie took me to visit a local woman who cooked for a white family whom she called Mr. and Mrs. Rainey. Let's call this lady Miss Virginia. She was skinny and weighed about eighty-five pounds soaking wet. Miss Virginia wore a red head-rag that day and walked on the back of some shoes, squashed down at the back.

Josie quietly nudged me to ask Virginia how she got the beautiful name for her daughter. Josie and others had heard this story many times. Miss Virginia proceeded to tell me the following. "When them pains commenced ta' hit me, I just see'd a bottle a' pa'nella [vanilla] flavor in dat windah. And tha' only thang I could thank of was pa'nella flavor. So I named her my beautiful Pa'nella."

And that's how Pa'nella got her name!

Folk

THE NEW RECTUM

from Daryl Cumber Dance, *Shuckin' and Jivin'*

These Old Sisters always came to church before anyone else and sat look-ing at everyone else as they came in [crosses arms and rolls eyes around, mimicking an Old Sister].

"I hear we got a new pastor," one says to the other.

"Yes, have you seen him?" the other asked.

"No, I sure haven't."

About that time a man walks in with eyeglasses with a chain hanging down from them [mimics the posture of a dignified, pompous man strolling down the aisle].

One hunched the other one: "Rachel, who is that?"

"I don't know," said Rachel, but she hunched her neighbor and asked, "Who is that pregnating looking man urinating down the aisle with gold testicles on?"

"That's the new rectum of the church," was the response.

Folk

STAYMAN

(Conversation between ladies at the bridge table)

I.

"Do you know Stayman?"

"I'm not sure. I think I may have met him, but I can't say I know him?"

II.

"Do you play Stayman?"
   "No, I just play bridge."

Folk

HURRY UP

Well, you know, these two old maids lived together, and they were in the bed one night, and a man was breaking into the house. He came into the bedroom, and he say, "Oh, hell, there's somebody in here." So he say, "Well, I'll just hypnotize these people," and he say, "Hocus-s-s-s . . . pocus-s-s-s . . . hocus-s-s-s . . . pocus-s-s-s. . . ."

   One of the old maids sat up in the bed and say, "Damn the *hocus,* hurry up and *poke* us."

Folk

PLAYING IN A BIG AUDITORIUM

This guy was getting a little piece, you know, and the girl said, "My what a small organ you have!"

   He say, "Naw, it ain't that my organ is so small. It's just that I'm playing in a big auditorium."

Ntozake Shange

SPELL #7 GEECHEE JIBARA QUIK MAGIC TRANCE MANUAL FOR TECHNOLOGICALLY STRESSED THIRD WORLD PEOPLE

ACT I

(there is a huge black-face mask hanging from the ceiling of the theater as the audience enters. in a way the show has already begun, for the members of the audience must integrate this grotesque, larger than life misrepresentation of life into their pre-show chatter. slowly the house lights fade, but the mask looms even larger in the darkness.

once the mask is all that can be seen, lou, the magician, enters. he is dressed in the traditional costume of Mr. Interlocutor: tuxedo, bow-tie, top hat festooned with all kinds of whatnots that are obviously meant for good luck, he does a few catchy "soft-shoe" steps & begins singing a traditional version of a black play song)

> lou *(singing)*
> 10 lil picaninnies all in bed
> one fell out and the other nine said:
> i sees yr hiney
> all black & shiny
> i see yr hiney
> all black & shiny/shiny

> *(as a greeting)*
> yes/ yes/ yes   isn't life wonderful

> *(confidentially)*
> my father is a retired magician
> which accounts for my irregular behavior
> everything comes outta magic hats
> or bottles wit no bottoms & parakeets
> are as easy to get as a couple a rabbits

or 3 fifty-cent pieces/ 1958
my daddy retired from magic & took
up another trade cuz this friend a mine
from the 3rd grade/ asked to be made white
on the spot

what cd any self-respectin colored american magician
do wit such an outlandish request/ cept
put all them razzamatazz hocus pocus zippity-doo-dah
thingamajigs away cuz
colored chirren believin in magic
waz becomin politically dangerous for the race
& waznt nobody gonna be made white
on the spot just
from a clap of my daddy's hands
& the reason i'm so peculiar's
cuz i been studyin up on my daddy's technique
& everything i do is magic these days
& it's very colored/ very now you see it/ now you
dont mess wit me

                              (boastfully)
                                        i come from a family of retired
sorcerers/ active houngans & pennyante fortune tellers
wit 41 million spirits/ critturs & celestial bodies
on our side
                    i'll listen to yr problems
                    help wit yr career/ yr lover/ yr wanderin spouse
                    make yr grandma's stay in heaven more
                    gratifyin
                    ease yr mother thru menopause & show yr son
                    how to clean his room

*(while lou has been easing the audience into acceptance of his appearance & the mask
(his father, the ancestors, our magic), the rest of the company enters in tattered field-
hand garb, blackface, and the countenance of stepan fetchit when he waz frightened.
their presence belies the magician's promise that "you'll be colored n love it," just as
the minstrel shows were lies, but lou continues)*

YES YES YES 3 wishes is all you get
   scarlet ribbons for yr hair
   a farm in mississippi
   someone to love you madly
all things are possible
but aint no colored magician in his right mind
gonna make you   white
i mean
       this is blk magic
you lookin at
& i'm fixin you up good/ fixin you up good & colored
& you gonna be colored all yr life
& you gonna love it/ bein colored/ all yr life/ colored & love it
love it/ bein colored. SPELL #7!

*(lou claps his hands, & the company which had been absolutely still til this moment/
jumps up. with a rhythm set on a washboard carried by one of them/ they begin a
series of steps that identify every period of afro-american entertainment: from acro-
bats, comedians, tap-dancers, calindy dancers, cotton club choruses, apollo theatre du-
wop groups, til they reach a frenzy in the midst of "hambone, hambone where ya
been"/ & then take a bow à la bert williams/ the lights bump up abruptly.*

*the magician, lou, walks thru the black-faced figures in their kneeling poses, arms out-
stretched as if they were going to sing "mammy." he speaks now [as a companion
of the mask] to the same audience who fell so easily into his hands & who were so
aroused by the way the black-faced figures "sang n danced")*

   lou
why dont you go on & integrate a german-american school in st. louis
mo./ 1955/ better yet why dont ya go on & be a red niggah in a blk
school in 1954/ i got it/ try & make one friend at camp in the ozarks in
1957/ crawl thru one a jesse james' caves wit a class of white kids waitin
outside to see the whites of yr eyes/ why dontcha invade a clique of working class italians trying to be protestant in a jewish community/ & come
up a spade/ be a lil too dark/ lips a lil too full/ hair entirely too nappy/ to
be beautiful/ be a smart child trying to be dumb/ you go meet somebody
who wants/ always/ a lil less/ be cool when yr body says hot/ & more/ be

a mistake in racial integrity/ an error in white folks' most absurd fantasies/ be a blk kid in 1954/ who's not blk enuf to lovingly ignore/ not beautiful enuf to leave alone/ not smart enuf to move outta the way/ not bitter enuf to die at an early age/ why dontchu c'mon & live my life for me/ since the dreams aint enuf/ go on & live my life for me/ i didnt want certain moments at all/ i'd give em to anybody . . . awright. alec.

[In the following scene Natalie, "a not too successful performer," fantasizes that she is a white woman in a conversation with Lou, Bettina, a chorus girl, and Lily, an unemployed actress who works as a chorus girl.]

bettina
you're still outta yr mind. ain't no apologies keeping us alive.

lou
what are you gonna do with white folks kneeling all over the country anyway/ man

(lou signals everyone to kneel)

lily
they say i'm too light to work/ but when i asked him what he meant/ he said i didnt actually look black. but/ i said/ my mama knows i'm black & my daddy/ damn sure knows i'm black/ & he is the only one who has a problem thinkin i'm black/ i said so let me play a white girl/ i'm a classically trained actress & i need the work & i can do it/ he said that wdnt be very ethical of him. can you imagine that shit/ not ethical

natalie
as a red-blooded white woman/ i cant allow you all to go on like that

(natalie starts jocularly)
cuz today i'm gonna be a white girl/ i'll retroactively wake myself up/ ah low & behold/ a white girl in my bed/ but first i'll haveta call a white girl i know to have some more accurate information/ what's the first thing white girls think in the morning/ do they get up being glad they aint niggahs/ do they remember mama/ or worry abt gettin to work/ do they

work?/ do they play isadora & wrap themselves in sheets & go tip toeing to the kitchen to make maxwell house coffee/ oh i know/ the first thing a white girl does in the morning is fling her hair/

so now i'm done with that/ i'm gonna water my plants/ but am i a po white trash white girl with a old jellyjar/ or am i a sophisticated & protestant suburbanite with 2 valiums slugged awready & a porcelain water carrier leading me up the stairs strewn with heads of dolls & nasty smellin white husband person's underwear/ if i was really protected from the niggahs/ i might go to early morning mass & pick up a tomato pie on the way home/ so i cd eat it during the young & the restless. in williams arizona as a white girl/ i cd push the navaho women outta my way in the supermarket & push my nose in the air so i wdnt haveta smell them. coming from bay ridge on the train i cd smile at all the black & puerto rican people/ & hope they cant tell i want them to go back where they came from/ or at least be invisible

i'm still in my kitchen/ so i guess i'll just have to fling my hair again & sit down. i shd pinch my cheeks to bring the color back/ i wonder why the colored lady hasnt arrived to clean my house yet/ so i cd go to the beauty parlor & sit under a sunlamp to get some more color back/ it's terrible how god gave those colored women such clear complexions/ it take em years to develop wrinkles/ but beauty can be bought & flattered into the world.

as a white girl on the street/ i can assume since i am a white girl on the streets/ that everyone notices how beautiful i am/ especially lil black & caribbean boys/ they love to look at me/ i'm exotic/ no one in their families looks like me/ poor things. if i waz one of those white girls who loves one of those grown black fellas/ i cd say with my eyes wide open/ totally sincere/ oh i didnt know that/ i cd say i didnt know/ i cant/ i dont know how/ cuz i'ma white girl & i dont have to do much of anything.

all of this is the fault of the white man's sexism/ oh how i loathe tight-assed thin-lipped pink white men/ even the football players lack a certain relaxed virility. that's why my heroes are either just like my father/ who while he still cdnt speak english knew enough to tell me how the niggers shd go back where they came from/ or my heroes are psychotic faggots who are white/ or else they are/ oh/ you know/ colored men.

being a white girl by dint of my will/ is much more complicated than i thought it wd be/ but i wanted to try it cuz so many men like white girls/ white men/ black men/ latin men/ jewish men/ asians/ everybody. so i thought if i waz a white girl for a day i might understand this better/ after all gertrude stein wanted to know abt the black women/ alice adams wrote *thinking abt billie*/ joyce carol oates has three different black characters all with the same name/ i guess cuz we are underdeveloped individuals or cuz we are all the same/ at any rate i'm gonna call this thinkin abt white girls/ cuz helmut newton's awready gotta book called *white women*/ see what i mean/ that's a best seller/ one store i passed/ hadda sign said/

> WHITE WOMEN
> SOLD OUT

it's this kinda pressure that forces us white girls to be so absolutely patho-logical abt the other women in the world/ who now that they're not all ser-vants or peasants want to be considered beautiful too. we simply krinkle our hair/ learn to dance the woogie dances/ slant our eyes with make-up or surgery/ learn spanish & claim argentinian background/ or as a real trump card/ show up looking like a real white girl. you know all western civi-lization depends on us/

    i still havent left my house. i think i'll fling my hair once more/ but this time with a pout/ cuz i think i havent been fair to the sisterhood/ women's movement faction of white girls/ although/ they always ask what do you people really want. as if the colored woman of the world were a strange sort of neutered workhorse/ which isnt too far from reality/ since i'm still waiting for my cleaning lady & the lady who takes care of my children & the lady who caters my parties & the lady who accepts quarters at the bath-room in sardi's. those poor creatures shd be sterilized/ no one shd have to live such a life. cd you hand me a towel/ thank-you caroline. i've left all of maxime's last winter clothes in a pile for you by the back door. they have to be cleaned but i hope yr girls can make gd use of them.

    oh/ i'm still not being fair/ all the white women in the world dont wake up being glad they aint niggahs/ only some of them/ the ones who dont/ wake up thinking how can i survive another day of this culturally con-doned incompetence. i know i'll play a tenor horn & tell all the colored artists i meet/ that now i'm just like them/ i'm colored i'll say cuz i have a struggle too. or i cd punish this white beleagered body of mine with the advances of a thousand ebony bodies/ all built like franco harris or peter tosh/ a thousand of them may take me & do what they want/ cuz i'm so sorry/ yes i'm so sorry they were born niggahs. but then if i cant punish myself to death for being white/ i certainly cant in good conscience keep waiting for the cleaning lady/ & everytime i attempt even the smallest venture into the world someone comes to help me/ like if i do anything/ anything at all i'm extending myself as a white girl/ cuz part of being a white girl is being absent/ like those women who are just with a man but whose names the black people never remember/ they just say oh yeah his white girl waz with him/ or a white girl got beat & killed today/ why someone will say/ cuz some niggah told her to give him her money & she said no/ cuz she thought he realized that she waz a white girl/ & he did know but he didnt care/ so he killed her & took the money/ but the cops knew she waz a white girl & cdnt be killed by a niggah especially/ when she had awready said no. the niggah was sposed to hop round the corner backwards/ you dig/ so the cops/ found the culprit within 24 hours/ cuz just like emmett till/ niggahs do not kill white girls.

i'm still in my house/ having flung my hair-do for the last time/ what with having to take 20 valium a day/ to consider the ERA/ & all the men in the world/ & my ignorance of the world/ it is overwhelming. i'm so glad i'm colored. boy i cd wake up in the morning & think abt anything. i can remember emmett till & not haveta smile at anybody.

M I M E O G R A P H E D   I T E M

Blacks Application for Employment

IT IS NOT NECESSARY TO
ATTACH PHOTO, SINCE YOU
ALL LOOK ALIKE.

DATE _____

NAME _____

ADDRESS_____
       If living in automobile, give make, model and license number

NAME OF MUTHA_____   NAME OF FATHA _____
                                              If known

NAME OF AUTO: (CHECK ONE) CADILLAC_____ LINCOLN _____

                         IMPERIAL _____ MERCEDES-BENZ_____

                         OTHER _____STOLEN_____

                         **FINANCED_____

**What is repossession date:_____

MARITAL STATUS: Common Law _____ Shack Up _____Other_____

APPROXIMATE ESTIMATE OF INCOME: Relief_____Welfare_____
   Unemployment _____   Theft _____

PLACE OF BIRTH: Charity Hospital_____ Free Public Hospital _____
                Cotton Patch_____ Back Alley_____Zoo ____ Other____

How many words do you jive a minute?_____

Check machines you can operate: Stereo____ Pinball___Crow Bar_____
                Straight Razor_____ Rubber Machine _____

Foods you like best: Bar B-Q____Coon____ Muskrat____Watermelon____
                Fish and Grits_____ All of the above_____

Check illinesses you may have had in the past year: Measles_____
                Mumps____VD ____ Food Stamp Poisoning____Other ____

Abilities: Gov't Employee____ Gossip Leader____Rapist_____ Pimp ____
           Unemployment Bureau_____Evangelist_____
           Used Hubcap Salesman____Waterbed Mattress Layer

How many children do you have? 1st wife____ 2nd wife ____
           3rd wife _____ Neighbor's wife_____ Shack-Ups ____

In 50 words or less list your greatest desire in life (other
   than a white girl).

MIMEOGRAPHED ITEM

Ebonics

Eighteen year old Leroy attends Oakland High School where Ebonics is taught. One of his homework assignments was to use the following words in sentences. Read them.

1) <u>Rectum:</u> I had two cars but my ole lady <u>rectum</u> both.

2) <u>Stain:</u> My friend axed if I were <u>stain</u> for dinner.

3) <u>Seldom:</u> I didn't need two tickets for the game so I <u>seldom</u>.

4) <u>Penis:</u> The doctor handed me a cup and said <u>penis</u>.

5) <u>Income:</u> I just got in bed with a hoe and <u>income</u> my wife.

6) <u>Fortify:</u> I asked the hoe, "How much?" She said "<u>fortify</u>"

7) <u>Disappointment:</u> If I miss <u>disappointment</u>, they gonna send me back to the big house.

8) <u>Foreclose:</u> If I pay alimony this month, I'll have no money "<u>foreclose</u>."

9) <u>Catacomb:</u> She looked at his hair and said, "someone should gib that <u>catacomb</u>.

10) <u>Undermine:</u> There is a fine lookin gal livin under the apartment <u>undermine</u>.

Needless to say—Leroy got an "A" God Bless America

Mama Sez

Monkey see, monkey do.

Act yo' age, not yo' color.

When the ax came into the forest, the trees said, "the handle is one of us."

> We ain't what we ought to be;
> We ain't what we want to be;
> We ain't what we gonna be;
> But, thank God, we ain't what we used to be.

Sister to Sister

There was wall-to-wall niggers at that party.

The party was suppose to start at ten, but you know they were operating on CPT [colored people's time].

She got about as much chance getting that job as a snowball in hell.

They piss poor.

They poor as church mice.

Money is as scarce round their house as hen's teeth.

They don't have a pot to piss in or a window to throw it out.

They don't have a pot to piss in or a bed to push it under.

They robbing Peter to pay Paul.

Quiet as it's kept, their son is robbing them blind.

When they come by my house, they greased back [ate heartily]!

They got a house full of crumbsnatchers.

I respect work like I do my mother, and wouldn't hit her a lick.

She sure bust the watermelon that time.

She look like a accident going somewhere to happen.

She look like homemade sin.

She look like something the dogs dragged home.

She's ugly as a monkey's uncle.

Ain't that just like a nigger.

A nigger ain't shit.

Look at her there crying those crocodile tears.

She talk out both sides o' her mouth at once.

Who the cap fit . . .

If the shoe fits, wear it.

When all those niggers got in that room, the funk was so thick you could cut it with a knife.

She always cutting the monkey/doing monkey shines for the white folks.

Don't make me act colored/show my color/get my colors up/act the nigger.

Don't mess wit' me today. I got up on the wrong side o' the bed.

I don't let noone call me outta my name.

She's so dumb she has to reach into her chest to count to two.

CHAPTER 10

Fight, Kick, Bite

DEALING WITH A RACIST AND SEXIST
AMERICA

The one doctrine of my mother's teaching which was branded upon my
senses was that I should never let anyone abuse me. "I'll kill you, gal, if
you don't stand up for yourself," she would say. "Fight, and if you can't
fight, kick; if you can't kick, then bite."
—anonymous former slave woman, Social Science Document No. 1,
Fisk University archives

The history of the black female in America began when she was captured or sold from home and family in Africa, branded, herded into the
filthy, dark, crowded holds of vessels, and chained in leg irons for the
most appalling voyage human beings have ever undergone. Upon her ar-
rival on these shores, she faced the ignominious slave block, where she was
sold to the highest bidder to serve him in whatever way he desired (his field
laborer, his cook, his nursemaid, his concubine, his breeder). Having been
stripped of home and family and even the acknowledgment of her humanity, she was then stripped of name and language—not to mention religion and culture.

For the next two hundred and some odd years she was regarded by
Supreme Court decree as having "no rights which the white man was
bound to respect." She was a pawn in a system that continued to trade in

human beings, separate families, brutalize individuals, and deny them any human rights.

The hopes that she held for a better life after Emancipation were quickly dashed. The Black Codes that were passed after the Civil War virtually reenslaved many blacks. State legislatures passed bills that made it impossible for freed men and women to go into commercial fields or work as artisans, to protect themselves and their families, or to achieve justice in Southern courts. They gave the white employers enormous control over all activities of their workers. They allowed the arrest of blacks under loose vagrancy and idleness statutes, and then authorized white landowners to force them to work off their sentences in their employ. They forbade blacks from holding office and voting, from serving on juries, or testifying in court against whites. These laws effectively put Negroes in a more vulnerable position than did slavery, since in slavery they sometimes had the protection of their white masters. Despite the response of the national government to these egregious attempts to in effect reenslave the Negroes, any relief was only temporary, and the restrictions of these laws were effectively enforced through a campaign of violence, terror, intimidation, and lynching by groups such as the Ku Klux Klan. Furthermore following the brief period of Reconstruction, most Southern states found various means to establish Jim Crow laws and to deny black males the vote (black women—black or white—had no right to vote). They used techniques such as the grandfather clause, white primaries, property requirements, poll taxes, and literacy tests, coupled with intimidation, well into the second half of the twentieth century. Throughout this time, of course, educational opportunities were nonexistent or severely limited.

Given her experience in this nation then, it is no wonder that at times the black woman feels that her life is spent reacting to white racism and sexism. Despite her political and economic powerlessness to effectively rectify her conditions, however, the black woman has always sought ways to empower herself and to resist, protest against, defeat, or at least embarrass the people and conditions that held her enslaved and tyrannized. Along with the black man, she has often contrived laughter as a means of appeasing, conciliating, and protesting against her masters and mistresses. Much early humor was based on shirking work, escaping a whipping, causing the master or mistress some physical harm or humiliating them. Similar tales of aggressiveness against white racism continue to serve the same

purposes for the African American woman today. The selections that follow illustrate how much the slave woman and her descendents relished accounts of defeating old master or mistress, any other white authority
figures, or the racist establishment generally (the landlord, the justice system, the social services system, etc.), embarrassing them, exposing them,
and switching the yoke and changing the joke (placing whites in the same
position that blacks usually endured). Indeed, the greatest pleasure from the
pieces in this chapter comes from the sense of revenge enjoyed by the storytellers. The psychological rewards of this type of humor are explained by
Sigmund Freud in "Wit and Its Relation to the Unconscious": "By belit-
tling and humbling our enemy, by scorning and ridiculing him, we directly
obtain the pleasure of his defeat by the laughter of the third person." The
black woman continues to adhere to the doctrine, "Fight, and if you can't
fight, kick; if you can't kick, then bite"—and if you can't do that, make
them and their foolish behavior the butt of your humor and hold them up
to the ridicule of the world.

Honey, hush!

Linda Brent

THE JEALOUS MISTRESS

from *Incidents in the Life of a Slave Girl*

I would ten thousand times rather that my children should be the half-
starved paupers of Ireland than to be the most pampered among the slaves
of America. I would rather drudge out my life on a cotton plantation, till
the grave opened to give me rest, than to live with an unprincipled master and a jealous mistress. The felon's home in a penitentiary is preferable.
He may repent, and turn from the error of his ways, and so find peace; but
it is not so with a favorite slave. She is not allowed to have any pride of
character. It is deemed a crime in her to wish to be virtuous.

Mrs. Flint possessed the key to her husband's character before I was
born. She might have used this knowledge to counsel and to screen the
young and the innocent among her slaves; but for them she had no sym-

pathy. They were the objects of her constant suspicion and malevolence. She watched her husband with unceasing vigilance; but he was well practised in means to evade it. What he could not find opportunity to say in words he manifested in signs. He invented more than were ever thought of in a deaf and dumb asylum. I let them pass, as if I did not understand what he meant; and many were the curses and threats bestowed on me for my stupidity. One day he caught me teaching myself to write. He frowned, as if he was not well pleased; but I suppose he came to the conclusion that such an accomplishment might help to advance his favorite scheme. Before long, notes were often slipped into my hand. I would return them, saying, "I can't read them, sir." "Can't you?" he replied; "then I must read them to you." He always finished the reading by asking, "Do you understand?" Sometimes he would complain of the heat of the tea room, and order his supper to be placed on a small table in the piazza. He would seat himself there with a well-satisfied smile, and tell me to stand by and brush away the flies. He would eat very slowly, pausing between the mouthfuls. These intervals were employed in describing the happiness I was so foolishly throwing away, and in threatening me with the penalty that finally awaited my stubborn disobedience. He boasted much of the forbearance he had exercised towards me, and reminded me that there was a limit to his patience. When I succeeded in avoiding opportunities for him to talk to me at home, I was ordered to come to his office, to do some errand. When there, I was obliged to stand and listen to such language as he saw fit to address to me. Sometimes I so openly expressed my contempt for him that he would become violently enraged, and I wondered why he did not strike me. Circumstanced as he was, he probably thought it was better policy to be forbearing. But the state of things grew worse and worse daily. In desperation I told him that I must and would apply to my grandmother for protection. He threatened me with death, and worse than death, if I made any complaint to her. Strange to say, I did not despair. I was naturally of a buoyant disposition, and always I had a hope of somehow getting out of his clutches. Like many a poor, simple slave before me, I trusted that some threads of joy would yet be woven into my dark destiny.

I had entered my sixteenth year, and every day it became more apparent that my presence was intolerable to Mrs. Flint. Angry words frequently passed between her and her husband. He had never punished me himself, and he would not allow any body else to punish me. In that respect, she was never satisfied; but, in her angry moods, no terms were too vile for her to bestow upon me. Yet I, whom she detested so bitterly, had far more pity for her than he had, whose duty it was to make her life happy. I never wronged her, or wished to wrong her; and one word of kindness from her would have brought me to her feet.

After repeated quarrels between the doctor and his wife, he announced his intention to take his youngest daughter, then four years old, to sleep in his apartment. It was necessary that a servant should sleep in the same room, to be on hand if the child stirred. I was selected for that office, and informed for what purpose that arrangement had been made. By managing to keep within sight of people, as much as possible, during the day time, I had hitherto succeeded in eluding my master, though a razor was often held to my throat to force me to change this line of policy. At night I slept by the side of my great aunt, where I felt safe. He was too prudent to come into her room. She was an old woman, and had been in the family many years. Moreover, as a married man, and a professional man, he deemed it necessary to save appearances in some degree. But he resolved to remove the obstacle in the way of his scheme; and he thought he had planned it so that he should evade suspicion. He was well aware how much I prized my refuge by the side of my old aunt, and he determined to dispossess me of it. The first night the doctor had the little child in his room alone. The next morning, I was ordered to take my station as nurse the following night. A kind Providence interposed in my favor. During the day Mrs. Flint heard of this new arrangement, and a storm followed. I rejoiced to hear it rage.

After a while my mistress sent for me to come to her room. Her first question was, "Did you know you were to sleep in the doctor's room?"

"Yes, ma'am."

"Who told you?"

"My master."

"Will you answer truly all the questions I ask?"

"Yes, ma'am."

"Tell me, then, as you hope to be forgiven, are you innocent of what I have accused you?"

"I am."

She handed me a Bible, and said, "Lay your hand on your heart, kiss this holy book, and swear before God that you tell me the truth."

I took the oath she required, and I did it with a clear conscience.

"You have taken God's holy word to testify your innocence," said she. "If you have deceived me, beware! Now take this stool, sit down, look me directly in the face, and tell me all that has passed between your master and you."

I did as she ordered. As I went on with my account her color changed frequently, she wept, and sometimes groaned. She spoke in tones so sad, that I was touched by her grief. The tears came to my eyes; but I was soon convinced that her emotions arose from anger and wounded pride. She felt that her marriage vows were desecrated, her dignity insulted; but she had no compassion for the poor victim of her husband's perfidy. She pitied herself as a martyr; but she was incapable of feeling for the condition of shame and misery in which her unfortunate, helpless slave was placed.

Yet perhaps she had some touch of feeling for me; for when the conference was ended, she spoke kindly, and promised to protect me. I should have been much comforted by this assurance if I could have had confidence in it; but my experiences in slavery had filled me with distrust. She was not a very refined woman, and had not much control over her passions. I was an object of her jealousy, and, consequently, of her hatred; and I knew I could not expect kindness or confidence from her under the circumstances in which I was placed. I could not blame her. Slaveholders' wives feel as other women would under similar circumstances. The fire of her temper kindled from small sparks, and now the flame became so intense that the doctor was obliged to give up his intended arrangement.

I knew I had ignited the torch, and I expected to suffer for it afterwards; but I felt too thankful to my mistress for the timely aid she rendered me to care much about that. She now took me to sleep in a room adjoining her own. There I was an object of her especial care, though not of her especial comfort, for she spent many a sleepless night to watch over me. Sometimes I woke up, and found her bending over me. At other times she whispered in my ear, as though it was her husband who was speaking to me, and listened to hear what I would answer. If she startled me, on such occasions, she would glide stealthily away; and the next morning she would tell me I had been talking in my sleep, and ask who I was talking to. At last, I began to be fearful for my life. It had been often threatened; and you can imagine, better than I can describe, what an unpleasant sensation it must produce to wake up in the dead of night and find a jealous woman bending over you. Terrible as this experience was, I had fears that it would give place to one more terrible.

My mistress grew weary of her vigils; they did not prove satisfactory. She changed her tactics. She now tried the trick of accusing my master of crime, in my presence, and gave my name as the author of the accusation. To my utter astonishment, he replied, "I don't believe it; but if she did acknowledge it, you tortured her into exposing me." Tortured into exposing him! Truly, Satan had no difficulty in distinguishing the color of his soul! I understood his object in making this false representation. It was to show me that I gained nothing by seeking the protection of my mistress; that the power was still all in his own hands. I pitied Mrs. Flint. She was a second wife, many years the junior of her husband; and the hoary-headed miscreant was enough to try the patience of a wiser and better woman. She was completely foiled, and knew not how to proceed. She would gladly have had me flogged for my supposed false oath; but, as I have already stated, the doctor never allowed any one to whip me. The old sinner was politic. The application of the lash might have led to remarks that would have exposed him in the eyes of his children and grandchildren. How often did I rejoice that I lived in a town where all the inhabitants knew each other! If I had been on a remote plantation, or lost among the multitude of a crowded city, I should not be a living woman at this day.

The secrets of slavery are concealed like those of the Inquisition. My master was, to my knowledge, the father of eleven slaves. But did the mothers dare to tell who was the father of their children? Did the other slaves dare to allude to it, except in whispers among themselves? No, indeed! They knew too well the terrible consequences.

My grandmother could not avoid seeing things which excited her suspicions. She was uneasy about me, and tried various ways to buy me; but the never-changing answer was always repeated: "Linda does not belong to *me*. She is my daughter's property, and I have no legal right to sell her." The conscientious man! He was too scrupulous to *sell* me; but he had no scruples whatever about committing a much greater wrong against the helpless young girl placed under his guardianship, as his daughter's property. Sometimes my persecutor would ask me whether I would like to be sold. I told him I would rather be sold to any body than to lead such a life as I did. On such occasions he would assume the air of a very injured individual, and reproach me for my ingratitude. "Did I not take you into the house, and make you the companion of my own children?" he would say. "Have I ever treated you like a negro? I have never allowed you to be punished, not even to please your mistress. And this is the recompense I get, you ungrateful girl!" I answered that he had reasons of his own for screening me from punishment, and that the course he pursued made my mistress hate me and persecute me. If I wept, he would say, "Poor child! Don't cry! don't cry! I will make peace for you with your mistress. Only let me arrange matters in my own way. Poor, foolish girl! you don't know what is for your own good. I would cherish you. I would make a lady of you. Now go, and think of all I have promised you."

I did think of it.

Linda Brent

MONTHS OF PERIL

from *Incidents in the Life of a Slave Girl*

[Linda finally ran away and was hidden by a friend in the neighborhood. In an effort to force her relatives to help him find her, Dr. Flint had her relatives, including her aunt, her brother, and her two children, jailed.]

Poor William! He also must suffer for being my brother. I took his advice and kept quiet. My aunt was taken out of jail at the end of a month, because Mrs. Flint could not spare her any longer. She was tired of being her own housekeeper. It was quite too fatiguing to order her dinner and eat it too. My children remained in jail, where brother William did all he could for their comfort. Betty went to see them sometimes, and brought me tidings. She was not permitted to enter the jail; but William would hold them up to the grated window while she chatted with them. When she repeated their prattle, and told me how they wanted to see their ma, my tears would flow. Old Betty would exclaim, "Lors, chile! what's you crying 'bout? Dem young uns vil kill you dead. Don't be so chick'n hearted! If you does, you vil nebber git thro' dis world."

Good old soul! She had gone through the world childless. She had never had little ones to clasp their arms round her neck; she had never seen their soft eyes looking into hers; no sweet little voices had called her mother; she had never pressed her own infants to her heart, with the feeling that even in fetters there was something to live for. How could she realize my feelings? Betty's husband loved children dearly, and wondered why God had denied them to him. He expressed great sorrow when he came to Betty with the tidings that Ellen had been taken out of jail and carried to Dr. Flint's. She had the measles a short time before they carried her to jail, and the disease had left her eyes affected. The doctor had taken her home to attend to them. My children had always been afraid of the doctor and his wife. They had never been inside of their house. Poor little Ellen cried all day to be carried back to prison. The instincts of childhood are true. She knew she was loved in the jail. Her screams and sobs annoyed Mrs. Flint. Before night she called one of the slaves, and said, "Here, Bill, carry this brat back to the jail. I can't stand her noise. If she would be quiet I should like to keep the little minx. She would make a handy waiting-maid for my daughter by and by. But if she staid here, with her white face, I suppose I should either kill her or spoil her. I hope the doctor will sell them as far as wind and water can carry them. As for their mother, her ladyship will find out yet what she gets by running away. She hasn't so much feeling for her children as a cow has for its calf. If she had, she would have come back long ago, to get them out of jail, and save all this expense and trouble. The good-for-nothing hussy! When she is caught, she shall stay in jail, in irons, for one six months, and then be sold to a sugar plantation. I shall see her broke in yet. What do you stand there for, Bill? Why don't you go off with the brat? Mind, now, that you don't let any of the niggers speak to her in the street!"

When these remarks were reported to me, I smiled at Mrs. Flint's saying that she should either kill my child or spoil her. I thought to myself there was very little danger of the latter. I have always considered it as one of God's special providences that Ellen screamed till she was carried back to jail.

That same night Dr. Flint was called to a patient, and did not return till near morning. Passing my grandmother's, he saw a light in the house, and thought to himself, "Perhaps this has something to do with Linda." He knocked, and the door was opened. "What calls you up so early?" said he. "I saw your light, and I thought I would just stop and tell you that I have found out where Linda is. I know where to put my hands on her, and I shall have her before twelve o'clock.' When he had turned away, my grandmother and my uncle looked anxiously at each other. They did not know whether or not it was merely one of the doctor's tricks to frighten them. In their uncertainty, they thought it was best to have a message conveyed to my friend Betty. Unwilling to alarm her mistress, Betty resolved to dispose of me herself. She came to me, and told me to rise and dress quickly. We hurried down stairs, and across the yard, into the kitchen. She locked the door, and lifted up a plank in the floor. A buffalo skin and a bit of carpet were spread for me to lie on, and a quilt thrown over me. "Stay dar," said she, "till I sees if dey know 'bout you. Dey say dey vil put thar hans on you afore twelve o'clock. If dey *did* know whar you are, dey won't know *now.* Dey'll be disapinted dis time. Dat's all I got to say. If dey comes rummagin 'mong *my* tings, dey'll get one bressed sarssin from dis 'ere nigger." In my shallow bed I had but just room enough to bring my hands to my face to keep the dust out of my eyes; for Betty walked over me twenty times in an hour, passing from the dresser to the fireplace. When she was alone, I could hear her pronouncing anathemas over Dr. Flint and all his tribe, every now and then saying, with a chuckling laugh, "Dis nigger's too cute for 'em dis time." When the housemaids were about, she had sly ways of drawing them out, that I might hear what they would say. She would repeat stories she had heard about my being in this, or that, or the other place. To which they would answer, that I was not fool enough to be staying round there; that I was in Philadelphia or New York before this time. When all were abed and asleep, Betty raised the plank, and said, "Come out, chile; come out. Dey don't know nottin 'bout you. 'Twas only white folks' lies, to skeer de niggers."

    Some days after this adventure I had a much worse fright. As I sat very still in my retreat above stairs, cheerful visions floated through my mind. I thought Dr. Flint would soon get discouraged, and would be willing to sell my children, when he lost all hopes of making them the means of my discovery. I knew who was ready to buy them. Suddenly I heard a voice that chilled my blood. The sound was too familiar to me, it had been too dreadful, for me not to recognize at once my old master. He was in the house, and I at once concluded he had come to seize me. I looked round in terror: There was no way of escape. The voice receded. I supposed the constable was with him, and they were searching the house. In my alarm I did not forget the trouble I was bringing on my generous benefactress. It seemed as if I were born to bring sorrow on all who befriended me, and that was the bitterest drop in the bitter cup of my life. After a while I heard approaching footsteps; the key was turned in my door. I braced myself against the wall to keep from falling. I ventured to look up, and there stood my kind benefactress alone. I was too much overcome to speak, and sunk down upon the floor.

"I thought you would hear your master's voice," she said; "and knowing you would be terrified, I came to tell you there is nothing to fear. You may even indulge in a laugh at the old gentleman's expense. He is so sure you are in New York, that he came to borrow five hundred dollars to go in pursuit of you. My sister had some money to loan on interest. He has obtained it, and proposes to start for New York to-night. So, for the present, you see you are safe. The doctor will merely lighten his pocket hunting after the bird he has left behind."

Nagueyalti Warren

BUTTER 'N' BREAD

[Dr. Warren informed me that the following poem "is based on a joke my grandmother told me that her grandmother told her from slavery days."]

> "Girl, we laughed until we cried
> 'Bout the way Miss Ann died."
>
> "Split our sides—cracked-up!"
>
> "Lord knows she'd have a fit
> If she knew we'd seen her tricks.
> Slippin' Jim in the back door—
> Him droppin' white bread &
> Butter on the floor."

"Yeah, Jim laughed about it too.
Old masser caught him near the big house
& want to know what's so funny.
Jim said, 'dropped my bread 'n' butter
& the butter side turned up.' "

"The woman was dead?"

"Dead as a door-nail!"

"Hush your mouth!"

Fannie Berry

US COLORED WOMEN HAD TO GO THROUGH A PLENTY

from Charles L. Perdue, Jr., et al., eds., *Weevils in the Wheat*

I wuz one slave dat de poor white man had his match. See Miss Sue? Dese here ol' white men said, "What I can't do by fair means I'll do by foul." One tried to throw me, but he couldn't. We tusseled an' knocked over chairs an' when I got a grip I scratched his face all to pieces; an dar wuz no more bothering Fannie from him; but oh, honey, some slaves would be beat up so, when dey resisted, an' sometimes if you'll 'belled [rebelled] de overseer would kill yo'. Us colored women had to go through a plenty, I tell you.

Fannie Berry

SUKIE

from Charles L. Perdue, Jr., et al., eds., *Weevils in the Wheat*

Sukie was her name. She was a big strappin' nigger gal dat never had nothin' to say much. She used to cook for Miss Sarah Ann, but ole Marsa was always tryin' to make Sukie his gal. One day Sukie was in the kitchen makin' soap. Had three gra' big pots o' lye jus' comin' to a bile in de fireplace when ole Marsa come in for to git arter her 'bout somep'n.

He lay into her, but she ain't answer him a word. Den he tell Sukie to take off her dress. She tole him no. Den he grabbed her an' pull it down off'n her shoulders. When he done dat, he fo'got 'bout whuppin' her, I guess, 'cause he grab hold of her an' try to pull her down on de flo'. Den dat black gal got mad. She took an' punch ole Marsa an' made him break loose an' den she gave him a shove an' push his hindparts down in de hot pot o' soap. Soap was near to bilin', an' it burnt him near to death. He got up holdin' his hindparts an' ran from de kitchen, not darin' to yell, 'cause he didn't want Miss Sarah Ann to know 'bout it.

Minnie Folkes

SERVES 'EM RIGHT

from *The Negro in Virginia*

Dis ole man, now, would start beatin' her nekked 'til the blood run down her back to her heels. I took an' seed de whelps an' scars fer my own self wid dese heah two eyes. (This whip she said, "was a whip like dey use to use on horses; it was a piece o' leather 'bout as wide as my han' f'om little finger to thumb.") After dey beat my mother all dey wanted, another overseer Lord, Lord, I hate white people and de flood waters gwine drown some mo'. Well honey, dis man would bathe her in salt an' water. Don' you know dem places was a hurtin'. Um! Um!

I asked mother, "what she done fer 'em to beat and do her so?" She said, "Nothin' tother t'dan 'fuse to be wife to dis man."

An' mother say, "If he didn' treat her dis way a dozen times, it wasn' nary one."

Mind you, now mother's master didn' know dis was goin' on. You know, ef slaves would tell, why dem overseers would kill 'em.

An' she sed dey use to have meetin's an' sing an' pray an' de ole paddy-rollers would heah dem; so to keep de soun' from goin' out, slaves would put a gra' big iron pot at de do' an' you know some times dey would fergit to put ole pot dar an' de paddyrollers would come an' horse whip ev'ry las' one o' dem, jes' 'cause de poor souls was prayin' to God to free 'em f'om dat awful bondage.

Ha! ha! ha! dar was one ole brudder who studies fer em' one day an' tol' all de slaves how to git even wid 'em. He tol' 'em to tie grape vines an' other vines 'cross de road. Den when de paddyrollers come galantin' wid dere horses, runnin' so fas' you see, dem vines would tangle 'em up an' cause de horses to stumble an' fall. An' lots o' times dey would break dere legs an' de horses too: one intervall one ole poor devil got tangled so an' de horses kept a carryin' him, 'til he fell off de horse an' nex' day a sucker was foun' in de road wher dem vines was win' aroun' his neck so many time jes' had choke' him, dey said, 'teetotally dead. Serve 'em right 'cause dem ole white folks treated us so mean.

Former Slave

NO OVERSEER EVER DOWNED HER

from B. A. Botkin, *Lay My Burden Down*

My mother had about three masters before she got free. She was a terrible working woman. Her boss went off deer hunting once for a few weeks. While he was gone, the overseer tried to whip her. She knocked him down and tore his face up so that the doctor had to 'tend to him. When Pennington came back, he noticed his face all patched up and asked him what was the matter with it. The overseer told him that he went down in the field to whip the hands and that he just thought he would hit Lucy a few licks to show the slaves that he was impartial, but she jumped on him and like to tore him up. Old Pennington said to him, "Well, if that is the best you could do with her, damned if you won't just have to take it."

Then they sold her to another man, named Jim Bernard. Bernard did a lot of big talk to her one morning. He said, "Look out there and mind you do what you told around here and step lively. If you don't, you'll get that bull whip." She said to him, "Yes, and we'll both be gitting it." He had heard about her; so he sold her to another man named Cleary. He was good to her; so she wasn't sold no more after that.

There wasn't many men could class up with her when it come to working. She could do more work than any two men. There wasn't no use for no one man to try to do nothing with her. No overseer never downed her.

Sophia Word

THE MEANEST NIGGER

from George P. Rawick, ed. *Kansas, Kentucky, Maryland, Ohio, Virginia, and Tennessee Narratives*, vol. 16 of *The American Slave*

The white folks said I was the meanest nigger that ever wuz. One day my Mistress Lyndia called for me to come in the house, but no, I wouldn't go. She walks out and says she is gwine make me go. So she takes and drags me in the house. Then I grabs that white woman, when she turned her back, and shook her until she begged for mercy. When the master comes in, I wuz given a terrible beating with a whip but I did'nt care fer I give the mistress a good'un too.

We lived off to the back of the masters house in a little log cabin, that had one winder in the side. We lived tobly well and didn't starve fer we had enough to eat but we didn't have as good as the master and mistress had. We would slip in the house after the master and mistress wuz sleeping and cook to suit ourselves and cook what we wanted.

The Mistress had an old parrot and one day I wuz in the kitchen making cookies, and I decided I wanted some of them so I tooks me out some and put them on a chair and when I did this the mistress entered the door, I picks up a cushion and throws over the pile of cookies on the chair and mistress came near the chair and the old parrot cries out, Mistress burn, Mistress burn, then the mistress looks under the cushion and she had me whupped but the next day I killed the parrot, and she often wondered who or what killed the bird.

Former Slave

IT'S A GOOD TIME TO DRESS YOU OUT

from B. A. Botkin, *Lay My Burden Down*

[Mistress] set me to scrubbing up the bar-room. I felt a little grum, and didn't do it to suit her; she scolded me about it, and I sassed her; she struck me with her hand. Thinks I, it's a good time now to dress you out, and damned if I won't do it. I set down my tools and squared for a fight. The first whack, I struck her a hell of a blow with my fist. I didn't knock her entirely through the panels of the door, but her landing against the door made a terrible smash, and I hurt her so badly that all were frightened out of their wits and I didn't know myself but what I'd killed the old devil.

Former Slave

CHILDHOOD

from Dorothy Sterling, ed., *We Are Your Sisters*

When the colored women has to cut cane all day till midnight come and after, I has to nurse the babies for them and tend the white children too. Some them babies so fat and big I had to tote the feet while 'nother gal tote the head. The big folks leave some toddy for colic and crying, and I done drink the toddy and let the children have the milk. I don't know no better. Lawsey me, it a wonder I ain't the biggest drunker in this here country, counting all the toddy I done put in my young belly!

Julia Frazier

CHARLIE

from *The Negro in Virginia*

[Charlie was the "rhymster" for the big house as well as the slave quarters, according to Mrs. Frazier, who provided the WPA interviewer the following illustration of his talent of "mak[ing] up songs 'bout anything."]

One day Charlie saw ole Marsa comin' home wid a keg of whiskey on his ole mule. Cuttin' 'cross de plowed field, de ole mule slipped an' Marsa come tumblin' off. Marsa didn't know Charlie saw him, an' Charlie didn't say nothin'. But soon arter a visitor come an' Marsa called Charlie to de house to show off what he knew. Marsa say, "Come here, Charlie, an' sing some rhymes fo' Mr. Henson." "Don' know no new ones, Marsa," Charlie answered. "Come on, you black rascal, give me a rhyme fo' my company— one he ain't heard." So Charlie say, "All right, Marsa, I give you a new one effen you promise not to whup me." Marsa promised, an' den Charlie sung de rhyme he done made up in his haid 'bout Marsa:

> Jackass rared
> Jackass pitch
> Throwed ole Marsa in de ditch.

Well, Marsa got mad as a hornet, but he didn't whup Charlie, not dat time anyway. An' chile, don' you know us used to set de flo' to dat dere song? Mind you, never would sing it when Marsa was roun', but when he wasn't we'd swing all roun' de cabin singin' 'bout how old Marsa fell off de mule's back. Charlie had a bunch of verses:

> Jackass stamped
> Jackass neighed
> Throwed ole Marsa on his haid.

Don' recollec' all dat smart slave made up. But ev'ybody sho' bus' dey sides laughin' when Charlie sung de las' verse:

Jackass stamped
Jackass hupped
Marsa hear you slave, you sho' git whupped.

Fannie Berry

FIRE STICKS

from *The Negro in Virginia*

Nother time Marse Tom come to me, an' say, "Fanny look here, look what I got." An' he had some little sticks wid yellow ends on em. I didn't know what dey was. So he took 'em over back of de barn an' drawed one cross a rock, an' it made a fire. So I said, "Marse Tom give me one dem." Well he ain't had but three, an' now he only got two left, but he give me one. I stuck it in my hair an' went on doin' what I been doin' till dat afternoon. Den I took it an' went inside de barn an' put some leaves down in de corner, an' struck dis piece of wood cross a rock jus' like Marse Tom done an' sho' nough it made a fire. An' I drap it in de leaves, an' run on out de barn down in de corn fiel' an' pretty soon de smoke come rollin' out, an' de flames show an' dar was de corner of de barn on fire.

It was gittin' bigger an' bigger an' I could hear it crackin'. Den I hear ev'body yellin' an' pretty soon ole Marse come runnin' an' shoutin' at ev'body. Well dey formed a chain an' passed water fum de well an' purty soon dey put it out. Den ole Marse called all de nigger chillun together an' tole em he gonna whup ev'y las' one of 'em cause he knows one of dem done made dat fire. An' he whupped 'em too till he got tired, whilst I lay dere in de corn fiel' not darin' to raise my head. Never did whup me. An' I never did play wid none dem fire sticks no mo'.

Hannah Prosser

from *The Southern Workman*

[This story is one of several of Hannah Prosser's tales collected and published by Ellen Dickson Wilson, a white woman who describes herself as "[Prosser's] literary executor, specially appointed by her." I have been reluctant to use accounts that have been written by whites, especially when they were published under their names, but some compromise must be made regarding material from slaves and former slaves. And despite what I expect is an exaggerated dialect (so prevalent at the time), I believe Ms. Wilson preserves some of the genuine humor of Mrs. Prosser in this anecdote.]

I'm jes' a co'n doctor 'ooman, Mis'. Dey got anudder name fer it, but you picked me up too late in de day, wid my teef all gone, to git my tongue twis'ed roun' dat high-soun'en talk. W'ite folks kin have it, but jes' plain co'n doctor 'ooman will hol' my time out.

Las' week a lady sont me a pos'cyard, an' she writ on it jes', "Dat Ole Cullud Co'n Doctor 'Ooman, Philadelphy." Dey sont dat cyard right up to Columbia. She was de ve'y same lady w'at ax me, "Auntie, will disyere co'n come back ag'n?" An' I tol' her, "No, honey, dat won' retu'n, but ef you don' quit dem foolishness shoes, anudder one will come right along fer to keep hit comp'ny." High heels an' p'inted toes—stan's to reason dey mus' suffer. An' I cyant larn 'em no wisdom. Dat lady was so easy in her min' w'en I lef' her wid her feet feelin' so pleasant, she didn't 'low de mis'ry 'd retu'n an' she fergot my name an' d'rections. How you reckon dey know'd whar to sen' dat pos'cyard? Well, Mis', ef dey fo'arded it to de Pos'massa Gin'ral, he'd s'picion "Ole Pross" (dats w'at dey all calls me) was de co'n doctor 'ooman dey was sarchin' fer. I tended his mudder, de bes' 'ooman ever I know'd, lookin' atter her 'tel she went to her rewa'd. But wedder hit wur de Pos'massa er de d'livery man w'at lan'ed dat cyard at my do', or nair one of 'em, I'm afeared to say. A pos'cyard startin' alone widout de pusson's name, er de town dey lives in, is mighty onreli'ble an' ap' fer to miss hit's connection, an' calls fer mo' wisdom dan you'll fin' in de pos'office. No, chile, I put's my 'pendance on de Almighty. Ef He's been countin' de wool on my ole black haid for eighty yeahs, He shorely wouldn' scorn to watch atter dat pos'cyard, fer it come f'om a mighty suff'rin' 'ooman.

You reckon I knows all dar is to larn 'bout feet? No Mis', my 'spe'ence don' reach so fur as to conclude all de wisdom dar is 'bout folks's feet. O law no, honey! Comin' 'long by Blair's drug sto' las' week, I met a doctor w'at's been knowin' me dis long time. "Good mornin', Aunt Hannah," says he, kind o' smilin' roun' at two doctors side uv 'im. W'en I see dat smile o' his'n, I 'gun fer to git cautious. "Aunt Hannah," says he, shakin' my han' mighty frien'ly. "I gwine out to de 'Versity nex' Chuesday to lectu'e to de young men consarnin' feet, an' I wan' you fer to come out an' go on de platfo'm wid me an' tell 'em all you knows on de subjec'." "Me!" says I, "me! no sir! you don' git me carryin' my ign'ance out dar. God knows you got 'nough o' dat dar now!" Yo' reckon he got riled wid me fer speakin' up so owdacious? Law no, honey, he ain' hol' it ag'in' me. Men is a heap mo' peacabler 'n 'oomans is; dey ain' allays cravin' fer to git de las' word.

Las' winter, w'en I fus' put on dese yere furs o' mine w'at you got tooken in de picture, I know'd de niggers would laugh. Dey cer' t 'ny is a mighty cur'us cut, an wool plush, but I made 'em myse'f, an' dey's good an' warm. I was comin' long Fo'th Street dis mornin' to take de cyar out to you, w'en I heerd a gen'leman—leas'wise I spose he was a gen'leman, he had de clo'es of a gen'leman. hit's ha'd work to tell dese days who's who—I heerd him say to de lady w'at was hangin' on his arm, "Look at dat nigger's furs." I walked kin' o' slow atter dat, an' by an' by dey cyan' he'p but pass me. "Auntie," says he, awful pleasan', "auntie, w'at's yo' furs trimmed wid?" I made a courtesy des as low as I could wid de stiffness o' my knees, an' I says. "Wid good manners, sir!"

Yes, honey, sometimes you fin's de right wo'd jes like as ef it was ef' on yo' tongue a pupp'ose. Dar was de time I was gwine to Media long befo' de wah. De cyars dem days had de stoves in de middle, an' up over de do' was a signbo'd wid writin' on it: "Cullud people will take de reah end of de passenger cayr, ur de fo'ard end ob de baggage cyar." Hit wur mighty col', so I sot down by de stove, like as ef dar wa'n't no signbo'd on top dat do'. D'rec'ly come a sassy little Jack-sparrer of a newsboy, an' he hollers at me, flingin' his imperdence 'bout cullud people, but I don' nuvver pay no 'tention to w'ite trash. Atter w'ile de conductor-man, he come in an' he pint up to de signbo'd over de do', an' says he, "Don' you see dat?" den, mighty cross, "Whar you gwine?" "Media, sir," says I. "All right," says he, "you mus' take de reah end o' de passenger cyar ur de fo'ard end ob de baggage car." I jumps right up an' collec's my basket jes as quick as I kin, an' I tole dat conductor-man I'm 'bleeged fer his kin'ness in warnin' me. I tol' him I done s'posed bof ends ob de cyar wen' to Media, but ef its only de reah end, in co'se I'll take it.

Dar ain' no use gittin' riled w'en folks is jes' havin' dey fun wid you. Why, dis ve'y mornin', comin' out on de train to you, I done had de spe'unce o' bein' spoke to jes' on 'count o' my quare ole black face. I was makin' a sheet. Yes Mis', I allays takes my sewin' wid me on de cyars. A good-lookin' young gen'leman sot an' stared at me. By an' by I puts down my sewin' an' looks up fer to ketch his eyes. Den he 'gun fer to laugh, an' says he, "Auntie, you mus' have been uncommon han'some in yo' youth." "Not a succumstance to w'at I is now, honey," says I.

Seems like ez ef folks was jes drawed to speak to me. Comin' long de road heah, a lady stopped her horses an' kerrage an' ax me, "Auntie, d'you know whar I kin fin' a good cook?" I tol' her, "No ma'am, no ma'am, sence de Paten' Office in Washin'ton been tu'nin' out so many 'ventions fer labor-savin' in de kitchen, de Almighty in Heaven has ceasted fer to tu'n out cooks."

W'at you say 'bout my bein' tired an' restin' 'tel atternoon? No, honey, I mus' be at de nex' place in a hour. Bless you, I ain' usen to scrimpin' my bus'ness 'ca'se I'se gittin' ole. I 'specs to keep right 'long at dis wuk 'twill my Ma'ster calls me home. I ain' in no hurry to go, an' I ain' cravin' to stay; eighty yeahs is 'bout long 'nough in dis campin' groun'.

Slave Song

OLD SATAN IS MAD

from John Lovell, Jr., ed., *Black Song: The Forge and the Flame*

Old Satan is mad an' I'm so glad, . . .
He missed de soul he thought he had,
Oh, sen'-a dem angels down.

Slave Song

MARCHING UP THE HEAVENLY ROAD

from John Lovell, Jr., ed., *Black Song: The Forge and the Flame*

Marching up the heavenly road,
Marching up the heavenly road,
I'm bound to fight until I die, . . .
My sister, have you got your sword and shield, . . .
I got 'em fo' I left the field,
Marching up the heavenly road.

Sarah Bradford

HARRIET, THE MOSES OF HER PEOPLE

[In the following selections from the biography of Harriet Tubman, famous for leading slaves to freedom, Ms. Bradford recounts lines from a song that Tubman would sing to alert slaves to an upcoming escape and recounts an incident of another of her methods for communicating with her cohorts.]

"When dat ar ole chariot comes,
I'm gwine to lebe you,
I'm boun' for de promised land,
Frien's, I'm gwine to lebe you."

———

"I'm sorry, frien's, to lebe you,
Farewell! oh, farewell!
But I'll meet you in de mornin',
Farewell! oh, farewell!

"I'll meet you in de mornin',
When you reach de promised land;
On de oder side of Jordan,
For I'm boun' for de promised land."

———

Jacob Jackson was a free negro, who could both read and write, and who was under suspicion just then of having a hand in the disappearance of colored "property." It was necessary, therefore, to exercise great caution in writing to him, on his own account as well as that of the writer, and those whom she wished to aid. Jacob had an adopted son, William Henry Jackson, also free, who had come North. Harriet determined to sign her letter with William Henry's name, feeling sure that Jacob would be clever enough to understand by her peculiar phraseology, the meaning she intended to convey.

Therefore, after speaking of indifferent matters, the letter went on: "Read my letter to the old folks, and give my love to them, and tell my brothers to be always *watching unto prayer,* and when *the good old ship of Zion comes along, to be ready to step on board."* This letter was signed "William Henry Jackson."

Jacob was not allowed to have his letters in those days, until the self-elected inspectors of correspondence had had the perusal of them, and consulted over their secret meaning. These wiseacres therefore assembled, wiped their glasses carefully, put them on, and proceeded to examine this suspicious document. What it meant they could not imagine. William Henry Jackson had no parents, or brothers, and the letter was incomprehensible. Study as they might, no light dawned upon them, but their suspicions became stronger, and they were sure the letter meant mischief.

White genius having exhausted itself, black genius was brought into requisition. Jacob was sent for, and the letter was placed in his hands. He read between the lines, and comprehended the hidden meaning at once. "Moses" had dictated this letter, and Moses was coming. The brothers must be on the watch, and ready to join her at a moment's warning. But Moses must hurry, for the word had gone forth that the brothers were to be sent South, and the chaingang was being collected.

Jacob read the letter slowly, threw it down, and said: "Dat letter can't be meant for me no how; I can't make head or tail of it." And he walked off and took immediate measures to let Harriet's brothers know that she was on the way, and they must be ready at the given signal to start for the North.

Sojourner Truth

WHILE THE WATER IS STIRRING I WILL STEP INTO THE POOL

from *Proceedings: First Anniversary of the American Equal Rights Association Held at the Church of the Puritans, New York, May 9 and 10, 1867*

[Following are excerpts from three speeches delivered by Sojourner Truth at the American Equal Rights Association Convention in New York City, in May 1867. As serious as her subject is, she characteristically uses humor to attack her foes and even to signify a bit on her friends and allies, the white women at the convention.]

My friends, I am rejoiced that you are glad, but I don't know how you will feel when I get through. I come from another field—the country of the slave. They have got their liberty—so much good luck to have slavery partly destroyed; not entirely. I want it root and branch destroyed. Then we will all be free indeed. I feel that if I have to answer for the deeds done in my body just as much as a man, I have a right to have just as much as a man. There is a great stir about colored men getting their rights, but not a word about the colored women; and if colored men get their rights, and not colored women theirs, you see the colored men will be masters over the women, and it will be just as bad as it was before. So I am for keeping the thing going while things are stirring; because if we wait till it is still, it will take a great while to get it going again. White women are a great deal smarter, and know more than colored women, while colored women do not know scarcely anything. They go out washing, which is about as high as a colored woman gets, and their men go about idle, strutting up and down; and when the women come home, they ask for their money and take it all, and then scold because there is no food. I want you to consider on that, chil'n. I call you chil'n; you are somebody's chil'n, and I am old enough to be mother of all that is here. I want women to have their rights. In the Courts women have no right, no voice; nobody speaks for them. I wish woman to have her voice there among the pettifoggers. If it is not a fit place for women it is unfit for men to be there. I am above eighty years old; it is about time for me to be going. I have been forty years a slave and forty years free and would be here forty years more to have equal rights for all. I suppose I am kept here because something remains for me to do; I suppose I am yet to help to break the chain. I have done a great deal of work; as much as a man, but did not get so much pay. I used to work in the field and bind grain, keeping up with the cradler; but men doing no more, got twice as much pay; so with the German women. They work in the field and do as much work, but do not get the pay. We do as much, we eat as much, we want as much. I suppose I am about the only colored woman that goes about to speak for the rights of the colored woman. I want to keep the thing stirring, now that the ice is cracked. What we want is a little money. You men know that you get as much again as women when you write, or for what you do. When we get our rights we shall not have to come to you for money, for then we shall have money enough in our own pockets; and may be you will ask us for money. But help us now until we get it. It is a good consolation to know that when we have got this battle once fought we shall not be coming to you any more. You have been having our right so long, that you think, like a slaveholder, that you own us. I know that it is hard for one who has held the reins for so long to give up; it cuts like a knife. It will feel all the better when it closes up again. I have been in Washington about three years, seeing about these colored people. Now colored men have the right to vote; and what I want is to have colored women have the right to vote. There ought to be equal rights now more than ever, since colored people have got their freedom. I am going to talk several times while I am here; so now I will do a little singing. I have not heard any singing since I came here.

————

I am glad to see that men are getting their rights, but I want women to get theirs, and while the water is stirring I will step into the pool. Now that there is a great stir about colored men's getting their rights is the time for women to step in and have theirs. I am sometimes told that "Women ain't fit to vote. Why, don't you know that a woman had seven devils in her: and do you suppose a woman is fit to rule the nation?" Seven devils ain't no account; a man had a legion in him. (Great laughter.)

[Discussing the "taxing" of women like herself, homeowners in Battle Creek, she also noted that they were "taxed" to build roads.]

They went on the road and worked. It took 'em a good while to get a stump up. (Laughter). Now, that shows that women can work. If they can dig up stumps they can vote. (Laughter). It is easier to vote than dig stumps. (Laughter).

Harriet E. Wilson

OUR NIG

[Recently documented as the first novel published by an African American woman and the first published in this country by an African American, *Our Nig* was until recently generally attributed to a white author. The autobiographical novel relates the story of Frado (Nig), who was abandoned by her white mother following her black father's death. Raised in the home of the Bellmonts, she was treated as a virtual slave by the cruel Mrs. Bellmont and her daughter Mary. Though other members of the family were often kind to Nig, her trials were great for she was almost constantly under the control of these two women. The following selection occurs when Nig is fourteen years old.]

It is impossible to give an impression of the manifest enjoyment of Mrs. B. in these kitchen scenes. It was her favorite exercise to enter the appartment noisily, vociferate orders, give a few sudden blows to quicken Nig's pace, then return to the sitting room with *such* a satisfied expression, congratulating herself upon her thorough house-keeping qualities.

    She usually rose in the morning at the ringing of the bell for breakfast; if she were heard stirring before that time, Nig knew well there was an extra amount of scolding to be borne.

No one now stood between herself and Frado, but Aunt Abby. And if *she* dared to interfere in the least, she was ordered back to her "own quarters." Nig would creep slyly into her room, learn what she could of her regarding the absent, and thus gain some light in the thick gloom of care and toil and sorrow in which she was immersed.

The first of spring a letter came from James, announcing declining health. He must try northern air as a restorative; so Frado joyfully prepared for this agreeable increase of the family, this addition to her cares.

He arrived feeble, lame, from his disease, so changed Frado wept at his appearance, fearing he would be removed from her forever. He kindly greeted her, took her to the parlor to see his wife and child, and said many things to kindle smiles on her sad face.

Frado felt so happy in his presence, so safe from maltreatment! He was to her a shelter. He observed, silently, the ways of the house a few days; Nig still took her meals in the same manner as formerly, having the same allowance of food. He, one day, bade her not remove the food, but sit down to the table and eat.

"She *will*, mother," said he, calmly, but imperatively; I'm determined; she works hard; I've watched her. Now, while I stay, she is going to sit down *here*, and eat such food as we eat."

A few sparks from the mother's black eyes were the only reply; she feared to oppose where she knew she could not prevail. So Nig's standing attitude, and selected diet vanished.

Her clothing was yet poor and scanty; she was not blessed with a Sunday attire; for she was never permitted to attend church with her mistress. "Religion was not meant for niggers," *she* said; when the husband and brothers were absent, she would drive Mrs. B. and Mary there, then return, and go for them at the close of the service, but never remain. Aunt Abby would take her to evening meetings, held in the neighborhood, which Mrs. B. never attended; and impart to her lessons of truth and grace as they walked to the place of prayer.

Many of less piety would scorn to present so doleful a figure; Mrs. B. had shaved her glossy ringlets; and, in her coarse cloth gown and ancient bonnet, she was anything but an enticing object. But Aunt Abby looked within. She saw a soul to save, an immortality of happiness to secure.

These evenings were eagerly anticipated by Nig; it was such a pleasant release from labor.

Such perfect contrast in the melody and prayers of these good people to the harsh tones which fell on her ears during the day.

Soon she had all their sacred songs at command, and enlivened her toil by accompanying it with this melody.

James encouraged his aunt in her efforts. He had found the *Saviour,* he wished to have Frado's desolate heart gladdened, quieted, sustained, by *His* presence. He felt sure there were elements in her heart which, transformed and purified by the gospel, would make her worthy the esteem and friendship of the world. A kind, affectionate heart, native wit, and common sense, and the pertness she sometimes exhibited, he felt if restrained properly, might become useful in originating a self-reliance which would be of service to her in after years.

Yet it was not possible to compass all this, while she remained where she was. He wished to be cautious about pressing too closely her claims on his mother, as it would increase the burdened one he so anxiously wished to relieve. He cheered her on with the hope of returning with his family, when he recovered sufficiently.

Nig seemed awakened to new hopes and aspirations, and realized a longing for the future, hitherto unknown.

To complete Nig's enjoyment, Jack arrived unexpectedly. His greeting was as hearty to herself as to any of the family.

"Where are your curls, Fra?" asked Jack, after the usual salutation.

"Your mother cut them off."

"Thought you were getting handsome, did she? Same old story, is it; knocks and bumps? Better times coming; never fear, Nig."

How different this appellative sounded from him; he said it in such a tone, with such a rogueish look!

She laughed, and replied that he had better take her West for a housekeeper.

Jack was pleased with James's innovations of table discipline, and would often tarry in the dining-room, to see Nig in her new place at the family table. As he was thus sitting one day, after the family had finished dinner, Frado seated herself in her mistress' chair, and was just reaching for a clean dessert plate which was on the table, when her mistress entered.

"Put that plate down; you shall not have a clean one; eat from mine," continued she. Nig hesitated. To eat after James, his wife or Jack, would have been pleasant; but to be commanded to do what was disagreeable by her mistress, *because* it was disagreeable, was trying. Quickly looking about, she took the plate, called Fido to wash it, which he did to the best of his ability; then, wiping her knife and fork on the cloth, she proceeded to eat her dinner.

Mattie J. Jackson

THE SOLDIERS, AND OUR TREATMENT DURING THE WAR

from *The Story of Mattie J. Jackson*

Soon after the war commenced the rebel soldiers encamped near Mr. Lewis' residence, and remained there one week. They were then ordered by General Lyons to surrender, but they refused. There were seven thousand Union and seven hundred rebel soldiers. The Union soldiers surrounded the camp and took them and exhibited them through the city and then confined them in prison. I told my mistress that the Union soldiers were coming to take the camp. She replied that it was false, that it was General Kelly coming to reenforce Gen. Frost. In a few moments the alarm was heard. I told Mrs. L. the Unionists had fired upon the rebels. She replied it was only the salute of Gen. Kelley. At night her husband came home with the news that Camp Jackson was taken and all the soldiers prisoners. Mrs. Lewis asked how the Union soldiers could take seven hundred men when they only numbered the same. Mr. L. replied they had seven thousand. She was much astonished, and cast her eye around to us for fear we might hear her. Her suspicion was correct; there was not a word passed that escaped our listening ears. My mother and myself could read enough to make out the news in the papers. The Union soldiers took much delight in tossing a paper over the fence to us. It aggravated my mistress very much. My mother used to sit up nights and read to keep posted about the war. In a few days my mistress came down to the kitchen again with another bitter complaint that it was a sad affair that the Unionists had taken their delicate citizens who had enlisted and made prisoners of them—that they were babes. My mother reminded her of taking Fort Sumpter and Major Anderson and serving them the same and that turn about was fair play. She then hastened to her room with the speed of a deer, nearly unhinging every door in her flight, replying as she went that the Niggers and Yankees were seeking to take the country. One day, after she had visited the kitchen to superintend some domestic affairs, as she pretended, she became very angry without a word being passed, and said—"I think it has come to a pretty pass, that old Lincoln, with his long legs, an old rail splitter, wishes to put the Niggers on an equality with the whites; that her children should never be on an equal footing with a Nigger. She had rather see them dead." As my mother made no reply to her remarks, she stopped talking, and commenced venting her spite on my companion servant. On one occasion Mr. Lewis searched my mother's room and found a picture of President Lincoln, cut from a newspaper, hanging in her room. He asked her what she was doing with old Lincoln's picture. She replied it was there because she liked it. He then knocked her down three times, and sent her to the trader's yard for a month as punishment. My mistress indulged some hopes till the victory of New Orleans, when she heard the famous Union song sang to the tune of Yankee Doodle:

The rebels swore that New Orleans never should be taken,
But if the Yankees came so near they should not save their bacon.
That's the way they blustered when they thought they were so handy,
But Farragut steamed up one day and gave them Doodle Dandy.

Ben Butler then was ordered down to regulate the city;
He made the rebels walk a chalk, and was not that a pity?
That's the way to serve them out—that's the way to treat them,
They must not go and put on airs after we have beat them.

He made the rebel banks shell out and pay the loyal people,
He made them keep the city clean from pig's sty to church steeple.
That's the way Columbia speaks, let all men believe her;
That's the way Columbia speaks instead of yellow fever.

He sent the saucy women up and made them treat us well
He helped the poor and snubbed the rich; they thought he was the devil.
Bully for Ben. Butler, then, they thought he was so handy;
Bully for Ben Butler then,—Yankee Doodle Dandy.

The days of sadness for mistress were days of joy for us. We shouted and laughed to the top of our voices. My mistress was more enraged than ever—nothing pleased her. One evening, after I had attended to my usual duties, and I supposed all was complete, she, in a terrible range, declared I should be punished that night. I did not know the cause, neither did she. She went immediately and selected a switch. She placed it in the corner of the room to await the return of her husband at night for him to whip me. As I was not pleased with the idea of a whipping I bent the switch in the shape of W, which was the first letter of his name, and after I had attended to the dining room my fellow servant and myself walked away and stopped with an aunt of mine during the night. In the morning we made our way to the Arsenal, but could gain no admission. While we were wandering about seeking protection, the girl's father overtook us and persuaded us to return home. We finally complied. All was quiet. Not a word was spoken respecting our sudden departure. All went on as usual.

———

On my return to St. Louis I met my old master, Lewis, who strove so hard to sell us away that he might avoid seeing us free, on the street. He was so surprised that before he was aware of it he dropped a bow. My mother met Mrs. Lewis, her old mistress, with a large basket on her arm, trudging to market. It appeared she had lived to see the day when her children had to wait upon themselves, and she likewise. The Yankees had taken possession, and her posterity were on an equality with the black man. Mr. Lewis despised the Irish, and often declared he would board at the hotel before he would employ Irish help, but he now has a dissipated Irish cook. When I was his slave I was obliged to keep away every fly from the table, and not allow one to light on a person. They are now compelled to brush their own flies and dress themselves and children. Mr. Lewis' brother Benjamin was a more severe slave master than the one who owned me. He was a tobacconist and very wealthy. As soon as the war commenced he turned Unionist to save his property. He was very severe in his punishments. He used to extend his victim, fastened to a beam, with hands and feet tied, and inflict from fifty to three hundred lashes, laying their flesh entirely open, then bathe their quivering wounds with brine, and, through his nose, in a slow rebel tone he would tell them "You'd better walk a fair chalk line or else I'll give yer twice as much." His former friends, the guerrillas, were aware he only turned Union to save his cash, and they gave those persons he had abused a large share of his luxury. They then, in the presence of his wife and another distinguished lady, tortured him in a most inhuman manner. For pretending Unionism they placed him on a table and threatened to dissect him alive if he did not tell them where he kept his gold. He immediately informed them. They then stood him against the house and fired over his head. From that, they changed his position by turning him upside down, and raising him two feet from the floor, letting him dash his head against the floor until his skull was fractured, after which he lingered awhile and finally died. There was a long piece published in the paper respecting his repentance, benevolence, & c. All the slaves who ever lived in his family admit the Lord is able to save to the uttermost. He saved the thief on the cross, and perhaps he saved him.

When I made my escape from slavery I was in a query how I was to raise funds to bear my expenses. I finally came to the conclusion that as the laborer was worthy of his hire, I thought my wages should come from my master's pocket. Accordingly I took twenty-five dollars. After I was safe and had learned to write, I sent him a nice letter, thanking him for the kindness his pocket bestowed to me in time of need. I have never received any answer to it.

When I complete my education, if my life is spared, I shall endeavor to publish further details of our history in another volume from my own pen.

Charlotte Forten

JOURNAL, OCTOBER 28, 1862*

Went into the Commissary's Office to wait for the boat which was to take us to St. Helena's Island which is about six miles from B [Beaufort]. T'is here that Miss Towne has her school, in which I am to teach, and that Mr.

---

*Ms. Forten's "Journal" is in folder 1816 of the Francis J. Grimké Papers, Boxes 40–45, Moorland-Spingarn Research Center, Howard University, Washington, D.C. Used by the permission of the Moorland-Spingarn Research Center.

Hunn will have his store. While waiting in the Office we saw several military gentleman [sic], *not* very creditable specimens, I sh'ld say. The little Commissary himself Capt. T is a perfect little popinjay, and he and a Colonel somebody who didn't look any too sensible, talked in a very smart manner, evidently for our especial benefit. The word "nigger" was plentifully used, whereupon I set them down at once as *not* gentleman [sic]. Then they talked a great deal about rebel attacks and yellow fever, and other alarming things, with significant nods and looks at each other. We saw through them at once, and were not at all alarmed by any of their representations. But if they are a fair example of army officers, I sh'ld pray to see as little of them as possible.

Annie L. Burton

MEMORIES OF CHILDHOOD'S SLAVERY DAYS

One day my master heard that the Yankees were coming our way, and he immediately made preparations to get his goods and valuables out of their reach. The big six-mule team was brought to the smoke-house door, and loaded with hams and provisions. After being loaded, the team was put in the care of two of the most trustworthy and valuable slaves that my master owned, and driven away. It was master's intention to have these things taken to a swamp, and there concealed in a pit that had recently been made for the purpose. But just before the team left the main road for the by-road that led to the swamp, the two slaves were surprised by the Yankees, who at once took possession of the provisions, and started the team toward Clayton, where the Yankees had headquarters. The road to Clayton ran past our plantation. One of the slave children happened to look up the road, and saw the Yankees coming, and gave warning. Whereupon, my master left unceremoniously for the woods, and remained concealed there for five days. The niggers had run away whenever they got a chance, but now it was master's and the other white folks' turn to run.

Armacie Adams

YOU'S FREE

from *The Negro in Virginia*

Guess I was 'bout 15 years ole when Marse come back from de fightin', mean as ever. Never did say nothin' 'bout de war, an' I didn't even know ef it's over or not. But one day Marse Bob, his son, was switchin' me in de woods playful like an' he say, "Whyn't you strike me back, Mici? You's free. Dat's what de war was fo', to free de niggers."

I took dat switch away an' beat him hard as I could 'cross de haid tell it busted. Den I run 'cross de fields to some colored folks 'bout 6 miles away. Dey name was Foremans, an' dey was free sho' 'nough. Dey tole me dat was right. I been free mo'n a year. Ain't never been back to dat place since.

Charlotte Brown

STOMP DOWN FREEDOM *

from *The Negro in Virginia*

De news come on a Thursday, an' all de slaves been shoutin' an' carryin' on tell ev'ybody was all tired out. 'Member de fust Sunday of freedom. We was all sittin' roun' restin' an' tryin' to think what freedom meant an' ev'ybody was quiet an' peaceful. All at once ole Sister Carrie who was near 'bout a hundred started in to talkin':

> Tain't no mo' sellin' today,
> Tain't no mo' hirin' today,
> Tain't no pullin' off shirts today,
> Its stomp down freedom today.
> Stomp it down!

*Courtesy of the Hampton University Archives.

An' when she says, "Stomp it down," all de slaves commence to shoutin' wid her:

> Stomp down Freedom today—
> Stomp it down!
> Stomp down Freedom today.

Wasn't no mo' peace dat Sunday. Ev'ybody started in to sing an' shout once mo'. Fust thing you know dey done made up music to Sister Carrie's stomp song an' sang an' shouted dat song all de res' de day. Chile, dat was one glorious time!

Fannie Berry

WE'S FREE*

from *The Negro in Virginia*

Niggers shoutin' an' clappin' hands an' singin'! Chillun runnin' all over de place beatin' tins an' yellin'. Ev'ybody happy. Sho' did some celebratin'. Run to de kitchen an' shout in de winder:

> Mammy don't you cook no mo'
> You's free! You's free!

Run to de henhouse an shout:

> Rooster, don't you crow no mo'
> You's free! You's free!
> Ol' hen, don't you lay no mo' eggs,
> You's free! You's free!

Go to de pigpen an' tell de pig:

*Courtesy of the Hampton University Archives.

Ol' pig, don't you grunt no mo'
You's free! You's free!

Tell de cows:

Ol' cow, don't you give no mo' milk,
You's free! You's free!

An' some smart alec boys sneaked up under Miss Sara Ann's winder an shouted:

Ain't got to slave no mo'
We's free! We's free!

Freedom Song

DONE WID DRIVER'S DRIBIN'

from John Lovell, Jr., *Black Song*

Done wid driber's dribin',
Done wid massa's hollerin', . . .
Done wide missus' scoldin', . . .
Roll, Jordan, roll

Priscilla Jane Thompson

A COMMON OCCURRENCE

from *Ethiope Lays*

Lucindy, who you 'spose I seed,
    Down at de mill, today?
I know you nebbah 'ud agreed,
    Dat he is, who he say.

It ain't no use to guess no mo',
    I'an' you's way off de track;
Dah, honey! 'twus one ub de Rowe's—
    Dat one dey all called Jack.

When we libed on his pappy's place,
    You know, he wus de one,
Dat al'ays had dat grinnin' face,
    And wrote ou' lettahs home.
Dat boy—de pictah ub his pap,
    Wid ha' all curled an' light;
Dat useta messmate wid ou' chaps,
    De same ef dey wus white.

    But mussy, honey! mussy me!
He's lurnt his propah place,
    Done climed dat des'-stool like a tree,
Specked eyes, an' frowned his face.
    An' crow-feet all about his eyes!
Looks fifty fo' uh pas';
    Dis fac' de white folks cain't deny:
Dey do git ole so fas'.

Dat's right Lucindy! he's ez ole,
    As ou'own Malachi;
But 'tis de trute dat I done tole,
    He looks mos' ole ez I.
"Hello dah, Petah!" loud he sed,
    (Done laid de 'uncle' by;)
"I'd knowed you, ef I done been dead,
    An' seed you in de sky."

"Guess I's becum a strangah, so,
    Mus' intahduce, I see;
Why, I am mistah Jackson Rowe—
    You use ta wuk fah me."
Yo' pappy, boy, you mus'ta mean;
    I wuked fah him a deal,

When you wus but a youngstah, lean,
    A sniv'lin' at his heel.

I looked wid all de eyes I hed;
    De pas' my brain did rack;
But spite ub all—it made me med,
    I couldn't fin' Rowe's Jack.
"Why, hab I changed dat much?" he sed,
    An' 'peared a little hu't;
It quickly cumed into my hed,
    I sed, "not fah de wus"

He sed, he'd bought sheers in dat mill;
    Lucindy, ain't you beat!
De house, wid his big voice wus fill,
    A-holl'rin' 'bout his wheat.
He'd boss de men in his employ,
    Den 'dress me as "my lad,"
De same ef I'd a-been a boy,
    An' he ole ez my dad.

He's got de 'big-he'd', dat's de fac';
    And got de 'big-he'd,' bed;
He made b'lieve, he'd fahgot my chaps—
    "Cain't place dem, Pete," he sed.
"Cain't min' my Malachi?" I sed;
    "An' all my uddah chaps?
You cain't keep ole times in yo' hed?'
    You's dif'unt f'om yo' pap.

An' den he spoke ub trabbling 'roun';
    Ub business keers, all days;
An' den his face put on dat frown,
    An' so I cumed away.
An' all along ez I cumed back,
    I thought, whut I thought fus:
"Dat, ef dis is Rowe's grinnin' Jack,
    He's pintly changed fah wus."

Julia Grovernor

I A I N ' T   K N O W   N U T T N '

from *Drums and Shadows*

[Though many of the former slaves were cooperative (at least to a degree) with the WPA interviewers, some of them were not very forthcoming, as can be seen with Julia Grovernor when they first approached her, as seen in the following brief summary of her responses to their questions. They later found her to be "sharp-witted."]

"No'm, I ain know nuttn. Ise feeble-minded. I bin weak in head sence I small chile. No'm, I ain know nuttn bout witches. I ain know nuttn bout root doctuhs. No'm, I ain nebuh heah uh cunjuh. No'm, I ain know nuttn bout spells. No'm, I ain kin tuh Katie Brown."

Folk

T H E   T A R   B A B Y

from Daryl Cumber Dance, *Shuckin' and Jivin'*

The animals were tryin' to *catch* Brer Rabbit; and Brer Rabbit would go down to the spring to get water. They thought that would be a good way to catch him. And so they made a Tar Baby and set it up at the spring 'cause Brer Rabbit was very inquisitive. And Brer Rabbit went down to drink, and he saw this Tar Baby; and he said, "Uh, who're you?" And he didn't say nothing, so then Brer Rabbit said, "You better tell me who you are!" And so the Tar Baby didn't say anything. So then Brer Rabbit went up there and say, "Well, I'll *slap* ya!" And the Tar Baby didn't say anything, so he slapped the Tar Baby, and his hand stuck, but the Tar Baby still didn't say anything. So then he say, "I'll kick ya!" And he kicked 'im and his foot stuck. So then he said, "Well, I got another foot; I'll kick ya with that!" And he kicked 'im and *that* foot stuck. And then he said, "Well, I got another hand— I'll slap ya." And so he slapped 'im with the other hand, and *that* stuck.

He said, "Now you think you smart, but I got a head—I'll butt ya!" So he butt 'im and *that* stuck. So when the animals came to catch him he was all stuck on the Tar Baby, and he say, "Oh-oh, oh! Turn me loose, turn me loose!"

They say, "We gotcha! We gotcha!"

He say, "Well, I tell you what you do. You throw me in the *briar* patch, because I don't like briar patches. You just throw me in the briar patch and you'll have me—then you kin keep me *forever.*"

So then they took him and throwed him in the briar patch, and he say, "O-o-oh!" when he got in the briar patch. "O-O-OH! This is where I was *born* and *raised*—right in the briar patch!"

Then he ran on down through the briars.

Folk

YOU GON' MAKE BREAD TODAY

from Daryl Cumber Dance, *Shuckin' and Jivin'*

On the side of a mountain once, the Lord summoned three people to help him with a project, one being a Black man, one being an Italian, and the other Jewish. And the Lord said, "I am simply looking for people to follow simple directions." And He said, "I simply want the three of you to go out and bring me back a stone, or as much stone as you'd like." And so the Black man, thinking that it was a timed thing, rushed right back with a pebble. The Italian took a couple of hours, and finally he came back with a wheelbarrow piled with crushed stone. And they waited until midnight. Finally they heard a rumbling. And the Jew was shoving a mountain. So the Lord in his patience blessed the stones and said, "These stones I will now turn into bread." Well, the Black man had a biscuit. The Italian had a wheelbarrow *filled* with loaves of bread. And the Jew had a bakery, of course.

So the next day, the Lord said, "Same gentlemen, same assignment. Go out and fetch stones." Well, the Black man was extremely happy for a second chance. So sometime later that evening, the Italian was the first one back, with his same wheelbarrow filled with stones. And the Jew took very long to come, but here he is with his mountain. And they waited until midnight. The Black man didn't show . . . Two A.M. . . . Three A.M. . . . Four A.M. . . . Well, just about dawn they heard a rumbling sound. And a whole avalanche of mountains and boulders—just everything—was being hurled at the Lord. And finally the Lord said, "Upon these rocks I'll build my church."

And the Black man said, "I be damned if you will. You gon' make *bread* today!"

Pauline Gay

TOO MANY UPS

from John A. Burrison, ed., *Storytellers*

I'm gonna tell you a story considerin' the farmer and his boss. In the year when slavery broke [ended], John didn't know what to do about the family situation. He got together and he talked it over with his wife. He was a farmer for his boss. Yet this didn't bring any income in to John and he felt like this would not be a good situation to raise his family on, since he was gonna have to be on his own and not get stuff from his boss. So he talked it over with his wife and he decided, "Well, slavery is broke now. I got to be on my own. I'll try to find something somewhere that my family might survive."

His boss came up to him one morning. He said, "John, I'm ready and it's time now for us to get started with our crop."

John was standin' there lookin' at him, and he was thinkin' all the time. John said, "Well, Boss," say, "let me tell you somethin'. Slavery time is over now, and I cannot make any crops anymore."

He said, "Why, John?" Said, "Didn't you have food when you were working for me?"

He say, "Yes suh, Boss," said, "but you see, hit's not like it used to be. Where I used to get my groceries from your table, I got to provide that now on my own."

He said, "Well, farmin' is a good situation, and you can be able to survive off o' that."

He say, "I was thinkin' and talkin' it over with my wife, just thinkin' about farmin'. It's just a little too many 'ups' in it."

Say, "What's that, John?"

"Well, when you get a farm you've got to start off *up.*"

Say, "How is that?"

Say, "When you lay down at night, arise the next morning, you got to get *up.* Then you got to go out to the barn, you got to feed *up.* After you feed the mule up, you got to take him out and water him *up.* Then after you water the mule up, you got to hook him *up.* Then after you hook him up, you go out into the farm, you got to plow the ground *up.* Then after you plow the ground up, Boss, I was just thinkin' all the way down the line, you got to plant it *up.* After you plant this ground up, then you got to gather it *up* when it make. And you gettin' on down through the year at this time. It's beginning to come down to a close. Well, when the end of the year come, after you gather your crop up, then I got to come *up* to you, Boss. When I come to you, you'll say, 'Well, John, I was just goin' over my book. You didn't clear anything this time.' I'll begin to scratch my head and I will be wondering. Say, 'Why not, Boss?' Say, 'I'm sorry, but you et it *up!*'"

So this ends the situation of the farmer and his boss.

Sarah and A. Elizabeth Delany

I WOULD RATHER DIE THAN BACK DOWN, HONEY

from *Having Our Say*

People learned not to mess with me from Day One. When I was small, a neighborhood girl started taunting me: "Bessie Delany, you scrawny thing. You've got the skinniest legs and the longest neck I ever did see." Now, this girl was a bully, and I had seen her technique before: She would say nasty things to other girls, and they'd burst into tears and run crying to their mama. She was a lot bigger than me, but I didn't care. I said, "Oh, why don't you shut up. You ain't so pretty yourself!" And she never bothered me again.

Papa used to say, "You catch more flies with molasses than vinegar." He believed you could get further in life by being nice to people. Well, this is easy for Sadie to swallow. Sadie is molasses without even trying! She can sweet-talk the world, or play dumb, or whatever it takes to get by without a fuss. But even as a tiny little child, I wasn't afraid of anything. I'd meet the Devil before day and look him in the eye, no matter what the price. If Sadie is molasses, then I am vinegar! Sadie is sugar, and I'm the spice.

You know, Sadie doesn't approve of me sometimes. She frowns at me in her big-sister-sort-of-way and says it's a wonder I wasn't lynched. Well, it's true I almost was. But I'm still here, yes, sir!

What worries me is that I know Sadie's going to get into Heaven, but I'm not so sure about me. I'm working on it, but it sure is hard to change. I've been trying to change for one hundred years without success, that's not so good, is it? I'm afraid when I meet St. Peter at the Gate, he'll say, "Lord, child, you were *mean!*"

I have trouble with the idea of forgiving and forgetting. You see, I can forgive, but I can't seem to forget. And I'm not sure the Lord would approve of that at all. I remember things that happened long, long ago that still make me madder than a hornet. I wish they didn't. Most of the things that make me mad happened to me because I am colored. As a woman dentist, I faced sexual harassment—that's what they call it today—but to me, racism was always a bigger problem.

Most of the people I'm still mad at are long dead. If I say something mean about them, Sadie will say, "Now Bessie, of the dead say nothing Evil." And I try to be good.

Sometimes I am angry at all white people, until I stop and think of the nice white people I have known in my life. OK, OK, there have been a few. I admit it. And my mother is part white, and I can't hate my own flesh and blood! There are good white people out there. Sometimes, they are hard to find, but they're out there, just look for them.

But the rebby boys tend to stand out, make themselves known. Rebby is what we used to call racist white men I guess it's short for rebel. I'll tell you, the way those rebby types treat colored folks—well, it just makes me sick. If I had a pet buzzard I'd treat him better than the way some white folks have treated me! There isn't a Negro this side of Glory who doesn't know exactly what I mean.

Why, the rebby boys start early in life learning to hate. I remember encountering some who weren't more than ten or twelve years old. They were cutting through the fields at Saint Aug's one day, and I had strayed a few yards from where I was supposed to be. I was about six years old. My little petticoat had slipped down a bit, and they made some nasty remarks about this little colored girl and her underpants. I'm not even sure I understood what they were saying, but I got their meaning.

The rebby boys don't give colored folks credit for a thing, not a single thing. Why, I think we've done pretty well, considering we were dragged over here in chains from Africa! Why, colored folks *built* this country, and that is the truth. We were the laborers, honey! And even after we were freed, we were the backbone of this country—the maids, cooks, undertakers, barbers, porters, and so on.

Those rebby types! What do they think, anyway? When we get to the Spirit World, do they think colored people are going to be waiting on their tables, pouring their tea? I think some of them are in for a big surprise. They're going to be pouring tea for *me.*

Now Sadie doesn't get all agitated like this. She just shrugs it off. It's been a little harder for me, partly because I'm darker than she is, and the darker you are, honey, the harder it is. But it's also been harder on me because I have a different personality than Sadie. She is a true Christian woman! I wish I were more like her but I'm afraid I am a naughty little darkey! Ha ha! I know it's not fashionable to use some of the words from my heyday, but that's who I am! And who is going to stop me? Nobody, that's who! Ain't nobody going to censor *me,* no, sir! I'm a hundred-and-one years old and at my age, honey, I can say what I want!

Now, don't go thinking that I'm *all* mean. I am not so angry that I cannot laugh at myself! One thing most Negroes learn early is how to laugh at their situation.

If you asked me the secret to longevity, I would tell you that you have to work at taking care of your health. But a lot of it's attitude. I'm alive out of sheer determination, honey! Sometimes I think it's my *meanness* that keeps me going.

———

Now, Georgia was a mean place—meaner than North Carolina. You know that song about Georgia, that sentimental song? Well, they can have it! They can have the whole state as far as I'm concerned.

In Georgia, they never missed a chance to keep you down. If you were colored and you tried on a hat or a pair of shoes, honey, you owned 'em. What a rebby state! To be fair, I can understand why they didn't want Negroes to try on hats without buying them because in those days, Negroes would grease their hair. And the store couldn't sell the hat if it got grease on it. So, to be fair, I think that was OK.

But it was on my way to my job in Brunswick in 1913 that I came close to being lynched. You see, I had to change trains in Waycross, Georgia. I was sitting in the little colored waiting room at the station, and I took my hair down and was combing it. I was fixing myself up. I was going to my new job, and I wanted to look nice.

Well, there I was with my long hair down when this white man opened the door to the colored waiting room. There was no one in there except me and two colored teachers from New York who were traveling with me to Brunswick. The white man stuck his head in and started, well, leering at me. He was drunk, and he smelled bad, and he started mumbling things. And I said, "Oh, why don't you shut up and go wait with your own kind in the white waiting room?"

What happened next was kind of like an explosion. He slammed the door and I could hear him shouting at the top of his lungs outside, "The nigger bitch insulted me! The nigger bitch insulted me!"

The two colored teachers traveling with me slipped out the back without a word and made a beeline for the woods. They hid in the woods! I guess I can't blame them. A colored porter came in to see what this was all about, and he whispered to me, "Good for you!" But then he ran out on me, too. He left me there by myself.

Well, I could see a crowd begin to gather on the platform, and I knew I was in big trouble. Papa always said, "If you see a crowd, you go the other way. Don't even hang around long enough to find out what it's about!" Now, this crowd was outside, gathering for *me*.

By now, there were dozens of white people in the crowd, and the white man kept yelling, "Nigger bitch insulted me!" I was just waiting for somebody to get a rope. Thousands of Negroes had been lynched for far less than what I had just done. But I just continued to sit on the bench, combing my hair, while that white man was a-carrying on! I realized that my best chance was to act like nothing was happening. You see, if you acted real scared, sometimes that spurred them on.

Two things saved me: That glorious, blessed train rounded the bend, breaking up the crowd and giving me my way to get on out of there. And it helped that the white man was drunk as a skunk, and that turned off some of the white people.

But I wasn't afraid to die! I know you ain't got to die but once, and it seemed as good a reason to die as any. I was ready. Lord, help me, I was ready.

You know what Sadie says? Sadie says I was a fool to provoke that white man. As if I provoked *him!* Honey, he provoked *me!* Sadie says she would have *ignored* him. I say, how do you ignore some drunk, smelly white man treating you like trash? She says, child, it's better to put up with it, and live to tell about it. She says at the very least I should have run off into the woods with those other two teachers. She says I am lucky to be alive. But I would rather die than back down, honey.

Alice Childress

LIKE ONE OF THE FAMILY

Hi Marge! I have had me one hectic day. . . . Well, I had to take out my crystal ball and give Mrs. C . . . a thorough reading. She's the woman that I took over from Naomi after Naomi got married. . . . Well, she's a pretty nice woman as they go and I have never had too much trouble with her, but from time to time she really gripes me with her ways.

When she has company, for example, she'll holler out to me from the living room to the kitchen: "Mildred dear! Be sure and eat *both* of those lamb chops for your lunch!" Now you know she wasn't doing a thing but tryin' to prove to the company how "good" and "kind" she was to the servant, because she had told me *already* to eat those chops.

Today she had a girl friend of hers over to lunch and I was real busy afterwards clearing the things away and she called me over and introduced me to the woman. . . . Oh no, Marge! I didn't object to that at all. I greeted the lady and then went back to my work. . . . And then it started! I could hear her talkin' just as loud . . . and she says to her friend, "We *just* love her! She's *like* one of the family and she *just adores* our little Carol! We don't know *what* we'd do without her! We don't think of her as a servant!" And on and on she went . . . and every time I came in to move a plate off the table both of them would grin at me like chessy cats.

After I couldn't stand it any more, I went in and took the platter off the table and gave 'em both a look that would have frizzled a egg. . . . Well, you might have heard a pin drop and then they started talkin' about something else.

When the guest leaves, I go in the living room and says, "Mrs. C . . . , I want to have a talk with you."

"By all means," she says.

I drew up a chair and read her thusly: "Mrs. C . . . , you are a pretty nice person to work for, but I wish you would please stop talkin' about me like I was a *cocker spaniel* or a *poll parrot* or a *kitten*. . . . Now you just sit there and hear me out.

"In the first place, you do not *love* me; you may be fond of me, but that is all. . . . In the second place, I am *not* just like one of the family at all! The family eats in the dining room and I eat in the kitchen. Your mama borrows your lace tablecloth for her company and your son entertains his friends in your parlor, your daughter takes her afternoon nap on the living room couch and the puppy sleeps on your satin spread . . . and whenever your husband gets tired of something you are talkin' about he says, 'Oh, for Pete's sake, forget it. . . .' So you can see I am not *just* like one of the family.

"Now for another thing, I do not *just* adore your little Carol. I think she is a likable child, but she is also fresh and sassy. I know you call it 'uninhibited' and that is the way you want your child to be, but *luckily* my mother taught me some inhibitions or else I would smack little Carol once in a while when she's talkin' to you like you're a dog, but as it is I just laugh it off the way you do because she is *your* child and I am *not* like one of the family.

"Now when you say, 'We don't know *what* we'd do without her' this is a polite lie . . . because I know that if I dropped dead or had a stroke, you would get somebody to replace me.

"You think it is a compliment when you say, 'We don't think of her as a servant. . . .' but after I have worked myself into a sweat cleaning the bathroom and the kitchen . . . making the beds . . . cooking the lunch . . . washing the dishes and ironing Carol's pinafores . . . I do not feel like no weekend house guest. I feel like a servant, and in the face of that I have been meaning to ask you for a slight raise which will make me feel much better toward everyone here and make me know my work is appreciated.

"Now I hope you will stop talkin' about me in my presence and that we will get along like a good employer and employee should."

Marge! She was almost speechless but she *apologized* and said she'd talk to her husband about the raise. . . . I knew things were progressing because this evening Carol came in the kitchen and she did not say, "I want some bread and jam!" but she did say, *"Please,* Mildred, will you fix me a slice of bread and jam."

I'm going upstairs, Marge. Just look . . . you done messed up that buttonhole!

Alice Childress

THE POCKETBOOK GAME

Marge . . . day's work is an education! Well, I mean workin' in different homes you learn much more than if you was steady in one place. . . . I tell you, it really keeps your mind sharp tryin' to watch for what folks will put over on you.

What? . . . No, Marge, I do not want to help shell no beans, but I'd be more than glad to stay and have supper with you, and I'll wash the dishes after. Is that all right? . . .

Who put anything over on who? . . . Oh yes! It's like this. . . . I been working for Mrs. E . . . one day a week for several months and I notice that she has some peculiar ways. Well, there was only one thing that really bothered me and that was her pocketbook habit. . . . No, not those little novels. . . . I mean her purse—her handbag.

Marge, she's got a big old pocketbook with two long straps on it . . . and whenever I'd go there, she'd be propped up in a chair with her handbag double wrapped tight around her wrist, and from room to room she'd roam with that purse hugged to her bosom. . . . Yes, girl! This happens every time! No, there's *nobody* there but me and her. . . . Marge, I couldn't say nothin' to her! It's her purse, ain't it? She can hold onto it if she wants to!

I held my peace for months, tryin' to figure out how I'd make my point. . . . Well, bless Bess! *Today was the day!* . . . Please, Marge, keep shellin' the beans so we can eat! I know you're listenin', but you listen with your ears, not your hands. . . . Well, anyway, I was almost ready to go home when she steps in the room hangin' onto her bag as usual and says, "Mildred will you ask the super to come up and fix the kitchen faucet?" "Yes, Mrs. E . . . ," I says, "as soon as I leave." "Oh, no," she says, "he may be gone by then. Please go now." "All right," I says, and out the door I went, still wearin' my Hoover apron.

I just went down the hall and stood there a few minutes . . . and then I rushed back to the door and knocked on it as hard and frantic as I could. She flung open the door sayin', "What's the matter? Did you see the super?" . . . "No," I says, gaspin' hard for breath, "I was almost downstairs when I remembered . . . *I left my pocketbook!*"

With that I dashed in, grabbed my purse and then went down to get the super! Later, when I was leavin' she says real timid-like, "Mildred, I hope that you don't think I distrust you because . . ." I cut her off real quick. . . . "That's all right, Mrs. E . . . , I understand. 'Cause if I paid anybody as lit- tle as you pay me, I'd hold my pocketbook too!"

Marge, you fool . . . lookout! . . . You gonna drop the beans on the floor!

Alice Childress

MRS. JAMES

Well Marge, you haven't heard anything! You should hear the woman I work for . . . she's really something. Calls herself "Mrs. James!" All the time she says "Mrs. James."

The first day I was there she come into the kitchen and says, "Mildred, Mrs. James would like you to clean the pantry." Well I looked 'round to see if she meant her mother-in-law or somebody and then she adds, "If any- one calls, Mrs. James is out shopping." And with that she sashays out the door.

Now she keeps on talking that way all the time, the whole time I'm there. That woman wouldn't say "I" or "me" for nothing in the world. The way I look at it . . . I guess she thought it would be too personal.

Now Marge, you know I don't work Saturdays for nobody! Well sir! Last Friday she breezed in the kitchen and fussed around a little . . . movin' first the salt and then the pepper, I could feel something brewin' in the air. Next thing you know she speaks up. "Mildred," she says, "Mrs. James will need you this Saturday." I was polishin' silver at the time but I turned around and looked her dead in the eye and said, "Mildred does not work on Saturdays."

Well, for the rest of the day things went along kind of quiet-like but just before time for me to go home she drifted by the linen closet to check the ruffle on a guest towel and threw in her two cents more. "Mildred," she says, "a depression might do this country some good, then some people might work eight days a week and be glad for the chance to do it."

I didn't bat an eyelash, but about 15 minutes later when I was headin' for home, I stopped off at the living room and called to her, "That's very true, but on the other hand some folks might be doin' their own house-work . . . don'tcha know." With that and a cool "goodnight" I gently went out the front door. . . .

Oh, but we get along fine now. . . . Just fine!

April Sinclair

NEVER TRUST A WHITE PERSON

[In the following section the speaker is the grandmother of the novel's young protagonist, Stevie. She is telling her granddaughter about the ways of white folk during her childhood in the South.]

I grew up with Kathy Jo. We even took baths together. That was common in the South. We couldn't sit together on the streetcar, but we could share the same bathwater. Figure that one out."

"Wow."

"The white man in the South is different from the white man in the North," Grandma continued. "In the South, a black person better not get too big, and in the North, a black person better not get too close."

"How's that, Grandma?"

"Kathy Jo's mother thought nothing of throwing her in the bed between me and my sister if she wanted my mother to keep Kathy Jo on a Saturday night. White folk in the South don't mind getting close to you as long as it's clear who works for who. White folk in the North don't care how big your house is, so long as you're not their neighbor."

"So, Grandma, did you trust Kathy Jo? Tell me what happened."

"Start mashing these sweet potatoes and I will."

Grandma handed me the masher. I started squishing and she sat down in a kitchen chair and started telling.

"It was Kathy Jo's tenth birthday and she was having a big party. It was all she talked about. For some reason I forgot that I was colored and thought that I would be invited. I dreamed about playing Pin the Tail on the Donkey and Musical Chairs and eating hot dogs and ice cream and chocolate cake. I bragged to my sisters and brothers that I was going to the party. Mama tried to warn me, but I wouldn't pay her any mind."

"Grandma, did you get an invitation?"

"Of course not," Grandma said. She stretched her legs out and I noticed her ankles were swollen again. Grandma had on a pair of Uncle Franklin's old house slippers. They kept her corns from acting up.

"I figured I ain't needed an invitation," Grandma explained. "Me and Kathy Jo was still sleeping together in the same bed sometimes. Well suh, my mother didn't ask Miss Mary if I could attend the party. She just let me put on my Sunday dress and go sashaying in there like I was rich and white, carrying my present. I'd made Kathy Jo a kite. She was nothing but a tomboy. The little white children looked at me like I was the boogey man, including Kathy Jo. Miss Mary turned beet red."

"What did you do?"

"I handed Kathy Jo the kite and asked her where she wanted me to sit. She took my present and told me to sit in the kitchen and they would call me if they needed anything."

"No, she didn't, Grandma."

"Yes, she did, chile. I looked into Kathy Jo's eyes and they were cold as blue ice."

"What did you do, Grandma?"

"I took back my kite and I took back my friendship."

"What Kathy Jo did was really cold, Grandma."

"I've never trusted a white person since. Oh, I might smile and act cordial, but I never let them touch the real me," Grandma said, pointing to her chest.

Grandma stood up and started adding eggs and sugar to the mashed sweet potatoes.

"So, Grandma, you think only a fool would try to be friends with a white woman, huh?"

Grandma laughed. "Chile, the only black women and white women who can be friends are hookers and bulldaggers."

"Bulldaggers?" I swallowed.

"Yes baby, bulldaggers, you know, funnies . . . lesbians."

"Lesbians." The word sent chills down my spine. I pretended to be cheerful as I poured the rich, orange mixture into the little tins covered with crust. But I felt scared and alone in the small kitchen with Grandma.

Folk

I'LL GO AS FAR AS MEMPHIS

from Daryl Cumber Dance, *Shuckin' and Jivin'*

This man had lived in Mississippi, and they were getting along so poorly during that particular time that he went up North, like a lot of people who migrated to the North to get out of the Deep South because they were being treated so badly. So he went up North and he was getting along *fine*. Oh, he got on top. So some of his friends asked him to come back down to Mississippi and help the others; and so then he said, "I'm going to talk to the Lord about it."

So he talked to the Lord about it, and his friend asked him, say, "Well, what did the Lord tell you?"

So he said, "I told the Lord my friends in Mississippi needed my help and asked Him if He would go back South with me, and the Lord told me, "I'll go as far as Memphis.""

Folk

GAINING RESPECT

I was always annoyed by whites calling blacks by their first names and requiring that blacks call them by a title. When I was a child, I was rebellious and would attack this practice every chance I got. I would call the home of the wealthy whites for whom my aunt worked and whom they called Bertha, and I would ask to speak to *Mrs.* Ballard, emphasizing my aunt's title. When the white insurance agent would come to our home, calling my parents by their first names, I would charge into the room and say to him, "Hi, *Longley.*"

When my mother and I would go to Thalhimers [the local department store], and the saleslady would ask. "May I help you girls?" my mother would respond, "How old do *girls* grow where you come from?"

Folk

'SIPPI

When Madame C. J. Van Morganstein saw Mary Lou, the new help that her housekeeper had hired, she asked her where she was from.

"Sippi," the girl drawled.

Puzzled, she questioned again, "Where?"

"Sippi," the girl repeated.

"Oh-h-h," Madame C. J. Van Morganstein smiled, "you mean *Misi—sippi.*"

"No, I said zackly what I meant—I'm from Sippi. I promised God and whoever else would listen when I left the Souf dat I'd never say Missus to *nobody* evah agin."

Moms Mabley

LISTEN, MAME

Last week, Mamie called me up, you know. She wanted me to come down and help her pack. They fixing to leave the White House. So I went down. So after breakfast we was sittin' in the East Room talking, me and her. I say, "Listen, Mame." She say, "Yes, Mrs. Mabley."

Kathryn L. Morgan

MAGGIE'S STORIES

[Following are sections of the stories told by Kathryn Morgan's grandmother, who was so fair that she was often mistaken for white. Her first time passing occurs when she was about sixteen and the white conductors took her bags, treated her nicely, and seated her in the white section of the train.]

So that's when I decided I would be white whenever I wanted to be, and colored whenever I wanted to be. They used to say that colored folks could tell other colored folks no matter what they looked like. I don't know if this is true or not: I know none of the colored folks ever gave me away if they did know.

How the Porter Almost Gave Up the Game

Well, I was sitting in the white car; did I tell you what happened? Well, we had gotten well out of Lynchburg when this man, this colored man from Lynchburg, you know; I knew him well . . . he was the porter who went through the white cars selling things, you know. Well, when he got to me, now I'm sitting there with all these white folks. He said, "Maggie! Maggie, what you doing here?" Well, I was too scared to open my mouth because all the white folks sitting around me started looking. So he caught on right away; he said, "Oh, I beg your pardon, Miss, I am sorry, I thought you was the daughter of the white lady I used to work for. I'm so sorry!" Well, I didn't say a word and the white folks went on back to whatever they were doing.

But every time he came through the car he was grinning and waiting on those folks and saying, "Yes, Ma'am," and stuff. And he said, "Anything I can get you, Ma'am?" I didn't have any money so I said, "No, thank you." And he said, "Yes, Miss," and went on just like we didn't know each other well. He was one of Prince's good friends and was in our house all the time.

Well, when I got off in Washington, D.C., he was standing in the station just grinning, watching those white conductors carrying my bags and stuff. Later on when I went home to visit we used to sit in the kitchen and laugh at that one. He said, "Maggie, I sure almost gave up the game that time!" I told him I didn't do it, the conductors did. He said, "Well, Maggie, I know one thing, I'll never make a mistake like that again, but I was some surprised to see you sitting in that white car!"

Maggie's best friend was an Italian who was married to a West Indian. Her name was Marie, and she is the only white person I know personally who tried to pass for black. She plays an important role in Maggie's accounts of "color" and "race." Maggie made us call her "aunt" and Marie told everybody that she was Maggie's sister. She and Maggie used to pass for white together to spite the segregation laws. I venture to speculate that Maggie also thought she was spiting the people in our neighborhood for their attitudes towards Marie. They were passing for white the night in 1938 when Joe Louis knocked out the German, Max Schmeling.

Joe Louis

You know, Marie and I used to go downtown to the movies any time we wanted, and we would always sit smack in the middle of the white section, downstairs. That's when the colored had to sit up in the peanut gallery, yes, right up here in Philadelphia, they had a peanut gallery, up in the attic of the theatre, and all the colored folks had to sit up there. Well honey, I remember this night, they stopped the show right in the middle, and a man walked out on the stage and announced that Joe Louis had knocked out Max Schmeling. Marie and I jumped up and down and started hollering and screaming and clapping our hands and hugging each other. All of a sudden we looked around and all the white folks were looking at us like we were crazy. Wasn't nobody hollering and screaming but us and the other niggers in the peanut gallery! That was something, I tell you. We sat down fast but we were as happy as we could be. We couldn't wait to get home and celebrate with the rest of the folks. I don't think we even stayed long enough to see the rest of the picture, we were so happy.

Ruby Dee

MARY HAD A LITTLE LAMB

from *My One Good Nerve*

Mary had a little lamb
Whose fleece was white as snow
It hooked up with the baa-baa black sheep
And fleece wasn't white any mo'!

Folk

SOME PEOPLE JUST CAN'T TELL JOKES

These old Black men used to sit around and tell jokes all the time. They had told the same jokes so much that they decided to save themselves some energy and time by just giving the jokes numbers. So one would say "Ninety-four!" and they'd all just bust out laughing. Another one would say "Seventy-two!" and they'd all split their sides. Then one would yell "One hundred and six!" and they'd crack up.

A White man was sitting around with them, and after a few days, he decided he would join the fun, so he yelled out, "Eighty-seven!" Silence. No reaction. Blank stares. Another one o' the old Black men yelled, "One hundred and four!" They all laughed for minutes. The White man tried another number, but again they all just looked at him like he was crazy.

So when he got a chance, the White man pulled one o' the men to the side, and he say, "Why is it that when anybody else says a number, everybody just cracks up, but nobody laughs at my numbers?"

The old Black man says to him, "Some people just can't tell jokes."

Folk

AT LEAST I KNOW WHERE I AM

A White man was driving a car in the Deep South when he found out he was lost. He saw a Black man in the field plowing and asked him several questions concerning how to get to his destination. Of course the nigger didn't know. The White man finally became disgusted and yelled, "Nigger, you don't know *nothing!*"

The nigger replied, "At least I know where I am."

Mama Sez

Every dog has his day.

I been in sorrow's kitchen, and I licked the pot clean.

All de justice in de world ain't fastened up in de cotehouse.

No wonder they call it a *criminal* justice system. When it comes to blacks, that's what it is—*criminal.*

Some smart folks can't tell a rotten rail widout sittin' on it.

Beware of Greeks bearing gifts, black men whispering sweet nothings in yo' ears, and whites who declare, "One of my best friends is a Negro."

Sister to Sister

P-I-D actually means pelvic inflammatory disease, but some doctors in emergency rooms use it to refer to black women who come in with pain in the lower abdominal region to mean "pussy in distress." [Holloway, *Codes,* 32]

I let those folks I work for know they better straighten up and fly right.

He makes his living by putting on white folks. And they just love him!

He sure does know how to play possum.

Sticks and stones may break my bones,
But words will never hurt me.

These White girls all got jungle fever.

White folks think they so fine,
But they raggedy drawers stink just like mine.

In response to the question about how she felt that Elvis Presley had made millions on a record that she had originally recorded and on which she had made only a few dollars, Big Mama Thornton responded, "I'm still here to spend mine."

CHAPTER 11

"From the Back of the Bus to the Back of the National Priority List"

THE CIVIL RIGHTS MOVEMENT, INTEGRATION, AND BEYOND

There are many ways to approach the question of how we moved from
the back of the bus to the back of the national priority list in
just one generation.
—Bonnie Allen, *We Are Overcome*

The only period in African American life that matched the hopeful enthusiasm of Emancipation was the period of the Civil Rights Movement, when blacks and whites joined together to once and for all
eradicate racial segregation in this nation. Though there had been a few
hopeful events after the initial recognition that Emancipation did not bring
with it equal opportunities for African Americans to enjoy the promise of
American equality (a few political advancements, a few legal victories, a few
cracks in the harsh wall of segregation); the possibility of the full enjoyment
of the promise of American democracy remained an unattainable goal
from shortly after Emancipation until 1954. The decision of the Supreme
Court in *Brown v. Board of Education of Topeka* offered the first real hope that
the nation might commit itself to providing equal access to education for
all of its citizens, despite the fact that that decree had little effect on racial

segregation in Southern schools for several years. Then the 1955 Alabama boycott and the ensuing sit-ins, freedom rides, marches, and other demonstrations of the sixties and seventies inspired additional hope as troops of committed warriors marched to the South—warriors both black and white, American and foreign, young and old—who were willing to give their time, energy, money, and lives to fight until all of the barriers came down, from bathrooms and water fountains to schoolhouses and statehouses. The federal government demonstrated its commitment: federal troops were dispatched, calls of encouragement were made from the White House, new laws were enacted, blacks were placed in cabinet positions, Thurgood Marshall was appointed to the Supreme Court. Soon blacks were winning local elections and receiving appointments to positions never before attained in the private and the public sector. They were dominating sports and making advances in the media. Some positive images of blacks were appearing in advertisements and TV shows and films. Blacks were anchoring the news and melodramatizing in soap operas. Alex Haley's *Roots* became the highest-rated TV drama in history. Black plays were running on Broadway. A black Miss America reigned (at least for a short while). A black man became a serious candidate for President and a black governor was elected in the heart of the Confederacy. A contributing factor to the optimism of this period was the winning of independence by African and Caribbean nations, all of which contributed to the growth of the Black Power Movement with its focus on Black Nationalism, self-defense, and self-pride, symbolized in the sporting of Afro hairstyles and African garb. Nationally and internationally, it appeared that Blacks were no longer restricted to the back of the bus.

Overnight it seems, however, a harsh reality burst the bubble of the black community as the nation's commitment to racial equality was not only called into question, but, at times it appeared, absolutely lost. One after one, John, Malcolm X, Martin, and Bobby were gunned down.[1] Thurgood held out as long as he could, but health and age finally forced him to retire from the Supreme Court; and the black community lamented that the Black Codes[2] had been reinstated when he was replaced with Clarence

1. Laments and songs, such as "Abraham, Martin, and John," often referred to these leaders familiarly by their first names.

2. Laws passed in Southern legislatures during 1865–66 to control the former slaves, which represented the beginning of a series of actions that finally resulted in the absolute segregation and virtual disenfranchisement of Negroes in the South.

Thomas, whose conservative views and reportedly sexist behavior, made it clear that this swing voter on the Supreme Court wouldn't be swinging the way of blacks and women. The Congress and state legislatures from the East Coast to the West Coast were passing laws that effectively undermined a number of the gains made during the Civil Rights Movement. Once hopeful terms such as *liberal, affirmative action, feminism, inclusive, multiculturalism, welfare, food stamps, racial quotas, war on poverty,* and *political correctness* became the bad words of the nineties, worse even it seems than formerly negative words such as *racism, sexism, segregation,* and *exclusion.* Conservatives no longer attacked Negroes as inferior through calling them niggers, but they used loaded words that came to imply only Negroes, words such as *welfare mothers, welfare cheats, teenage pregnancy, inner city slums, projects, food stamps, criminals.* The backlash had set in; a movement was begun to restore America to its "former greatness," which implicitly signified a return to its exclusively white cultural and political domination. Not only was the Ku Klux Klan rising again, but hate groups, such as the Aryan Nations and Nazi Skinheads with their even more frightening agendas, were multiplying and preparing for war throughout America. As upwardly mobile blacks witnessed door after door being slammed in their faces and came up against glass ceilings, last hired/first fired, and redlining, they looked around them and realized that the majority of the black community had not profited from the Civil Rights Movement as they had. The social, educational, and economic situation of the majority of African Americans seemed in many cases to have worsened, especially when one looks at unemployment, the disproportionate incarceration of black men, broken families, illegitimate births, and inferior schools that serve a predominantly black student body. Aids, crack, and crime reigned supreme in black communities throughout the nation. The most dominant symbol of the true status of blacks in America in the nineties was the rash of attacks (some of them videotaped) upon blacks being pulled from their cars and sometimes beaten and killed by police. Unknown blacks in inner cities, famous stars in Hollywood, and even the noted physician and astronaut, Dr. Mae Jemison in Texas, were among the victims; but the most infamous attack of all, of course, was that on Rodney G. King, whose beating by white Los Angeles police officers became a familiar image all over the world of racist American police brutality. The subsequent acquittal of the police officers involved sparked the biggest riot since the explosions of the sixties. But that riot in Los Angeles did not spawn others across the country as it might have in earlier decades: Bertice Berry, incensed by the verdict, observes in *The World According to Me:* "I was enraged. I tried to riot, but I was in upstate New York and I couldn't find five other Black people." Seeing Rodney King writhing on the ground, witnessing the police officers walk out of court exonerated, and hearing people defend the beating and the acquittal on TV talk shows brought about the final awareness that the position and aspiration of blacks in America had seriously deteriorated.

Whether on the back of the bus or the back of the national priority list, however, African American women (and men) can be heard, not only complaining, but laughing about everything from the sit-ins to Rodney King. Some of the most hilarious commentary about this period of reversal comes from the biting satire of Bonnie Allen, from whose work I borrow the title of this chapter. Much of it comes from the poets and novelists who have come to prominence during these years. But most of it comes from the ordinary African American women who come together to reflect on how far we haven't come in this man's country as we move toward the twenty-first century.

Bonnie Allen

WE ARE OVERCOME

When I was growing up in Oakland, California, in the fifties and sixties, being an African-American was a simple issue. Neighborhoods were redlined. Employment was segregated. Banks discriminated. You never asked a police officer for assistance, for fear of death and dismemberment. Other than that, you were free. God bless America.

I've been trying to put my finger on when the racial situation got a little more complicated. It seems like it was sometime after Kunta Kinte discovered America but before Lee Atwater discovered Willie Horton. One minute we were all holding hands, Blacks and whites together, overcoming and what all. The next thing I know, the melanin-impaired segment of the population is signing a contract asking Newt Gingrich to erase the Congressional Black Caucus from the face of the earth and turn back the clock to the good old days of Ike, Doris Day, Pat Boone, Amos, Andy, and Beulah. (Please note: I have seen the good old days, and once was more than enough. I do not do windows.)

There are many ways to approach the question of how we moved from the back of the bus to the back of the national priority list in just one generation. If I was an academic, I would probably do it with a heavily footnoted, fact-filled, thoroughly detailed tome. Fortunately for you, nobody's ever accused me of being an academic.

I am taking a completely different tack to look at who we are and how we got to where we are (particularly since, on many levels, we hadn't planned to pass this way again). If after reading this book you still feel a niggling urge for more facts, more concrete data, more *just plain information,* go out and volunteer at a homeless shelter. Obviously, you have been floating too close to the glass ceiling and you need to get a quick blast of humanity before you tip over the edge.

Lorraine Hansberry

A RAISIN IN THE SUN

BENEATHA (*At the phone*) Hay lo . . . (*Pause, and a moment of recognition*) Well—when did you get back! . . . And how was it? . . . Of course I've missed you—in my way . . . This morning? No . . . house cleaning and all that and Mama hates it if I let people come over when the house is like this . . . You *have?* Well, that's different . . . What is it— Oh, what the hell, come on over . . . Right, see you then.

(*She hangs up*)

MAMA (*Who has listened vigorously, as is her habit*) Who is that you inviting over here with this house looking like this? You ain't got the pride you was born with!

BENEATHA Asagai doesn't care how houses look, Mama—he's an intellectual.

MAMA *Who?*

BENEATHA Asagai—Joseph Asagai. He's an African boy I met on campus. He's been studying in Canada all summer.

MAMA What's his name?

BENEATHA Asagai, Joseph. Ah-sah-guy . . . He's from Nigeria.

MAMA Oh, that's the little country that was founded by slaves way back . . .

BENEATHA No, Mama—that's Liberia.

MAMA I don't think I never met no African before.

BENEATHA Well, do me a favor and don't ask him a whole lot of ignorant questions about Africans. I mean, do they wear clothes and all that—

MAMA Well, now, I guess if you think we so ignorant 'round here maybe you shouldn't bring your friends here—

BENEATHA It's just that people ask such crazy things. All anyone seems to know about when it comes to Africa is Tarzan—

MAMA (*Indignantly*) Why should I know anything about Africa?

BENEATHA Why do you give money at church for the missionary work?

MAMA Well, that's to help save people.

BENEATHA You mean save them from *heathenism*—

MAMA (*Innocently*) Yes.

BENEATHA I'm afraid they need more salvation from the British and the French.

————

(BENEATHA, *herself profoundly disturbed, opens the door to admit a rather dramatic-looking young man with a large package*)

ASAGAI Hello, Alaiyo—

BENEATHA (*Holding the door open and regarding him with pleasure*) Hello . . . (*Long pause*) Well—come in. And please excuse everything. My mother was very upset about my letting anyone come here with the place like this.

ASAGAI (*Coming into the room*) You look disturbed too . . . Is something wrong?

BENEATHA (*Still at the door, absently*) Yes . . . we've all got acute ghetto-itus. (*She smiles and comes toward him, finding a cigarette and sitting*) So—sit down! How was Canada?

ASAGAI (*A sophisticate*) Canadian.

BENEATHA (*Looking at him*) I'm very glad you are back.

ASAGAI (*Looking back at her in turn*) Are you really?

BENEATHA Yes—very.

ASAGAI Why—you were quite glad when I went away. What happened?

BENEATHA You went away.

ASAGAI Ahhhhhhhh.

BENEATHA Before—you wanted to be so serious before there was time.

ASAGAI How much time must there be before one knows what one feels?

BENEATHA (*Stalling this particular conversation. Her hands pressed together, in a deliberately childish gesture*) What did you bring me?

ASAGAI (*Handing her the package*) Open it and see.

BENEATHA (*Eagerly opening the package and drawing out some records and the colorful robes of a Nigerian woman*) Oh, Asagai! . . . You got them for me! . . . How beautiful . . . and the records too! (*She lifts out the robes and runs to the mirror with them and holds the drapery up in front of herself*)

ASAGAI (*Coming to her at the mirror*) I shall have to teach you how to drape it properly. (*He flings the material about her for the moment and stands back to look at her*) Ah—Oh-pay-gay-day, oh-gbah-mu-shay. (*A Yoruba exclamation for admiration*) You wear it well . . . very well . . . mutilated hair and all.

BENEATHA (*Turning suddenly*) My hair—what's wrong with my hair?

ASAGAI (*Shrugging*) Were you born with it like that?

BENEATHA (*Reaching up to touch it*) No . . . of course not.

(*She looks back to the mirror, disturbed*)

ASAGAI (*Smiling*) How then?

BENEATHA You know perfectly well how . . . as crinkly as yours . . . that's how.

ASAGAI And it is ugly to you that way?

BENEATHA (*Quickly*) Oh, no—not ugly . . . (*More slowly, apologetically*) But it's so hard to manage when it's, well—raw.

ASAGAI And so to accommodate that—you mutilate it every week?

BENEATHA It's not mutilation!

ASAGAI (*Laughing aloud at her seriousness*) Oh . . . please! I am only teasing you because you are so very serious about these things. (*He stands back from her and folds his arms across his chest as he watches her pulling at her hair and frowning in the mirror*) Do you remember the first time you met me at school? . . . (*He laughs*) You came up to me and you said—and I thought you were the most serious little thing I had ever seen—you said: (*He imitates her*) "Mr. Asagai—I want very much to talk with you. About Africa. You see, Mr. Asagai, I am looking for my *identity!*"

(*He laughs*)

BENEATHA (*Turning to him, not laughing*) Yes—
   (*Her face is quizzical, profoundly disturbed*)
ASAGAI (*Still teasing and reaching out and taking her face in his hands and turning her profile to him*) Well . . . it is true that this is not so much a profile of a Hollywood queen as perhaps a queen of the Nile—(*A mock dismissal of the importance of the question*) But what does it matter? Assimilationism is so popular in your country.
BENEATHA (*Wheeling, passionately, sharply*) I am not an assimilationist!
ASAGAI (*The protest hangs in the room for a moment and* ASAGAI *studies her, his laughter fading*) Such a serious one. (*There is a pause*) So—you like the robes? You must take excellent care of them—they are from my sister's personal wardrobe.
BENEATHA (*With incredulity*) You—you sent all the way home—for me?
ASAGAI (*With charm*) For you—I would do much more . . . Well, that is what I came for. I must go.
BENEATHA Will you call me Monday?
ASAGAI Yes . . . We have a great deal to talk about. I mean about identity and time and all that.
BENEATHA Time?
ASAGAI Yes. About how much time one needs to know what one feels.
BENEATHA You never understood that there is more than one kind of feeling which can exist between a man and a woman—or, at least, there should be.
ASAGAI (*Shaking his head negatively but gently*) No. Between a man and a woman there need be only one kind of feeling. I have that for you . . . Now even . . . right this moment . . .
BENEATHA I know—and by itself—it won't do. I can find that anywhere.
ASAGAI For a woman it should be enough.
BENEATHA I know—because that's what it says in all the novels that men write. But it isn't. Go ahead and laugh—but I'm not interested in being someone's little episode in America or—(*With feminine vengeance*)—one of them! (ASAGAI *has burst into laughter again*) That's funny as hell, huh!
ASAGAI It's just that every American girl I have known has said that to me. White—black—in this you are all the same. And the same speech, too!
BENEATHA (*Angrily*) Yuk, yuk, yuk!

ASAGAI It's how you can be sure that the world's most liberated women are not liberated at all. You all talk about it too much!

(MAMA *enters and is immediately all social charm because of the presence of a guest*)

BENEATHA Oh—Mama—this is Mr. Asagai.

MAMA How do you do?

ASAGAI (*Total politeness to an elder*) How do you do, Mrs. Younger. Please forgive me for coming at such an outrageous hour on a Saturday.

MAMA Well, you are quite welcome. I just hope you understand that our house don't always look like this. (*Chatterish*) You must come again. I would love to hear all about—(*Not sure of the name*)—your country. I think it's so sad the way our American Negroes don't know nothing about Africa 'cept Tarzan and all that. And all that money they pour into these churches when they ought to be helping you people over there drive out them French and Englishmen done taken away your land.

(*The mother flashes a slightly superior look at her daughter upon completion of the recitation*)

ASAGAI (*Taken aback by this sudden and acutely unrelated expression of sympathy*) Yes . . . yes . . .

MAMA (*Smiling at him suddenly and relaxing and looking him over*) How many miles is it from here to where you come from?

ASAGAI Many thousands.

MAMA (*Looking at him as she would* WALTER) I bet you don't half look after yourself, being away from your mama either. I spec you better come 'round here from time to time and get yourself some decent home-cooked meals . . .

ASAGAI (*Moved*) Thank you. Thank you very much. (*They are all quiet, then*—) Well . . . I must go. I will call you Monday, Alaiyo.

MAMA What's that he call you?

ASAGAI Oh—"Alaiyo." I hope you don't mind. It is what you would call a nickname, I think. It is a Yoruba word. I am a Yoruba.

MAMA (*Looking at* BENEATHA) I—I thought he was from—

ASAGAI (*Understanding*) Nigeria is my country. Yoruba is my tribal origin

BENEATHA You didn't tell us what Alaiyo means . . . for all I know, you might be calling me Little Idiot or something . . .

ASAGAI Well . . . let me see . . . I do not know how just to explain it . . . The sense of a thing can be so different when it changes languages.

BENEATHA You're evading.

ASAGAI No—really it is difficult . . . *(Thinking)* It means . . . it means One for Whom Bread—Food—Is Not Enough. *(He looks at her)* Is that all right?

BENEATHA *(Understanding, softly)* Thank you.

MAMA *(Looking from one to the other and not understanding any of it)* Well . . . that's nice . . . You must come see us again—Mr.—

ASAGAI Ah-sah-guy . . .

MAMA Yes . . . Do come again.

ASAGAI Good-bye.

(He exits)

MAMA *(After him)* Lord, that's a pretty thing just went out here! *(Insinuatingly, to her daughter)* Yes, I guess I see why we done commence to get so interested in Africa 'round here. Missionaries my aunt Jenny!

(She exits)

BENEATHA Oh, Mama! . . .

(She picks up the Nigerian dress and holds it up to her in front of the mirror again. She sets the headdress on haphazardly and then notices her hair again and clutches at it and then replaces the headdress and frowns at herself. Then she starts to wriggle in front of the mirror as she thinks a Nigerian woman might)

Fannie Lou Hamer

SICK AND TIRED OF BEING SICK AND TIRED

from Kay Mills, *This Little Light of Mine*

[Civil Rights activist Fannie Lou Hamer had a sense of humor that was always evident. Below are a few of her sayings, the first her most famous one, the last sentence of which is engraved on her tombstone. To help the protesters deal with the very real dangers they faced, she also frequently created songs, adapting relevant lyrics to a familiar tune as she did in the second passage, sung in the tune of "Oh, Mary."]

I.

All my life I've been sick and tired. Now I'm sick and tired of being sick and tired.

II.

If you miss me in the Freedom fight
And you can't find me nowhere,
Come on over to the graveyard
I'll be buried over there.

III.

In response to the accusation, "Fannie Lou, you must be with the Left group," she retorted, "Yes, I've been left four hundred years. Left *out.*"

Michele Wallace

BLACK MACHO AND THE MYTH OF THE SUPERWOMAN

[In her often caustic account of the sexism of the black revolutionary movement, Michele Wallace issued some controversial indictments of black males, such as the two that follow.]

Come 1966, the black man had two pressing tasks before him: a white woman in every bed and a black woman under every heel.

And when the black man went as far as the adoration of his own genitals could carry him, his revolution stopped. A big Afro, a rifle, and a penis in good working order were not enough to lick the white man's world after all.

Ruby Dee

JACK AND JILL

from *My One Good Nerve*

Jack and Jill
Moved up on a hill
To get away from the slaughter
And things were going real swell until
A minority married their daughter.

Carolyn M. Rodgers

YEAH, I IS UH SHOOTIN OFF AT THE MOUTH, YEAH, I IS UH FAIRY TALE OR YEAH, I IS UH REVOLUTIONIST!

from *Songs of a Black Bird*

i is uh revolutionist
i has uh blue newport dashiki
and uh solid gold tiki.
my girlfriend, she got uh natural
and i does too
my mother, she go tuh breadbasket
ev'ry sat. morning
and we is saving to buy as many
Black businesses as we can.
i is uh revolutionist
cause i don't eat pig no mo
cause i dun read Fanon &
Malcolm and i quote LeRoi &
Karenga & my brotha—he be-

long to the Black Panther
Party!
yeah, i is uh revolutionist
and i belongs to uh revolutionary
group What GOT FuNDED(!) (and we is got some guns)
and was tellin the wite folks (out in whatchamacallit)
what we was gon do tuh them.
i gives the fist everytime i
see uh brotha, i speak swa-
hili 1/2% of the time and i
stay on the wite boys and
negroes case
i write poetry since day befo yesterday
and i use words like muthafucka & goddamn to show
that i'm bad—i listens to coltrane ev'ry morning
when i take my shower and i dream about sun-ra & the
cosmos, yeah, i is uh revolutionist, yeah YOU BET!
                    i IS uH ReVoLuTioNiST!!!
                              BOOOOOOOOOOM
Ladies & Gentlemen—We are sorry to announce that
our REVOLUTIONIST for this week's
installment of AESOP'S FAIRY TALES
just shot his mouth off with
his tongue. . . . . . .

Carolyn M. Rodgers

AND WHEN THE REVOLUTION CAME

(for Rayfield and Lillie and the whole rest)

from *Songs of a Black Bird*

and when the revolution came
the militants said
niggers wake up

you got to comb yo hair
the natural way
              and the church folks say oh yeah? sho 'nuff . . .
and they just kept on going to church
gittin on they knees and praying
and tithing and building and buying

and when the revolution came
the militants said
niggers you got to change
the way you dress
and the church folk say oh yeah?
              and they just kept on going to church
with they knit suits and flowery bonnets
and gittin on they knees and praying
and tithing and building and buying

and when the revolution came
the militants said
you got to give up
white folks and the
                  church folk say oh yeah? well?
never missed what we never had
and they jest kept on going to church
with they nice dresses and suits and
praying and building and buying

and when the revolution came
the militants say you got to give up
pork and eat only brown rice and
health food and the
                    church folks said uh hummmm
and they just kept on eating they chitterlings and
going to church and praying and tithing and
building and buying

and when the revolution came
the militants said
all you church going niggers
got to give up easter and christmas
and the bible
cause that's the white man's religion
and the church folks said well well well well well

and then the militants said we got to
build black institutions where our children
call each other sister and brother
and can grow beautiful, black and strong and grow in black grace
and the church folks said yes, lord Jesus we been calling each other
sister and brother a long time

and the militants looked around
after a while and said hey, look at all
these fine buildings we got scattered throughout
the black communities some of em built wid schools and nurseries
who do they belong to?

and the church folks said, yeah.
we been waiting fo you militants
to realize that the church is an eternal rock
now why don't you militants jest come on in
we been waiting for you
we can show you how to build
     anything that needs building
and while we're on our knees, at that.

Carolyn M. Rodgers

THE REVOLUTION IS RESTING

from *how i got ovah*

The revolution is dead said little willie to joe

just like a balloon thats been flying high the revolution's
gone and lost all its air and fell on the ground
Folks done stomped   it so its almost buried in the dirt

I tell you, Joe, little Willie said,
Black is as tired as it is beautiful.

The "revolutionaries" is whispering so low
you cant git over   or   under em
Looks like to me the women, pimps and dope fiends
is gon run it
I tell you, the revolution is dead, my man, dead.

   Naw, said Joe the revolution aint dead
Sometimes when you be flying in the sky in them airplanes,
you move so fast dont seem like you be moving at all/
And you go up and down hitting air pockets, you dig?
You be hitting hard like a boxer
like a heavyweight boxer that the wite folks got in
   a monkey ring
boxing wid a different person every hour of the day
now you'd be tired, Little Willie if they had you in that bag,
   wouldn't you?
You'd have to either stop fighting altogether, or ease up
   change or tighten your strategy or you'd fall out from
   pure exhaustion.

Naw Little Willie, Joe said
I looks at it this way, my man . . .
the Revolution aint dead
its tired,
and jest resting.

Opal J. Moore

GIT THAT GAL A RED DRESS: A CONVERSATION BETWEEN FEMALE FACULTY AT A STATE SCHOOL IN VIRGINIA

First Female Professor: [complaining of administrative policies that favor spending state funds on new buildings and new furniture rather than on supporting existing people and their needs]: They will spend six million dollars on a sports arena named after the President, but they won't be able to *afford* a security system, so that women will have a *new* place where they can be assaulted in dim hallways and locker rooms . . . and if a woman protests being assaulted, she will find she has no redress—

Second Female Professor: [taking on the voice of a cracker public relations staffer]: A red dress? Ya say she won't have a red dress? Sam! Git that little gal there a red dress! [Aside] Some thangs nevah change. There ain' no gal-problem cain't be solved with a red dress.

First Female Professor: She's the devil with the blue dress on.

Second Female Professor: Ah said a *red* dress. Blue don't suit 'em.

Ethel Morgan Smith

COME AND BE BLACK FOR ME

I dread January and February. January is Martin Luther Kings's birthday month, and February is Black History Month.

I'm the only African-American professor in my university department of fifty-odd faculty members. I reside in a world that is predominately white and male: a land grant, research state university with twentysomething thousand students, about 5 percent of whom are African-Americans. And it is those six weeks that everyone is looking for me, or rather, anyone who can come and be black for them.

Those six weeks begin after the holiday season. I come into my office early to work through my mail. My mailbox is overstuffed. Four other mail baskets have been placed on top of our boxes for me. I make two trips downstairs to the main office to collect it all. Most of the mail will be requests for me to represent "my people" for some worthwhile organization during the month of February and February only. Sometimes the tone is pleasant. I generally accept those. Most often the tone is not pleasant.

In my office I begin the process of grouping my mail into categories of "accept for sure," "decline for sure," "maybe," and "I'll get back to you." The first of my correspondence to go into the recycling bin is the letters that point out (if not in so many words) that their tax dollars pay my salary and they rightfully deserve a piece of me. The least I can do, these letter imply, is come and be black for them. The requests that conflict with events that I must attend because it's part of my job are the next to go into the bin. If those requests aren't too many, I write a note expressing my disappointment.

My phone rings. A pleasant woman from the arts council needs someone to attend her luncheon/bookclub meeting at her house. One of my colleagues, whom I haven't had the pleasure of meeting, gave her my telephone number. Her group is thinking of including a black writer on their reading list next year. She knows that I teach on Tuesdays and Thursdays. Wednesday is the day of the luncheon. I thank her and accept her pleasant invitation. It doesn't conflict with my calendar. I can be black that Wednesday.

The phone rings again. A student from last semester wants to talk to me about her grade. I give her my office hours and thank her for calling.

Someone knocks on my door. A graduate student, white male, wants me to be a member of his thesis committee. A portion of his writing will be on the impact of contemporary African-American women authors on American literature. He's a good student. I accept and thank him for thinking of me. I want to know when I can expect some of his work to begin reading.

Someone knocks on my door again. An African-American female student can't decide if she's angry with me or not. Last semester I thought she was being self-righteous (like I think many students are) when she screamed at me in class for selecting a novel whose protagonist, a black man, was married to a white woman. The student said that the protagonist wasn't really black because he was married to a white woman. I blew up at her in class and asked her who made her God of Blackness? I don't think I apologized to her. She wants to talk about what to do with the rest of her life. I suggest improving her grades. She leaves before I can thank her for coming.

The telephone rings. Someone is soliciting money for the United Way. I tell her that I already gave.

My mail is dwindling. Two more baskets. I begin a pile of work for photocopying. In this stack of mail three students have asked me to write letters of recommendation for graduate school and five more organizations have submitted requests for me to come (and be black). I'm getting hungry, but it's too much trouble to go out in the rain for lunch. I take a break and eat an apple and two rice cakes. I can't find any more food in my office. I continue to work through my mail. Two reject letters for two of my short stories are hidden in the pile of my junk mail. I'm disappointed. I'll decide what to do about them later.

The phone rings again. Wrong number.

Someone knocks on my door. It's two white students, male and female from last semester's African-American literature class. They (well he, since the male speaks for the female) liked my class and learned a lot, but thought that they would offer me some advice for the future so that my classes could be even better. He tells me that the black kids, all four of them, wanted to speak too much when I asked for comments or specific questions about the text. I remind them that everyone was given ample opportunity to speak. The student tells me that it was also annoying that "they" always sat together. I point out that all of the white students sat together as well. They leave before I can thank them for coming.

Someone knocks on my door. It's my colleague whose office is down the hall. He calls himself a folklorist. He too wants me to come and be black for his group even if it's in the month of March. He's sensitive to how I get exploited during black history month, but I should be thankful. I could be like him and never get exploited. I thank him but decline his offer.

Two years ago I did accept one of his offers. I was new. He coordinates one of the oldest conferences sponsored by the University. My folklorist colleague telephoned me at home that summer to extend an invitation to me to moderate the panel on "The African-American Experience in Film and Literature."

I go to the bathroom. Then I go downstairs to make photocopies and drop off some mail. The staff gives me candy. I'm glad. My rice cakes and apple lunch has left me hungry. After the candy I go back to my office and drink a tall glass of water.

The phone rings. It's the bookstore. Two of my required texts are out of print, but due to be rereleased next term. I tell her that I'll get back with substitutes. I'll have to rethink my syllabus. When I first started teaching African-American literature I began my classes by telling the students how I couldn't get at least two of the required texts every semester. What did they think about that? I stopped when students wrote on my evaluations that they wished I'd select books that they could get without problems. It was part of my job to do so. They thought that I should take some responsibility.

A week after my folklorist colleague called to invite me to participate in his conference, he telephoned again. This time he wanted to point out exactly what my job was—I was to keep time for the presenters so that the conference would run according to schedule. And I was to be lively. He said the real work of the conference was done by the scholars who were presenting papers.

Someone knocks on my door. A white male student with a long red ponytail wants to bow to me for the rest of his life. I gave him Toni Morrison's

Sula semester before last. He has read all of Morrison's books now. I tell him he has discovered one of America's greatest writers. I like him now that he knows I'll only discuss literature. I thank him for coming.

Someone knocks on my door. An African-American female student wants to know why I always pick novels that make the "brothers" look bad, books like Alice Walker's *Third Life of Grange Copeland*. I tell her that I'm sure Ms. Walker didn't have her "brothers" in mind when she wrote the novel. I thank her for coming by.

My telephone rings. Another request to come and speak. I decline. It's a conflict.

I file some of my papers. I find a box of raisins. They are old. I eat them anyway and drink another glass of water.

The panel I moderated for my colleague had an active audience of ten members hailing from California, Connecticut, New Mexico, Tennessee, Vermont, and Virginia. Three presenters were scheduled to read papers. One presented. Two were absent. My colleague wasn't present after he'd promised that he'd be there because the conference was really taking a chance by including a panel on "my people." The one presenter's paper was about playing the "dozens" in the film *White Men Can't Jump*. The paper was titled "Fresh Toast and Jam: New Images of the 'Dozens.' "

Someone knocks on my door. A friendly colleague and I exchange holiday stories. And we gossip about the newest divorce in the department.

Someone knocks on my door. Two African-American male students from last semester tell me that they didn't appreciate me calling "brother Mike" a criminal in class last semester. I point out that technically Mike Tyson is a criminal. I thank them for dropping by.

The phone rings. The audio visual division of the library has just received *Roots—The Next Generation*. I could expect the original *Roots* any day now. I thank the caller.

As a moderator I had to make the panel work with one presenter whose paper was based on a movie I had not seen. I introduced myself and talked about the kind of issues I come upon in my classes on African-American literature. I talked about texts and how students responded to some of them. I then asked each person to introduce him/herself and talk about their interest in the subject. A retired literature professor, from Virginia, wanted me to know that he was glad to be there and happy that I was moderating the panel, and that he didn't have a racist bone in his body. He'd climbed mountains with pure Africans and was proud to call them friends. I welcomed him to our University and thanked him for taking part in the conference.

Someone knocks on my door. It's another colleague, a white male who's fascinated by Africa and wants me to know that if I have any interest in going to see my homeland, he is the man to help me get there. I tell him that Alabama is my homeland. He leaves before I can thank him for coming.

The phone rings. One of the secretaries wants to know which committee of the graduate faculty council I'll be willing to serve on. I'd forgotten to give her my form. I apologize and ask which committee met the least during the term. She tells me and I agree to serve on that committee.

Someone knocks on my door. A white female student returns three books of poetry by Gwendolyn Brooks, Lucille Clifton, and Nikki Giovanni. She enjoyed them and wants to borrow more. I point to the poetry section of my library. We exchange a few pleasantries. She thanks me and leaves.

The audience blasted the presenter for using the film *White Men Can't Jump* to make her point. Only one member of the audience had seen this film. They were sure there were more sophisticated ways of her presenting her scholarship. They weren't sure that a film called *White Men Can't Jump* was scholarly enough. I thought I did a good job of not allowing everyone to attack her at the same time.

Someone knocks on my door. An African-American female student from semester before last wants me to write a letter of recommendation for her. She's applying for jobs. I ask if she had considered graduate school. She says not now. She is tired of school. She wants to live in a city. I ask her to drop off her resume and addresses of places to send my letter. She thanks me. I wish her well.

My telephone rings. A student from last semester didn't receive a grade from me. I check my record and tell the student that I turned in a grade.

If she wants me to call records and admissions I'd be happy to do so. She'll get back to me after she speaks with her adviser. She thanks me for my help.

Someone knocks on my door. A white male student from last semester wants me to write him a letter of recommendation. I point out to him that he received a C in my class. He tells me that was the best grade he received. I ask what he wants me to say in my letter. He thanks me and leaves.

In my mail there are five other requests for me to come and speak. I stack all of the catalogues for new textbooks in a pile. Will go through them later. I check my calendar to consider the five other requests. I accept two.

I go to the bathroom and wash my face.

Someone knocks on my door. An African-American male student wants to know why I taught a book like *Giovanni's Room*. I tell him that James Baldwin is one of the most important writers of our time, and that I know of no other book written with more dignity and honesty. The student tells me teaching books about homosexuality should be against the law. I tell him we're all better for reading *Giovanni's Room*. He leaves before I can thank him for coming.

The presenter, close to tears, told the audience that she's really an apple—white on the inside and red on the outside—Native American. And the only reason she was working in African-American literature was because Native American literature was too painful for her. The audience was silent. The retired professor from Virginia shook his head. I spoke longer than I should have about the main problem I have with teaching African-American literature, that students have such a problem placing texts in a historical context. The presenter excused herself. The audience and I continued to talk about history and African-American literature.

Someone knocks on my door. A student, white male, wants a list of the books I'll be teaching in the spring. He tells me that everyone in his family is racist and this is the first opportunity he has had to learn about blacks. I tell him I'm glad he's learning. I give him the list and thank him for coming.

Someone knocks on my door. An African-American female student from last semester who owes me a paper wants me to know that she's happy that I'm on the faculty here. She identifies with me since I embrace feminism and appear to be a "real sister." I tell her the way I dress and wear my hair is purely fashion. I want to know when I can expect her paper. She says soon and leaves before I can thank her for coming.

Someone knocks on my door. My boss wants me to be part of a new task force on diversity. I accept and thank him for thinking of me.

I have to get home. It's the beginning of come-and-be-black-for-me season and I need my rest.

Ann Petry

THE BONES OF LOUELLA BROWN

Old Peabody and Young Whiffle, partners in the firm of Whiffle and Peabody, Incorporated, read with mild interest the first article about Bedford Abbey which appeared in the Boston papers. But each day thereafter the papers printed one or two items about this fabulous project. And as they learned more about it, Old Peabody and Young Whiffle became quite excited.

For Bedford Abbey was a private chapel, a chapel which would be used solely for the weddings and funerals of the Bedford family—the most distinguished family in Massachusetts.

What was more important, the Abbey was to become the final resting-place for all the Bedfords who had passed on to greater glory and been buried in the family plot in Yew Tree Cemetery. These long-dead Bedfords were to be exhumed and reburied in the crypt under the marble floor of the chapel. Thus Bedford Abbey would be officially opened with the most costly and the most elaborate funeral service ever held in Boston.

As work on the Abbey progressed, Young Whiffle (who was seventy-five) and Old Peabody (who was seventy-nine) frowned and fumed while they searched the morning papers for some indication of the date of this service.

Whiffle and Peabody were well aware that they owned the oldest and the most exclusive undertaking firm in the city; and having handled the funerals of most of the Bedfords, they felt that, in all logic, this stupendous funeral ceremony should be managed by their firm. But they were uneasy.

For Governor Bedford (he was still called Governor though it had been some thirty years since he held office) was unpredictable. And most unfortunately, the choice of undertakers would be left to the Governor, for the Abbey was his brain-child.

A month dragged by, during which Young Whiffle and Old Peabody set an all-time record for nervous tension. They snapped at each other, and nibbled their fingernails, and cleared their throats, with the most appalling regularity.

It was well into June before the Governor's secretary finally telephoned. He informed Old Peabody, who quivered with delight, that Governor Bedford had named Whiffle and Peabody as the undertakers for the service which would be held at the Abbey on the twenty-first of June.

When the Bedford exhumation order was received, Old Peabody produced an exhumation order for the late Louella Brown. It had occurred to him that this business of exhuming the Bedfords offered an excellent opportunity for exhuming Louella, with very little additional expense. Thus he could rectify a truly terrible error in judgment made by his father, years ago.

"We can pick 'em all up at once," Old Peabody said, handing the Brown exhumation order to Young Whiffle. "I want to move Louella Brown out of Yew Tree Cemetery. We can put her in one of the less well-known burying places on the outskirts of the city. That's where she should have been put in the first place. But we will, of course, check up on her as usual."

"Who was Louella Brown?" asked Young Whiffle.

"Oh, she was once our laundress. Nobody of importance," Old Peabody said carelessly. Though as he said it he wondered why he remembered Louella with such vividness.

Later in the week, the remains of all the deceased Bedfords, and of the late Louella Brown, arrived at the handsome establishment of Whiffle and Peabody. Though Young Whiffle and Old Peabody were well along in years, their research methods were completely modern. Whenever possible they checked on the condition of their former clients and kept exact records of their findings.

The presence of so many former clients at one time—a large number of Bedfords and Louella Brown—necessitated the calling in of Stuart Reynolds. He was a Harvard medical student who did large-scale research jobs for the firm, did them well, and displayed a most satisfying enthusiasm for his work.

It was near closing time when Reynolds arrived at the imposing brick structure which housed Whiffle and Peabody, Incorporated.

Old Peabody handed Reynolds a sheaf of papers and tried to explain about Louella Brown, as tactfully as possible.

"She used to be our laundress," he said. "My mother was very fond of Louella, and insisted that she be buried in Yew Tree Cemetery." His father had consented—grudgingly, yes, but his father should never have agreed to it. It had taken the careful discriminatory practices of generations of Peabodys, undertakers like himself, to make Yew Tree Cemetery what it was today—the final home of Boston's wealthiest and most aristocratic families. Louella's grave had been at the very tip edge of the cemetery in 1902, in a very undesirable place. But just last month he had noticed, with dismay, that due to the enlargement of the cemetery, over the years, she now lay in one of the choicest spots—in the exact center.

Before Old Peabody spoke again he was a little disconcerted, for he suddenly saw Louella Brown with an amazing sharpness. It was just as though she had entered the room—a quick-moving little woman, brown of skin and black of hair, and with very erect posture.

He hesitated a moment and then he said, "She was—uh—uh—a colored woman. But in spite of that, we will do the usual research."

"Colored?" said Young Whiffle sharply. "Did you say 'colored'? You mean a black woman? And buried in Yew Tree Cemetery?" His voice rose in pitch.

"Yes," Old Peabody said. He lifted his shaggy eyebrows at Young Whiffle as an indication that he was not to discuss the matter further. "Now, Reynolds, be sure and lock up when you leave."

Reynolds accepted the papers from Old Peabody and said, "Yes, sir. I'll lock up." And in his haste to get at the job he left the room so fast that he stumbled over his own feet and very nearly fell. He hurried because he was making a private study of bone structure in the Caucasian female as against the bone structure in the female of the darker race, and Louella Brown was an unexpected research plum.

Old Peabody winced as the door slammed. "The terrible enthusiasm of the young," he said to Young Whiffle.

"He comes cheap," Young Whiffle said gravely. "And he's polite enough."

They considered Reynolds in silence for a moment.

"Yes, of course," Old Peabody said. "You're quite right. He is an invaluable young man and his wages are adequate for his services." He hoped Young Whiffle noticed how neatly he had avoided repeating the phrase "he comes cheap."

" 'Adequate,' " murmured Young Whiffle. "Yes, yes, 'adequate.' Certainly. And invaluable." He was still murmuring both words as he accompanied Old Peabody out of the building.

Fortunately for their peace of mind, neither Young Whiffle nor Old Peabody knew what went on in their workroom that night. Though they found out the next morning to their very great regret.

It so happened that the nearest approach to royalty in the Bedford family had been the Countess of Castro (nee Elizabeth Bedford). Though neither Old Peabody nor Young Whiffle knew it, the countess and Louella Brown had resembled each other in many ways. They both had thick glossy black hair. Neither woman had any children. They had both died in 1902, when in their early seventies, and been buried in Yew Tree Cemetery within two weeks of each other.

Stuart Reynolds did not know this either, or he would not have worked in so orderly a fashion. As it was, once he entered the big underground workroom of Whiffle and Peabody, he began taking notes on the condition of each Bedford, and then carefully answered the questions on the blanks provided by Old Peabody.

He finished all the lesser Bedfords, then turned his attention to the countess.

When he opened the coffin of the countess, he gave a little murmur of pleasure. "A very neat set of bones," he said. "A small woman, about seventy. How interesting! All of her own teeth, no repairs."

Having checked the countess, he set to work on Louella Brown. As he studied Louella's bones he said, "Why how extremely interesting!" For here was another small-boned woman, about seventy, who had all of her own teeth. As far as he could determine from a hasty examination, there was no way of telling the countess from Louella.

"But the hair! How stupid of me. I can tell them apart by the hair. The colored woman's will be—" But it wasn't. Both women had the same type of hair.

He placed the skeleton of the Countess of Castro on a long table, and right next to it he drew up another long table, and placed on it the skeleton of the late Louella Brown. He measured both of them.

"Why, it's sensational!" he said aloud. And as he talked to himself he grew more and more excited. "It's a front page story. I bet they never even knew each other and yet they were the same height, had the same bone structure. One white, one black, and they meet here at Whiffle and Peabody after all these years—the laundress and the countess. It's more than front page news, why, it's the biggest story of the year—"

Without a second's thought Reynolds ran upstairs to Old Peabody's office and called the *Boston Record*. He talked to the night city editor. The man sounded bored, but he listened. Finally he said, "You got the bones of both these ladies out on tables, and you say they're just alike. Okay, be right over—"

Thus two photographers and the night city editor of the *Boston Record* invaded the sacred premises of Whiffle and Peabody, Incorporated. The night city editor was a tall, lank individual, and very hard to please. He no sooner asked Reynolds to pose in one position than he had him moved, in front of the tables, behind them, at the foot, at the head. Then he wanted the tables moved. The photographers cursed audibly as they dragged the tables back and forth, turned them around, sideways, lengthways. And still the night city editor wasn't satisfied.

Reynolds shifted position so often that he might have been on a merry-go-round. He registered surprise, amazement, pleasure. Each time the night city editor objected.

It was midnight before the newspapermen said, "Okay, boys, this is it." The photographers took their pictures quickly and then started picking up their equipment.

The newspaperman watched the photographers for a moment, then he strolled over to Reynolds and said, "Now—uh—sonny, which one of these ladies is the countess?"

Reynolds started to point at one of the tables, stopped, and let out a frightened exclamation. "Why—" His mouth stayed open. "Why—I don't know!" His voice was suddenly frantic. "You've mixed them up! You've moved them around so many times I can't tell which is which—nobody could tell—"

The night city editor smiled sweetly and started for the door.

Reynolds followed him, clutched at his coat sleeve. "You've got to help me. You can't go now," he said. "Who moved the tables first? Which one of you—" The photographers stared and then started to grin. The night city editor smiled again. His smile was even sweeter than before.

"I wouldn't know, sonny," he said. He gently disengaged Reynolds' hand from his coat sleeve. "I really wouldn't know—"

It was, of course, a front page story. But not the kind that Reynolds had anticipated. There were photographs of that marble masterpiece, Bedford Abbey, and the caption under it asked the question that was later to seize the imagination of the whole country: "Who will be buried under the marble floor of Bedford Abbey on the twenty-first of June—the white countess or the black laundress?"

There were photographs of Reynolds, standing near the long tables, pointing at the bones of both ladies. He was quoted as saying: "You've moved them around so many times I can't tell which is which—nobody could tell—"

When Governor Bedford read the *Boston Record,* he promptly called Whiffle and Peabody on the telephone and cursed them with such violence that Young Whiffle and Old Peabody grew visibly older and grayer as they listened to him.

Shortly after the Governor's call, Stuart Reynolds came to offer an explanation to Whiffle and Peabody. Old Peabody turned his back and refused to speak to, or look at, Reynolds. Young Whiffle did the talking. His eyes were so icy cold, his face so frozen, that he seemed to emit a freezing vapor as he spoke.

Toward the end of his speech, Young Whiffle was breathing hard. "The house," he said, "the honor of this house, years of working, of building a reputation, all destroyed. We're ruined, ruined—" he choked on the word. "Ah," he said, waving his hands, "Get out, get out, get out, before I kill you—"

The next day the Associated Press picked up the story of this dreadful mix-up and wired it throughout the country. It was a particularly dull pe riod for news, between wars so to speak, and every paper in the United States carried the story on its front page.

In three days' time Louella Brown and Elizabeth, Countess of Castro, were as famous as movie stars. Crowds gathered outside the mansion in which Governor Bedford lived; still larger and noisier crowds milled in the street in front of the offices of Whiffle and Peabody.

As the twenty-first of June approached, people in New York and London and Paris and Moscow asked each other the same question: Who would be buried in Bedford Abbey, the countess or the laundress?

Meanwhile Young Whiffle and Old Peabody talked, desperately seeking something, anything, to save the reputation of Boston's oldest and most expensive undertaking establishment. Their talk went around and around in circles.

"Nobody knows which set of bones belongs to Louella and which to the countess. Why do you keep saying that it's Louella Brown who will be buried in the Abbey?" snapped Old Peabody.

"Because the public likes the idea," Young Whiffle snapped back. "A hundred years from now they'll say it's the black laundress who lies in the crypt at Bedford Abbey. And that we put her there. We're ruined—ruined—ruined—" he muttered. "A black washerwoman!" he said, wringing his hands. "If only she had been white—"

"She might have been Irish," said Old Peabody coldly. He was annoyed to find how very clearly he could see Louella. With each passing day her presence became sharper, more strongly felt. "And a Catholic. That would have been equally as bad. No, it would have been worse. Because the Catholics would have insisted on a mass, in Bedford Abbey, of all places! Or she might have been a foreigner—a—a—Russian. Or, God forbid, a Jew!"

"Nonsense," said Young Whiffle pettishly. "A black washerwoman is infinitely worse than anything you've mentioned. People are saying it's some kind of trick, that we're proving there's no difference between the races. Oh, we're ruined—ruined—ruined—" Young Whiffle moaned.

As a last resort, Old Peabody and Young Whiffle went to see Stuart Reynolds. They found him in the shabby rooming house where he lived.

"You did this to us," Old Peabody said to Reynolds. "Now you figure out a way, an acceptable way, to determine which of those women is which or I'll—"

"We will wait while you think," said Young Whiffle, looking out of the window.

"I *have* thought," Reynolds said wildly. "I've thought until I'm nearly crazy."

"Think some more," snapped Old Peabody, glaring.

Peabody and Whiffle seated themselves on opposite sides of the small room. Young Whiffle glared out of the window and Old Peabody glared at Reynolds. And Reynolds couldn't decide which was worse.

"You knew her, knew Louella, I mean," said Reynolds. "Can't you just say, this one's Louella Brown, pick either one, because, the body, I mean, Whiffle and Peabody, they, she was embalmed there—"

"Don't be a fool!" said Young Whiffle, his eyes on the windowsill, glaring at the windowsill, annihilating the windowsill. "Whiffle and Peabody would be ruined by such a statement, more ruined than they are at present."

"How?" demanded Reynolds. Ordinarily he wouldn't have argued but being shut up in the room with this pair of bony-fingered old men had turned him desperate. "Why? After all, who could dispute it? You could get the embalmer, Mr. Ludastone, to say he remembered the neck bone, or the position of the foot—" His voice grew louder. "If you identify the black woman first, nobody'll question it—"

"Lower your voice," said Old Peabody.

Young Whiffle stood up and pounded on the dusty windowsill. "Because black people, bodies, I mean the black dead—"

He took a deep breath. Old Peabody said, "Now relax, Mr Whiffle, relax. Remember your blood pressure."

"There's such a thing as a color line," shrieked Young Whiffle. "You braying idiot, you, we're not supposed to handle colored bodies, the colored dead, I mean the dead colored people, in our establishment. We'd never live down a statement like that. We're fortunate that so far no one has asked how the corpse of Louella Brown, a colored laundress, got on the premises in 1902. Louella was a special case but they'd say that we—"

"But she's already there!" Reynolds shouted. "You've got a colored body or bones, I mean, there now. She *was* embalmed there. She *was* buried in Yew Tree Cemetery. Nobody's said anything about it."

Old Peabody held up his hand for silence. "Wait," he said. "There is a bare chance—" He thought for a moment. He found that his thinking was quite confused, he felt he ought to object to Reynolds' suggestion but he didn't know why. Vivid images of Louella Brown, wearing a dark dress with white collars and cuffs, added to his confusion.

Finally, he said, "We'll do it, Mr. Whiffle. It's the only way. And we'll explain it with dignity. Speak of Louella's long service, true she did laundry for others, too, but we won't mention that, talk about her cheerfulness and devotion, emphasize the devotion, burying her in Yew Tree Cemetery was a kind of reward for service, payment of a debt of gratitude, remember that phrase, 'debt of gratitude.' And call in—" he swallowed hard, "the press. Especially that animal from the *Boston Record,* who wrote the story up the first time. We might serve some of the old brandy and cigars. Then Mr. Ludastone can make his statement. About the position of the foot, he remembers it—" He paused and glared at Reynolds. "And as for you! You needn't think we'll ever permit you inside our doors again, dead or alive."

Gray-haired, gray-skinned Clarence Ludastone, head embalmer for Whiffle and Peabody, dutifully identified one set of bones as being those of the late Louella Brown. Thus the identity of the countess was firmly established. Half the newspapermen in the country were present at the time. They partook generously of Old Peabody's best brandy and enthusiastically smoked his finest cigars. The last individual to leave was the weary gentleman who represented the *Boston Record.*

He leaned against the doorway as he spoke to Old Peabody. "Wonderful yarn," he said. "Never heard a better one. Congratulations—" And he drifted down the hall.

Because of all the stories about Louella Brown and the Countess of Castro, most of the residents of Boston turned out to watch the funeral cortege of the Bedfords on the twenty-first of June. The ceremony that took place at Bedford Abbey was broadcast over a national hook-up, and the news services wired it around the world, complete with pictures.

Young Whiffle and Old Peabody agreed that the publicity accorded the occasion was disgraceful. But their satisfaction over the successful ending of what had been an extremely embarrassing situation was immense. They had great difficulty preserving the solemn mien required of them during the funeral service.

Young Whiffle and Old Peabody both suffered slight heart attacks when they saw the next morning's edition of the *Boston Record.* For there on the front page was a photograph of Mr. Ludastone, and over it in bold, black type were the words "child embalmer." The article which accompanied the picture, said, in part:

> Who is buried in the crypt at Bedford Abbey? The countess, or Louella the laundress? We ask because Mr. Clarence Ludastone, the suave gentleman who is head embalmer for Whiffle and Peabody, could not possibly identify the bones of Louella Brown, despite his look of great age. Mr. Ludastone, according to his birth certificate (which is reproduced on this page) was only two years old at the time of Louella's death. This reporter has questioned many of Boston's oldest residents but he has, as yet, been unable to locate anyone who remembers a time when Whiffle and Peabody employed a two-year-old child as embalmer . . .

Eighty-year-old Governor Bedford very nearly had apoplexy when he saw the *Boston Record*. He hastily called a press conference. He said that he would personally, publicly (in front of the press), identify the countess, if it was the countess. He remembered her well, for he had been only thirty-five when she died. He would know instantly if it were she.

Two days later the Governor stalked down the center aisle of that marble gem—Bedford Abbey. He was followed by a veritable hive of newsmen and photographers. Old Peabody and Young Whiffle were waiting for them just inside the crypt.

The Governor peered at the interior of the opened casket and drew back. He forgot the eager-eared newsmen, who surrounded him, pressed against him. When he spoke he reverted to the simple speech of his early ancestors.

"Why they be nothing but bones here!" he said. "Nothing but bones! Nobody could tell who this be."

He turned his head, unable to take a second look. He, too, someday, not too far off, how did a man buy immortality, he didn't want to die, bones rattling inside a casket—ah, no! He reached for his pocket handkerchief, and Young Whiffle thrust a freshly laundered one into his hand.

Governor Bedford wiped his face, his forehead. But not me, he thought. I'm alive. I can't die. It won't happen to me. And inside his head a voice kept saying over and over, like the ticking of a clock: It will. It can. It will. It can. It will.

"You were saying, Governor," prompted the tall thin newsman from the *Boston Record*.

"I don't know!" Governor Bedford shouted angrily. "I don't know! Nobody could tell which be the black laundress and which the white countess from looking at their bones."

"Governor, Governor," protested Old Peabody. "Governor, ah—calm yourself, great strain—" And leaning forward, he hissed in the Governor's reddening ear, "Remember the press, don't say that, don't make a statement, don't commit yourself—"

"Stop spitting in my ear!" roared the Governor. "Get away! And take your blasted handkerchief with you." He thrust Young Whiffle's handkerchief inside Old Peabody's coat, up near the shoulder. "It stinks, it stinks of death." Then he strode out of Bedford Abbey, muttering under his breath as he went.

The Governor's statement went around the world, in direct quotes. So did the photographs of him, peering inside the casket, his mouth open, his eyes staring. There were still other photographs that showed him charging down the center aisle of Bedford Abbey, head down, shoulders thrust forward, even the back of his neck somehow indicative of his fury. Cartoonists showed him, in retreat, words issuing from his shoulder blades, "Nobody could tell who this be—the black laundress or the white countess—"

Sermons were preached about the Governor's statement, editorials were written about it, and Congressmen made long-winded speeches over the radio. The Mississippi legislature threatened to declare war on the sovereign State of Massachusetts because Governor Bedford's remarks were an unforgiveable insult to believers in white supremacy.

Many radio listeners became completely confused and, believing that both ladies were still alive, sent presents to them, sometimes addressed in care of Governor Bedford, and sometimes addressed in care of Whiffle and Peabody.

Whiffle and Peabody kept the shades drawn in their establishment. They scuttled through the streets each morning, hats pulled low over their eyes, en route to their offices. They would have preferred to stay at home (with the shades drawn) but they agreed it was better to act as though nothing had happened. So they spent ten hours a day on the premises as was their custom, though there was absolutely no business.

Young Whiffle paced the floor, hours at a time, wringing his hands, and muttering, "A black washerwoman! We're ruined—ruined—ruined—!"

Old Peabody found himself wishing that Young Whiffle would not speak of Louella with such contempt. In spite of himself he kept dreaming about her. In the dream, she came quite close to him, a small, brown woman with merry eyes. And after one quick look at him, she put her hands on her hips, threw her head back and laughed and laughed.

He was quite unaccustomed to being laughed at, even in a dream; and the memory of Louella's laughter lingered with him for hours after he woke up. He could not forget the smallest detail of her appearance: how her shoulders shook as she laughed, and that her teeth were very white and evenly spaced.

He thought to avoid this recurrent visitation by sitting up all night, by drinking hot milk, by taking lukewarm baths. Then he tried the exact opposite—he went to bed early, drank cold milk, took scalding hot baths. To no avail. Louella Brown still visited him, each and every night.

Thus it came about that one morning when Young Whiffle began his ritual muttering: "A black washerwoman—we're ruined—ruined—ruined—" Old Peabody shouted: "Will you stop that caterwauling? One would think the Loch Ness monster lay in the crypt at Bedford Abbey." He could see Louella Brown standing in front of him, laughing, laughing. And he said, "Louella Brown was a neatly built little woman, a fine woman, full of laughter. I remember her well. She was a gentlewoman. Her bones will do no injury to the Governor's damned funeral chapel."

It was a week before Young Whiffle actually heard what Old Peabody was saying, though Peabody made this same outrageous statement, over and over again.

When Young Whiffle finally heard it, there was a quarrel, a violent quarrel, caused by the bones of Louella Brown—that quick-moving, merry little woman.

By the end of the day, the partnership was dissolved, and the ancient and exclusive firm of Whiffle and Peabody, Incorporated, went out of business.

Old Peabody retired; after all, there was no firm he could consider associating with. Young Whiffle retired, too, but he moved all the way to California, and changed his name to Smith, in the hope that no man would ever discover he had once been a member of that blackguardly firm of Whiffle and Peabody, Incorporated.

Despite his retirement, Old Peabody found that Louella Brown still haunted his dreams. What was worse, she took to appearing before him during his waking moments. After a month of this, he went to see Governor Bedford. He had to wait an hour before the Governor came downstairs, walking slowly, leaning on a cane.

Old Peabody wasted no time being courteous. He went straight to the reason for his visit. "I have come," he said stiffly, "to suggest to you that you put the names of both those women on the marble slab in Bedford Abbey."

"Never," said the Governor. "Never, never, never!"

He is afraid to die, Old Peabody thought, eying the Governor. You can always tell by the look on their faces. He shrugged his shoulders. "Every man dies alone, Governor," he said brutally. "And so it is always best to be at peace with this world and any other world that follows it, when one dies."

Old Peabody waited a moment. The Governor's hands were shaking. Fear or palsy, he wondered. Fear, he decided. Fear beyond the question of a doubt.

"Louella Brown visits me every night and frequently during the day," Peabody said softly. "I am certain that unless you follow my suggestion, she will also visit you." A muscle in the Governor's face started to twitch. Peabody said, "When your bones finally lie in the crypt in your marble chapel, I doubt that you want to hear the sound of Louella's laughter ringing in your ears—till doomsday."

"Get out!" said the Governor, shuddering. "You're crazy as a loon."

"No," Old Peabody said firmly. "Between us, all of us, we have managed to summon Louella's spirit." And he proceeded to tell the Governor how every night, in his dreams, and sometimes during the day when he was awake, Louella came to stand beside him, and look up at him and laugh. He told it very well, so well in fact that for a moment he thought he saw Louella standing in the room, right near Governor Bedford's left shoulder.

The Governor turned, looked over his shoulder. And then he said, slowly and reluctantly, and with the uneasy feeling that he could already hear Louella's laughter, "All right." He paused, took a deep unsteady breath. "What do you suggest I put on the marble slab in the crypt?"

After much discussion, and much writing, and much tearing up of what had been written, they achieved a satisfactory epitaph. If you ever go to Boston and visit Bedford Abbey you will see for yourself how Old Peabody propitiated the bones of the late Louella Brown. For after these words were carved on the marble slab, Louella ceased to haunt Old Peabody:

HERE LIES

ELIZABETH, COUNTESS OF CASTRO

OR

LOUELLA BROWN, GENTLEWOMAN
1830 1902
REBURIED IN BEDFORD ABBEY JUNE 21, 1947

"They both wore the breastplate of faith and love;
And for a helmet, the hope of salvation."

Lani Guinier

FEMALE GENTLEMAN

[The following is the beginning and the ending of Professor Guinier's introduction of Professor Mari Matsuda, who was speaking at a symposium on Race, Gender and Free Speech held in Philadelphia on March 24 and 25, 1994.]

When I was a law student at Yale Law School, I had a white male professor in Business Units One (the name Yale gave to Corporations) who called each of us: "gentleman." Every morning at ten minutes after the hour, he would enter the classroom and greet the upturned faces: "Good morning gentlemen." He explained this ritual the first day. He was a creature of habit. He had been teaching for many years. For him, "gentlemen" was a neutral term, an asexual term. After all, law school trained lawyers to be "gentlemen of the bar" who have neither a race nor a gender. In his mind, the term was a form of honorific. If we were not already, we would all soon become gentlemen.

As a "female gentleman" of Business Units One, I never once spoke out. I never once raised my hand to ask a question. I took his greeting for its implicit message—I was admitted but not accepted. I had been welcomed into the so-called mainstream even as I was reminded that I was not a part of its flow. My presence was conditioned on my silence. I was present. But I was without a voice.

That was twenty years ago.

————

When I was considering whether to leave the practice of law and join the academy, I thought about my experience as a female gentleman. I thought about the larger-than-life portraits that dominated not only the walls of my classroom but the norms of my lessons. And then I read *Looking To The Bottom*.* It spoke to me. It said, you, too, matter. You have an important point of view. Mari Matsuda spoke to me as a voice for the voiceless in the tradition of the poet Nikki Giovanni. Nikki Giovanni tells us that the purpose of leadership is to speak until the people gain a voice. Mari Matsuda dared me to be more outspoken when she told personal stories of resistance and struggle and then incorporated those stories into her own teaching of Torts and American Legal History.

Mari Matsuda taught me that I have a voice. I did not have to become a female gentleman, a social male. Nor should I strive to become someone else in order to be heard.

It is with great pride, admiration, and deep personal affection that I introduce Professor Mari Matsuda, who gave me permission to speak in my own voice. (And, as most of you have probably noticed, with a brief exception one spring not too long ago, I haven't stopped speaking since.)**

————

*The reference is to Mari J. Matsuda, *Looking to the Bottom: Critical Legal Studies and Reparations,* 22 HARV. C.R.-C.L.L. Rev. 323, 335n. 50 (1987).

**Professor Guinier refers to the period of controversy in April 1993 after President Clinton picked her for the job of Assistant Attorney General in the Justice Department's Civil Rights Division. He later withdrew her name after the storm of protests raised by conservatives who attacked her as a radical.

Shirley Chisholm

I DIDN'T COME HERE TO PLAY

When Congressman Chisholm was appointed to the Agricultural Sub-committee on Forestry and Rural Villages rather than the Education and Labor Committee, which she had sought, she responded, "Apparently all they know here in Washington about Brooklyn is that a tree grew there. I can think of no other reason for assigning me to the House Agriculture Committee."
—*New York Times,* January 30, 1969

In response to an invitation to the male-only Gridiron Dinner in 1972, she fired off a classic response, "Guess who's not coming to dinner."
—*Washington Post,* June 6, 1982

Angered by the debate on abortion in 1980 she was heard to mention "mandatory vasectomies."
—*Washington Post,* June 6, 1982

Recalling her early days in Congress, she said to her Congressional colleagues who unrelentingly revealed their dislike for her: " 'Look, since you resent my being here, when you see me coming just get out of the way. I'm on a mission. I didn't come here to play.' I had to make it very clear that I would not stand for any of the negative patterns of social behavior directed toward me. After that, the rest of my stay in Congress was marvelous. In fact, when I left, some cried. Along with speaking up, I had a sense of humor. I can laugh at myself and laugh at others."
—*St. Petersburg Times,* February 13, 1990

Bertice Berry

GETTING TO KNOW ME

from *The World According to Me*

Hi, my name is Bertice Berry. I know, you're thinking that I look like that other Black woman with dreadlocks. She's beautiful, but I'm not her. All Black women do not look alike.

The other day I got on the bus and this woman said, "You look just like Whoopi Goldberg."

I told her, "You're fat and White, but you don't look like Mama Cass."

Bertice Berry

CHANGING THE TAPES

from *The World According to Me*

A lot of comedy comes from conversations I have with myself about all the things in the world that make me angry or despairing. I try to find the irony in life. Alice Walker has said there's a point at which even grief becomes absurd. At that point laughter gushes up to retrieve the sanity. I cultivate that laughter. My humor is not based on hatred; it comes from realizing how stupid other people can be. Not stupid as in Forrest Gump (by the way, didn't it bother anyone else that he was named after the founder of the Ku Klux Klan?). But stupid as in they haven't read a book in years or talked to anyone who's life doesn't revolve around soap operas or get his news from talk shows.

Herein lies the possibility to create change.

Now, I usually fly first-class, not because I have a lot of money, but because I fly so often to comedy gigs that I can get upgraded for free. Once when I had just taken a seat on a plane, the flight attendant came up to me and said, "You must be in the wrong seat. Somebody named *Doctor* Berry is supposed to be sitting there." I took a deep breath and fought back the urge to punch her in her implants.

I pursed my lips and batted my eyes and said, "Oh, I can understand your mistake. It's because I look so—young." Girlfriend spent the whole flight trying to give me every peanut on the plane.

Nikki Giovanni

CAMPUS RACISM 101

from *Racism 101*

There is a bumper sticker that reads: TOO BAD IGNORANCE ISN'T PAINFUL. I like that. But ignorance is. We just seldom attribute the pain to it or even recognize it when we see it. Like the postcard on my corkboard. It shows a young man in a very hip jacket smoking a cigarette. In the background is a high school with the American flag waving. The caption says: "Too cool for school. Yet too stupid for the real world." Out of the mouth of the young man is a bubble enclosing the words "Maybe I'll start a band." There could be a postcard showing a jock in a uniform saying, "I don't need school. I'm going to the NFL or NBA." Or one showing a young man or woman studying and a group of young people saying, "So you want to be white." Or something equally demeaning. We need to quit it.

I am a professor of English at Virginia Tech. I've been here for four years, though for only two years with academic rank. I am tenured, which means I have a teaching position for life, a rarity on a predominantly white campus. Whether from malice or ignorance, people who think I should be at a predominantly Black institution will ask, "Why are you at Tech?" Because it's here. And so are Black students. But even if Black students weren't here, it's painfully obvious that this nation and this world cannot allow white students to go through higher education without interacting with Blacks in authoritative positions. It is equally clear that predominantly Black colleges cannot accommodate the numbers of Black students who want and need an education.

Is it difficult to attend a predominantly white college? Compared with what? Being passed over for promotion because you lack credentials? Being turned down for jobs because you are not college-educated? Joining the armed forces or going to jail because you cannot find an alternative to the streets? Let's have a little perspective here. Where can you go and what can you do that frees you from interacting with the white American mentality? You're going to interact; the only question is, will you be in some control of yourself and your actions, or will you be controlled by others? I'm going to recommend self-control.

What's the difference between prison and college? They both prescribe your behavior for a given period of time. They both allow you to read books and develop your writing. They both give you time alone to think and time with your peers to talk about issues. But four years of prison doesn't give you a passport to greater opportunities. Most likely that time only gives you greater knowledge of how to get back in. Four years of college gives you an opportunity not only to lift yourself but to serve your people effectively. What's the difference when you are called nigger in college from when you are called nigger in prison? In college you can, though I admit with effort, follow procedures to have those students who called you nigger kicked out or suspended. You can bring issues to public attention without risking your life. But mostly, college is and always has been the future. We, neither less nor more than other people, need knowledge. There are discomforts attached to attending predominantly white colleges, though no more so than living in a racist world. Here are some rules to follow that may help:

Go to class. No matter how you feel. No matter how you think the professor feels about you. It's important to have a consistent presence in the classroom. If nothing else, the professor will know you care enough and are serious enough to be there.

Meet your professors. Extend your hand (give a firm handshake) and tell them your name. Ask them what you need to do to make an A. You may never make an A, but you have put them on notice that you are serious about getting good grades.

Do assignments on time. Typed or computer-generated. You have the syllabus. Follow it, and turn those papers in. If for some reason you can't complete an assignment on time, let your professor know before it is due and work out a new due date—then meet it.

Go back to see your professor. Tell him or her your name again. If an assignment received less than an A, ask why, and find out what you need to do to improve the next assignment.

Yes, your professor is busy. So are you. So are your parents who are working to pay or help with your tuition. Ask early what you need to do if you feel you are starting to get into academic trouble. Do not wait until you are failing.

Understand that there will be professors who do not like you; there may even be professors who are racist or sexist or both. You must discriminate among your professors to see who will give you the help you need. You may not simply say, "They are all against me." They aren't. They mostly don't care. Since you are the one who wants to be educated, find the people who want to help.

Don't defeat yourself. Cultivate your friends. Know your enemies. You cannot undo hundreds of years of prejudicial thinking. Think for yourself and speak up. Raise your hand in class. Say what you believe no matter how awkward you may think it sounds. You will improve in your articulation and confidence.

Participate in some campus activity. Join the newspaper staff. Run for office. Join a dorm council. Do something that involves you on campus. You are going to be there for four years, so let your presence be known, if not felt.

You will inevitably run into some white classmates who are troubling because they often say stupid things, ask stupid questions—and expect an answer. Here are some comebacks to some of the most common inquiries and comments:

Q: What's it like to grow up in a ghetto?
A: I don't know.

Q: (from the teacher): Can you give us the Black perspective on Toni Morrison, Huck Finn, slavery, Martin Luther King, Jr., and others?
A: I can give you *my* perspective. (Do not take the burden of 22 million people on your shoulders. Remind everyone that you are an individual, and don't speak for the race or any other individual within it.)

Q: Why do all the Black people sit together in the dining hall?
A: Why do all the white students sit together?

Q: Why should there be an African-American studies course?
A: Because white Americans have not adequately studied the contributions of Africans and African-Americans. Both Black and white students need to know our total common history.

Q: Why are there so many scholarships for "minority" students?
A: Because they wouldn't give my great-grandparents their forty acres and the mule.

Q: How can whites understand Black history, culture, literature, and so forth?
A: The same way we understand white history, culture, literature, and so forth. That is why we're in school: to learn.

Q: Should whites take African-American studies courses?
A: Of course. We take white-studies courses, though the universities don't call them that.

Comment: When I see groups of Black people on campus, it's really intimidating.
Comeback: I understand what you mean. I'm frightened when I see white students congregating.

Comment: It's not fair. It's easier for you guys to get into college than for other people.
Comeback: If it's so easy, why aren't there more of us?

Comment: It's not our fault that America is the way it is.
Comeback: It's not our fault, either, but both of us have a responsibility to make changes.

It's really very simple. Educational progress is a national concern; education is a private one. Your job is not to educate white people; it is to obtain an education. If you take the racial world on your shoulders, you will not get the job done. Deal with yourself as an individual worthy of respect, and make everyone else deal with you the same way. College is a little like playing grown-up. Practice what you want to be. You have been telling your parents you are grown. Now is your chance to act like it.

Barbara Brandon

WHERE I'M COMING FROM

Bonnie Allen

AMERICA: THE BOARD GAME

from *We Are Overrcome*

BACKGROUND

The year is 1981. Some people claim it's morning in America, but to you it looks like high noon. The Forces of Evil are amassing in their oval-shaped headquarters, ready to turn back the clock to the glory days when

Rock Hudson was a sex symbol, Pat Boone was a rock star, Norman Vincent Peale was the only self-help guru, Donna Reed wore spike heels while vacuuming, all religions were Christian, and, according to the enemy's telegenic but slightly vacant leader, *nobody* knew racism existed.

You are facing a daunting challenge. Your opponents have Congress, the Justice Department, the press, and, according to rumor, God on their side. All you have is a job obtained through affirmative action and a two-bedroom home bought with a HUD loan. The odds, not to mention history, are against you, but this may be your last chance to beat the enemy at its own game.

Are you up to the challenge? Can you fight the world's most daunting public-relations machine without protection from the Justice Department? Can you stop a legislative steamroller without support from either the media or public opinion? Does it bother you that even if you win, you'll probably end up a loser? If your response is, Hey, that's the way things go in AMERICA [:the Board Game], then get ready to play!

Number of Players

If there are only two players, one plays a single black marker while the other plays nine white markers. No matter the number of players, there should always be nine white markers for every one black marker on the board in order to keep the odds even.

Equipment

10 black markers, 90 white markers
1 pair loaded dice
$4 trillion in unmarked bills
Just My Luck cards
Fat Chance cards

One board with a fifty-square perimeter, which is clearly separated from a large inner-city square by white picket fences topped with barbed wire. Outer squares are called Wall Street, Rodeo Drive, Park Avenue, Lakeshore

Drive, and so on. The inner square is surrounded by an eight-lane highway named Dr. Martin Luther King, Jr., Boulevard, which has no exits to
the outer squares. (There is also a thin, grayish, dying area called Middle
America between the inner and outer squares. Although it is affected by
everything that happens in the game, and players pay lip service to it, it can
be treated as if it is not there.)

OBJECT OF THE GAME

The primary goal of black-marker players is to stay in place without losing ground. Their other goal is to avoid landing in the inner-city square,
which operates like a roach motel: You can get in, but you can't get out. If
this occurs, black-marker players automatically forfeit.

The goal of white-marker players is to amass as much cash as possible
without being forced to share.

TO SET UP

One white-marker player is designated as the banker. At the start, the
banker gives out 98 percent of the cash on hand to 2 percent of the players, leaving the remainder to be fought over by everyone else. (Please note:
If a black-marker player is accidentally included in the larger share, the
game ends immediately.) It is the banker's job to make sure no money
passes between the outer squares and the inner-city square.

If, during play, the banker needs more money, he mints it and makes a
notation in the deficit column of his ledger.

TO PLAY

To determine who goes first, the players each toss the dice; the highest
number leads off. (It should be noted that because the dice are loaded, the
leader will be a white-marker player under all circumstances.)

White-marker players move forward.

Black-marker players move backward.

White-marker players proceed around the board as quickly as possible, collecting cash whenever available and cheating when the opportunity arises. Since black-marker players are simply trying to stay in place, white-marker players assist them by denying them two out of three of their designated turns.

Just My Luck Cards

Randomly placed around the board are spaces requiring black-marker players to pick a card. At the top of each card is a black cat walking under a ladder, with instructions such as:

> Trickle-down economy isn't trickling in your direction. Go back 3 spaces.

> Your son's school lunch program calls catsup a vegetable and substitutes it for broccoli. Go back 1 space.

> Deregulation means your small business can be legally bankrupted by a large conglomerate. Go back 24 spaces.

[Ms. Allen continues the description of the game, which also includes "Fat Chance Cards" that only black players draw, all detailing opportunities that obviously won't benefit them. These are contrasted with the "Bonus Opportunities" cards that only White players draw. Everything in the game is designed to defeat the black players, but Ms. Allen concludes that "The rules will have to change eventually."]

Benilde Little

THE INTERVIEW

From *Good Hair*

[Alice, the protagonist of *Good Hair,* is an attractive and well-educated African American born into an upper middle class family. Because she was so privileged, she often did not fit into certain areas of the black world. Because she is black she doesn't fit into the white world. In this scene she is confronting that world—in a job interview.]

I had a second interview set up today with a magazine called *View*. On a whim, a few weeks before I had taken the time off from the *Beacon-Herald*, I'd sent them my résumé. They had called me immediately, and I had had an interview one day on my way to work. They'd seemed quite hot for me, and while I knew this wasn't my dream job, I needed to leave the *Beacon-Herald*. The work was no longer fulfilling and didn't pay enough. I had a $15,000 Visa bill—accumulated while buying Miles expensive presents and clothes for myself that I couldn't afford. *View* would mean a $10,000 increase plus a thousand-a-month expense account. Also, I figured my anxiety level would be much lower at this job, since I would be doing mostly fashion and my most taxing writing challenge would be coming up with lots of synonyms for "hot."

I poured mocha coffee into my favorite blue-and-white ceramic mug, stirred in the half-and-half, and waited a few seconds for the coffee to cool. I lingered over the paper, sipping my coffee, savoring my mood. I actually felt happy. I was glad to be back home with Jack.

I stood before my closet, deciding what to wear on my interview. My black Armani jacket with the charcoal wool skirt always worked. It had cost me two months' rent. I had been seriously depressed when I bought it.

Holly Thomasson looked as though she were born to be a New York magazine editor. A natural brunette who had successfully converted herself into a blonde. I would never understand White folks' obsession with blond hair. Mention that a woman is blond, and that immediately translates into beautiful and desired. The paler the hair, the better, it seemed. I guess the idea was that it was the farthest from dark. She was also superthin, another ruling-class obsession. Thin was the only standard of beauty for women's magazine editors and their subjects. Her uniform was a starched white cotton shirt with a little black skirt and square-toed, chunky heeled loafers. She wore tiny gold hoop earrings and no signet ring this time, but she did have the requisite large round diamond abutted by equally hefty dark blue sapphires on her left ring finger.

"Alice, hi, it's so nice to see you again, come on in. Do you want some coffee?"

Holly emphasized every syllable of every word, as if she were speaking to someone who didn't understand English. Unconsciously I started speaking that way back to her.

"Yes, it's nice to see you, too. I'd love some coffee," I heard myself say even though I was still shaking from overdoing the morning's dose. I should've asked for tea or decaf, but I didn't. Good corporate soldiers drank coffee and did not upset the corporate culture. I followed her into her corner office, which was decorated tastefully in shades of mauve. We sat on the sofa, and she crossed her legs and leaned in to me.

"So, your résumé is very impressive. You went to Holyoke? I went to Simmons."

We were about to play White Girl Poker. Worse than Negro Geography was White Girl Poker. Holyoke is more celebrated than Simmons, so she had to raise me, asking personal questions, referring to my résumé for more info to best me.

"So you live on the East Side? So do I." To make sure it wasn't Yorkville, she asked, "You're on Eighty-fifth between . . . ?"

When I told her Madison and Park, she ended the game. Not revealing her address meant I'd won the round. If I'd been wearing a wedding ring, she would have moved on to husband roulette, as in "What does your husband do?" But she, by dint of birth, won the set.

An overdressed Black woman reeking of Obsession and carrying a silver-plated tray with two china cups and saucers filled with coffee, a creamer, and a sugar dish came into my view. She was Holly's secretary. She gingerly placed it in front of us on the Lucite coffee table and left. I tried unsuccessfully to make eye contact with her.

"Thanks, Gloria," Holly yelled after her. "So, what do you think of our little setup?" she said, handing me a cup and saucer.

I was in my best interview mode: up but not perky, cool but not aloof. "The offices are great, and people seem happy," I said.

"So do you think you'd be interested in working at *View*?"

What I wanted to know was would I have an office with a window.

At least she was direct. I liked that. It could be fun, I told myself, maybe I could even get Gloria, Holly's secretary, to look me in the eye.

"Yes, I think it would be a challenge to come here," I heard myself say. I'd say just about anything now to get away from the paper.

"Well, great. We'd love to have you as soon as you can come aboard.

Your references looked good, but we will need a few more, maybe five in addition to the ten you already gave us. Is that okay?"

Fifteen references. If I were a White girl, even one who had gotten her degree through a matchbook correspondence course, five references would've been sufficient. I knew, and she knew I knew, that this reference thing was saved just for us—Black people. Even though I don't fit the stereotype of a gun-toting, drug-selling ghetto dweller, I was still Black and had to prove that I could fit in. It wasn't about doing the job. The issue was, what kind of Negro was I? Was I agreeable or angry? I knew I had to grin and bear it, because it was just part of the Black tax, part of why Lucas checked out.

"Sure, five more, that's not a problem," I said.

"Well, great. I still need for one other editor to meet you, but I'm sure she'll think you're just terrif, too."

Terrif? What was I getting myself into? I looked around the office and wondered if it was too late to ask for an additional ten thousand. Holly called the other editor to tell her we were coming by. After a brief meeting with the production editor, a humorless woman in Birkenstocks, Holly walked me to the reception area. She shook my hand enthusiastically and said she was looking forward to working with me.

When I got to the elevator Gloria was standing there. This time she looked me in the eye and said hi.

"Hi, I'm Alice."

The elevator opened before us, she got in first, and we were alone.

"So, Gloria, have you worked here long?"

"Mmm, yeah, almost ten years."

"Ten years, really? So, I guess you like it here?"

"It's all right. These girls is a trip, but they okay. You gonna be workin' here?"

"Um, it looks like it. Unless one of my five additional references says that I'm really an ax murderer."

The elevator had delivered us to the lobby, but Gloria seemed to want to continue the conversation. "How many references they ask you for?"

"Well, first ten, and today they asked for five more. Why?"

"Man, that's the kinda shit I'm talkin' about. They don't do that for them White girls, three references is all they ever ask them for."

"Really? Are you sure?"

"Hell, yeah. Who you think has to Xerox all that shit, résumés and whatnot? I know where everybody went to school, they grades, reference letters, everything—"

I felt sick, like I wanted to throw up, but it was tempered with gratitude that I felt for what Gloria had confirmed, what I'd always believed but couldn't prove. Another standard, a higher hoop to jump through, if you're Black. In that split second, though, I knew I was still going to take the job, so I had to be careful not to let any editor come by and see me talking with Gloria as if we were old homies.

"Listen, Gloria, I appreciate the information. I'll take you to lunch—"

"You still gone take the job?"

"Oh, yeah, I'm taking the job."

"You go, that's right, don't let that stupid shit keep you from taking it. We need some color up there. Maybe we'll finally get some color in the magazine."

"Yeah, well, that's the plan. Take care, Gloria. I'll see you."

"Awright."

On the turnpike on my way to the paper the car phone rang. One of the few perks was having a car phone.

"So how'd the interview go?"

"Hi, sweetie. It was great, they made me an offer."

"Oh, that's terrific. Congratulations, sweetheart. When do you start?"

"In a few weeks. I still have to give them five more references."

"Well, that's no biggie. Is it?"

"It's not what they ask White folks, but—"

"How do you know what they usually ask—"

"A Black woman who works there told me, one of the secretaries."

"A secretary, Alice? How would she know?"

"The secretaries always know, Jack."

"Yeah, I guess you're right. Anyway, I gotta go, but let's celebrate tonight, okay? I should be home for dinner."

"Okay."

"Love you—"

I hung up and began composing my resignation speech in my head. One went like this: "Sam, I want you to know that the last five years that I've worked here have been a complete waste of time. You have no idea what you could have had in me and in the other Black reporters you have here, who you use only as translators for ghettoese. You are a racist dog and I quit."

It was so much fun imagining all the things I could finally say to him that by the time I got to the paper, I was in quite a happy mood.

Jill Nelson

WE WILL LIVE THE LIFE OF THE COSBYS

from *Volunteer Slavery*

[Jill Nelson, like the persona in Benilde Little's *Good Hair,* was born into a well-to-do black family and was a well-educated journalist. In the following scene from her autobiography, she recounts her job interview with the *Washington Post* and her decision to join their staff.]

By the time my day of infamy, er, interviews is over, Ben has communicated his feelings to the editors—probably by talking about himself—and I've been offered a job on the Sunday magazine. I have no feeling left in my feet, and I'm just about brain dead.

I feel as if thousands of cornea-sized holes have been burned into the back of my dress from the discreet scrutiny of the voiceless reporters who may soon become my colleagues.

Lovinger walks me to the elevator.

"Well, what do you think? We'd really like you to be a part of the magazine."

"I'm interested, but I'd like a few days to think about the offer and talk to my daughter," I say.

"Why? Is there a problem?" He looks at me with a mixture of surprise, annoyance, and panic, as if the thought that I might not want to join this particular family is heretical. He needs me, black and breasted, to complete his staff.

A Jew who grew up in the housing projects of Manhattan, Jay Lovinger's come to the *Post* via *People* magazine and is desperate to make the magazine work, and to prove himself—poor, Jewish, a college dropout—worthy of membership in the *real* white boys club, the WASP one. It isn't enough that he's making big money and working for the number-two newspaper in the country (after *The New York Times*) without benefit of even the most mediocre college education. No, he wants to truly belong. Doesn't he know that without Harvard his efforts are futile?

Belonging isn't what I crave; I'm after money and a larger audience. But as we used to say in the 1960s, I don't like the vibes around here. No one makes eye contact, no one speaks, everyone watches. In nearly eight hours, the only people who've said squat to me besides editors are Joyce and Margo, the sisters at the switchboard. I am not optimistic about the future.

I am so whipped after being on all day that I don't even have the energy to smile superficially. Since ten in the morning I've hobbled from cubicle to cubicle, white male to white male, being interrogated. I feel like a felon up for parole trying to cop a plea with the commissioners.

I've also been doing the standard Negro balancing act when it comes to dealing with white folks, which involves sufficiently blurring the edges of my being so that they don't feel intimidated, while simultaneously holding on to my integrity. There is a thin line between Uncle Tomming and Mau-Mauing. To fall off that line can mean disaster. On one side lies employment and self-hatred: on the other, the equally dubious honor of unemployment with integrity. Walking that line as if it were a tightrope results in something like employment with honor, although I'm not sure exactly how that works.

I keep getting this creepy feeling that the *Washington Post* is doing me some kind of favor. It's as if, as an African-American, female, freelance writer, I'm a handicapped person they've decided to mainstream. The words to "Look at Me I'm Walking," the theme song of the annual Jerry Lewis Muscular Dystrophy Telethon, pop into my head.

The thought of all those bills being pledged to a good cause makes me think about my favorite cause—me—and my interview with Tom Wilkinson, the money man. As far as I can tell, all he does is talk to people about money and deliver bad news.

"There're not many reporters here who've just been freelancers. This is a tough institution. Most of our people have worked their way up from smaller papers. Do you think you'll be able to fit in, handle the demands of working for a daily newspaper?" he asks me.

"I think freelancers, people who work for themselves, work harder than people who have job-jobs," I say, trying not to sound as exhausted and bor-

derline sullen as I am. My college friend Adrienne, who went off to teach
in St. Thomas and never came back, coined the term "job-job." We met in
a class on black women writers at City College and first connected when
the teacher, an African-American woman, announced that she didn't know
what racism was until she was twenty-five. Adrienne and I found this statement both hilarious and outrageous, and said so. We've been tight ever
since. "Job-job" is the phrase Adrienne used to differentiate working for
someone else from working for yourself. "Have you ever noticed," she'd say,
"How the 'J' in job looks just like a hook?"

"We hope you'll come and work here. Everyone liked you," Wilkinson
says. Here we go again with the popularity contest. I'm glad I wore the
turquoise dress. I smile, cross my legs. Then I recross them.

"Now. Let's talk about salary. How much money did you make last
year?" I stare at him. He sits, a thin, intense man in his forties with a weasel-
like face, waiting for a response. I do what everyone does in salary negotiations. I lie.

"About $40,000."

"We can offer you $42,500," he spits out.

"Well, the editor mentioned a salary of—"

"$45,000," he interrupts. I feel like a damaged urn under bid at a
Sotheby's auction. Get me off the block fast and maybe no one will notice
the cracks.

"I was thinking more in terms of—"

"Without newspaper experience, I think that is a good starting salary. Of
course, if things work out well, there'll be raises and that sort of thing."

"I understand that," I say, "But I'll be moving both myself and my
daughter from New York, she has to go to school and—"

He looks at me with what I think is exasperation, then glances at his
wrist. Clearly, I am taking up too much time. I feel myself slipping off that
tightrope. I also feel like a troublemaker, a subversive for not being properly grateful for the chance to work at the *Washington Post,* whatever the
salary. I also feel out of my league. Mommy and Daddy never fully explained to me that I'd have to support myself when I grew up. They certainly never mentioned salary negotiations.

I have the feeling that even though I'm doing the right thing, I'm also
somehow in bad taste, a familiar feeling for African-Americans. It's like I'm
the first black woman to become Miss America and instead of feeling

thankful I refuse to put on the tiara because the rhinestones are of such lousy quality. Instead of being happy I'm an ingrate.

"All right, $50,000," he snaps. I can almost hear a voice saying, "Going once, going twice, gone." I'm not sure anymore which way is which.

"Fine. But I need a few days to think about it." Now he looks really annoyed, but what the hell? Last year I made about $20,000, so $50,000 would be a hefty raise. So why do I have a feeling of impending doom? I try to talk myself out of it, but I can't think of what to say.

Then I hear my mother's voice from the day before.

"I think it's a great opportunity even though if you move I'll miss you and Misu you'll be making good money and the *Post* is a good liberal newspaper after all they brought down Nixon that son of a bitch you're getting older and have to start thinking about college for your daughter and retirement some security you can't be a vagabond all your life what about health insurance . . ."

Enough. I shut her off. My mind begins to wander to boutiques, malls, bookstores, liposuctionists, all the places I can spend the *Post*'s money. I don't notice Wilkinson standing by the door waiting to usher me out until he says, "Nice meeting you." I want to ask him, "But do you like me, really *like* me?" Instead, I leave.

"Please let me know your decision as soon as possible," Lovinger says as I leave, sticking his long neck and nearly bald head inside the elevator doors. "We'd like you to be a part of what we're trying to do." It's as if I'm being recruited to join a crusade, but no one will tell me its objective.

"I will," I say. The doors close. I fall back against the wall and do some deep yogic breathing. What I'd really like to do is scream. My pantyhose feels like a girdle, slowly cutting off the circulation from feet to waist. I barely manage to cross the street to The Madison Hotel, where my daughter Misu, age thirteen, awaits me.

As I am soon to discover is true of much of Washington, The Madison Hotel is a warped facsimile, an unknowing parody of something that probably never was real. It has cachet because Washington is a city of pretension and nostalgia. Whites yearn for the time when the city was run by a cabal of presidentially appointed commissioners and not a black mayor; for the good old days when D.C. was a cultural backwater but there were no traffic jams; for the bygone era when there was no race problem because genteel segregation reigned. Black people yearn for the 1960s, before the riots, when it really did seem things would change. They yearn for Marion Barry in his first two—sober—terms, for D.C.B.C., before crack. Organizations have their own specific nostalgia; at the *Post,* it is for the boom days of Richard Nixon and Watergate.

The Madison, with its faux tapestry-upholstered loveseats, neo Japanese flower arrangements, bad food, and obsequious Central American waiters, is a wannabee's vision of the life of the powerful WASP. Aspiring yuppies, brought to Washington by a job in corporate or political middle-management, lunch at The Madison and declare themselves important, in the know, powerbrokers. This is a town where importance and longevity are connoted by having a capital "The" in front of everything.

"Hi, Misu. I'm back." My daughter sits propped up on one of the two double beds, watching television. She is brown, thin, wears braces. The debris of room service—trays, frilly paper things, silverware, and the smell of grease—surrounds her.

"Sorry I took so long." My daughter, a hotel abuser from way back, shrugs. Being left alone in a room she doesn't have to clean up, with television and room service, is a significant element in her vision of nirvana.

"That's okay, Mom. How'd it go?"

"Okay. But really weird," I say, yanking off my shoes and stockings in one effective but less than fluid movement. I walk into the bathroom, turn on the water, and begin scraping mascara and eyeliner from my face before I'm blinded.

"I don't really think the *Washington Post* is the place for me—" I begin, shouting to be heard above the roar of Madison water.

"I like it here, Mom. I think we should move here," my daughter says.

"Why?" I ask, drying my face. "What do you like about it here?" I try to keep my tone neutral.

"The buildings are small. The people are nice. And it's clean," she says. "If we lived here, we'd live in a house, right? Then we could have a car and lots of cats and a dog and all that stuff, like the Cosbys, couldn't we?"

I open my mouth to point out that the Cosbys don't have cats or dogs, that they have a father, that they live in New York. Then I look at the dreamy expression on my daughter's face, and close my mouth again. Abruptly, it all becomes clear to me.

My daughter is tired of being a leftist. She is tired of eccentric clothes, artists, vegetarian diets, the New York subway, and living in an apartment.

The culturally rich and genteel poverty in which she was raised is played out. Deep in her little African-American heart, she yearns to be Vanessa Huxtable, her age cohort in the television Cosby clan. With a perfect room, in a perfect house, with perfect parents and lots of perfectly hip clothes in the closet. She is sick of my Sixties class-suicide trip, of middle-class Mommy's vow of poverty in pursuit of the authentic Negro experience. She is tired, simply, of hanging in there with my trip.

She's got a point. I'm tired, too. Taking the job would not only fulfill some of her fantasies, it would provide me with a ready-made escape from New York, Ed Koch and his soul mate, subway gunman Bernhard Goetz, not to mention my life there. Let's face it. I'm burnt out and dread answering the telephone. I'm dating a mortician who's about to lose his business, which is located in the heart of the area with the most liquor stores and highest death rate in the city. At thirty-four, post-divorce, I am again living with my own Mommy. How much worse could Washington be? Still, I have a stress stomachache and the feeling that I'm about to make the wrong decision for all the right reasons. I had the same feeling the night before I got married.

"It might be fun to live here for a while, Mom. Not forever. What do you think?"

"We'll see," I say, falling back on every parent's favorite meaningless expression in a desperate bid for time. "What'd you do today?"

"Watched television and ordered lunch. You know what I like about Washington? When I ordered my lunch they didn't have shakes on the menu. So when I called I asked the lady, 'Do you have milkshakes?' And the woman said, 'My dear, this is The Madison. We have everything.' Having everything. Isn't that great?"

My fate is sealed. We will move to Washington. I will go to work for the *Washington Post*. We will live the life of the Cosbys, sans Daddy. I feel I owe my daughter stability, bourgeoisdom, charge accounts at Woodies, a chance to join the mainstream. I will be the Cosmo mom, the queen of having it all, and my daughter a Cosby clone. For 50,000 smackeroos, how bad could it be?

Three months later we move to Washington. In the four and a half years I work at the *Post,* my daughter never has another milkshake at The Madison.

MIMEOGRAPHED ITEM
Affirmative Action in Heaven

An OFFCP Desk Audit revealed an under-representation of Blacks in Heaven.

OFFCP and the Lord entered into a conciliation agreement whereby, 20 percent of all entering Heaven had to be black.

After extensive good faith recruitment efforts by Gabriel Jones, EEO Coordinator, Black representation in Heaven increased tremendously.

Black representation in Heaven resulted in problems that Gabriel could not handle. He took his burden to the Lord.

"Lord, I don't know what I'm going to do; Niggers don't want to wear the pearly white robes; they don't want to wear sandles; they insist on wearing these nappy afros, and you know Lord, halos don't fit over nappy hair; they want the best jobs; they're picking the gold off the street; they're swinging on the pearly gates; they stole my trumpet to start a jazz combo; and they've got watermelon seeds all over the place."

The Lord said, "Tell those Niggers to go to hell." The Lord thought about this for a minute and remembered his conciliation agreement with the OFFCP and said, "No, wait a minute Gabriel. The problem is, we don't have any experience in this area, so in order to document our good faith efforts, let's place a call to the devil as a community consultant."

So the Lord called the devil. "Hello devil, this is the Lord."

The devil said, "Oh hey Lord, what's happening?" and the Lord said, "Devil, we're encountering all kinds of problems with these niggers up here in Heaven." The devil interrupted and said, "Lord, could you hold on for a minute, I'll be right back."

The Lord held on, and moments later the devil came back on the line. "Lord, I'm back, now; what's the problem?" The Lord proceeded once again to begin telling the devil about the problem, and once again the devil put him on hold. The devil came back again to the phone and said, "Sorry about that Lord, now; what's the problem?" The Lord proceeded to relate the problem for the third time. The devil interrupted again and said, "Lord, I'm going to have to call you back later, these damn Niggers down here are putting out my fire."

OFFCP = Office of Freedom and Fairness for Colored People
EEO = Equal Employment Opportunity

Sarah and A. Elizabeth Delany

I KNOW A RASCAL WHEN I SEE ONE

from *Having Our Say*

Oh my, what fun
In Washington
I bettya every coon
From coontown will be there
Oh my, what fun
In Washington
When the coon sits in that presidential chair.

See, I think white people would rather die than vote for a Negro president. I predict there will be a white woman president before there is a Negro president. And if a Negro is elected president? That person will be a Negro *woman*.

How do I know this? I'm a little psychic. Like with that Clarence Thomas mess, the Supreme Court nomination. He's lying. That girl, Anita Hill, is telling the *truth*. And Sadie says, "How do you know?" Well, I'll tell you something: Honey, I know a rascal when I see one!

Sadie and I watched the whole thing on the TV, and when I saw all those silly old white men asking those stupid questions I almost got myself on a train and went down to Washington. I could have straightened out that whole Clarence Thomas mess in ten minutes, yes, sir! I should have gotten myself on a train and gone on down there, but Sadie wouldn't let me.

So you see that I still have the urge to change the world. The truth is, you're born a certain way and there's some things you can change, and some things you can't.

Barbara Brandon

WHERE I'M COMING FROM

Sister to Sister

I went in this restaurant and the woman told me, "I'm sorry, but we don't serve Negras." I said, "And I don't eat 'em."

Since integration, you can't find no good soul food nowhere. The Negroes were so happy to go to these white restaurants that all the black places done gone outta business.

Yeah, I know bout Reagan's Trickle Down Theory. I'm just waiting for some of it to trickle down to *me*.

Clarence Thomas got the right name. He ain't nothing but a Uncle Tom.

Clarence Thomas got the right name. He ain't nothing but a Bigger Thomas.

Be aware of the Establishment's CON Game (Control-of-Niggers).★

★This acronym comes from Flo Henderson, *Color Me Flo*, 13.

CHAPTER 12

Tidbits from the Laughing Barrel

There is a popular old joke in the black community that Negroes in Southern towns were prohibited from laughing in the street. If they felt a laugh coming on, they had to rush and stick their heads into the laughing barrel marked "For colored" in order to protect whites from their loud, uproarious, and corrupting behavior. When overcome by the urge to laugh, people who rushed to stick their heads in the laughing barrel didn't necessarily feel constrained to conform to any set themes. This concluding chapter is, therefore, a potpourri of humor, though some of the selections treat similar subjects; they were not, however, numerous enough for a complete chapter.

The first group of tidbits in this chapter deals with the manner in which creative women, (artists, poets, intellectuals, singers) survive and remain productive in this society. These women are producing against the odds.

Most of them have had to expend so much energy just to stay alive, earn a living, and raise their children that one wonders where they find the energy and the leisure to create. Their husbands, other family members, and communities often do not understand and support them in their artistic endeavors. The larger society certainly hasn't expected and by no means supported their creativity. The demands on their time certainly do not allow them time for the leisurely pursuit of their craft. One would expect that these frustrations and obstacles would leave them too exhausted, despairing, and bitter to value and pursue aesthetics. But like Celie in *The Color Purple,* who started sewing to keep from killing her husband, they somehow find themselves with "a needle and not a razor in my hand." Creativity is an outlet that has similarly proven a life raft for Alice Walker, who has declared, "Writing poems is my way of celebrating with the world that I have not committed suicide the evening before." The battle does not end after they produce their works, however. A number of the artists have had to fight against an army of publishers, managers, agents, directors, professional critics, patrons who often try to force them into certain molds. The same determination that brought them to this point empowers them to resist such pressures. Typical of their resistance is the following response of Billie Holiday, who when her manager ordered her, "Speed up the tempo, you gotta sing hot stuff," retorted, "Look, you son of a bitch, you sing it. I'm going to sing my way, you sing your way."[1]

A significant portion of this chapter consists of the X-rated tales, jokes, and mimeographed items of folk humor. Among every group, humor is largely motivated by the enjoyment of forbidden themes. In "Wit and Its Relation to the Unconscious," Sigmund Freud explains the appeal of obscene humor:

> It makes possible the gratification of a craving (lewd or hostile) despite a hindrance which stands in the way; it eludes the hindrance and so derives pleasure from a source that has been inaccessible on account of the hindrance. . . . Owing to the repression brought about by civilization many primary pleasures are now disapproved by the censorship and lost. But the human psyche finds renunciation very difficult; hence we discover that tendency-wit furnishes us with a means to make the renunciation retrogressive and thus to regain what has been lost.

[1]Donald Clarke, *Wishing on the Moon,* 104.

Other selections here include games, comments on contemporary events, such as the O. J. Simpson trial, philosophical reflections on life, and ethnic jokes. I have no doubt that my readers will be grateful that I dug around in the laughing barrel for these choice tidbits that might otherwise have fallen through the cracks.

Johnnetta B. Cole

SISTER PRESIDENT

[Affectionately dubbed "Sister President" by Spelman College students, Dr. Cole is the most familiar face among all black women college presidents (perhaps among all college presidents of any race or gender), having graced the covers of numerous magazines and having constantly received frequent other media attention. Following are some of her reflections on her job kindly given to me specifically for this anthology.]

There are not many of us African American Sister Presidents, and those of us who are in this field do not have an easy time of it. Why the story goes that one Black woman college president died and went to hell, and it was two weeks before she realized that she wasn't still on the job.

How well I recall the day when a visitor rang the doorbell at the President's Home on the Spelman College campus, and said: "Is the President in? I would like to meet him."
I responded: "Here she is, and you are welcome to meet her."

I am fond of saying that if you are an African American woman at the helm of a college or university, you are doing the Lord's work, and she's got a mighty lot of it for you to do!

I think that our historically Black colleges and universities do a lot of righteous work. Why we often make heroes and sheroes out of young folks who live in a society that does so much to challenge their sense of themselves and their people.

When it comes to the question of community service, I agree with Spelman College's distinguished alumna, Marian Wright Edelman: Doing for others is just the rent you must pay for living on this earth.

Toni Cade Bambara

A SORT OF PREFACE

from *Gorilla, My Love*

It does no good to write autobiographical fiction cause the minute the book hits the stand here comes your mama screamin how could you and sighin death where is thy sting and she snatches you up out your bed to grill you about what was going down back there in Brooklyn when she was working three jobs and trying to improve the quality of your life and come to find on page 42 that you were messin around with that nasty boy up the block and breaks into sobs and quite naturally your family strolls in all sleepy-eyed to catch the floor show at 5:00 A.M. but as far as your mama is concerned, it is nineteen-forty-and-something and you ain't too grown to have your ass whipped.

And it's no use using bits and snatches even of real events and real people, even if you do cover, guise, switch-around and change-up cause next thing you know your best friend's laundry cart is squeaking past but your bell ain't ringing so you trot down the block after her and there's this drafty cold pressure front the weatherman surely did not predict and your friend says in this chilly way that it's really something when your own friend stabs you in the back with a pen and for the next two blocks you try to explain that the character is not her at all but just happens to be speaking one of her lines and right about the time you hit the laundromat and you're ready to just give it up and take the weight, she turns to you and says that seeing as how you have plundered her soul and walked off with a piece of her flesh, the least you can do is spin off half the royalties her way.

So I deal in straight-up fiction myself, cause I value my family and friends, and mostly cause I lie a lot anyway.

Opal J. Moore

A HAPPY STORY

"What's this story about?" Everett leans over my shoulder. He really wants to ask "when will dinner be ready?" But he will not have it spread about that he is a traditionalist.

"It's about a woman," I say as he inspects the contents of pots with an air of disapproval. I continue. "Intelligent. Attractive. Educated. A career is possible if she plays her cards right." Everett has thrown open the refrigerator door, is standing, feet apart, fists on hips, as if silently demanding that certain foods present themselves for his until-dinner-gets-ready snacking. I continue. "But one morning she wakes up to realize that despite her efforts, she is living the same life her mother led. She feels desperate at this idea—"

Everett is desperately opening up foil wrappers. Finds one cold pork chop.

"—and in that moment, she begins to plan her own suicide."

"Why?" mumbles Everett around a mouthful of pork chop. "I thought she was so intelligent."

"Maybe she's intelligent enough—" I say to his back as he returns to his armchair enclave, "—intelligent enough to wonder if surviving is worth the trouble."

Everett rattles his newspaper. The TV drones. I sweep up crumbs from the table and deposit the abandoned pork chop foil wrapper in the trash can. Slowly I recover my thoughts, make a few scribbles on my yellow pad.

"Why don't you ever write a *happy* story?" Everett says, moments later, newspaper crumpling in his lap. I pretend I don't hear him, wish that I hadn't.

"Angel? Didja hear me? Why can't you write a *happy* story for a change?" I don't even look up.

"You know one?" I say. "Tell me a happy story and I'll use it," I say. When I do look up, his eyes are waiting. We look at each other. I smile, feeling some triumph. "Tell me," I say, "and I'll write it."

Everett is a determined optimist; I call it self-delusion. I am a realist; he calls it "bad disposition." I say that he pretties up life with pretense. He says that I don't consider the cloud's silver lining. I say you're liable to be struck by lightning standing in a thunderstorm looking for a silver lining. He says I live for bad news. "Tell me a happy story," I persist. "I can't wait to write it."

His tongue is working inside of one cheek; maybe he's thinking . . . or maybe he's just after a sliver of pork chop caught between his teeth. He seems to regard me with infinite patience and pity. But now, his unflagging optimism comes to rescue his face from furrows of doubt. I see firm determination light his eyes. He will, now as ever, rescue me from myself. I am caught off guard by my own laughter; it comes snorting unladylike from my nose.

"Come on," I say, "Lay this fairy tale on me."

It has to be a fairy tale. All stories with nice happy endings are—either that, or gothic romance. But I prefer fairy tales. At least they don't pretend to be in any way real—just morality tales cloaked in an entertainment. Snow White bites the poison apple but does not die—she lives happily ever after (and the bad queen dies a horrible death). An ancient wish for moral justice, but certainly no reflection of life, where victims don't sleep but die, and bad queens suffer fame and millions made on the Vegas circuit.

The problem with fairy tales is that they end just where true stories begin. What if the story of Snow White continued beyond the grand wedding, and her prince carried her to a land called Newark, to a tenement castle subdivided for multiple family dwelling? And what if his princely income waned, and his ardor, as her body sagged with childbearing, and the mirror chanted a different tune, and Prince Charming—whipping up his trusty steed—stumbled across a younger damsel in distress upon the urban glade? And the matronly Snow White became the poison toting neglected wife. . . .

It would not take much to convince me that happiness *is* the darker side of life: suburban housewife pushing husband and kiddies off to work and day care just to crawl back into illicit daydreaming; the unrequited lover tasting the most profound ecstasy at the lip of the poison cup. . . . I try to return to my *own* thoughts, abandon this tired academic problem of art vs. life. But Everett has been pondering.

"You could write a story about my mother," he says.

"Your mother's story is not happy," I say.

"My mother is a saint," he says.

"Saints do not happy stories make. Saints are tragic," I point out. "In order to even qualify for sainthood, one must suffer inordinately and die pathetically for the purpose of inspiring pity, guilt, and other behavior inhibiting emotions. Not a prescription for a truly happy story."

"But it's their triumph over suffering," he says, "That's the happy part."

"The happy part is that it was *their* suffering and not *yours.*" I think this, but I don't say it. Everett can't stand being *always* wrong. So I nod at his last protest even if I don't agree. Because nobody overcomes hardships; we merely survive them, like car wrecks, to haul the scars around with us until we die. But I nod as if the saintly mother story is a possibility to consider. Heartened by this, Everett continues:

"... And mama has spent her whole life trying to help other people. As hard as her life has been, she could always find something to give. Isn't that happy?" Everett pauses. Studies my face which I make sure is giving away nothing. He waits for my acquiescence on his last point; I can't give it. So I tell him flat out, "That's the saddest story there is. Along with being the oldest." Everett's face tightens. The words sound harsh. Maybe the truth will go better with a musical accompaniment. So I toss aside my writing, flip through albums for something mellow—something sad.

I wouldn't object to writing his mother's story if, in her old age, she had put hard times behind her and was now enjoying some ease and peace of mind. But Everett's mother is living in the same two-story walkup of her childhood—the same, but different, because it's older, more decrepit. The beams are termite riddled, the front porch is a hazard, and her new neighbors are young acid heads who don't know the difference between sleep and death. It is not triumph but the height of tragedy—the final kick: sacrifice rewarded with pain. Maybe it is irreverent to say that her story is the oldest story on record, but it is: a mother sacrificing body and mind for children who will eventually spurn her (or idealize her) but never recognize what was traded for their lives. It is old. It is sad. . . . It is true. It is not happy. And now I hope that Everett can realize the magnitude of the thing he has so frivolously proposed. It's easy to *say* "write a happy story," but when you get down to the brass tacks of it, the task is formidable.

Of course I could manufacture happy tales unending if I made them out of wish instead of life: flawlessly beautiful men and women living lives full of satisfaction; modern episodes of Ozzie and Harriet; heroic tales of John Wayne justice, Right prevailing over Wrong; evil creatures disarmed with a fortuitous bucket of water—

The stove hisses vehemently.

"Your pot is boiled over," says Everett cocking one eye to the stove, then to me. I cross the kitchen, deliberately slow, watching the foaming white water smear down the sides of the saucepan, sizzle into the hot recesses of the stove where it will congeal into an impossible to remove glue.

"What about Alice?" says Everett.

I think about my friend Alice, now a very big costume jewelry magnate on the East coast. She *is* a success story.

"Is Alice happy?"

"She made more money last year than most people ever see—outside a Monopoly game," Everett says.

I swab the stove top with a soppy dishcloth. "Is she happy, you think?" Everett doesn't answer. I stir pots.

"What's *this* story about?"

"Alice's happy story fragment. It's not finished."

"How much've you got?"

"I've got:

"At seven, Alice was a pretty girl. Everyone always said so. Especially her uncle, her mother's step-brother, who had Sunday dinner with them every week without fail.

"But they were poor, so Alice's mother had no chicken for Sunday pots, but depended on her step-brother to bring fish that he caught at the lake. He always brought an extra fish for Alice who hated fish but was always made to thank her uncle for her extra portion with a kiss.

" 'You see Alice, a pretty girl will always get more,' he whispered to her every Sunday without fail, and endlessly, like the smell of fish that she came to associate, not with a meal, but with her uncle. With his breath, his shirt, his fingers that squeezed her quick and rough whenever she had to kiss him.

"Men told Alice she was pretty. Alice's mother said, 'You must think you're cute, or somethin',' and slapped her when she was angry. But Alice loved her mother. She knew the slaps were not from lack of love, but because her mother hated fish also. So Alice gathered pretty trash, lost buttons, bright chips of glass, and strung them for her mother who wore them on 'chicken days'—Christmases and Easters—to make Alice smile."

"That's happy?" Everett asks incredulous.

"Well . . . ," I say, "She never went hungry."

"The uncle is a lech."

"She overcomes that hardship," I say. But Everett has heard enough.

"Alice never had any uncles like that," he says.

"How do you know?"

"And she was never poor."

"This is fiction, not biography," I say. "Besides, a story should be universal. Every girl has an uncle, or *some*body, like that."

"Did you?"

"This is fiction, not autobiography," I say.

Everett takes a deep exaggerated breath. "Alice's family was well-off, she went to college, majored in Business Administration. She married, had two sons, and in her spare time, she blasted her way into the costume jewelry market and made a killing." The world according to Everett.

I amend. "Alice was a neglected child who hung around college campuses, married a rich man's son, had two sons right quick, divorced the rich man's son, sued for humongous alimony, bought herself a nanny, and a costume jewelry business," and reality reigns once again.

"You don't have to put it like that. You could emphasize the success part," says Everett.

I sweep gleaming vegetables from the chopping board into the skillet. The hot butter gives a long sigh. "So," I say. "A happy story is a story with the sad parts snipped away. And writing is an aberrant form of—cosmetology?"

I don't agree with this dishonesty, but I have to admire Everett's clear vision, a man for whom happiness is attainable through good sound planning—or a good pearl eraser. Later, as I clear and wash up from dinner, I wonder if he isn't right about Alice. With one son in jail, the other a part-time hairdresser, and her series of interesting but impermanent men, she was surely, I had thought, in pure agony. I scrub pots. Ironic that Everett would be the one to suggest that a woman's happiness could exist despite the failures of children and men.

Everett seems to have lost interest in this quest for the happy story, but I am tortured by it. The problem is the thing itself—happiness. What is it? The attainment of what I *think* I want, or just the absence of grief? Who has it? How did they get hold of it? Hang onto it? Or is it just mind control—looking for the bright side while constantly living in the dark? Is it the predictable routine of Everett's mother's last years, whose whole life was spent in flux? Is her happiness the mere absence of the awful unexpected, the knowledge that there are no new disasters? That her own death is no longer frightening—that it is a not altogether unpleasant prospect? The idea that every eventuality can be met? The reason that she can refuse to be rescued from the dilapidation of life, finally insist upon having some things her own way and not worry about the consequences? There might be a certain satisfaction in this.

Still, how sad if happiness boiled down to a kind of good-natured fatalism. I wanted my happiness to be more perfect, even if that made it impossible to obtain. Even if it had to remain the property of childhood ignorance, or of memory.

"Are you trying to say you've never been happy?" says Everett.

"I would never say that."

"What was the happiest time of your life?"

"Happiest?" I repeat, balancing a stack of plates to a high shelf. "It's so hard to speak in degrees. . . ."

"Give me one time," he says. "When?"

"When?" I repeat.

When. Everett's voice is like the crossed arms of my old piano teacher, Mrs. Poindexter. One hand always gripping a ruler. "Give me the time," she would say, smacking the ruler against her narrow backside for the tempo. And I played, struggling to meet the demand. Everett waits. I rifle through my life, days, and years, in search of a single convincing moment. I think it must be something wholly selfish and completely satisfying—

Like the time two nickels bought me two whole Big Time candy bars to eat all by myself and *not* share. It had taken me all day to shake little sisters and supervision. The city air had smelled sweet to me as I ran, full tilt, without stopping, to the basement store. The agony, sweet, of impossible choices: candy necklaces or candy mint juleps or "wine" candy sours. But I had already known I wanted the Big Times that were hurt-yourself good and never enough when you had to split one two ways, or three, or four. But I had two nickels and a little bit of time. . . . Except I remember the candy didn't taste as good as I had expected. Maybe they were stale. Or maybe it was because I ate them so fast, afraid of being discovered, afraid of the sudden cry of: "dibs dibs!" our unrefusable demand to share. Or worse, some unexpected adult demanding to know "—and where'd you get the money for that?" Because a nickel for candy was unusual, and two was rare if not completely unheard of. And the nickels were "borrowed" from my grandmother's mantel. No, this was not a happy memory. The selfish moment is always spoiled by guilt.

A happy moment would, evidently, have to be some occasion of selfless generosity or sacrifice. When I was oh, maybe ten years old, my sisters and I had saved a wool sock full of money. A collection of nickels, quarters and even some dollar bills. We counted it constantly, thoroughly excited at our thrift. We discussed what to do with the money, but could think of no purchase exciting or satisfying enough to justify spending all of that money, close to thirteen dollars. It must have been Palm Sunday, or some other special occasion. It could not have been an ordinary Sunday when we carried our treasure in its black wool "bank" to Sunday school, and we decided to give a whole dollar in offering. Our Sunday School master must have smelled our excitement, or our money, because she kept on begging and prodding, saying: "Oh, our class has never won the distinction of best offering. A little bit more, and we might earn a special blessing." (One more dollar). And: "Oh! wouldn't it be something if the children of the Sunday School outshined the adults in their offering to God?" (*Two* more dollars). And: "I just checked and we're still five dollars lower than the Elders' collection plate." In defeat, we emptied the entire remains of our sock savings into the plate. . . . And, in a moment, a great cry rose up in the church. Three daughters had given thirteen dollars to the collection plate. Wasn't that a wonderment! Wasn't that the spirit of God at work! But there was jealousy in the House of God because a rally cry went up. The adults reached into their deep pockets and came forth with dollar after dollar. Even so, we almost earned our special blessing, which was little enough reward I thought, when my own father came forward with five dollars in his hand. The adults grinned. I wept. No. Selfless generosity was, and always had been, for the birds. How could I have forgotten that even joyful giving *must* offer *some* small reward.

The last possibility: happiness must be some simple uncomplicated moment when your purposes—no matter how unambitious—go unthwarted.

Like I had my own house once. And once, I had a certain recognition for particular kinds of Saturday afternoons, early dusk, mild uneventful

days. Yes, summer Saturdays, early dusk, just as the worst of the midday heat
has dissipated, and every window is thrown open to the deepening air, the
beginning breeze; rooms stretch out infinite in growing shadows. I am part
of the shadows, sweaty, rank. But every surface is scrubbed, rubbed to
gleaming. Leisurely, slow, I lean in to every doorway and everything is perfect order: perfumed linen, gleaming glass, dark scent of wax and incense
burning into dusk. And jazz saxophone mellow on the box—Standing
sour and damp, old clothes sticking to me, scalp pricking sweat, lifting my
shirtfront to the breath of a breeze, knowing I am the only imperfection
within this small perfection made by me. And I, for the moment, am my
own creation. It is not the weekly grind of housework that satisfies, but
purposes being met without interference. Completion. The signature on
the painting. The flourish at the end of the performance.

"Climbing into the wonderful world of Calgon is bliss," I say to Everett.
"I have been happy."

"Taking a bath is happiness for you?" he says, voice cracking. His look
is scorching. I guess I have missed a beat somewhere. I suppose I ought to
include *him* in it somehow.

I return to myself in an incredibly hot bath, so hot I am floating up like
the mist, so perfect my thoughts burst open like the bubbles I nudge with
my toe. I can dissolve into the sweat of mirrors that multiply me, disappear
into the yellow brilliance of saxophone straining toward the treble—a single superb note the horn blower discovers at the top of the riff. He blows,
bending at the knees until his chest caves—holding it . . . holding on. . . .
It is the uncertainty of the moment that inspires absorption: knowing the
sweetness of the bath can't last, knowing how hot dissipates to tepid, knowing that the record will end. That the silence will be broken . . . by a faint
sound—the deadbolt sliding back under the key. Joy is the prior regret for
the sweet ending of an irretrievable moment. I tell Everett that his returning home from an absence and I'm brand new in the bathtub is an intensely
exquisite experience.

Everett considers this—tongue busy. But I'm dissatisfied. What is this
feeling I'm looking for, so fleet, like a bubble I burst with my toe? Why
should it be that I can recall injuries and slights no end, have at my disposal
infinite evidence of the world's injustice, malice, casual cruelty. And disappointments: like discovering that there *is* no magic—no benevolent and

timely fairy godmother to rescue us from the daily cinders and rubble; that the bread crumbs strewn to show us the way are *always* food for birds, or the hustling industrious ants, leaving us all standing, faces tipped, staring up into a knit of blankness. Where are the matching memories of joy so powerful, so engulfing, enough to muffle the continuous pummeling of life?

This is a happy story with a dole of sadness, like the surplus bread handed out to the poor. Like the rich man whose joy in his richness is tainted with a worry that the poor might get too much. . . .

My neighborhood church is a dispensary to the poor. I volunteer to hand out surplus food to the needy. Sometimes cheese, sometimes bread. The Reverend Lester hands out religion. "Jesus fed the multitude with five loaves and two fish," he preaches a popular sermon.

"You givin' out fish too, Rev'rend?" a young woman asks.

"They given out fish," someone passes it on.

"*Some* folks got fish," another says, dissatisfied. "They run out."

The people stand in lines. I think of fish dinners, back yard fish fries, slapping mosquitoes on summer nights, pungent hot sauces, cold beer and lemonade. Mountains of catfish, perch, fried golden, crisp, the hot steam trapped inside the skin. How it would take all day to get ready with errands and cleaning the fish, and sweeping stray children from underfoot. The air full of expectation and no one too impatient.

A woman stands in front of me, her hands held forth for her portion. Her expression is sour. She looks at the smooth blocks of cheese thinking of fish. She takes the cheese, hands the large weight of it to her small child standing beside her. The child wobbles with the burden.

"There never was any fish," I say to her.

"Sure," she says.

"It was just a rumor," I say, but she stalks off. She wants to know who is in charge. My eyes are met by the direct stare of the woman standing behind her. She is elderly; her skin is smooth like rubbed, cured wood. After a moment, she smiles.

"The good Lord didn't need fish nor bread to do what he done. Don't never call *that* no rumor," she tells me, mocking-stern. "God bless," she says, receiving the cheese into her arms carefully. "I gives some of this to my nephew," she says. "He don't qualify. He earn $10.00 over the limit." Her smile is full of yellow gold, a bright chip drawing the vague light of the dim room to a single brilliant mite. She leaves me with my own smile.

"The happiest day of my life was the day we were married," Everett confesses to me, then waits. Then he says, "What about you?"

"I'm still working on it," I say.

"You weren't happy on our wedding day?" he says.

"Well," I say, "I didn't want to take *your* happiest day."

"But it *was* the happiest? So far? Right?"

Everett no longer asks me about my stories. Now I *make* him listen.

"This is a story about happiness," I say. "It's not finished." Everett says nothing. "This is what I have so far," I say.

"Alice always loved weddings. So, as a young girl, she resolved to have several. Each one would be more beautiful than the last, each husband more beautiful than his predecessor. Therefore, the spareness of her first wedding and the sparsity of beauty in the face and form of her first husband did not disturb her excessively. When the aged preacher misread a few of the vows, it was not devastating to Alice who, later, had to console her new husband's anger regarding the matter.

" 'You didn't plan to keep all those promises anyway,' she chided him, laughing, teasing. The accusation shocked him at first, as he did not expect her to know this, and he protested the fidelity of his heart. But, a day later, when Alice found her husband's eyes wandering behind an unfamiliar woman, he smiled, licked his lips and resolved to be more careful.

"His name was Cheever. Cheever did not have good looks but knew 'how to make him some money.' He said this often and Alice, who was always agreeable, agreed.

"But Alice did not despise Cheever for his lack of handsomeness. She felt genuinely grateful to him—he'd been her escape route from home, from her uncle's fish smell. She was satisfied with her marriage and learned how to keep house out of magazines, cooked out of books, and drew designs with colored pencils which she pinned all over her walls until they lived inside a montage of faint scribbly color. She even pinned the light designs to the bedboard above their heads. And sunny mornings when she woke to Cheever thrusting love at her from behind, matter-of-factly like a drowsy bear rubbing an itch against a slender bark, she had only to lift her eyes to study the outlines of dreams, outside the sudden odor of private lust.

"One day, when Cheever had gone, Alice crawled back into the spoiled sheets that held her daydreams. And behind her lids grew a tree supple and bending beneath the jewels that budded on the tips of its branches. She plucked one red fruit and made it disappear inside the warm dark of her palm."

"She's living in a dream world," says Everett. "Her husband is selfish and inconsiderate. *And* ugly. Where does the happy part come in?"

"It's coming," I say.

I am still writing the story of the woman—intelligent, ambitious, attractive, educated. Did I say intelligent? Because she is no longer planning her suicide, realizing it was a waste of her time since death is already scripted and requires no additional preparation. Realizing that her mother's life contained some moments of joy because she was a woman who worked towards the completion of tasks small and large and always spoke of her life without excluding any of its parts.

Nikki Giovanni

LORRAINE HANSBERRY: AN EMOTIONAL VIEW

from *Those Who Ride the Night Winds*

It's intriguing to me that "bookmaker" is a gambling . . . an underworld . . . term somehow associated with that which is both illegal . . . and dirty . . . Bookmakers . . . and those who play with them . . . are dreamers . . . are betting on a break . . . a lucky streak . . . that something will come . . . their way—something good . . . something clean . . . something wonderful . . . We who make books . . . we who write our dreams . . . confess our fears . . . and witness our times are not so far . . . from the underworld . . . are not so far . . . from illegality . . . are not so far from the root . . . the dirt . . . the heart of the matter.

Writers . . . I think . . . live on that fine line between insanity and genius . . . Either scaling the mountains . . . or skirting the valleys . . . Riding that lonely train of truth . . . with just enough of the player in us . . . to continue to hope . . . for the species . . . Writers are . . . perhaps . . . congenital hypocrites . . . I don't think preachers . . . priests . . . rabbis . . . and ayatollahs are hypocritical . . . because they have tubular vision . . . are indeed . . . myopic . . . They know the answer . . . before you ask the question . . . But the writer . . . the painter . . . the sculptor . . . the creator . . . those who work . . . with both the mind . . . and the heart of mankind . . . have no reason . . . to be hopeful . . . We have . . . in fact . . . no right to write the happy ending . . . or the love poem . . . no reason . . . to sculpt David . . . or paint . . . like Charles White . . . We who have seen . . . all sides of the coin . . . the front . . . the back . . . and the ribbed edge . . . know what the ending . . . will surely be . . . Yet we speak . . . to and of . . . courage . . . love . . . hope . . . something better . . . in mankind . . . When we are perfectly honest . . . with ourselves . . . we cannot justify . . . our faith . . . Yet faith we do have . . . and continue to share.

Bookmaking is shooting craps . . . with the white boys . . . downtown on the stock exchange . . . is betting a dime you can win . . . a hundred . . . Making books is shooting craps . . . with God . . . is wandering into a casino where you don't even know the language . . . let alone the rules of the game . . . And that's proper . . . that's as it should be . . . If you wanted to be safe . . . you would have walked into the Post Office . . . or taken a graduate degree in Educational Administration . . . If you want to share . . . a vision . . . or tell the truth . . . you pick up . . . your pen . . . And take your chances . . . This is not . . . after all . . . tennis . . . where sets can be measured by points . . . or football . . . where games run on time . . . or baseball . . . where innings structure the play . . . It is life . . . open-ended . . . And once the play has begun . . . the book made . . . time . . . is the only judge.

Time . . . to the Black American . . . has always been . . . a burden . . . from 1619 to now . . . we have played out our drama . . . before a reluctant time . . . We were either too late . . . or too early . . . No people on Earth . . . in all her history . . . has ever produced so many people . . . so generally considered . . . "ahead of their time." . . . From the revolts in Africa . . . to our kidnapping . . . to the martyrs of freedom today . . . our people have been burdened . . . by someone else's sense . . . of the appropriate . . . There are . . . of course . . . all the jokes . . . about C. P. time . . . and there are the reminders . . . by the keepers of our souls . . . that God "is never late . . . but He always comes . . . on time." . . . To be Black . . . in America . . . is to not at all understand . . . time . . . Little Linda Brown was told . . . her school would be desegregated . . . "with all deliberate speed" . . . and twenty-five years later . . . this is still . . . untrue . . . Dr. King was told . . . in Montgomery . . . he was pushing too hard . . . going too fast . . . expecting too much . . . I wish we had been enslaved . . . at the same rate we are being set . . . free . . . It would be . . . an entirely different story . . . I wish the battleships . . . had sailed down the Mississippi River . . . when Emmett Till was lynched . . . at the same speed they sped to Cuba . . . during the missile crisis . . . I wish food . . . had been airlifted . . . to the sharecroppers in Tennessee . . . when they were pushed off the land . . . for exercising their right to vote . . . at the same speed . . . it was airlifted . . . to West Berlin . . . at the ending of World War II . . . But I'm only a colored poet . . . and my wishes . . . no matter which star I choose . . . do not come true . . . But I'm also a writer . . . and I know . . . that the Europeans aren't the only ones . . . who keep time . . . some of the time is going . . . to be my time . . . too . . .

Life teaches us not to regret . . . not to spend too much time on what might have been . . . It is neither emotionally . . . nor intellectually possible . . . for me to dwell on might-have-beens . . . I have a great love of history and antiques . . . the past is there to instruct us . . . I am socially retarded . . . so I hold on . . . to old friends . . . I like to be surrounded . . . by that which is warm and familiar . . . yet I'm sorry . . . I never met Lorraine Hansberry . . . I vividly understand that a writer is not the book she made . . . any more than a child is the print of his parents . . . Many of us are personally paranoid . . . generally uncommunicative . . . and basically unnice . . . just like most people . . . But I think Lorraine must have been one . . . of those wonderful humans who . . . seeing both sides of the dilemma . . . and all sides of the coin . . . still called "Heads" . . . when she tossed . . . And in her gamble . . . never came up snake eyes . . . It's not that she wrote . . . beautifully . . . and truthfully . . . though she did . . . It's not just that she anticipated

... our people and their reactions ... though she did ... She also ... when reading through ... and between the lines ... possessed that quality of courage ... to say what had to be said ... to those who needed to hear it ... If writers are visionary ... her ministry was successful ... She made it ... possible for all of us ... to look ... a little ... deeper.

Rita Dove

NEXUS

from *The Yellow House on the Corner*

I wrote stubbornly into the evening.
At the window, a giant praying mantis
rubbed his monkey wrench head against the glass,
begging vacantly with pale eyes;

and the commas leapt at me like worms
or miniature scythes blackened with age.
The praying mantis screeched louder,
his ragged jaws opening onto formlessness.

I walked outside;
the grass hissed at my heels.
Up ahead in the lapping darkness
he wobbled, magnified and absurdly green,
a brontosaurus, a poet.

Flo Kennedy

TO WHOM IT CONCERNS

from *Color Me Flo*

[The following is a paper that Ms. Kennedy wrote in 1946 for a creative writing class at Columbia University.]

"To whom it concerns:

"I am one of those thousands of people whose head is swimming with unwritten books: novels, short stories, articles, and non-fictional outbursts of every imaginable sort. Naturally, I'm goose-pimply to write the inevitable autobiography.

"I'm thirty, and what with working eight hours a day as a dreary (even if rebellious) clerical in the U.S. Treasury Department and taking eleven units of extension work as a pre-law student at Columbia, my chances seem sickeningly slim. From where I sit, it looks as if I'll be older and much grayer before I have either the time to write, or enough money saved to quit work and—you know the story.

"I've done publicity for organizations in Kansas City—articles and accounts written in this connection have appeared in the *Kansas City Call,* a weekly. I am completing a course in professional writing at school, where I have a lot of fun, but have rather made a fool of myself.

"I think the folks in my writing class all love me, but they (especially my friends) can't help laughing at my long, tumbling, "wordy" sentences (see above and below), my crazy ideas. (I don't believe in marriage, horizontal romance or religion, church, and/or the Bible; I love the hiccups, words, and fighting; I do not smoke, except other people's, and I don't drink because I don't like the flavor of alcohol.)

"I'm very poor, very proud, and a Negro—but I don't think very much about it, and I run like everything to keep out of organizations.

"I can't say anything about quality, as regards my writing, but I suffer from an acute case of word diarrhea, and there has never been a time when I couldn't write on and on about almost anything. The only thing is that no one ever agrees with what I write, although it makes perfectly good sense to me."

Zora Neale Hurston

THE MAP OF DIXIE ON MY TONGUE

from *Dust Tracks on a Road: An Autobiography*

I was a Southerner, and had the map of Dixie on my tongue. . . . It was not that my grammar was bad, it was the idioms. . . . [The] average Southern child, white or black, is raised on simile and invective. They know how to call names. It is an every day affair to hear somebody called a mullet-headed, mule-eared, wall-eyed, hog-nosed, 'gator-faced, shad-mouthed, screw-necked, goat-bellied, puzzle-gutted, camel-backed, butt-sprung, battle-hammed, knock-kneed, razor-legged, box-ankled, shovel-footed, unmated so-and-so! . . . They can tell you in simile exactly how you walk and smell. They can furnish a picture gallery of your ancestors, and a notion of what your children will be like. What ought to happen to you is full of images and flavor. . . . they take their comparisons right out of the barnyard and the woods.

Folk

HOW YOU DOING?

[The following responses were collected from black folk by the Hampton Folk-Lore Society and published in *Southern Workman* 27 (July 1898). They are typical of the humorous and colorful language preferred by a people who frequently disdain a bland, direct response to an inquiry such as, "How are you doing?" These responses reveal more of what Hurston called "The Map of Dixie" that characterizes the vivid imagery and imaginative love of wordplay that is representative of much Southern black folk speech.]

"I ain't many."
"I'm much behine, but I have to keep on gwine."
"Right smart."

"Mighty peart."
"I'm kickin' but not high."
"Tough up and tolable."
"When you are half dead and runnin' I'll be up and a comin'."
"Kinder so-so."
"Sorter tolable."
"I'm fat but don't show it."
" 'Twixt the middlin's and the hams."
"I'm barkin' but I won't bite."
"I'm fat an' fine."
"W'ite folks calc'latin' to keep me behin'."
"I'm middlin', considerin'."
"I'm hangin' an' draggin' like an ole shoe."
"T'ank de Lawd I'm spa'ed."

Marilyn Nelson Waniek

EMILY DICKINSON'S DEFUNCT

She used to
pack poems
in her hip pocket.
Under all the
gray old lady
clothes she was
dressed for action.
She had hair,
imagine,
in certain places, and
believe me
she smelled human
on a hot summer day.
Stalking snakes

or counting
the thousand motes
in sunlight
she walked just
like an Indian.
She was New England's
favorite daughter,
she could pray
like the devil.
She was a
two-fisted woman,
this babe.
All the flies
just stood around
and buzzed
when she died.

Sibby Anderson-Thompkins

EPITAPH FOR WILLIE OR LITTLE BLACK POET WITH NO FUTURE

today
i will b
a
poet
i
will writ of
beautiful blck people
ancient egypt
and fantastik aventures
in distant lands

p.s. for lack of refrence
i will have ta git
back
ta y

Whoopi Goldberg

FONTAINE

[Fontaine bops in, walking that special cool street walk, exaggerated by his constant bobbing. He is the stereotypical stoned junkie, with a scarf tied around his head. He is clearly high, and in a world of his own as he enters, singing:] Around-d-d the world in eighty mothafuckin days. Da dubby do-o-o, da dubby do-o-o, da dubby do-o-o, da dubby, dubby, dub, du wah! Around-d-d the world in eighty mothafuckin days. Da dubby do-o-o, da dubby do-o-o, da dubby do-o-o, da dubby, dubby, dub, du wah-ah-ah-ah-ahhh! [picking up the pace] Around the world in eighty days. Da dubby da. [picking up the pace] Around, shuwhopp de whop, shuwhopp, the mothafuckin world, dubby, dubby, dubby dubby wah-ah-ah-ah in eigh-ty— [pauses, looks around, suddenly aware of the audience, grabs crotch (throughout, Fontaine's hand will frequently be clutching his genitalia), and looks towards audience].

What's happening? What's happening? Hey, Look yawl, I say, "What's happening," yawl say "everything is everything. . . ."*—whatever the fuck you say. O.K. So we gon try the shit again.

Around-d-d the world in eighty motha-fucking days. Da duppy do-o-o, da duppy do-o-o, da dubby-dubby-dubby-du-du-wah-ah-ah-ah-h-h-h-h-h.

What's happening?
[Audience responds loudly]
That wasn't shit!

---

*I have used spaced periods throughout to indicate pauses in the monologue rather than omissions from it. Actual omissions are indicated by bracketed summaries.

What's happening, Cute-tay [speaking to woman in audience]? Looking *good!* Shit. My name is Fontaine, and *love* is my game. And when I kiss the girls, hey! they all aflame. Come on let me kiss your hand. . . . No, the one with the *diamonds* on it. Looking *good* too. Glad to see you here. Yeah! I'm glad you was cool enough to play. I notice you didn't clutch your *pocketbook.* Yeah, Mon, a lot of people can't handle me. I don't understand it. Cause like I feel like I'm a friendly person. But you know some people's attitudes nearly drove me out the country at one point. No . . . they did, Mon, but I got the kinda gig that allows me the freedom to cruise. Because *I* am a *thief.* It's the all-American traditional gig. Some people always got something, some people always want something. I provide a *service.* Yeah. I service my ass right on up to the upper Eastside too. Checked out these bad apartments. Found these gold plated digital *escargot* forks. Yeah, Mon. Cashed those mothafuckers in, picked up some cash. Went on down to JFK. Cause you know on T.V. they always tell you, "Come on down and pick up your ticket to Europe." So that's what I did, you know. And I said to the dude real politely, "Hey! Where is my mothafuckin ticket to Europe at?" Yeah, you know. And that man looked at me like I farted on his best suit. But, he wrote the ticket out. I mean he handed it to me, you know. I took it and walked away. He come runnin' up behind me, talkin' 'bout I had to *pay* for it first. I say, "What! I mean you really expect me to pay *before* I fly?" You know, because I'm a business person, o.k. And if I have a product I want you to buy from me, I'm gon' give you a taste first—just so *you* know I *stand* behind my product, you know, because that's good business, you know. But the airlines, they don't feel like that. They get your money, get you up in the air, and then they drop your ass. But you know, the dude say he was gon' call the police on me and shit. I said fuck it, you know. I gave 'im the nine hundred and fifty-six dollars, and I walked ten steps away over to this chick who is standin' there, looking at me like this: [imitating an exaggerated and artificial grin showing all of her teeth]. I say, "Bitch what *are* you grinning at?" You know. . . . You know?

And she looks at me talkin' 'bout [artificial grin], "We have a bit of a problem. Now what's happened is we've oversold this flight. Now, what that means is we have one hundred seats on the plane, but we sold tickets to *three* thousand people [artificial grin and pause]. . . . So I guess you're not going anywhere, are you?" [big grin]

So you know, I pulled some shit outta my hip, you see—just in case you find yourself in the same position. Cause I got down in her *face,* I said, "Hey!" [Whoopi's grin is a threatening one] I say, "I been through your pocketbook and I know where you *live. . . . "* And needless to say, I got me a seat on the plane. That's right, Mon, checked my bags through and shit.

And like just as I was goin' out the door, I pass this big dude walkin' around in circles wit' a picket sign, talking about stop abortions. I say, "Motherfucka, when was the last time *you* was *pregnant?"* And he looks at me, he say [indignant tone], "I don't have to discuss that with you." I said, "Oh but you should because I have the *answer* to abortion." He say [interested], "What is it?" I say, "Shoot your dick!" Hey, Mon, I did, I tol' 'im. I say "Take that tired piece a meat down to the ASPCA, and let 'em put it to sleep." And then, hey, I'd feel better then cause then I'd know he put his money where his mouth is.

[After a hilariously recounted plane trip, Whoopi lands in Amsterdam and goes to the Anne Frank House] And I noticed a small staircase leadin' up to a big bookcase—and I'm into books, you know. I got a Ph.D. in literature from *Columbia.* So I . . . [shocked that he is interrupted by laughter]. I know you don't think I was *born* a junkie. . . . No, I have an education. I got a Ph.D. I can't do shit with, you know, so I stay high so I don't get *mad!*

So I went on up the stairs cause, you know, cause I wanted to see this one book. So I like pulled on the book, and when I did that the bookcase opened up. And on the other side was a whole other room. Now, wasn't nobody up there sayin' "Don't go in"—ain't nah one a dem signs. So I walked in. [After browsing around for a while Fontaine discovers where he is.] I happened to turn my head and see the skylight. And I say, oh my, I'm in the room where Anne Frank and the family is. And that kinda like threw me, you know. Cause this ain't somethin' I'm really on top of, you know, in terms of, . . . [pauses in response to audience] no it wasn't, you know, in terms of history. My forte is American history from the twenties to the present time, you know [pauses again in shock at the audience's laughter]. . . . Now why is that hard to believe, Mon? I mean I know I'm a junkie but I'm not stupid!

So, like I was checking out, you know, the differences. Because, like, *here* we *knew* what was happening—things like the Civil Rights Movement, but it was a little bit different over in Europe, Mon. Cause the Jews wasn't ready. See they been livin' there *integrated* into these areas—as well as they could be. They thought of themselves as Germans, or Austrians, or whatever. And when these people *changed* on 'em. Start callin' them nasty names and turnin' em in—they turn around say, "Well, hey, we been through this kind o' thing before. You know, this is goin' to pass." And when they *realized* what was happening was *real,* it was too late. And they ended up in the camps. Leavin' and goin' into hiding, and that kind of blew me away too. Cause like I always thought when you went into hiding, it was like moving from one apartment to another. Yeah, cause everybody I ever knew who went into hiding, *I knew* where they were. The only people who didn't know was the *police*—you know what I'm saying? These folks were stuck in this room for two years. And it wasn't like they was *living.* They got in there. They had twenty hours a day of nonmovement, Mon. Non-movement. No noise. They sat with no sound . . . [long pause of perhaps a minute, and the audience begins to get restless].

Nerve wracking ain't it? Yeah! And I discovered just like you just did that I couldn't do it. See, I'd a had to make some noise and *mess* up, you know. And I realize that that was really a stupid way to do things. Yeah, cause why cut off your nose to spite your face? And when that hit me, so did the fact that I was in an empty room . . . *cryin'.* See wasn't nobody in there sayin' they was goin' to kick my ass. You know, wasn't nothin' in there threatening me. I say, no this don't have nothing to do with me. Get me *out!* And I ran to the door. but I got stopped by a big *sign* that said, "In spite of everything, I still believe people are good at heart." I say, What? I mean, who put this up? Why would they put it in this room, Mon? I-I just couldn't understand it, you know. So I copped an attitude. Decided to write a letter to the author of the quote. So I got up close enough to see the author's name, . . . and my jaw dropped, cause it say Anne Frank. And I thought this is too childish for *words,* Mon. You know, what *are* you talkin' about? You . . . you didn't even make it. And as soon as I said that it made perfect sense. Of course Anne Frank *could* say that. She *was* a child. She was a kid. And, you know, no matter what you do to children, they're always able to still see some good in you. Cause, you see, they got that ability to see the light at the end of the tunnel. I don't have it. I'm what you call . . . jaded. And I say, Yeah, Mon, you know, what can I say?

And I started examinin' my own shit. You know, what are my day-to-day worries? I mean, what grinds my ass to the bone on a daily basis, Mon? Things like *why* can't I get an American Express Card, you know?

Oh, yeah! Why can't I find a hairdresser to mess with my coif? You know, these are my big day-to-day worries, Mon. But *then*, you know, you go into a *room* like this and you hold your coif and your card up against life and death, and you know the true meaning of trivial pursuit.

I decided what I was goin' to do, you know. I figured what I should do is try to adopt this philosophy somehow, you know, this "in spite of every-thing . . . ," cause it might help me in case I got home and I caught some mothafucka in my *house* rippin' off my stereo. Yes, I will still break their legs but I will remember that, in spite of everything, this person is still good at heart and that will save their life. O.K. So yeah, and somethin' told my ass it was time to go home, you know.

And like on the way home it was kind of tense for me, you know, cause I happen to be looking out the mothafuckin window and I noticed that it was all *black*. And on the other side the plane, was all blue and shit. And I say, now somethin' *wrong* with this picture. And I realize that the wing was smoking. So I said to the stewardess, you know—I didn't want to panic or nothing—I say [false calm in voice], "I beg your pardon, but it seem as though the *wing* is *smoking!*" She turn around talkin' 'bout, "Shhhh." I say [hysterical now], "Hey bitch, the wing is on fire!"

You got two choices in this kind of situation. Now, I mean that's true. You can take this shit like a man or a woman, or you can freak out. Guess which venue I took. . . . Yeah, I *freaked!* I freaked up and down the plane, felt like Daffy Duck [waving arms wildly and screaming] Whaaahhhh, Whaaahhhh! I freaked while the plane was landin' in New York, Mon. I freaked while they was pulling my ass off the plane, putting me in that muthafuckin' straitjacket, threw my ass in the ambulance, goin' to Bellevue. That's right, and they let me out. I freaked from the street *into* the hospital, *into* my room, you know. Yeah, Mon, yeah. I freaked for 'bout *ten* weeks. . . . I just got out *yesterday.*

Yeah, but, you know, I had a lot of time to think, you know, in between freak bouts. Cause it turns out, you know, I'm one of those people, you know, if you don't speak English, don't come up to me in the street and ask me where shit is.

Yeah, you the same way, right? [Mockingly] "Yeah, go talk to somebody who know what the hell you talkin 'bout; come over here and take my job." Yeah, well, you know it's real hard to be that cold once you've been the alien. See cause once you've been the alien, you find out how *hard* it is to have to ask somebody where some shit is. And then you find out what it take to be able to tell 'em. Cause it don't take nothin' but a little bit o' graciousness, Mon. That's it, you know. Just a little bit. And that coupled wit' everything else that happened to me kinda freaked me out, you know. Cause I realize that life is a constant thing. It's constant live and learn. Never get over that shit. Not even a junkie. Not even a junkie.

[Fontaine slowly turns and leaves the stage, still bopping and still holding his crotch with his hand. In the distance sirens can be heard.]

M I M E O G R A P H E D   I T E M
Bill Clinton's Advisers and Cabinet

DEPT. OF TRANSPORTATION	TED KENNEDY
DEPT. OF HOUSING	LEONA HELMSLEY
DEPT. OF LABOR	ANITA HILL
DEPT. OF DEFENSE	RODNEY KING
SECY. OF TREASURY	CHARLES KEATING
SECY. OF HEALTH	MAGIC JOHNSON
DIR. OF THE C.I.A.	H. ROSS PEROT
DIR. OF THE F.B.I.	HILLARY CLINTON
HEAD OF NASA	JERRY BROWN
VETERANS AFFAIRS	JANE FONDA
SURGEON GENERAL	DR. JACK KEVORKIAN
DRUG ENFORCEMENT AGENCY	MARION BARRY
SPECIAL ADVISER ON FAMILY AFFAIRS	WOODY ALLEN

MIMEOGRAPHED ITEM

How You Can Tell When It's Going To Be A Rotten Day

You wake up face down on the pavement.

You put your bra on backward and it fits better.

You call Suicide Prevention and they put you on hold.

You see a <u>60 Minutes</u> news team waiting in your office.

Your birthday cake collapses from the weight of the candles.

Your son tells you he wishes Anita Bryant would mind her own business.

You want to put on the clothes you wore home from the party and there aren't any.

You turn on the news and they're showing emergency routes out of the city.

Your twin sister forgot your birthday.

You wake up and discover your waterbed broke and then realize that you don't have a waterbed.

Your car horn goes off accidentally and remains stuck as you follow a group of Hell's Angels on the freeway.

Your wife wakes up feeling amorous and you have a headache.

Your boss tells you not to bother to take off your coat.

The bird singing outside your window is a buzzard.

You wake up and your braces are locked together.

You walk to work and find your dress is stuck in the back of your pantyhose.

You call your answering service and they tell you it's none of your business.

Your blind date turns out to be your ex-wife.

Your income tax check bounces.

You put both contact lenses in the same eye.

Your pet rock snaps at you.

Your wife says, "Good morning, Bill" and your name is George.

Author Unknown . . . But Troubled . . .

Folk

O . J .   I S   C H I L L Y

[When on June 12, 1994, Nicole Brown Simpson, the wife of famed athlete O. J. Simpson, was found brutally stabbed along with a male friend, America and the world turned its attention to Los Angeles. Viewers first watched minute by minute the televised low-speed automobile chase, during which O.J. was followed by police who were attempting to take him into custody. Then they watched the trial daily for nine months, with night shows offering recaps and providing "experts" to analyze the events of the day's proceedings. An unprecedented number of books were written about the family and the trial, and numerous commentators, lawyers, talk-show hosts, and formerly unknown friends built a career around the case. The names of lawyers, judges, friends of those involved, and even Nicole Simpson's dog became so well known that they were discussed without the need to fully identify them. Cochran in the selection below is Johnnie Cochran, the lead attorney for O. J. Simpson. Ito is Judge Lance Ito. Key evidence in the case included a cap, gloves, and socks found either at the scene of the crime or at Simpson's home with hair or blood samples that purportedly connected him to the crime.]

Cochran asked Judge Ito to please turn the air-conditioning down—O.J. was getting chilly, and he has done so well without catching a cold before now.

    Ito say "Awright." And he went on with something else.

    Cochran went to him again, and he say, "Judge, yo' honor, *please,* can you turn it down? It is really annoying him now and he's beginning to shiver."

    The man ignored him again. So the third time, Ito say [impatient voice], "Listen, if you gon ask me about the air, something else takes precedence over that. Just forget it."

    Cochran say, "Well then, he wants to know, can he have his cap, his gloves, and his socks back."

Folk

APPROACH THE BENCH

Judge Ito said, "Okay, everybody approach the bench!"
So everybody ran to Marcia Clark.★
The Judge said, "I said the *bench*—not the *bitch!*

Barbara Brandon

WHERE I'M COMING FROM

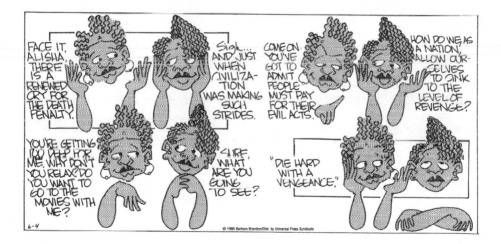

★Marcia Clark was the lead prosecuting attorney in the trial.

Folk

WAIT ON DE LORD

from Daryl Cumber Dance, *Shuckin' and Jivin'*

This Buzzard went and he lit on a dead pine tree. And he was sittin' all up there like he ain't got *nobody* in the worl'. So a Hawk come 'long, say, "Hey, Mr. Buzzard," say, "you look you ain't got *nobody* in de worl'." Old Buzzard ain't say a *mumblin'* word. After while, a little sparrow pranced along down below the Buzzard; a little sparrow come along and went underneath the fence to get out. Old Hawk tried to ketch him, you know, and Hawk like to eat everything fresh. He tried to ketch the little sparrow, and he run through that wire; he hang up in the wire. So the old Buzzard ain't said nothin' *yet*. After a while the old Hawk started to smellin' and the old Buzzard fly down; "It's a good t'ing to wait on de Lord."

I tell them around home, I say, "Who? I'm a buzzard; I gon' wait on de Lord."

Folk

IS THE COAST CLEAR?

This man had just come home from a two-week business trip, and he had missed his wife so much, you know, couldn't wait to get in the bed. As soon as they got in the bed, the telephone rang. He reached over and picked it up, frowned, and hung up.

His wife say, "Who was it, dear?"

He say, "Nothin' but some fool tryin' to get the weather bureau—want to know if the coast is clear?"

M I M E O G R A P H E D   I T E M
Retirement Policy

TO: ALL PERSONNEL

FR: MANAGEMENT

SUBJECT: NEW RETIREMENT POLICY/ADDITIONAL TRAINING

As a result of the reduction in money budgeted for division purposes, we are going to cut down our number of personnel.

Under the new plan, older employees will go on early retirement, thus permitting the retention of younger people who represent our future plans.

Therefore, a program to phase out older personnel by the end of the current fiscal year via early retirement will be placed into effect immediately. The program shall be known as RAPE (Retired Aged Personnel Early).

Employees who are RAPED will be given the opportunity to seek other jobs within the system, provided that while they are being RAPED they request a review of their employment records before actual retirement takes place. This phase of the operation is called SCREW (Survey of Capabilities of Retired Early Workers).

All employees who have been RAPED or SCREWED may also apply for a trial review. This will be called SHAFT (Study by Higher Authority Following Termination).

Program policy dictates employees may be RAPED once and SCREWED twice, but may get the SHAFT as many times as the company deems appropriate.

It is now and always has been the policy of this company to assure its employees that they are well trained. Through our Special High Intensity Training Program (SHIT), we have given our employees more SHIT than any other company in the area.

Any employee feeling that he or she does not receive enough SHIT on this job, or that he or she could advance to another, position by taking more SHIT, see your supervisor.

Our people are especially trained to assure you that you will get all the SHIT you can handle.

MNGE

Folk

TEACHERS ON THE THIRD FLOOR

This woman decided she was gon' open this whorehouse—so she got this *three*-story building, and she put her ad in the paper for the people to come and work in it. So, she got just *all* sorts of responses from *every* walk of life— just all sorts of responses. Just all sorts of professional women responded to the ad. So she had enough people to fill up the whole place. But she said, "Now *who* are we going to put on the third floor? Cause we don't want to make our best men customers walk *all* the way up to the third floor once they get here, . . . you know. . . . We'll just put the worst ones up on the third floor."

So they say, "Well, we'll put the *teachers* on the third floor."

So the men came, and all of 'em start askin' to go up on the third floor. They want to go up there and be with the *teachers.*

So they say, "We just can't understand it. We just felt like the teachers are just so conservative and so straight-laced that they just would not want the teachers. They would be the last choice."

So finally one came in, and they say, "Now will you just tell us what is it up there on the third floor that makes yawl want to go up on the third floor."

He say, "One thing bout those teachers up there—they make you do it and do it again until you git it right."

MIMEOGRAPHED ITEM
Senior Citizens Beat Inflation

A couple, age 67, went to the doctor's office. The doctor asked, "What can I do for you?" The man said, "Will you watch us have sexual intercourse?" The doctor looked puzzled but agreed. When the couple had finished, the doctor said, "There is nothing wrong with the way you have intercourse," and he charged them $32.00. This happened several weeks in a row. The couple would make an appointment, have intercourse, pay the doctor and leave. Finally the doctor asked, "Just exactly what are you trying to find out?" The old man said, "We're not trying to find out anything, She is married and we can't go to her house. I am married and we can't go to my house. The Holiday Inn charges $60.00. The Hilton charges $78.00, we do it here for $32.00 and I get back $28.00 from Medicare for a visit to the doctor's office."

Jacqueline Brice-Finch

SAFE SEX

PROTECTION I

Trojans are a hard
fit when excitement and no
practice meet head on.

PROTECTION II

Which side of latex
will scroll the organ right
before the ardor cools.

Flo Kennedy

WOMEN'S MOVEMENT

Commenting on the women's movement, Flo Kennedy declared, "If it's a movement, I sometimes think it needs a laxative."
—*Des Moines Sunday Register,* April 7, 1974

MIMEOGRAPHED ITEM

West Virginia Medical Terminology for the Layman

Artery	The study of fine paintings.
Barium	What you do when C.P.R. fails.
Benign	What you be after you be eight.
Caesarean section	A district in Rome.
Colic	A sheep dog.
Coma	A punctuation mark.
Congenital	Friendly.
Denial	A large river in Egypt.
Dilate	To live longer.
Fester	Quicker.
Grippe	A suitcase.
G.I. Series	Baseball games between teams of soldiers.
Hangnail	A coathook.
Medical staff	A doctor's cane.
Minor Operation	Coal digging.
Morbid	A higher offer.
Nitrate	Lower than the day rate.
Node	Was aware of (I node it).
Organic	Church musician.
Outpatient	A person who has fainted.
Post-operative	A letter carrier.
Protein	In favor of young people.
Secretion	Hiding something.
Serology	Study of English knighthood.
Tablet	A small table.
Tumor	An extra pair.
Urinalysis	What you get from your psychiatrist.
Urine	Opposite of you're out.
Vagina	A state just south of Maryland.
Varicose veins	Veins that are very close together.

Folk

MY SYMPATHY

New mother: (in a somewhat haughty and fervent tone, as she looks at and proudly caresses her baby): "Well, you know, he has his father's complexion. And he has my eyes. And everybody can see he's got his grandfather's nose. And he has my sister's lips. And, and—"

Listener: "And he has my sympathy."

MIMEOGRAPHED ITEM
The Birth of a Candy Bar

One Pay Day Mr. Good-bar wanted a Bit-A-Honey. So he took Mrs. Hershey behind the Power House on Fifth Avenue he began unstriping her Reese Cups and started feeling Mounds which turned out to be pure Almond Joy, then he went up her Milky Way. She screamed OhHenry and squeezed his Nutty Butty and the result was a Baby Ruth.

Moms Mabley

THE GREATEST MAN

from *Moms Mabley Onstage*

A Jewish fellow and a Chinaman were standing on the corner arguing about who was the greatest man that ever lived. And an Irishman walked up. He said, "If you tell me who the greatest man that ever lived I'll give you five hundred dollars in cash."

The lil' Chinaman say, "Chiang Kai-shek."

He say, "Nah!"

The lil' Jewish fellow say, "St. Patrick!"

He say, "You're right." Reached his hand in his pocket, give 'im the $500.00. He walked away.

The lil' Jewish fellow looked at the $500. He say, "I had *Moses* in mind, but *business* is business."

MIMEOGRAPHED   ITEM

Best Rum Cake Ever

1 or 2 quarts Rum	Baking Powder
1 cup butter	1 teaspoon soda
1 teaspoon sugar	Lemon Juice
2 large eggs	Brown sugar
1 cup dried fruit	Nuts

Before you start, sample the rum to check for quality. Good, isn't it? Now go ahead. Select a large mixing bowl, measuring cup, etc. Check the rum again. It must be just right. To be sure rum is of the highest quality, pour one level cup of rum into a glass and drink it as fast as you can. Repeat.

With an electric mixer, beat 1 cup of butter in a large fluffy bowl. Add 1 seaspoon of thugar and beat again. Meanwhile, make sure that the rum is of the finest quality. Try another cup. Open second quart if necessary. Add 2 arge leggs, 2 cups fried druit and beat until high. If druit gets stuck in beaters, just bry it loose with a drewscriver. Sample the rum again, testing for tonscisticity. Next sift 3 cups of pepper or salt (it really doesn't matter). Sample the rum again. Sift 1/2 pint of lemon juice. Fold in chopped butter and strained nuts. Add 1 babblespoon of brown thugar, or whatever color you can find. Wix mell. Grease oven and turn cake pan to 350 gredees. Now pour the whole mess into the coven and ake. Check the rum again, and bo to ged.

Moms Mabley

HELEN HUNT

from *Moms Mabley Onstage*

Oh, I like to forgot it. The manager told me to announce that some lady in the house by the name of Miz Helen Hunt has found somebody's pocketbook. So, if you want your pocketbook, go to Helen Hunt [Hell and hunt] for it.

Kate Rushin

IN ANSWER TO THE QUESTION: HAVE YOU EVER CONSIDERED SUICIDE?

from *The Black Back-Ups*

Suicide??!!
Gurl, is you crazy?
I'm scared I'm not gonna live long enough
As it is

I'm scared to death of high places
Fast cars
Rare diseases
Muggers
Drugs
Electricity
And folks who work roots

Now what would I look like
Jumping off of something
I got everything to do

And I ain't got time for that
Let me tell you
If you ever hear me
Talking about killing my frail self
Come and get me
Sit with me until that spell passes
Cause it will
And if they ever
Find me laying up somewhere
Don't let them tell you it was suicide
Cause it wasn't

I'm scared of high places
Fast-moving trucks
Muggers
Electricity
Drugs
Folks who work roots
And home-canned string beans

Now with all I got
To worry about
What would I look like
Killing myself

Mama Sez

Run that by me one more time. [This is not just a request to repeat something, but a reminder to reflect on what you have said.]

One hand washes the other.

She give up the ghost [died].

It's raining while the sun is shining, so you know the Devil is beating his wife.

Don't measure my bushel by your pint.

You got to root, hog, or die.

She's up the creek widout a paddle.

Sister to Sister

What do you call two skunks who practice oral sex? Odor eaters.

What's the difference between the accountant and the computer? The computer is friendlier [you know the computer is user-friendly].

She ran through here like a bat outta hell.

It's as cold in here as a witch's titty.

Money is as scarce in this house as hen's teeth.

It was so quiet in there you could hear a rat piss on cotton.

It was so quiet in there you could hear a gnat piss fifty feet away.

She sure can burn [cook]!

Don't that just take the cake!

Here she comes in her Sunday-go-to-meeting clothes.

Excuse my French [profanity]!

[In response to Gloria Wade-Gayles, who asked a woman whose parents and other family members had been slaughtered by whites how she felt about white people.] "Some of them is too nice to be white people" [*Pushed Back to Strength,* 187].

I been down so long that down looks like up.

When I told her that, she like to had a duck fit.

They were laughing to beat the band.

Adams, Armacie (c. 1850–?)

Armacie Adams was one of the former Virginia slaves interviewed by the WPA interviewers, whose account appears in *The Negro in Virginia* (1940). She was born in Gates County, North Carolina. After her mother's death when Armacie was three years old, she was raised, she says, by "white folks" in Huntersville, Virginia (near Norfolk). She told the interviewers that her master was cruel: "I ain't plannin' on meetin' him in heaven." She was not told that slavery was over and continued to be held in bondage until she discovered several months later that she was free.

Allen, Bonnie (b. 1946)

Bonnie Allen was born and grew up in Oakland, California. A nationally published film and television critic, she has contributed to several magazines. Ms. Allen now lives in New York City, where she writes for a number of magazines.

Anderson-Thompkins, Sibby

Born in Greenville, North Carolina, Sibby Anderson-Thompkins completed a B.A. and M.A. in speech communication at the University of North Carolina at Chapel Hill, where she worked as Assistant Dean of Students.

Angelou, Maya (b. 1928)

Born in St. Louis, Missouri, on April 4, 1928, and raised in Stamps, Arkansas, by her grandmother, Maya Angelou has become one of the most popular teachers, lecturers, autobiographers, poets, actresses, talk-show guests, and overall entertainers of our times. Her works include *I Know Why the Caged Bird Sings* (1970), *Just Give Me a Cool Drink of Water 'fore I Die* (1971), *Gather Together in My Name* (1974), *Oh Pray My Wings Are Gonna Fit Me Well* (1975), *Singin' & Swingin' & Gettin' Merry Like Christmas* (1976), *And Still I Rise* (1978), *The Heart of a Woman* (1981), *Shaker, Why Don't You Sing?* (1983), and *All God's Children Need Travelling Shoes* (1986). She read her popular *On the Pulse of Morning,* composed for the inauguration of President Clinton in 1993. In 1996 she recorded an album, *Been Found,* in which she melds comments on love and hope with the melodies of Ashford and Simpson. Since 1982 she has been Reynolds Professor at Wake Forest University.

Ansa, Tina McElroy (b. 1949)

Born and raised in Macon, Georgia, Tina McElroy was educated at Spelman College and went on to work as a journalist for *The Charlotte Observer* and *The Atlanta Journal-Constitution.* She also taught at Clark College and Spellman College. She is the author of three novels: *Baby of the Family* (1989), *Ugly Ways* (1993), and *The Hand I Fan With* (1996), all of which are set in her fictional small town of Mulberry, Georgia. Her first novel was named a Notable Book of the Year by the *New York Times* in 1989. She lives on St. Simons Island, off the coast of Georgia.

Bambara, Toni Cade (1939–1996)

Born and raised in New York City, Toni Cade Bambara received a B.A. from Queens College and an M.A. from City College of New York. She also studied theater, dance, and film in the United States and abroad. She worked as a social investigator and a director of recreation before going on to teach in several colleges and universities, including Rutgers University, City College of New York, Duke University, and Spelman College. She edited *The Black Woman: An Anthology* (1970) and *Tales and Stories for Black Folks* (1971). Her writings include two collections of short stories: *Gorilla, My Love* (1972) and *The Sea Birds Are Still Alive* (1977), and the novel *The Salt Eaters* (1980). She also produced a number of documentary films, including *The Bombing of Osage Avenue* (treating the bombing of the MOVE group in Philadelphia in 1985) and *W. E. B. Du Bois—a Biography in Four Voices*. She won the American Book Award for *The Salt Eaters*.

Berry, Bertice (b. 1960)

The sixth of seven children, Bertice Berry grew up in a poor family headed by an alcoholic mother in Wilmington, Delaware. She persevered in school, despite the fact that she was told she wasn't college material. After earning a Ph.D. in sociology from Kent State University, Dr. Berry taught sociology there until she became a stand-up comedienne, a popular lecturer, a television talk-show host (*The Bertice Berry Show* premiered in 1993), and a singer. She is the author of *The World According to Me* (1996).

Berry, Fannie (1841–?)

Born into slavery, Fannie Berry's earliest recollections are of living in Appomattox County. Her oral account of her life in slavery was collected by WPA interviewers in Petersburg, Virginia in 1937. She notes that she was "a reg/lar debbil" during her youth, though she did later marry a preacher (*The Negro in Virginia*, 92).

Binford, Virgie M. (b. 1924)

Born in Tralake, Mississippi, Virgie M. Binford went on to study at Virginia State College and Virginia Polytechnic Institute and State University. After a prominent career as a classroom teacher, a college teacher, and an administrator, she continues to be a popular educational consultant, lecturing and conducting workshops throughout the United States and abroad. Dr. Binford is the author of several pedagogical works, including *Helping Them Succeed by Meeting Their Needs* (1987) and *The Wind Beneath Their Wings: Self-Esteem Builders for Students and Teachers* (1992). In the fall of 1996 she was honored for her years of volunteer service to the juvenile court system by having the education wing of the new Oliver W. Hill Juvenile Courts Building in Richmond, Virginia, named after her.

Birtha, Becky (b. 1948)

Born in Hampton, Virginia, Becky Birtha moved to California in 1969. She earned a degree in children's studies from The State University of New York at Buffalo and studied in the Master of Fine Arts in Writing Program at Vermont College. Birtha is the author of two collections of short stories, *For Nights Like This One: Stories of Loving Women* (1983) and *Lovers' Choice* (1987), and one collection of poetry, *The Forbidden Poems* (1991). Her works focus on the lives of women and their relationships (often lesbian) in a moving, poignant, and distinctive voice. In 1988 she won a National Endowment for the Arts Creative Writing Fellowship and the Pushcart Prize.

Bowen-Spencer, Michele (b. 1957)

Born and raised in St. Louis, Missouri, Michele Bowen-Spencer received the B.A., M.F.A., and M.Ed. degrees from Washington University in St. Louis. She also holds an M.P.H. and an M.A. in history from the University of North Carolina at Chapel Hill. She has worked in health and human services and is now serving as Executive Director of the Wright/Hurston Foundation and completing *Churchfolk,* a novel about the black church. She lives in Richmond, Virginia.

Boyd, Julia A.

A psychotherapist whose work has appeared in numerous professional journals and books, Julia Boyd is the author of *In the Company of My Sisters: Black Women and Self-Esteem* (1993), *Girlfriend to Girlfriend: Everyday Wisdom and Affirmations from the Sister Circle* (1995), and *Embracing the Fire: Sisters Talk About Sex & Relationships* (1996 or 1997). She received the African American Women's Achievement Award for 1994.

Brandon, Barbara (b. 1960)

Barbara Brandon was born in Brooklyn. Her father, Brumsic Brandon, Jr., created *Luther,* a comic strip about an inner city youth, which was syndicated by a *Los Angeles Times* Syndicate from 1969 to 1984. Brandon graduated from Syracuse University's College of Visual and Performing Arts and worked for *Essence* magazine. Her cartoon, *Where I'm Coming From,* which began running in the *Detroit Free Press* in June 1989, is the first cartoon by a black woman to be syndicated nationally. It features the heads and arms of a number of single black women of every complexion and hairstyle in their twenties and thirties talking on the phone about a number of issues. Only the women's heads are shown in order to keep the emphasis on their minds and not their bodies, Brandon notes that "cleavage [and] hot pants"* will not be shown in her cartoon. Nor are men present, though sometimes they are voices on the other end of the phone. Her goal is "to show what I, as a black woman, find funny" ("New Cartoonist Has Lots of Character," *Detroit Free Press,* June 11, 1989).

Brent, Linda (pseudonym of Harriet Jacobs, 1818–1896)

Though born into a slave family, Harriet Jacobs knew few deprivations during her early life because of the industry of her father and the connections of her family, some of whom had earned their freedom. As she reached maturity, however, she suffered immensely because of the determination of her owner to seduce her. Rather than submit to him after he refused to allow her to marry the free black man of her choice, she allowed herself to become impregnated by a powerful white man. Her account of her trials and her escape, which involved hiding in a cramped attic for seven years, was published in her *Incidents in the Life of a Slave Girl: Written by Herself* (1861), using the pseudonym Linda Brent.

Brewington, Louise (born in the first decade of the twentieth century)

Louise Brewington was a resident of Atlanta, Georgia, when her tales were recorded by Ruth Cipolla, a student of John Burrison's at the University of Georgia.

Brice-Finch, Jacqueline (b. 1946)

A native of Washington, D. C., Jacqueline Brice-Finch received a B.A. from Howard University, an M.A. from Indiana University, Bloomington, and a Ph.D. from the University of Maryland, College Park. She has contributed poetry and prose to several publications and is currently Professor

---

*quoted in Lisa Jones, *bulletproof diva,* 89.

of English at James Madison University where she teaches courses in Caribbean and African American literature.

Brooks, Sonya (b. 1967)

Born in Berkeley, California, this performing poet and writer received her B.A. in English from Spelman College in 1989. She teaches at Arrowsmith Academy and lives in Richmond, California.

Brown, Charlotte (c. 1855–?)

Charlotte Brown was one of the former Virginia slaves interviewed by the WPA interviewers, whose account appears in *The Negro in Virginia* (1940). She was interviewed in Woods Crossing, Virginia.

Burrell, Savilla

Savilla Burrell was a former South Carolina slave whose account of her life in slavery was recorded by the WPA interviewers and published in *Before Freedom: 48 Oral Histories of Former North and South Carolina Slaves,* ed. Belinda Hurmence.

Burton, Annie L. (1860–?)

A former slave, Annie L. Burton published her *Memories of Childhood's Slavery Days* in 1909. Though she recalls pleasant childhood days, after slavery ended her mother had to sneak her children away from the plantation. She moved to the North in 1879, living in Boston and New York. She later returned the South.

Butterbeans and Susie (Joe/Jody [1895–1967] and Susie Edwards [1896–1963])

The vaudeville team of Butterbeans and Susie was one of the most popular on the black circuit where they entertained for more than thirty-five years. They met in 1916 when they were performing in Alabama, and later married on the stage in Greenville, South Carolina. Butterbeans and Susie produced a number of hit recordings, including *A to Z Blues, Construction Gang,* and *A Married Man's a Fool If He Thinks His Wife Don't Love Nobody Else but Him.* Zora Neale Hurston, in her discussion of the unsuccessful efforts of white and black performers in New York to copy the essence of Negro expression, declared, "Butterbeans and Susie, Bo-Jangles and Snake Hips are the only performers of the real Negro school it has ever been my pleasure to behold in New York" ("Characteristics of Negro Expression," *Negro: An Anthology,* ed. Nancy Cunard and Hugo Ford).

Campbell, Bebe Moore (b. 1950)

Born into a middle-class family in Philadelphia, Pennsylvania, Bebe Moore Campbell was influenced during her formative years by the Civil Rights Movement. After receiving her B.A. from the University of Pittsburgh, she taught school for six years and then turned to journalism, contributing to periodicals such as *Essence, Ebony, Ms.,* the *New York Times,* and the *Washington Post.* Campbell has written several works of nonfiction: *Old Lady Shoes* (which she rewrote into a radio play, 1987), *Successful Women, Angry Men: Backlash in the Two-Career Marriage* (1987), and *Sweet Summer: Growing Up With and Without My Dad* (1989); and two popular novels, *Your Blues Ain't Like Mine* (1992) and *Brothers & Sisters* (1994). A regular commentator for *Morning Edition* on National Public Radio, her work has also appeared in numerous popular magazines. She won a National Endowment for the Arts award in 1980 and an NAACP Image Award in 1994. She now lives in Los Angeles.

Childress, Alice (1920–1994)

Alice Childress was born in Charleston, South Carolina, but moved to Harlem when she was five years old to live with her grandmother. Largely self-educated, she dropped out of high school after three years, and received a graduate medal from the Radcliff Institute in 1968. Some of the best known of her many plays are *Trouble in Mind* (1955), *Wedding Band* (1966), and *Wine in the Wilderness* (1969). Her novels include *A Hero Ain't Nothin' but a Sandwich* (1973), *A Short Walk* (1979), *Rainbow Jordan* (1981), and *Those Other People* (1989). Her masterpiece, however, is her collection of vignettes about a domestic, *Like One of the Family* (1956). Among her many awards was an Obie for *Trouble in Mind* in 1956.

Chisholm, Shirley (b. 1924)

Born in New York City, Shirley Chisholm received a B.A. degree from Brooklyn College and an M.A. from Columbia University. During her political career she served as a New York State Legislator, a United States Congresswoman, and a United States Ambassador to Jamaica. Ms.

Chisholm was the first woman to ever actively run for President of the United States. She is the author of an autobiography, *Unbought and Unbossed* (1970). In addition to receiving numerous honorary degrees, she was the recipient of Clairol's Woman of the Year Award for outstanding achievement in public affairs in 1973, and she was on the Gallop Poll's list of ten most admired women in the world for three years.

Coco (c. 1974)

Coco, one of the contributors to *Love Awaits,* ed. by Courtney Long, is identified only as a twenty-one-year-old dancer.

Cole, Johnnetta B. (b. 1936)

Born into a highly respected and well-educated family of teachers and businessmen/women, Johnnetta Betsch entered Fisk at the age of fifteen. She went on to complete her college degree at Oberlin and to earn the M.A. and Ph.D. degrees at Northwestern University. A renowned anthropologist, educator, and lecturer, she was appointed in 1987 as the first African American woman president of Spelman College, a historically black college for women. Her *All-American Women: Lines That Divide, Ties That Bind* (1986), *Anthropology for the Eighties,* and *Anthropology for the Nineties* are used widely in classrooms in anthropology and women's studies. Her most recent book, *Conversations: Straight Talk with America's Sister President* (1993), is a discussion she had with her African American sisters. She sits on numerous boards and is the recipient of more than thirty-five honorary degrees. Dr. Cole has announced her plans to retire from Spelman in 1997 and take a position as a professor at Emory University.

Cox, Ida (1896–1967)

Born Ida Prather in Toccoa, Georgia, this famous blues singer ran away from home when she was fourteen years old and worked in the minstrel shows and on the vaudeville circuit. She was the first of the "classic" blues singers to record on the Paramount label.

Dawson, Hattie Mae (b. 1919)

Hattie Mae Dawson was a resident of Atlanta who told stories that she had heard at Gibson, Glascock County, Georgia, to Pamela Roberts, a student of John Burrison at the University of Georgia.

Dee, Ruby (b. 1924)

Born Ruby Ann Wallace in Cleveland, Ohio, Ruby Dee grew up in Harlem, her parents having moved North in the quest for better job opportunities. Under the guidance of her mother, a schoolteacher, Ruby and her siblings read poetry in the evenings, contributing no doubt to her lifelong love of and devotion to poetry. She earned her B.A. from Hunter College. This famed actress and author has starred in scores of plays and films, including *A Raisin in the Sun; Purlie Victorious; Buck and the Preacher; Roots, the Next Generation; Wedding Band;* and *Boesman and Lena.* Through their company, Emmelyn Enterprises, she and her equally famous husband, Ossie Davis, produced or coproduced *Martin Luther King: The Dream; The Drum: A Walk Through the 20th Century with Bill Moyers; Countdown at Kusini;* and *Today Is Ours.* They also coproduced for three seasons the critically acclaimed series, *With Ossie and Ruby.* Her writings include *Zora Is My Name!* (which she wrote and starred in at the American Playhouse; the video was released in 1989), *My One Good Nerve* (1987, a compilation of some of her short stories, humor, and poetry), *Two Ways to Count to Ten* (1989, an adaptation of an African folktale), *Tower to Heaven* (1991, an adaptation of an African folktale), and *Glowchild and Other Poems* (1972, a collection of poetry by and for young people). Her numerous awards include an Emmy, an Obie, and the NAACP Image Award, and she has been inducted into the Theater Hall of Fame. She won the Literary Guild Award for *Two Ways to Count to Ten.*

Delany, A. Elizabeth (1891–1995)

Annie Elizabeth (Bessie) Delany came to national attention in 1993 when she and her sister Sarah (Sadie) published *Having Our Say: The Delany Sisters' First 100 Years,* the first of their two books. Annie was 101, Sarah, 103. That best-selling memoir was followed in 1994 with *The Delany Sisters' Book of Everyday Wisdom.* The country was mesmerized by the gentile background of these ladies, their independence, their professional success (Dr. Bessie was a dentist), their family commitment, their sense of humor, and their daily routine, which consisted of rising early, doing yoga (managing positions many young people couldn't achieve), eating garlic, praying, and reading. Born and raised in Raleigh, North Carolina, on the campus of St. Augustine's College, where their father was chaplain, they both moved on to New York where Bessie earned a Doctor of Dental

Surgery degree from Columbia University in 1923, thus becoming the first black female dentist in New York. When her mother became ill, she gave up her dental practice to care for her. Bessie and her sister knew and were friends with many of the figures prominent in the Harlem Renaissance.

Delany, Sarah (b. 1889)

Sarah (Sadie) Delany earned a B.A. in 1920 and a master's degree in education from Columbia University in 1925. She went on to teach in the New York Public Schools, supplementing her salary by selling her homemade cakes and lollipops. In 1930 she became the first colored teacher to teach domestic science on the high school level in New York. She retired in 1960. After her sister's death, she wrote *On My Own at 107: Reflections of Life Without Bessie* (1996 or 1997).

Derricotte, Toi (b. 1941)

Born in Detroit, Michigan, Toi Derricotte was educated in Catholic schools in that city, and then went on to receive a B.A. from Wayne State University, and an M.A. from New York University. She taught in public schools in Detroit, Michigan, and Teaneck, New Jersey, before becoming a university professor, first at Old Dominion University in Norfolk, Virginia, and later at the University of Pittsburgh. She has published several collections of poetry, including *Empress of the Death House* (1978), *Natural Birth* (1983), *Captivity* (1989), and *The Black Notebooks* (1997). Among Derricotte's numerous awards are two NEA grants, a United Black Artists, Inc., Distinguished Pioneering of the Arts Award, a Pushcart Prize, The Lucille Medwick Memorial Award from the Poetry Society of America, and the Folger Shakespeare Library Poetry Book Award.

Dove, Rita (b. 1952)

Noted poet Rita Dove was born in Akron, Ohio. She earned a B.A. from Miami University of Ohio and her M.F.A. from the University of Iowa. Her publications include the poetry collections *The Yellow House on the Corner* (1980), *Museum* (1983), *Thomas and Beulah* (1986), *Grace Notes* (1989), *Selected Poems* (1993), and *Mother Love* (1995); the short story collection *Fifth Sunday* (1985), the novel *Through the Ivory Gate* (1992), the verse drama *The Darker Face of the Earth* (1994), and essays *The Poet's World*

(1995). In 1987 she received the Pulitzer Prize in poetry, and from 1993 to 1995 she served as Poet Laureate of the United States and Consultant in Poetry at the Library of Congress. She is Commonwealth Professor of English at the University of Virginia.

Drake, Jeannette (b. 1941)

Jeanette Drake received a B.A. from Hampton University, and an M.S.W. and M.F.A. from Virginia Commonwealth University. She has worked as a tutor, social worker, family therapist, and adjunct college instructor. She frequently conducts writing workshops and poetry readings. Her publications include *Daughter of Abraham, Bulletin!* and *Pods and Peas,* all published in 1996.

Edwards, Susie. *See Butterbeans and Susie*

Fauset, Jessie Redmon (1882–1961)

Born into a well-to-do family in Philadelphia, Pennsylvania, Jessie Fauset received her A.B. from Cornell and her M.A. from the Sorbonne. After teaching for several years in Washington, D.C., she joined the staff of *The Crisis* in New York, where she played a prominent role in the Harlem Renaissance. She wrote four novels: *There Is Confusion* (1924), *Plum Bun: A Novel without a Moral* (1928), *The Chinaberry Tree: A Novel of American Life* (1931), and *Comedy: American Style* (1933).

Folkes, Minnie (c. 1860–?)

Born in Chesterfield, Virginia, Minnie Folkes was one of the former slaves interviewed by WPA workers in Virginia. Her memorates appear in *The Negro in Virginia.* She married when she was fourteen years old and had eleven children.

Fordham, Mary Weston (c. 1845–1905)

Born free and privately tutored in Charleston, South Carolina, Mary Weston Fordham herself established a school for Negroes during the Civil War in defiance of South Carolina law. She later taught in South Carolina in the American Missionary Association School. She is the author of *Magnolia Leaves* (1897).

Forten, Charlotte (1838–1914)

Born into a well-to-do family of free blacks in Philadelphia, Charlotte Forten was tutored at home and then sent to school in Salem, Massachusetts. She was an ardent abolitionist and was closely associated with many prominent activists of the time, including John Greenleaf Whittier, Wendell Phillips, William Lloyd Garrison, Colonel T. W. Higginson, and Colonel Robert Gould Shaw. During the Civil War she went to the South and taught on St. Helena Island, a Sea Island off the coast of South Carolina. In 1878 she married Francis J. Grimké, a distinguished minister. Her journal, which she kept from 1854 to 1864, offers unique insight into the life of a black lady of her class and time.

Frazier, Julia (1854–?)

Born in Spottsylvania County, Virginia, Julia Frazier was one of the former Virginia slaves interviewed by the WPA interviewers; her account appears in *The Negro in Virginia* (1940). Frazier notes that she learned her ABC's when she was eleven and learned to write when she was seventeen. After emancipation her family moved to Fredericksburg, Virginia.

Fullen-Collins, Marilyn (b. 1954)

Marilyn Fullen-Collins was born in Los Angeles, California. She moved to Seattle in 1983 and pursues her passion for justice issues as a social worker for The Church Council of Greater Seattle, where she works with homeless single parents and their children and through her writing of children's books. *Pathblazers, Eight People Who Have Made a Difference,* was published by Open Hand Publishing Company in 1992, and was designed to introduce young readers to African Americans who have made a difference, but have not received the kind of recognition accorded sports figures and rappers. *Pathblazers II* will be published in late 1997.

Gay, Pauline

Pauline Gay was a resident of Atlanta, Georgia, when her tales were collected by LeAnn Hulsey, a student in the class of John Burrison at the University of Georgia.

Giovanni, Nikki (b. 1943)

Born in Knoxville, Tennessee, Yolande Cornelia Giovanni moved to Knoxville in 1957 to live with her maternal grandparents. She was educated at Fisk University and the University of Pennsylvania. One of the most popular poets to arise during the Black Arts Movement, she continues to have a large and enthusiastic following among her earlier devotees from the sixties and seventies as well as their children and even grandchildren. A prolific writer, she has to her credit several volumes of poetry, including *Black Judgement* (1969), *Black Feeling, Black Talk/Black Judgement, Re: Creation* (1970), *Spin a Soft Black Song* (1970), *My House* (1972), *Ego Tripping and Other Poems for Young Readers* (1973), *The Women and the Men* (1975), *Cotton Candy on a Rainy Day* (1978), *Those Who Ride the Night Winds* (1983), and *Love Poems* (1996). Her autobiography, *Gemini,* was published in 1971. Other works include *A Dialogue: James Baldwin and Nikki Giovanni* (1972), *A Poetic Equation: Conversations Between Nikki Giovanni and Margaret Walker* (1974), and *Sacred Cows . . . And Other Edibles* (essays, 1988). She edited *Night Comes Softly* (1970), an anthology of poetry by black women. Ms. Giovanni has also released several popular recordings of her reading her poetry.

Ms. Giovanni has taught at Queens College, Rutgers University, Ohio State University, and College of Mount St. Joseph on the Ohio. She is currently a Professor of English at Virginia Polytechnic Institute and State University (Virginia Tech) in Blacksburg, Virginia. The recipient of numerous honors, citations, and awards, Ms. Giovanni has received honorary doctorates from Wilberforce University (1974), Ripon University (Wisconsin, 1976), University of Maryland (1977), Smith College (1978), Mount St. Joseph (1985), Fisk University (1988), Indiana University (1991), and Otterbein College (Westerville, Ohio [1992]).

Goldberg, Whoopi (b. 1955)

Born Caryn E. Johnson in New York City, Whoopi Goldberg always knew she wanted to be a performer. When she was eight, she acted in children's plays at the Hudson Guild Theater. As a teenager, she became involved in the drug culture and dropped out of high school. By the time she was twenty and a mother, she had cleaned herself up and moved to California to pursue her dreams. After some difficult years, including some on welfare, she came to prominence as a stand-up commedienne in 1984 with the one-woman Broadway show from which "Fontaine" was taken and which she revived at Carnegie Hall twelve years later in 1996. She has gone on to become one of the highest-paid actresses ever. She established herself as an actress in *The Color Purple,* for which she received a Golden

Globe Award and an Academy Award nomination. She received a Best Supporting Actress Oscar for her role in *Ghost*. She has also starred in twenty-one other films, including *Sister Act, Clara's Heart, The Associate, Bogus,* and *Ghost of Mississippi.* In February 1997 she returned to the Broadway stage as Pseudolus in *A Funny Thing Happened on the Way to the Forum.* Goldberg has served twice as emcee of the Academy Awards telecast and she has hosted the Grammy Awards. She also received a 1985 Grammy Award for Best Comedy Recording of the Year and NAACP Image Awards in 1985 and 1990. She is the author of *Alice,* a children's book.

Goodman, Hazelle. *See Hazelle*

Grovernor, Julia

Julia Grovernor was a former slave on Sapelo Island, off the coast of Georgia, whose recollections of slavery were collected by the WPA interviewers and published in *Drums and Shadows,* ed. Guy Johnson.

Guinier, Lani (b. 1950)

Born into a family of lawyers (her grandfather and father were lawyers), Lani Guinier attended public schools in New York City and went on to earn a B.A. from Radcliffe College in 1971 and a J.D. from Yale Law School in 1994. A distinguished lawyer and a prominent law professor, Guinier was thrust into the national spotlight when President Clinton picked her for the job of Assistant Attorney General in the Justice Department's Civil Rights Division in April 1993 and then withdrew her name when the conservatives attacked her as a radical, using excerpts from some of her legal writings to paint her as an extremist. She is currently a professor of law at the University of Pennsylvania.

Guntharpe, Violet (c. 1854–?)

Violet Guntharpe was born a slave in Fairfield County, South Carolina. Her recollection of slavery is a part of the WPA collection of interviews with former slaves and is published in *Before Freedom: 48 Oral Histories of Former North and South Carolina Slaves,* ed. Belinda Hurmence.

Hamer, Fannie Lou (1917–1977)

Born in Montgomery County, Mississippi, Fannie Lou Hamer had only six years of schooling. She came to prominence as an activist in the Civil

Rights movement, noted not only for her courage and eloquence, but also for her sense of humor. In 1964 she became the first black female to run for Congress from Mississippi. In 1968 she led a delegation to the Democratic Convention in an effort to win seats from the all-white Mississippi delegation. Popular as a speaker she raised considerable funds which she used to build a 680-acre farm community to house the needy and to establish a day care center for the children of working mothers.

Hansberry, Lorraine (1930–1965)

Lorraine Hansberry was born in Chicago to a well-to-do family. Her father, a black activist who worked with the Urban League and the NAACP, was jailed for protesting housing discrimination. As she grew up she met many prominent blacks, including African students and exiles who visited her home. Thus her sense of racial pride and political activism was developed early. Hansberry's classic *A Raisin in the Sun* (1959) was the first play on Broadway by an African American woman. She was the first black and the youngest American to receive the New York Drama Critics Circle Award for the best play of the year, winning over plays by Tennessee Williams, Eugene O'Neill, and Archibald MacLeish. *Raisin* is probably the most influential play in black dramatic history, being the first highly acclaimed serious drama and the most memorable one for a number of later playwrights who recall that seeing *Raisin* was a turning point in their lives. Other works by Hansberry include *The Sign in Sidney Brustein's Window* (1964), *Les Blancs: The Collected Last Plays of Lorraine Hansberry* (1972), edited by her widower, Robert Nemiroff; and *To Be Young, Gifted, and Black* (1969), a posthumous autobiography assembled from her words.

Harper, Frances Ellen Watkins (1825–1911)

Born free in Baltimore, Ms. Harper was orphaned at three and raised by her aunt and uncle, the latter of whom was an abolitionist who ran an academy for black youths, in which Frances was educated. After working as a seamstress and a teacher, she went on to become an active antislavery lecturer and member of the Underground Railroad. She was a prolific writer of poetry, letters, essays, and fiction. She published a prose volume, *Forest Leaves,* in 1845 and is credited with publishing the first short story by an African American writer, "The Two Offers," which appeared in the *Anglo-African Magazine* in 1859. Her poetry includes *Poems on Miscellaneous Sub-*

jects (1854), *Moses, a Story of the Nile* (1870), *Poems* (1870), *Sketches of South-ern Life* (1872), *Atlanta Offering* (1895), and *Martyr of Alabama* (1895). She also wrote the novels *Sowing and Reaping: A Temperance Story* (serialized in 1867), *Trial and Triumph* (1888), and *Iola LeRoy* (1892).

Harris, Trudier (b. 1948)

Noted literary critic Trudier Harris, was born in Mantua, Alabama. She was educated at Stillman College (B.A.) and Ohio State University (M.A. and Ph.D.). Her numerous critical works include *From Mammies to Mili-tants: Domestics in Black American Literature* (1982), *Exorcising Blackness: His-torical and Literary Lynching and Burning Rituals* (1984), *Black Women in the Fiction of James Baldwin* (1985), *Fiction and Folklore: The Novels of Toni Mor-rison* (1991), and *In the African Southern Vein: Narrative Strategies in Works by Zora Neale Hurston, Gloria Naylor, and Randall Kenan* (1996). The recipient of numerous grants, awards, and fellowships, she is currently a fellow at the National Humanities Center (1996–97). She has taught at The College of William and Mary, the University of Arkansas, Ohio State University, and Emory University. Presently, she is the J. Carlyle Sitterson Professor of English at the University of North Carolina, Chapel Hill.

Hazelle (b. 1967)

Born in Trinidad and raised in Brooklyn, Hazelle (Goodman) earned her B.A. degree in drama from the City College of New York. Her 1995 HBO Special, *Hazelle,* from which "Not Going to Stop til I Make It to de Top" was taken, received unprecedented ratings for a newcomer and was nom-inated for two Cable Ace Awards—Best Comedy Special and Best Per-former. Committed to building children's self-esteem, the comedienne was first discovered performing her children's show, "Hold on to Your Dreams." The show originated from her childhood experiences of being treated dif-ferently for her darker complexion and Caribbean heritage. Ironically, these differences have now become the cornerstone of her success as well as her trademark beauty. When at home in New York, she enjoys performing at Cami Hall ("my sandbox") where she brings her collage of risky, sassy, and hilarious characters to life. Currently, Hazelle is filming her first costarring role with Woody Allen in New York.

Holiday, Billie (Lady Day, 1915–1959)

Born in Baltimore, Maryland, Billie Holiday went on to become one of the world's best known jazz vocalists, one who is, unfortunately, most often recalled for her tragic life, most notably her problems with drugs. Those who know her best, however, attest to the fact that her sense of humor, molded in the black community, never left her. Bill Duffy, a journalist at the *NY Post,* tells of her having him "on the floor with laughter, as usual. To me she was quite simply the funniest lady who ever lived. Her stinging Afro-Irish wit raised profanity and gutter grammar to the level of poetry."*

Holloway, Karla F. C. (b. 1949)

Born in Buffalo, New York, Karla Holloway received a B.A. degree from Talledega College, and the M.A. and Ph.D. degrees from Michigan State University. She is the author of *The Character of the Word* (1987), *Moorings and Metaphors: Figures of Culture and Gender in Black Women's Literature* (1992), and *Codes of Conduct: Race, Ethics and the Color of Our Character* (1995). She coauthored with Stephanie A. Demetrakopoulos *New Dimensions of Spirituality: A Biracial and Bicultural Reading of the Novels of Toni Morrison* in 1987. Her forthcoming book is about death and dying in African American culture. She is Professor of English and Director of African American Studies at Duke University.

Hurston, Zora Neale (1891–1960)

Born in the all-colored town of Eatonville, Florida, Zora Neale Hurston went on to study at Morgan Academy, Howard University, and Barnard College and to become a prominent if controversial participant in the Harlem Renaissance movement. Her major works include four novels, *Jonah's Gourd Vine* (1934), *Their Eyes Were Watching God* (1937), *Moses, Man of the Mountain* (1942), and *Seraph on the Suwannee* (1948); two folklore collections and studies, *Mules and Men* (1935) and *Tell My Horse* (1938); and an autobiography, *Dust Tracks on a Road* (1942). One of the earliest trained black anthropologists, Hurston did pioneering work in the South and the Caribbean. She also wrote a number of plays, one of them, *Mule Bone,* with Langston Hughes.

*cited in Donald Clarke, *Wishing on the Moon,* 395.

As a personality, a novelist, a playwright, a folklorist, and a spokeswoman, Hurston was controversial throughout her often tragic life. She died destitute in Florida in 1960 and was buried in an unmarked grave. She is now regarded as a major novelist and anthropologist, one whose work has had a greater influence on contemporary scholars and writers than that of any of her contemporaries, except, arguably Langston Hughes. She is a model and a heroine for most contemporary black female writers, whose discovery of the voice and feminism of Hurston was a turning point in their lives.

Jackson, Mattie J. (c. 1846–?)

A St. Louis, Missouri, native, Mattie J. Jackson was twenty when she dictated her autobiography to Dr. L. S. Thompson, herself a black woman. That autobiography, *The Story of Mattie J. Jackson: Her Parentage—Experience of Eighteen Years in Slavery—Incidents During the War—Her Escape from Slavery: A True Story,* was published in 1866.

Jacobs, Harriet. *See Linda Brent*

Johnson, Maggie Pogue

Born in Fincastle, Virginia, Maggie Pogue Johnson attended what is now Virginia State University. Her dialect poetry, reminiscent of that of her better-known contemporaries Paul Laurence Dunbar and Daniel Webster Davis, appeared in *Virginia Dreams/Lyrics for the Idle Hours: Tales of the Time Told in Rhyme* (1910). She lived in Covington, Virginia, where she was President of the Covington Literary and Debating Society.

Jones, Lisa (b. 1961)

The daughter of famed poet and dramatist Amiri Baraka (formerly LeRoi Jones), Lisa Jones was born in New York, New York, and educated at Yale University and New York University's Graduate School of Film and Television. A staff writer for *The Village Voice,* she has produced several radio and stage plays and is the author of *bulletproof diva.* She has also coauthored with Spike Lee three companion pieces to his movies: *Uplift the Race: The Construction of "School Daze," Do the Right Thing: The New Spike Lee Joint,* and *Variations on the Mo' Better Blues.*

Kennedy, Flo (b. 1916)

Born in St. Louis, Missouri, Florynce Rae Kennedy received the B.A. and J.D. degrees from Columbia University. A lawyer, political activist, and humorist, whose career has been one long and extended attack on racism, sexism, and varied other forms of prejudist, she was active from its beginning in the National Organization for Women (NOW). She later became disillusioned with NOW and went on to found the Feminist Party. In addition to her autobiography, *Color Me Flo,* which was published in 1976, Flo Kennedy has coauthored *Abortion Rap* (1971, with Diane Schulder) and *Sex Discrimination in Employment: An Analysis and Guide for Practitioner and Student* (1981, with William F. Pepper).

Little, Benilde (b. 1959)

Born and raised in Newark, New Jersey, Benilde Little graduated from Howard University and went on to do graduate work at Northwestern University. A former *Essence* magazine editor and *People Magazine* reporter, she lives in New Jersey. *Good Hair* (1996) is her first novel.

Lorde, Audre (1934–1992)

Born Audrey Geraldine Lorde in Harlem to Gradanian parents, Audre Lorde attended the University of Mexico, received a B.A. from Hunter College, and earned an M.L.S. from Columbia University. She worked as a librarian before going on to teach at City University of New York, Tougaloo College, Herbert Lehman College, Hunter College, and Atlanta University. In addition to eight volumes of poetry, she is the author of *The Cancer Journals* (1980), a recounting of her struggles with breast cancer; *Zami: A New Spelling of My Name* (1982), a work that she described as "biomythography," a fictionalized account of her coming to terms with her lesbianism, and *Sister Outsider* (1984). Her many honors and awards include two NEA grants and two Creative Artists Public Service grants, and the Borough of Manhattan President's Award for Literary Excellence. *From a Land Where Other People Live* won her a National Book Award nomination for poetry in 1974. She was also honored as the 1991 Poet Laureate of the State of New York.

Mabley, Moms (1894?–1975)

Jackie Moms Mabley was born Loretta Mary Aiken in Brevard, North Carolina. Her father, a highly successful and respected entrepreneur, was killed in an accident when Loretta was eleven. She was raped twice—at the age of eleven (by an elderly black man) and thirteen (by the white sheriff)—and impregnated each time. Her grandmother encouraged her to leave Brevard, go out into the world, and seek her fortune; and at fourteen she left home to join the minstrel shows, where she impressed Butterbeans and Susie, who made her a part of their show. Despite her popularity in Negro theaters and clubs, stage life was difficult and the economic rewards meager for a black woman in show business. The T.O.B.A. (Theater Owners Booking Association), the segregated booking association for which she performed until its demise during the Depression, was often called the chitlin' circuit and the Tough on Black Asses Circuit. She persisted, however, for more than sixty years, finally achieving a modicum of mainstream success in the 1960s, when she appeared on television shows and began drawing bigger pay for her stage shows. Twenty-five recordings were made of her performances, and one, *Moms Mabley: The Funniest Woman in the World,* went Gold. She always appeared as a toothless old motherly figure, comically dressed in a large housedress, a floppy hat, long socks, and shoes too big for her feet, and addressed her audience as "children."

McMillan, Terry (b. 1951)

Born in Port Huron, Michigan, novelist Terry McMillan received her B.A. from the University of California at Berkeley and her M.F.A. from Columbia University. She has worked as a journalist for the *New York Times, Atlanta Constitution,* and *Philadelphia Inquirer,* and has taught at the University of Wyoming, the University of Arizona, and Stanford University. Her best-selling (and often controversial) novels include *Mama* (1987), *Disappearing Acts* (1989), *Waiting to Exhale* (1992), and *How Stella Got Her Groove Back* (1996). *Waiting to Exhale* was made into a popular movie. She also edited *Breaking Ice: An Anthology of Contemporary African-American Fiction* (1990).

Marshall, Paule (b. 1929)

Distinguished novelist, short story writer, lecturer, and educator, Paule Marshall was born in Brooklyn to Barbadian parents. She received a B.A. from Brooklyn College and later studied at Hunter College. Her novels include *Brown Girl, Brownstones* (1959), *The Chosen Place, The Timeless People* (1969), *Praisesong for the Widow* (1983), and *Daughters* (1991). Her two collections of short prose are *Soul Clap Hands and Sing* (1961), and *Reena and Other Stories* (1983). The numerous prestigious awards, prizes, and grants that have been bestowed upon her include an American Book Award,

NEH, Ford, Rosenthal, Guggenheim, MacArthur, and John Dos Passos Prize for Literature. A popular lecturer who has been the featured speaker at conferences around the world, she has taught at the University of California, the University of Iowa, the University of Massachusetts, Columbia University, Virginia Commonwealth University, and (currently) New York University.

Martin, Sarah (1884–?)

Born in Louisville, Kentucky, Sarah Martin worked in vaudeville from 1915 to 1931. She began recording blues songs in 1923 and recorded well over one hundred tracks. After 1931 she devoted herself to the church and her work in a nursing home in Louisville.

Meriwether, Louise (b. 1923)

Born in Haverstraw, New York, to parents who had migrated from their native South Carolina, Louise Jenkins Meriwether moved with her parents and four siblings to Brooklyn and later to Harlem. She received a B.A. in English from New York University and an M.A. in journalism from the University of California. She has worked as a secretary, bookkeeper, real-estate salesperson, newspaper reporter, and story analyst at Universal Studios. Her *oeuvre* includes two novels: *Daddy Was a Number Runner* (1970) and *Fragments of the Ark* (1994), the latter of which is a historical novel based upon the life of Robert Smalls (1839–1915), who stole a Confederate ship from Charleston Harbor and sailed to freedom in the North with his family and friends; and three children's books based upon the lives of important African Americans: *The Freedom Ship of Robert Smalls* (1971), *The Heart Man: Dr. Daniel Hale Williams* (1972), and *Don't Ride the Bus on Monday: The Rosa Parks Story* (1973). Her first novel was selected by the *New York Times* and *Library Journal* as one of the major books of 1970.

Miles, Lizzie (Elizabeth Mary Landreaux, 1895–1963)

Born in New Orleans, blues singer Lizzie Miles worked in tent shows and on the vaudeville circuit, finally achieving fame in the 1920s when she recorded with some of the major bands of the period. She performed in Paris where she was known as "La Rose Noir." She disappeared from public view as blues singing went out of fashion in the 1940s and was rediscovered in the sixties, when she began entertaining again.

Miller, Norma (b. 1919)

Born in New York, New York, Norma Miller has performed as a dancer and comic. She coauthored with Redd Foxx *The Redd Foxx Encyclopedia of Black Humor* in 1977.

Moore, Opal J. (b. 1953)

Born in Chicago, Illinois, Opal Moore received a B.F.A. from Wesleyan and an M.A. and M.F.A. from the University of Iowa. Her fiction and poetry have appeared in a variety of journals and anthologies, and she has published a number of critical and pedagogical essays, in which she frequently focuses on literature for children. Moore is currently working on a collection of short stories titled *Going to Kingdom Come*. She was a Fulbright Lecturer at Johannes Gutenberg-Universität in Mainz, Germany, in 1994 and the Jessie Ball duPont Visiting Scholar at Hollins College in 1995. Currently Associate Professor of English at Radford University, she will join the faculty at Spelman College in fall 1997.

Morgan, Katherine (b. in the 1920s)

Katherine Morgan, who was born in the 1920s, grew up in Philadelphia, hearing the tales of her family's history, which she has published as *Children of Strangers: The Stories of a Black Family* (1980). A folklorist educated at the University of Pennsylvania and the University of California at Berkeley, Katherine Morgan taught at Swarthmore College.

Moss, Thylias (b. 1954)

Thylias Moss grew up in Cleveland, Ohio, and graduated from Oberlin College; she went to graduate school at the University of New Hampshire. Now an associate professor of English at the University of Michigan, Ann Arbor, she has five books of poetry to her credit: *Hosiery Seams on Bowlegged Woman, Pyramid of Bones, At Redbones, Rainbow Remnants in Rock Bottom Ghetto Sky* (1991), and *Small Congregations,* as well as the children's book, *I Want to Be* (1993). Among her awards are the Whiting Writer's Award, the Witter Bynner Prize, and the MacArthur Foundation Fellowship.

Mother Love

Jo Anne Hart, AKA Mother Love, AKA The Queen of Advice, grew up in the Cleveland projects. A single mother and a school bus driver, she went on to become a popular guest on national talk shows, a regular on *The Home Show,* a guest star on *Murphy Brown* and *Married with Children,* a spokesperson for a national full-figured clothing line, and a stand-up comic. This author (with Connie Church) of *Listen Up, Girlfriends! Lessons on Life from the Queen of Advice* now lives in Southern California.

Naylor, Gloria (b. 1950)

Born in New York City to parents who had recently migrated from Mississippi, Gloria Naylor received her B.A. from Brooklyn College and her M.S. from Yale University. She has served as visiting professor at George Washington University, New York University, Princeton University, Boston University, and Cornell University. She has authored four highly acclaimed novels: *The Women of Brewster Place* (1982), *Linden Hills* (1985), *Mama Day* (1988), and *Bailey's Cafe* (1992). Her first novel was made into a movie and then became a television series; her last novel was made into a play that premiered at the Hartford Stage Company in April 1994. Her numerous honors include an American Book Award in 1983, a National Endowment for the Humanities Fellowship in 1985, and a Guggenheim Fellowship in 1988.

Ndegeocello, Me'shell (b. 1970)

Born into an army family in Berlin, Me'Shell Ndegeocello was raised in the Washington, D.C., area. She studied jazz at the Duke Ellington School of the Arts and Howard University. A popular hip-hop song stylist/composer/rapper/bassist, she titled her first album *Plantation Lullabies,* "plantation" being a metaphor for ghettos and shantytowns. After living in New York for a few years she moved to California, where she has made a video with John Mellencamp, scored a John Singleton film, and recorded songs with Herbie Hancock and Chaka Khan.

Neely, Barbara (b. 1941)

Barbara Neely grew up in Labanon, Pennsylvania, where she was the only Negro in the Catholic schools that she attended. Though she never acquired an undergraduate degree, she earned a master's degree in urban and regional planning from the University of Pittsburgh in 1971. A novelist and short story writer whose fiction has appeared in numerous anthologies, Barbara Neely's first book, *Blanche on the Lam* (1992), has been hailed as the first mystery novel by a black woman to be published by a major publishing house. That well received novel was followed up by *Blanche Among the Talented Tenth* (1994). Neely lives in Jamaica Plains, Massachusetts.

Nelson, Jill (b. 1952)

Born in New York City into a prosperous family—her father was a dentist and her mother a businesswoman and librarian—Jill Nelson enjoyed a privileged childhood, attending private schools and spending the summers in her family's summer home in Martha's Vineyard. Educated at City College of New York (B.A.) and the Columbia School of Journalism (M.A.), Ms. Nelson has worked for a number of years as a journalist; from 1986 to 1990 she was a staff writer at the *Washington Post* and a contributing editor for *Essence, Village Voice,* and other magazines. She became nationally known with the publication of her 1993 autobiography, *Volunteer Slavery: My Authentic Negro Experience.*

Petry, Ann (b. 1908)

Born in Old Saybrook, Georgia, Ann Petry went on to receive a Ph.D. from the University of Connecticut in 1931. She worked as a pharmacist until 1938, when she took a position with the *Amsterdam News,* later moving on to the *People's Voice.* Her first novel, *The Street,* was published in 1946. This classic novel was followed by a number of other novels, short stories, and historical works: *Country Place* (1947), *The Drugstore Cat* (1949), *The Narrows* (1953), *Harriet Tubman: Conductor on the Underground Railroad* (1955), *Tituba of Salem Village* (1964), *Legends of the Saints* (1970), and *Miss Muriel and Other Stories* (1971). The recipient of several honorary degrees, Dr. Petry also was a Houghton Mifflin Literary Fellow and the winner of a 1994 Distinguished Writer Award.

Prosser, Hannah (1812–1895)

Born a slave on Passuie Island, Maryland, Hannah Prosser and her slave husband Thomas Prosser, purchased their freedom in 1841 and moved to Columbia, Pennsylvania. Her stories were recorded by Ellen Dickson Wilson.

Rodgers, Carolyn M. (b. 1945)

Born in Chicago, Illinois, Carolyn M. Rodgers studied at The University of Illinois and went on to receive a B.A. from Roosevelt University. She is the author of several volumes of poetry, notably *Paper Soul* (1968), *Songs of a Black Bird* (1969), *how i got ovah* (1976), and *The Heart as Ever Green* (1978). She has served as writer-in-residence at Columbia College, Malcolm X College, University of Washington, University of Indiana, and Albany State College. Among her awards are the first Conrad Kent Rivers Writing Award (1969); a National Endowment for the Arts Award (1970), and The Poet Laureate Award of the Society of Midland Authors (1970). *How i got ovah* was nominated for the National Book Award in 1976. Ms. Rodgers continues to live in Chicago.

Rushin, Kate (b. 1951)

Kate Rushin received a B.A. in Theater and Communications from Oberlin College and an M.F.A. in Creative Writing from Brown University. She has been active on the Boston literary and political scene. Her work has been anthologized widely and recently collected in her major publication, *The Black Back-ups* (1993). She received the Groller Poetry Prize in 1988 and received a scholarship to the Bread Loaf Writers' Conference in 1976.

Saar, Betye (b. 1926)

Betye Saar, who grew up in Watts, received her B.A. from the University of California at Los Angeles. Her artwork has been exhibited throughout the United States and abroad. She began in the late 1960s to use derogatory commercial images of blacks in her work in order to expose the racism those images conveyed. *The Liberation of Aunt Jemima,* which is reprinted in this anthology, converts the stereotypical mammy figure into a gun-toting warrior. She received National Endowment of the Arts Awards in 1974 and 1984. The film, *Spirit Catcher: The Art of Betye Saar,* was a part of the Women in the Arts Series of WNET-TV in New York.

Sanders, Dori (b. 1935)

Born and raised on a farm in York, South Carolina, Dori Sanders was the eighth of ten children. She says that she began writing in order to preserve for her nieces and nephews some of the wonderful aspects of the farm experience. She continued to farm and to sell produce at a roadside shed even after she began writing well received novels as a senior citizen. Her works include *Clover* (1990) and *Her Own Place* (1993). *Clover* won the Lillian Smith Award in 1990. She also published *Dori Sanders' Country*

Cooking: Recipes and Stories from the Family Farm Stand (1995), an autobiographical cookbook.

Shange, Ntozake (b. 1948)

Born Paulette Williams in Trenton, New Jersey, Ntozake Shange moved with her family to St. Louis, Missouri, when she was eight years old. There she was a part of the first group of black students who integrated previously segregated Southern schools. This experience both embittered and strengthened her. Her family returned to New Jersey when she was thirteen. Shange graduated from Barnard College and went on to complete an M.A. at the University of Southern California. The 1976 Broadway production of her choreopoem *for colored girls who have considered suicide/when the rainbow is enuf* brought her to national attention and controversy. Her other works include *Sassafrass: A Novella* (1977), *Nappy Edges* (1978), *spell #7: geeche jibara quik magic trance manual for technologically stressed third world people* (1978), *Sassafrass, Cypress, and Indigo* (1982), *A Daughter's Geography* (1983), *From Okra to Greens* (1984), *See No Evil: Prefaces, Essays and Accounts, 1976–1983* (1984), *Betsy Brown* (1985), *Ridin the Moon in Texas: Word Paintings* (1987), *The Love Space Demands* (1991), *I Live in Music* (1994, nonfiction), and *Liliane: Resurrection of the Daughter.* Shange won Obie Awards for *for colored girls* and *Mother Courage and Her Children* (1980). Other awards include an Outer Critics Circle Award, a Guggenheim, and an Excellence Medal from Columbia University.

Shanté, Roxanne (b. 1969)

Born Lolita Gooden, Roxanne Shanté established herself as an important force in rap music with her first record, the 1984 "Roxanne's Revenge." Her first album, *Bad Sister,* was released in 1989.

Sinclair, April

The author of two well-received novels, *ain't gonna be the same fool twice* (1994) and *Coffee Will Make You Black* (1996), Ms. Sinclair has won the 1994 Book of the Year (Young Adult Fiction) from the American Library Association and the Carl Sandburg Award in Fiction from the Friends of the Chicago Public Library.

Smith, Amanda Berry (1837–1915)

Born to slave parents in Long Green, Maryland, Amanda Berry knew little of the trials of slavery because her father purchased her when she was quite young and because her mistress spoiled her so, not even allowing her mother to whip her. She did not realize at the time that she was treated so kindly because she was being prepared for the market. Twice married and the mother of four children, Ms. Smith had a long career as an evangelist and missionary of the AME Church. From 1878 to 1890 she served as a missionary in England, Ireland, Scotland, India, Liberia, and Sierra Leone. Moved by the plight of black orphans, she opened a school for the care of colored children in Harvey, Illinois, using the proceeds from *An Autobiography: The Story of the Lord's Dealings with Mrs. Amanda Smith, the Colored Evangelist* (published in 1893) and contributions from wealthy donors. The Amanda Smith School was destroyed by fire in 1918, three years after the death of its founder.

Smith, Bessie (1898?–1937)

Born into a poor family in Chattanooga, Tennessee, Bessie Smith lost her father soon after her birth and her mother when she was nine, at which age she entered show business, singing in the streets and performing at Chattanooga's Ivory Theater. When she was eleven years old, famous blues singer Ma Rainey heard her sing and took her into her troupe. She began recording in the early 1920s and recorded 180 songs for Columbia Records between 1921 and 1933. She was the biggest star on the T.O.B.A., and is generally regarded as the world's greatest blues singer. She was killed in an automobile accident near Coahoma, Mississippi, a death that resulted, many claim, because she was denied medical treatment because of her race and that motivated Edward Albee's play, *The Death of Bessie Smith*.

Smith, Ethel Morgan (b. 1952)

Born and raised in Louisville, Alabama, Ethel Morgan Smith is a graduate of the Hollins Creative Writing Program. She has taught creative writing at Virginia Polytechnic Institute and State University and (currently) at West Virginia University in Morgantown. She is the recipient of fellowships from Hollins College, Bread Loaf Writers' Conference, The Virginia Center for Creative Arts, The Virginia Foundation, and The National Endowment for the Humanities. She will be a Fulbright Lecturer in Germany during the 1997–98 school year.

Smith, Mary Carter (b. 1919)

Born in Birmingham, Alabama, Mary Carter Smith received a B.S. from Coppin State College in Baltimore, Maryland, and went on to do graduate study at New York University, Johns Hopkins University, University of Maryland, and Catholic University. She worked as a teacher/librarian in the Baltimore School System. A folklorist and storyteller, she has produced a number of videocassettes. Smith is a coauthor of *The Griot's Cookbook,* 1982. She currently lives in Baltimore, Maryland.

Thomas, Joyce Carol (b. 1938)

Poet, playwright, novelist Joyce Carol Thomas was born in Ponca City, Oklahoma, and educated at San Jose State University (B.A.) and Stanford University (M.A.). She has taught at Purdue University and the University of Tennessee. Her oeuvre includes six novels: *Marked by Fire* (1982), *Bright Shadow* (1983), *The Golden Pasture* (1986), *Water Girl* (1986), *Journey* (1988), and *When the Nightingale Sings* (1992); a multicultural anthology, *A Gathering of Flowers: Stories About Being Young in America* (1990); and two best-selling collections of poems, *Brown Honey in Broomwheat Tea* (1993) and *Gingerbread Days* (1995). She has won many prestigious awards for her poetry, plays, and novels, including the National Book Award for her first novel *Marked by Fire.*

Thompson, Priscilla Jane (1871–1942)

Born to former slaves from Virginia, Priscilla Jane Thompson prepared for a career as a teacher, but because of health problems she could not follow that vocation. She wrote poetry and gave poetry readings. Her published works include *Ethiope Lays* (1900) and *Gleanings of Quiet Hours* (1907). She was a member of a family of poets: her brother, Aaron Belford Thompson, and her sister, Clara Thompson, also published books of poetry.

Truth, Sojourner (1797?–1883)

Born Isabella Baymfree in Ulster County, New York, Sojourner Truth remained a slave until 1827, when she claimed her freedom on the basis of the manumission laws in New York and renamed herself Sojourner Truth. Though illiterate, this tall and commanding woman was an eloquent, forceful, and charismatic orator. She traveled extensively, speaking out for the abolition of slavery, for women's rights, and for temperance. During the Civil War she spoke and sang to raise money for the cause, and she served as a nurse. After the war, she worked to help former slaves in Washington,

D.C., find jobs and housing, and she petitioned Congress to give land in the West to former slaves. Though criticized for what some saw as her acceptance of demeaning treatment by her white friends and associates, Truth became the most famous black woman of her times, even having an audience with President Abraham Lincoln on November 26, 1883. A recent study, Nell Irvin Painter's *Sojourner Truth: A Life, A Symbol* (1996), deflates somewhat the legendary heroine, revealing, among other things, that Truth probably never uttered the phrase for which she is best known at the 1851 Women's Rights Convention in Akron, Ohio, "Ain't I a Woman."

Tubman, Harriet (c. 1821–1913)

Born a slave in Bucktown, Maryland, Harriet Tubman intervened in a confrontation between a slave and an overseer and was struck in the head by the overseer, an injury that caused her to suffer from narcolepsy the rest of her life. Fearing that she was about to be sold years later when her slave master died, she decided in 1849 to escape. She returned South at least fifteen times to assist other slaves to escape, establishing herself as the "Moses" of her people and leading approximately three hundred others to freedom, including her parents. Rewards of up to $40,000 were offered for her capture, but this did not deter the clever, courageous, resourceful, and dedicated freedom fighter. She was active during the Civil War as a spy, scout, nurse, and cook. After the Civil War she settled in Auburn, New York, and became involved in a number of causes, including the women's suffrage movement. Denied a military pension, she lived in poverty until thirty years later Congress passed a special bill to award her a pension, which she used to established a home for orphans and a home for indigent and aged colored people. When she died from complications of pneumonia in her early nineties, she was an internationally known figure.

Wade-Gayles, Gloria (b. 1938)

Born in Memphis, Tennessee, Gloria Wade-Gayles earned a B.A. from LeMoyne College, an M.A. from Boston University, and a Ph.D. from Emory University. After teaching briefly at Howard University, Morehouse College, Emory University, and Talledega College, she joined the faculty at Spelman College in 1984, where she continues as Professor of English and Women's Studies. She is the author of the collection of poetry, *Anointed to Fly* (1991), the critical study, *No Crystal Stair: Visions of Race and Sex in*

Black Women's Fiction (1984), and the autobiographical essays, *Pushed Back to Strength: A Black Woman's Journey Home* (1993) and *Rooted Against the Wind: Personal Essays* (1996).

Walker, Alice (b. 1944)

Born in Eatonton, Georgia, the eighth child of sharecropping parents, Alice Walker left home with a scholarship to Spelman College. After two years there she went on to Sarah Laurence College, from which she graduated in 1965. Returning to the South to participate in the Civil Rights Movement, she worked with voter registration in Georgia and Headstart in Mississippi. One of America's best-known novelists, poets, essayists, and biographers, her works include *Once* (1968), *The Third Life of Grange Copeland* (1970), *In Love and Trouble* (1973), *Revolutionary Petunias* (1973), *Meridian* (1976), *Goodnight, Willie Lee, I'll See You in the Morning* (1980), *The Color Purple* (1982), *In Search of Our Mothers' Gardens* (1983), *You Can't Keep a Good Woman Down* (1981), *Langston Hughes, American Poet, Temple of My Familiar* (1989), *Living by the Word: Selected Writings 1973–1987* (1989), *Possessing the Secret of Joy* (1992), and *Same River Twice: Honoring the Difficult: A Meditation on Life, Spirit, Art, and the Making of the Film, The Color Purple, and Ten Years Later* (1996). In 1979 she edited *I Love Myself When I Am Laughing . . . and then Again When I Am Looking Mean and Impressive: A Zora Neale Hurston Reader* (1979). She coauthored with Pratibha Parmar *Woman's Marks: Female Genital Mutilation and the Sexual Blinding of Women* (1993). The first black woman to win the Pulitzer Prize for fiction, for *The Color Purple* in 1983, Walker also won The National Book Award that same year.

Walker, Margaret (b. 1915)

Born in Birmingham, Alabama, Margaret Walker received her B.A. from Northwestern University and her M.A. and Ph.D. from the University of Iowa. She has taught briefly at Livingston College, West Virginia State College, and Northwestern University, but most of her long and illustrious teaching career has been spent at Jackson State College. Her first volume of poetry, *For My People* (1942), won a place in the Yale Series of Younger Writers. Her historical novel, *Jubilee* (1966), won a Houghton Mifflin literary award. Her other works include *Ballad of the Free* (1966), *Prophets for a New Day* (1966), *How I Wrote Jubilee* (1972), *October Journey* (1973), *A Poetic Equation: Conversations Between Nikki Giovanni and Margaret*

Walker (1974), *The Daemonic Genius of Richard Wright* (1987), *This Is My Century: New and Collected Poems* (1989), and *How I Wrote Jubilee and Other Essays on Life and Literature* (ed. Maryemma Graham, 1990).

Wallace, Michele (b. 1952)

Born into a middle-class family in Harlem, New York, Michele Wallace earned B.A. and M.A. degrees from City College of the City University of New York. Ms. Wallace sprang on the national scene with the publication of the controversial *Black Macho and the Myth of the Superwoman* in 1979, a work that, along with Shange's *For Colored Girls,* sparked an angry backlash from black males to black feminism/womanism. Recent works include *Invisibility Blues: From Pop to Theory* (1990) and *Black Popular Culture: A Project by Michele Wallace* (1992). She is currently teaching at City College of New York and the City University of New York Graduate Center.

Waniek, Marilyn Nelson (b. 1946)

Born in Cleveland, Ohio, Marilyn Nelson Waniek was educated at the University of California at Davis (B.A.), the University of Pennsylvania (M.A.), and the University of Minnesota (Ph.D.). After teaching English in various places, she has been on the faculty at the University of Connecticut at Storrs since 1978. With Pamela Espeland she published *The Cat Walked Through the Casserole and Other Poems for Children* (1984). Her volumes of poetry include *For the Body* (1978), *Mama's Promises* (1985), *Homeplace* (1990), and *Magnificat* (1994).

Ward, Val (b. 1932)

Born and reared in Mound Bayou, Mississippi, the second oldest all-black town in American, Ms. Ward moved to Chicago in 1951. She later attended Wilson Junior College there. An internationally known actress, producer, and theater personality who has made major contributions to the cultural life of Chicago and America through her work as a dramatist and actor, and as founder and artistic director of the Kuumba Theater, Val Ward's productions include *Gwendolyn Brooks Tribute* (1969), *The Life of Harriet Tubman* (1971), and *The Heart of the Blues* (1984). She now lives in Syracuse, New York.

Warren, Nagueyalti (b. 1947)

Nagueyalti Warren was born in Atlanta, Georgia, but grew up in Los Angeles. She earned a B.A. in English from Fisk University, an M.A. in Afro-American Studies at Boston University, an M.A. in English from Simmons College, and a Ph.D. in English from the University of Mississippi. In 1992 her first book of poetry, *Lodestar and Other Night Lights,* was published. Currently she is Assistant Dean and Adjunct Associate Professor of African American Studies at Emory University in Atlanta, Georgia.

Waters, Ethel (1896–1977)

Born in Chester, Pennsylvania, to a twelve-year-old mother who had been raped by a white musician whose name she took, Ethel Waters was raised by her maternal grandmother, a live-in domestic. In 1917 Waters began singing blues in a Philadelphia saloon and went on to become a vaudeville regular. On the T.O.B.A. circuit, she was popularly known as Sweet Mama Stringbean because she was tall and thin. A singer, dancer, comedienne, and actress, Waters went on to become one of the most popular and highest paid black performers of her day.

Welsing, Frances Cress (b. 1935)

Born in Chicago into a family line of physicians (her paternal grandfather and her father), Frances Cress Welsing went on to complete a B.S. at Antioch and an M.D. at Howard University School of Medicine, where she taught from 1968 to 1975. A psychiatrist, Dr. Welsing is best known for her controversial theories of race and racism, first formulated in 1996 in *The Cress Theory of Color Confrontation and Racism.*

Wesley, Valerie Wilson (b. 1948)

Valerie Wilson Wesley received a degree in philosophy from Howard University, a master's degree in early childhood education from Banks Street College, and a master's degree in journalism from Columbia University. She has worked as a freelance writer and is currently an executive editor of *Essence* magazine. Her works include *When Death Comes Stealing* (1994), *Devil's Gonna Get Him* (1995), and *Where Evil Sleeps* (1996).

West, Dorothy (b. 1907)

Born in Boston into a comfortable middle-class family, Dorothy West attended Girls Latin School and began writing as a teenager. When she was only seventeen years old, she shared the coveted *Opportunity* short-story prize with Zora Neale Hurston and later moved to New York where she became associated with the Harlem Renaissance. West studied journalism and philosophy at Columbia University. The founder and editor of two literary magazines: *The Challenge* and *New Challenge*, she has lived on Martha's Vineyard since 1943. Her works include *The Living Is Easy* (1948), *The Wedding* (1995), and *The Richer, the Poorer: Stories, Sketches and Reminiscences* (1995).

Williams, Patricia J. (b. 1951)

Born in Boston to a middle-class family, Patricia Joyce Williams earned a B.A. from Wellesley College and a J.D. from Harvard Law School. After working for five years in the Office of the City Attorney in Los Angeles and as a staff attorney for the Western Center on Law and Poverty in Los Angeles, Williams began her career in academia. She has been a Professor of law at the City University of New York Law School at Queens College, Stanford University, Duke University, University of Wisconsin at Madison, and Columbia University. She also served as visiting professor of women's studies for one year at Harvard University. Patricia J. Williams is author of *The Alchemy of Race and Rights: Diary of a Law Professor* (1991) and *The Rooster's Egg: On the Persistence of Prejudice* (1995).

Williams, Penny

Penny Williams, an ex-slave, was seventy-six years old and living in Raleigh, North Carolina, when she talked with the WPA interviewers and told them of the deprivations and hardships she had suffered while a slave on a large plantation just outside of Raleigh.

Wilson, Harriet E. (1828[?]–1870)

Very little is known about the early years of Harriet E. Wilson. Birth dates listed for her range from 1807 to 1828. By 1850 Wilson, who may have been born in Fredericksburg, Virginia, was living with a white family in Milford, New Hampshire. In 1859 she published the autobiographical novel, *Our Nig: or Sketches from the Life of a Free Black, in a Two-Story House, North, Showing That Slavery's Shadows Fall Even There*. Having been abandoned by her husband, she explained that the novel was written for the express purpose of raising money to help care for her child, who died five months later. She also expressed her intention of indicting indenture and racism in the North (see subtitle)—and in this case especially, the racism of a white woman.

Word, Sophia (1837–?)

Sophia Word, who was held in slavery for nineteen years and nine months, was ninety-nine years old when she talked with the WPA interviewers.

Workman, Alison (b. 1970)

Born in the United Kingdom, Alison Workman spent her earliest formative years on a farm in the remote English countryside. She moved to the United States as a child and has lived in New York, Maine, and Virginia. She earned a B.A. in English from Virginia State University (1995) and an M.A. in English from the University of Richmond (1997).

BIBLIOGRAPHY

Abrahams, Roger D. "Negotiating Respect: Patterns of Presentation Among Black Women." *Journal of American Folklore* 88 (1975): 58–80.

Albertson, Chris. *Bessie.* New York: Stein and Day, 1972.

Allen, Bonnie. *We Are Overcome.* New York: Crown, 1995.

Andrews, William L., ed. *Sisters of the Spirit: Three Black Women's Autobiographies of the Nineteenth Century.* Bloomington: Indiana University Press, 1986.

———, ed. *Six Women's Slave Narratives.* New York: Oxford, 1988.

Angelou, Maya. *And Still I Rise.* New York: Random House, 1978.

Ansa, Tina McElroy. *Ugly Ways.* New York: Harcourt Brace, 1993.

Armstrong, M. F. and Helen W. Ludlow. *Hampton and Its Students: with Fifty Cabin and Plantation Songs, Arranged by Thomas P. Fenner.* New York: G. P. Putnam's Sons, 1875.

Arnez, Nancy Levi, and Clara B. Anthony. "Contemporary Negro Humor as Social Satire." *Phylon* 29 (winter, 1968): 339–46.

Bibliography

Ashe, Bertram D. " 'Why don't he like my hair?': Constructing African-American Standards of Beauty in Toni Morrison's *Song of Solomon* and Zora Neale Hurston's *Their Eyes Were Watching God.*" *African American Review* 29 (winter 1995): 579–92.

Bambara, Toni Cade. "Searching for the Mother Tongue" (an interview with Kalamu ya Salaam). *First World* 2 (1980): 48–53.

Banks, Frank D. "Plantation Courtship." *Southern Workman* 24 (January 1895): 14–15.

Barreca, Regina. *They Used to Call Me Snow White . . . But I Drifted: Women's Strategic Use of Humor.* New York: Viking, 1991.

Bell, Bernard W. *The Afro-American Novel and Its Tradition.* Amherst: The University of Massachusetts Press, 1987.

Bennett, D. J. "The Psychological Meaning of Anti-Negro Jokes." *Fact* (March–April, 1964): 53–59.

Bergler, Edmund. *Laughter and the Sense of Humor.* New York: Intercontinental Medical Book Corp, 1956.

Bergson, Henri. *Laughter: An Essay on the Meaning of the Comic.* 1911. London: Macmillan and Co., 1913.

Berry, Bertice. *The World According to Me.* New York: Scribner, 1996.

Bier, Jesse. *The Rise and Fall of American Humor.* New York: Holt, Rinehart, and Winston, 1968.

Blount, Roy, Jr., ed. *Roy Blount's Book of Southern Humor.* New York: W. W. Norton, 1994.

Bogle, Donald. *Toms, Coons, Mulattoes, Mammies, and Bucks: An Interpretive History of Blacks in American Films.* New York: Viking, 1973.

Boskin, Joseph. " 'How Fast Is Slow, Baby?' Good-by, Mr. Bones." *New York Times Magazine,* May 1, 1966: 30, 31, 84, 86, 88, 90, 92.

Botkin, B. A., ed. *Lay My Burden Down: A Folk History of Slavery.* Chicago: University of Chicago Press, 1945.

Boyd, Julia A. *Girlfriend to Girlfriend: Everyday Wisdom and Affirmations from the Sister Circle.* New York: Penguin Books, 1995.

Bradford, Sarah. *Harriet, The Moses of Her People.* Secaucus, New York: Citadel Press, 1974.

Braxton, Joanne M. *Black Women Writing Autobiography: A Tradition Within a Tradition.* Philadelphia: Temple University Press, 1989.

Brent, Linda. *Incidents in the Life of a Slave Girl.* Boston: Thayer & Eldredge, 1861.

Brooks, A. Russell. "The Comic Spirit and the Negro's New Look. *CLAJ* 6 (September 1962): 35–43.

Brooks, Gwendolyn. *Maud Martha.* New York: Harper, 1953.

Bunkers, Suzanne L. "Why Are These Women Laughing? The Power and Politics of Women's Humor." *Studies in American Humor* [New Series] 4, nos. 1, 2 (spring/summer 1985): 82–93.

Burma, John H. "Humor as a Technique in Race Conflict." *American Sociological Review* 2 (1946): 710–15.

Burrison, John A., ed. *Storytellers: Folktales & Legends from the South*. Athens: University of Georgia Press, 1989.

"Butterbeans and Susie: Oldest Negro Song and Dance Celebrates Its 35th Anniversary in Show Business." *Ebony* 7 (April 1952): 59–63.

Cade, Toni. *The Black Woman: An Anthology*. New York: New American Library, 1970.

Callahan, John F. "Frequencies of Memory: A Eulogy for Ralph Waldo Ellison (March 1, 1914–April 16, 1994)." *Callaloo* 18 (spring, 1995): 298–309.

Campbell, Bebe Moore. *Sweet Summer: Growing Up With and Without My Dad*. New York: The Putnam Publishing Group, 1989.

Cantor, Joanne R. "What Is Funny to Whom?" *Journal of Communication* 26 (summer 1976): 164–72.

Chesnutt, Charles. *The Wife of His Youth and Other Stories of the Color Line*. New York: Houghton Mifflin, 1899.

Clarke, Donald. *Wishing on the Moon: The Life and Times of Billie Holiday*. New York: Viking, 1994.

Cullen, Countee. *One Way to Heaven*. New York: Harper, 1932.

Dance, Daryl Cumber. *Shuckin' and Jivin': Folklore from Contemporary Black Americans*. Bloomington: Indiana University Press, 1978.

Davies, Christie. *Ethnic Humor Around the World: A Comparative Analysis*. Bloomington: Indiana University Press, 1990.

Davis, Ossie, "Purlie Victorious," *American Ethnic Writing: Speaking for Ourselves*, ed. Lillian Faderman and Barbara Bradshaw. Glenview, Illinois: Scott, Foresman and Company, 1969. 98–145.

DeCosta-Willis, Miriam, Reginald Martin, and Roseann P. Bell, eds. *Erotique Noire/Black Erotica*. New York: Doubleday, 1992.

Dee, Ruby. *My One Good Nerve*. Chicago: Third World Press, 1987.

Delany, Sarah, and A. Elizabeth Delany (with Amy Hill Hearth). *Having Our Say: The Delany Sisters' First 100 Years*. New York: Kodansha America, Inc., 1993.

Dove, Rita. *Through the Ivory Gate: A Novel*. New York: Pantheon Books, 1992.

Drums and Shadows: Survival Studies Among the Georgia Coastal Negroes. Foreword by Guy B. Johnson. New York: Doubleday, 1972.

Dundes, Alan, ed. *Mother Wit from the Laughing Barrel: Readings in the Interpretation of Afro-American Folklore*. Englewood Cliffs: Prentice-Hall, 1973.

Dundes, Alan, and Carl R. Pagter. *Urban Folklore from the Paperwork Empire.* Austin, Texas: The American Folklore Society, 1975.

———. *When You're up to Your Ass in Alligators . . . : More Urban Folklore from the Paperwork Empire.* Detroit: Wayne State University Press, 1987.

Ellison, Ralph. *Shadow and Act.* New York: Vintage Books, 1972.

Esar, Evan. *The Humor of Humor.* New York: Horizon Press, 1952.

Fanon, Frantz. *The Wretched of the Earth.* Trans. Constance Farrington. New York: Grove Press, 1968.

Farrer, Claire R. *Women and Folklore.* Austin: University of Texas Press, 1975.

Fauset, Jessie. "The Gift of Laughter." *Black Expression: Essays by and about Black Americans in the Creative Arts.* Ed. Addison Gayle. New York: Weybright and Talley, 1969. 159–65.

———. "Mary Elizabeth." *The Crisis* 19 (December 1919): 51–56.

Feinberg, Leonard. *Introduction to Satire.* Ames, Iowa: The Iowa State University Press, 1967.

Finney, Gail, ed. *Look Who's Laughing: Gender and Comedy.* Langhorne, Pennsylvania: Gordon and Breach, 1994.

"Folk-lore and Ethnology." *Southern Workman* 25 (October 1896): 205–6.

Fordham, Mary Weston. *Magnolia Leaves: Poems by Mary Weston Fordham.* Charleston: Walker, Evans & Cogswell Co., 1897.

Forten, Charlotte. Journal. Folder 1816 of the Francis J. Grimké Papers, Boxes 40–45. Moorland-Spingarn Research Center, Howard University, Washington, D.C.

Foster, Frances Smith. *Written by Herself: Literary Production by African American Women, 1746–1892.* Bloomington: Indiana University Press, 1993.

Foxx, Redd, and Norma Miller. *The Redd Foxx Encyclopedia of Black Humor.* Pasadena, California: Ward Ritchie Press, 1977.

Frazier, E. Franklin. *Black Bourgeoisie: [The Rise of a New Middle Class in the United States].* Glencoe, Illinois: Free Press, 1957.

Freud, Sigmund. *The Basic Writings of Sigmund Freud.* New York: The Modern Library, 1938.

———. *Jokes and Their Relation to the Unconscious.* Trans. and ed. James Strachey. New York: W. W. Norton, 1960.

Gaines, Patrice. *Laughing in the Dark: From Colored Girl to Woman of Color: A Journey from Prison to Power.* New York: Anchor Books/Doubleday, 1994.

Gale, Stephen H., ed. *Encyclopedia of American Humorists.* New York: Garland, 1988.

Gates, Henry Louis, Jr. *The Signifying Monkey.* New York: Oxford University Press, 1988.

Gilman, Sander L. *Difference and Pathology: Stereotypes of Sexuality, Race, and Madness.* Ithaca, New York. Cornell University Press, 1985.

Goldberg, Whoopi. Foreword. *True Beauty: Secrets of Radiant Beauty for Women of Every Age and Color.* By Beverly Johnson. New York: Warner Books, Inc., 1994.

Golden, Marita, ed. *Wild Women Don't Wear No Blues: Black Women Writers on Love Men and Sex.* New York: Doubleday, 1993.

Goldman, Morris. "The Sociology of Negro Humor." Diss. New School for Social Research, New York, 1960.

Grier, William H., and Price M. Cobbs. *Black Rage.* New York: Bantam Books, 1969.

Harper, Frances Ellen Watkins. *Sketches of Southern Life.* Philadelphia: Ferguson Bros., 1891.

Hemenway, Robert, ed. *Dust Tracks on a Road* by Zora Neale Hurston. 1942. Urbana: University of Illinois Press, 1984.

Highet, Gilbert. *The Anatomy of Satire.* Princeton: Princeton University Press, 1962.

Holloway, Karla F. C. *Codes of Conduct: Race, Ethics, and the Color of Our Character.* New Brunswick, New Jersey: Rutgers University Press, 1995.

Hudson, Arthur P., ed. *Humor of the Old Deep South.* Port Washington, New York: Kennikat Press, 1936. 2 volumes.

Hughes, Langston. *The Book of Negro Humor.* New York: Dodd, Mead, 1966.

———. "Jokes Negroes Tell on Themselves." *Negro Digest* 9 (June 1951): 21–25.

Hughes, Langston, and Zora Neale Hurston. *Mule Bone: A Comedy of Negro Life.* 1931. New York: Harper Perennials, 1991.

Hurmence, Belinda, ed. *Before Freedom: 48 Oral Histories of Former North and South Carolina Slaves.* Winston-Salem, North Carolina: John F. Blair Publisher, 1990.

Hurston, Zora Neale. "Characteristics of Negro Expression." *Negro: An Anthology.* Ed. Nancy Cunard and Hugo Ford. London: Wishart, 1934. 39–46.

———. *Dust Tracks on a Road.* Philadelphia: J. P. Lippincott, 1942.

———. "The Gilded Six-Bits." *Story Magazine* 3 (August 1933): 60–70.

———. *Jonah's Gourd Vine.* Philadelphia: J. P. Lippincott, 1934.

———. *Mules and Men.* Philadelphia: J. P. Lippincott, 1935.

———. "Spirituals and Neo-Spirituals," in *Negro: An Anthology.* Ed. Nancy Cunard and Hugo Ford. London: Wishart, 1934. 359–61.

———. *Tell My Horse.* New York: J. P. Lippincott, 1935.

———. *Their Eyes Were Watching God.* 1937. Urbana: University of Illinois Press, 1978.

Jackson, Bruce. *"Get Your Ass in the Water and Swim Like Me": Narrative Poetry from Black Oral Tradition.* Cambridge: Harvard University Press, 1974.

Jackson, Mattie J. *The Story of Mattie J. Jackson: Her Parentage—Experience of Eighteen Years in Slavery—Incidents During the War—Her Escape from Slavery: A True Story.* Written and arranged by Dr. L. S. Thompson. Lawrence, Kansas: Printed at Sentinel Office, 1866.

Jacobs, Harriet. (see Brent, Linda)

Jenkins, Ron. *Subversive Laughter: The Liberating Power of Comedy.* New York: The Free Press, 1994.

Johnson, Beverly. *True Beauty: Secrets of Radiant Beauty for Women of Every Age and Color.* New York: Warner Books, Inc., 1994.

Johnson, James Weldon. *The Book of American Negro Poetry.* New York: Harcourt Brace, 1922.

Johnson, Maggie Pogue. *Virginia Dreams/Lyrics for the Idle Hour: Tales of the Time Told in Rhyme.* N.p. Copyright 1910 by John M. Leonard.

Jones, Lisa. *bulletproof diva.* New York: Doubleday, 1994.

Jordan, Rosan A. and Susan J. Kalcik, eds. *Women's Folklore, Women's Culture.* Philadelphia: University of Pennsylvania Press, 1985.

Kaufman, Gloria, and Mary Kay Blakely, eds. *Pulling Our Own Strings: Feminist Humor & Satire.* Bloomington: Indiana University Press, 1980.

Kennedy, Florynce R. *Color Me Flo.* Englewood Cliffs: Prentice-Hall, 1976.

Kernan, Claudia Mitchell. (see Mitchell, Claudia I.)

Killens, John Oliver. *"Rappin' with Myself."* Amistad 2. Ed. John A. Williams and Charles F. Hann. New York: Random House, 1971.

Larsen, Nella. *Quicksand.* New York: Knopf, 1928.

Levine, Lawrence W. *Black Culture and Black Consciousness: Afro-American Folk Thought from Slavery to Freedom.* New York: Oxford University Press, 1977.

Lewis, Samella. *Art: African American.* New York: Harcourt Brace, 1978.

Locke, Alain. *The Negro and His Music: Negro Art: Past and Present.* New York: Arno Press, 1969.

Long, Courtney, ed. *Love Awaits.* New York: Bantam Books, 1995.

Lovell, John, Jr. *Black Song: The Forge and the Flame: The Story of How the Afro-American Spiritual Was Hammered Out.* New York: Paragon House, 1972.

Lowe, John. *Jump at the Sun: Zora Neale Hurston's Cosmic Comedy.* Urbana: University of Illinois Press, 1994.

McGhee, Paul E. *"The Role of Laughter and Humor in Growing Up Female."* Becoming Female: Perspectives on Development. Ed. Claire B. Kopp. New York: Plenum Press, 1979. 183–206.

McMillan, Terry. *Waiting to Exhale.* New York: Viking, 1992.

Major, Clarence, ed. *Juba to Jive: A Dictionary of African-American Slang.* New York: Penguin, 1994.

Metcalf, George R. *Up from Within: Today's New Black Leaders.* New York: McGraw-Hill, 1971.

Mills, Kay. *This Little Light of Mine: the Life of Fannie Lou Hamer.* New York: Dutton, 1993.

Mitchell, Carol. "Some Differences in Male and Female Joke-Telling." *Women's Folklore, Women's Culture.* Ed. Rosan A. Jordan and Susan J. Kalcik. Philadelphia: University of Pennsylvania Press, 1985. 163–86.

Mitchell [Kernan], Claudia I. "Language Behavior in a Black Urban Community." Diss. University of California, Berkeley, 1970.

Monroe, Barbara. "Courtship, Comedy, and African-American Expressive Culture in Zora Neale Hurston's Fiction." *Look Who's Laughing.* Ed. Gail Finney. Langhorne, Pennsylvania: Gordon and Breach, 1994. 173–88.

Morrison, Allan. "Negro Humor: An Answer to Anguish." *Ebony* 22 (May 1967): 99, 100, 102, 104–106, 108, 110.

Morrison, Toni. *The Bluest Eye.* New York: Holt, Rinehart and Winston, 1970.

———. *Jazz.* New York: Alfred A. Knopf, 1992.

———. *Song of Solomon.* New York: Alfred A. Knopf, 1978.

Mother Love [Jo Anne Hart], with Connie Church. *Listen Up, Girlfriends!* New York: St. Martin's Press, 1995.

Neal, Angela M., and Midge L. Wilson. "The Role of Skin Color and Features in the Black Community: Implications for Black Women and Therapy." *Clinical Psychology Review* 9 (1989): 323–33.

Neely, Barbara. *Blanche Among the Talented Tenth.* New York: St. Martin's Press, 1994.

———. *Blanche on the Lam.* New York: St. Martin's Press, 1992.

The Negro in Virginia: Compiled by Workers of the Writers' Program of the Work Projects Administration in the State of Virginia. New York: Hastings House Publishers, 1940.

Nelson, Jill. *Volunteer Slavery: My Authentic Negro Experience.* Chicago: The Noble Press, Inc., 1993.

O'Brien, John. "Alice Walker." *Interviews with Black Writers.* New York: Liveright, 1973.

Painter, Nell Irvin. *Sojourner Truth: A Life, A Symbol.* New York: W. W. Norton, 1996.

Patterson, Ruth Polk. *The Seed of Sally Good'n: A Black Family of Arkansas 1833–1953.* Lexington, Kentucky: University Press of Kentucky, 1985.

Percelay, James, Ivey Monteria, and Stephan Dweck. *Snaps.* New York: William Morrow, 1994.

Perdue, Charles L., Jr., Thomas E. Barden, and Robert K. Phillips, eds. *Weevils in the Wheat: Interviews with Virginia Ex-Slaves.* Charlottesville: University Press of Virginia, 1976.

Pickens, William. *American Aesop: Negro and Other Humor.* Boston: The Jordan & More Press, 1926.

Prange, Arthur J., Jr., and M. M. Vitols. "Jokes Among Southern Negroes: The Revelation of Conflict." *Journal of Nervous and Mental Disease* 136 (1963): 162–67.

Proceedings: First Anniversary of the American Equal Rights Association Held at the Church of the Puritans, New York, May 9 and 10, 1867. New York: Robert J. Johnston, Printer, 1867.

Rapp, Albert. *The Origins of Wit and Humor.* New York: Dutton, 1951.

Rawick, George P., ed. *Kansas, Kentucky, Maryland, Ohio, Virginia, and Tennessee Narratives.* Vol. 16 of *The American Slave: A Composite Autobiography.* 1941. Westport, Connecticut: Greenwood, 1972.

————. *North Carolina Narratives.* Vol. 15 of *The American Slave: A Composite Autobiography.* 1941. Westport: Greenwood, 1972.

Reed, Ishmael. *Mumbo Jumbo.* New York: Doubleday, 1972.

Reid, Mark A. *Redefining Black Film.* Berkeley: University of California Press, 1993.

Roberts, Diane. *The Myth of Aunt Jemima: Representations of Race and Region.* New York: Routledge, 1994.

Robinson, Debra J. *I Be Done Was Is.* 60-minute film, distributed by Women Make Movies. New York: 1983.

Robinson, William H., ed. *Nommo: An Anthology of Modern Black African and Black American Literature.* New York: Macmillan, 1972.

Russell, Kathy, Midge Wilson, and Ronald Hall. *The Color Complex: The Politics of Skin Color Among African Americans.* New York: Harcourt Brace Jovanovich, 1992.

Sanders, Dori. *Clover.* Chapel Hill, North Carolina: Algonquin Books, 1990.

————. *Her Own Place.* Chapel Hill, North Carolina: Algonquin Books, 1993.

Sapphire, "Queen of the ABC's," *Push.* New York: Alfred A. Knopf, 1996.

Schechter, William. *The History of Negro Humor in America.* New York: Fleet Press, 1970.

Schipper, Mineke, ed. *Unheard Words: Women and Literature in Africa, the Arab World, Asia, the Caribbean and Latin America.* New York: Allison & Busby, 1985.

Senghor, Leopold. "African–Negro Aesthetics." In *The Ideology of Blackness*. Ed. Raymond F. Betts. Lexington, Massachusetts: D. C. Heath, 1971: 110–25.

Sexton, Adam, ed. *Rap on Rap: Straight-Up Talk on Hip-Hop Culture*. New York: Dell, 1995.

Sherman, Charlotte Watson, ed. *Sisterfire: Black Womanist Fiction and Poetry*. New York: Harper, 1994.

Sinclair, April. *Ain't Gonna Be the Same Fool Twice*. New York: Hyperion, 1994.

———. *Coffee Will Make You Black*. New York: Hyperion, 1996.

Smith, Amanda. *An Autobiography: The Story of the Lord's Dealings with Mrs. Amanda Smith, the Colored Evangelist, Containing an Account of Her Life Work of Faith, and Her Travels in America, England, Ireland, Scotland, India and Africa, as an Independent Missionary*. Chicago: Meyer & Brother, Publishers, 1893.

Smith, Barbara, ed. *Home Girls: A Black Feminist Anthology*. New York: Kitchen Table: Women of Color Press, 1983.

Smith, Faye McDonald. *Flight of the Blackbird*. New York: Scribner, 1996.

Smitherman, Geneva. *Talkin and Testifyin: The Language of Black America*. Detroit, Michigan: Wayne State University Press, 1977.

Sochen, June, ed. *Women's Comic Visions*. Detroit, Michigan: Wayne State University Press, 1991.

Souljah, Sister. *No Disrespect*. New York: Times Books, 1994.

Southern, Eileen. *The Music of Black Americans: A History*. New York: W. W. Norton, 1971.

Spalding, Henry D., ed. *Encyclopedia of Black Folklore and Humor*. Middle Village, New York: Jonathan David Publishers, 1990.

Stearns, Marshall and Jean Stearns. "Frontiers of Humor: American Vernacular Dance." *Southern Folklore Quarterly* 30 (1966): 227–35.

Sterling, Dorothy, ed. *We Are Your Sisters: Black Women in the Nineteenth Century*. New York: W. W. Norton, 1984.

Stetson, Erlene, ed. *Black Sister: Poetry by Black Women, 1746–1980*. Bloomington: Indiana University Press, 1981.

Stockard, Janice Lynn. *The Role of the American Black Woman in Folktales: An Interdisciplinary Study of Identification and Interpretation*. Diss. Tulane University, 1979. Ann Arbor: University of Michigan Press, 1984. 8019435.

Taft, Michael. *Blues Lyric Poetry: An Anthology*. New York: Garland, 1983.

Taylor, Clyde. "The Language of Hip: from Africa to What's Happening Now." *First World* (January/February 1977): 25–32.

Taylor, Patrick. *The Narrative of Liberation: Perspectives on Afro-Caribbean Literature, Popular Culture, and Politics*. Ithaca, New York: Cornell University Press, 1989.

Thompson, Priscilla Jane. *Ethiope Lays.* Rossmoyne, Ohio: privately printed, 1900.

Toth, Emily. "Female Wits." *Massachusetts Review* 22 (1981): 783–93.

———. "Forbidden Jokes and Naughty Ladies." *Studies in American Humor* [New Series] 4, nos. 1, 2 (spring/summer 1985): 7–17.

Truth, Sojourner. ["While the Water Is Stirring I Will Step into the Pool"]. *Proceedings: First Anniversary of the American Equal Rights Association Held at the Church of the Puritans, New York, May 9 and 10, 1867.* New York: Robert J. Johnston, Printer, 1867. 20–21, 63.

Vanzant, Iyanla. *The Value in the Valley: A Black Woman's Guide through Life's Dilemmas.* New York: Simon & Schuster, 1995.

Wade-Gayles, Gloria. *Pushed Back to Strength: A Black Woman's Journey Home.* Boston: Beacon Press, 1993.

———. *Rooted Against the Wind: Personal Essays.* Boston: Beacon Press, 1996.

Walker, Alice. *The Color Purple.* New York: Harcourt Brace Jovanovich, 1982.

Walker, Margaret. *This Is My Century: New and Collected Poems by Margaret Walker.* Athens, Georgia: University of Georgia Press, 1989.

Walker, Nancy. *A Very Serious Thing: Women's Humor and American Culture.* Minneapolis: University of Minnesota Press, 1988.

Wallace, Michele. *Black Macho and the Myth of the Superwoman.* New York: The Dial Press, 1978.

Warren, Nagueyalti. *Lodestar and Other Night Lights.* New York: Mellen, 1992.

Washington, Mary Helen, ed. *Black-Eyed Susans: Classic Stories by and about Black Women.* New York: Anchor Press, 1975.

———. *Invented Lives: Narratives of Black Women 1860–1960.* Garden City: Doubleday, 1987.

Waters, Donald J., ed. *Strange Ways and Sweet Dreams: Afro-American Folklore from the Hampton Institute.* Boston: G. K. Hall, 1983.

Watkins, Mel. *On the Real Side: Laughing, Lying, and Signifying—the Underground Tradition of African-American Humor That Transformed American Culture, from Slavery to Richard Pryor.* New York: Simon & Schuster, 1994.

Wesley, Valerie Wilson. *Devil's Gonna Get Him.* New York: G. P. Putnam's Sons, 1995.

———. *When Death Comes Stealing.* New York: G. P. Putnam's Sons, 1994.

———. *Where Evil Sleeps.* New York: G. P. Putnam's Sons, 1996.

West, Dorothy. *The Living Is Easy.* 1948. Old Westbury: The Feminist Press, 1982.

———. *The Wedding.* New York: Doubleday, 1995.

White, Deborah Gray. *Ar'nt I a Woman? Female Slaves in the Plantation South.* New York: W. W. Norton, 1987.

Williams, Elsie Griffin. "Jackie Moms Mabley: African American, Woman, Performer." Diss. University of Maryland, 1992. 2 vol.

Williams, Patricia J., "A Rare Case Study of Muleheadedness and Men, or How to Try an Unruly Black Witch, with Excerpts from the Heretical Testimony of Four Women, Known to be Hysterics, Speaking in Their Own Voices, as Translated for This Publication by Brothers Hatch, Simpson, DeConcini, and Specter," in Toni Morrison's *Race-ing Justice, En-gendering Power: Essays on Anita Hill, Clarence Thomas, and the Construction of Social Reality.* New York: Pantheon, 1992. 159–64.

Wilson, Ellen Dickson, "Aunt Hannah Introduces Herself." *The Southern Workman* (January 1912): 40–48.

Wilson, Harriet E. *Our Nig: or Sketches from the Life of a Free Black, in a Two-Story House, North, Showing That Slavery's Shadows Fall Even There.* Boston: Printed by Geo. C. Rand & Avery, 1859.

Wright, Howard E. "Racial Humor: A Value Analysis." Diss. Ohio State University, 1946.

CREDITS

Adams, Armacie. See *The Negro in Virginia*.

Allen, Bonnie, from "Introduction," "Your attitude is politically correct if . . . ," and "America: The Board Game," from *We Are Overcome* by Bonnie Allen. Copyright © 1995 by Bonnie Allen. Reprinted by permission of Crown Publishers, Inc.

Anderson-Thompkins, Sibby, "Epitaph for Willie: Or Little Black Poet With No Future," from *In the Tradition: An Anthology of Young Black Writers,* ed. Kevin Powell and Ras Baraka, 1992. Published for Harlem River Press by Writers and Readers Publishing, Inc. Reprinted by permission of Deborah Cowell, Editor, Writers and Readers.

Angelou, Maya, from *I Know Why the Caged Bird Sings.* Copyright © 1969 by Maya Angelou. Reprinted by permission of Random House, Inc.

Ansa, Tina McElroy, Chapter Four from *Ugly Ways.* Copyright © 1993 by Tina McElroy Ansa. Reprinted by permission of Harcourt Brace & Company.

Bambara, Toni Cade, "A Sort of Preface," "The Lesson," and selection from "The Johnson Girls," from *Gorilla, My Love* by Toni Cade Bambara. Copyright © 1972 by Toni Cade Bambara. Reprinted by permission of Random House, Inc.

Berry, Bertice, selections from *The World According to Me.* Copyright © 1996 by Bertice Berry Productions. Reprinted with the permission of Scribner, a Division of Simon & Schuster from *Bertice: The World According to Me* by Bertice Berry.

Binford, Virgie, "Quilting Time." Reprinted with permission of the author.

Birtha, Becky, "Johnnieruth," from *Lovers' Choice.* Copyright © 1987 by Becky Birtha. Reprinted by permission of Seal Press (Seattle, Washington).

Bowen-Spencer, Michele. "A Fool, a Girlfriend, a Husband and a Wife," an excerpt from *Churchfolk* (a novel in progress). Used by permission of author.

Boyd, Julia A., from *Girlfriend to Girlfriend: Everyday Wisdom and Affirmations from the Sister Circle.* New York: Penguin Books, 1995.

———. Selections from Chapter 16, "Got a Job to Do," *In the Company of My Sisters: Black Women and Self-Esteem.*

Brandon, Barbara, *Where I'm Coming From.* Copyright © Barbara Brandon. Distributed by Universal Press Syndicate. Reprinted with permission. All rights reserved.

Brewington, Louise. See John Burrison.

Brice-Finch, Jacqueline, "English 'Umor" and "Safe Sex." Copyright © 1996 by Jacqueline Brice-Finch. Used by permission of author.

Brooks, Sonya, "Grandma Talk," from *In the Tradition: An Anthology of Young Black Writers,* ed. Kevin Powell and Ras Baraka, 1992. Published for Harlem River Press by Writers and Readers Publishing, Inc. Reprinted by permission of Writers and Readers.

Burrison, John A., "Preacher Tells a Lie," "The Laziest Man," "The Prayer John Gets Paid By," and "Too Many Ups," from *Storytellers: Folktales & Legends from the South.* Copyright © 1989 by University of Georgia Press. Reprinted by permission of The University of Georgia Press.

Butterbeans and Susie, "I Wanna Hot Dog (For My Roll)," words and music by Tosh Hammed and Clarence Williams. Copyright © 1935 by MCA Music Publishing, a division of Universal Studios, Inc. Copyright renewed. International copyright secured. All rights reserved. Used by permission.

Campbell, Bebe Moore, "Black Men, White Women: A Sister Relinquishes Her Anger," from the *New York Times* of August 23, 1992. Copyright © 1992 by the *New York Times* Co. Reprinted by permission of the *New York Times* and Bebe Moore Campbell.

————, Chapter 5 of *Sweet Summer: Growing Up With and Without My Dad*. Copyright © 1989 by Bebe Moore Campbell. Reprinted by permission of The Putnam Publishing Group.

Childress, Alice, "Like One of the Family, "The Pocketbook Game," and "Mrs. James," from *Like One of the Family: Conversations from a Domestic's Life*. Copyright © 1956. Copyright renewed © 1984 by Alice Childress. Used by permission of Flora Roberts, Inc.

"Coco," from *Love Awaits* by Courtney Long. Copyright © 1995 by Courtney Long. Used by permission of Bantam Books, a division of Bantam Doubleday Dell Publishing Group, Inc.

Cole, Johnnetta, "Sister President." Used by permission of Johnnetta Cole.

Cox, Ida, "Wild Women Don't Have No Blues." Paramount, 1924. We have made every effort to find the copyright holder for this selction. If you have information regarding the copyright holder, please write to W. W. Norton, 500 Fifth Avenue, New York, NY 10110 (Attn: Amy Cherry).

Dance, Daryl Cumber, "Ball It Up and Throw It to Me," "Upon This Rock," "How Blacks Got to America," "I Raised Hell," "Shall We Gather at the River," "He Remembered," "The New Rectum," "Gone to Meddling," "Tongue and Teeth," "How'd You Make Out," "Plenty Fire in the Furnace," "The Tar Baby," "I'll Go as Far as Memphis," The Tar Baby," "How?," "Wait on de Lord," and "Over the Hill," from *Shuckin' and Jivin': Folklore from Contemporary Black Americans*. Copyright © 1978 by Daryl Cumber Dance. Reprinted by permission of Indiana University Press.

Dee, Ruby, "Jack and Jill," "Mary Had a Little Lamb," and "To Pig or Not to Pig," from *My One Good Nerve*. Chicago: Third World Press. Copyright © 1987 by Ruby Dee. Used by permission of the author.

Delany, Sarah and A. Elizabeth, with Amy Hill Hearth, selections from *The Delany Sisters' Book of Everyday Wisdom*. New York: Kodansha, 1994. Copyright © 1994. Reprinted by permission of Kodansha America, Inc.

————, selections from *Having Our Say*. New York: Kodansha, 1993. Copyright © 1993. Reprinted by permission of Kodansha America, Inc.

Dericotte, Toi, "Dildo." Copyright © by Toi Dericotte. Reprinted by permission of the author.

Dove, Rita, "Nexus," from *The Yellow House on the Corner: Poems* by Rita Dove. Pittsburgh, Carnegie-Mellon University Press, copyright © 1980 by Rita Dove. Reprinted by permission of the author.

————, from *Through the Ivory Gate* by Rita Dove. Copyright © 1992 by Rita Dove. Reprinted by permission of Pantheon Books, a division of Random House, Inc.

Drake, Jeannette, "Conflict," from *Pods and Peas* (Richmond, Va.: Creative Works Publishing). Copyright © 1996 by Jeannette Drake. Reprinted by permission of author.

———, "Yes M'am," from *Daughter of Abraham*. Richmond: Creative Works Publishing. Copyright © 1996 by Jeannette Drake. Reprinted by permission of author.

Fullen-Collins, Marilyn, "Mama." Copyright © 1990 by Marilyn Fullen-Collins. Reprinted from *Over the Transom* (Earth's Daughters) by permission of author.

Gay, Pauline, "Too Many Ups." See Burrison, *Storytellers*.

Giovanni, Nikki, "Ego Tripping," *Re: Creation* (Detroit: Broadside Press). Copyright © 1970 by Nikki Giovanni. Reprinted by permission of the author.

———, "Campus Racism 101," from *Racism 101*. New York: William Morrow. Copyright © 1994 by Nikki Giovanni. Reprinted by permission of the author.

———, "Even Now, Hoorah for the Black Woman." Reprinted by permission of the author.

———, "Lorraine Hansberry," from *Those Who Ride the Night Winds*. New York: William Morrow. Copyright © 1983 by Nikki Giovanni. Reprinted by permission of the author.

Goldberg, Whoopi, from "Direct from Broadway." Reprinted by permission of Whoopi Goldberg. Ms. Goldberg retains full and absolute ownership of "Direct from Broadway" and the elements and/or character(s) contained therein.

Guinier, Lani, "Female Gentleman," from "Introduction of Professor Mari Matsuda." Reprinted with permission from *Temple Political & Civil Rights Law Review*. Vol. 3 (1993).

Hansberry, Lorraine. From *A Raisin in the Sun* by Lorraine Hansberry. Copyright © 1958 by Robert Nemiroff, as an unpublished work. Copyright © 1959, 1966, 1984 by Robert Nemiroff. Reprinted by permission of Random House, Inc.

Harris, Trudier, "The Overweight Angel," from *Obsidian: Black Literature in Review* 1 (summer 1975): 56–61. Copyright © 1975 by Alvin Aubert, editor of *Obsidian*. Permission to reprint from Alvin Aubert and Trudier Harris.

Hazelle (Hazelle Goodman), "Not Going to Stop til I Make It to de Top" from *HBO Presents Hazelle,* Home Box Office, 1995. Copyright © 1995 by Hazelle Goodman. Reprinted by permission of Hazelle Goodman.

Holloway, Karla F. C., excerpts from "Nice Girls" and "The Long Way Home," from *Codes of Conduct: Race, Ethics, and the Color of Our Character,* copyright © 1995 by Karla F. C. Holloway. Reprinted by permission of Rutgers University Press.

Hurston, Zora Neale, excerpts from *Jonah's Gourd Vine*. Copyright © 1934 by Zora Neale Hurston. Copyright renewed © 1962 by John C. Hurston. Reprinted by permission of HarperCollins Publishers, Inc.

————, from "Story in Harlem Slang," as taken from *The Complete Stories by Zora Neale Hurston*. Introduction copyright © 1995 by Henry Louis Gates, Jr., and Sieglinde Lemke. Compilation copyright © 1995 by Vivian Bowden, Lois J. Hurston Gaston, Clifford Hurston, Lucy Ann Hurston, Winifred Hurston Clark, Zora Mack Goins, Edgar Hurston, Sr., and Barbara Hurston Lewis. Afterword and Bibliography copyright © 1995 by Henry Louis Gates, Jr. "Story in Harlem Slang" was originally published in *The American Mercury*, July 1942. Reprinted by permission of HarperCollins Publishers, Inc.

————, excerpts from *Their Eyes Were Watching God* by Zora Neale Hurston. Copyright © 1937 by Harper & Row, Publishers, Inc. Copyright renewed © 1965 by John C. Hurston and Joel Hurston. Reprinted by permission of HarperCollins Publishers, Inc.

Jones, Lisa, "Corporate Boys," from *bulletproof diva* by Lisa Jones. Copyright © 1994 by Lisa Jones. Used by Permission of Doubleday, a division of Bantam Doubleday Dell Publishing Group, Inc.

Kennedy, Flo, excerpts from *Color Me Flo*. Copyright © 1976 by Florynce R. Kennedy. Reprinted by permission of Simon & Schuster from *Color Me Flo: My Hard Life & Good Times* by Flo Kennedy.

Little, Benilde. Excerpts from *Good Hair: A Novel*. Copyright © 1996 by Benilde Little. Reprinted by permission of Simon & Schuster.

Lorde, Audre, "Naturally," from *The Collected Poems of Audre Lorde*. Copyright © 1997 by The Audre Lorde Estate. Reprinted by permission of W. W. Norton & Company, Inc.

Mabley, Moms, selections from "Moms Mabley On Stage," recorded during her performance at the Tioli Theatre Chicago, Chess MCA Records, Inc., 1984. We have made every effort to find the copyright holder of this selection. If you have information regarding the copyright holder, please write to W. W. Norton, 500 Fifth Avenue, New York, NY 10110 (Attn: Amy Cherry).

McMillan, Terry, selections from *Waiting to Exhale*. Copyright © 1992 by Terry McMillan. Used by permission of Viking Penguin, a division of Penguin Books USA, Inc.

Marshall, Paule, excerpts from *Brown Girl, Brownstones*. New York: Random. Copyright © 1959 by Paule Marshall. Reprinted by permission of the author.

Meriwether, Louise, "A Happening in Barbados." Copyright © 1968 by Louise Meriwether. Reprinted by permission of Louise Meriwether.

Mitchell [Kernan], Claudia I., selection from "Language Behavior in a Black Urban Community" (Diss. University of California, Berkeley, 1970). Reprinted by permission of Claudia Mitchell Kernan.

Moore, Opal, "The Fence," from *African American Review* 29 (spring, 1995). Copyright © 1995 by Opal Moore. Reprinted by permission of the author.

———, "Git That Gal a Red Dress." Reprinted by permission of Opal Moore.

———, "A Happy Story," from *Callaloo* 12 (spring, 1989). Copyright © 1989 by The Johns Hopkins University Press. Reprinted by permission of The Johns Hopkins University Press and Opal Moore.

Morgan, Kathryn L., excerpt from *Children of Strangers: The Stories of a Black Family.* Philadelphia: Temple University Press. Copyright © 1980 by Temple University Press. Reprinted by permission of Temple University Press.

Moss, Thylias, "A Reconsideration of the Blackbird" and "Lessons from a Mirror," from *Pyramid of Bone* by Thylias Moss. Charlottesville: University Press of Virginia, 1989. Reprinted by permission of the University Press of Virginia.

Mother Love [Jo Anne Hart], with Connie Church, excerpts from *Listen Up, Girlfriends!* by Mother Love with Connie Church. Copyright © 1995 by Mother Love. Reprinted by permission of St. Martin's Press, Incorporated.

Naylor, Gloria. Excerpt from *Mama Day.* Copyright © 1988 by Gloria Naylor. Reprinted by permission of Ticknor & Fields/Houghton Mifflin Company. All rights reserved.

———. Excerpt from *Linden Hills.* Copyright © 1985 by Gloria Naylor. Reprinted by permission of Ticknor & Fields/Houghton Mifflin Company. All rights reserved.

Ndegeocello, Me'shell, selection from "Soul on Ice," by Me'shell Ndegeocello. Copyright © 1993 WB Music Corp. (ASCAP), Askia Music (ASCAP) & Maverick Music Company (ASCAP). All rights administered by WB Music Corp. All Rights reserved. Used by permission Warner Brothers Publications U.S., Inc.

Neely, Barbara, from *Blanche Among the Talented Tenth* by Barbara Neely. Copyright © 1994 by Barbara Neely. Reprinted by permission of St. Martin's Press Incorporated.

The Negro in Virginia. New York: Hampton University, 1940. Excerpts from the Minnie Folkes, Julia Frazier, Armacie Adams, Fannie Berry, and Charlotte Brown selections and "Freedman's Bureau" were reprinted by permission of Hampton University Archives.

Nelson, Jill, "We Will Live the Life of the Cosbys," from *Volunteer Slavery: My Authentic Negro Experience.* Copyright © 1993 by Jill Nelson. Reprinted by permission of the author.

Perdue, Charles L., Jr., Thomas E. Barden, and Robert K. Phillips, eds. *Weevils in the Wheat: Interviews with Virginia Ex-Slaves.* Charlottesville: University Press of Virginia, 1976. "Ol' Enough," "Us Colored Women Had to Go Through Plenty," "Sukie," and "Fire Sticks," from *Weevils* were reprinted by permission of the University Press of Virginia.

Petry, Ann. "The Bones of Louella Brown," from *Miss Muriel and Other Stories.* Copyright © 1947 by National Urban League; copyright renewed © in 1975 by Ann Petry. Reprinted by the permission of Russell & Volkening as agents for the author.

———. ["When I Mourns, I Mourns All Over,"] from *The Narrows.* Copyright © 1953 by Ann Petry; copyright renewed © in 1981 by Ann Petry. Reprinted by the permission of Russell & Volkening as agents for the author.

Rodgers, Carolyn M., "Jesus must have been some kind of dude," Part IV of "Living Water," "It Is Deep II," and "For Sistuhs Wearin Straight Hair," from *how i got ovah.* New York: Doubleday, 1975. Copyrights © 1969 and 1970 by Carolyn M. Rodgers. Reprinted by permission of author.

———, "and when the revolution came," "The Revolution Is Resting," and "Yeah, I Is Uh Shootin Off at the Mouth, . . ." from *Songs of a Black Bird.* Chicago: Third World Press. Copyright © 1970 by Carolyn M. Rodgers. Reprinted by permission of the author.

Rushin, Kate, "In Answer to the Question: Have You Ever Considered Suicide?" and "The Tired Poem: Last Letter from a Typical Unemployed Black Professional Woman," from *The Black Back-ups: Poetry.* Ithaca, New York: Firebrand Books. Copyright © 1993 by Kate Rushin. Used by permission of Firebrand Books.

Saar, Betye. "The Liberation of Aunt Jemima," 1972. Reprinted by permission of the University of California, Berkeley Art Museum; purchased with the aid of funds from the National Endowment for the Arts.

Sanders, Dori, excerpts from *Her Own Place* by Dori Sanders. Copyright © 1993 by the author. Reprinted by permission of Algonquin Books of Chapel Hill, a division of Workman Publishing.

Shange, Ntozake, "lady in red," from *for colored girls who have considered suicide/when the rainbow is enuf.* Copyright © 1975, 1976, 1977 by Ntozake Shange. Reprinted with the permission of Simon & Schuster.

———, from *spell # 7,* from *Three Pieces* by Ntozake Shange. Copyright © 1981 by Ntozake Shange. Reprinted by permission of St. Martin's Press, Incorporated.

Shanté, Roxanne, "Have a Nice Day," by Antonia Hardy and Marlon Williams. Copyright © 1987 Cold Chillin' Music Publishing (ASCAP) and WB Music Corp. (ASCAP) All rights o/b/o Cold Chillin' Music Publishing administered by WB Music Corp. All Rights Reserved. Used by permission Warner Bros. Publications U.S. Inc., Miami, FL, 33014.

Sinclair, April, from *ain't gonna be the same fool twice.* Copyright © 1994 April Sinclair. Reprinted by permission of Hyperion.

———, from *Coffee Will Make You Black.* Copyright © 1996 April Sinclair. Reprinted by permission of Hyperion.

Smith, Bessie. "Backwater Blues." By Bessie Smith. Copyright © 1927. Renewed © 1974 Frank Music Corp. All rights reserved.

Smith, Ethel Morgan, "The Spelling Bee." Copyright © by Ethel Morgan Smith. Reprinted by permission of the author.

———, "Come and Be Black for Me." Copyright © by Ethel Morgan Smith. Reprinted by permission of the author.

Smith, Mary Carter, "Cindy Ellie, a Modern Fairy Tale." Copyright © 1982 by Mary Carter Smith. Published by permission of Mary Carter Smith. Previously published in *The Griot's Cookbook,* by Alice McGill, Mary Carter Smith, and Elmira M. Washington, C. H. Fairfax Co., Columbia, Md., 1982.

Thomas, Joyce Carol, "Young Reverend Zelma Lee Moses," from *A Gathering of Flowers.* New York: Harper Collins. Copyright © 1990 by Joyce Carol Thomas. Reprinted by permission of HarperCollins Publishers and Joyce Carol Thomas.

Wade-Gayles, Gloria, excerpt from "Who Says an Older Woman Can't/Shouldn't Dance?" from *Rooted Against the Wind* by Gloria Wade-Gayles. Copyright © 1996 by Gloria Wade-Gayles. Reprinted by permission of Beacon Press, Boston.

Walker, Alice, excerpt from *The Color Purple.* Copyright © 1982 by Alice Walker. Reprinted by permission of Harcourt Brace & Company.

Walker, Margaret, "Kissie Lee," from *This Is My Century: New and Collected Poems by Margaret Walker.* Copyright © 1989 by Margaret Walker Alexander. Used by permission of the University of Georgia Press, Athens, Georgia.

Waniek, Marilyn Nelson, "Emily Dickinson's Defunct." Copyright © 1978 by Marilyn Nelson Waniek. Reprinted by permission of Louisiana State University Press from *For the Body* by Marilyn Nelson Waniek.

Ward, Val. "Pa'nella." Copyright © by Val Ward. Reprinted by permission of the author.

Warren, Nagueyalti. "Butter 'n' Bread." Copyright © by Nagueyalti Warren. Reprinted by permission of the author.

———. "Down Home Sunday Blues" and "Funny," from *Lodestar and Other Night Lights.* New York: Mellen. Copyright © 1992 by Nagueyalti Warren. Reprinted by permission of the author.

Waters, Ethel. From *His Eye Is on the Sparrow* by Ethel Waters with Charles Samuels. Copyright © 1951 Ethel Waters and Charles Samuels. Used by permission of Doubleday, a division of Bantam Doubleday Dell Publishing Group, Inc.

Wooley, Valerie Wilson. From *Devil's Gonna Get Him* by Valerie Wilson Wesley. Copyright © 1995 by Valerie Wilson Wesley. Reprinted by permission of The Putnam Publishing Group.

West, Dorothy. Excerpts from *The Living Is Easy*. New York: The Feminist Press at The City University of New York, 1982 (originally published in 1948). Copyright © 1948, 1975 by Dorothy West. Reprinted by permission of Dorothy West.

————. From *The Wedding*. Copyright © 1995 by Dorothy West. Used by permission of Doubleday, a division of Bantam Doubleday Dell Publishing Group, Inc.

Williams, Patricia J. excerpt from "In Search of Pharaoh's Daughter," originally published in *Out of the Garden: Women Writers on the Bible* by Christine Buchman and Celine Speigel, 1994, and subsequently published in *The Rooster's Egg: On the Persistence of Prejudice* by Patricia Williams, Cambridge, Mass.: Harvard University Press. Copyright © 1995 by the President and Fellows of Harvard College. Reprinted by permission of Harvard University Press.

Workman, Alison, "Grease," from *Tapestry: The Literary Magazine of Virginia State University*. Petersburg, Va.: Department of Languages and Literature at Virginia State University, Spring 1995. Copyright © by Alison Workman. Reprinted by permission of the author.